State Succession to International Responsibility

Theory and Practice of Public International Law

Series Editor

Vincent Chetail

VOLUME 9

The titles published in this series are listed at *brill.com/tppi*

State Succession to International Responsibility

Second Edition

By

Patrick Dumberry

BRILL | NIJHOFF

LEIDEN | BOSTON

Library of Congress Cataloging-in-Publication Data

Names: Dumberry, Patrick, author.
Title: State succession to international responsibility / Patrick Dumberry.
Description: Second edition. | Leiden ; Boston : Brill/Nijhoff, 2024. |
Series: Theory and practice of public international law, 2405-6847 ; volume 9 | Includes index. | Summary: "In the context of the break-up of the Soviet Union and Yugoslavia, the independence of Montenegro and the unification of Germany, can a new State be held responsible for wrongful acts committed before its independence by the predecessor State? This book is the most comprehensive analysis of State practice, case law and scholarship identifying the factors and circumstances under which the rights and obligations arising from wrongful acts committed before independence can be transferred to a new State. This updated and revised second edition covers new developments, including the recent works of the International Law Commission and the Institute of International Law"– Provided by publisher.
Identifiers: LCCN 2024017877 (print) | LCCN 2024017878 (ebook) | ISBN 9789004703803 (hardback) | ISBN 9789004703810 (ebook)
Subjects: LCSH: State succession. | Government liability (International law) | International obligations.
Classification: LCC KZ4024 .D86 2024 (print) | LCC KZ4024 (ebook) | DDC 341.26–dc23/eng/20240509
LC record available at https://lccn.loc.gov/2024017877
LC ebook record available at https://lccn.loc.gov/2024017878

Typeface for the Latin, Greek, and Cyrillic scripts: "Brill". See and download: brill.com/brill-typeface.

ISSN 2405-6847
ISBN 978-90-04-70380-3 (hardback)
ISBN 978-90-04-70381-0 (e-book)
DOI 10.1163/9789004703810

Contents

PART 2
Succession of States to the Obligation to Repair

Foreword to the First Edition (2007)

State succession became a neglected topic of international law after the most important wave of decolonisation had reached its peak towards the end of the 1960s. The subject of State succession attracted again the interest of scholars after the fall of the Berlin Wall with the emergence of new States, mainly as a result of the collapse of federal "Socialist" States, such as the Soviet Union and Yugoslavia, or the unification of other States, such as Germany and Yemen. However, less attention was given by authors to the emergence of two so-called "newly independent States" (Namibia in 1990 and Timor Leste in 2002).

The subject of succession of States has been analysed by the International Law Commission (ILC) and partially codified by two treaties: the Vienna Convention of 1978, dealing with State succession in respect to treaties and the Vienna Convention of 1983 concerning State property, archives, and debts. In 1993, soon after the end of the Cold War, the ILC undertook the study of the issue of State succession to matters of nationality of natural and legal persons. Even then, little interest was paid in the literature (with some significant exemptions, however) to the interaction between the issue of State succession and another topic, which had been thoroughly analysed by the ILC: State responsibility. Indeed, in the context of the ILC's *Articles on State Responsibility*, Special Rapporteur James Crawford highlighted the difficulties and uncertainties surrounding the issue of State succession to international responsibility: "[i]t is unclear whether a new State succeeds to any State responsibility of the predecessor State with respect to its territory".[1] Patrick Dumberry's remarkable book fills this important analytical gap and sheds some most welcomed light into a controversial subject, which had until now not received all the attention it deserved.

The book I have the great pleasure to introduce is a Ph.D. thesis which was submitted by the author to the Graduate Institute of International Studies of Geneva in 2006. The first merit of the book is that it correctly addresses the interaction between State succession and State responsibility for internationally wrongful acts. Thus, the relevant question does not involve any succession of States with respect to *responsibility per se*, but instead deals with whether or not there is succession to the *rights and obligations arising from internationally*

1 ILC, *Commentaries to the Draft Articles on Responsibility of States for Internationally Wrongful Acts Adopted by the ILC at Its Fifty-Third Session* (2001), ILC Report, 53rd sess. Official Records of the GA, 56th sess., Suppl. No. 10 (A/56/10), 119, para 3 (hereinafter "ILC, Commentaries, State Responsibility, 2001").

wrongful acts committed or suffered by the predecessor State. In other words, the issue is whether or not the successor State has (after the date of succession) an obligation to repair or a right to reparation in relation to unlawful acts committed before the date of succession. This clear perspective adopted by the author avoids at the outset simplistic solutions proposed by some writers such as the existence of a general rule of non-succession based on the so-called *intuitu personae* character of responsibility for wrongful acts.

The book's second major merit is its systematic analysis of State practice which takes into account the different types of succession of States (dissolution, separation, unification, etc.). Indeed, the different types of succession of States require separate analysis and are subject to specific solutions. For instance, the fact that the predecessor State continues to exist after the date of succession has important consequences with respect to the determination of whether there is any succession to international responsibility. The author also analyses different factors and circumstances and concludes that they lead to distinct solutions of succession. For instance, he examines in detail factors such as the acceptance by the successor State of its responsibility, the fact that the act was committed by an insurrectional movement or by an autonomous government (which subsequently became an independent State), the enrichment of a State as a result of the act, etc.

Finally, I should mention that the book is the only existing comprehensive study which examine in detail both ancient and contemporary international (and municipal) case law and State practice. In fact, some of the examples analysed by Dr. Dumberry have never been dealt with previously by scholars. The extensive research undertaken by the author makes this book a major source of information for all practitioners and scholars interested in issues of State succession.

The book is presented in a clear and straightforward manner. The introductory part of the book contains a general introduction delimitating the scope of the study and outlining the author's perspective on State succession and international responsibility. The book is divided in two parts, the first dealing with State succession to the obligation to repair and the second concerning State succession to the right to reparation. Both parts follow the same scheme: a comprehensive presentation of the doctrinal positions on each issue which is followed by the examination of State practice and case law (which is examined separately for each different types of State succession). Finally, the author presents different factors and circumstances which are relevant to determine whether or not there is succession to international responsibility. An impressive and precious bibliography, including references to case law and national and international documents, completes this excellent picture.

The fact that the author concludes that there is no general rule on the issue of State succession to the obligation to repair and that, in fact, specific solutions prevail depending on the different types of succession involved (as well as on a variety of different factors and circumstances), does not prevent him from ultimately presenting a systematic and all-embracing conclusion. He highlights three fundamental principles with respect to the obligation to repair: 1) that an international wrongful act must not remain unpunished simply because of the application of the mechanisms of State succession, 2) that the actual wrongdoer State should be the one responsible for the obligations arising from commission of the wrongful act and 3) that the State that has beneficiated from the consequences arising from an international wrongful act should be responsible for the obligations resulting from such act. The author considers that the other question of succession to the right to reparation is much more straightforward and favours succession. In sum, the general trend observed by the author is the acceptance by States of the principle of succession to rights and obligations arising from the commission of internationally wrongful acts. The great merit of this book is that it disproves the view generally held in doctrine in favour of non-succession. The author's conclusion is that the doctrine of strict and automatic non-succession is simply not representative of contemporary State practice and case law. The author's comprehensive analysis of State practice also leads him to conclude that several rules of customary international law have developed.

In conclusion, this is a timely and fascinating book. The need for a comprehensive study of the issue of State succession to international responsibility is illustrated by the fact that in 2003, the *Institut de droit international* has set up a commission in charge of addressing this topic (i.e. while Dr. Dumberry was working on his Ph.D. doctoral thesis). I believe that this book will be of extraordinary help to the work of the *Institut*.

The book "*State Succession to International Responsibility*" does a great service to the doctrine of international law and will undoubtedly become an indispensable reference in the field of State succession.

Marcelo G. Kohen
Professor of International Law
Graduate Institute of International Studies, Geneva
19 January 2007

Acknowledgments to the Second Edition

The first edition of this study was a slightly modified version of my Ph.D. thesis submitted in February 2006 to the Graduate Institute of International Studies in Geneva, Switzerland. I will be forever indebted to my thesis supervisor, Professor Marcelo G. Kohen. He provided me with not only invaluable comments, guidance, and extraordinary support, but also timely and constructive criticisms. Marcelo continues to be a role model and a mentor for me throughout all these years, ever since I met him in 1998. I would also like to thank Professor Brigitte Stern and Professor Jean Salmon, who sadly passed away in 2022, for their very useful comments and suggestions.

I decided in 2023 to publish a second edition of this study. Since its publication in 2007, this study has received favourable comments from scholars. It has also been used by States in their pleadings before international tribunals and referred to by judges in judgments. Since 2007, the question of State succession to responsibility, which had been rarely addressed by scholars in the past, has been thoroughly examined by two major international law institutions. First, the Institute of International Law, under the rapportership of Professor Kohen, published in 2015 its resolution on "State Succession in Matters of State Responsibility". The author of this book and Marcelo Kohen published in 2019 an article-by-article commentary explaining the scope and content of that resolution (Marcelo G. Kohen & Patrick Dumberry, *The Institute of International Law's Resolution on State Succession and State Responsibility: Introduction, Text and Commentaries,* Cambridge UP 2019). Second, in 2017, the ILC placed the topic of "Succession of States in respect of State Responsibility" on its current programme of work and appointed Professor Pavel Šturma as Special Rapporteur. ILC Special Rapporteur Šturma issued five Reports from 2018 to 2022. In 2022, almost all of the provisions of the Guidelines (except for one related to the "content and forms" of reparation) had been provisionally adopted by the ILC and the commentary to these provisions had also been approved. But in 2023 the ILC decided to establish a Working Group to determine what would be the outcome of its work. A final decision was taken at the 75th session (2024). The Working Group recommended drafting a report that 'would contain a summary of the difficulties that the Commission would face if it were to continue its work on the topic and explain the reasons for the discontinuance of such work' (ILC, 'Report of the Working Group', 12 July 2024, A/CN.4/L.1003, para. 23).

These two parallel works of codification are of the greatest importance to the study of the question of State succession to responsibility. Their findings are included in the second edition of this book. The new edition also takes into account scholarship published in the last 15 years on the topic as well as several new decisions rendered by international tribunals and domestic courts dealing with the issue. I would like to thank Brill (Marie Sheldon, Beth Derr, Dove Morissette and others) for agreeing to publish this second edition.

Finally, I would like to dedicate this book to my mother, my two beautiful, adorable and intelligent children, Ophelie and Florent, and to Fatima for her love and support throughout this journey.

Patrick Dumberry
Montreal, Canada
January 2024

Abbreviations

1978 Vienna Convention	*Vienna Convention on Succession of States in Respect of Treaties*, signed on 23 August 1978, entered into force on 6 November 1996, ST/LEG/SER.E/10, in: 17 *I.L.M.*, 1978, 1488
1983 Vienna Convention	*Vienna Convention on Succession of States in Respect of State Property, Archives and Debts*, signed on 8 April 1983, not yet in force, in: 22 *I.L.M.*, 1983, 306
AD	Annual Digest of Public International Law Cases: Being a Selection from the Decisions of International and National Courts and Tribunals, ed. by Sir Hersch Lauterpacht, Longmans, Green & Co., 1919–1949
AFDI	Annuaire français de droit international
AJIL	American Journal of International Law
Annuaire IDI	Annuaire de l'Institut de Droit international (Institute of International Law)
ASDI	Annuaire suisse de droit international
Atlam	Hazem M. Atlam, *Succession d'Etats et continuité en matière de responsabilité internationale*, doctoral thesis, Université de droit, d'économie et des sciences d'Aix-Marseille (France), 1986, 526 p
Barde	Jacques Barde, *La notion de droit acquis en droit international public*, Publ. univ. de Paris, 1981
Bardonnet	D. Bardonnet, *La succession d'Etats à Madagascar: succession au droit conventionnel et aux droits patrimoniaux*, LGDJ, 1970
Bedjaoui	Mohammed Bedjaoui, "Problèmes récents de succession d'Etats dans les Etats nouveaux", *Rec. des cours*, t. 130, 1970–II
Bernhardt	R. Bernhardt (ed), *Encyclopaedia of Public International Law*, v. 10, North Holland, Max Planck Institute, 1984
BGBl.	Bundesgesetzblatt (German Federal Law Gazette)
Bijelić case	*Bijelić v. Montenegro and Serbia,* ECHR App no 19890/05, Judgment, 11 June 2009
Booysen	Hercules Booysen, "Succession to Delictual Liability: A Namibian Precedent", 24 *Comp. & Int'l L.J. S. Afr.*, 1991,
Brockman-Hawe	Benjamin E. Brockman-Hawe, "Succession, the Obligation to Repair and Human Rights; The European Court of Human Rights Judgment in the Case of Bijelić v. Montenegro and Serbia", 59(3) *ICLQ* 2010

Buser	A. Buser, "Colonial Injustices and the Law of State Responsibility: The CARICOM Claim for Reparations" 77 *Heidelberg JIL* 2017, 409–446, KFG Working Paper No. 4
BverfGE	Bundesverfassungsgericht
Cavaglieri, Effets	Arrigo Cavaglieri, "Effets juridiques des changements de souveraineté territoriale", in: *Annuaire I.D.I.*, 1931–I
Cavaglieri, Règles	Arrigo Cavaglieri, "Règles générales du droit de la paix", *Rec. des cours*, v. 26, 1929–I
CIS	Commonwealth of Independent States
Comp. & Int'l l.j. s. Afr.	Comparative & International Law Journal of Southern Africa
Cotran	Eugene Cotran, "Some Legal Aspects of the Formation of the United Arab Republic and the United Arab States", 8 *ICLQ* 1959
Crawford, State Responsibility	J. Crawford, *State Responsibility: The General Part,* CUP, 2013
Crawford, Brownlie's	J. Crawford, *Brownlie's Principles of Public International Law,* 8th ed., OUP, 2013
Croatia Genocide Convention case	*Application of the Convention on the Prevention and Punishment of the Crime of Genocide* (*Croatia v. Serbia*), Judgment of 3 February 2015, ICJ Rep. 2015
CUP	Cambridge University Press
Czaplinski	Wladyslaw Czaplinski, "State Succession and State Responsibility", 28 *Canadian Y.I.L.*, 1990, 339–359
D'Argent	Pierre D'Argent, *Les réparations de guerre en droit international public,* Bruylant, 2002
Degan	Vladimir D. Degan, "Création et disparition de l'Etat (à la lumière du démembrement de trois fédérations multiethniques en Europe)", *Rec. des cours*, t. 279, 1999
Dumberry, Rebellions	P. Dumberry, *Rebellions and Civil Wars: State Responsibility for the Conduct of Insurgents,* CUP 2021
Dupuy & Kerbrat	P.-M. Dupuy & Y. Kerbrat, *Droit international public*, 15th ed., Dalloz, 2020
ECHR	European Court of Human Rights
E.C. Bull.	Bulletin des communautes europeennes

Eisemann, Emprunts russes	Pierre Michel Eisemann, "Emprunts russes et problèmes de succession d'Etats", in: P. Juillard & B. Stern, (eds), *Les emprunts russes et le règlement du contentieux financier franco-russe*, Paris, Cahiers internationaux n°16, 2002
Eisemann & Koskenniemi	Pierre Michel Eisemann & Martti Koskenniemi (Dir.), *La succession d'Etats: la codification à l'épreuve des faits / State Succession: Codification Tested Against the Facts*, Hague Academy of International Law, Martinus Nijhoff Publ., 2000
EJIL	European Journal of International Law
EuGRZ	*Feilchenfeld* Europäische Grundrechte-Zeitschrift Ernst H. Feilchenfeld, *Public Debts and State Succession*, Macmillan, 1931
FLN	Front de libération nationale
FOCP	United Kingdom Foreign Office Confidential Paper
For. Rel.	American State Papers, Foreign Relations, Foreign Relations (United States)
FRG	Federal Republic of Germany
FRY	Federal Republic of Yugoslavia
Gabčíkovo-Nagymaros case	*Case Concerning the Gabčíkovo-Nagymaros Project* (Hungary v. Slovakia), Judgment of 25 September 1997, *ICJ Reports* 1997, 3
Ga.J.Int'l.& Comp.L.	Georgia Journal of International and Comparative law
GDR	German Democratic Republic
Geo. Wash. Int'l L. Rev.	George Washington International Law Review
GPO	Government Printing Office (United States)
Gruber	Annie Gruber, *Le droit international de la succession d'Etats*, Publ. faculté de droit de l'Université René Descartes (Paris V) & Bruylant, 1986
Guggenheim	Paul Guggenheim, *Traité de Droit international public*, v. 1, Librairie de l'Université, 1953
Hawaiian Claims case	*F.H. Redward and Others (Great Britain) v. United States*, US-Great Britain Arbitral Commission, Award of 10 November 1925, in: *UNRIAA* vol. 6, 157; in: 20 *A.J.I.L.*, 1926, 382; in: *Annual Digest*, 1925–1926, case no. 59, 80
HJLP	Hawaiian Journal of Law and Politics
Hyde	Charles Cheney Hyde, *International Law Chiefly as Interpreted and Applied by the United States*, vol. 1, 2nd ed., Little, Brown & Co., 1945
Hurst	Cecil J.B. Hurst, "State Succession in Matters of Tort", 5 *British Y.I.L.*, 1924, 163–178

ICJ	International Court of Justice
ICJ Rep.	International Court of Justice Reports of Judgments, Advisory Opinions and Orders
ICLQ	International and Comparative Law Quarterly
IIL or Institute	Institute of International Law
IIL, Final Report, Kohen	Institute of International Law, "Final Report" on "State Succession in Matters of State Responsibility", Rapporteur Marcelo G. Kohen, 28 June 2015, in: (2015) 76 *Annuaire de l'Institut de Droit international*, 511ff
IIL, Resolution 2015	Institute of International Law, *State Succession in Matters of State Responsibility*, 14th Commission, Rapporteur. M.G. Kohen, Resolution, 28 August 2015
IIL, State Succession in Matters of Property, 2001	Institute of International Law, *State Succession in Matters of Property and Debts*, Resolution, Session of Vancouver, 2001, in: 69 *Annuaire I.D.I*, 2000–2001
ILA	International Law Association
ILC	International Law Commission
ILC's *Articles on State Responsibility*, 2001	Titles and Texts of the Draft Articles on Responsibility of States for Internationally Wrongful Acts Adopted by the Drafting Committee on Second Reading, *26 July 2001, A/CN.4/L.602/Rev.1*
ILC, Commentaries, State Responsibility, 1996	Commentary to the Draft Articles on State Responsibility Adopted by the Commission on First Reading, Report of the ILC on the Work of its Forty-eighth Session, 1996, A/51/10, chap. III, in: *Yearbook ILC*, 1996, vol. II (Part Two), 58–65
ILC, Commentaries, State Responsibility, 2001	Commentaries to the Draft Articles on Responsibility of States for Internationally Wrongful Acts Adopted by the International Law Commission at its Fifty-Third Session (2001), November 2001, Report of the ILC on the work of its Fifty-third Session, Official Records of the General Assembly, Fifty-sixth Session, Supplement No. 10 (A/56/10), ch. IV.E.2), 59ff.
ILC, Commentaries, 2019	"Text of the Draft Guidelines and Commentaries", provisionally adopted, in ILC, "Report on the Work of its 71st Session", 2019, A/74/10, 2019, chap. VII

ILC, Commentaries, 2021	"Text of the Draft Guidelines and Commentaries", provisionally adopted, in: ILC, "Report on the Work of its 72th Session", 2021, A/76/10, 2021, chap. VII
ILC, Commentaries, 2022	"Text of the Draft Guidelines and Commentaries", provisionally adopted, in ILC, "Report on the Work of its 73rd Session", 2022, A/77/10, chap. VII
ILC, Draft Articles on Nationality	*Draft Articles on Nationality of Natural Persons in Relation to the Succession of States*, adopted by the ILC on second reading in 1999, ILC Report, A/54/10, 1999, chp. IV, paras. 44 and 45, in: *Yearbook ILC*, 1997, vol. II, 13
ILC, Ninth Report Bedjaoui, 1977	"Ninth Report on Succession of States in Respect of Matters Other than Treaties", M. Bedjaoui, Special Rapporteur, 28th session, 1977, A/CN.4/301 and Add.1, ILC Report, A/32/10, 1977, ch. III(A)(1), par. 49, in: *Yearbook ILC*, 1977, vol. II, 45
ILC Report, 70th Session, 2018	"Report on the Work of its 70th Session", 2018, A/73/10, chap. X, at para. 255
ILC, Second Report Bedjaoui, 1969	"Second Report on Succession of States in Respect of Matters Other Than Treaties", Mohammed Bedjaoui, Special Rapporteur—Economic and Financial Acquired Rights and State Succession, A/CN.4/216/Rev.1, in (1969) II *Yearbook ILC*
ILC Special Rapporteur Šturma, First Report, 2017	"First Report on Succession of States in Respect of State Responsibility', Special Rapporteur Pavel Šturma, 69th sess., 31 May 2017, A/CN.4/708
ILC Special Rapporteur Šturma, Second Report, 2018	"Second Report on Succession of States in Respect of State Responsibility", Special Rapporteur Pavel Šturma, 70th sess. April 2018, A/CN.4/719
ILC Special Rapporteur Šturma, Third Report, 2019	"Third Report on Succession of States in Respect of State Responsibility", Special Rapporteur Pavel Šturma, 71st sess., 2 May 2019, A/CN.4/731

ILC Special Rapporteur Šturma, Fourth Report, 2020	"Fourth Report on Succession of States in Respect of State Responsibility", Special Rapporteur Pavel Šturma, 72nd sess., 7 March 2020, A/CN.4/743
ILC Special Rapporteur Šturma, Fifth Report, 2022	"Fifth Report on Succession of States in Respect of State Responsibility", Special Rapporteur Pavel Šturma, 73rd sess., 1 April 2022, A/CN.4/751
ILC, Statement, Grossman Guiloff, 2019	Succession of States in respect of State responsibility, "Statement, Chair of the Drafting Committee, Claudio Grossman Guiloff", 31 July 2019
ILC, Statement, Galvão Teles, 2021	Succession of States in respect of State responsibility, "Statement, Chair of the Drafting Committee, Patrícia Galvão Teles", 28 July 2021
ILC, Statement, Park, 2022	Succession of States in respect of State responsibility, "Statement of the Chair of the Drafting Committee Mr. Ki Gab Park", 14 July 2022
ILM	International Legal Materials
ILR	International Law Reports
Int'l Law.	International Lawyer.
Jakubowski, State Succession	Jakubowski, A., *State Succession in Cultural Property*, OUP, 2015
Jap. AIL	Japanese Annual of International Law
JDI	Journal du droit international (Clunet)
Jenning & Watts	Sir Robert Jenning & Sir Arthur Watts, *Oppenheim's International Law*, vol. I (Peace: Introduction and Part 1), 9th ed., Longman
J. Trib.	Journal des Tribunaux (Belgium)
JORF	Journal Officiel de la République Française (France)
Kaplane	A. Kaplane, "Succession of States in Respect of State Responsibility: Towards Yet Another Vienna Convention?", *Riga Graduate School of Law Research Papers*, No. 23
Keith	A.B. Keith, *The Theory of State Succession with Specific Reference to English and Colonial Law*, 1907

Kohen, Succession of States	M.G. Kohen, "Succession of States in the Field of International Responsibility: The Case for Codification", in: M.G. Kohen, R. Kolb, & D. Tehindrazanarivelo (dir.), *Perspectives of International Law in the 21st Century. Liber amicorum Professor Christian Dominicé in Honour of His 80th Birthday* (M. Nijhoff 2011)
Kohen & Dumberry	Marcelo G. Kohen & Patrick Dumberry, *The Institute of International Law's Resolution on State Succession and State Responsibility: Introduction, Text and Commentaries*, CUP 2019
La.L.Rev.	Louisiana Law Review
Lighthouse Arbitration case	*Sentence arbitrale en date des 24/27 juillet 1956 rendue par le Tribunal d'arbitrage constitué en vertu du Compromis signé à Paris le 15 juillet 1932 entre la France et la Grèce,* French-Greek Arbitral Tribunal, Award of 24/27 July 1956, in: *UNRIAA* vol. 12, 155; in: 9 *R.H.D.I.*, 1956, 176; in: 23 *I.L.R.*, 1956, 81
LNTS	League of Nations Treaty Series
*MAT*s	Mixed Arbitral Tribunals
Malloy	William M. Malloy, *Treaties, Conventions, International Acts, Protocols and Agreements between the United States of America and other Powers, 1776–1909,* several volumes, GPO, 1910–1938.
Marek	Krystyna Marek, *Identity and Continuity of States in Public International Law*, Librairie Droz, 1968,
Mikulka, State Succession	V. Mikulka, 'State Succession and Responsibility', in: J. Crawford, A. Pellet & S. Olleson (eds), *The Law of International Responsibility,* OUP 2010
Md.L.Rev.	Maryland Law Review
Monnier	Jean Philippe Monnier, "La succession d'Etats en matière de responsabilité internationale", 8 *AFDI*, 1962, 65–90
Moore, Digest	John Bassett Moore, *A Digest of International Law*, several volumes, GPO, 1906.
Moore, History	John Bassett Moore, *History and Digest of the International Arbitrations to which the United States has been a Party*, several volumes, GPO, 1898

Mwandinghi case, Namibia, Supreme Court	*Minister of Defence, Namibia v. Mwandinghi,* Supreme Court of Namibia, 25 October 1991, in: 1992 (2) *SA* 355 (NmS), in: 91 *I.L.R.*, 358
Mwandinghi case, Namibia, High Court	*Mwandinghi v. Minister of Defence, Namibia*, High Court, 14 December 1990, in: 1991 (1) *SA* 851 (Nm), in: 91 *I.L.R.*, 343
Nielsen	Fred K. Nielsen, *American and British Claims Arbitration, Report*, GPO, 1926
NJW	Neue Juristische Wochenschrift
NYU JIL & Pol.	New York University Journal of International Law & Politics
Oeter	Stefan Oeter, "German Unification and State Succession", 51(2) *ZaöRV,* 1991
O'Connell, The Law of State Succession, 1956	D.P. O'Connell, *The Law of State Succession*, CUP 1956
O'Connell, Recent Problems	D.P. O'Connell, "Recent Problems of State Succession in Relation to New States", *Rec. des cours*, t. 130, 1970–II
O'Connell, State Succession, vol. I	D.P. O'Connell, *State Succession in Municipal Law and International Law*, vol. I, CUP, 1967
ÖBGBl.	Österreichische Bundesgesetzblatt (Austrian Federal Law Gazette
OUP	Oxford University Press
ÖZöR	Österreichische Zeitschrift für öffentliches Recht
ÖZöRV	Österreichische Zeitschrift für öffentliches Recht und Völkerrecht (Austrian Journal of Public and International Law)
Pablo Nájera case	*Pablo Nájera (France) v. Mexico*, Decision no. 30–A, 19 October 1928, in: *UNRIAA* v. V, 466, *Annual Digest*, 1927–1928, 52
Pajnkihar	Grega Pajnkihar, *State Succession to Responsibility for Internationally Wrongful Acts*, Brill, 2023
Panevezys-Saldutiskis Railway case	*Panevezys-Saldutiskis Railway* case, Judgment of 28 February 1939, PCIJ, *Series A/B*, no. 76
PCA	Permanent Court of Arbitration
PCIJ	Permanent Court of International Justice

Peterschmitt	Miriam Peterschmitt, *La succession d'Etats et la responsabilité internationale pour fait illicite*, Mémoire de DES, Université de Genève/ Institut Universitaire de hautes études internationales (Switzerland), 2001, 87 p
RAACE	Recueil des arrêts et avis du Conseil d'Etat (Belgium)
RBDI	Revue belge de droit international
Rec. des Cours	Collected Courses of the Hague Academy of International Law
RDH	Revue des droits de l'homme
RDI	Rivista de diritto internazionale
RDILC	Revue de droit international et de législation comparée
R.E. Brown case	*R.E. Brown (United States) v. Great Britain*, US-Great Britain Arbitral Commission, Award of 23 November 1923, in: *UNRIAA* vol. 6, 120; in: 5 *British Y.I.L.*, 1924, 210; in: *A.J.I.L.*, 1925, 193; in: *Annual Digest*, 1923–1924, case no. 35, 69
Rec. Lebon	Recueil des décisions du Conseil d'Etat (France)
RDTAM	Recueil des décisions des tribunaux arbitraux mixtes institués par le Traité de Paix, 10 vols., Librairie de la société du recueil sirey, 1922–1930
REDI	Revista Española de Derecho Internacional
RFDA	Revue française de droit administratif
RGDIP	Revue générale de droit international public
RHDI	Revue hellénique de droit international
RJDA	Recueil de jurisprudence du droit administratif et du Conseil d'Etat (Belgium)
RJPUF	Revue juridique et politique de l'Union française
Rousseau	Charles Rousseau, *Droit international public*, several volumes, Sirey, 1977
Ruy & Baecke	Tom Ruy & Tomas Baecke, "Haunted by The Past? Belgium's international responsibility for the atrocities of the Congo Free State and the question of State succession in matters of international responsibility", Grili Working Paper No. 6 (also in: (2021) *Revue belge de droit international*, 477)
Samos case	*Samos (Liability for Torts) Case*, Greece, Court of the Aegean Islands, 1924, N° 27, in: *Thémis*, vol. 35, 294, in: *Annual Digest*, 1923–1924, at 70
Sastry	T.S.N. Sastry, *State Succession in Indian Context*, Dominant Publ. & Dist., 2004
SFRY	Socialist Federal Republic of Yugoslavia
Shaw	Malcolm Shaw, *International Law*, 8th ed., CUP, 2021
SJ Res.	Senate Joint Resolution (United States)

Stern, Concluding Remarks	B. Stern, "General Concluding Remarks", in: Brigitte Stern (ed), *Dissolution, Continuation and Succession in Eastern Europe*, Martinus Nijhoff Publ., 1998
Stern, Responsabilité	Brigitte Stern, "Responsabilité internationale et succession d'Etats", in: Laurence Boisson De Chazournes & Vera Gowlland-Debbas (eds), *The International Legal System in Quest of Equity and Universality/L'ordre juridique international, un système en quête d'équité et d'universalité. Liber amicorum Georges Abi-Saab*, M. Nijhoff, 2001, 327–355
Stern, Succession	Brigitte Stern, "La succession d'Etats", *Rec. des cours*, t. 262, 1996
Šturma, State Succession	Pavel Šturma, "State Succession in Respect of International Responsibility", (2016) 48 *George Washington ILR*
Schwarzenberger	Georg Schwarzenberger, *International Law as Applied by International Courts and Tribunals*, v. I, 3rd ed., Steven & Sons 1957
Trb.	Tractatenblad van het Koninkrijk der Nederlanden (Treaty Journal of the Kingdom of the Netherlands)
UCLA JILFA	University of California in Los Angeles Journal of International Law & Foreign Affairs
Udina	Manlio Udina, "La succession des Etats quant aux obligations internationales autres que les dettes publiques", *Rec. des cours*, t. 44, 1933–II,
UK	United Kingdom
UKTS	United Kingdom Treaty Series
UN	United Nations
UNCC	United Nations Compensation Commission
UNTS	United Nations Treaty Series
USSR	Union of Soviet Socialist Republics
USTS	United States Treaty Series
UST	United States Treaties and Other International Agreements
U.Ill.L.Rev.	University of Illinois Law Review
UNRIAA	United Nations Reports of International Arbitral Awards
TIAS	Treaties and Other International Acts Series
Vergara Lamadrid	Ana Paola Vergara Lamadrid, *La obligación de reparar en el marco de una sucesión de Estados*, Thesis, Pontificia Universidad Católica Del Perú, Lima, 2022

Versailles Treaty	*Versailles Treaty*, signed on 28 June 1919, entered into force on 10 January 1920, in: *The Treaties of Peace 1919–1923*, Carnegie Endowment for International Peace, 1924; in: *U.K.T.S.* 1919, No. 8 (Cmd. 223)
Verzijl	J.H.W. Verzijl, *International Law in Historical Perspective, t. VII (State Succession)*, A.W. Sijthoff, 1974
Verzijl, Jurisprudence	J.H.W. Verzijl, *The Jurisprudence of the World Court: A Case by Case Commentary*, vol. I, A.W. Sijthoff, 1965
Weston & Lillich	Burns H. Weston & Richard B. Lillich, *International Claims: Their Settlement by Lump Sum Agreements*, Univ. Press of Virginia, 1975
Weston et al.	Burns H. Weston, Richard B. Lillich & David J. Bederman, *International Claims: Their Settlement by Lump Sum Agreements, 1975–1995*, Transnational Publ., 1999
VfSlg	Sammlung der Erkenntnisse und wichtigsten Beschlüsse des Verfassungsgerichtshofes" (Compendium of Judgments and Most Important Decisions of the Constitutional Court, Austria)
VRU	Verfassung und Recht in Ubersee (Law and Politics in Africa, Asia and Latin America)
Volkovitsch	Michael John Volkovitsch, "Righting Wrongs: Toward a New Theory of State Succession to Responsibility for International Delicts", 92(8) *Colum. L.Rev.*, 1992, 2162–2214
VVDStRL	Veroffentlichungen der Vereinigung der Deutschen Staatsrechtslehrer
W. Va. LR	West Virginia Law Review
Yale Stud.World PO	Yale Studies in World Public Order
Yearbook ILC	Yearbook of the International Law Commission
ZaöRV	Zeitschrift für ausländisches öffentliches Recht und Völkerrecht

PART 1

General Introduction

General Introduction of Part 1

1 The Issue Addressed in This Study

Succession of States (or "State succession") is defined as "the replacement of one State by another in the responsibility for the international relations of territory".[1] Both *Vienna Conventions*[2] and the instruments adopted by Institute of International Law ("Institute" or "IIL") and the International Law Commission ("ILC") only cover situations of succession which are considered *legal* under international law.[3] Since the end of the Cold War, problems of State succession have been the object of significant developments. This area of research is vast and complex, and it is undoubtedly also one of the most controversial and disputed areas in international law. It has recently been the object of tremendous attention by scholars.[4] The rarity (at least before the 1990s) and the great variety of events involving succession of States account for both a contradictory practice and different and mutually exclusive theories in scholarship. State practice is thus largely based on political opportunity rather than on the

1 See, definition in: Art. 2(1)b), *1978 Vienna Convention on Succession of States in Respect of Treaties*, ST/LEG/SER.E/10, 17 *ILM* 1978, 1488 (hereinafter "1978 *Vienna Convention*"); Art. 2(1)a), *1983 Vienna Convention on Succession of States in Respect of State Property, Archives and Debts*, 22 *ILM* 1983, 306 (hereinafter "1983 *Vienna Convention*"); Art. 2, *Draft Articles on Nationality of Natural Persons in Relation to the Succession of States*, adopted by the ILC on second reading in 1999, ILC Report, A/54/10, 1999, chp. IV, paras 44 and 45, *Yearbook ILC*, 1997, v. II, 13 (hereinafter "*Draft Articles on Nationality*"). The same definitions were also adopted by the more recent works of the Institute and the ILC.

2 Art. 6, 1978 *Vienna Convention*, ibid; Art. 3, 1983 *Vienna Convention*, ibid; Art. 3, *Draft Articles on Nationality*, ibid.

3 See, Art. 2(2), Institute of International Law, *State Succession in Matters of State Responsibility*, 14th Commission, Rapporteur. M.G. Kohen, Resolution, 28 August 2015 (hereinafter "IIL, Resolution 2015"); Marcelo G. Kohen & Patrick Dumberry, *The Institute of International Law's Resolution on State Succession and State Responsibility: Introduction, Text and Commentaries* (CUP 2019) (hereinafter "Kohen & Dumberry"), 25–28. See, Guideline 3 and ILC, "Second Report on Succession of States in Respect of State Responsibility", Special Rapporteur Pavel Šturma, 70th sess. April 2018, A/CN.4/719 (hereinafter "ILC Special Rapporteur Šturma, Second Report, 2018"), paras 22–41.

4 See: F. Markx-Veldhuijzen, *State Succession: Codification Tested against the Facts*, Center for Studies and Research of the Hague Academy of International Law, 1996, updated in: Pierre Michel Eisemann & Martti Koskenniemi (Dir), *La succession d'Etats: la codification à l'épreuve des faits/State Succession: Codification Tested Against the Facts* (Hague Academy of International Law, Martinus Nijhoff 2000) (hereinafter "Eisemann & Koskenniemi") 929–968.

 | DOI:10.1163/9789004703810_002

strict observation of legal concepts.[5] Only very few issues relating to State succession can be qualified as norms of customary international law.[6] There is no *general* rule on State succession, and any attempt to define a *general* theory of State succession is by definition bound to be uncertain.[7] As explained by one author: "Les diverses situations de mutations territoriales sont tellement riches de conséquences qu'elles excluent a priori la possibilité de l'apparition de règles juridiques simples et uniformes en matière de succession d'Etats".[8]

The study of the many problems arising from the process of succession of States is usually divided into several different aspects: succession to treaties, to debts, to assets, to archives, to international organisations, etc. The present study addresses one specific question of succession of States: whether there is a succession to the *consequences of international responsibility* arising from an internationally wrongful act committed before the date of succession. More specifically, the question is whether there is a succession of States to the *rights and obligations arising from the commission of an internationally wrongful act.* Contrary to other areas of succession of States, the question addressed in the present study had, until recently, not been the object of great attention by past and contemporary legal scholars.

The issue analysed in the present study arises from the commission of an "internationally wrongful act"[9] *before* the "date of succession".[10] The present study will examine what are the consequences of an internationally wrongful act committed *by the predecessor State* against another State.[11] Before the date of succession, the predecessor State is the *debtor of an obligation to repair* towards the injured third State. The present study will also address the opposite situation, when an internationally wrongful act was committed by a State *against the predecessor State.* In such case, before the date of succession, the

5 D.P. O'Connell, *The Law of State Succession* (CUP 1956) (hereinafter "O'Connell, The Law of State Succession, 1956"), 272; D.P. O'Connell, "Recent Problems of State Succession in Relation to New States", *Rec. des cours*, v. 130, 1970–II (hereinafter "O'Connell, Recent Problems"), 117–118, 199.

6 See Brigitte Stern, "La succession d'Etats", *Rec. des cours*, v. 262, 1996 (hereinafter "Stern, Succession") 164–173, examining these customary norms.

7 D.P. O'Connell, "Reflections on the State Succession Convention", 39(4) *ZaöRV*, 1979, 726.

8 Vladimir D. Degan, "Création et disparition de l'Etat (à la lumière du démembrement de trois fédérations multiethniques en Europe)", *Rec. des cours*, v. 279, 1999 (hereinafter "Degan") 300.

9 The concept of an "internationally wrongful act" is further explained: Part 1, Section 4.4.

10 Art. 2(1)e), 1978 *Vienna Convention* defines the "date of the succession of States" as "the date upon which the successor State replaced the predecessor State in the responsibility for the international relations of the territory to which the succession of States relates".

11 Art. 2(1)c), 1978 *Vienna Convention* defines the "predecessor State" as "the State which has been replaced by another State on the occurrence of a succession of States".

predecessor State is the creditor of the *right to reparation* against the State responsible for the commission of the internationally wrongful act. The question at the heart of the present study is what happens in the context of a succession of States to the *rights and obligations* arising from an internationally wrongful act committed before the date of succession. In other words, what happens to those rights and obligations *after* that date.

There are essentially two questions which arise from the commission of an internationally wrongful act in the context of succession of States:

(a) Which of the predecessor State or the successor State(s)[12] should be held responsible for the obligations arising from an internationally wrongful act committed by the predecessor State *against a third State*? In other words, which of the predecessor State or the successor State(s) is the debtor of the *obligation to repair* towards the injured third State?[13]
(b) Which of the predecessor State or the successor State(s) should have the right to claim reparation as a consequence of an internationally wrongful act committed *by a third State* against the predecessor State? The issue is then, which of the predecessor State or the successor State(s) is the creditor of the *right to reparation* against the third State?[14]

The answers to these two questions revolve around the other essential question whether or not international law allows for the "transfer" from the predecessor State to the successor State(s) of the rights and the obligations arising from an internationally wrongful act committed before the date of succession.[15] Here again this issue is twofold:

12 Art. 2(1)d), 1978 *Vienna Convention* defines the "successor State" as "the State which has replaced another State on the occurrence of a succession of States".

13 This is what Brigitte Stern, "Responsabilité internationale et succession d'Etats", in: Laurence Boisson de Chazournes & Vera Gowlland-Debbas (eds), *The International Legal System in Quest of Equity and Universality. Liber amicorum Georges Abi-Saab* (M. Nijhoff 2001) 327–355 (hereinafter "Stern, Responsabilité") 335, refers to as "la responsabilité internationale active".

14 The "responsabilité internationale passive" according to Stern, ibid 353.

15 The concept of the "transfer" of obligations arising from the commission of internationally wrongful acts is expressed in scholarship in different ways. Thus, Jean Philippe Monnier, "La succession d'Etats en matière de responsabilité internationale", 8 *AFDI* 1962 (hereinafter "Monnier") 66, speaks of "droits et obligations dérivant de la responsabilité internationale". Stern, Responsabilité, 338, refers to the "transmission des conséquences de la responsabilité". In *Sentence arbitrale en date des 24/27 juillet 1956 rendue par le Tribunal d'arbitrage constitué en vertu du Compromis signé à Paris le 15 juillet 1932 entre*

(a) Whenever an internationally wrongful act is committed by the predecessor State *against a third State,* can the *obligation to repair*, for which the predecessor State is the debtor before the date of succession, be "transferred" to the successor State(s)?[16]

(b) Whenever an internationally wrongful act is committed *by a third State* against the predecessor State, can the *right to reparation*, for which the predecessor State is the creditor before the date of succession, be "transferred" to the successor State(s)?[17]

In the words of Crawford, "the standard answer to this question is no".[18] This is, at least, the answer which was typically given for decades. There is one essential point that is the object of much controversy and misunderstanding in scholarship and which needs to be mentioned at this early juncture. This study does not seek to address the question whether or not the successor State(s) should be "*responsible*" for internationally wrongful acts committed by the predecessor State before the date of succession. As a matter of principle, the successor State(s) cannot be *liable for* internationally wrongful acts committed by *another State* (the predecessor State).[19] The issue central to the present

la France et la Grèce, UNRIAA v. 12, 155 (hereinafter "*Lighthouse Arbitration* case") 197, the Arbitral Tribunal used the concept of "transmission of responsibility". Michael John Volkovitsch, "Righting Wrongs: Toward a New Theory of State Succession to Responsibility for International Delicts", 92(8) *Colum. L.Rev.* 1992 (hereinafter "Volkovitsch") 2173, uses the concept of "transfer".

16 In the words of Monnier, 67: "L'Etat successeur assume-t-il l'*obligation* de réparer qui incombait à l'Etat prédécesseur, auteur de la violation de la norme internationale?" (emphasis in the original). Hazem M. Atlam, *Succession d'Etats et continuité en matière de responsabilité internationale*, Thesis, Université d'Aix-Marseille (France), 1986 (hereinafter "Atlam") 24, indicates "quel serait le sort des obligations internationales engendrées par une action de responsabilité internationale dirigée contre l'Etat prédécesseur".

17 Monnier, 67 ("[l]'Etat successeur peut-il faire valoir contre l'Etat à qui est imputé l'acte illicite le *droit* qu'avait l'Etat prédécesseur, lésé par cet acte de demander réparation?" emphasis in the original); Atlam, 24 ("quel serait le sort des droits de réclamations reconnus à l'Etat prédécesseur à raison d'un fait internationalement illicite mettant en cause la responsabilité internationale d'un autre sujet tiers de l'ordre juridique international?").

18 J. Crawford, *State Responsibility: The General Part* (CUP 2013) (hereinafter "Crawford, State Responsibility") 435.

19 Grega Pajnkihar, *State Succession to Responsibility for Internationally Wrongful Acts* (Brill 2023) (hereinafter "Pajnkihar") 298: "In this way, the IDI and the ILC effectively circumvented the first provision of the ARSIWA, according to which "[e] very internationally wrongful act of a State entails the international responsibility of *that* State." The wrongdoing State remains internationally responsible because international responsibility stays with it even after the date of succession; only the rights and obligation are succeeded to".

analysis is whether obligations (as well as rights) *arising from* the commission of an internationally wrongful act may (in some circumstances) be "transferred" to the successor State(s). In other words, the issue is not one of transfer of *responsibility* for internationally wrongful acts *per se*, but of transfer of the *consequences* of international responsibility (i.e. international rights and obligations) *arising from* the commission of such acts. The same approach has also been adopted by both the work of the Institute and the ILC[20] and many writers since then.[21] These are two fundamentally different questions which have often not been treated as such in scholarship. The failure to make this essential distinction blurs the analysis by many authors of the issue. It should be noted that the expression State succession to "international responsibility" will nevertheless be used throughout this study to facilitate the reading.

Part 2 of the present study deals with the question of succession of States to the *obligation to repair*, while Part 3 will address the other issue of succession of States to the *right to reparation*. Part 1 is a general introduction to this study.

2 The Objective of This Study

The aim of the present study is to provide a general framework of analysis of the issue of State succession to international responsibility. The intention is, however, not to advance any *general theory* which will encompass this question entirely. The development of such a *general theory*, as in any other areas of succession of States, would be both uncertain and unsatisfactory.[22] This is clearly expressed by the Arbitral Tribunal in the *Lighthouse Arbitration* case:

20 ILC, "First Report on Succession of States in Respect of State Responsibility", Special Rapporteur Pavel Šturma, 69th sess., 31 May 2017, A/CN.4/708 (hereinafter "ILC Special Rapporteur Šturma, First Report, 2017"), para 33: the text "does not envisage the succession of States in respect of State responsibility as a transfer of the responsibility as such but as a transfer of rights and obligations arising from international responsibility of a (predecessor) State". On this point, see: Institute of International Law, "Final Report" on "State Succession in Matters of State Responsibility", Rapporteur Marcelo G. Kohen, 28 June 2015, para 31, 76 *Annuaire IDI* 2015 511ff (hereinafter "IIL, Final Report, Kohen").

21 Crawford, State Responsibility, 439; Tom Ruy & Tomas Baecke, "Haunted by The Past? Belgium's international responsibility for the atrocities of the Congo Free State and the question of State succession in matters of international responsibility", *Grili Working Paper* No. 6 (also in: *RBDI* 2020, 477) (hereinafter "Ruy & Baecke"), 21; Ana Paola Vergara Lamadrid, *La obligación de reparar en el marco de una sucesión de Estados*, Thesis, Pontificia Universidad Católica Del Perú, Lima, 2022, 223 p (hereinafter "Vergara Lamadrid"); Pajnkihar, 298.

22 P.M. Eisemann, "Rapport du Directeur de la section de langue française du Centre", in: Eisemann & Koskenniemi, 64: "Le phénomène de la succession d'Etats n'est nullement

> [T]he question of the transmission of responsibility in the event of a territorial change presents all the difficulties of a matter which has not yet sufficiently developed to permit solutions which are both certain and applicable equally in all possible cases.[23]
>
> It is impossible to formulate a general, identical solution for every imaginable hypothesis of territorial succession, and any attempt to formulate such a solution must necessarily fail in view of the extreme diversity of cases of this kind.[24]

In clear, the present study does not intend to build a strict and self-contained general theory either *in favour* of or *against* the *automatic transfer* of the right to reparation and the obligation to repair from the predecessor State to the successor State(s). Such generalisation is impossible to make, and any attempt in that direction is bound to be inconsistent with the much more complex reality of the issue. This point is supported in scholarship.[25] The 2015 IIL Resolution also discarded the application of a general and an all-encompassing rule of "non-succession". As noted by Rapporteur Kohen in his Final Report, "the purpose of ensuring that obligations stemming from the commission of internationally wrongful acts must be carried out even in cases of State succession must not lead to the adoption of an opposite, general rule of succession to these obligations in all cases".[26] In other words, the Institute did not support the opposite rule of automatic succession whereby the successor State *always* takes over the consequences of wrongful acts committed by the predecessor State. The same approach was adopted by ILC Special Rapporteur Šturma, indicating that "he does not suggest replacing one highly general theory of non-succession by another similar theory in favour of succession", adding that

---

rebelle au droit mais il conduit naturellement vers des solutions spécifiques adaptées à la variété des situations plutôt que vers l'application automatique de règles générales".

23 *Lighthouse Arbitration* case, 23 *ILR* 1956, 91. J.H.W. Verzijl, *International Law in Historical Perspective*, v. VII (A.W. Sijthoff 1974) (hereinafter "Verzijl") 223, who was acting as President of the Arbitral Tribunal in the *Lighthouse Arbitration* case, expressed the same opinion in subsequent writings.

24 Ibid.

25 This is, for instance, the position of D.P. O'Connell, *State Succession in Municipal Law and International Law*, v. I (CUP 1967) 482–493 (hereinafter "O'Connell, State Succession, v. I"), 486, for whom "there is no universal criterion for distinguishing claims which may be made against the successor State from those which may not". Similarly, according to Volkovitsch, 2198–2199, the "application of any single, rigid rule in every possible circumstance is doomed to produce results that are at times inherently inequitable and ultimately untenable". The same view is held by Atlam, 15, 235–236.

26 IIL, Final Report, Kohen, 534.

"instead, a more flexible and realistic approach is needed".[27] As further examined below, this issue would become highly contentious during the work of the ILC.

Again, quoting the Arbitral Tribunal in the *Lighthouse Arbitration* case:

> It is no less unjustifiable to admit the principle of transmission as a general rule than to deny it. It is rather and essentially a question of a kind the answer to which depends on a multitude of concrete factors.[28]

Indeed, many different factors must be taken into account in order to determine whether the transfer of any rights and obligations arising from the commission of an internationally wrongful act is possible under contemporary international law.

The analysis of the relevant State practice and international (and municipal) case law will be based on the essential distinction between the *different types* of succession of States (i.e. separation, the creation of "Newly Independent States", dissolution of State, unification of States, integration of State and cession and transfer of territory). The basic assumption is that one solution to the question of State succession to rights and obligations arising from the commission of internationally wrongful acts which may very well be appropriate for one type of succession of States may, however, not be adapted to another. This approach has since then been endorsed by writers.[29] It was also adopted by ILC Special Rapporteur Šturma: "at best, it is possible to conclude that it was succession in certain cases" and that "the transfer or not of obligations or rights arising from State responsibility in specific kinds of succession needs to be proved on a case-by-case basis".[30] The starting point for both the ILC and

---

27 ILC Special Rapporteur Šturma, Second Report, 2018, para 16. See also, ILC Special Rapporteur Šturma, First Report, 2017, para 83; ILC, "Third Report on Succession of States in Respect of State Responsibility", Special Rapporteur Pavel Šturma, 71th sess., 2 May 2019, A/CN.4/731 (hereinafter "ILC Special Rapporteur Šturma, Third Report, 2019") para 35 ("The approach of the Special Rapporteur to the topic excludes both the (automatic) extinction of responsibility and the automatic transfer of responsibility in cases of succession of States").

28 *Lighthouse Arbitration* case, 23 *ILR* 1956, 91. See also: Verzijl, 223; Atlam, 239.

29 M.G. Kohen, "Succession of States in the Field of International Responsibility: The Case for Codification", in: M.G. Kohen et al. (eds), *Perspectives of International Law in the 21st Century. Liber amicorum Professor Christian Dominicé in Honour of His 80th Birthday* (Martinus Nijhoff 2011) (hereinafter "Kohen, Succession of States") 168.

30 ILC Special Rapporteur Šturma, First Report, 2017, para 83. See also, ILC Special Rapporteur Šturma, Second Report, 2018, para 16: "the outcome might well be a confirmation of

the IIL[31] was that the solution adopted for one specific type of succession may very well not be appropriate for other instances of succession.[32] I will examine State practice and international case law to determine whether there exists any set of rules and principles for each different type of succession of States. Both the ILC and the Institute also examined six types of succession separately.[33]

Another important goal of the present study is to determine the *factors and circumstances* (other than the different types of succession of States) used in State practice and international case law, and referred to in scholarship, to justify the transfer of the obligation to repair and of the right to reparation from the predecessor State to the successor State(s). As previously observed, there is no *general solution* which may resolve *all questions* in the context of State succession to international responsibility. The basic assumption is that *specific problems* of State succession to rights and obligations will indeed require *specific solutions*. The aim of the present study is therefore to determine whether there exists any such set of *specific rules and principles* for some of these *specific problems*. This approach has since then been endorsed by many writers.[34] Similarly, the Institute's Resolution also considered several different factors and circumstances (including the "organ" and "direct link" elements, further discussed below) to determine whether there should be succession to obligations and rights.

3 Relevance of This Study When I Wrote the First Edition of This Book

The need for a comprehensive survey of the issue of succession of States to international responsibility arises from the fact that this topic had, until recently, not been the object of any general study by the ILC or by any international

non-succession in certain legal relations arising from State responsibility and a formulation of special rules (or possible exceptions) on succession in others". See also: ibid, paras 16, 167.

31 Kohen & Dumberry, 15.

32 See, for instance, ILC Special Rapporteur Šturma, First Report, 2017, para 84.

33 The structure adopted by the Institute's Resolution is however different insofar as it contains a provision for each six categories of State succession (Articles 11 to 16), each dealing with both questions of succession to rights and obligations. The ILC Guidelines examine the question of succession to rights and obligations separately.

34 Kohen, Succession of States, 168; A. Kaplane, "Succession of States in Respect of State Responsibility: Towards Yet Another Vienna Convention?", *Riga Graduate School of Law Research Papers* No. 23, 2020 (hereinafter "Kaplane") 37.

law scientific institution. At the time when I wrote the first edition of this book (2007), the topic had also only rarely been addressed in scholarship. At the time, no comprehensive survey of State practice and international (and municipal) case law had been published.

3.1 *The Question Had Never Been Addressed by the ILC or by Any International Law Scientific Institution*

Until recently, the ILC had never dealt with the question of succession of States to international responsibility.[35] The work of the ILC on the codification of questions of State succession first started in 1963. Interestingly, at that time, the issue of State responsibility for "torts" was included by Lachs as one of the topics for discussion.[36] However, when in 1967 the work of codification of the Commission was further defined, the topic was left aside.[37]

Thus, at that time three different areas of research were proposed.[38] The first one was the question of State succession in respect of treaties, which eventually led to the adoption of the 1978 *Vienna Convention on Succession of States in Respect of Treaties*.[39] Article 39 of this Convention specifically indicates that the question of succession of States to responsibility is reserved.[40] The second area of research to be undertaken by the ILC was State succession in respect

35 See, comments by Wladyslaw Czaplinski, "State Succession and State Responsibility", 28 *Canadian YIL* 1990 (hereinafter "Czaplinski") 353–355.

36 ILC, "Report by Mr Manfred Lachs, Chairman of the Sub-Committee on Succession of States and Governments", A/CN.4/160, ILC Report, A/5509 (A/18/9), 1963, annex II, ch. IV(B), para 56, *Yearbook ILC*, 1963, v. II, 261 (see in particular Annex II: Memoranda submitted by members of the Sub-Committee, "Delimitation of the Scope of Succession of States and Governments" by T.O. Elias, 282).

37 The reason given was that the topic of "torts" was one of municipal law rather than international law: ILC, "Report by Mr Roberto Ago, Chairman of the Sub-Committee on State Responsibility", A/CN.4/152, ILC Report A/5509 (A/18/9), 1963, annex I, chp. IV, paras 51–55, *Yearbook ILC*, 1963, v. II, 187, 287, para 10.

38 ILC Report, 19th sess. 1967, A/6709/Rev.1 (A/22/9), 1967, chp. III(A)(1), paras 36–41, *Yearbook ILC*, 1967, v. II. The ILC appointed Sir Humphrey Waldock as Special Rapporteur to deal with State succession in respect of treaties and Mr Mohammed Bedjaoui as Special Rapporteur on the topic of succession in respect of rights and duties resulting from sources other than treaties.

39 1978 *Vienna Convention*.

40 Art. 39 reads as follows: "The provisions of the present Convention shall not prejudge any question that may arise in regard to the effects of a succession of States in respect of a treaty from the international responsibility of a State or from the outbreak of hostilities between States". See, O. Corten, "Article 39", in G. Distefano, G. Gaggioli & A. Hêche (eds), *La Convention de Vienne de 1978 sur la succession d'État en matière de traités: Commentaire article par article et études thématiques*, v. 2 (Bruylant 2015) 1306ff.

to membership in international organisations, which was never the object of a convention. Finally, the ILC decided to address another issue generally defined as "succession of States in respect of matters other than treaties". Special Rapporteur Bedjaoui later decided to concentrate the effort of the ILC on the question of succession to State property, archives and debts, which led to the adoption of the 1983 *Vienna Convention on Succession of States in Respect of State Property, Archives and Debts*.[41] Subsequently, the issue of nationality was the object of the work of the ILC and led to the adoption of a Declaration.[42] The issue of State succession with respect to State responsibility was therefore left aside by the ILC. Only very sporadic mention of the question is found in the codification work of the ILC on State succession.[43]

Similarly, the work of the ILC on State responsibility for internationally wrongful acts refrained from addressing the question of State succession to the consequences arising from the commission of internationally wrongful acts. The applicability of these Articles in situations of State succession essentially rests on the consequences to a State in term of international responsibility *after* the date of succession. Yet, some situations where internationally wrongful acts are committed *before* the date of succession were, in fact, addressed by the Articles.[44] For instance, internationally wrongful acts committed by an "insurrectional movement" (or other "movement") leading to the subsequent creation of a new State (Article 10(2)),[45] and internationally wrongful acts having a continuing character occurring both before and after the date of

41 1983 *Vienna Convention*.

42 *Draft Articles on Nationality*.

43 See, for instance: ILC Report, 29th sess. A/32/10, 1977, chp. III, paras 32–60, ("Summary Records of the 1421st Meeting"), *Yearbook ILC*, 1977, v. I, 27–28; ILC, "Sixth Report on Succession of States in Respect of Matters Other than Treaties", Mohammed Bedjaoui, Special Rapporteur, 25th Session, 1973, A/CN.4/267, ILC Report, A/9090/Rev.1 (A/28/10), 1973, chp. III(A)(1)(c), paras 71–77, *Yearbook ILC*, 1973, v. II, 3, 19.

44 Kaplane, 41, referring to two provisions (Arts 10 and 14) and indicating that "the ARSIWA are not completely silent on succession" and that "there are possibilities to hold the successor state accountable under the existing legal rules".

45 This principle is examined in detail below: Part 2, Chapter 3, Section 6. However, the work of the ILC does not envisage the devolution of responsibility from the successful rebels to the new State based on the mechanism of succession of States but rather, from the perspective of State responsibility: "[These wrongful] acts committed by agents of the insurrectional movement before the movement takes power are attributed to the state because there is continuity between the apparatus of the insurrectional movement and the new governmental apparatus of the state, *not a succession of the state as one subject of international law to the insurrectional movement as another*" (emphasis added) (ILC Report, 27th sess. 1975, A/10010/Rev.1, *Yearbook ILC*, 1975, v. II, 47, 101, para 8).

succession (Article 14(2)).[46] Apart from these two questions, further examined below, the work of the ILC contains only a few references to the issue of State succession to international responsibility.[47] One such reference is found in the ILC's 2001 Commentaries by Special Rapporteur Crawford:

> In the context of State succession, it is unclear whether a new State succeeds to any State responsibility of the predecessor State with respect to its territory.[48]

It is precisely because this issue was, in the words of Special Rapporteur Crawford, "unclear" that the present study was relevant in 2007. It should be added, as further discussed below, that in his subsequent book, Crawford analysed the issue thoroughly.[49]

In 2017, the ILC placed the topic "Succession of States in respect of State responsibility" on its current work programme and appointed Pavel Šturma as Special Rapporteur. ILC Special Rapporteur Šturma issued five Reports.[50] As further explained below, while he had all along favoured draft articles with commentaries,[51] he was later "convinced" "to propose a change of form" to "draft guidelines".[52] In 2022, the ILC provisionally adopted, with commentaries, draft guidelines 1 to 15 bis which had been provisionally adopted by the Drafting Committee in previous sessions. Only one provision (guideline 15ter) had not been approved.[53] The mandate of Special Rapporteur Šturma ended in

46 IIL, Final Report, Kohen, 8.

47 But, as noted by IIL, ibid 8, the work of the ILC on diplomatic protection does cover one question relevant to this study: the exercise of diplomatic protection in relation to acts committed against the predecessor State. The question is examined below in detail: Part 3, Ch. 6.

48 ILC, Commentaries, State Responsibility, 2001, 119, para 3.

49 Crawford, State Responsibility, 447ff.

50 ILC Special Rapporteur Šturma, First Report, 2017; ILC Special Rapporteur Šturma, Second Report, 2018; ILC Special Rapporteur Šturma, Third Report, 2019; ILC, "Fourth Report on Succession of States in Respect of State Responsibility", Special Rapporteur Pavel Šturma, 72nd sess., 7 March 2020, A/CN.4/743 (hereinafter "ILC Special Rapporteur Šturma, Fourth Report, 2020"); ILC, "Fifth Report on Succession of States in Respect of State Responsibility", Special Rapporteur Pavel Šturma, 73rd sess., 1 April 2022, A/CN.4/751 ("ILC Special Rapporteur Šturma, Fifth Report, 2022").

51 ILC Special Rapporteur Šturma, First Report, 2017, para 28.

52 ILC, "Provisional Summary Record of the 3583rd Meeting", 73rd sess., 17 May 2022, A/CN.4/SR.3583.

53 Guideline 15 *ter* deals with restitution, compensation and satisfaction. This provision is outside the scope of this book. For a detailed analysis, see, ILC Special Rapporteur Šturma, Fourth Report, 2020; Pajnkihar, 299ff., 325ff.

2022. At its 74th session (2023), the ILC decided to establish a Working Group with August Reinisch as Chair. Many options were apparently on the table, including "continue developing a text in the Drafting Committee and proceed to conclude the first reading of the draft guidelines".[54] At the end, the Working Group decided to recommend that the Commission "continue its consideration of the topic, but not proceed with the appointment of a new Special Rapporteur" and that "a decision on such a way forward would be taken" at the next session on the basis of a working paper prepared by the Chair.[55] A final decision was taken at the 75th session (2024). The Working Group recommended drafting a report that "would contain a summary of the difficulties that the Commission would face if it were to continue its work on the topic and explain the reasons for the discontinuance of such work" (ILC, "Report of the Working Group", 12 July 2024, A/CN.4/L.1003, para. 23). In other words, the ILC will not formally adopt the "Guidelines".

International organisations[56] and academic institutions such as the Institute and the ILA have addressed many issues of State succession but had, until recently, never dealt specifically with the question of State succession to responsibility.[57] However, the Institute decided at its 2003 Bruges session that the question of "State Succession in matters of State Responsibility" would be the object of a study by a Commission set up to examine the question (the 14th Commission).[58] The "Final Report" by Rapporteur Marcelo Kohen was issued on 28 June 2015,[59] and the Institute adopted the Resolution that same year (the "Institute's Resolution").[60] In 2019, this book's author and Marcelo Kohen

54 ILC Report, 74th sess., 2023, A/78/10, chap. IX, paras 231ff, at para 237.

55 Ibid, paras 240–243.

56 For instance, no mention is made of the problem of succession of States to responsibility in the pilot project of the Council of Europe: Jan Klappers (ed), *State Practice Regarding State Succession and Issues of Recognition* (Kluwer 1999) 147–153.

57 For instance, see IIL, "Resolution on State Succession in Matters of Property and Debts", sess. Vancouver, 2001, 69 *Annuaire. IDI*, 2000–2001 (hereinafter "IIL, State Succession in Matters of Property, 2001") 713ff. See also, IIL, "Les effets des changements territoriaux sur les droits patrimoniaux", 44–II *Annuaire IDI* 1952, 471. See also, the work of the ILA by the Committee on "Aspects of the Law of State Succession".

58 71(2) *Annuaire IDI*, 59 & 354. See the comments by V.-D. Degan, 65 & 73, and S. Torres Bernardez, 66, both expressing great reservation as to whether this issue should be the object of a study by the Institute. On the contrary, J. Salmon, 73, who was at the origin of the proposition to investigate this question, was of the view that the topic should be studied because it has rarely been addressed in case law and never been dealt with by the ILC. The proposition to create a Commission to study this topic was finally adopted (see ibid 74) with 35 votes in favour, 2 against and 5 abstentions.

59 IIL, Final Report, Kohen.

60 IIL, Resolution 2015.

published an article-by-article commentary explaining the scope and content of that resolution.[61]

3.2 *The Doctrinal Analysis Was Very Limited and Generally Unsatisfactory*

When I wrote the first edition of this book, very few scholars had directly and thoroughly tackled the issue. Thus, at the time no book had been published on the issue, and only five articles,[62] one doctoral thesis[63] and one master's thesis[64] had directly focused on this question. Since then, the question has been addressed not only by the Institute and the ILC but by several writers in articles,[65] a few thesis[66] and one book published in 2023.[67] In 2007, only a

61 Kohen & Dumberry.

62 Stern, Responsabilité, 327–355; Cecil J.B. Hurst, "State Succession in Matters of Tort", 5 *British YIL* 1924 (hereinafter "Hurst") 163–178; Monnier, 65–90; Czaplinski, 339–359; Volkovitsch, 2162–2214. See also: Dimitrijević Duško, "Sukcesija država u odnosu na deliktnu odgovornost" (in Serbian, State Succession to International Responsibility), 87 (2–3) *Arhiv za pravne i društvene nauke*, 2001, 187–214.

63 Atlam.

64 Miriam Peterschmitt, *La succession d'Etats et la responsabilité internationale pour fait illicite*, Mémoire de DES, Université de Genève/Institut Universitaire de hautes études internationales, 2001, 87 pp (hereinafter "Peterschmitt").

65 V. Mikulka, "State Succession and Responsibility", in: J. Crawford, A. Pellet & S. Olleson (eds), *The Law of International Responsibility* (OUP 2010) 291–296 (hereinafter "Mikulka, State Succession"); V. Mikulka, "Succession of States in Respect of Rights of an Injured State", ibid 965–967; Kohen, Succession of States, 161–174; Pavel Šturma, "State Succession in Respect of International Responsibility", 48 *George Wash. ILR* 2016, 653–678 (hereinafter "Šturma, State Succession"); P. Dumberry & M. Kohen, "State Succession and State Responsibility in the context of Investor-State Dispute Settlement", 37(1–2) *ICSID Rev.* 2022, 85–100; I. Reyes Gajardo, "State Succession in Regard to State Responsibility: Succession to Obligations Where the Predecessor State Ceases to Exist", 10(19) *Rev. Tribuna Internacional* 2021, 71–87 (hereinafter "Reyes Gajardo"); E. Sargsyan, "Issues of State Responsibility for Committing an Internationally Wrongful Act by the Predecessor State", 2(2) *Russian JCL* 2014, 80–90; Leonardo Flach Aurvalle & Isadora Brondani, "State Succession to International Responsibility", 8 *UFRGS Model United Nations*, 2021, 449–489; Mohsen Abdolahi & Mona Karbalaye Amini, "The Inadequacy of the doctrine of Non-Succession in respect of the International Responsibility of States", 52(1) *Public Law Studies Quarterly*, 2022, 121–143. M.V. Keshner, "Development of the Concept of State Responsibility in Succession Situations in the Light of Draft Articles of the UN International Law Commission", 4 *Moscow JIL* 2019, 114–132; Ana Paola Vergara Lamadrid, "Nada se destruye, todo se transforma: la exigibilidad de la obligacion de reparar en el marco de una sucesion de Estados", 40 *Agenda Internacional* 2022, 89–110.

66 Vergara Lamadrid, 240 p; Kaplane, 44 p.

67 Pajnkihar.

handful of general international law textbooks were properly addressing this issue,[68] while most of them simply devoted a few lines to it.[69]

The Arbitral Tribunal in the *Lighthouse Arbitration* case stressed the unsatisfactory nature of the theoretical analysis of this issue, speaking of the "chaotic state of authoritative writings".[70] In 2007, I argued that the doctrinal analysis suffered from two serious shortcomings.

The first shortcoming concerned the limited investigation of State practice and international and municipal case law. The very few scholars who have tackled the issue at the heart of the present study usually refer to only three international arbitral decisions[71] and a very limited number of municipal law cases. The research that I conducted in 2007 led to the "discovery" (or rather the rediscovery) of a great number of other relevant international arbitration cases and municipal law decisions which had either been previously overlooked in scholarship or simply never been referred to. Similarly, most of the examples of State practice examined in the present study had never been analysed in scholarship (in the context of State succession to international responsibility). Importantly, the recent work of both the Institute and the ILC have examined State practice in detail. For instance, the ILC Secretariat published a comprehensive and very useful survey of agreements dealing with succession to responsibility.[72]

The second shortcoming concerned methodology. It is generally agreed in scholarship and by international arbitration tribunals that State practice and international and municipal case law are confused and contradictory.[73] For

68 See, for instance: O'Connell, State Succession, v. I, 482–493; Verzijl, 219–228; Charles Rousseau, *Droit international public*, v. III (Sirey 1977) (hereinafter "Rousseau") 504–511.

69 A complete list of writers who briefly mention the issue is provided in Part 2, Chapter 1, Section 2.1.

70 *Lighthouse Arbitration* case, 23 *ILR* 1956, 91.

71 Ibid 155; *R.E. Brown* (US v. Great Britain), Award, 23 November 1923, *UNRIAA* v. 6, 129 (hereinafter "*R.E. Brown* case"); *F.H. Redward and Others* (Great Britain v. US), Award, 10 November 1925, *UNRIAA* v. 6, 158 (hereinafter "*Hawaiian Claims* case"), 157.

72 ILC, "Succession of States in respect of State responsibility, Information on treaties which may be of relevance to the future work of the Commission on the topic", Memorandum by the Secretariat, A/CN.4/730*, 20 March 2019.

73 This assessment is made by the Arbitral Tribunal in the *Lighthouse Arbitration* case, 23 *ILR* 1956, 91: "The variety of possible hypotheses of territorial succession, the political considerations which often govern the solution of juridical problems relative thereto, and the rarity of arbitral or judicial decisions resolving the problem in a really clear and unequivocal manner after convincing argument heard, explain both the vagaries of international practice and the chaotic state of authoritative writings". See also, Volkovitsch, 2172: "The relative lack of attention is a scattered, often confused, and sometimes contradictory jurisprudence from which it is extremely difficult to extract a coherent doctrine".

instance, O'Connell concluded that it is "exasperating not to be able to propose a synthetic structure of State succession doctrine which can accommodate the problem of torts".[74] This may be a consequence of the methodology generally used to conduct the investigation. Thus, back in 2007 scholars did not usually conduct their analysis based on the two fundamental assumptions adopted in the present study.[75]

First, until recently the doctrinal analysis of both State practice and international and municipal case law was generally not conducted in the light of the essential distinction between different *types* of succession of States. Most authors did not seem to base their research on the fundamental assumption that for each type of State succession there will exist different specific solutions to the issue of succession to responsibility. In my view, no general principle can apply indiscriminately to all types of succession of States. Second, another shortcoming of the doctrinal analysis was the fact that it did not base its research on another fundamental assumption (which is adopted in the present study): solutions to questions of State succession to responsibility will largely depend on a variety of factors and circumstances. The assumption adopted in this book is that *specific problems* of State succession will require *specific solutions*. As mentioned above, the same approach has since then been adopted by both the Institute and the ILC as well as by recent scholarship.[76]

The present study shows that, based on these two fundamental assumptions, State practice and international case law is not chaotic and confused. Quite the contrary, the present study demonstrates the existence of some basic rules and principles depending on the different types of succession of States and different circumstances.

74 O'Connell, Recent Problems, 164.

75 This comment does *not* apply to the research conducted at the time by Stern, Peterschmitt and Atlam.

76 For instance, ILC Special Rapporteur Šturma, First Report, 2017, para 36 (indicating that the work of the ILC "calls for flexibility to allow for the tailoring of different solutions to different situations"); Crawford, State Responsibility, 447–8 ("The most expansive analysis of the state practice surrounding succession to responsibility has been undertaken by Dumberry, who concludes that aside from specific situations where the successor has agreed to answer for the delicts of the predecessor, the landscape produced by state practice reflects the position taken in Lighthouses Arbitration, namely 'the solution adopted in State practice (…) essentially depends on the different types of mechanism of succession of States involved'", quoting my 2007 book); Vergara Lamadrid, 224.

4 Scope of This Study

At this juncture, it is important to define the actual scope of the present study. In doing so, I will determine some aspects of the issue which will not be covered by this study.

4.1 *Meaning of State Succession*

Situations of State succession need to be clearly distinguished from other situations where there is a *continuity* of State.[77] Thus, a State may be affected by important changes, but its legal identity can nevertheless remain intact.[78] One example is a change of government, which is *not* to be considered an example of succession. The present study does *not* deal with cases where the State remains identical and where no question or debate arises as to the continuity of its rights and obligations. While some authors[79] have downplayed, the importance of distinguishing between identity/continuity and State succession, it remains essential. During the recent work of the ILC, some States seem to have doubted the relevance of this distinction.[80] The distinction between cases of dissolution and separation is clear on paper and seems easily assessable. Yet,

77 A. Zimmermann, "Continuity of States", *Max Planck Encyclopedia of Public International Law* (OUP online 2006), para 6 ("As a matter of principle, State continuity and State succession are mutually exclusive concepts"). On these concepts, see: Anne Østrup, "Conceptions of State Identity and Continuity in Contemporary International Legal Scholarship", *Legal Studies Research Paper Series* (U. Copenhagen) no. 2016–15.

78 On the concept of "identity" of State, see: Krystyna Marek, *Identity and Continuity of States in Public International Law* (Droz 1968) (hereinafter "Marek"); G. Cansacchi, "Identité et continuité des sujets de droit international", *Rec. des cours*, v. 130(1) 1970 1–94; Matthew C.R. Craven, "The Problem of State Succession and the Identity of States under International Law", 9(1) *EJIL* 1998, 142–163; Stern, Succession, 39–87; I. Ziemele, "Is the Distinction between State Continuity and State Succession Reality or Fiction? The Russian Federation, the Federal Republic of Yugoslavia and Germany" 1 *Baltic YIL* 2001, 191, 215.

79 Tai-Heng Cheng, *State Succession and Commercial Obligations* (Transnational 2006) 50.

80 Turkey, letter sent to the UN GA Sixth Commission, Rep. 73rd sess. 2018: "It should be underlined that the continuity and succession of massive political and legal consequences are not definitely extricated from each other in legal terms yet, and are largely intertwined in many aspects. Each case of transition throughout the history emerged as a result of peculiar conditions and turned out contingently, with a lot of varieties from each other by specific political and legal arrangements. The arrangements are far from having commonalities and thus far from being apt so as to be conceptualized. Those terms themselves are not clear-cut enough, doubtful in their legal or political characteristic, as well. Rather, they are still at the level of theoretical debate over political theses". See also, Turkey, ibid, Rep. 76th sess. Oct–Nov. 2021.

the question of the continuity of the international legal personality of a given State involved in an event of succession of States "is often a matter of broader political consideration, rather than that of application of objectively assessable criteria", which "involves a large degree of voluntarism".[81] For instance, non-legal reasons are the primary explanation why other States have accepted Russia's claim to continuity to the USSR, while the FRY's claim to be same State as Yugoslavia was rejected.[82] I have explained elsewhere what are the important criteria which should be examined to determine whether there is State identity or not.[83]

One observation which needs to be made at the outset is that the very term "State succession" is somewhat misleading.[84] In the context of the present study, the term "State succession" makes reference to "the replacement of one State by another in the responsibility for the international relations of territory".[85] Therefore, the term "State succession" should *not* be understood as meaning that the successor State "becomes invested with all the juridical consequences of its predecessor's acts".[86] These two very distinct ideas should not be mixed.[87] Professor Stern rightly distinguishes the first situation as a

81 ILC Special Rapporteur Šturma, Third Report, 2019, para 47.

82 Stern, Succession, 78–79: "Si l'on compare ainsi l'éclatement de l'URSS et celui de la Yougoslavie, il n'y a guère de différences objectives dans le processus de dislocation de l'Etat préexistant. Simplement, les nécessités stratégiques et géopolitiques dans le cas de la Russie, et les prises de position éthiques et juridiques dans le cas de la RFY engagée dans une politique de 'nettoyage ethnique' en Bosnie-Herzégovine, ont conduit la communauté internationale à analyser différemment les deux processus: sécessions des différentes républiques de l'URSS ayant laissé subsister la Russie en tant qu'Etat continuateur; dissolution de la RSFY faisant théoriquement naître des Etats successeurs tous placés sur le même plan par rapport à l'ancien Etat".

83 See, P. Dumberry, *A Guide to State Succession in International Investment Law* (Elgar 2018) 11–25; P. Dumberry, "Is Turkey the "Continuing" State of the Ottoman Empire under International Law?", 59(2) *Netherlands ILR* 2012, 235–262, examining the elements of territory, government, population, a country's name, the concept of the essential portion of a State and recognition.

84 In the words of Mohammed Bedjaoui, "Problèmes récents de succession d'Etats dans les Etats nouveaux", *Rec. des cours*, v. 130, 1970–II (hereinafter "Bedjaoui") 463, the expression State succession "recèle surtout une ambiguïté dans le fond, le terme employé suggérant toujours une *continuité* de situation là où la pratique des Etats enregistre parfois une *rupture*. On entendrait ainsi exprimer certaines réalités par un terme porteur d'un signe contraire" (emphasis in the original).

85 Art. 2(1)a), 1978 *Vienna Convention* and 1983 *Vienna Convention*. The same definition can also be found in Art. 2 of the *Draft Articles on Nationality*.

86 O'Connell, State Succession, v. I, 3.

87 According to Hans Kelsen, "Théorie générale du droit international public. Problèmes choisis", *Rec. des cours*, v. 42, 1932–IV, 314–315: "On entend donc par succession des Etats

"succession in fact" and the second as a "succession in law".[88] Similarly, ILC Special Rapporteur Šturma explained that "the term 'succession' is used both to describe the factual situation of replacement of one State by another on the given territory and the legal regime (legal succession) in a sense of the transfer of rights and obligations from one State to another State, as a result of the territorial change".[89] The Commentary makes it clear that the term "succession of States" is used to refer only to the *factual* situation and that the term "does not imply an automatic transfer of rights or obligations" and that such transfer "is only possible under certain circumstances and according to the rules set forth in the draft articles".[90]

In the course of this study, the term "State succession" will only refer to succession "in fact". I will use words such as "transfer" or "pass" to describe a "succession in law" where the rights and obligations of the predecessor State(s) are taken over by the successor State(s).

4.2 *Classification of the Different Types of Succession of States*

As previously explained, the present study intends to analyse the relevant State practice and case law based on the essential distinction between the *different types* of succession of States. It is thus assumed that specific solutions to the issue of State succession to international responsibility will prevail depending on the different types of succession of States. It is therefore essential to establish at this juncture a classification of the different types and to define them. There is support for the importance of making such distinction between these different types.[91] Both the ILC and the Institute also followed this approach.

---

aussi bien cette succession juridique que constitue la modification territoriale elle-même que la succession juridique qui intervient à la suite de ladite modification. Mais il s'agit là de deux phénomènes distincts". See also: J. Basdevant, *Dictionnaire de la terminologie du droit international* (Sirey 1960), 587; Manlio Udina, "La succession des Etats quant aux obligations internationales autres que les dettes publiques", *Rec. des cours*, v. 44, 1933–II, 679 (hereinafter "Udina").

88 Stern, Succession, 90.

89 ILC Special Rapporteur Šturma, Third Report, 2019, para 28, referring to J. Salmon (ed), *Dictionnaire de droit international public* (Bruylant 2001) 1059.

90 ILC, "Text of the draft guidelines and commentaries thereto provisionally adopted by the Commission at its seventy-third session", ILC Report, 71th sess., 2019, A/74/10, chap. VII (hereinafter "ILC, Commentaries, 2019"), para 118, Art. 2, sub-para 2.

91 Crawford, State Responsibility, 447–8; Kay Hailbronner, "Legal Aspects of the Unification of the Two German States", 2(1) *EJIL* 1991, 33. This is also the view of O'Connell, Recent Problems, 164, who, however, indicates in another publication (D.P. O'Connell, "Reflections on the State Succession Convention", 39(4) *ZaöRV* 1979, 730–731) that the different types of succession of States as established in the Vienna Convention "are sometimes only formally distinguishable" from each other. See also, Vergara Lamadrid, 224. *Contra*: Sir

Such distinction is especially relevant in the context of State succession to responsibility.[92] This is the conclusion reached by the Arbitral Tribunal in the *Lighthouse Arbitration* case.[93] In contrast, the opposite position was taken by the US-Great Britain Arbitral Commission in the *Hawaiian Claims* case.[94]

The first essential distinction concerns the consequences that an event may have *on the predecessor State*. There are cases where the predecessor State will *continue to exist* following the event affecting its territorial integrity and should therefore be considered to be the "continuing" State. The concept of "continuing" State will be used in the present study to refer to such situations. This is the term most often used in scholarship and by the ILC.[95] In the 2007 *Genocide* case between Bosnia-Herzegovina and Serbia-Montenegro, the ICJ used the

---

Robert Jenning & Sir Arthur Watts, *Oppenheim's International Law*, v. I (9th edn, Longman 1996) (hereinafter "Jenning & Watts") 209, for whom these different types of succession of States are not "terms of art with them carrying clearly established legal consequences".

92 This is, for instance, the position of Atlam, 15, 235–236, 268ff; Verzijl, 219–220. Stern, Succession, 110, has some doubts concerning the relevance of the distinction between cases of separation and dissolution but not in the field of succession to responsibility where she believes this difference remains necessary. The position of Volkovitsch is more ambiguous. He first indicates (at 2164) that "the rule to be applied in any particular case may be determined by the kind of transformation that State has experienced, be it separation, merger, or decolonization". However, later in his paper (at 2191–2192) he expresses doubts on any rule which determines an outcome based on a categorisation between different types of succession of States. This is so because he sees the distinction between the different types of succession as "largely formalistic, at once masking the significant similarity between States in different categories and ignoring the substantial diversity of States of any one type". He is also of the view that "it is almost impossible to conceive of all of the possible factual permutations in advance of their occurrence".

93 According to the Arbitral Tribunal in the *Lighthouse Arbitration* case, 23 ILR 1956, 93, these different types of succession of States "cannot but exercise a decisive influence on the solution of the problem of State succession even in cases of delictual obligation". The Tribunal indicated (at 91): "Is it a matter of the complete dismemberment of a pre-existing State, of the secession of a colony or of a part of a State, or is it rather a matter of the merger of two previously independent States, of the incorporation of one State in another? To what point, in the last-mentioned hypothesis, should one, in order to resolve the problem, take into account the more or less close relationship between the incorporating State and the incorporated State, or the voluntary or involuntary nature of their union?".

94 *Hawaiian Claims* case, 158, where the Arbitral Commission concluded that there was no "valid reason" to distinguish between these different types of succession of States, since in all cases "the legal unit which did the wrong no longer exists, and legal liability for the wrong has been extinguished with it".

95 See, e.g. ILC Special Rapporteur Šturma, First Report, 2017, para 51; ILC Special Rapporteur Šturma, Second Report, 2018, paras 90, 87 (speaking of the "question whether Russia should be considered as the continuing State (or 'continuator') of the USSR").

term "continuator" State.[96] The work of the Institute also refers to this term.[97] Both terms have the exact same meaning. On the contrary, in other cases the predecessor State will *cease to exist*. This distinction is recognised in scholarship;[98] it is sometime referred to as "partial" and "total" State succession.[99] The second essential distinction between different types of succession of States concerns the question whether or not the events affecting the territorial integrity of the predecessor State lead to the *creation of a new State*.[100] These two fundamental distinctions are further examined in the following paragraphs.

When the predecessor State *ceases to exist* following an event affecting its territorial integrity, there are *three* different scenarios which need to be differentiated (and which will be analysed separately in this study).

Firstly, the extinction of the predecessor State may result in the *creation of one new State*. This is the case of a *unification of States*, whereby (at least) *two* existing States will merge to form a new State. It is different from cases of "union of States" where each State will typically keep its international personality and where no new State emerges.[101] The most recent case of unification is that of Yemen in 1990.[102] Another case, which will often be referred to in this study, is the unification of Egypt and Syria into a single State in 1958 (the United Arab Republic).

Secondly, the extinction of the predecessor State may result in the *creation of many new States* on its original territory. This is the case of *dissolution of*

96 *Application of the Convention on the Prevention and Punishment of the Crime of Genocide (Bosnia and Herzegovina v. Serbia and Montenegro)*, Judgment 26 February 2007, ICJ Rep. 2007, paras 71, 75, 80, 81, 106, 130, 131.

97 IIL, Final Report, Kohen, paras 31, 78–8, 127, etc. But the work of Kohen & Dumberry uses the term "continuing State".

98 Stern, Succession, 111–112; Stern, Responsabilité, 335; Udina, 677–678. Volkovitsch, 2164–2165, refers to this distinction as the most significant one to be made. See also: Degan, 300–301.

99 Jenning & Watts, 209; Yilma Makonnen, "State Succession in Africa: Selected Problems", *Rec. des cours*, v. 200, 1986–V, 102–103; O'Connell, State Succession, v. I, 4.

100 Stern, Succession, 111–112.

101 Cases of union of States are analysis by: Rousseau, v. II, 114–115; Massimo Pilotti, "Les unions d'Etats", *Rec. des cours*, v. 24, 1928–IV, 445–546.

102 The Yemen Arab Republic (North Yemen) and the People's Democratic Republic of Yemen (South Yemen) merged on 22 May 1990 to form a unified Republic of Yemen. Art. 1 of the *Agreement on the Establishment of the Republic of Yemen and the Organisation of the Thirty-Month Interim Period*, 22 April 1990, in force on 21 May 1990, 30 *ILM* 1990, 820, indicates that: "There shall be established between [the two Yemen] ... a full and complete union, based on a merger, in which the international personality of each of them shall be integrated in a single international person called 'the Republic of Yemen'".

State. Modern examples of dissolutions are those of Czechoslovakia and the Socialist Federal Republic of Yugoslavia (SFRY).

Thirdly, the extinction of the predecessor State sometimes results not in the creation of a new State but in the *enlargement of the territory of an existing State*. This is the case of *incorporation* (or "absorption") of State where the territory of a State (the successor State) is enlarged as a result of the integration of the *entirety* of the territory of the predecessor State. There are also very few examples where the extinction of the predecessor State resulted in the enlargement of the territory of not *one* existing State but of *many* States.[103] The most recent example of an incorporation of State is when in 1990 the German Democratic Republic ceased to exist as an independent State and its territory comprising five *Länder* was integrated into the already existing Federal Republic of Germany.

In cases where the predecessor State *continues to exist* following an event affecting its territorial integrity, there are *three* different scenarios which also need to be differentiated (and which will be analysed separately in this study).

Firstly, the event affecting the territorial integrity of the predecessor State may result in the *creation of a new State*. This is the case of separation, where a new State emerges from the break-up of an already existing State which nevertheless continues its existence after the loss of part of its territory. Recent examples include those of Montenegro (2006) and South Sudan (2009). There is some controversy as to the proper terminology that should be used to make reference to this phenomenon and whether the term "secession" should not be used instead.[104] In scholarship, the two terms are sometimes used as distinct concepts describing different situations. Thus, for some writers, the term "secession" should be reserved more specifically to describe instances where the removal of one part of the territory is made *without the consent* of the predecessor State.[105] An example of secession where the predecessor State later

103 This is, for instance, the case of the extinction of Poland in 1775. The former territory of Poland was divided among Austria, Prussia and Russia.

104 Art. 34, 1978 *Vienna Convention* and Art. 17, 1983 *Vienna Convention* use the term "separation". This is also the case of the *Draft Articles on Nationality*.

105 Making such a distinction: Marcelo G. Kohen, "Le problème des frontières en cas de dissolution et de séparation d'Etats: quelles alternatives?", in: Olivier Corten et al., *Démembrement d'Etats et délimitations territoriales: L'uti possidetis en question(s)* (Bruylant 1999) 368–369; Marcelo G. Kohen, "Introduction", in: Marcelo G. Kohen (ed), *Secession: International Law Perspectives* (CUP 2006) 2–3; James Crawford, *The Creation of States in International Law* (Clarendon 1979) 247; James Crawford, "State Practice and International Law in Relation to Secession", *British YIL* 1998, 85. Similarly, O'Connell, State Succession, v. II, 88, speaks of "revolutionary secession" and "evolutionary secession". See also, ILC Special Rapporteur Šturma, First Report, 2017, para 25: "It is still important

recognised the newly created State is that of Bangladesh which separated from Pakistan in 1971 and was recognised by the latter in 1974.[106] Writers use the term "separation" to refer instead to those instances where the removal is *accepted* by the predecessor State.[107] One example is the separation of Singapore from Malaysia in 1965.[108] What matters in the context of this study is that in both cases of "separation" and "secession" result in the *creation of a new State* and the continuity of the existence of the predecessor State. The Institute used the term "separation". While ILC Special Rapporteur Šturma used both expressions as synonymous,[109] Guideline 9 adopted in 2022 refers to "separation".[110] The present study will use the term "separation" in its general sense.

Secondly, there is another type of succession of States which is similar to cases of separation insofar as the events affecting the territorial integrity of the predecessor State results in the creation of a new State while the predecessor State continues to exist. This is the case of the creation of "Newly Independent States" in the context of decolonisation. It is generally admitted that the territory of a colony should not be considered part of the territory of the colonial State administrating it.[111] In that sense, a "Newly Independent State" is a

---

to distinguish between negotiated and contested (revolutionary) secession. Negotiated secession creates better conditions for agreement on all aspects of succession, including in respect of responsibility".

106 Soon after, Bangladesh was admitted to the UN: GA Res. 3203 (1974), 17 September 1974.

107 It should be noted that other writers use the term "separation" in the context of unitary State, while "secession" is used for cases involving federal States. For instance, see: Jacques Brossard & Daniel Turp, *L'accession à la souveraineté et le cas du Québec* (2nd edn, Presse U. Montréal 1995) 94; Daniel Turp, *Le droit de choisir: Essais sur le droit du Québec à disposer de lui-même/The Right to Choose: Essays on Québec's Right of Self-Determination* (Thémis 2001) 22.

108 *Agreement Relating to the Separation of Singapore from Malaysia as an Independent and Sovereign State*, 7 August 1965, 563 *UNTS*, no. 8206, 89.

109 ILC Special Rapporteur Šturma, Second Report, 2018, 21, sect. on "Secession (separation of parts of a State)", and Draft Article 7 entitled "Separation of parts of a State (secession)". See also, ILC Special Rapporteur Šturma, Second Report, 2018, para 79 ("For the purpose of the present topic, there are no different meanings given to these terms. Therefore, they can be used interchangeably").

110 ILC, "Text of the Draft Guidelines and Commentaries", provisionally adopted, 72th session, ILC Report, 2021, A/76/10, 2021, chap. VII (hereinafter "ILC, Commentaries, 2021"), at para 165, Art. 9, sub-para 1, referring to "separation".

111 "Declaration of Principles of International Law Concerning Friendly Relations and Co-Operation Among States in Accordance with the Charter of the United Nations", adopted by UN GA Res. 2625 (XXV), 24 October 1970.

new State which, however, cannot be said to have "seceded" from the colonial power to the extent that its territory was never formally part of it.[112]

There is some controversy as to whether Newly Independent States should at all be viewed as a distinct type of succession of States.[113] Supporters of the distinction rely on the specific circumstances of decolonisation and the fact that different rules of State succession should apply to these States in order for them to freely exercise their right to self-determination and to break the vicious circle of economic domination.[114] The work of the ILC on State succession, including the recent ILC Guidelines adopted in 2023,[115] has recognised the specificity of this category of State succession.[116] Both Vienna Conventions on matters of State succession have thus adopted different rules applicable to Newly Independent States.[117] The ILC Draft Articles on nationality in relation

112 Zidane Meriboute, *La codification de la succession d'États aux traités: décolonisation, sécession, unification* (PUF 1984) 174.

113 Some writers do not view Newly Independent States as a distinct category: Degan, 298–299. See also: *Restatement (Third), Foreign Relations Law of the United States*, v. I (American Law Inst. 1987) § 210, Rep. notes no. 4 (at 113).

114 See, for instance, the position held by Yilma Makonnen, "State Succession in Africa: Selected Problems", *Rec. des cours*, v. 200, 1986–V, 130–131, for whom "the guiding principles governing the consequences of State succession are the complete elimination of 'colonialism' in all form and manifestation and creating the conditions for the realization of the right to self-determination by the newly independent States". Similarly, the position of Bedjaoui, 468–469: "Un Etat nouveau, pour remplir sa mission interne et sa fonction internationale, doit s'affermir et s'affirmer en tant que tel, faute de quoi son indépendance serait pleine d'illusion et sa viabilité, d'artifice. L'objectif essentiel consiste à purger les rapports anciens de leur contenu inégalitaire. Cela, on le pressent, doit conférer une tonalité spécifique à la succession d'Etats par décolonisation, par rapport à la succession du type classique où ne décelait pas l'existence de liens de subordination". See also, at 530: "L'impératif catégorique pour l'Etat nouveau demeure l'élimination des causes réelles de la colonisation ou de la colonisabilité par la suppression du sous-développement. Le droit de la succession d'Etats peut y contribuer ou non selon qu'il intègre les principes nouveaux, notamment de la Charte des Nations unies, ou qu'il demeure l'expression des intérêts impériaux".

115 ILC Special Rapporteur Šturma, Second Report, 2018, paras 124ff; Guideline 9. See, critical comment on this point by Austria, letter sent to the UN GA Sixth Commission, rep. 73rd sess., 30 Oct. 2018.

116 This is discussed in: Zidane Meriboute, *La codification de la succession d'États aux traités: décolonisation, sécession, unification* (PUF 1984) 29–30, 49, 56, 63.

117 Thus, Art. 16 of the 1978 *Vienna Convention* indicates that treaties entered into by the predecessor State are not binding on a Newly Independent State, while other new States emerging from a dissolution of State or separation/secession are bound by such treaties (Art. 34). Art. 38 of the *1983 Vienna Convention* indicates that, in principle, and without any agreement to the contrary, debts of the predecessor State do not pass to the Newly Independent State. A different regime applies to cases of unification of States (where debts pass to the successor State, Art. 39) and cases of separation and dissolution of State

to State succession did not.[118] The Institute's Resolution contains a specific clause dealing with this type.[119] A modern example of a Newly Independent State, which will be discussed at length in this study, is the independence of Namibia in 1990. The most recent case is that of the independence of Timor Leste in 2002.

Thirdly, the event affecting the territorial integrity of the predecessor State may sometimes result not in the creation of a new State but in the enlargement of the territory of an existing State. This is the case of the *cession or transfer of territory* from one existing State to another existing State. The term "cession" refers to cases where the territorial change is made pursuant to a treaty to which the predecessor State is a party. The concept of "transfer" applies to situations where there is no agreement between the predecessor State and the successor State. This semantic distinction having been explained, it remains that both cases of cession and transfer of territory will be analysed in this study as *a single* type of succession of States. This type of territorial transformation is somewhat different compared to other mechanisms of State succession insofar as it results neither in the extinction of a State nor in the creation of a new State.[120] It is nevertheless clearly a distinct type of State succession.[121] It is analysed as such by the work of the ILC on matters of State succession,[122]

(where an "equitable share" of the predecessor State's debts pass to the new State(s), Art. 40 and 41).

118 The Commentary to the Articles recognises the theoretical distinction between Newly Independent States and "separation of part or parts of the territory". However, it also indicates that the "substantive rules" established for cases of separation (i.e. Art. 24 to 26) would be applicable *mutatis mutandis* to any remaining cases of decolonisation in the future. Therefore, no separate section was included in the Draft Articles to deal specifically with Newly Independent States.

119 IIL, Resolution, 2015, Art. 16, See, discussion in Kohen & Dumberry, 129ff; IIL, Final Report, Kohen, para 18.

120 There is one main difference between cases of "cession" of territory and cases of "incorporation". Cases of cession of territory only deal with *part of a territory* of a State which passes to another State, while cases of incorporation involve the *whole territory* of the State which is integrated into another State. Another difference is that in the context of cession of territory, the predecessor State is not extinguished as a result of the loss of part of its territory.

121 This is emphasised by Stern, Succession, 105.

122 Art. 15 of the 1978 *Vienna Convention* does not use the concept of "cession" but refers instead to the situation "[w]hen part of the territory of a State, or when any territory for the international relations of which a State is responsible, not being part of the territory of that State, becomes part of the territory of another State". See also, Art. 14, *1983 Vienna Convention*; Art. 20, *Draft Articles on Nationality*.

including the recent Guidelines,[123] and that of the Institute.[124] A classic example of cession of territory dealt with in this study is that of Alsace-Lorraine from Germany to France in 1919. A more recent example is that of the cessions of Hong Kong from Great Britain to China (1999) and that of Macao from Portugal to China (1997).

The relevant State practice and international case law will be examined *separately* for the following six different types of succession of States:[125]

- Unification of States;
- Dissolution of State;
- Incorporation of State;
- Separation;
- Creation of Newly Independent States; and
- Cession and transfer of territory.

This typology is by no means authoritative, and many different ones have been used in the past.[126] For instance, the two Vienna Conventions on succession of States and the ILC Draft Articles on nationality in relation to State succession have adopted their own typologies. Yet, the absence of any distinction in these Conventions between dissolution and separation is problematic.[127] Scholarship is also rich with a great variety of such typologies.[128] The recent work of both the Institute and the ILC have adopted a similar typology (minor variations will be discussed below).

4.3 *Fundamental Principles of State Responsibility in International Law*

Since the present study deals with the issue of State succession to international responsibility, it is appropriate to briefly examine the regime of State responsibility in international law. The basic rule of the regime is provided in Article 1 of the ILC's *Articles on Responsibility of States for Internationally Wrongful Acts*

123 ILC Special Rapporteur Šturma, Second Report, 2018, 36; ILC, Commentaries, 2019, at para 165, Art. 9, sub-para 1.

124 IIL, Resolution, 2015, Art. 11.

125 It should be noted, however, that State practice and case law will not be examined separately for the different types of succession of States in the context of succession to the right to reparation for damage affecting new nationals of the successor State (Part 3, Chapter 6). This is because of the limited number of examples of State practice and case law.

126 This typology is essentially based on the work of Stern, Succession, 113. Degan, 298–299, uses a similar typology with the exception of Newly Independent States, which are not analysed as a distinct category.

127 On this point, See Kohen & Dumberry, 78.

128 A survey of some typologies used can be found in: Stern, Succession, 104–116; Annie Gruber, *Le droit international de la succession d'Etats* (Bruylant 1986) (hereinafter "Gruber") 17–18.

adopted by the Drafting Committee on Second Reading on 26 July 2001: "Every internationally wrongful act of a State entails the international responsibility of that State".[129] According to the ILC, this principle "is one of the principles most strongly upheld by State practice and judicial decisions and most deeply rooted in the doctrine of international law".[130] It goes without saying that this principle applies to every internationally wrongful act committed *by every* State. Thus, no State is immune from engaging its international responsibility.

Article 1 refers to two concepts, "internationally wrongful act" and "international responsibility", which will each be examined in the next sections.

International wrongful act. Article 2 of the ILC's *Articles on Responsibility of States for Internationally Wrongful Acts* indicates what are the conditions required to establish the existence of an "internationally wrongful act". The constituent elements of an "internationally wrongful act" consist of a "subjective" and an "objective" element. There is an "internationally wrongful act" of a State when conduct consisting of an action or an omission:

(a) is attributable to that State under international law; and
(b) constitutes a breach of an international obligation of that State.[131]

These two elements are the only necessary components of an internationally wrongful act; there is no general requirement of the existence of a material (or moral) "damage".[132]

The first requirement (the "objective" element) is the commission by a State of a breach of an "international obligation" by an action or an omission. Liability arises from the commission of "internationally wrongful acts" and not from acts not prohibited under international law. It also needs to be a breach of an "international" obligation and not merely the failure of a State to fulfil an obligation imposed by its own legal system (Article 3). A State also cannot escape liability for the breach of an obligation imposed by international law based on the ground that such conduct is in conformity with its domestic law. Since the *Articles on State Responsibility* deal only with the "secondary" rules

129 ILC, "Titles and Texts of the Draft Articles on Responsibility of States for Internationally Wrongful Acts Adopted by the Drafting Committee on Second Reading", 26 July 2001, A/CN.4/L.602/Rev.1. (hereinafter "ILC's *Articles on State Responsibility*, 2001").

130 ILC, "Commentary to the Draft Articles on State Responsibility Adopted by the Commission on First Reading", ILC Report, 48th sess., 1996, A/51/10, chp. III, *Yearbook ILC*, 1996, v. II–2, 58–65 (hereinafter "ILC, Commentaries, State Responsibility, 1996").

131 It should be noted that a State commits an "internationally wrongful act" only to the extent that there are no circumstances precluding wrongfulness.

132 ILC, "First Report on State Responsibility (*addendum* no. 4)", Special Rapporteur James Crawford, 26 May 1998, A/CN.4/490/Add.4, para 116.

of State responsibility, and not with the "primary" rules, they do not "attempt to define the content of the international obligations breach of which gives rise to responsibility".[133] The Articles only determine the "general conditions under international law for the State to be considered responsible for wrongful actions or omissions" and the consequences arising from such violation.[134] Article 12 states that an international obligation is breached by a State "when an act of that State is not in conformity with what is required of it by that obligation".

The second requirement (the "subjective" element) for the existence of an "internationally wrongful act" is that the breach of an international obligation can be "attributable" to a State. Since the State is an organised entity which cannot act in itself but only through its agents and representatives, the question of attribution needs to be answered by considering "which persons should be considered as acting on behalf of the State, i.e. what constitutes an act of the State for the purposes of State responsibility".[135]

International responsibility. According to Article 1 of the ILC's Articles, the commission of an internationally wrongful act by a State entails its international responsibility.[136] The commission of such act gives rise to new international legal relations characterised by a subjective legal situation distinct from that which existed before the act took place.[137] The new legal relations "are grouped under the common denomination of international responsibility".[138] A State that committed an internationally wrongful act is nevertheless under the continuous obligation to perform the obligation breached (Article 29). The responsible State is also obliged to cease the wrongful conduct or, in

133 ILC, Commentaries, State Responsibility, 2001, 59, para 1. See also: "[I]t is one thing to define a rule and the content of the obligation it imposes, and another to determine whether that obligation has been violated and what should be the consequences of the violation" (ILC Report, 22nd sess., 1970, A/8010/Rev.1 (A/25/10), 1970, chp. IV. paras 64–83, *Yearbook ILC*, 1970, v. II, 271, 306, para 66 (c).

134 Ibid.

135 Ibid 71, para 5. According to Art. 4 of the Articles, the conduct of a State "shall be considered an act of that State under international law, whether the organ exercises legislative, executive, judicial or any other functions, whatever position it holds in the organization of the State, and whatever its character as an organ of the central government or of a territorial unit of the State".

136 A special regime prevails in cases where the internationally wrongful act constitutes a "serious breach" by a State of an obligation arising under a peremptory norm of general international law. The particular legal consequences of a breach of such an obligation are set out in Art. 41.

137 ILC, Commentaries, State Responsibility, 1996, 173–176, paras 4–6.

138 ILC, Commentaries, State Responsibility, 2001, 123.

some circumstances, to offer appropriate assurances and guarantee of non-repetition (Article 30).

The responsible State has to make full reparation for the injury caused by the internationally wrongful act (Article 31). The present study will constantly refer to the "obligation to repair" as well as to the "right to reparation" arising from internationally wrongful acts committed before the date of succession. In the present context, the "reparation" will often take the form of *compensation*. However, instances where the proper means of reparation will be *restitution* or *satisfaction* should not be excluded. There may even be cases where counter measures may be an appropriate form of reparation.[139]

4.4 *The Term "Internationally Wrongful Act" Should Be Used instead of "Tort"*

The present study will use the term "internationally wrongful act" to refer to the illegal act committed by a State against another State. As previously observed, this is the expression used by the ILC in its Articles.[140] In the work of the ILC, this expression is preferred to other terms such as delinquency or torts. Both the Institute's Resolution and the ILC Guidelines also use that term.

It is, indeed, important to differentiate the concept of "internationally wrongful act" from the common law notion of "torts".[141] The two concepts have different meanings. Thus, the concept of "internationally wrongful act" includes *all types* of breaches of international obligations, whatever their sources (treaty, contract, rule of customary international law, general principle of law). In common law, the concept of tort is limited to "extra contractual liability". There is no distinction in international law between "contractual" (*ex contractu*) and "tortious" (*ex delicto*) responsibility; the same legal regime of State responsibility applies for both.[142]

---

139 See, ILC Guideline 15 *ter*, dealing with restitution, compensation, satisfaction. See, ILC Special Rapporteur Šturma, Fourth Report, 2020; Lena Raxter, "Responsibility After Succession: The Work of the International Law Commission and Its Application for Seeking Redress After the Breach of Investor-State Agreements", 88(3) *Int. J. Arb., Med. Disp. Manag.* 2022, 372ff.

140 ILC's *Articles on State Responsibility*, 2001.

141 This important distinction is made by writers such as: O'Connell, State Succession, v. 1, 482–483; Czaplinski, 356; Volkovitsch, 2167; Ernest H. Feilchenfeld, *Public Debts and State Succession* (Macmillan 1931) (hereinafter "Feilchenfeld"), 688; Crawford, State Responsibility, 436.

142 *Case Concerning the Difference Between New Zealand and France Concerning the Interpretation or Application of two Agreements, concluded on 9 July 1986 Between the two States and which Related to the Problems Arising from the Rainbow Warrior Affair*, [*The*

Another essential distinction is that an "internationally wrongful act" is defined and exists solely under international law, while "torts" are rooted in municipal law.[143] Earlier writing on State succession used the expression "torts".[144] The use of such term creates great confusion, as it is not clear whether the proposition advanced by some authors that there is no succession to "torts" is in fact a reference to the limited scope of the concept under common law or to the more general notion of "internationally wrongful act".[145] This confusion in terminology makes uncertain the analysis of some of the older scholarship on the question at the heart of this study.[146] The Institute also excludes municipal "torts" from the scope of its resolution.[147]

4.5 *This Study Does Not Deal with the Regime of State Responsibility for Breaches of Rules of State Succession*

Another important remark that should be made at the outset is that the present study does not deal with the *interaction* between "State succession" and "State responsibility", which are two fundamentally different areas of international law. Thus, the present study *does not* deal with the legal consequences of the breach of rules of State succession by a new State *after its independence*. It

Rainbow Warrior II case] (*New Zealand v. France*), Award, 30 April 1990, *UNRIAA* v. XX, 217, at para 75.

143 The importance of the distinction is highlighted by O'Connell, State Succession, v. 1, 482; Volkovitsch, 2167. Torts also generally survive changes of sovereignty only to the extent that the successor State adopts its predecessor's municipal law without any changes. A tort in municipal law may, however, also constitute an "internationally wrongful act" as in the case of the wrongful deprivation (without any reparation) by a State of private property owned by aliens.

144 For instance, Hurst; A.B. Keith, *The Theory of State Succession with Specific Reference to English and Colonial Law* (1907) (hereinafter "Keith"), 74.

145 Thus, some writers, such as Feilchenfeld, 688, endorse a rule of non-succession to "torts" in the common law sense of "delictual liability" (*ex delicto*) as opposed to "contractual" acts. Other writers, such as Arrigo Cavaglieri, "Règles générales du droit de la paix", *Rec. des cours*, v. 26, 1929–I (hereinafter "Cavaglieri, Règles"), 374, refers, however, to the notion of "torts" in the sense of international wrongful acts. This issue is further discussed by O'Connell, Recent Problems, 164.

146 Similarly, Czaplinski, 356, states that "the most important difficulty is that usually responsibility for international delicts is not correctly distinguished from liability for torts in municipal law". For O'Connell, State Succession, v. 1, 482, "this failure to characterise the event properly has produced a defective jurisprudence". He concludes (O'Connell, Recent Problems, 164) that the "obvious intellectual confusion" of the analysis "has prompted the question whether the proposition that there is no succession to torts is not, perhaps, spurious".

147 See, Kohen & Dumberry, 25.

will not determine the legal consequences of such violation under the appropriate rules of State responsibility.[148] The present study deals with the situation where an internationally wrongful act was committed *before* the date of succession and examines the legal consequences in the event that the State perpetrator or victim of such an act is *subsequently* affected by State succession. The same approach has also been adopted by the Institute in its Resolution.[149]

4.6 *This Study Does Not Deal with the Issues of "Odious Debts" and "War Damage" between the Predecessor State and the Successor State*

As a matter of principle, the focus of the present study is on the question of rights and obligations arising from internationally wrongful acts suffered by or caused by *third States*. The question of reparation for damage *between* the predecessor State and the successor State, or even *between* the different new successor States (such as in the case of dissolution) will not be addressed *per se* in the course of the present study. The principal reason being that in such cases the issue at stake only deals with problems of State responsibility *per se* and not with any questions of State succession. Yet, I will nevertheless refer to some examples involving reparation claims between the predecessor and the successor States such as, for instance, in the context of the independence of Algeria. Whenever this is the case the specific nature of the example will be highlighted.

So-called "odious debts" and "war damage" will therefore not be addressed specifically in the present study. Odious debts include war debts contracted by the predecessor State in its war effort against the successor State and "enslavement" debts, which are debts contracted with the aim of the colonisation of a territory.[150] It is only to the extent that such "odious debts" actually refer to third States (as the victim or the perpetrator of the wrong) that they will be taken into account in this study. I will briefly examine below the different, but related, question of succession to odious "acts".[151]

---

148 Bedjaoui, 531: "La succession d'Etats n'a pour objet que de déterminer l'existence ou non d'une obligation internationale mise à la charge de l'Etat successeur. Elle laisse à la matière de la responsabilité le soin d'assurer le relai et d'étudier la possibilité, la nature et la mise en jeu des sanctions d'une violation de ce devoir international s'il existe".

149 See, IIL, Final Report, Kohen, para 23; Kohen & Dumberry, 25.

150 There is support for the principle that "odious debts" are non-transmissible from the predecessor State to the successor State as a matter of customary international law: Stern, Responsabilité, 341; B. Stern, "General Concluding Remarks", in: Brigitte Stern (ed), *Dissolution, Continuation and Succession in Eastern Europe* (Martinus Nijhoff 1998) (hereinafter "Stern, Concluding Remarks") 205; Gruber, 120.

151 See, Part 2, Chapter 3, Section 12.1.

Similarly, questions of "war damage" *between* the predecessor State and the successor State (or between the different new successor States in the context of dissolution) will not be addressed *per se* in the course of the present study. Questions of war damage are generally excluded from the analysis of issues of State succession.[152] In the context of the aftermath of the Yugoslav civil war in the 1990s, Slovenia and Croatia, co-chairing the Peace Conference, asked the Badinter Arbitral Commission to determine whether any amounts owed by one or more States in the form of war damage could affect the distribution of the debts and assets of the former Yugoslavia.[153] The former Republics were divided on this issue depending on whether or not they had been the victims of such damage.[154] In its Decision no. 13, the Commission decided that the question of State succession to debts and assets and the other question of reparation for war damage were governed by two distinct fields of international law:

> The rules applicable to State succession, on the one hand, and the rules of State responsibility, on which the question of war damages depends, on the other, fall within two distinct areas of international law.[155]

152 This is, for instance, the position of Stern, Responsabilité, 342–343; Udina, 751.

153 The question is further examined in: M. Mrak (ed), *Succession of States* (Martinus Nijhoff 1999) 189ff.

154 Stern, Responsabilité, 342–343. Thus, Slovenia, which had suffered only minor war damage as a result of a short period of conflict with the federal authorities of Yugoslavia, refused that the question be included in the negotiations leading to a comprehensive agreement on pending questions of State succession. On the other hand, Bosnia, undoubtedly the victim of many war exactions, was, for obvious reasons, strongly in favour of the inclusion of the question of war damage in the negotiations. The position of Bosnia is explained in this negotiation document: "Principles and Attitudes Regarding Drawing Up the Contract on Succession of the Property, Archives and Debts of Former SFRY" (see at point no. 20), 24 December 1990, in: Snezana Trifunovka, *Former Yugoslavia Through Documents—From Its Dissolution to the Peace Settlement* (Martinus Nijhoff 1999) 1280–1286. A similar view was also held by Croatia stating that "as principal victims [with Bosnia] of the aggression" it "cannot agree to an overall settlement that would not take into account the reparation of war damages inflicted on them and their population": "Statement to the Working Group on Succession Issued of the ICFY by the Delegation of Croatia" attached to a letter dated 17 May 1994 from the Head of the Delegation of Croatia to the Working Group on Succession Issued of the ICFY addressed to the Co-Chairman of the International Conference, S/1994, 624, Annex, in: Trifunovka, ibid 1260–1267.

155 Arbitration Commission, "Opinion no. 13", 16 July 1993, *ILM* 1993, 1592. The Commission nevertheless acknowledged the possibility that the transfer of debts and assets could be set off against war damage: "The possibility cannot be excluded in particular of setting off assets and liabilities to be transferred under the rules of State succession on the one hand against war damage on the other".

In the *Agreement on Succession Issues* (2001)[156] entered into between the successor States to the former Yugoslavia, questions of war damage were deliberately excluded from other issues of State succession.[157]

4.7 *This Study Does Not Deal with Internationally Wrongful Acts Committed by the Predecessor State against Its Own Nationals/ Corporations*

The present study focuses on internationally wrongful acts committed by a State *against other States* (and nationals/corporations of other States). It does not intend to treat in great detail the other situation of acts committed by the predecessor State against *its own* nationals before the date of succession. Therefore, the basic aim of this study is not to address human rights abuses committed by the predecessor State or to examine the question of whether the successor State is bound to provide reparation for such wrongful acts committed against its new nationals. The same approach has also been adopted by the Institute in its Resolution.[158] It also seems to be the position followed by the ILC Special Rapporteur.[159]

156 *Agreement on Succession Issues*, 29 June 2001, 41 *ILM* 2002, 3.

157 This is the position of Professor Vladimir-Djuro Degan, who participated in the negotiations leading to this Agreement as a representative of Croatia. In a reply to a letter sent by me, Degan explained (letter, 21 October 2002, on file with the author) that the reference in Art. 7 of the Agreement to "certain other non-succession matters" was a clear reference to questions of war damage that the successor States deliberately decided to exclude from this Agreement on issues of State succession. In a letter (13 November 2002, on file with the author) sent to the present author, Sir Arthur Watts, who was the "Special Negotiator for Succession Issues" and under whose supervision the Agreement was signed, indicated that issues of war damage were not included in the negotiations but were, nevertheless, very much present in the background as they "coloured the attitudes of the negotiating States whenever the words 'international responsibility' cropped up". The present author was given permission from Professor Degan and Sir Arthur to refer to the content of these letters in the context of the present study.

158 See, Kohen & Dumberry, 25.

159 This question is examined in: Ruy & Baecke, 17ff, indicating that "it remains uncertain to what extent the findings and draft articles put forth by the ILC Special Rapporteur are also applicable in respect of wrongful acts committed by the predecessor State against its own nationals". Thus, on the one hand, "the reports of the Special Rapporteur do not explicitly exclude such situations from the scope of the ILC's work". Yet, "on closer scrutiny then, the ILC project appears to be aimed exclusively at the question of international responsibility at the inter-State level, with the issue of responsibility for internationally wrongful act committed by the predecessor State against its own nationals (esp. human rights violations) falling between the cracks".

The difference between these two types of claims has been highlighted by the UK's High Court in the *Mutua* case.[160] The Judge noted that claims dealing with the "succession of states in respect of obligations assumed to *other states*" have "nothing to do with liability of a newly independent state under municipal law for torts of a previous government committed on *private individuals*".[161] However, he added that "decisions of domestic courts on claims made by private individuals or entities against former colonial powers" were relevant to this claim dealing with wrongs committed by the UK, the colonial power, against the local population before Kenya's independence.[162]

It should be added that many of the municipal court decisions examined in this study involve cases where internationally wrongful acts were committed by a State against its nationals before the date of succession and where such nationals subsequently became nationals of another State. Throughout this study, these cases will be identified as such and distinguished from those other cases involving *international* responsibility for internationally wrongful acts committed against other States (or nationals of other States). The reasons for treating them differently is that the solution adopted by local courts will often be dictated by the successor State's own *internal political agenda* which has little to do with any international law considerations. The fact that the damage was suffered by a successor State's new national, as opposed to a foreigner, may have also played a role in the conclusion reached by some municipal courts.

4.8 *This Study Does Not Deal with Wrongs Committed by Non-State Actors*

The present study focuses on internationally wrongful acts *committed by a State* against another State or a national of that State. It does not cover wrongs committed by a non-State actor, such as individuals, corporations etc. The only exception (discussed in the next paragraph) is regarding wrongs committed by an "insurrectional movement" in the context of its fight to create a new State.

The scope of the Institute's Resolution is different. Article 2(1) of the Resolution refers to "another subject of international law" as the possible perpetrator or victim of a wrongful act. A similar reference is also found in other provisions of the Resolution.[163] The Commentary explained who these

160 *Mutua et al. v. The Foreign and Commonwealth Office*, 21 July 2011, High Court of Justice, Judgments of Justice McCombe, [2011] EWHC 1913 (QB) and of 5 October 2012, [2012] EWHC 2678 (QB).

161 Ibid para 89, emphasis added.

162 Ibid para 90.

163 See, for instance, IIL, Resolution, 2015, Art. 3, 4, 5, 6 and 7.

non-State actors are ("national liberation movements", "people entitled to self-determination", etc.) and in which context their acts are relevant for the purpose of the application of the resolution.[164] One concrete illustration of an internationally wrongful act committed prior to the date of succession *by* a non-State actor (subject of international law) against another State is found in Article 16(3) of the Resolution. Under this provision, the conduct of a "national liberation movement" before the date of succession which "succeeds in establishing a newly independent State shall be considered the act of the new State under international law". In other words, the new State takes over the consequences of a wrongful act initially committed by a "national liberation movement".[165] Article 16(4) of the Institute's Resolution covers the situation where an internationally wrongful act is committed prior to the date of succession by the predecessor State specifically *against* a "people entitled to self-determination". Under that provision, the right to reparation arising from such an act will pass to the Newly independent State "created by that people".[166] While this study focuses on wrongs committed against a State (or one of its nationals), I will briefly examine this question below.[167] Another issue which will be examined below is what happens when there exists a "direct link" between the consequences of the internationally wrongful act committed by a State and the territory *or the population* of the new State. Under Article 5(2) of the Institute's Resolution whenever an injury caused by such an act affects "persons" which, after the date of succession, "are under the jurisdiction of a successor State", that State can request reparation. Thus, wrongful acts committed against non-State actors will be relevant when addressing the question of State succession to the right to reparation in Part 3.

On the contrary, the ILC Guidelines do not refer to other subjects of international law.[168] Yet, the ILC Report noted that "the draft articles should also address subjects other than States as possible injured subjects".[169] There are some passages in the Special Rapporteur's reports where "the injured State or

164 Kohen & Dumberry, 23ff.

165 The question is examined in: Part 2, Chapter 3, Section 6.

166 The question is examined in Kohen & Dumberry, 139.

167 See, Part 3, Chapter 5, Section 3.4.1.

168 It should be added that the expression was found in Draft Articles 3 (Relevance of the agreements to succession of States in respect of responsibility), 4 (Unilateral declaration by a successor State), and 6 (general rule) of an earlier draft attached to ILC Special Rapporteur Šturma, Second Report, 2018. These provisions were later either deleted or modified. See ILC Special Rapporteur Šturma, Fifth Report, 2021, paras 71–76.

169 ILC Report, 70th sess., 2018, A/73/10, chap. X, paras 219–266, at para 261.

subject" are mentioned.[170] With the exception of movements ("insurrectional or other") mentioned in Guideline 7, the final text contains no reference to non-State actors as a perpetrator of a wrongful act.

170 ILC Special Rapporteur Šturma, Third Report, 2019, para 36; ILC Special Rapporteur Šturma, Second Report, 2018, paras 48, 73, 74, 145. See also: ILC Report, 70th sess., 2018, A/73/10, chap. X (hereinafter "ILC Report, 70th sess., 2018"), para 255; ILC Report, 71st sess., 2019, A/74/10, 2019, chap. VII, para 261 ("In the Special Rapporteur's view, the draft articles should also address subjects other than States as possible injured subjects"). This question is examined in Vergara Lamadrid, 134.

PART 2

Succession of States to the Obligation to Repair

General Introduction of Part 2

This second Part explores the issue of State succession to the *obligation to repair*.[1] The issue analysed in this Part arises from the commission of an internationally wrongful act by the predecessor State against another State. Before the date of succession, the predecessor State is thus the debtor of the *obligation to repair* towards the injured third State. The question addressed in this Part is what happens to the obligations arising from the commission of the internationally wrongful act in the context of a succession of States. In other words, after the date of succession, who from the predecessor State or the successor State should be held responsible for the obligations arising from the commission of the internationally wrongful act. Can the obligation to repair, for which the predecessor State is the debtor before the date of succession, be "transferred" to the successor State? It is undisputed that nothing in international law prevents a successor State from freely deciding to take over the internationally wrongful acts committed by the predecessor State before the date of succession.[2] The other question, which remains "unclear", to paraphrase the ILC Special Rapporteur Crawford,[3] is the situation prevailing *in the absence* of such consent by the successor State.[4] This is the topic addressed in the present Part.

The first chapter (Chapter 1) of this Part explores the theoretical dimension of the question whether the transfer of the obligation to repair from the predecessor State to the successor State is accepted in international law. It examines in detail (at Section 1) the legal arguments advanced by many writers for whom there can be no succession to international responsibility. It also explores the criticisms and challenges which have been expressed by scholars against this strict doctrine of non-succession (Section 2).

The next chapter (Chapter 2) examines the relevant State practice and international and municipal case law where questions of State succession to responsibility arose. Such analysis will be made separately for the different types of

1 The other question of State succession to the *right to reparation* is examined in the next Part (Part 3).

2 This question is analysed: Part 2, Chapter 3, Section 4.

3 ILC, Commentaries, State Responsibility, 2001, 119, para 3.

4 L. Caflisch, "The Law of State Succession: Theoretical Observations", *Netherlands ILR* 1963, 358, noting that "the doctrinal controversy concerning the eventual succession to tortious liabilities" "has never been clarified".

 | DOI:10.1163/9789004703810_003

succession of States. It also examines the position of scholars on which of the principles of succession or non-succession should apply for each situation.

Based on this investigation of State practice and case law, this Part examines (in Chapter 3) specific factors and circumstances (other than the different types of succession of States, discussed in Chapter 2) that are relevant to determine which of the principles of succession or non-succession should apply. There are, indeed, specific issues of State succession to obligations, which will be resolved by specific solutions.

CHAPTER 1

Analysis of Scholarship

1 Introduction

This chapter analyses scholarship on the question whether the "transfer" of the obligation to repair from the predecessor State to the successor State(s) is accepted in international law. Section 2 examines the legal arguments advanced by the doctrine of non-succession, according to which there can be no transfer of the obligation to repair to the successor State. This section critically assesses the soundness of these arguments. Section 3 deals with the criticisms and challenges that have been expressed in scholarship against this strict principle of non-succession.

2 The Doctrine of Non-succession

2.1 *General Overview of the Doctrine*

As already mentioned, the issue of succession of States to responsibility is rarely addressed in general textbooks of international law and, when it is, only a few lines are usually devoted to the question. In almost all of these general textbooks, the applicable "rule" is stated as being the principle of non-succession, whereby the successor State is not bound by internationally wrongful acts committed by the predecessor State before the date of succession.[1]

---

1 For example, see the following writers: Peter Malanczuk, *Akehurst's Modern Introduction to International Law* (7th edn, Routledge 1997) 169; Paul Guggenheim, *Traité de Droit international public*, v. I (Librairie de l'Université 1953) (hereinafter "Guggenheim") 474; H. Lauterpacht, *Oppenheim's International Law*, v. I (Longmans Green 1955) 162; Cavaglieri, Règles, 374; Georg Schwarzenberger, *A Manual of International Law*, v. I (4th edn, Stevens & Sons 1960) 81; Louis Cavare, *Le droit international positif*, v. I (2nd edn, Pedone 1961) 379; J.L. Brierly, *The Law of Nations, An Introduction to the International Law of Peace* (Clarendon 1928) 89–90; J.L. Brierly, "Règles générales du droit de la paix", *Rec. des cours*, v. 58, 1936–IV, 69; Bin Cheng, *General Principles of Law as Applied by International Courts and Tribunals* (Stevens & Sons 1953) 167–168; A. Verdross, *Völkerrecht* (4th edn, Springler 1959) 198; A. Verdross & B. Simma, *Universelles Völkerrecht, Theorie und Praxis* (Dunker & Humblot 1984) 633–634; Hans Kelsen, *Principles of International Law* (2nd edn, by Robert W. Tucker, Holt, Rinehart & Winston 1966) 419; Lord Mcnair, *International Law Opinions*, v. I (CUP 1956) 166. Charles De Visscher, *Théories et réalités en droit international public* (Pedone 1953) 210; Coleman Phillipson, *Termination of War and Treaties of Peace* (E.P. Dutton 1916) 331; Louis Delbez, *Principes généraux du droit*

 | DOI:10.1163/9789004703810_004

Similarly, in 2007, other books and articles more specifically related to the study of questions of State succession also generally supported this principle of non-succession.[2] Those writers are referred to collectively as the doctrine

---

international public (3rd edn, LGDJ 1964) 275; John O'Brien, *International Law* (Cavendish 2001) 604; Jackson H. Ralston, *The Law and Procedure of International Tribunals (Supp. to 1926 rev. ed.)* (Stanford UP 1936) 146–147; Louis Henkin et al., *International Law, Cases and Materials* (3rd edn, West 1993) 293; Herbert W. Briggs, *The Law of Nations: Cases, Documents, and Notes* (F.S. Crofts 1947) 132; Angelo Piero Sereni, *Diritto Internazionale*, v. 2 (Giuffré 1958) 399; J.P. Müller & L. Wildaber, *Praxis des Völkerrechts* (2nd edn, Stämpfli 1982) 172; Emile Giraud, "Arbitrage international", in: A. de Lapradelle & J.-P. Niboyet, *Répertoire de droit international*, v. I (Sirey 1929) 687; Hugh M. Kindred (ed), *International Law Chiefly as Interpreted and Applied in Canada* (5th edn, E. Montgomery 1993) 71; Green Haywood Hackworth, *Digest of International Law*, v. I (GPO 1940) 560–561; Suzanne Bastid, *Droit international public, Principes généraux*, Fasc. II (Univ. de Paris les Cours de droit 1966–1967) 170; R.C. Hingorani, *Modern International Law* (2nd edn, Oceana 1984) 109; Wesley L. Gould, *An Introduction to International Law* (Harpers & Bro. 1957) 428; David Ruzié, *Droit international public* (14th edn, Dalloz 1999) 90; Georg Dahm, *Völkerrecht*, v. 1 (W. Kohlhammer 1958) 121; Marcel Sinkondo, *Droit international public* (Ellipses 1999) 327; Oscar Svarlien, *An Introduction to the Law of Nations* (McGraw-Hill 1955) 119; Kurt Von Schuschnigg, *International Law: An Introduction to the Law of Peace* (Bruce 1959) 158; Charles Cheney Hyde, *International Law Chiefly as Interpreted and Applied by the United States*, v. I (2nd edn, Little, Brown & Co. 1945) (hereinafter "Hyde") p. 437 (the author is, however, also quite critical of this rule which "leaves something to be desired"); John Dugard, *International Law; a South African Perspective* (2nd edn, Juta 2000) 232–233.

2 For example, see: D. Bardonnet, *La succession d'Etats à Madagascar: succession au droit conventionnel et aux droits patrimoniaux* (LGDJ 1970) (hereinafter "Bardonnet") 315–316; Michel Waelbroeck, "Arrêt no. 8160 du Conseil d'Etat Belge, note d'observations", *RJDA* 1961, no. 1, 35 (making an exception for unjust enrichment); Marek, 1, 11, 189; Konrad G. Bühler, "State Succession, Identity/Continuity and Membership in the United Nations", in: Eisemann & Koskenniemi, 193–194; Oskar Lehner, "The Identity of Austria 1918/19 as a Problem of State Succession", 44 *ÖZöRV* 1992, 76; Isaac Paenson, *Les conséquences financières de la succession d'Etats (1932–1953)* (Domat-Montchrestien 1954) 19; Max Huber, *Die Staatensuccession: völkerrechtliche und staatsrechtliche Praxis im XIX. Jahrhundert* (Duncker & Humblot 1898) 65–66; Keith, 74–75, 77; H.A. Wilkinson, *American Doctrine of State Succession* (Johns Hopkins Press, 1934) 463; W. Schönborn, *Staatensuccession, Handbuch des Völkerrechts*, v. 2 (1913) 49; Matthew C.R. Craven, "The Problem of State Succession and the Identity of States under International Law", 9(1) *EJIL* 1998, 149–150; Natalino Ronzitti, *La successione internazionale tra stati* (Giuffrè 1970) 216; Ulrich Fastenrath, "Der deutsche Einigungsvertrag im Lichte des Rechts der Staatennachfolge", 44 *ÖZöRV* 1992, 39; Florian Drinhausen, *Die Auswirkungen der Staatensukzession auf Verträge eines Staates mit privaten Partnern* (Peter Lang 1995) 151; Eugene Cotran, "Some Legal Aspects of the Formation of the United Arab Republic and the United Arab States", 8 *ICLQ* 1959, 368 (hereinafter "Cotran"); S.K. Agrawala, "Law of Nations as Interpreted and Applied by Indian Courts and Legislature", 2 *Indian JIL* 1962, 431, 442; Zyade Motala, "Under International Law, Does the New Order in South Africa Assume the Obligations and Responsibilities of Apartheid Order? An Argument for Realism over Formalism", 30 *Comp. & Int'l L.J. S. Afr.* 1997, 291–292; Neville Botha, "To Pay or Not to Pay?: Namibian Liability for South African Delicts", 16 *South African YIL* 1990–91,

of non-succession. In his reports, ILC Special Rapporteur Šturma refers to this approach as the "traditional" thesis or doctrine of non-succession,[3] an expression I have also used elsewhere,[4] and which has since then been adopted by others, including Crawford.[5]

Supporters of this doctrine of non-succession can be found among all the different schools of thought on State succession.

Writers who support the "universal succession theory" ("*théorie de la succession universelle de droit privé*") based on Roman law generally believe that all rights and obligations of the "defunct" State automatically pass to the successor State. This theory goes back to Grotius and was the leading doctrine of State succession up until the 19th Century.[6] However, an exception is made with respect to internationally wrongful acts of the predecessor State based on the fact that under Roman law *ex delicto* liability does not pass from the *cujus* to the heirs. A good example of that approach is the work of Lauterpacht.[7]

162; Hercules Booysen, "Succession to Delictual Liability: a Namibian Precedent", 24 Comp. & ILJ S. Afr. 1991 (hereinafter "Booysen") 207; Jiri Malenovsky, "Problèmes juridiques liés à la partition de la Tchécoslovaquie", 39 *AFDI* 1993, 334; Lauri Mälksoo, *Illegal Annexation and State Continuity: The Case of the Incorporation of the Baltic States by the USSR* (Martinus Nijhoff 2003) 257 (stating that the principle of non-succession is a rule of customary international law); Volinka Reina, "Iraq's Delictual and Contractual Liabilities: Would Politics or International Law Provide for Better Resolution of Successor State Responsibility?", 22 *Berkeley JIL* 2004, 583, 595.

3 E.g, ILC Special Rapporteur Šturma, First Report, 2017, paras 83, 78; ibid, Second Report, 2018, paras 10, 44, 160, 166.

4 P. Dumberry, "The Controversial Issue of State Succession to International Responsibility in Light of Recent State Practice", 49 *German YIL* 2006, 415.

5 Crawford, State Responsibility, 437. See also, Andreas Zimmermann & James G Devaney, "State Succession in Matters Other Than Treaties" in Rüdiger Wolfrum (ed), *Max Planck Encyclopedia of Public International Law* (OUP online 2019), para 33, calling it the "orthodox position in international law".

6 H. Grotius, *De jure belli as pacis*, lib. 2, chap. IX, no. 12; E. de Vattel, *Le droit des gens ou les principes de la loi naturelle*, v. II, xii, no. 191; Samuel Pufendorf, *De jure naturae et gentium*, 1698, lib. VIII, chap. 5; W.E. Hall, *A Treatise on International Law* (8th edn, A. Pearce Higgins, Clarendon 1924) 114–115; H. Wheaton, *Elements of International Law* (8th edn, R.H. Dana, 1866) pt. I, sect. 29; William Oke Manning, *Commentaries on the Law of Nations* (by Sheldon Amos, 1875), 91; Robert Phillimore, *Commentaries on International Law* v. I (2nd edn, 1871) 168; F. De Martens, *Traité de droit international* (Marescqains, 1883) 369; F. Desparget, *Cours de droit international public* (4th edn, Sirey 1910) 117; E. Nys, *Le droit international: les principes, les théories, les faits*, v. II (2nd edn, Castaigne 1904) 31; H.W. Hallek, *International Law* v. I (Kegan 1893) 91; A. Merignhac, *Traité de droit international public*, v. II (LGDJ 1907) 14; T.D. Woolsey, *Introduction to Study of International Law* (6th edn, 1899) 38–39. Other writers are mentioned in: O'Connell, State Succession, v. I, 10.

7 H. Lauterpacht, *Private Law Sources and Analogies of International Law* (Longmans 1927) 131–132, 283.

Supporters of the theory of "organic substitution" ("*théorie de la succession universelle de droit public*") are also of the opinion that the rights and obligations of the defunct State do not simply disappear as a result of State succession.[8] This doctrine has received much support both from classical doctrine[9] and modern writers.[10] However, based on the maxim *actio personalis moritur cum persona*,[11] they argue that internationally wrongful acts are considered to be too "personal" to the predecessor State for them to be the object of any transfer to another State at the time of succession.[12]

Finally, scholars supporting the "negative school" of State succession, quite logically, also refute any transfer of the consequences of international responsibility from one State to another.[13] For the supporters of this theory, the principle of sovereignty implies that upon its arrival on the international scene, a new State is free of any obligations incumbent upon the predecessor State; it starts with a clean slate (*tabula rasa*). This voluntarist theory was largely supported in classical doctrine by the end of the 19th Century.[14] The classical

---

8 According to J.C. Bluntschli, *Das Modern Völkerecht der civilisierten Staaten* (Nördlingen 1878, trans. *Le droit international codifié*, Lib. Guillaunin 1895) 75: "Lorsqu'un Etat est annexé à un autre Etat, le premier cesse d'exister, ainsi son anéantissement n'entraîne pas nécessairement l'extinction de ses droits et de ses obligations vis-à-vis des autres Etats, parce que le peuple et le territoire de cet Etat continuent en substance à exister et n'ont fait que passer dans l'autre Etat. Ces droits et obligations passeront même à l'autre Etat, toutes les fois que le maintien sera possible et pourra être concilié avec le nouvel ordre des choses". See also: P. Fiore, *Le droit international codifié et sa sanction juridique* (Pedone 1911) no. 137, 141.

9 Max Huber, *Die Staatensuccession: völkerrechtliche und staatsrechtliche Praxis im XIX. Jahrhundert* (Duncker & Humblot 1898) 3, 18, 24, 73; John WestLake, *International Law* (CUP 1904) 69; A. Rivier, *Principes du droit des gens*, v. I (A. Rousseau 1896) 70; H. Appleton, *Des effets des annexions sur les dettes de l'Etat démembré ou annexé* (L. Larose 1894) no. 14ff; P. Pradier-Fodere, *Traité de droit international public européen et américain*, v. I (Biblio. Internationale et diplomatique 1885) no. 160, 276; S. Kiatibian, *Conséquence juridiques des transformations territoriales des Etats sur les traités* (Giard & Brière 1892).

10 For instance: Marco G. Marcoff, *Accession à l'indépendance et succession d'Etats aux traités internationaux* (Ed. Univ. 1969) 19–20.

11 This point is further discussed in Section 2.2.2.

12 This is the case, for instance, of Max Huber, *Die Staatensuccession: völkerrechtliche und staatsrechtliche Praxis im XIX. Jahrhundert* (Duncker & Humblot 1898) 65, who makes a specific exception for "torts".

13 This is clearly the position of Monnier, 86: "Comme la notion de succession universelle ne trouve pas application en droit international positif lors de la substitution d'un ordre juridique étatique à un autre sur un territoire déterminé, il suit que l'Etat nouveau ne succède pas, sauf convention contraire, aux obligations incombant à l'Etat antérieur à raison de ses actes contraires au droit". See also, A. Verdross, *Völkerrech* (4th edn, Springler 1959) 198.

14 Cavaglieri, Règles, 15–16.

clean slate theory was subsequently adopted by Newly Independent States in the context of decolonisation in the 1960s: they argued that any other solution would undermine their newly attained self-determination by maintaining a relationship of dependence with the former colonial State.[15]

When examining these old debates, one should not lose sight of the fundamental fact that the successor State does not derive its sovereignty from the predecessor State, but from international law.[16] The new State "establishes its sovereignty as its own original sovereignty, in accordance with international law".[17] This is reflected in the definition of State succession found in the codification instruments adopted by the ILC, speaking of the "replacement of one State by another" in the responsibility for the international relations in a territory rather than to the "transfer" of any such responsibility between them. In

15 An illustration of this approach is Bedjaoui, 493: "A la base de la création de l'Etat nouveau se trouve le principe d'autodétermination. L'atteinte à un tel droit que suppose nécessairement la protection de tous les intérêts et privilèges de l'ancienne puissance colonial, reviendrait à hypothéquer ce droit même qui a été l'agent de la création de cet Etat. Cela reviendrait à la remise en cause de l'indépendance et de la souveraineté de l'Etat nouveau. Or, donner et retenir ne vaut. Accorder l'indépendance et la confisquer ensuite par le jeu de prétendues règles conventionnelles ou autres de succession d'Etats, ne paraît pas licite". See also, the author's analysis (485, 503–504, 519–527) of the issue of succession to treaties and his conclusion (526) that there is succession *ipso jure* to treaties reinforcing international cooperation between States and a rule on non-succession for treaties contrary to the principle of self-determination.

16 ILC, "Second Report on Succession of States in Respect of Matters Other Than Treaties", Mohammed Bedjaoui, Special Rapporteur—Economic and Financial Acquired Rights and State Succession, A/CN.4/216/Rev.1, *Yearbook ILC* 1969, v. II, 76–77 (hereinafter "ILC, Second Report Bedjaoui, 1969"): "The successor State does not derive its sovereignty from the predecessor State, but from international law and from its own statehood. In other words, there is not a *transfer* of one sovereignty, but a *substitution* of sovereignties by the extinction of one and the creation of another. The successor State possesses its own sovereignty because it has acceded to the dignity of statehood. (…) Sovereignty is an attribute of public international law which attaches to statehood. The new State does not derive its sovereignty from the predecessor State, but from international law. Furthermore, if sovereignty is necessarily derived only from a predecessor, from whom then did the very first sovereign, at the beginning of a long chain of succession, derive his sovereignty?" (emphasis in the original). See also: Bedjaoui, 537; Stern, Succession, 117–8 ("lorsqu'un nouvel État apparaît sur la scène internationale, à la suite d'un processus de succession d'États, c'est un État souverain différent de l'État souverain prédécesseur. Cette souveraineté lui est reconnue par le droit international, et ne lui vient évidemment pas de l'État prédécesseur"); Erik Castren, "Aspects récents de la succession d'États", *Rec. des Cours*, v. 78, 1951–I, 388.

17 ILC Special Rapporteur Šturma, Third Report, 2019, para 32.

the words of O'Connell, "the successor State in no sense 'continues' the sovereignty of its predecessor".[18]

Consequently, the rights and the obligations of the predecessor State before the date of succession cannot *automatically* be "transferred" to the new State.[19] However, given the fact that a new State is "sovereign", should it be concluded that such rights and obligations should *never* be imposed on that entity? While such a conclusion would undoubtedly be logical,[20] it remains, as noted by Bedjaoui, that such a "mechanical" application of the principle of the equality and sovereignty of States would not take "any account of the special situation of the successor State".[21] For him, such an approach "would be more idealistic than realistic"[22] given the fact that "the successor State has not been established *ex nihilo,* any more than it has come from outer space to lodge in a corner of the Earth".[23] Thus, because the new State derives its sovereignty from international law, "it cannot disengage itself from pre-existing rules and situations, or at least it cannot do so immediately and forever".[24] As rightly noted by O'Connell, "one may subscribe to the view that changes of sovereignty is not a transfer of sovereignty (…) and still reach the conclusion that the successor State is entitled to exercise the predecessor's rights and is obliged to discharge

---

18 O'Connell, State Succession, v. I, 26.

19 Bedjaoui, 537.

20 Stern, Succession, 118: "Sur le plan de la théorie du droit, l'idée même d'une succession est considérée par certains comme incompatible avec le concept de souveraineté. La succession d'États s'analysant en une substitution d'une souveraineté à une autre, on ne peut imaginer grever la souveraineté nouvellement apparue d'une obligation juridique de reprise des droits et obligations de l'État prédécesseur. Il devrait en résulter en bonne logique qu'un État souverain ne devrait être tenu d'aucune des obligations de son prédécesseur, et que devrait donc s'appliquer ce que l'on a appelé le principe de la '*table rase*'".

21 ILC, Second Report Bedjaoui, 1969, 75–76: "As a first approach, it may be argued that in the matter of acquired rights nothing should be imposed on the successor State that would not be imposed on any other State. The emphasis is on statehood, which the successor State possesses like any other State. If we stopped at this concept, however, the principle of the equality and sovereignty of States would be applied mechanically, without taking any account of the special situation of the successor State. That would be tantamount to denying the existence not only of acquired rights but also of all State succession. The successor State would be merely a State, no different from the other members of the international community and not governed by a special regime, that of State succession, which would cease to exist in public international law".

22 Ibid 76.

23 Ibid.

24 Ibid 6.

the predecessor's duties, *because international law so directs*".[25] As explained by Bedjaoui, "the obligation of the predecessor State does not survive, but is replaced by an international duty deriving solely from international law".[26]

O'Connell identifies the "ultimate question" as being "whether international law contains rules for regulating the disposition of public rights and duties as a consequence of a succession of States, and how these rules are to be established".[27] Indeed, he believes that international law does impose *some* obligations upon the new States regarding different aspects of State succession. However, he rejects the extreme approaches that have been adopted in the past by writers whereby the new State is either bound by *all* rights and obligations or by *none* of them. The basic assumption of his work is that "the solution lies in a presumption of continuity which concrete analysis may rebut (…) and not in a universal touchstone of succession or non-succession".[28] For Stern, international law imposes obligations upon the successor States based on the application of the principle of "coherence" of the international legal order.[29] New States are indeed *automatically* bound by rules of customary international law.[30]

2.2 *The Arguments Invoked in Support of the Doctrine*

This section critically analyses in detail the two most important legal theories which have been invoked by writers supporting the establishment of a "rule"

---

25 O'Connell, State Succession, v. I, 32–33 (emphasis added). See also, Gruber, 97: "on ne voit pas pourquoi il faudrait évacuer le principe d'une norme juridique qui imposerait ce respect au successeur en vertu du droit international. Ce n'est pas en tant qu'obligation dérivée et personnalisée qu'il convient en effet de traiter le respect des droits acquis, mais en tant que norme du droit international public".

26 ILC, Second Report Bedjaoui, 1969, 100. It should be added that he is critical regarding the existence of any such duties.

27 O'Connell, State Succession, v. I, 32–33.

28 Ibid 35.

29 Stern, Succession, 119: "Ce que j'appelle ici le principe de cohérence est le principe selon lequel un État successeur en accédant au statut d'État devient partie intégrante du système international préexistant, dont il doit respecter l'intégrité et la cohérence. De même qu'un individu entrant dans une maison doit en respecter l'agencement, un État successeur en entrant dans la communauté internationale doit en reconnaître l'ordonnancement. En d'autres termes, la table rase n'est pas un corollaire incontournable du principe de souveraineté, si l'on veut bien ne pas oublier qu'en accédant au statut d'État souverain le nouvel État s'insère dans une société internationale qui précisément lui confère une souveraineté, telle que définie par le droit international, c'est-à-dire soumise par exemple au respect des règles coutumières existantes".

30 ILA, "Rapport Final sur la Succession en matière de traités", New Delhi Conference 2002, 24.

of non-succession.[31] Two other justifications, which are clearly outdated and not representative of contemporary international law, will not be analysed in detail.

One such outdated theory was developed by Hurst, for whom "what the conqueror annexes is the territory of the former state, not the State itself, still less its government" and, consequently, "it is impossible to hold the conqueror liable for the torts of the government which he has displaced, because the torts were the torts of the government and not the torts of the territory".[32] This theory is undoubtedly influenced by the "theory of property" (*Eigentumstheorie*, "*théorie de l'objet*"), according to which the territory was part of the patrimonial property of the prince and could be exchanged between sovereigns in contracts or as part of a succession as a mere property, an object, dissociated from the State and without any relationship with the concept of sovereignty.[33] This "theory of property" is, however, clearly outdated.[34] The modern interpretation of the element of territory in international law is represented by the *Kompetenztheorie* ("*théorie de la competence*"), according to which the territory is where the State exercises its jurisdiction.[35] This theory is largely accepted by scholars.[36] Modern international law therefore rejects State succession as *a mere transfer of territory* from one State to another.[37]

31 These arguments are briefly examined in: ILC Special Rapporteur Šturma, First Report, 2017, paras 30ff; IIL, Final Report, Kohen, para 27; Šturma, State Succession, 656.

32 Hurst, 178.

33 Verzijl, 298ff. In the past, many writers supported this theory: Paul Fauchille, *Traité de droit international public*, v. I (8th edn, A. Rousseau 1922) 450; W.E. Hall, *A Treatise on International Law* (8th edn, A. Pearce Higgins 1924) 125; T.J. Lawrence, *The Principles of International Law* (7th edn, MacMillan 1925) 136.

34 Stern, Responsabilité, 329. See also: Volkovitsch, 2197.

35 See, Julio A. Barberis, "Les liens juridiques entre l'Etat et son territoire: perspectives théoriques et évolution du droit international", *AFDI* 1999, 132–147.

36 W. Schoenborn, "La nature juridique du territoire", *Rec. des cours,* v. 30, 1929–V, 124; L. Delbez, "Du territoire dans ses rapports avec l'Etat", *RGDIP* 1932, 712; Guggenheim, 374; Rousseau, v. II, 51; Charles De Visscher, *Theory and Reality in Public International Law* (Princeton UP 1957) 197; Verzijl, 12–13; Oppenheim, *International Law*, v. 1 (8th edn, 1955) 452.

37 For Udina, 680, in the context of a succession of States "il y a substitution matérielle d'un Etat à l'autre dans le territoire donné et non pas transfert du territoire, car le territoire ne peut être matériellement transféré". Similarly, Verzijl, 11–13, speaks of the transfer not of a "real" right of a proprietary nature but of "the aggregate of public competencies respecting the territory and its inhabitants which the ceding State used, or was entitled under international law, to exercise until the cession". In other words, for Verzijl, what is transferred is the "total of State competencies inherent in the concept of territorial sovereignty". See also, Monnier, 87–89.

Another theory that has been put forward is deeply rooted in the age of colonialism, when the use of force was still lawful and when the annexation of "backward" States was still considered legitimate.[38] For Hurst, the imposition of a rule of succession to responsibility upon the "better governed and more advanced" States would discourage them from intervening in "backward States" to put an end to the "anarchy and misrule" existing in such countries; such rule would set a "premium on misgovernment".[39] Hurst, who acted as Counsel to Great Britain, made use of the same argument in the *R.E. Brown* case.[40] Another scholar, Hyde, writing in 1947, argued that one positive consequence of the establishment of a rule of succession in this context would be to

38 This theory is examined by Stern, Responsabilité, 329; Monnier, 88; Volkovitsch, 2185.

39 Hurst, 178: "A principle which would render a conqueror liable for damages for all the unliquidated claims based on wrongful acts of the State he is driven to subdue would be neither just nor reasonable, and would entail consequences which would be fruitful of mischief. Such a principle would enable a small and backward State to withstand all pressure from a better governed and more advanced neighbour, and would act as a direct encouragement to any such backslider among the family of nations to render itself secure from intervention and absorption by perpetuating anarchy and misrule within its borders. The more the condition of such a State cried aloud for intervention for the sake of the inhabitant of the country, whether native of foreign, the more would neighbouring Governments be held back for necessary action by the contemplation of the burdens it might entail. In short, if there were any such rule of international law, it would merely set a premium on misgovernment".

40 "Brief", US, *R.E. Brown* case, in: Fred K. Nielsen, *American and British Claims Arbitration, Report* (GPO 1926) (hereinafter "Nielsen") 165ff, 184. In relation to the possibility he raised during the pleading that European Powers could invade newly Communist Russia to stop the atrocities committed there at that time, he stated that any rule of succession to responsibility would make "Governments hesitate long before they set out to redress very grievous wrongs that may be committed in any particular part of the world". In its pleading in the *R.E. Brown* case, Great Britain provides this other example: "Supposing the Ruler of Government of a country is grossly extravagant, is wasting the substance of the people in some riotous form of spending, and it is creating trouble and the Government of one of the big Powers says: This must stop, we cannot allow this to go on, it is a danger to civilization and we are going to stop it, if, in such circumstances, a country or several countries in alliance, stepped in and tried to provide good and decent and proper Government in that particular State that was behaving wrongly, can it be said that they would have to pay all the damages that had been wrongfully incurred by the country that, at the time they took it over, had rendered itself bankrupt and helpless so far as money matters are concerned? I submit that would be wrong; I submit it would not be in the interests of civilization, and certainly it would not be moral in the circumstances. If one comes to deal with the subject, and think it out, I submit there can obviously be no general rule regard to State succession" ("Answer", UK, *R.E. Brown* case, 253–256, quoted in: "Brief", US, *Hawaiian Claims* case, Nielsen, 95ff, 97).

"diminish the interest of strong powers in seeking to annex and so obliterate the statehood of weaker and backward neighbours".[41]

2.2.1 A State Is Only Responsible for Its Own Internationally Wrongful Acts and Not for Those Committed by Other States

The central argument of the doctrine of non-succession is that a State is generally not responsible for acts committed by other States. This has, in fact, been described as the *only* relevant theoretical justification for this doctrine.[42] This is, for instance, the position of Cavaglieri:

> Quelle que soit la source d'une obligation internationale, celle-ci est presque toujours déterminée par des circonstances et des situations, qui appartiennent à l'Etat, qui les a contactées et qui par conséquent doivent nécessairement s'éteindre avec lui … Il est absurde de penser qu'un Etat puisse être tenu responsable d'un délit, commis par un autre Etat.[43]

This fundamental principle that a State is generally not responsible for acts committed by other States is said to be based on the principle of the independence of States[44] and on the principle of the equality of States.[45] It has also been argued, more simply, that the successor State should not take over the consequences of internationally wrongful acts committed by the predecessor State because the two States do not have the same "international legal personality".[46]

---

41 Hyde, 438.

42 Monnier, 89.

43 Arrigo Cavaglieri, "Effets juridiques des changements de souveraineté territoriale", *Annuaire IDI* 1931–I (hereinafter "Cavaglieri, Effets") 190.

44 Michel Waelbroeck, "Arrêt no. 8160 du Conseil d'Etat Belge, note d'observations", *RJDA* 1961, no. 1, 35.

45 Louis Cavare, *Le droit international positif*, v. I (2nd edn, Pedone 1961) 415–416: "En D.I.P. la responsabilité délictuelle ou quasi-délictuelle du fait d'autrui est exceptionnelle. L'égalité juridique des Etats rend chacun d'entre eux pleinement capable et en conséquence seul responsable. Sauf exception, un Etat ne répond pas des actes dommageables d'un autre. Voilà du moins ce qu'implique la logique". Cavare also indicates (408) that "ces droits ont existé ou ces obligations ont été conclues en fonction des circonstances spéciales à l'Etat disparu et ne se conçoivent pas d'une façon indépendante de lui". See also, Monnier, 89.

46 Atlam, 487: "Notion indissociable du droit successoral, la personnalité internationale est, selon nous, l'un des paramètres qui doivent être toujours présents lors de l'appréciation des implications de la réalisation d'une transformation territoriale sur les prérogatives de la responsabilité internationale du sujet du droit international—Etat ou mouvement révolutionnaire—affecté par la succession d'Etats". See also, this comment (289–290): "[L]es conséquences que l'on pourrait éventuellement tirer de la notion de

Only the State which has actually committed an internationally wrongful act should be responsible for it.[47] This basic principle does not create any difficulty when the predecessor State continues to exist after the changes affecting its former territory have occurred; it should, in principle, remain responsible for its own internationally wrongful acts.[48] In the event that the predecessor State ceases to exist (such as in cases of dissolution, unification and incorporation of States), the legal liability for internationally wrongful acts would be extinguished at the same time.[49] This was the position taken by the US-Great Britain Arbitral Commission in the *Hawaiian Claims* case: "[T]he legal unit which did the wrong no longer exists, and legal liability for the wrong has been extinguished with it".[50]

The argument is no doubt logically sound. This basic rule is stipulated in Article 1 of the ILC's *Articles on State Responsibility*.[51] According to Special Rapporteur Crawford, this provision "affirms the basic principle that each State

---

personnalité internationale sur le plan de l'identité ou de la rupture dans la qualité internationale du sujet juridique affecté par la succession d'Etats doivent être notamment présentes lors de l'appréciation du sort devant être retenu quant aux prérogatives de la responsabilité internationale de ce dernier". Atlam argues (283–284) that in cases of dissolution of State, where there is no *identity* of the international legal personality between the predecessor State and the successor States, there should, consequently, be no transfer of the obligation to repair to the new States: "La reconnaissance de la rupture dans la personnalité internationale entre l'Etat démembré et les Etats successeurs issus de son démembrement constituerait ici le prélude à l'application de la règle de la table rase à l'égard du passif de la responsabilité internationale du premier".

47 Nguyen Quoc Dinh, Patrick Daillier & Alain Pellet, *Droit international public* (6th edn, LGDJ 1999) 550: "Les principes généraux de la responsabilité internationale, en particulier les règles sur l'attribution des faits internationalement illicites, excluent toute idée de continuité en matière de responsabilité passive et active" (However, the 8th edition, by Daillier, Forteau, Pelet, 618–9, indicates that the practice of the 1990s shows that successor States have in general taken over such obligations). See also, Jiri Malenovsky, "Problèmes juridiques liés à la partition de la Tchécoslovaquie", 39 *AFDI* 1993, 334; P.-M. Dupuy & Y. Kerbrat, *Droit international public* (15th edn, Dalloz 2020) (hereinafter "Dupuy & Kerbrat") 84–5; Rousseau, v. III, 505; Charles De Visscher, *Théories et réalités en droit international public* (Pedone 1953) 210; Louis Delbez, *Principes généraux du droit international public* (3rd edn, LGDJ 1964) 275; Marcel Sinkondo, *Droit international public* (Ellipses 1999) 327; Atlam, 285.

48 Monnier, 67; Czaplinski, 357; Nguyen, ibid; Dupuy, ibid; Rousseau, v. III, ibid.

49 Marcel Sinkondo, *Droit international public* (Ellipses 1999) 327; Wesley L. Gould, *An Introduction to International Law* (Harpers & Bro. 1957) 428; W.K. Wilburn, "Filing of U.S. Property Claims in Eastern Germany", *Int'l Law.* 1991, 660–661.

50 *Hawaiian Claims* case, 158.

51 ILC's *Articles on State Responsibility*, 2001.

is responsible for its own wrongful conduct".[52] It is indeed true that, as a matter of principle, the successor State should not be "responsible" for any internationally wrongful act committed by *another State*.[53]

This argument (however correct it may be) is nevertheless beside the point. Thus, as already explained, the question dealt with in the present study is *not* whether the successor State should be *"responsible"* for internationally wrongful acts it has not itself committed. As explained by Verhoeven: "Il va de soi que la responsabilité n'est pas celle de l'Etat successeur, auquel aucune faute ne peut être directement imputée. C'est ce qui fait la spécificité du problème de succession d'Etats".[54] Thus, the successor State cannot be liable for internationally wrongful acts committed by another State. This is undisputed.

What matters in the context of the present study is whether the *obligations resulting* from an internationally wrongful act committed by the predecessor State can, in some circumstances, be "transferred" to the successor State. Rousseau rightly speaks of the question whether there is in international law a principle imposing on the successor State "l'obligation de prendre à sa charge la réparation des actes illicites imputables à l'Etat prédécesseur".[55] Similarly, Stern refers to the issue as being that of the "transmission des conséquences de la responsabilité, plus que de transmission de la responsabilité elle-même".[56]

---

52 ILC, "First Report on State Responsibility (*addendum* no. 4)", Special Rapporteur James Crawford, 26 May 1998, A/CN.4/490/Add.4, para 110. It should be noted that the ILC Articles envisage two exceptional cases where an internationally wrongful act committed by a State entails the responsibility of another State (Arts 17, 18).

53 Thus, writers who reject the transferability of the obligation to repair to the successor State base such a conclusion on the fact that the successor State cannot be responsible for *the acts of another State*. This is clear from these few quotations: Guggenheim, 474 ("[l]'Etat successeur n'est pas responsable des actes illicites commis par l'Etat auquel il succède"); Dupuy & Kerbrat, 84–5 ("[l]e principe général découlant des règles gouvernant l'imputabilité des actes illicites internationaux est celui de la non transmissibilité de la responsabilité de l'Etat prédécesseur à l'Etat successeur"); Louis Delbez, *Principes généraux du droit international public* (3rd edn, LGDJ 1964) 275 ("l'Etat nouveau n'est pas tenu de réparer les suites dommageables des actes imputables à l'Etat disparu"); Louis Cavare, *Le droit international positif*, v. I (2nd edn, Pedone 1961) 415–416 (speaking of "la responsabilité délictuelle … du fait d'autrui"); Monnier, 89, ("[l]'Etat n'est pas responsable, en principe, pour le fait d'autrui"). See also: Suzanne Bastid, *Droit international public, Principes généraux* (Fasc. II, Univ. les Cours de droit, 1966–1967) 170.

54 Joe Verhoeven, *Droit international public* (Larcier 2000) 189, who criticises the argument of the doctrine of non-succession based on the said impossibility to attribute the internationally wrongful acts of the predecessor State to the successor State.

55 Rousseau, v. III, 505. He is of the view that there exists no such general principle of succession to obligations arising from the commission of internationally wrongful acts.

56 Stern, Responsabilité, 338. See also, Peterschmitt, 10, 72.

In other words, the *responsibility* for the commission of an internationally wrongful act remains with the predecessor State; it is the only State which is "responsible" for such act.[57] The other question, which is at the heart of this study, is whether the successor State can take over the obligations *arising from responsibility* for an internationally wrongful act committed before the date of succession.[58] This distinction has been endorsed by the work of the Institute,[59] ILC Special Rapporteur Šturma,[60] and Judge Kreća, in his separate opinion in the *Croatia Genocide Convention* case.[61]

2.2.2 Actio personalis moritur cum persona

Many writers have based their support for the principle of non-succession on the so-called "personal character" of internationally wrongful acts which would not enable their transfer from one State to another: *actio personalis moritur cum persona*.[62] This position is well-illustrated by these two quotations, the first from Cavaglieri and the second by Udina:

57 Pajnkihar, 298.

58 See, the different position adopted by Reyes Gajardo, 83: "What happens is that the successor State assumes obligations of its predecessor, but this does not mean that the obligations that the successor assumes have always been legally its own. These obligations arising from the internationally wrongful act become extinct with the disappearance of the wrongdoer predecessor State, and 'new obligations' or the 'same previously existing obligations' are re-created and imposed upon the successor State. Such extinctions of the obligations arising from an internationally wrongful act committed by the predecessor State can be explained by, as already mentioned the *"intuitu personae"* character of the international responsibility in international law enshrined in Article 1 of ARSIWA".

59 Kohen & Dumberry, 10, 21–22.

60 ILC Special Rapporteur Šturma, First Report, 2017, para 75 ("the report does not envisage the succession of States in respect of State responsibility as a transfer of the responsibility as such but as a transfer of rights and obligations arising from international responsibility of a (predecessor) State").

61 *Application of the Convention on the Prevention and Punishment of the Crime of Genocide* (*Croatia v. Serbia*), Judgment, 3 February 2015, ICJ Rep. 2015 (hereinafter "*Croatia Genocide Convention* case"), sep. op. Judge Kreća, para 65.4: "Succession to responsibility *in personam* is not *strict sensu* legally possible. (…) Even if responsibility of a State for acts or omissions of another State is established on the basis of consented succession to responsibility, it is not *strict sensu* a matter of succession to responsibility as subjective, of the *intuit personae* category, but of assuming the *consequences* of responsibility in a proper form" (emphasis in the original).

62 This concept was introduced by Max Huber, *Die Staatensuccession: völkerrechtliche und staatsrechtliche Praxis im XIX. Jahrhundert* (Duncker & Humblot 1898) 65, 95. It was subsequently adopted at the beginning of the 20th Century by many authors: W. Schönborn, *Staatensuccession, Handbuch des Völkerrechts*, v. 2, Part. 5 (1913) 49, 76, 95; Georg Dahm, *Völkerrecht*, v. 1, (W. Kohlhammer 1958) 121; A. Verdross, *Völkerrech* (4th edn, Springler 1959) 198. A number of contemporary scholars still rely on this argument to support their

> En ce qui concerne les obligations du droit international … il n'y a pas, suivant la *communis opinio*, de transmission à l'Etat annexant. Il s'agit de rapports si personnels, si étroitement liés à la situation, aux qualités, aux intérêts de l'Etat disparu, si conclus *intuitu personae*, qu'il est parfaitement logique qu'ils cessent d'exister avec lui.[63]
>
> [Il] est évident, étant donné le caractère strictement personnel des droits et obligations découlant de ces délits ou quasi-délits, qu'ils ne peuvent faire l'objet d'une succession. Les auteurs et la pratique internationale sont unanimes en ce sens.[64]

These writers draw a parallel with the concept of succession under Roman law, where liability for an action *ex delicto* does not pass to the heir.[65] This is

---

position in favour of non-succession: A. Verdross & B. Simma, *Universelles Völkerrecht, Theorie und Praxis* (Dunker & Humblot 1984) 633–634; Peter Malanczuk, *Akehurst's Modern Introduction to International Law* (7th edn, Routledge 1997) 169; Wilfred Fiedler, "State Succession", in: R. Bernhardt (ed), *Encyclopaedia of Public International Law*, v. 10 (Max Planck Institute 1984) (hereinafter "Bernhardt"), 454; Bardonnet, 316; Ulrich Fastenrath, "Der deutsche Einigungsvertrag im Lichte des Rechts der Staatennachfolge", 44 *ÖZöRV* 1992, 39; J. Crawford, *Brownlie's Principles of Public International Law* (8th edn, OUP 2013) (hereinafter "Crawford, Brownlie's") 442; I. Seidl-Hohenveldern, *Völkerrecht* (Carl Heymanns 1987) 288; Knut Ipsen, *Völkerrecht: ein Studienbuch* (4th edn, C.H. Beck 1999) 322 (quoted in: Peterschmitt, 10); Nguyen Quoc Dinh, *Droit international public* (LGDJ 1975) 434 (this argument is no longer found in subsequent editions of the textbook, such as in: Nguyen Quoc Dinh, Patrick Daillier & Alain Pellet, *Droit international public* (6th edn, LGDJ 1999); Louis Delbez, *Principes généraux du droit international public* (3rd edn, LGDJ 1964) 275; Volinka Reina, "Iraq's Delictual and Contractual Liabilities: Would Politics or International Law Provide for Better Resolution of Successor State Responsibility?", 22 *Berkeley JIL* 2004, 583, 587.

63 Cavaglieri, Règles, 374. His position is also clearly expressed in: "Rapport sur les effets juridiques des changements de souveraineté territoriale", *Annuaire IDI* 1931–I, 189: "Les obligations internationales de l'Etat disparu, d'après l'opinion la plus rependue et la plus conforme à la pratique, disparaissent en principe avec lui. Il s'agit, en effet, de rapports conclus *intuitu personae* … La nature de ces rapports et des obligations, qui en découlent, est en opposition avec l'idée de la succession, laquelle suppose des droits et des devoirs doués d'une autonomie qui leur permet de survivre et de continuer malgré le changement de leur sujet". See also: Arrigo Cavaglieri, "Note in materia di successione di Stato a Stato", 16 *RDI* 1924, 26 34–37.

64 Udina, 767. See also, 690.

65 The Institutes of Justinian, Book IV, Title 12: "Actions which will lie against a man under either the civil or the praetorian law will not always lie against his heir, the rule being absolute that for delict—for instance, theft, robbery, outrage, or unlawful damage—no penal action can be brought against the heir" (J.B. Moyle, *The Institutes of Justinian Translated into English* (3rd edn, Clarendon 1913).

the position which was adopted by Great Britain in its pleadings in the *R.E. Brown* case:

> I need not to remind you that so far as individuals are concerned under Roman Law the successor was never liable for torts; under our English law and American law for torts the successor was never liable, or with very rare exceptions, so rare as to say, I think, never is liable for the torts of the dead person. The liability for torts dies with the person, and it would be an extraordinary thing, in my submission, if it were found that in International law, there was a law which did not exist when you are dealing with local law as applied to individuals.[66]

The US-Great Britain Arbitral Commission in the *Hawaiian Claims* case relied (at least partially) on the private law doctrine of non-succession for action *ex delicto* to refute any transfer of the obligation to repair to the successor State:

> The analogy of universal succession in private law, which is much relied upon by those who argue for a large measure of succession to liability for obligations of the extinct State, even if admitted (and the aptness of the analogy is disputed), would make against succession to liability for delicts.[67]

This theory of the personal character of the internationally wrongful act is, however, contested.[68] It has been depicted as being "based on erroneous generalisation"[69] and "overly simplistic".[70] It is even rejected by scholars who are

66 "Synopsis of Argument", UK, *R.E. Brown* case, in: Nielsen, 185–186.

67 *Hawaiian Claims* case, 158.

68 Pierre D'Argent, *Les réparations de guerre en droit international public* (Bruylant 2002) (hereinafter "D'Argent") 814; Vahagn Avedian, "State Identity, Continuity, and Responsibility: The Ottoman, the Republic of Turkey and the Armenian Genocide", 23 *EJIL* 2012, 802; Mikulka, State Succession, 293 (the argument "no longer appear convincing").

69 Feilchenfeld, 690. It should be noted, however, that he is not referring to "internationally wrongful acts" but to "torts" in common law. He believes that "torts debts" are not necessarily personal obligations and that it all depends on whether they are described as such *under the laws of the debtor State*. If the "torts debts" are deemed to be personal obligations under the laws of the debtor State, the writer is of the view that "they would frequently be excluded from international law protection in case of State succession, not because of any specific rule of international law applying to tort debts, but because, according to the laws under which they were created, such debts could not survive the destruction of the debtor". On the contrary, he adds that if "the debtor is not destroyed by the territorial change, these debts would remain valid as long as the debtor continues to exist".

70 Volkovitsch, 2196.

strong supporters of the doctrine of non-succession.[71] There are, indeed, at least two reasons to reject this theory.

The first reason to reject the theory of the personal character of the internationally wrongful act is the analogy it draws between private law and international law.[72] This is, for instance, the position of the "universal succession theory", which resolves problems of State succession by making reference to the situation prevailing for individuals under private law.[73]

It has been rightly submitted that the consequences of the extinction of an individual and a State are simply not comparable.[74] Thus, if the death of an individual is a *sine qua non* prerequisite to the application of the rule of succession under private law, the same cannot be transposed automatically into the field of succession of States.[75] Thus, as a result of a change in its territory, a State does not necessarily lose its international legal personality.[76] Territorial losses *per se* do not affect a State's identity and do not necessarily result in its

71 Hurst, 177–178; Monnier, 87.

72 See, H. Lauterpacht, *Private Law Sources and Analogies of International Law* (Longmans 1927) 129–130; Booysen, 208–210. *Contra*: Monnier, 87: "Une construction reposant sur une analogie avec une institution propre au droit privé interne n'a pas, en effet, sa place naturelle sur le terrain du droit international public, où une terminologie recouvre une situation tout à fait différente".

73 Paul Fauchille, *Traité de droit international public*, v. I (8th edn, Rousseau 1922) 391: "Quand un Etat est absorbé par un autre, il se produit une succession du premier au profit du second, en tous points assimilable à celle du droit privé: l'extinction d'un Etat est, dans la mesure où elle se produit, une mort comparable à celle d'un particulier; et, comme un individu, l'Etat défunt a un successeur qui continu sa propre personnalité: le gouvernement en faveur de qui a lieu la cession est à l'égard du gouvernement cédant un véritable héritier, un successeur à la personne".

74 Stern, Succession, 37–38; Volkovitsch, 2196; Crawford, State Responsibility, 440; Vergara Lamadrid, 224–5; Pajnkihar, 306–7.

75 Gruber, 30, 35.

76 W. Schoenborn, "La nature juridique du territoire", *Rec. des cours*, v. 30, 1929–V, 119 ("une autorité ne subit aucun changement dans sa nature propre et particulière lorsque sa compétence locale est étendue ou restreinte"); L. Delbez, "Du territoire dans ses rapports avec l'Etat", *RGDIP* 1932, 719 ("[l]a modification territoriale aura bien entendu pour effet de déplacer les bornes de la compétence étatique, le sol national se trouvant agrandi ou restreint. Mais l'autorité de l'Etat ne se trouvera pas, par cela même, atteint dans sa nature. Aucun changement ne sera apporté dans l'identité de l'Etat. Il est clair en effet qu'une autorité ne subit aucune modification dans sa nature lorsque sa compétence territoriale est étendue ou restreinte"). See also: D. Anzilotti, *Cours de droit international public* (Sirey 1929) 183–184.

"death".[77] Indeed, some types of State succession (for instance, separation and cession and transfer of territory) do not involve the "death" of a State but only the loss of part of its territory. Therefore, and contrary to the situation prevailing in private law, the complete disappearance (or "death") of a State is not a formal condition to the application of the rules of State succession.[78]

In any event, it would also be wrong to qualify the extinction of a State as a "death" comparable to one affecting individuals.[79] This is well-explained by the "theory of organic substitution".[80] If it is unquestionable that a State losses its legal personality as a result of its extinction (its "death"), it remains that its "organic forces" or its "constitutive elements" (its territory and its population) survive such disintegration.[81] The constitutive elements of a State are only *affected*, to different degrees, by the process of State succession; they are not extinguished as a result of this fundamental change.[82] This is the position prevailing in doctrine.[83] In the words of Crawford, "even if a state somehow loses

77 Stern, Succession, 38; Erik Suy, "Réflexions sur la distinction entre la souveraineté et la compétence territoriale", in: R. Marcic et al. *Internationale Festschrift für Alfred Verdross* (Wilhem Fink 1971) 494.

78 Gruber, 33.

79 Verzijl, 129 ("The 'person' the State is quite another entity than a human being. In various cases, the State which succeeds in the sovereignty of a territory continues for all purposes the personality of its predecessor"); Vergara Lamadrid, 224–5.

80 This theory is influenced by the work of O. von Gierke, *Die Genossenschaftstheorie und die deutsche Rechtsprechung* (1887) 876, for whom the State is conceived as a "social organism", which, as any organism, rarely disappears as a result of death. Max Huber, *Die Staatensuccession: völkerrechtliche und staatsrechtliche Praxis im XIX. Jahrhundert* (Duncker & Humblot 1898) 3, subsequently imported this theory into the analysis of questions of State succession.

81 Stern, Succession, 38. The three constitutive elements of the State are the territory, the population and the government. It was first stated in Art. 1, *Montevideo Convention on the Rights and Duties of States,* 26 December 1933, in force on 26 December 1934; 28 *AJIL* 1934, Supp. 75). The Badinter Arbitration Commission in its "Opinion no. 1" (29 November 1991, 92 *ILR* 1993, 166) also recognised the three constitutive elements of the State in the context of the dissolution of Yugoslavia.

82 The only situation which could be envisaged where the constitutive elements of a State would be extinguished is if an Island-State simply disappeared from the face of the Earth, for instance, as a result of climate changes.

83 A good explanation is also found in: Marco G. Marcoff, *Accession à l'indépendance et succession d'Etats aux traités internationaux* (Ed. Univ. 1969) 15: "Contrairement à ce qu'on constate à la suite de la mort d'une personne physique, L'Etat qui 'meurt' ne disparaît pas totalement; ce n'est que sa personnalité morale qui prend fin, mais les autres éléments qui composent son 'corps matériel' n'en continuent pas moins à exister. L'Etat ancien continue de vivre dans le territoire et le peuple de l'Etat nouveau; il ne recueille donc pas la personnalité de l'Etat antérieur, mais les éléments—un ou plusieurs—qui le constituent". See also, this other comment (257): "Si la mort signifie, en droit, l'extinction totale de la

its legal personality, its constituent elements—that is, its territory, property and population—persist".[84] This position was however rejected by Judge Kreća for whom this theory "contains an element of legal absurdity" since it "portrays new States as a specific mix of the successor State and the continuator State expressed in percentage share, because each of them possesses a part of the territory and population of the predecessor State".[85]

Even if one were to accept the analogy with private law, it remains that modern private law rules of succession no longer follow the principle of Roman Law of non-succession of the heirs for "personal" delictual acts of the *cujus*. This is the situation under English law.[86] This argument is made by Volkovitsch.[87] It has also been expressed by the Arbitral Tribunal in the *Lighthouse Arbitration* case as follows:

> If that argument did in truth set out a general principle of law, it ought to be equally valid in civil law, but that is far from being the case. On the contrary, delictual obligations of private individuals, which appear to present the same 'highly personal' nature, normally pass to the heirs. That is not to say that the principles of private law are applicable as such

personne physique du défunt, l'extinction d'un Etat, même en cas de *debellatio* (à l'exception du cas purement hypothétique de la disparition physique d'une entité étatique), ne déclenche pas la perte de tous les éléments constituants la personnalité de l'Etat. L'organisation juridique antérieure disparaît, mais le territoire et les personnes humaines qui en constituaient le *substratum* réel resteront. Ce sont eux qui représenteront, avec l'organisation politique et juridique nouvelle après l'indépendance, l'Etat nouveau".

84 Crawford, State Responsibility, 440. See also, Pajnkihar, 306–7.

85 *Croatia Genocide Convention* case, sep. op. Judge Kreća, para 65.4: "It appears that the concept of 'organic substitution' fails to take into account the element of legal identity and continuity as the very substance of international personality in the frame of territorial changes. It reduces the State to its physical attributes (territory, population), which are also possessed by territorial non-State entities devoid of the quality of subjects in terms of international law".

86 See: P.H. Winfield, *Textbook of the Law of Tort* (3rd edn, Sweet & Maxwell 1946) 178ff; R.W.M. Dias & B.S. Markesinis, *Tort Law* (Clarendon 1984) 416ff.

87 Volkovitsch, 2196. For the author, "modern case law and code provisions have almost universally reversed the very Roman doctrine on which the personality theory was based". He maintains (2211) that "almost all states [are] now providing for the survivability of actions against deceased tortfeasors, in both common law and civil law countries". The writer analyses the reversal of the rule on the survivability of torts actions as a shift "from a system centered on the punishment of tortfeasors to one that focuses on the compensation of the victims and the avoidance of incidents". For him this shift is relevant to the question of the survival of internationally wrongful acts in international law because it involves the same "competing equities"; the situation prevailing in private law can illuminate the solution to be adopted in international law. See also: Crawford, State Responsibility, 441.

> in cases of State succession, but only that the one argument which is sometimes invoked against the transmission of delictual obligations is without force.[88]

The second reason for rejecting the theory of the personal character of the internationally wrongful act is that it is founded on the outdated concept of *culpa* ("*faute*") in State responsibility.[89] For those writers who maintain that a *faute* needs to be proven for a State to engage its international responsibility,[90] an internationally wrongful act has conceivably a "personal character". However, it is generally recognised that the element of *faute* is not a necessary condition to determine the liability of a State under contemporary international law.[91] The work of the ILC on State responsibility no longer makes use of the concept of *culpa*.[92]

It has rightly been observed by Stern that when international responsibility is conceived as an *objective* concept rather than a *personal* internationally wrongful act involving culpa or intention, the transferability of the obligation to repair to the successor State becomes possible:

> Il n'est pas exclu, en particulier, que ces analyses [of the doctrine of non-succession rejecting any transfer of obligations] restent liées à une conception ancienne de la responsabilité, dans laquelle l'idée de *culpa* était forte, et ne prennent pas en compte l'évolution de concept de la responsabilité internationale vers une plus grande objectivation: on ne voit pas, dans une conception de la responsabilité internationale fondée

88 *Lighthouse Arbitration* case, 23 *ILR* 1956, 93.

89 Stern, Responsabilité, 335; Crawford, State Responsibility, 441; Mikulka, State Succession, 294; Vergara Lamadrid, 224–5; Peterschmitt, 10. Ian Brownlie, *State Responsibility,* Part 1 (Clarendon 1983) 44–45, describes the notion of "fault" in the following words: "In the more general sense the fault principle rests upon the proof of intention (dol, dolus) or negligence (faute, culpa). The term faute (or culpa) is used to describe types of blameworthiness based upon reasonable forseeability, or foresight without desire of the consequences (recklessness, culpa lata)".

90 See, for instance, Udina, 767, for whom "c'est toujours la faute de l'Etat qui donne lieu à sa responsabilité internationale". See also, Charles De Visscher, *Théories et réalités en droit international public* (Pedone 1953) 210.

91 Ian Brownlie, *State Responsibility,* Part 1 (Clarendon 1983) 39.

92 ILC, "First Report on State Responsibility (*addendum* no. 4)", Special Rapporteur James Crawford, 26 May 1998, A/CN.4/490/Add.4, para 122. However, the ILC, Commentaries, State Responsibility, 2001, 70, also indicates that the Articles lay down no general standards with respect to the question whether State responsibility in some context involves some degree of fault, culpability, negligence or want of due diligence.

> sur l'existence d'un acte illicite, compris comme violation objective du droit positif existant, de raison majeurs conduisant à exclure la transmission des obligations naissant d'une telle responsabilité dans le cadre d'une succession d'Etats.[93]

3 Challenges and Criticisms of the Doctrine of Non-succession

For the most part of the 20th Century, very few authors challenged the doctrine of non-succession to responsibility. In fact, the rule seemed so well-established, that O'Connell, who was critical about this theory, opened the chapter on the topic in his 1967 two-volumes book by stating that "it has been taken for granted that a successor State is not liable for the delicts of its predecessor".[94] Thus, as previously mentioned, until recently, almost all general international law textbooks adopted the position of non-succession.[95] In fact, in their pleadings before the ICJ in the 1997 *Gabčíkovo-Nagymaros* case,[96] both Slovakia and Hungary made reference to the "widely accepted"[97] and "well-established"[98] principle of non-succession.

Feilchenfeld was probably one of the first to express a dissenting voice in this apparent unanimity. According to him, a successor State cannot reject its responsibility for a "tort" committed by the predecessor State solely on the ground that this "tort" is not strictly speaking a "debt".[99] He concluded that "the rule of maintenance of tort claims" after a succession of States had "not been excluded by the growth of a general new custom" and that it was "not justified by the theories which are advanced in favour of such exclusion".[100] His

93 Stern, Responsabilité, 335. See also: Stern, Succession, 174, indicating that the rule of non-succession "ne tient pas nécessairement compte des évolutions contemporaines concernant le concept de responsabilité internationale".

94 O'Connell, State Succession, v. 1, 482.

95 The list of those scholars is provided in Section 2.1.

96 *Case Concerning the Gabčíkovo-Nagymaros Project* (*Hungary v. Slovakia*), Judgment, 25 September 1997, ICJ Rep. 1997, 3 (hereinafter "*Gabčíkovo-Nagymaros* case").

97 "Counter-Memorial", Slovakia, v. 1, 5 December 1994, para 3.59. Slovakia even referred to "the practically unanimous view of the doctrine" on this question (ibid para 3.60).

98 "Reply", Hungary, v. 1, 20 June 1995, para 3.163. Hungary also added that there would exist one "key exception" where the successor State, by its *own* conduct, continues the wrongful act committed by its predecessor.

99 Feilchenfeld, 689, 728. It should be noted, however, that he is not referring to "internationally wrongful acts" but to "torts" in the common law sense of the term.

100 Ibid 690. He rejects the theory of the personal character of the internationally wrongful act.

conclusion is that the right to reparation of injured States is "protected in case of State succession in the same way as other debts".[101]

Hyde was critical about the doctrine of non-succession because it disassociates State responsibility from the territory affected by State succession.[102] He favours instead a principle under which there would be a "connection between the territory as such and certain forms of conducts committed thereon as to cause the [new State] to afford under some conditions a means of redress regardless of a change of sovereignty that marks the extinction of the tort feasor".[103]

The issue was also mentioned by the Tripartite Claims Commission set up under a 1924 Treaty entered into by the US, Hungary and Austria to determine the amount of reparation to be paid by the last two States (considered to be "continuators" of the Austria-Hungary Dual Monarchy) to US nationals as a result of internationally wrongful acts committed by Austria-Hungary during the First World War.[104] The Commission acknowledged that scholars were divided on the question whether there was succession to obligations arising from the commission of internationally wrongful acts.[105]

The 1956 award of the Arbitral Tribunal in the *Lighthouse Arbitration* case[106] appears to be a milestone in that respect.[107] It clearly rejects the position of non-succession traditionally taken by scholarship:

101 Ibid. He notes (689, footnote 46) that the work of Gentilis, Grotius, Pufendorf and de Vattel does not make any exception for "torts" claims.

102 Hyde, 437–438.

103 Ibid.

104 *Agreement between the United States and Austria and Hungary for the Determination of the Amount to be Paid by Austria and Hungary in Satisfaction of their Obligations under the Treaties Concluded by the United States with Austria on August 24, 1921, and with Hungary on August 29, 1921*, 26 November 1924, *LNTS* v. 48, 70, *UNRIAA* v. VI, 199.

105 This is the relevant quote from *Administrative Decision no. 1*, Tripartite Claims Commission, 25 May 1927, *UNRIAA* v. VI, 203; 21 *AJIL* 1927, 599: "The answer must be found in the provisions of the Treaties of Vienna and of Budapest. It will not be profitable to examine the divergent views maintained by European continental writers on continental law as compared of Great Britain and the US with respect to the liability of a Successor State for the obligations either ex contractu or ex delicto of a dismembered State. It is, however, interesting to note in passing that while one group maintains that such obligations pass with succession and are apportioned between the Successor States, and while the other group maintains that the obligations do not pass with succession, neither group maintains that a joint liability rests upon two or more Successor States where the territory of a dismembered State has been divided between them".

106 *Lighthouse Arbitration* case, 23 *ILR* 1956, 81. This case is examined in detail at Part 2, Chapter 2, Sections 5.2.5 and 5.3.1.

107 For Volkovitsch, 2190, this case "represents a clear evolution of doctrine from the imperialism-tainted decisions" of the *R.E. Brown* case and the *Hawaiian Claims*. See

> The thesis, one of theory rather than of practice, that there can never be a question of transmission—or more accurately, of transfer ... is not, in general, well founded.[108]
>
> Certain tendencies among writers clearly necessitate reconsideration by reason of the different kinds of possible delictual obligations and the diversity of possible hypotheses of territorial succession.[109]

In subsequent writing, Verzijl, who acted as the President of the Arbitral Tribunal in the *Lighthouse Arbitration* case, has also expressed very strong criticisms of this doctrine of non-succession. He stated that "public international law is haunted by [this] unyielding and wide-spread thesis" which is "unacceptable as a general rule" as it tends "to become, as a result of unjustified generalisation, an assertedly unassailable dogma though it is in fact no more than a legal myth".[110] The author therefore rejects the principle of non-succession in its "absolute variant, because there are situations conceivable in which its application would be unreasonable".[111]

Another similar approach is that of O'Connell, who refutes the strict theory of non-succession on the ground that "there is no great intellectual incubus behind this supposed rule of international law"[112] and that "the net is too widely cast if it is proposed that there can be no succession to international delicts".[113] He also notes that any comprehensive theory would be impossible to the extent that "there is no universal criterion for distinguishing claims which may be made against the successor State from those which may not".[114] The same position is adopted by Atlam,[115] who

also: Atlam, 248; Crawford, State Responsibility, 443 ("A juridical break of sorts with the absolutist position was achieved" by that case), 445 (the case "is notable, however, for its articulated critique of absolutist solutions both for and against succession with respect to responsibility").

108 *Lighthouse Arbitration* case, 23 *ILR* 1956, 92.

109 Ibid 93.

110 Verzijl, 219–220. See also, J.H.W. Verzijl, "Droit de la mer et succession d'Etats", in: *Hommage d'une génération de juristes au président Basdevant* (Pedone 1960) 523–524.

111 Verzijl, 219–220.

112 O'Connell, Recent Problems, 162.

113 O'Connell, State Succession, v. I, 486. See also, ibid 164, where he indicates that any proposition of non-succession to obligations arising from the commission of internationally wrongful acts (as opposed to "torts" in the common law sense of the term) would be "patently erroneous".

114 Ibid.

115 Atlam, 15, 235–236. However, he does not deny altogether the relevance of the doctrine of non-succession. For instance (see 281ff), he adopts the principle of non-succession for

devoted a doctoral thesis to the subject. Czaplinski is more prudent in his conclusion.[116]

Volkovitsch is undoubtedly the most outspoken critical commentator on the doctrine of non-succession, which he believes:

> Lacks the necessary foundation in practice and theory to be accepted as a customary norm of international law. Both the provisions of international agreement and the history of diplomatic practice on the subject are inconsistent and have been frequently misunderstood. Nor do the varied decisions of international tribunals or municipal courts provide sufficient support for a theory of nonsuccession. Moreover, the various theoretical bases proposed for such a principle are each plagued by fundamental flaws.[117]

Thus, not only does he reject the existence of any customary norm in favour of the principle of non-succession but he goes a step further in advocating "a customary norm of international law providing for a rebuttable presumption of succession to liability".[118]

Stern is particularly critical of the doctrine of non-succession insofar as an internationally wrongful act committed by the predecessor State would simply disappear along with its perpetrator.[119] She denies the existence of any strict "rule" of non-succession:

---

cases where the predecessor State ceases to exist (such as dissolution of State) but accepts the rule of succession in cases of unification of States (see 274, 286–288).

116 Czaplinski, 356. For him, State practice, judicial decisions (which are said to be "neither clear nor unanimous" (346)) and the writings of scholars on the issue "[do] not provide a sufficient basis on which to formulate the principles governing succession in respects of delictual responsibility".

117 Volkovitsch, 2198. See also, 2172–2173.

118 Ibid 2162. See also, 2172–2173. He believes (2198) that "sufficient support exists in jurisprudential theory and in evolving diplomatic and judicial practice of sovereign states" for the establishment of such a presumption, which is also the "most practical and logically consistent solution". For him (see 2198), such a presumption is also supported by a "series of well-established principle of both international and municipal law, including the concept of acquired rights, the linkage between rights and obligations, the doctrine of international servitudes, the principle of unjust enrichment, and the principle of responsibility for torts". He is of the view (see 2199–2200) that a *strict rule* of transfer of the obligation to repair to the successor State, which could not be rebutted in any circumstances, should apply in some specific cases. He also provides (2100–2103) several examples where, on the contrary, no such transfer should apply.

119 Stern, Responsabilité, 336: "Une absence systématique de succession en matière de responsabilité choque cependant l'esprit de justice".

> Sans pour autant affirmer, en l'absence de précédents significatifs, qu'existe une règle générale de transmission de la responsabilité, je souhaite tout de même souligner qu'il est facilement concevable de considérer que certaines obligations financières, en quoi se résout le plus souvent la réparation, pourraient être transmises au moment d'une succession d'Etats de l'Etat prédécesseur à l'Etat successeur de la même façon que le sont les dettes d'Etats. On pourrait parler des transmissions des conséquences de la responsabilité, plus que de transmission de la responsabilité elle-même.[120]

It can therefore safely be concluded that earlier statements making reference to the "unanimity" of scholars against the principle of State succession to responsibility are no longer valid.[121] At the timing of writing the first edition of my book, I noted that several modern writers had rejected the application of a strict principle of non-succession and adopted the view that succession to obligations may be an acceptable solution in some circumstances.[122] Many

---

120 Ibid 338. In her conclusion (355), Stern affirms the existence of a rebuttable presumption of succession to obligations arising from the commission of internationally wrongful acts. In a previous general study on the question of succession of States (Stern, Succession, 173–174), she concluded that the principle of non-succession was a rule "dont l'existence en droit international contemporain reste à prouver". See also, Peterschmitt, 72, for whom there is no general "rule" providing for the non-transferability of the consequences of international responsibility.

121 See, for instance, statements made in 1933 by Udina, 767, and in 1961 by Monnier, 86.

122 This is the case of D'Argent, 814 (rejecting the principle of non-transferability "dans sa formulation absolue" but indicating that there is probably no presumption of succession to obligations arising from the commission of internationally wrongful acts); Pierre Michel Eisemann, "Emprunts russes et problèmes de succession d'Etats", in: P. Juillard & B. Stern (eds), *Les emprunts russes et le règlement du contentieux financier franco-russe* (Cahiers internationaux n°16 2002) (hereinafter "Eisemann, Emprunts russes") 60–62, 77 ("le droit international contemporain admet la succession à la responsabilité internationale"); Mark Thompson, "Finders Weepers Losers Keepers: United States of America v. Steinmetz: the Doctrine of State Succession, Maritime Finds, and the Bell of the C.S.S. Alabama", 28 *Conn.L.Rev.* 1996, 481 ("although opinions diverge greatly, a significant body of case law and commentary would require a power in succession to assume the obligations of the predecessor, including its liability for international torts"); Joe Verhoeven, *Droit international public* (Larcier 2000) 189–190 (criticising the arguments developed by the doctrine of non-succession and concluding that it cannot be totally excluded that responsibility can be transferred from the predecessor State to the successor State); Oscar Schachter, "State Succession: the Once and Future Law", 33(2) *Va. JIL* 1993, 256 ("the old view that such responsibility should not be transferable to successor is by no means self-evident and persuasive arguments based on general principles of law (including unjust enrichment) can be made to support succession of liability in some situations"); Ivan A. Shearer, *Starke's International Law* (11th edn, Butterworths 1994) 303 (stating that

more have adopted this approach since then.[123] One example is Mikulka's

"there is no general principle of succession to delictual responsibility" but also expressing doubts as to whether this rule should be considered to be an "invariable proposition" and concluding that "it may in some circumstances be reasonable to bind the successor State to respect the unliquidated claim against its predecessor"); Andreas Zimmermann, *Staatennachfolge in völkerrechtliche Verträge: Zugleich ein Beitrag zu den Möglichkeiten und Grenzen völkerrechtlicher Kodifikation* (Springer 2000) 68 (indicating that there is no automatic succession but also referring to some more recent State practice which suggests that increasingly there is an assumption by the successor State that there is a transfer of the obligation to repair); H.A. Strydom, "Namibian Independence and the Question of the Contractual and Delictual Liability of the Predecessor and Successor Governments", 15 *South African* YIL 1989–1990, 112 ("in absolute terms, neither of [the theories rejecting or accepting succession to obligations arising from the commission of internationally wrongful acts] is compatible with the complex variety of legal relationships and corresponding liabilities usually associated with territorial transfers"); Naomi Roht-Arriaza, "Reparations Decisions and Dilemmas", 27 *Hastings Int'l & Comp. L. Rev.* 2004, 157, 212 ("[i]n cases where the State or Government under whose authority the violation occurred is no longer in existence, the State or Government successor in title should provide reparation to the victims"); Gregory Townsend, "The Iraq Claims Process: A Progress Report on the United Nations Compensation Commission & U.S. Remedies", 17 *Loy.L.A.Int'l & Comp.L.Rev.* 1995, 973, 979–980 ("[m]any members of the international community would like to see a change in Iraq's government or even the partition of Iraq into several smaller states, including a Kurdish one. A new Iraqi government or subsequent successor state, however, still would be responsible for paying the claims against Iraq under international law"); Ineta Ziemele, "State Continuity, Succession and Responsibility: Reparations to the Baltic States and their Peoples" 3 *Baltic* YIL 2003, 176 ("[i]t is therefore not excluded that through the joint efforts of third States, in some cases a new State is considered to be bound by some international obligations and bear responsibility thereof"). See also, the analysis made by Michael Silagi, *Staatsuntergang und Staatennachfolge: mit besonderer Berücksichtigung des Endes der* DDR (Peter Lang, 1996, 352ff, 372–373.

123 Kohen, Succession of States, 161–174; Šturma, State Succession, 653–678; Jakubowski, State Succession, 265–270, 330–1 ("the recent developments of international practice and legal scholarship have shown that traditional concepts on non-transferability of obligations arising from internationally wrongful act do not correspond with state practice nor with the general principles of justice and equity. However, the existence of precise rules of succession in such obligations under general international law remains debatable"); Andrzej Jakubowski, "Cultural Heritage and State Succession", in F. Francioni & A.F. Vrdoljak (ed), *The Oxford Handbook of International Cultural Heritage Law* (OUP 2020) 600 (referring to legal scholarship which have "led to widespread criticism of the negative succession rule" and that "These new trends clearly favour a more equitable approach to State succession and international responsibility, based on analysing the factual and legal contexts of a given case in light of the principles of international justice as well as the stability and security of international legal relations"); Benjamin E. Brockman-Hawe, "Succession, the Obligation to Repair and Human Rights; The European Court of Human Rights Judgment in the Case of Bijelić v. Montenegro and Serbia", 59(3) ICLQ 2010 (hereinafter "Brockman-Hawe") 866; Marcel Szabó, "State Succession and the Jurisprudence of the European Court of Human Rights", in: Christina Binder & Konrad Lachmayer (eds), *The European*

nuanced position.[124] Another interesting feature is that some authors who had supported the doctrine of non-succession in the past have since then adopted a much more nuance view.[125]

Court of Human Rights and Public International Law: Fragmentation or Unity? (Nomos 2014) 139; European Commission for Democracy through Law (Venice Commission), *amicus* brief in *Bijelić v. Montenegro and Serbia*, ECHR, 11 June 2009, Application no. 11890/05 (opinion no. 495/2008, CDL-AD (2008)021, 20 Oct. 2008, para 33, 41ff); Vahagn Avedian, "State Identity, Continuity, and Responsibility: The Ottoman, the Republic of Turkey and the Armenian Genocide", 23 *EJIL* 2012, 801ff; M. Milanovic, "Territorial Application of the Genocide Convention and State Succession", in: Paola Gaeta (ed), *The UN Genocide Convention: A Commentary* (OUP 2009) 19 (paper version) ("the clean slate rule that is applicable to state succession to treaties should not apply to state succession to international responsibility"); Marko Milanovic, "The Spatial Dimension: Treaties and Territory", in: C.J. Tams et al., (eds), *Research Handbook on the Law of Treaties* (Cheltenham 2014) 219; M. Bracke, *The Rules of State Succession Applied to a Hypothetical Flemish Independence*, Master thesis, Ghent Univ. 2019–2020, 49, 54; A. Buser, "Colonial Injustices and the Law of State Responsibility: The CARICOM Claim for Reparations" 77 *Heidelberg JIL* 2017 (hereinafter "Buser") 409–446; Vergara Lamadrid, 224; Pajnkihar, 298ff, 308 ("international law, and in particular the law of international responsibility, does not preclude the institution of succession to international responsibility but allows it at least in certain circumstances, among which *consent to assume responsibility* stands out in particular", emphasis in the original), 338 ("succession to secondary rights and obligations does not in itself contradict the principles of the law of international responsibility of States").

124 Mikulka, State Succession, 292, first indicating that "Neither practice nor doctrine provide a uniform answer to the question whether, and if so, in what circumstances a successor State may be held responsible for an internationally wrongful act of its predecessor". He later mentions that the *Gabcíkovo-Nagymaros* case "falls within the period of time when international law evolved towards broader acceptance of continuity of international obligations for successor States". For him, "In view of the link which exists between the primary obligation and secondary obligations arising from its breach, the presumption of succession in respect of responsibility may be stronger or weaker depending on the outcome of succession in respect of the primary obligation itself. Any hypothesis formulated on this basis could, however, be verified only in the light of further State practice and jurisprudence in this field". See also: Ruy & Baecke, 22, stating "in more recent decades, legal doctrine has become increasingly critical of the theory of non-succession to State responsibility, and has instead found growing support for continuity in State practice and case-law", but also adding that "the picture remains nuanced" and that "in particular, the observed trend away from a general doctrine of non-succession—important as it is—cannot alter the fact that it is a relatively recent phenomenon only, the impact of which remains somewhat uncertain".

125 Malcolm Shaw, *International Law* (4th edn, CUP 1997) 713. In the 8th edition (2021), 876–7, he noted that the topic was of "considerable uncertainty" and that the "general principle" which "has often been stated", i.e. non-succession, was to "state that matter too baldly", citing the *Lighthouse Arbitration* case, the work of O'Connell and the Institute's 2015 Resolution. He concluded that the "matter will depend upon the particular circumstances of the case and it may be premature to assert that a presumption one way or another has now established as a proposition of international law".

A good example of such evolution is reflected in the ILC's work on State responsibility. Thus, in its "First Report on State Responsibility (addendum no. 5)" (1998), Special Rapporteur Crawford mentioned that "there is a widely held view that a new State does not, in general, succeed to any State responsibility of the predecessor State with respect to its territory".[126] However, in the 2001 Commentaries, he indicated that it was "unclear whether a new State succeeds to any State responsibility of the predecessor State with respect to its territory".[127] ILC Special Rapporteur Šturma highlighted the evolution of Crawford's point of view: "from a refusal in 1998 to a partial acceptance in 2001".[128] In fact, in his 2013 book, Crawford stated that "there has been a certain shift in consensus, from what Dumberry refers to as the 'traditional' or 'absolute' approach of non-succession (…) to a more nuanced view that focuses on the facts of the succession in question".[129] This is the approach he prefers.[130] The landscape has significantly changed in the last 15 years. As mentioned above, the Institute's Resolution discarded the application of both a general rule of non-succession and the opposite principle of automatic succession:[131]

> The sort of 'clean slate' rule applicable to all cases of State succession in the field of international responsibility (…) would result in numerous situations where the consequences of illegality would simply be erased and unaccounted for. Such an outcome flies in the face of the requirement for stability in international relations as well as the very idea of equity and justice. Such an outcome would also be contrary to the interests of all States affected by an event of State succession (…). One of the most fundamental goals guiding the Resolution, as mentioned in the Final Report,

126 ILC, "First Report on State Responsibility (*addendum* no. 5)", Special Rapporteur James Crawford, 22 July 1998, A/CN.4/490/Add.5., para 282.

127 ILC, Commentaries, State Responsibility, 2001, 119, para 3.

128 ILC Special Rapporteur Šturma, First Report, 2017, paras 10, 35.

129 Crawford, State Responsibility, 437.

130 Ibid 455: "the fact-sensitive approach" to the issue "promoted in the *Lighthouse Arbitration*, and advanced by O'Connell, Verzijl and Dumberry, seems preferable to the negative succession rule posited by *R.E. Brown, Hawaiian Claims* and the commentators such as Hurst".

131 IIL, Final Report, Kohen, para 54: "the purpose of ensuring that obligations stemming from the commission of internationally wrongful acts must be carried out even in cases of State succession must not lead to the adoption of an opposite, general rule of succession to these obligations in all cases".

> is to 'prevent situations of State succession from leading to an avoidance of the consequences of internationally wrongful acts, particularly in the form of the extinction or disappearance of the obligation to repair, by virtue of the mere fact of the State succession.' One of the Resolution's central themes is therefore to discard the application of a general strict non-succession 'clean slate' solution for matters involving State succession to the consequences of international responsibility.[132]

The same approach was adopted by Special Rapporteur Šturma. He indicated that "he does not suggest replacing one highly general theory of non-succession by another similar theory in favour of succession", adding that "instead, a more flexible and realistic approach is needed".[133] As further examined below, this issue would become highly contentious during the ILC's work.

While the Court in the *Croatia Genocide Convention* case did not formally take position on the issue, it did not reject the possibility for a new successor State to be held responsible for obligations arising from the commission of wrongful acts by the predecessor State before the date of succession.[134] In fact, a number of judges (in their individual opinions) have considered the Court's reasoning on this issue to be based upon a *presumption* in favour of succession to international responsibility.[135] Both Judges Skotnikov[136] and Kreća[137] clearly rejected the possibility of any such succession to responsibility. Their views will be further discussed below.[138]

A review of relevant State practice and international and municipal case law in the next chapter shows that, despite some earlier claims of near unanimity

132 Kohen & Dumberry, 10–11, quoting IIL, Final Report, ibid para 53.

133 ILC Special Rapporteur Šturma, Second Report, 2018, para 16. See also, ibid First Report, 2017, para 83; ibid Third Report, 2019, para 35 ('The approach of the Special Rapporteur to the topic excludes both the (automatic) extinction of responsibility and the automatic transfer of responsibility in cases of succession of States").

134 Kohen & Dumberry, 11; ILC Special Rapporteur Šturma, First Report, 2017, para 54 ("the judgment seems to be the most recent pronouncement in favour of the argument that the responsibility of a State might be engaged by way of succession"), para 58 ("It is worth mentioning that the Court did not refuse and thus accepted the alternative argument of Croatia as to its jurisdiction over acts prior to 27 April 1992"). See also: ibid Second Report, 2018, para 179.

135 *Croatia Genocide Convention* case, Decla. Judge Xue, para 22; Sep. op. Judge Skotnikov, para 5; Sep. op. Judge Kreća, paras 60–61. See also, Sep. op. Judge Sebutinde, paras 9, 13.

136 Ibid Sep. op. Judge Skotnikov, paras 4–5.

137 Ibid Sep. op. Kreća, paras 60ff.

138 See, Part 2, Chapter 2, Section 4.3.3.5.

in scholarship for the "rule" of non-succession,[139] the actual practice is much more diversified. The *strict and automatic* principle of non-succession is not representative of contemporary international law practice.

139 For instance, see: Monnier, 86; Rousseau, v. III, 507.

CHAPTER 2

Analysis of State Practice and Case Law

1 Introductory Remarks on the Doctrinal Analysis of State Practice

Supporters of the doctrine of non-succession usually refer to two international arbitral awards which were decided in the context of incorporation of State: the *R.E. Brown* case[1] and the *Hawaiian Claims* case.[2] Some scholars consider these international decisions to be strong authorities in support of the doctrine of non-succession.[3]

Other writers have been more critical in their assessment of these two precedents, referring to them as "neither clear nor unanimous".[4] It has also been suggested that these two arbitral awards were "relatively outdated"[5] and "obsoletes",[6] that their authority was "doubtful",[7] and that they ultimately echoed the age of colonialism in international relations.[8] This is, for instance, the position

1 *R.E. Brown* case, 129. This case is further discussed in Chapter 2, Section 2.1.4.

2 *Hawaiian Claims* case, 157. See, Chapter 2, Section 2.1.5.

3 Scholars writing at the time recognised the importance of the awards in support of the rule of non-succession: Hurst, 165; H. Lauterpacht, *Private Law Sources and Analogies of International Law* (Longmans, 1927), 283, 131–132. See also, many years later: Monnier, 86 ("l'homogénéité que présente la jurisprudence internationale en cette matière ne se retrouve en effet dans aucun des autres domaines où se pose le problème de la succession d'Etats", adding "sans doute les décisions rendues ici sont-elles peu nombreuses. Mais ce fait est sans importance tant il est vrai que la valeur normative de la jurisprudence est moins fonction de décisions qui la composent que de leur cohérence"); Rousseau, v. III, 507 (speaking of a "unanimité impressionnante" concerning these decisions).

4 Czaplinski, 346. Similarly, for Volkovitsch, 2182, these decisions "cannot be characterised as either unanimous or definitive" and do not establish a customary rule in favour of a principle of non-succession. He believes (2186) that the fact that the US and the UK advocated diametrically opposite positions in these two cases prove the non existence of a rule of non-succession. See also, Verzijl, 219, referring to these cases as a "few isolated precedents". This is also the position of Eisemann, Emprunts russes, 60, for whom the so-called rule of non-succession (the existence of which he disputes) is based on an incorrect reading of these two cases.

5 Czaplinski, 356.

6 Sir Robert Jenning, "General Course on Principles of International Law", *Rec. des cours*, v. 121, 1967–II, 449. See also, Peterschmitt, 11.

7 The *Restatement (Third), Foreign Relations Law of the United States*, v. I (American Law Inst. 1987) § 209, Rep. notes no. 7, 108.

8 Ibid 107–108: "These cases date from the age colonialism when colonial powers resisted any rule that would make them responsible for the delicts of States which they regarded as

 | DOI:10.1163/9789004703810_005

of Volkovitsch, for whom "if international law is to have any relevance, it must abjure rhetoric and the pernicious theories on which it rests by denying such decisions any persuasive authority".[9] These two decisions rendered by the same international tribunal will be examined later in this chapter.[10] A somewhat different reading of these cases will be proposed. In any event, there is no doubt that these awards were influenced by the view held by many ancient scholars for whom responsibility is an *intuitu personae* phenomenon.[11] The present study is not concerned with the question of succession to responsibility per se, but rather with the issue of succession to rights and obligations arising as a consequence of responsibility.[12] Another case of great importance which will be analysed in this chapter is the *Lighthouse Arbitration* case.[13] A number of other awards rendered by international tribunals will also be examined in this chapter.

In scholarship, reference is also often made to decisions of municipal courts that had to directly tackle the issue of State succession to responsibility.[14] Writers are generally divided on the significance and the weight to be given to these judicial precedents before national courts and on whether they actually support the doctrine of non-succession.[15] One writer decided to exclude their examination from his study.[16] This chapter will examine in detail all relevant municipal court decisions, many of which have simply never been analysed by

---

uncivilized". Similarly, for Volkovitsch, 2185, these two arbitral awards are "representative of the ideology of the Great Power at the height of the imperialist era" and that "the basic rationale of these decisions was simply that a civilized nation should never be responsible for the delicts of a backward state". The passage seems to be approved in: ILC Special Rapporteur Šturma, First Report, 2017, para 39. See also, Mikulka, State Succession, 294.

9 Volkovitsch, 2186. See also, Mark Thompson, "Finders Weepers Losers Keepers: United States of America v. Steinmetz: the Doctrine of State Succession, Maritime Finds, and the Bell of the C.S.S. Alabama", 28 *Conn. L.Rev.* 1996, 542, for whom these two arbitral awards "should not be the basis for a per se rule rejecting succession to predecessor delicts".

10 See, Sections 2.1.4 and 2.1.5.

11 Kohen & Dumberry, 117.

12 IIL, Final Report, Kohen, paras 27ff.

13 *Lighthouse Arbitration* case, 23 *ILR* 1956, 81. See, Sections 5.2.5 and 5.3.1.

14 Hurst, 173–177; O'Connell, State Succession, v. I, 492–493; Verzijl, 224–227; Czaplinski, 346–351; Volkovitsch, 2192–2195; Rousseau, v. III, 510; Atlam, 217–222.

15 Czaplinski, 346, 351, indicates that the impact of these decisions is somewhat limited and does not establish the existence of any customary rule. Volkovitsch, 2193–2195, maintains that the "contemporary precedents demonstrate the development and reinforcement of a customary norm in favour of succession".

16 This is the reasoning of Monnier, 72: "Les raisons qui ont conduit les juges nationaux tantôt à admettre, tantôt à nier la responsabilité de l'Etat successeur sont si diverses et, très souvent, si éloignées du droit international qu'il serait vain de vouloir y chercher des précédents". He concludes that these decisions should not be considered "comme la traduction répétée d'une pratique étatique générale ou d'un usage créateur de droit".

scholars. Some of these cases will prove to be a very valuable source of information which has, unfortunately, often been discarded in the past by writers. Yet, it should be added that some of them do not involve matters of international responsibility regarding wrongs committed against *third* States.

Scholars supporting the doctrine of non-succession generally make reference to State practice.[17] It has been suggested that these examples of State practice do not permit to draw any clear, positive or negative conclusions.[18] This chapter will analyse several relevant examples of State practice.

As previously observed, a proper analysis of State practice and case law can only be made taking into account the different *types* of State succession involved.[19] It should be recalled here the statement of the Arbitral Tribunal in the *Lighthouse Arbitration* case: "It is impossible to formulate a general, identical solution for every imaginable hypothesis of territorial succession, and any attempt to formulate such a solution must necessarily fail in view of the extreme diversity of cases of this kind".[20] The Tribunal concluded: "All these differences cannot but exercise a decisive influence on the solution of the problem of State succession even in cases of delictual obligation".[21]

In the following sections, relevant State practice and international and municipal case law will be examined for the following different types of succession of States:[22]

- Incorporation of State;
- Unification of States;
- Dissolution of State;
- Cession and transfer of territory;
- Separation; and
- Creation of Newly Independent States.

17 See, Hurst; Rousseau, v. III, 505; Atlam, 204, 216.

18 For Czaplinski, 343, State practice "shows a tendency to transfer delictual liability, but it is not consistent" and that "the conclusion is that this practice does not prove the existence of a customary rule concerning the succession in respect of delictual obligations". See also, Monnier, 73, for whom these precedents of State practice must be "jugés avec une certaine prudence en raison des considérations extra-juridiques qui, le plus souvent, ont poussé les Etats à assurer ou au contraire à rejeter les obligations de la responsabilité internationale des Etats auxquels ils ont succédé".

19 The other factors and circumstances calling for specific solutions to specific problems of State succession to responsibility are examined in Chap. 3, below.

20 *Lighthouse Arbitration* case, 23 *ILR* 1956, 91.

21 Ibid.

22 The classification of the different types of succession of States has already been examined in Part 1, Section 4.2.

2 Incorporation of State

There are several examples of State practice and international and municipal case law where the question of succession to responsibility arose in the context of incorporation of State. Two principles emerge from this analysis:

- Older cases of "annexation" of States support the principle that the successor State is *not* responsible for the obligations arising from internationally wrongful acts committed by the predecessor State (Section 2.1);
- Modern practice tends to support the principle that the successor State *is* responsible for the obligations arising from internationally wrongful acts committed by the predecessor State (Section 2.3).

I will also explain the position adopted in this Study and that of the Institute and the ILC (Section 2.2).

2.1 *Older Examples of Annexation of States Support the Principle of Non-succession*

Many of the older examples of State practice and international and municipal case law can be assimilated to cases of annexation of States characterised by the use of force. As a consequence of the general prohibition of the use of force in international relations following the adoption of the *Charter of the United Nations* (Article 2(4)), annexation of territory is illegal.[23] The 1978 *Vienna Convention on Succession of States in Respect of Treaties* specifically indicates at its Article 6 that the Convention does not apply to cases of annexation.[24]

---

23 See also, *Declaration of Principles of International Law Concerning Friendly Relations and Co-Operation Among States in Accordance with the Charter of the United Nations*, UN GA Res. 2625 (XXV), 24 October 1970: "The territory of a State shall not be the object of acquisition by another State resulting from the threat or use of force. No territorial acquisition resulting from the threat or use of force shall be recognized as legal". Art. 5(3), *Definition of Aggression*, UN GA Res. 3314 (XXIX), 14 December 1974: "No territorial acquisition or special advantage resulting from aggression is or shall be recognized as lawful".

24 Art. 6, 1978 *Vienna Convention* indicates that the Convention only applies "to the effects of a succession of States occurring in conformity with international law and, in particular, the principles of international law embodied in the Charter of the United Nations". Same provision: Art. 3, 1983 *Vienna Convention*, Art. 3, *Draft Articles on Nationality*. The debate leading to the adoption of this provision is discussed in: Zidane Meriboute, *La codification de la succession d'États aux traités: décolonisation, sécession, unification* (PUF 1984) 177–178.

Both the Institute's Resolution and the ILC Guidelines only cover situations of succession which are considered *legal* under international law.[25]

State practice in the context of older cases of annexation of States clearly supports the principle that the successor State is *not responsible* for the obligations arising from internationally wrongful acts committed by the predecessor State prior to the annexation. This is also the view held in scholarship.[26] Such practice is clear in the context of the unity of Italy (1860–1861), in the context of the annexation of Burma by Great Britain (in 1886), the annexation of Madagascar by France (in 1896) and the annexation of the Boer Republic of South Africa by Great Britain (in 1902).[27] However, it should be noted that in the last three instances the successor States have nevertheless made some payments to the injured third State, but only on an *ex gratia* basis without any formal acceptance of the principle of responsibility. Some writers have argued that such payments in fact undermine the principle of non-succession.[28]

It should be added that two writers have recently examined how the rules of succession to responsibility could potentially be used in the context of the complicated history of the incorporation of the "Congo Free State" to Belgium in 1908.[29] On that date, Congo formally became a colony of Belgium. Under Article 1 of the Treaty, King Leopold II declared to cede, together with these territories, "all the rights and obligations attached to them" and, in turn, Belgium declared "to accept this cession, and to accept as its own the obligations of

25 See, Art. 2(2), IIL, Resolution, 2015. For an analysis of the controversy surrounding this provision: Kohen & Dumberry, 25–28. See, Guideline 3 and ILC Special Rapporteur Šturma, Second Report, 2018, paras 22–41, explaining the reasons for adopting the same text.

26 Hyde, 437; Czaplinski, 342.

27 Hurst, 166–167, refers to other cases of annexation supporting the principle of non-succession.

28 Volkovitsch, 2181.

29 In 1876, King Léopold II of Belgium founded the African International Association which was transformed in 1882 into the International Association of the Congo. At the 1884–85 Berlin Conference, the different European Powers separately recognised King Léopold II's International Association of the Congo which shortly afterward became (in 1885) the "Congo Free State". The Conference recognised King Léopold II as sovereign of the "new State". The Congo Free State had a "personal union" with Belgium. It is only in 1908 that the Congo Free State became formally a colony of Belgium: *Traité de Cession de l'Etat indépendant du Congo à la Belgique*, approved by *Loi sur le gouvernement du Congo belge*, 18 October 1908, *Pasicrisie belge*, 1908, no. 265. See, Roger Brunet, *L'annexion du Congo à la Belgique et le droit international*, thesis, Bordeaux, 1911; Paul De Visscher, "Le problème de la succession d'Etats envisagé dans l'histoire diplomatique du Congo", 11 *Comunicazioni e studi* 1960–1962, 53–83; Suzanne Bastid, "La succession du Congo belge aux obligations de l'Etat indépendant du Congo", *RJPUF* 1957, 356ff.

the [Congo Free State], as detailed in Annex A".[30] In other words, "Belgium effectively succeeded in the rights and obligations of the Congo Free State".[31] While the issue is disputed, these two authors consider that the language of the treaty covered internationally wrongful acts which had been committed by the Congo Free State.[32] They consider that this example is an illustration of the transfer of the obligation to repair to the successor State.[33]

Decisions of municipal law courts and international tribunals in the context of annexation of States have also adopted the principle of non-succession. This is, for instance, the position of English courts in the context of the annexation of the Boer Republic of South Africa.[34] This principle of non-succession was also applied on two occasions by an arbitral commission, the US-Great Britain Arbitral Commission. In the *R.E. Brown* case (1923), the Arbitral Commission made statements which constitute the very first *dictum* of an international tribunal in support of the principle of non-succession to responsibility.[35] It indicated that it could not endorse a doctrine based on "an assertion that a succeeding state acquiring a territory by conquest without any undertaking to assume such liabilities is bound to take affirmative steps to right the wrong by the former state".[36] In the *Redward* case (better known as the *Hawaiian Claims* case, 1925), the same arbitral commission followed its own precedent in the *R.E. Brown* case and held that there was no general principle of succession to international responsibility.[37]

30 Treaty of cession and annexation, ibid.

31 Ruy & Baecke, 24.

32 Ibid 26–7, referring to the different position adopted by P. De Visscher, "Le problème de la succession d'Etats envisagé dans l'histoire diplomatique du Congo", 11 *Comunicazioni e studi* 1960–1962, 64.

33 Ibid 33: "While it remains doubtful whether that approach can be regarded as extant customary law, the provisions of the 1907 Treaty of Cession provide a powerful argument to conclude that Belgium has effectively succeeded in the obligations flowing from the wrongful conduct of the Congo Free State. Inasmuch as the Treaty were to leave room for doubt, additional factors related to the Belgian involvement (financial and other) in the Congo Free State enterprise, the continuity of certain practices (esp. the system of compulsory labour) and institutions (such as the Force Publique) post 1907, and the 'unjust enrichment' resulting from the cession, conclusively tilt the balance in favour of succession in this case".

34 *West Rand Central Gold Mining Company Ldt. v. The King*, 1 June 1905, LR 1905, 2 KB, 391. Other cases are discussed in: O'Connell, State Succession, v. I, 487–488.

35 *R.E. Brown* case, 130.

36 Ibid.

37 *Hawaiian Claims* case, 158.

The position adopted by these tribunals was in line with the views of scholars at the time. To the best of my knowledge, all scholars (with one exception[38]) writing from 1900 to 1930 also favored the rule of non-succession.[39] In fact, in a 1933 article, Udina speaks of the "unanimity" of scholars in favour of this rule.[40] At the time, the most outspoken supporter of the rule was certainly Hurst who devoted a whole article to the question.[41] As mentioned above, the central argument put forward by these writers was that a State is generally not responsible for acts committed by another State.[42] These writers also argued that based on the Roman law principle *actio personalis moritur cum persona*, the "personal character" of wrongful acts does not allow for their transfer from one State to another.[43] Just like an individual is "never liable for the torts of the dead person",[44] a State conquering another State should never be responsible for anything done by what has become a "dead" State. This is indeed the conclusion reached by the Arbitral Commission in the *Hawaiian Claims* case: "the

38 Feilchenfeld, 689–690.

39 See, *inter alia*, Phillipson, *Termination of War and Treaties of Peace* (E.P. Dutton & Cie. 1916), 331 ("an acquiring State is not bound to recognize the claims of subjects for damages due to the tortious acts or omissions generally of the preceding Government, and Claims based on war losses, in particular to the belligerent operations prior to the annexation of the territory"); I.J.L. Brierly, "Règles générales du droit de la paix", *Rec. des cours*, v. 58, 1936–IV, 69 ("En ce qui concerne les obligations délictuelles de l'Etat prédécesseur, il est certain qu'aucune règle existe qui oblige l'Etat successeur à les reprendre"); W.E. Hall, *A Treatise on International Law* (8th edn, A. Pearce Higgins, Clarendon 1924) 125; *Wheaton's Elements of International Law* (6th ed. By Keith, vol. I, Stevens & Sons, 1929), 70–72; Keith, 77 ("There is no difficulty, then, in understanding that liability for torts does not pass over to the successor, while at the same time it is easy to see why, though contractual obligations equally do not pass in law, it is more often expedient for a government to recognise contractual obligations than obligations ex delicto"); H.A. Wilkinson, *American Doctrine of State Succession* (Johns Hopkins Press 1934), 463 ("However, even after eliminating this particular type of case, the obligation placed upon the succeeding state to protect and secure individual rights cannot be construed so broadly as to burden the new state either with the duty of correcting wrongs committed by the preceding sovereign, or with an obligation to indemnify the inhabitants for losses caused by the transfer itself"); Max Huber, *Die Staatensuccession: völkerrechtliche und staatsrechtliche Praxis im XIX. Jahrhundert* (Duncker & Humblot, 1898), 65.

40 Udina, 767.

41 Hurst, 178, arguing that the Commission in the *R.E. Brown* case had "definitely laid it down that the liability (…) never passed to or was assumed by the British Government, and thereby establishes the rule that the conquest and annexation of the territory of a State does not render the annexing State liable for the torts of the State which it has displaced".

42 Cavaglieri, Effets, 190.

43 Udina, 767.

44 "Synopsis of Argument", UK, in: Nielsen, 185–186.

legal unit which did the wrong no longer exists, and legal liability for the wrong has been extinguished with it".[45]

2.1.1 The Unity of Italy (1860–1861)

The formation of the unity of Italy is considered in scholarship as a series of annexations of States by the Kingdom of Piemont-Sardagna.[46] Hurst makes reference to several cases which were decided by Italian courts in the context of its unity which, according to him, do not "support the proposition that a State annexing territory is bound to pay unliquidated claims arising out of internationally wrongful acts on the part of the Government which is extinguished".[47] It should be mentioned that these cases do not deal with any question of succession to *international* responsibility; they only concern claims submitted by *Italian nationals* (who became nationals of Italy as a result of annexations).[48]

The Court of Cassation of Rome held in an 1885 decision that since the predecessor State (the Dutchy of Este) had declined to admit any liability for an alleged wrong committed before the annexation, Italy (the successor State) should also have no liability for it.[49] In its pleading in the *R.E. Brown* case,[50] Great Britain analysed this case as supporting the principle of non-succession.[51]

45 *Hawaiian Claims* case, 158.

46 Rousseau, v. III, 340. See, list of Italian writers supporting this proposition.

47 Hurst, 176–177. See also: Keith, 74–75; Atlam, 221. These cases are also discussed in: John Westlake, *International Law* v. I (2nd edn, CUP 1910) 79–80. For other cases, see: "Brief", US, *Hawaiian Claims* Case, in: Nielsen, 115. O'Connell, State Succession, v. I, 483, refers to one Italian municipal court decision where it was decided that the successor State was held liable for acts committed by the predecessor State.

48 The reasons for treating these types of cases differently have been explained in Part 1, Section 4.7.

49 This is the relevant quote from the decision of the Court (in: Hurst, 175): "Seeing that the reinstated Government of Este declared that it did not recognize that the Commune of Capri was entitled to be compensated for the supplies furnished by it to the volunteers of the Provisional Government, it will be clear to everyone that by the annexation of the Duchy of Este by the Italian State, an obligation to which even the late preceding Government was not subject in civil law could not be transmitted to that State. There cannot be any doubt that the Government of Este, being eminently absolute and despotic, by the fact of not acknowledging that it was bound as against the commune with respect to the above-mentioned claim, established in a judicial manner that the commune did not posses the legal right of action for claiming from the State the payment for the supplies: it is therefore equally evident that if it was not entitled to such action during the Ducal Government, it cannot acquire such right by the political reunion of the Province of Modena with the Italian Government which has taken place".

50 *R.E. Brown* case, 120.

51 "Answer", UK, *R.E. Brown* case, 14–16 (quoted in: "Brief", US, *Hawaiian Claims* case, in: Nielsen, 114–115). Great Britain argued that this case was not "support[ing] the

In a decision by the Court of Appeal of Florence in the *Walter v. Minister of War* case, it was held that the principle of succession to obligations arising from the commission of internationally wrongful acts constituted only a "moral obligation".[52] In the context of the annexation of Venice to Italy, it was decided in the case of *Orti-Manara v. Italian Government and Austrian Government* that the consequences of an expropriation of land committed by Austria before the date of succession should not pass to Italy.[53]

On the contrary, in the case of *Orcesi v. The Ministry of War*, the Court of Cassation of Florence held that the Italian government was liable to pay compensation for damage which occurred before the annexation and for which the predecessor State (Parma) had already admitted its responsibility (but had

contention that Great Britain is liable to pay compensation for the torts of the South African Republic" since "the claim had been definitely rejected by an autocratic Government which was supreme within its territory, and there was, therefore, no claim in the existence at the time of the annexation".

52 *Walter v. Minister of War*, 1871, Court of Appeal of Florence, *Monitore dei tribunali*, 1872, 133, in "Brief", US, *Hawaiian Claims* case, in: Nielsen, 115–116. This is the relevant quote from the decision of the Court: "The claim that Walter has stated against the Italian Government as successor to the preceding Bourbon Government would certainly never have been the subject of a civil proceeding within the competence of the courts, for even if the principle can be admitted as true that the Government succeeding another is bound to satisfy the obligations of the preceding, it is likewise true that the indicated principle constitutes nothing more than a moral obligation, for the fulfilment of which the courts are not competent to entertain an action".

53 *Orti-Manara v. Italian Government and Austrian Government*, 1877, Court of Appeal of Venice, *Giurisprudenza Italiana*, v. 30, Part 1, Section 2, column 1, in: "Brief", US, *Hawaiian Claims* case, in: Nielsen, 119. This is the relevant quote from the decision of the Court: "It is certainly a fact that the damages complained of in the petition were done to the lands of the claimant while the Austrian Government, ruling those provinces, had the Verona-Brescia railway line constructed for its own account, and the thought immediately occurs that the liability naturally rests on that Government and that the alleged responsibility of the national [Italian] Government would not depend upon an act of its own, would not be direct, but only indirect and consequence upon its succeeding to all the obligations of the Austrian Government or at least to the special obligation here dealt with. Now, nothing could be added to these conclusions unless on the basis of the maxims of public international law or by reason of special express stipulations, which in this case would have to be found either in the treaty of peace of October 3, 1866, approved by the Act of April 25, 1867, n°3665, or in the relative financial conventions approved by Act of March 23, 1874, n°137. But the alleged responsibility of the national Government towards the claimant emanates from neither of these sources. The very fact that the two Governments made special agreements on the subject with a view to precisely regulate along financial lines the succession of one to the other is against the hypothesis of a general and absolute succession of the second to the first".

paid no compensation).[54] Hurst explains the decision of the Court by the fact that "the claim had been admitted [by the predecessor State] and had become a debt".[55] The same explanation was given by Great Britain in its pleading in the *R.E. Brown* case.[56] A similar conclusion was reached by the Court of Cassation of Florence in the case of *Verlengo v. Finance Department*.[57]

2.1.2 Burma (1886)

The State of Burma was annexed by Great Britain in 1886 to become part of the British Empire of India.[58] This example supports the principle of non-succession.[59] After the annexation, France and Italy made claims to Great Britain (as the successor State) for internationally wrongful acts committed by the Burmese government against their nationals during the war which took place prior to the annexation.[60] Great Britain refused to be held responsible

54 *Orcesi v. The Ministry of War*, Court of Cassation of Florence, 21 December 1881, in: Hurst, 177.

55 Hurst, ibid.

56 "Answer", UK, *R.E. Brown* case, 14–16 (quoted in: "Brief", US, *Hawaiian Claims* case, in: Nielsen, 114–115).

57 *Verlengo v. Finance Department*, 1878, Court of Cassation of Florence, *Giurisprudenza Italiana*, 3rd Series, v. 30, Part 1, Section 1, col. 1206, in: "Brief", US, *Hawaiian Claims* case, in: Nielsen, 119–120. The Court held that "whereas, assuming that Austria, through the expropriation in question, had contracted and assumed the obligation to the indemnity Verlengo, it can not seriously be denied that this obligation is now transferred to the Italian Government. Moreover, even Article VIII of the treaty of peace of October 3, 1866, does not lead to a different conclusion".

58 Great Britain annexed portions of the territory of Burma in 1826 and in 1852 (the "Second Anglo-Burmese War"). In 1862, some of these territories were united to form British "Lower" Burma (part of British India). As a result of the "Third Anglo-Burmese War", which started in 1885, the remnant of the Kingdom of Awa (known as "Upper Burma") was conquered by Great Britain on 1 January 1886. On 26 February 1886, it was annexed to British India (a colony of Great Britain). This example is discussed in: O'Connell, State Succession, v. I, 486–487; Rousseau, v. III, 506; Hurst, 170–172; Atlam, 206; Monnier, 75.

59 See, O'Connell, State Succession, v. I, 486–487; Czaplinski, 342; Rousseau, v. III, 506; Hurst, 170–172. *Contra*: Volkovitsch, 2181, for whom the fact that *ex gratia* payments were made by the successor State undermines the rule of non-succession.

60 One such claim was submitted by an Italian national (Mr Fea), a naturalist who was working for an Italian museum, for the seizure of his collection of specimens by the Burmese government during the War. Another claim was submitted by two traders, a French national (Mr Rey) and an "Eurasian" (Mr Calogreedy), who's property had been seized and destroyed by the Burmese government and who had been arrested, imprisoned and compelled to pay certain sum to secure the favour of their jailors. Finally, another French national (Mr D'Avera) claimed for the taking of his house by the local authorities.

for the acts of the predecessor State based on a legal opinion by the Solicitor of the Government of (British) India in which he indicated that he was not aware:

> [O]f any such proposition of law as renders a new government responsible for losses caused by depredations committed by or under the orders of the former government when in a state of war or otherwise.[61]

However, it should be mentioned that some payments were made by Great Britain to an Italian national, but only on an *ex gratia* basis without any acceptance of responsibility.[62]

Two US missionaries (Mr Freiday and Mr Roberts) claimed compensation for the taking of their properties and that of their mission by the Burmese army. Great Britain refused to be held responsible for the acts of the predecessor State but agreed to pay compensation on an *ex gratia* basis on grounds of equity:[63]

> The British Government cannot undertake to compensate people for losses they may have suffered at the hands of robbers, or at the hands of Burmese troops during or in consequence of the war. But in view of the fact that these reverend and self-denying missionaries have suffered great losses, that the losses occurred mainly in consequence of the war, and that the missionaries may be trusted to spend anything granted to them on the rehabilitation of their churches and missions, the Chief Commissioner advises that a sum of Rs. 10,000 be granted to the Bishop for the repair of his churches and mission buildings, it being made clear that the British Government admits no liability to pay for injuries done by dacoits, or for loss inflicted by the Burmese soldiery.[64]

---

61 Letter of the Solicitor to the Government of India to the Chief Commissioner, 30 January 1886 (in: O'Connell, State Succession, v. I, 486–487).

62 Hurst, 171.

63 Rousseau, v. III, 506. On the contrary, Hurst, 172, and O'Connell, State Succession, v. I, 487, indicate that Great Britain rejected the claim and declined to pay compensation, even on an *ex gratia* basis.

64 Communication of 8 June 1886 by Mr H. Thirkell White (Secretary of Upper Burma to the Chief Commissioner) to the Secretary to the Government of India, Foreign Department (in: Annex VI, "Answer", UK, *R.E. Brown* case, 140; "Brief", US, *Hawaiian Claims* case, in: Nielsen, 112).

2.1.3 Madagascar (1896)

Another example of annexation is that of Madagascar by France on 6 August 1896.[65] It supports the view that a State annexing another should not be held accountable for internationally wrongful acts committed before the annexation.[66]

France rejected the only claim submitted by a foreign government (Great Britain) for an internationally wrongful act committed by the authorities of Madagascar before the formal annexation in 1896.[67] However, it should be noted that France rejected the claim based on the ground that it was of a private nature and that it should have been directed against the individuals which committed the internationally wrongful act and not against the previous government, which had nothing to do with it.[68] France did not reject the claim based on any theory of non-succession. A few years prior to the annexation, a debate emerged in France between the partisans of the status of protectorate for Madagascar and those supporting its annexation.[69] At the time, some had argued that in the case of annexation France would not have to pay any compensation for illegal acts committed by the local authorities, based on the ground that the former State would no longer exist.[70] France finally agreed to pay some compensation to Mr Warrick on an *ex gratia* basis; it nevertheless refused to assume any responsibility for the acts committed by the predecessor State.[71] Apparently, the payment

65 Bardonnet, 311–316. See also, Atlam, 208; Volkovitsch, 2181; Rousseau, v. III, 506.

66 Bardonnet, 311–316; Czaplinski, 342; Rousseau, ibid; Hurst, 172. *Contra*: Volkovitsch, 2181, for whom the *ex gratia* payments made by the successor State in this case undermines the rule of non-succession.

67 In 1890 (i.e. before the annexation), Mr Warrick, a British national, submitted a claim to the local authorities of Madagascar for several "torts" (robberies) which, as it turned out after an enquiry, involved the participation of army personnel. After the annexation, the claim was espoused by Great Britain and directed against France as the successor State. This case is discussed in: Bardonnet, 307; *Archives nationales, section d'outre mer, Mad.* 427 (1143).

68 Bardonnet, 312ff.

69 Ibid 304. For an overview of the debate: "Chronique des faits internationaux", *RGDIP* 1897, 228, 243ff.

70 The argument is developed by Mr Le Myre De Vilers, "Le traité hova", *La Revue de Paris*, 15 November 1895, and was summarised as follows in: "Chronique des faits internationaux", ibid 248: "Le maintien de la personnalité de l'Etat malgache aurait ce résultat que celui-ci, et par voie de conséquence le protecteur, devrait payer des indemnités aux étrangers lésés par la guerre; en cas d'annexion, la France n'aurait rien à payer".

71 Bardonnet, 307.

made by France was almost the equivalent of a complete satisfaction of the claim.[72]

In another case, a French national (Mr Orville) had suffered from tortious acts committed by the authorities of Madagascar during the war of rebellion of 1894–1895 against France. Following the annexation in 1896, Mr Orville submitted a claim to France for compensation. The matter was finally settled out of court. The French government did not, however, consider itself responsible for the acts attributable to the predecessor State, and the amount of compensation paid to the claimant was apparently solely based on equitable principles.[73]

2.1.4 Boer Republic of South Africa (1902)

The Boer Republic of South Africa was annexed to the British Empire in 1902 at the end of the Boer War (1899–1902).[74] In the context of this annexation, there are several examples of State practice and one municipal court case where the question of succession to obligations arising from the commission of internationally wrongful acts arose.[75] The British government rejected any responsibility for internationally wrongful acts committed by the conquered State before the annexation.[76] These examples will be briefly examined in the next paragraphs.

72 Ibid 311–312, indicating that the claimant originally sought an amount of US$ 926 in compensation and was finally given US$ 816.

73 Ibid 310.

74 In 1877 Great Britain annexed the Transvaal. After a revolt, Great Britain restored its independence in 1881. In 1889, the Cape colony and the Orange Free State joined in a customs union but the Transvaal (led by Mr Paul Kruger) refused to take part. In 1896, the Transvaal and the Orange Free State formed an alliance. In 1899, they declared war on Great Britain. The so-called Boer War ended in 1902 with the victory of Great Britain. The Afrikaners settlements (the Boer Republic of South Africa) were then annexed to the British Empire. In 1910, the Union of South Africa, with Dominion status, was established by Great Britain.

75 A few words should be said about another case: *Union Bridge Co. (US) v. Great Britain*, US-Great Britain Arbitral Tribunal, Award of 8 January 1924, *UNRIAA* v. VI, 138; *AD* 1923–1924, 170. See, Verzijl, 221. This case dealt with the internationally wrongful acts committed by officials of the Orange Free State against a US company. The US invoked diplomatic protection for the company on the ground of the succession of Great Britain to contractual liability of the Orange Free State. This position was soon abandoned. The US pursued its claim instead on the ground of Great Britain's direct liability for acts committed *after* the annexation. The Tribunal therefore did not discuss any issue of State succession.

76 Czaplinski, 342; Atlam, 220. *Contra*: Volkovitsch, 2181, for whom the fact that *ex gratia* payments were made by Great Britain in some cases undermines the rule of non-succession.

2.1.4.1 *State Practice and Case Law*

In one case, an English company was the holder of a concession from the Boer Republic of South Africa and was subject to a judgment debt in its favour against the Republic.[77] After the annexation, the company requested that the British government takes over the debt. The Government replied that it was a tortious debt and that therefore no liability should be admitted.[78] Reference is also made in scholarship to a similar attitude adopted by the British government with respect to the claim submitted by an Italian company.[79]

O'Connell also refers to claims that Great Britain made on behalf of its nationals against the Boer Republic of South Africa for tortious acts committed by the latter before the war.[80] After the annexation, the claimants sought reimbursement from the British government. Great Britain provided compensation to certain claimants on an *ex gratia* basis. The reasoning of the British government concerning one of these claims by a British national is found in a communication of the Law Officers dated 21 December 1900:

> It has never been laid down that the conquering State takes over liabilities for wrongs which have been committed by the Government of the conquered Country and any such contention appears to us to be unsound in principle.[81]

Similarly, in another communication of the Law Officers, dated 27 November 1901, dealing with another claim of a British national for torts committed by the predecessor State, it is indicated that the "assumption of the liabilities of the extinct [South African] Government is a matter of international usage, but cannot be enforced in Municipal Courts".[82] Reference is also made of the fact that Great Britain "ought to recognize any legal obligation arising out of the contract of the late Government of the South African Republic with the company", but that "if it was a mere tort of which the South African Republic was guilty, His majesty's Government would not be liable".[83]

---

77 Discussed in: O'Connell, State Succession, v. I, 487–488; Rousseau, v. III, 507; Volkovitsch, 2179; Monnier, 75; Keith, 76ff; Atlam, 209.

78 FOCP no. 8144, 6, 7 (in: O'Connell, State Succession, v. I, 488). See also, Keith, ibid.

79 O'Connell, ibid.

80 Ibid.

81 FOCP, no. 8144, Annex no. 2 (in: ibid 488).

82 FOCP, no. 8144, Annex no. 3 (in: ibid).

83 Ibid.

In the case of *West Rand Central Gold Mining Company Ltd. v. The King*, the High Court of Justice of England dealt with a case where before the outbreak of the Boer War gold produced in a mine in the Republic of Transvaal owned by the claimant had been confiscated by officials acting on behalf of the Government of that Republic.[84] The claimant argued that the Republic was liable to return the gold or its value. It further claimed that as a result of the conquest and annexation of the territories of the Republic by Great Britain, such obligation was now binding upon the successor State based on a presumption in favour of the transfer of liabilities.[85] Counsel for Great Britain argued, on the contrary, that there was "no principle of international law by which a conquering State becomes *ipso facto* liable to discharge all the contractual obligations of the conquered State".[86]

Lord Alverstone C.J., writing for the Court, rejected the application by the claimant. He indicated that the proposition submitted by the claimant "that by international law the conquering country is bound to fulfil the obligations of the conquered" could not be sustained.[87] He added that: "When making peace the conquering Sovereign can make any conditions he thinks fit respecting the financial obligations of the conquered country, and it is entirely at his option to what extent he will adopt them".[88] The Lord Justice also indicated that there was no "reason at all why silence should be supposed to be equivalent to a promise of universal novation of existing contracts with the Government of the conquered State".[89] The decision was summarised as follows in the headnote of the case:

84 *West Rand Central Gold Mining Company Ltd. v. The King*, 1 June 1905, King's Bench, *LR*, 1905, 2 *KB* 391 [1905], in: 1(1) *AJIL* 1907, 217. The case is discussed in: Hurst, 173; "Answer", UK, *R.E. Brown* case, 13 (in: "Brief", US, *Hawaiian Claims* case, in: Nielsen, 113–114).

85 This is the full quotation of the argument developed by Counsel for the claimant: "The Sovereign has, it is admitted, power when annexing a conquered State to impose what terms and conditions he pleases as to the taking over of the obligations of the conquered State; but if nothing is said about a particular obligation then it must be deemed to have been taken over, and it can be enforced in the municipal Courts of the conquering State". Counsel for the claimant also submitted that "by international law, where one civilized State after conquest annexes another civilized State, the conquering State, in the absence of stipulations to the contrary, takes over and becomes bound by all the contractual obligations of the conquered State, except liabilities incurred for the purpose of or in the course of the particular war".

86 1(1) *AJIL* 1907, 220.

87 Ibid 226.

88 Ibid.

89 Ibid 227.

> There is no principle of international law by which, after annexation of conquered territory, the conquering State becomes liable, in the absence of express stipulation to the contrary, to discharge financial liabilities of the conquered State incurred before the outbreak of war.[90]

At the time, scholars considered this case as a clear example of the rule of non-succession.[91]

2.1.4.2 *The* R.E. Brown *Case* (1923)

The decision by the US-Great Britain Arbitral Commission in the *R.E. Brown* case was the first statement of an international tribunal in support of the principle of non-succession to responsibility.[92]

The *R.E. Brown* case involves a US national who had "pegged out" in 1895 some 1,200 mining claims for gold mining concessions in the Boer Republic of South Africa at the time it was still an "independent" republic. The Government of the Boer Republic of South Africa later made three proclamations by which it rejected Mr Brown's applications for these concessions. Mr Brown alleged that he had been deprived of his licence rights to which he believed he was entitled. He subsequently brought an unsuccessful lawsuit before the High Court of the Boer Republic of South Africa.

After the Boer Republic of South Africa was annexed by Great Britain in 1902, the US presented a claim in 1903 on behalf of its national to Great Britain. Great Britain rejected any responsibility for the alleged internationally wrongful acts. Thus, in a letter addressed to the US Ambassador, Lord Lansdowne, Chief of the British Foreign Office, noted that he was not aware of any rule of international law whereby "the conquering State takes over liabilities for wrongs which have been committed by the Government of the conquered country and any such construction appears to be unsound in principle".[93] It

90 Ibid 217–8.

91 Keith, 75 ("In the case of English jurisprudence the rule is that the state itself recognises no liability for tort, and therefore if it succeeds another state it equally recognises no liability for the tort of its predecessor, whether or not its predecessor by its laws admitted liability in tort"); W.E. Hall, *A Treatise on International Law* (8th ed. by A.P. Higgins, Clarendon Press, 1924), 125 ("the Court decided unequivocally that there is no principle of international law by which, after annexation of conquered territory the conquering state becomes liable in the absence of express stipulation to the contrary to discharge financial liabilities of the conquered state incurred before the outbreak of war").

92 *R.E. Brown* case. For documents about the case, see: Nielsen, 187–202.

93 Letter dated 14 November 1903 of Lord Lansdowne, Chief of the British Foreign Office, to the US Ambassador, in: Nielsen, 197.

was only much later (in 1923) that the claim was brought before the US-Great Britain Arbitral Commission, which had been set up in 1910 to deal with pecuniary outstanding claims between the two States following the "Boer War" (1899–1902).[94]

It should be noted that the US did not clearly and definitively invoke as an argument the principle of succession to international responsibility to convince the Arbitral Commission that Great Britain should take over the Boer Republic of South Africa's (alleged) responsibility. At the start of the proceedings, the US did invoke the argument, as shown from this extract of its written submission:

> [I]nasmuch as Great Britain has acquired the entire and complete territory of the South African Republic by conquest, and has succeeded to and holds the full and entire sovereignty thereof, thereby replacing and substituting itself for the South African Republic which has by such acts wholly ceased to exist, Great Britain is bound to pay the debts of the defunct Republic, and especially so when such debts are in the nature of judgement debts.[95]

The US, however, later decided to drop the argument.[96] The US thus conceded that, generally speaking:

> The broad rule stated by eminent authorities and supported with forceful reasons, relative to the inheritance by an absorbing State of all the obligations of an extinguished State are not conceded to be an established rule of international law.[97]

The US in fact even admitted at a later stage of the proceedings that there was no "general liability for torts of a defunct state".[98] Instead, the US based its argumentation on the so-called "acquired rights" of Mr Brown which, it was argued, Great Britain had the obligation to respect after its annexation of the

94 *Special Agreement for the Submission to Arbitration of Pecuniary Claims Outstanding between the United States and Great Britain*, signed on 18 August 1910, in: Nielsen, 3; Hurst, 168.

95 "Memorial", US, in: Hurst, 164.

96 Hurst, 165.

97 "Brief", US, in: Nielsen, 182.

98 *R.E. Brown* case, 130, referring to "Transcript of the 17th Sitting", 9 November 1923, 339.

Boer Republic of South Africa. This is the relevant passage of the brief filed by the US:

> International law requires that, when a nation absorbs another nation through conquest, the absorbing State shall respect and safeguard rights of person and of property in the conquested State.[99]
>
> … it is well-established that appropriate judicial acts of an extinguished State, defining such rights, should not be disregarded by the absorbing State.[100]

The US also maintained that Great Britain should be liable for acts committed *after* the annexation by its own officials against Mr Brown. Finally, the US argued that Great Britain should also be held accountable for the acts committed by the local authorities of the Boer Republic of South Africa because of the peculiar relation of suzerainty which it maintained in the region at the time of the commission of the illegal acts.

Great Britain's contention was that Mr Brown had actually never acquired such rights because of the wrongful acts committed by local authorities of the Boer Republic of South Africa. It maintained that it had no control at the time over the local South African authorities and that it should therefore not be held responsible for the obligations arising from the commission of such wrongful acts.

According to Hurst, who acted as Counsel for Great Britain in this case, Great Britain also dealt with the question of the transfer of the consequences of international responsibility and showed that "the proposition that liability passed in such circumstances was unsound, that the rules of international law embodied no such principle and that it would be contrary to justice and to reason".[101] The general background to the whole question was described as follows by Great Britain in its written submission:

> During the period in which Brown was engaged in difficulties with authorities of the South African Republic, that country was a free and independent State. To establish Brown's right to compensation as against Great Britain, it is necessary for the United States to show not only that there was an obligation on the part of the South African Republic to pay compensation in respect to the injury suffered by Brown, but also

99 "Brief", US, in: Nielsen, 167.
100 Ibid 180.
101 Hurst, 165.

> that liability for such failure of duty on the part of the Government of a conquested State passed to the conqueror upon annexation of the conquested State.[102]

On the specific problem of succession to internationally wrongful acts, Counsel for Great Britain made this observation:

> [I]f you look through all the authorities which deal with State succession you do find expressions of opinion I agree in individual writers that the doctrine of State succession applies to claims for tort or in tort, but I have been unable to find, and I have made a careful search, a single case where in practice that has been carried into effect. It may be that in some case by special agreement the Governments of one or another country have dealt with claims that arise out of tort, but in those cases I venture to submit in every case, if you look carefully into the subject, it has been an *ex gratia* payment, and not one in which right has been admitted at all, and if you come to think of the subject a little carefully, in my submission, that position must be correct; there can not be State succession, treating it, first of all, as a broad rule with regard to torts.[103]

In order to illustrate his position, Counsel for Great Britain gave the example of Soviet Russia, where the Government "has done some dreadful things during the last five or six years" and where "hundreds of foreigners have been murdered, and the property of thousands of foreigners confiscated and dealt with, and improperly deal with, by that government".[104] Counsel then discussed the possibility that some European States could decide to invade Russia in order to stop the atrocities committed by the Soviet government. He then asked the question whether it could be said that "any country who took possession of Russia under these circumstances would be liable to provide damages for all the torts committed by the Soviet Government".[105] For Counsel, the answer was obviously in the negative. He further added that such solution would "make Governments hesitate long before they set out to redress very grievous wrongs that may be committed in any particular part of the world".[106]

102 "Synopsis of Argument", UK, in: Nielsen, 183.
103 Ibid 183–184.
104 Ibid 184.
105 Ibid.
106 Ibid.

The most important theoretical argument advanced by Great Britain in support of its claim of non-succession was based on the Roman law doctrine of the personal character of "torts" (*actio personalis moritur cum persona*):

> I need not remind you that so far as individuals are concerned under Roman Law the successor was never liable for torts; under our English law and American law for torts the successor was never liable, or with very rare exceptions, so rare as to say, I think, never is liable for the torts of the dead person. The liability for torts dies with the person, and it would be an extraordinary thing, in my submission, if it were found that in international law, there was a law which did not exist when you are dealing with local law as applied to individuals.[107]

Great Britain summarised its position on the matter as follows:

> [T]here is no rule of international law imposing liability for the wrongful acts of the government of the extinct State upon a State which conquers and annexes the territory of another. Such a theory is supported by no precedents and would be contrary to sound principle and mischievous in effect.[108]

The Arbitral Commission came to the conclusion that Mr Brown had indeed acquired a right and that the authorities of the Boer Republic of South Africa had denied his right. It however followed Great Britain's line of argumentation and decided that Mr Brown had suffered a "denial of justice" from the Government of the Boer Republic of South Africa but not from the British authorities after annexation.[109] Consequently, no damages were awarded. In an important passage of its decision, the Arbitral Commission stated that:

> If there had never been any war, or annexation by Great Britain, and if these proceedings were directed against the South African Republic, we should have no difficulty in awarding damages on behalf of the claimant

107 Ibid 185–186.

108 "Answer", UK, 19, in: O'Connell, State Succession, v. 1, 489.

109 The Arbitral Commission also rejected the US contention on British suzerainty over the Boer Republic of South Africa. Thus, according to the Commission, the British government did not have "any rights to interest herself in the internal administration of the country, legislative, executive of judicial; nor is there any evidence that Great Britain ever did undertake to interfere in this way": *R.E. Brown* case, 131.

> … We are equally clear that this liability never passes to or was assumed by the British Government. Neither in the terms of peace granted at the time of the surrender of the Boer Forces, nor in the Proclamation of Annexation, can there be found any provision referring to the assumption of liabilities of this nature.[110]

This decision is important because, as previously mentioned, it is the first statement of an international tribunal on the issue of State succession to responsibility. According to Hurst, who acted as Counsel for Great Britain, the decision "shows that liability for the torts of the Government of a former State does not pass to a State conquering and annexing its territory".[111]

The importance to be given to this Award as supporting the principle of non-succession to responsibility is, however, undermined by two factors.[112] The first one is the fact that the claimant (the US) did not base its argumentation on the existence of any doctrine of non-succession. The Arbitral Commission's Award is clear on this point when it states that "[n]or is there, properly speaking any question of State succession here involved".[113] Another inherent limitation of this Award is that the often-quoted passage of the decision supporting the principle of non-succession is in fact a mere *obiter dictum*, where the Arbitral Commission only notes that it could not endorse a doctrine based on "[a]n assertion that a succeeding state acquiring a territory by conquest without any undertaking to assume such liabilities is bound to take affirmative steps to right the wrong by the former state".[114] In other words, the Arbitral Commission did not decide the issue before it by resorting in any way

110 Ibid 129.

111 Hurst, 165. See also, 178, arguing that the Commission in the *R.E. Brown* case had "definitely laid it down that the liability (…) never passed to or was assumed by the British Government, and thereby establishes the rule that the conquest and annexation of the territory of a State does not render the annexing State liable for the torts of the State which it has displaced". See also, H. Lauterpacht, *Private Law Sources and Analogies of International Law* (Longmans, 1927), 283 ("The case is of interest because of the concordant opinion of both parties and of the tribunal to the effect that there is no liability in international law for the torts of a defunct State"), 131–132 (speaking of the "exclusion of responsibility for tortious acts of the predecessor State"). The same opinion was expressed many years later by Czaplinski, 345; Monnier, 85.

112 Volkovitsch, 2184; Eisemann, Emprunts russes, 61.

113 *R.E. Brown* case, 129.

114 Ibid 130.

to the doctrine of non-succession to responsibility.[115] Yet, there is also no doubt that the Commission endorsed this doctrine.

2.1.5 The *Hawaiian Claims* Case (1925) in the Context of the Annexation of Hawaii by the United States (1898)

A few years after having rendered its decision in the *R.E. Brown* case, the same Arbitral Commission (the US-Great Britain Arbitral Commission) had to deal with a case of a similar nature, only with the position of the parties reversed. In the *Redward* case, better known as the *Hawaiian Claims* case,[116] a group of British nationals were illegally detained and expelled from Hawaii by the "Republic of Hawaii" in 1895 before the Islands were formally annexed by the US in 1898. Great Britain exercised its diplomatic protection for its nationals and claimed damages against the "Republic of Hawaii", which rejected such claim on 17 December 1897. After the annexation, Great Britain submitted the same claim, but this time against the US. The claim was rejected by the US in 1898. Finally, in 1925, the claim was brought before the Arbitral Commission.[117]

The argument submitted by Great Britain was partly based on an analogy with company partnership in private law:

> [A]nnexation surely entails the continuation of the life of the State under new auspices. In a sense, the State to which the territory is ceded has taken in a new partner, and in taking in a new partner surely the obligations of the individual person who is taken in would become the obligation of the firm into which he entered into partnership.[118]

Great Britain admitted that no support could be found in State practice or in scholarship on this point: "there is very little authority on the question of obligation arising out of tortious acts" and "most writers and most of the decision are completely silent".[119] It seems that Great Britain ultimately based its argument on principles of equity and justice:

115 Mark Thompson, "Finders Weepers Losers Keepers: United States of America v. Steinmetz: the Doctrine of State Succession, Maritime Finds, and the Bell of the C.S.S. Alabama", 28 *Conn.L.Rev.* 1996, 542.

116 *Hawaiian Claims* case, 157. For documents about the case, see: Nielsen, 382–402.

117 The Commission was set up in 1910 to deal with pecuniary outstanding claims between the two States: *Special Agreement for the Submission to Arbitration of Pecuniary Claims Outstanding between the United States and Great Britain*, 18 August 1910, in: Nielsen, 3; Hurst, 168.

118 "Synopsis of Argument", UK, *Hawaiian Claims* case, in: Nielsen, 94.

119 Ibid 88–89.

> What I am contending here is that one must look at the circumstances, the political circumstances of the coalition [between the US and the independent Republic of Hawaii], and then consider the question really from the point of view of common sense, equity, and justice.[120]
>
> It is surely unjust and inequitable to the highest degree that all obligations should simply perish. Surely it is repugnant to natural justice when a person has a perfectly just claim against the Hawaiian Government that it simply be extinguished because that Government and the US choose to enter into a voluntary union.[121]

One of the arguments put forward by Great Britain was that the present case had to be distinguished from the *R.E. Brown* case. Thus, Great Britain contended that in the *R.E. Brown* case, the Republic of South Africa was annexed "by force", while in the present case of the "Republic of Hawaii" it was a "voluntary cession" to the US. For the British government, in case of "voluntary cession", the principle of succession to obligations applied:

> I suggest that the US by acquiring the territory of Hawaii has acquired with it the obligations which Hawaii … is bound to pay. I suggest that in case of this sort, where there has been a voluntary coalition of two States in the union, all obligations pass whether they arise out of contract or out of tort.[122]

The US first stated that there were "practically no rules of international law defining obligations of a State that absorbs another State".[123] The main argument advanced was that "support for a rule such as that on which the British Government must rely to fix liability on the US for wrongful acts of a defunct state is not found in any of the sources of evidence of international law".[124] In other words, "an absorbing State is of course not guilty of wrongs committed by a defunct State towards another State".[125] The US lastly argued that even if the Commission was to conclude that it was required under international law to pay compensation for the imprisonment of British subjects by the authorities of the "Hawaiian Republic", the claims should nevertheless be

120 Ibid 88.
121 Ibid 92.
122 Ibid 91.
123 "Brief", US, in: Nielsen, 95.
124 Ibid 100.
125 Ibid 107.

rejected "because no claims valid under international law ever arose against the Republic of Hawaii on account of the imprisonment of the claimants".[126]

The Arbitral Commission rejected the argument put forward by Great Britain and concluded that:

> We are unable to accept such distinction contended for. In the first place, it assumes a general principle of succession to liability for delicts, to which the case of succession of one State to another through conquest would be an exception. We think there is no such principle. It was denied in the Brown case and has never been contended for to any such extent ... nor do we see any valid reason for distinguishing termination of a legal unit of international law through conquest from termination by any other mode of merging in, or swallowing up by, some other legal unit. In either case the legal unit which did the wrong no longer exists, and legal liability for the wrong has been extinguished with it.[127]

The Arbitral Commission therefore followed its own precedent in the *R.E. Brown* case and held that there was no general principle of succession to liability for internationally wrongful acts. It decided that the US (as successor State) could not be held responsible for obligations arising from the internationally wrongful acts committed by a legal entity that no longer existed.[128]

In my opinion, there are reasons to argue that the Arbitral Commission could have found the US responsible for the acts committed by the "Republic of Hawaii" on two different grounds, which were not at all discussed in the Award.

The first reason is that in the present case the wrongful acts were not committed by the predecessor independent State (Hawaii), but by the so-called "Republic of Hawaii", a US-installed and controlled "puppet" government which had taken power in a coup d'État in 1893.[129] Hawaii was an independent State prior to its annexation in 1898.[130] In 1893, a group of conspirators

126 Ibid 132.

127 *Hawaiian Claims* case, 158.

128 Ibid.

129 For an overview of the issue: Matthew Craven, "Hawai'I, History and International Law", 1 *HJLP* 2004, 6–22; Matthew Craven, "Continuity of the Hawaiian Kingdom", Legal brief provided for the acting Council of Regency, 12 July 2002, 1 *HJLP* 2004, 453–489.

130 Hawaii was recognised by several States, including the US (in 1842). It also ratified several treaties with more than 20 States (see: <http://www.alohaquest.com/archive/treaties.htm>). Hawaii also became a member of the Universal Postal Union in 1882. In the case of *Lance Larsen v Hawaiian Kingdom*, PCA case no. 99–001, Award, 5 February 2001, 119 *ILR* 566, 581, the Arbitral Tribunal (presided by James Crawford) recognised the existence of Hawaii as an independent State prior to its annexation (see para 7.4 of

led by US nationals and supported by US military representatives proclaimed the establishment of a "provisional" government, without the consent of the local native population. The ultimate goal of the conspirators was the annexation of the Islands to the US.[131] The new US President recognised the illegality of the acts and called for the restoration of the Hawaiian Monarchy.[132] Notwithstanding the official position of the US government, the "provisional" government declared itself a "Republic of Hawaii" in 1894 and was eventually recognised as the *de facto* government by the US.[133] In the midst of the

---

the Award). See, Patrick Dumberry, "The *Hawaiian Kingdom Arbitration Case* and the Unsettled Question of the Hawaiian Kingdom's Claim to Continuity as an Independent State under International Law", 2 *Chinese JIL* 2002, 655–684.

131 At that time, a treaty of annexation was even signed by this US led provisional government and the US Secretary of State; the treaty was submitted to the US Senate for ratification.

132 A change of government in the US led to the establishment of an official investigation on the events surrounding the insurrection. The conclusion reached by the investigation was that US diplomatic and military representatives were responsible for the coup and the overthrow of the lawful government in Hawaii: "Report of US Special Commissioner James Blount to US Secretary of State Walter Gresham", 17 July 1893, *Executive Documents, US House of Representatives*, 53D Congress, 1894–95, Appendix II, For. Rel. (1894), 567; also 1 HJLP, 2004, 136–192. In a message to Congress on 18 December 1893, US President Cleveland described the US government's actions as an "act of war, committed with the participation of a diplomatic representative of the US and without authority of Congress". He also emphasised that the "provisional" government did not have "the sanction of either popular revolution or suffrage" and that it was "neither a government de facto nor de jure". See, "Message to the Joint Houses of Congress", 18 December 1893, in: James D. Richardson, *A Compilation of the Messages and Papers of the Presidents: 1789–1908*, v. IX (Bureau of National Literature and Art 1909) 5, 12, 18, 26; 1 *HJLP* 2004, 201–213. See, analysis: J.B. Moore, *A Digest of International Law*, v. I (GPO 1906) (hereinafter "Moore, Digest") 501. The interpretation of events has since been confirmed by the US government in its *Apology Resolution* of 23 November 1993, whereby the US Congress and Senate admitted that elements of the US government had "conspired with a small group of non-Hawaiian residents of the Hawaiian Kingdom, including citizens of the US, to overthrow the indigenous and lawful Government of Hawaii" (*Apology Bill*, Joint Resolution of the US Congress of 23 November 1993, Public Law 103–105, *SJ Res.* 19, 103rd Congress, 107 Stat. 1510, 1993, 7; 1 *HJLP* 2004, 235–240). See, Francis A. Boyle, "Restoration of the Independent Nation State of Hawaii under International Law", 7 *St. Thomas LR* 1995, 723–756.

133 *For. Rel.* 1894, 358–360. The new US President, Mr William McKinley, even entered into a second treaty of annexation with the "Republic of Hawaii" on 16 June 1897: *American-Republic of Hawaii Treaty of Annexation*, 16 June 1897, 1 *HJLP* 2004, 224–225. The preamble to the Treaty reads as follows: "The US and the Republic of Hawaii, in view of the natural dependence of the Hawaiian Islands upon the US, of their geographical proximity thereto, of the preponderant share acquired by the US and its citizens in the industries and trade of said Islands and of the expressed desire of the government of the Republic of Hawaii that those Islands should be incorporated into the US as an integral part thereof and under its sovereignty, have determined to accomplish by treaty an object so important to

Spanish-American War, the US Congress passed a Joint Resolution on 6 July 1898, which was duly signed by US President McKinley the following day, purporting to finally annex[134] the "Republic of Hawaii" to the US.[135]

The fact that the internationally wrongful acts were committed by the so-called "Republic of Hawaii" is clear in the Award.[136] At the time the events took place, the US was no doubt exercising a political domination over this "puppet" government. In accordance with Article 17 of the ILC *Articles on State Responsibility*, a State which "directs and controls another State in the commission of an internationally wrongful act" is held internationally responsible for this act.[137] This principle of law certainly existed at the time of the events

their mutual and permanent welfare". The Queen of Hawaii transmitted an official protest to the US. The Treaty of annexation was not ratified by the US Senate.

134 Verzijl, v. II, 129, believes that this is not a case of annexation but a process of voluntary merger between the "Republic of Hawaii" and the US.

135 *U.S. Congress Joint Resolution no. 55* (to Provide for Annexing the Hawaiian Islands to the US; the "Newlands" Resolution), 6 July 1898, 30 Stat. 750; 2 Supp. R.S. 895 12, 20; in: G.F. De Martens, *Nouveau recueil général de traités*, 2nd series, v. XXXII, 72; 1 *HJLP* 2004, 230. As a result of the Joint Resolution passed before the US Congress, the self-proclaimed "Republic of Hawaii" ceded sovereignty over the Hawaii Islands to the US without the consent of the native population or any compensation in return. The Resolution mentioned that the Republic of Hawaii consented "to cede absolutely and without reserve to the US all rights of sovereignty of whatsoever kind". Similarly, President McKinley subsequently indicated that "by that resolution the Republic of Hawaii as an independent nation was extinguished, its separate sovereignty destroyed, and its property and possessions vested in the US" (President McKinley, "Third Annual Message", 5 December 1899, in: Moore, Digest, v. I, 511). In 1900, the US Congress passed the Organic Act (*Organic Act, An Act to Provide a Government for the Territory of Hawaii*, US Congress, 30 April 1900, C 339, 31 Stat 141) establishing Hawaii as an "incorporated territory" of the US. In 1946, Hawaii (and other territories such as Alaska, the Philippines, Puerto Rico, American Samoa and Guam) was placed under Art. 73(e) of Chapter XI of the *UN Charter* as a "non-selfgoverning territory" administered by the US. As a result of an overwhelming vote in a Special Election in favour of a proposition, Hawaii was officially admitted as the 50th State of the Union on 21 August 1959 by Proclamation no. 3309.

136 *Hawaiian Claims* case, 157–588, referring to acts committed by "the authorities of the Hawaiian Republic prior to the annexation by the US" which occurred during a "monarchist rebellion in Hawaii on January 6, 1895". Similarly, Nielsen, 85, described the events as follows: "On January 6 [1895] open rebellion broke out in that Country [i.e. Hawaii], the purpose of the uprising being to overthrow the existing republican form of government and to restore the former monarchy. An attack was begun outside the city of Honolulu by an armed force of natives. On January 7, martial law was proclaimed by the President of the Republic, and military forces promptly proceeded to arrest persons suspected of implication in the attempt to overthrow the government. Approximately 200 persons, including the claimants, were arrested and imprisoned".

137 ILC's *Articles on State Responsibility*, 2001.

(the end of the 19th Century).[138] Therefore, it can be argued that the US should have been held accountable for the acts committed by the so-called "Republic of Hawaii" against British nationals based on the application of this basic principle of State responsibility.

There is also another reason for suggesting that the US could have been held responsible for the acts committed by the "Republic of Hawaii" prior to the annexation. The measures taken by this puppet government can be assimilated to those of rebels which were aimed at having the Islands of Hawaii annexed to the US. There is a well-recognised principle of State responsibility (which will be examined below) whereby the successor State is responsible for obligations arising from internationally wrongful acts committed by rebels in their fight to achieve independence.[139]

2.2 *The Position Adopted in This Study and That of the Institute and the ILC*

In my view, in the context of *modern* cases of incorporation (further examined in the next section), the successor State should be held responsible for the obligations arising from internationally wrongful acts committed by the predecessor State. This solution is adopted by some writers.[140] One reason invoked by them is that the successor State will undoubtedly benefit (at least to some extent) from the incorporation of a formerly independent State within its territory. A successor State should not, as a matter of principle, benefit from some rights enjoyed by the predecessor State without equally taking

138 *Affaire des biens britanniques au Maroc Espagnol* (Great-Britain v. Spain), Award of Umpire Huber, 23 October 1924, *UNRIAA* v. II, 639, 648–649.

139 This principle is examined in detail: Part 2, Chapter 3, Section 6. See, Dumberry, *Rebellions and Civil Wars: State Responsibility for the Conduct of Insurgents* (CUP 2021) (hereinafter "Dumberry, Rebellions") 365–6. The application of this principle is however problematic and uncertain in the specific context of an incorporation of State where the actions of rebels are committed with the aim of annexing a territory to an already existing State. See, P. Dumberry, "State Responsibility of New States for Wrongful Acts Committed by Rebels in the Context of Civil Wars: Does the Rule Apply to Cases Other than Secession?", in: Jorge Viñuales, Andrew Clapham, Laurence Boisson de Chazournes & Mamadou Hébié (eds), *The International Legal Order in the XXIst Century; Essays in Honour of Professor Marcelo Gustavo Kohen* (Brill 2023) 556–570.

140 Peterschmitt, 67–69; Buser, 437; Pajnkihar, 340 ("In the case of incorporation and unification, the successor State succeeds to all the secondary rights and obligations arising from the international responsibility of the predecessor State(s)"). See also: Ruy & Baecke, 17, affirming the principle, but later (21–22) indicating that "In the end, whether existing custom prescribes a binding rule of succession in situations where the predecessor State ceases to exist, as suggested by both the IDI and the ILC Special Rapporteur, ultimately remains to be confirmed in further practice and case-law".

over some of its international obligations. In the words of Reuter, "les droits et les obligations vont de pair" and "l'on ne peut recueillir les uns et rejeter les autres".[141] Ultimately, any other solution would lead to the following unfair consequence: An internationally wrongful act committed before the date of succession would remain unpunished and the injured State would be left (after the date of succession) with no debtor against whom it could file a claim for reparation. The application of the principle of succession in the context of incorporation prevents such an unjust result. The same solution was adopted under Article 14 of the Institute's Resolution: the obligations arising from an internationally wrongful act committed by the predecessor State "pass to the successor State".[142]

ILC Special Rapporteur Šturma adopted the same view in Draft Article 10(2).[143] He considered this principle a "presumption" finding application "unless the States concerned, including an injured State, otherwise agreed".[144]

The affirmative language contained in ILC Draft Article 10(2) (obligations "pass to the successor State") was later removed in Guideline 10 *bis,* which the ILC provisionally adopted at its seventy-third session.[145] The provision (which was never formally adopted by the ILC) now indicated that "the injured State and the incorporating State should agree on how to address the injury".[146] This language is the result of a compromise stemming from opposing views by

141 Paul Reuter, *Droit International Public* (4th edn, PUF Thémis 1973) 155. Similarly, for Volkovitsch, 2206, a successor State which finds it desirable "to exercise certain of its predecessor's rights bring with it the obligation to fulfil related responsibilities".

142 See, Kohen & Dumberry, 114ff.

143 ILC Special Rapporteur Šturma, Second Report, 2018, paras 147, 157ff.

144 Ibid para 164. See also, ILC Report, 70th sess., 2018, para 265: "draft article 10 created a rebuttable presumption rather than a rule of automatic succession replacing that of non-succession in all circumstances".

145 ILC, "Text of Draft Articles 10, 10 bis and 11", provisionally adopted, Drafting Committee, 72nd sess., 19 July 2021, A/CN.4/L.954.

146 It should be noted that while earlier Draft Article 10(2) used the terms "successor State" to describe the State which has enlarged its territory, Guideline 10(1) *bis* refers to the term "incorporating State". Also, when it was decided in 2022 to adopt Guidelines rather than draft articles, the Drafting Committee replaced the word "shall" by "should". Another point to mention is that Guideline 10 *bis* (2) provides that when a wrongful act has been committed before the incorporation "by a State prior to incorporating another State" (i.e. the "incorporating State") its responsibility "is not affected" by the incorporation. In other words, the incorporating State continues to be responsible for its own wrongful acts committed before the date of succession. That rule is not controversial. In fact, it was probably not necessary to include this second paragraph given that Guideline 6 already provides for the same rule. This question was discussed by the Drafting Committee: ILC, Succession of States in respect of State responsibility, "Statement, Chair of the Drafting

Committee members.[147] The Commentary makes it clear that the "obligations arising from the internationally wrongful act do not pass automatically to the incorporating State".[148] It also adds that it is "incumbent" on the parties concerned "to pursue an agreement" and that "the obligation to negotiate in good faith is also relevant here".[149] In my view, by putting the injured State and the successor State on an equal footing and by merely letting them decide "how to address the injury", Guideline 10 *bis* leaves the door open to the possibility that a wrong remains unpunished. This solution is clearly not the most effective to protect the injured State's interests.[150]

2.3 *Modern State Practice Supports the Principle of Succession*

There are several examples of State practice in the context of the incorporation of the German Democratic Republic (GDR) into the Federal Republic of Germany (FRG). In all three relevant examples, the FRG (the successor State) decided to take over the obligations arising from internationally wrongful acts committed by the GDR (the predecessor State) before the date of succession.[151]

Before studying these examples in the following sections, a few words should be said about another example mentioned by ILC Special Rapporteur Šturma in his Second Report.[152] He refers to the interesting example of the 1963 incorporation of Singapore, a British colony, into the Federation of Malaya (an independent State since 1957). The Agreement provides that "the Colonies of North Borneo and Sarawak" and "the State of Singapore" (but it was still a British colony at the time[153]) "shall be federated with the existing States of the Federation of Malaya" and the country be called Malaysia.[154] The Agreement

Committee, Patrícia Galvão Teles", 28 July 2021 (hereinafter "ILC, Statement, Galvão Teles, 2021") 8.

147 ILC, Statement, Galvão Teles, 2021, 7.

148 ILC, Commentaries, 2022, para 89, Art. 10 bis, sub-para 3.

149 Ibid sub-para 3.

150 This question is further examined in Part 4, Section 5.

151 This principle that the successor State is always free to take over responsibility for obligations arising from wrongful acts committed by the predecessor State is further discussed in Chapter 3, Section 4.

152 ILC Special Rapporteur Šturma, Second Report, 2018, para 162.

153 The Special Rapporteur refers to this example in a section of his report dealing with incorporation, even if it could be considered an example of a transfer of territory between two existing States (the UK and Malaya). On this question, see: L.C. Green, "Malaya/Singapore/Malaysia: Comments on State Competence, Succession and Continuity", 4 *Canadian YIL* 1966, 33.

154 *Agreement relating to Malaysia (with annexes, including the Constitutions of the States of Sabah, Sarawak and Singapore, the Malaysia Immigration Bill and the Agreement between*

explicitly refers to the transfer of responsibility from Singapore to the successor State.[155]

It should be added that all examples examined in this Section involve the successor State *agreeing* to take over liabilities of the predecessor State. I have not found any example of State practice where the successor State refused the transfer of such obligations. I have also not found any example where a judicial body, or any other authority, *imposed* the solution of succession to a reluctant successor State.

2.3.1 The Integration of the German Democratic Republic into the Federal Republic of Germany (1990)

At the end of the Second World War, the US, France, the UK and the USSR occupied militarily the defeated German Reich. In 1949 two German States were established: the GDR (East Germany) and the FRG (West Germany). The official position taken by the FRG was that it did not constitute a new State and that it had the same international legal personality as the German Reich.[156] Therefore, questions of State succession to responsibility for internationally wrongful acts committed during the Second World War and *before 1949* do not arise in the context of the FRG since there is a legal continuity between the German Reich and West Germany.[157]

On 31 August 1990 the *Treaty on the Establishment of German Unity* was signed between the GDR and the FRG, providing for the "unification" of the two States by 3 October 1990.[158] On that date, the GDR ceased to exist as an independent

the Governments of the Federation of Malaya and Singapore on common market and financial arrangements), 9 July 1963, *UNTC*, v. 75, no. 10760. See, Art. 1.

155 Ibid. See, Annex A (Malaysia Bill), Art. 76: "(1) All rights, liabilities and obligations relating to any matter which was immediately before Malaysia Day the responsibility of the government of a Borneo State or of Singapore, but which on that day becomes the responsibility of the Federal Government, shall on that day devolve upon the Federation, unless otherwise agreed between the Federal Government and the government of the State".

156 This was confirmed by the Constitutional Court of the FRG: *Re Treaty on the Basis of Relations between the Federal Republic of Germany and the German Democratic Republic*, 31 July 1973, Case no. 2 *BVerfG* 1/73, 78 *ILR* 149. On the question of the legal status of the two Germany after WWII, See: G. Ress, "Germany, Legal Status after World War II", in: Bernhardt, 191ff.

157 Issues of succession to responsibility in the context of the "secession" of the GDR in 1949 are examined in Chapter 2, Section 6.2.3.

158 *Vertrag zwischen der Bundesrepublik Deutschland und der Deutschen Demokratischen Republik über die Herstellung der Einheit Deutschlands* (Treaty between the Federal Republic of Germany and the German Democratic Republic on the Establishment of German Unity), 31 August 1990, *BGBl.* 1990–II, 885; 30 *ILM* 1991, 463. For documents on the German "unification", see: 51(2) *ZaöRV* 1991, 494. On the constitutional aspects of

State and its territory comprising five *Länder* was *integrated* into the already existing Federal Republic of Germany. In other words, the GDR acceded to the Federal Republic under Article 23 of the Basic Law (the Constitution of the FRG).[159] Therefore, one cannot speak of a merger of States, since no new State was created in the process. The term "unification" (or "reunification"), which has been widely used to describe the process, should not be regarded as the proper legal definition. This is a case of the "integration" of one State (East Germany) into another already existing State (West Germany), which continued its legal personality under international law.[160] This is the view held in scholarship.[161] There is therefore a continuity of State between the FRG before and after the accession of the *Länder* forming the GDR.[162] The present section of this study therefore only deals with questions of international responsibility in the context of the integration of East Germany into West Germany.[163]

---

the unification, see: Peter E. Quint, "The Constitutional Law of German Unification", 50 *Md.L.Rev.* 1991, 475.

159 Before the "unification", Art. 23 of the Basic Law contemplated the possibility that "other parts" of Germany (a clear reference to the former GDR) could join the Federal Republic.

160 Thus, Art. 1, *Treaty on the Establishment of German Unity*, provides that "upon the accession of the German Democratic Republic to the Federal Republic of Germany … the *Länder* of [the German Democratic Republic] shall become *Länder* of the Federal Republic of Germany".

161 Kay Hailbronner, "Legal Aspects of the Unification of the Two German States", 2(1) *EJIL* 1991, 33; Ulrich Fastenrath, "Der deutsche Einigungsvertrag im Lichte des Rechts der Staatennachfolge", 44 *ÖZöRV* 1992, 1–54; Stefan Oeter, "German Unification and State Succession", 51(2) *ZaöRV* 1991 (hereinafter "Oeter") 351–352; ILC Special Rapporteur Šturma, Second Report, 2018, para 157.

162 Jochen A. Frowein, "Die Verfassungslage Deutschlands im Rahmen des Volkerrechts", 49 *VVDStRL* 1990, 25–26.

163 On State succession issues in the context of the "unification" of Germany, see, *inter alia*: Wladyslaw Czaplinski, "Quelques aspects juridiques de la réunification de l'Allemagne", *AFDI* 1990, 89–105; F. Elbe, "Resolving the External Aspects of German Unification: The 'two-plus-four' Process", 36 *German YIL* 1993, 371–384; U. Fastenrath, "Der Deutsche Einigungsvertrag im Lichte des Rechts der Staatennachfolge", 44 *ÖZöRV* 1992, 1–54; U. Fastenrath, "Die Regelungen uber die Staatennachfolge bei der Vereinigung der beiden deutschen Staaten", 25 *VRU* 1992, 67–83; Jochen A. Frowein, "Current Development: The Reunification of Germany", 86 *AJIL* 1992, 152–163; T. Giegerich, "The European Dimension of German Reunification: East Germany's Integration into the European Communities", 51 *ZaöRV*, 1991, 384–450; Note "Taking Reichs Seriously: German Unification and the Law of State Succession", 104 *Harv.L.Rev.* 1990, 588–606; K. Heilbronner, "Legal Aspects of the Unification of the Two German States", 2 *EJIL* 1991, 18–41; Oeter; C. Tomuschat, "A United Germany Within the European Community", 27 *Common Market L.R.* 1990, 415–436; F.G. Von Der Dunk, & P.H. Kooijmans, "The Unification of Germany and International Law", 12 *Michigan JIL* 1991, 510–557; R. Wittowski, "Die Staatensukzession in volkerrechtliche

2.3.1.1 Article 24(1) of the *Treaty on the Establishment of German Unity*

The *Treaty on the Establishment of German Unity* contains a provision, Article 24(1), which reads as follows:

> Insofar as they arise from the monopoly on foreign trade and foreign currency or from the performance of other state tasks of the German Democratic Republic vis-à-vis foreign countries and the Federal Republic of Germany up to 1 July 1990, the settlement of the claims and liabilities remaining when the accession takes effect shall take place under instruction from, and under the supervision of, the Federal Minister of Finance.[164]

This provision indicates that the FRG will endorse claims of third States regarding "claims and liabilities" arising from "the performance of State tasks" by the GDR. It has rightly been interpreted by scholars (and the ILC Special Rapporteur[165]) as the acceptance by the FRG of obligations arising from wrongful acts committed by the former East Germany.[166] This would certainly cover illegal expropriation undertaken by the GDR, whereby Germany would have to offer compensation in return.[167] This aspect is further discussed in the following section.

Vertrage unter besonderer Berucksichtigung der Herstellung der staatlichen Einheit Deutshlands", 48 *Schriften Zum Staats- und Volkerrecht* 1992.

164 Treaty on the Establishment of German Unity, 31 August 1990, 30 ILM 1991, 457.

165 ILC Special Rapporteur Šturma, First Report, 2017, para 61. See, however ibid, Second Report, 2018, para 159, stating that the "controversy remains as to whether this provision also indicates and could be interpreted as acceptance by the FRG of obligations arising from internationally wrongful acts committed by the GDR" (citing writers taking different positions on this point).

166 This is the position of the following authors: Crawford, State Responsibility, 449–450; Oeter, 381; Volkovitsch, 2177; Mikulka, State Succession, 293; Stern, Responsabilité, 352. *Contra*: Florian Drinhausen, *Die Auswirkungen der Staatensukzession auf Verträge eines Staates mit privaten Partnern* (Peter Lang 1995) 151 (who approves the position of non-transfer of obligations he believes the FRG adopted). For Ulrich Fastenrath, "Der deutsche Einigungsvertrag im Lichte des Rechts der Staatennachfolge", 44 *ÖZöRV* 1992, 39, the Treaty does not contain any provision dealing with the question of succession to responsibility. Similarly, Peter E. Quint, "The Constitutional Law of German Unification", 50 *Md.L.Rev.* 1991, 534 (footnote no. 217), seems to limit the scope of this provision to "international contractual obligations".

167 This is the position of Oeter, 381; L. Horn, "Völkerrechtliche Aspekte der deutschen Vereinigung", *NJW* 1990, 2176.

2.3.1.2 *Restitution/Compensation for Expropriated Property in the* GDR

At the time of the "unification", one very important pending legal issue was the status of many years of expropriation and nationalization of property which took place in the territory of the former East Germany. Acts of expropriation and nationalization had been committed by the Nazi regime,[168] by the Soviet Union during its military occupation (1945–1949)[169] and by the GDR after 1949.[170] For many decades, the GDR refused to provide any compensation for acts of nationalization which it committed.[171]

Faced with such a long history of unlawful expropriation against both German nationals and foreigners, the first changes started to occur in the GDR just before its integration into the Federal Republic of Germany.[172] On

168 When the Nazi regime was in power in Germany (from 30 January 1933 to 8 May 1945), the German government passed many laws which prohibited, *inter alia*, Jewish ownership of property. As a result, their properties were subject to forced sale, confiscation and other types of seizure.

169 See, for instance, the Soviet Military Administration Command no. 124 (30 October 1945) and no. 126 (31 October 1945) which focused on government and Nazi properties as well as those of war enemies and "other persons identified by the Soviet Command". Soon after, the Soviet Military Administration carried out an important "land reform", whereby many properties were expropriated.

170 It should be noted that Art. 23 of the GDR's Constitution of 1949 specifically declared that fair compensation should be paid in return for measures of expropriation taken by the Government. The different laws passed by the GDR are described in: Jonathan J. Doyle, "A Bitter Inheritance: East German Real Property and the Supreme Constitutional Court's 'Land Reform' Decision of April 23, 1991", 13 *Michigan JIL* 1992, 834ff.

171 It should be noted, however, that the GDR concluded some lump sum agreements with several States for compensation resulting from expropriation: Denmark (*Abkommen zwischen der Regierung des Königreichs Dänemark und der Regierung der Deutschen Demokratischen Republik zur Regelung vermögensrechtlicher und finanzieller Fragen*, 3 December 1987, in: G. Fieberg & H. Reichenbach (eds), *Enteignung und Offene Vermögensfragen in der ehemaligen DDR*, v. II (1991) sect. 5.5), Austria (*Vertrag zwischen der Republik Österreich und der Deutschen Demokratischen Republik zur Regelung offener vermögensrechtlicher Fragen*, 21 August 1987, *Bundesgesetzblatt* v. 12. 1. 1988, S. 128ff; text in: Fieberg, ibid, sect. 5.4) and Sweden (*Abkommen zwischen der Regierung des Königreichs Schweden und der Regierung der Deutschen Demokratischen Republik*, 24 October 1986, text in: Fieberg, ibid, sect. 5.3). Other treaties were also entered into with Finland and Yugoslavia. According to Andreas Zimmermann, *Staatennachfolge in völkerrechtliche Verträge: Zugleich ein Beitrag zu den Möglichkeiten und Grenzen völkerrechtlicher Kodifikation* (Springer 2000) 270, unified Germany continued the obligations arising out of these treaties after the accession of East Germany. This is, however, a question of succession to treaties more than an issue of succession to responsibility.

172 See, Andreas Zimmermann, "Restitution of Property after German Reunification", in: R.W. Piotrowicz & S.K.N. Blay (eds), *Unification of Germany in International and Domestic Law* (Rodopi 1997) 103ff; O. Passavent & G. Nosser, "The German Reunification: Legal Implications for Investment in East Germany", *Int'l Law*. 1991, 875ff;

12 January 1990, the GDR amended its Constitution and removed the prohibition against private ownership. It also enacted many laws for the restitution of private property expropriated *after 1949*. One such law was the *Law for the Settlement of Open Property Questions* (*Property Act*) of 29 June 1990.[173] This Property Act, which later became part of German law,[174] was the object of several subsequent amendments.[175] This body of laws stipulates that assets which had been confiscated, expropriated or taken by the authorities of the former GDR (during the years 1949–1990) should be restored to their former owners. Some categories of cases were, however, excluded from restitution.[176] The law also provides that in some circumstances restitution of property to the owners is replaced by compensation.[177]

On 15 June 1990, a *Joint Declaration* on the settlement of outstanding issues of property rights was entered into by the FRG and the GDR.[178] It was

---

A. Elinger, "Expropriation and Compensation: Claims to Properly in East Germany in Light of German Unification", *Emory Int'l L.Rev.* 1992, 215ff; Peter E. Quint, "The Constitutional Law of German Unification", 50 *Md.L.Rev.* 1991, 475ff; W.K. Wilburn, "Filing of U.S. Property Claims in Eastern Germany", *Int'l Law.* 1991, 649ff; Jonathan J. Doyle, "A Bitter Inheritance: East German Real Property and the Supreme Constitutional Court's 'Land Reform' Decision of April 23, 1991" 13 *Michigan JIL* 1992, 832–865.

173 *Gesetz zur Regelung offener Vermögensfragen* (*Vermögensgesetz*) (Law for the Settlement of Open Property Questions (Property Act)) *BGBl.*, 1990, v. II, 1159.

174 It was incorporated as Annex II to the *Treaty on the Establishment of German Unity* (Ch. III, Sect. B. I, No. 5 to the Treaty).

175 *Gesetz zur Beseitigung von Hemmnissen bei der Privatisierung von Unternehmen und zur Förderung von Investitionen* (Hemmnisbeseitigungsgesetz) (Investment Acceleration Law), 22 March 1991, *BGBl.*, 1991, v. I, 766. See also, the *Zweites Vermögensrechtsänderungsgesetz* (Second Investment Priority Law), 14 July 1992, *BGBL.*, 1992, v. I, 1257. Other changes can also be found in the *Gesetz über besondere Investitionen in der DDR* (*Law on Certain Investments in the GDR*), 26 June 1990, *BGBl.*, 1990, v. II, 1157, which was included in the *Treaty on the Establishment of German Unity* (as Annexe II, ch. III, Sect. B, para I (4)).

176 These exclusions are discussed in: Andreas Zimmermann, "Restitution of Property after German Reunification", in: R.W. Piotrowicz & S.K.N. Blay (eds), *Unification of Germany in International and Domestic Law* (Rodopi 1997) 103ff. One such exception is for individuals who had already been compensated by the GDR for loss of property under the relevant laws of the GDR. Another exception is for foreigners who had also been compensated through the lump sum agreements entered into by the GDR and several States.

177 These different exceptions, as well as the restitution procedures, are analysed in: A.B. Shingleton, V. Ahrens & P. Ries, "Property Rights in Eastern Germany: An Overview of the Amended Property Law", 21 *Ga.J.Int'l.& Comp.L.* 1991, 345–57; David B. Southern, "Restitution or Compensation. The Land Question in East Germany", 42(3) *ILCQ* 1993, 690–697; Dorothy A. Jeffress, "Resolving Rival Claims on East German Property Upon German Unification", 101(2) *Yale LJ* 1991, 527–549.

178 *Gemeinsame Erklärung der Regierungen der Bundesrepublik Deutschland und der Deutschen Demokratischen Republik zur Regelung offener Vermögensfragen* (Joint

later incorporated as an integral part of the laws of the Federal Republic of Germany.[179] Section 4 of the *Joint Declaration* indicates that property confiscated *after 1949* should be returned to the original owner.[180] However, under Section 2 of the *Joint Declaration*, expropriations which occurred on the territory of the GDR during the period of Soviet military occupation (1945–1949) should not be reversed and restitution should not take place (only an "equalization" payment could be received).[181] The legality of such an exclusion was addressed by the German Constitutional Court in its "Land Reform" decision of 23 April 1991.[182] It was decided that "unified" Germany could not assume responsibility for actions undertaken by the Soviet Union before the Basic Law had come into force in 1949. The Court did not, however, view the question in light of principles of State succession.[183] The same

---

Declaration between the Governments of the FRG and the GDR on the Settlement of Outstanding Issues of Property Rights), 15 June 1990, *BGBl.* 1990, v. II, 1237.

179 The Declaration was made part of the *Treaty on the Establishment of German Unity* (Annex III). Under Art. 41(3), the FRG is under the obligation not to enact legislation contrary to the contents of the Declaration.

180 ILC Special Rapporteur Šturma, First Report, 2017, para 61, indicates that this example "may be mostly interpreted as a matter of delictual liability (torts) rather than that of State responsibility".

181 It should be noted that the text of the *Joint Declaration* is the result of a compromise between not only the FRG and the GDR, but also the USSR. In fact, with respect to the question of the measures to be taken regarding property expropriated before 1949, the *Joint Declaration* explicitly states that the Soviet Union and the GDR "see no possibility of revising the measures that were taken" during the period of Soviet occupation. In the Declaration, the FRG only "takes note of this [result] in light of the historical development" but also declares "a final decision over possible government compensation payments must remain reserved for a future all-German parliament".

182 *Land Reform*, German Federal Constitutional Court (First Senate), 23 April 1991, *BVerfGE* 84, 90, 18 *EuGRZ*, 1991, 121, 94 *ILR* 42. See, Jonathan J. Doyle, "A Bitter Inheritance: East German Real Property and the Supreme Constitutional Court's 'Land Reform' Decision of April 23, 1991" 13 *Michigan JIL* 1992, 842ff; Charles E. Stewart, "The Land Reform Decision", 85 *AJIL* 1991, 690–696.

183 It has been suggested, however, that the refusal of "unified" Germany (as the successor State) to take over the obligations arising from acts committed by the *occupant* (the USSR) during that period (1945–1949) was based on the principle of non-succession to international responsibility. See, Jonathan J. Doyle, "A Bitter Inheritance: East German Real Property and the Supreme Constitutional Court's 'Land Reform' Decision of April 23, 1991" 13 *Michigan JIL* 1992, 858 ("well accepted principles of public international law dictate that one nation State takes over the territory of another without being bound by any legal strictures whatever, so that West Germany was free to assume or deny any or all prior obligations incurred by the East German government", quoting Walter Leisner, "Das Bodenreform-Urteil des Bundesverfassungs-gerichts", 1991, *NJW*, 1570).

conclusion was reached in a case decided by the European Court of Human Rights.[184]

The question of State succession regarding acts of expropriation committed by East Germany was addressed in a decision of 1 July 1999 by the Federal Administrative Court.[185] The Court rejected, as a matter of principle, the responsibility of the FRG for obligations arising from internationally wrongful acts (expropriation of property) committed by the former GDR against a Dutch national. However, the Court also stated that because the expropriated property was now part of "unified" Germany, the unfulfilled obligations of the GDR to pay compensation to the injured individual had now passed to the successor State. The Court stated that the successor State's obligation would be limited to the payment of compensation and not extend to the restitution of property.[186] As noted by the Special Rapporteur, "this case provides an exception to the traditional approach of non-succession".[187] Other writers agree.[188]

These different laws, which were first passed by the GDR and were subsequently incorporated as part of the laws of "unified" Germany, are all examples where the successor State (Germany) decided to take over the obligations arising from internationally wrongful acts committed by the predecessor State (the GDR) between 1949 and 1990.[189] One can truly speak of succession to

184 In its decision of 2 March 2005, the Court declared inadmissible the applications made in the cases of *von Maltzan et al v. Germany* (appl. no. 71916/01), *von Zitzewitz et al v. Germany* (appl. no. 71917/01) and *Man Ferrostaal and Alfred Töpfer Stiftung v. Germany* (appl. no. 10260/02). The Court held that Germany did not have any responsibility for acts committed by the Soviet occupying forces (1945–1949) or for those perpetrated by another State against its own nationals. The Court indicated that any right to restitution had been expressly ruled out by the *Joint Declaration* of 15 June 1990 and that the Federal Constitutional Court had confirmed that the exclusion of any right to restitution did not breach the Basic Law.

185 German Federal Administrative Court, Decision of 1 July 1999, *BVerwG* 7 B 2.99, 52 *NJW* 1999, 3354.

186 It should be noted that the claim was ultimately dismissed by the Court on the ground that the injured Dutch national had already received some sort of compensation for his lost property by the GDR. To the extent that the victim had no valid claim for expropriation against the GDR *before the date of succession*, the Court simply decided that no such valid claim also existed against the FRG after the date of succession.

187 ILC Special Rapporteur Šturma, Second Report 2018, para 160. See also: Šturma, State Succession, 668–9.

188 Crawford, State Responsibility, 449–451; Kohen & Dumberry, 115–6.

189 This is the position of the following writers: Šturma, State Succession, 669; Oeter, 381; L. Horn, "Völkerrechtliche Aspekte der deutschen Vereinigung", *NJW* 1990, 2176; A. Elinger, "Expropriation and Compensation: Claims to Properly in East Germany in Light of German Unification", *Emory Int'l L.Rev.* 1992, 250 ("the claims resulting from forty years of East German refusal to compensate claimants for its expropriatory acts, are being paid

obligations arising from *international* responsibility, since these different laws apply not only to all German nationals (whether or not from the former East Germany) but to foreigners as well.

2.3.1.3 *The 1992 Agreement for the Settlement of Property Claims between the Federal Republic of Germany and the United States*

The question of expropriated property of US nationals in the territory of the former GDR remained unresolved for many years after the Second World War. In 1974, the US and the GDR established diplomatic relations and agreed to enter into negotiation "for the settlement of claims and other financial and property questions which remained unsolved".[190] These claims were to include property questions which arose prior to or since 1945.

Since no agreement was reached with the GDR on the question of compensation, the US decided in 1976 to pass legislation creating a "Claim Program" under which the US Foreign Claims Settlement Commission would process outstanding GDR property claims.[191] By 1981, the US Foreign Claims Settlement Commission had formally recognised the validity of 1,899 claims by US individuals, corporations, and trusts (worth approximately some US$ 78 million).[192] The US and the GDR having failed to enter into a lump sum settlement, these

by the unified Germany"); Cynthia Day Wallace, *The Multinational Enterprise and Legal Control Host State Sovereignty in an Era of Economic Globalization* (2nd edn, Martinus Nijhoff 2002) 1000 ("with German reunification, the Federal Republic undertook to honour the outstanding GDR obligations, involving both domestic and foreign claims"). *Contra*: Florian Drinhausen, *Die Auswirkungen der Staatensukzession auf Verträge eines Staates mit privaten Partnern* (Peter Lang 1995) 151, for whom this legislation does not indicate that the FRG has accepted the obligations of the predecessor State.

190 *Agreed Minutes on Negotiations Concerning the Establishment of Diplomatic Relations, with Exchange of Notes*, 4 September 1974, 25 *UST*, 2597; *TIAS* no. 7937, in: W.K. Wilburn, "Filing of U.S. Property Claims in Eastern Germany", *Int'l Law.* 1991, 650. See also, 27 *Int'l Law.* 1993, 220–221.

191 The legislation (US Public Law 94–542 of 18 October 1976, 90 Stat. 2509–25111 (1976), codified as 22 USC no. 1644a-1644m (1982)) led to the enactment of "Subchapter VI: Claims against German Democratic Republic" of the "International Claims Settlement Act" of 1949 (22 USC 1621–1627, (1982)). Under this legislation, the US Foreign Claims Settlement Commission was to "receive and determine in accordance with applicable substantive law, including international law, the validity and amounts of claims by nationals of the US against the GDR for losses arising as a result of the nationalization, expropriation, or other taking of (or special measures directed against) property, including any rights or interests therein, owned wholly or partially, directly or indirectly, at the time by nationals of the US whether such losses occurred in the GDR or in East Berlin".

192 These figures are taken from W.K. Wilburn, "Filing of U.S. Property Claims in Eastern Germany", *Int'l Law.* 1991, 651.

claims remained unsettled until the incorporation of the GDR into the FRG in 1990.

An agreement was finally signed on 13 May 1992 by the FRG and the US concerning "the settlement of certain property claims". The Agreement was for an amount of up to US$ 190 million (with an initial payment of US$ 160 million).[193] It provided that:

> The Agreement shall cover claims of nationals of the US (including natural and judicial persons) arising from any nationalization, expropriation, intervention, or other taking of, or special measures directed against, property of nationals of the US before October 18, 1976, covered by the US German Democratic Republic Claim Program established by the US Public Law 94–542 of October 18, 1976.

The Agreement only covers internationally wrongful acts committed by the GDR between 1949 and 1976.[194] It does not cover expropriation committed during the period of occupation by the Soviet Union (1945–1949).[195] In an exchange of diplomatic notes in April 1997 between the US and Germany, the amount of the final transfer was settled at some US$ 102 million.[196]

In this Agreement, the FRG (the successor State) expressed its willingness to provide compensation for obligations arising from internationally wrongful acts committed by the GDR before 1976 with regard to lost properties of

193 *Agreement between the Government of the Federal Republic of Germany and the Government of the United States of America Concerning the Settlement of Certain Property Claims*, 13 May 1992, *TIAS* no. 11959; 1911 *UNTS* 27; also in: Burns H. Weston, Richard B. Lillich & David J. Bederman, *International Claims: Their Settlement by Lump Sum Agreements, 1975–1995* (Transnational 1999) 333 (hereinafter "Weston et al.").

194 Thus, the Agreement indicates that it covers claims of US nationals arising from any nationalisation which are "covered by the US German Democratic Republic Claim Program established by the US Public Law 94–542 of October 18, 1976". Under Art. 3(7) of the Agreement, the expropriation claims of US nationals arising on or *after* 18 October 1976 are to be treated as any other claims by German nationals or any other foreigners.

195 Thus, Sect. 1644a of the "Subchapter VI: Claims Against German Democratic Republic" defines the term "property" as including those which were "nationalized, expropriated, or taken" by the GDR. It makes no reference to acts committed by the Soviet occupant from 1945 to 1949.

196 US Foreign Claims Settlement Commission, "Annual Report, 2000". Under Art. 2(9) of the Agreement, the US is responsible for the distribution of the transferred amount. US nationals whose properties had been expropriated by the GDR authorities could choose between accepting the payment awarded by the Commission in the context of this Agreement, or to pursue their claims under the German property claims program (Art. 3(1)).

nationals of the US. This is an example where the successor State accepted to take over the obligations arising from internationally wrongful acts committed by the predecessor State against a third State.[197]

3 Unification of States

3.1 *The Position Adopted in This Study and That of the Institute and the ILC*

In the context of unification of States, succession to international responsibility is the solution usually adopted in scholarship,[198] as well as by ILC Special Rapporteur Bedjaoui.[199] Underlying this principle is the fact that as the successor State may have found it desirable to exercise the rights which were those of its predecessor States, it should equally have to fulfil their responsibilities and obligations.[200] The application of the principles of good faith and equity

197 ILC Special Rapporteur Šturma, Second Report 2018, para 161; Šturma, State Succession, 669; Crawford, State Responsibility, 451; Kohen & Dumberry, 115–6; Peterschmitt, 68. The position of W.K. Wilburn, "Filing of U.S. Property Claims in Eastern Germany", *Int'l Law.* 1991, 660–661 (the article was published *before* the 13 May 1992 Agreement) was that unified Germany could decide not to recognise the obligations of the GDR with respect to the outstanding 1,899 claims by US nationals based on the ground that a State should not be responsible for the internationally wrongful acts committed by another State.

198 This is, for instance, the position of Verzijl, 219–220, giving the following example: "One single State emerges from the voluntary fusion of two separate States, one or both of which have previously been guilty of an international wrong committed to the detriment of a third State". In such cases of merger, the author believes that "it would really be absurd to assume that the successor State can nevertheless take shelter behind the argument put forward by the dominant doctrine, according to which the offences of its predecessor(s) do not regard it". Crawford, Brownlie's, 442, indicates that his general position on the question (i.e. the application of the principle of non-succession) "clearly cannot have general application and is less cogent in relation to voluntary merger". See also: T.S.N. Sastry, *State Succession in Indian Context* (Dominant 2004) (hereinafter "Sastry") 209. Volkovitsch, 2200, believes that in cases of unification of States, a non-rebutable *strict rule* of succession to obligations should apply. This is also the position of Peterschmitt, 67–69; Buser, 437. On the contrary, Jenning & Watts, 218, believe that there is "good authority" for the rule of non-succession to unliquidated damages in cases of merger of States.

199 ILC, "First Report on Succession of States in Respect of Rights and Duties Resulting from Sources other than Treaties", Mohammed Bedjaoui, Special Rapporteur, 20th sess., 1968, A/CN.4/204, ILC Report, A/7209/Rev.1 (A/23/9), 1968, chp. III(C)(a), paras 45–50, *Yearbook ILC*, 1968, v. II, 94, 101, para 47: "The two merging State have decided to join forces in the future and the liabilities of each are fully assumed by the new political entity they have created".

200 Volkovitsch, 2206. Czaplinski, 357, also believes that in cases of merger the transfer of obligations should occur in situations where "the successor State takes over all rights of

would also certainly call for the transfer of the obligations arising from the commission of internationally wrongful acts to the extent that cases of unification of States are the result of an *agreement* between them.[201] In such scenario, the injured third States' right to compensation should be respected by the successor State.[202] A similar argument based on the voluntary nature of the agreement was developed by Great Britain in its pleadings in the *Hawaiian Claims* case (which Great Britain viewed as one example of a merger of States and not a case of annexation[203]).[204]

Ultimately, any other solution would lead to the unfair consequence that an internationally wrongful act committed before the date of succession would remain unpunished and the injured State victim of such an act would be left (after the date of succession) with no debtor against whom it could file a claim for reparation. As in the context of incorporation, the application of the principle of succession for unification prevents such an unjust result. The same position was adopted under Article 13 of the Institute's Resolution. Since the predecessor States cease to exist as a consequence of the unification, it follows that the obligations arising from an internationally wrongful act committed by one of the two predecessor States "pass to the successor State".[205]

---

the predecessors and thus obtains measurable advantages from the delicts", and that "in these cases delictual obligations should be treated as contractual debts".

201 Peterschmitt, 33. For Atlam, 286, the obligation of the unified State to provide compensation to injured States is based on the "volonté unificatrice librement et effectivement exprimée par l'infrastructure réelle de celui-ci" and on the general principle of good faith (289). However, he comes to this conclusion based on a (questionable) assumption. For him (274, 286–288), a unification of States is simply a territorial mutation on the whole of the territory of the predecessor States, whereby the predecessor States keep their own international legal personality intact. There is no creation of a new State in cases of unification (76–78). Therefore, the question of any transfer of the obligation to repair simply does not arise. He is of the view (287–288) that the unified State should always remain liable for the commission of "its" own internationally wrongful acts based on rules of State responsibility (and not rules of State succession).

202 Peterschmitt, 33.

203 This case, which is undoubtedly one of annexation (and not a case of unification), was discussed in detail in Chapter 2, Section 2.1.5.

204 "Synopsis of Argument", UK, *Hawaiian Claims* case, in: Nielsen, 92: "It is surely unjust and inequitable to the highest degree that all obligations should imply perish. Surely it is repugnant to natural justice when a person has a perfectly just claim against the Hawaiian Government that it simply be extinguished because that Government and the US choose to enter into a voluntary union".

205 See, Kohen & Dumberry, 111ff.

ILC Special Rapporteur Šturma adopted the same solution in Draft Article 10(1).[206] In fact, in his Second Report, he speaks of the application of a "presumption" of the transfer of obligations in the context of unification.[207] This is because in this situation "the wrongdoing State does not exist any longer, but the consequences of its international wrongful acts continue".[208] For him, "the application of the general rule of non-succession" here "would mean that no State incurs obligations arising from internationally wrongful acts", adding that "such a solution would be hardly compatible with the objectives of international law, which include equitable and reasonable settlement of disputes".[209] The clear and affirmative language contained in that provision (i.e. obligations "pass to the successor State") is no longer present in Guideline 10, which the ILC provisionally adopted at its seventy-third session, in 2022.[210] The new provision (which was never formally adopted by the ILC) indicated instead that in the context of "uniting of States",[211] "the injured State and the successor State should agree on how to address the injury".[212] How did the content of this provision changed so radically?

The clause was modified because of criticisms by some ILC members which considered the earlier draft as an endorsement of a general presumption of succession[213] or a rule of "automatic

206 ILC Special Rapporteur Šturma, Second Report, 2018, paras 149ff. See, Draft Article 10(1): "When two or more States unite and form a new successor State, the obligations arising from an internationally wrongful act of any predecessor State pass to the successor State".

207 Ibid para 164: "it seems appropriate to accept the presumption that obligations arising from an internationally wrongful act of the predecessor State pass to the successor State, unless the States concerned (which include an injured State) otherwise agreed". See also, at para 148.

208 Ibid para 147.

209 Ibid.

210 ILC, "Text of Draft Articles 10, 10 bis and 11", provisionally adopted, Drafting Committee, 72nd sess., 19 July 2021, A/CN.4/L.954.

211 See, ILC, Statement, Galvão Teles, 2021, 6, explaining why the term was chosen instead of "merger" or "unification".

212 The word "should" eventually replaced "shall" when the Drafting Committee decided in 2022 to adopt guidelines instead of articles.

213 ILC Report, 70th sess., 2018, para 236: "Several members cautioned against replacing a general theory of non-succession to State responsibility with a similarly general presumption of succession. It was noted that some of the draft articles proposed by the Special Rapporteur in fact espoused such a presumption of succession, especially in relation to cases where the predecessor State no longer existed. In the view of several members, such proposals were based on policy grounds rather than State practice, and were more in the nature of progressive development, or de lege ferenda, rather than codification of existing international law". See also, at para 249.

succession".[214] They were also critical of the position adopted by the Institute on the matter.[215] Their views are clearly reflected in the Commentary to Draft Guideline 10 explaining that "the provision is not to be interpreted as a rule of automatic succession, as rights and obligations do not automatically transfer from a predecessor State to a successor State".[216] In contrast, other members were concerned that the new clause would amount to adopting the clean slate approach and "would risk leaving the injured State without remedy".[217] Their views are also reflected in the Commentary.[218] The Chair explained that the final wording adopted by the Drafting Committee in 2021 was the "result of a compromise between the various divergent positions" ("a middle ground between these formulations") insofar as it "does not articulate a 'clean slate' rule or an automatic succession rule".[219] Special Rapporteur Šturma made the same comment in his last report.[220]

The last version of the provision (never formally adopted by ILC) calls for a few observations.

First, in my view, the wording "should" (or even "shall") "agree on how to address the injury" is clearly not strong enough. In fact, the Chair indicated that some members of the Drafting Committee favored "formulating the obligation to address the injury in stronger terms, and thereby avoiding the impression that the 'clean slate' rule applied to the circumstance contemplated in the draft article".[221] She referred to several drafting examples (such as "shall reach an agreement") that were discussed and stipulated that the injured

214 See, ILC, Statement, Galvão Teles, 2021, 3. See also, at 5: "several members who were concerned that such formulation, and in particular the reference to obligations 'passing' to a successor State, effectively amounted to a rule of automatic succession. In their view, succession in respect of responsibility in cases of merger could only take place subject to the consent of the successor State, and they proposed that the provision expressly say so".

215 Ibid 4: "The view was expressed that the Institute of International Law's decision to provide for the responsibility of the successor State in cases of merger was not based on sufficient State practice, but rather on a policy decision to avoid leaving the internationally wrongful act unrepaired".

216 ILC, "Text of the Draft Guidelines and Commentaries", provisionally adopted, 72th sess., in ILC Report, 73rd sess., 2022, A/77/10, chap. VII (hereinafter "ILC, Commentaries, 2022") para 89, Art. 10, sub-para 3.

217 ILC, Statement, Galvão Teles, 2021, 3ff. See also, at 5 ("other members of the Drafting Committee emphasized that draft article 10 should ensure that States cannot evade their international responsibility by forming a new State").

218 ILC, Commentaries, 2022, para 89, Art. 10, sub-para 3 ("the provision should not be viewed as an expression of the clean slate principle either, as that would risk leaving the injured State without a remedy").

219 ILC, Statement, Galvão Teles, 2021, 5.

220 ILC Special Rapporteur Šturma, Fifth Report, 2022, para 6.

221 ILC, Statement, Galvão Teles, 2021, 4.

State and the successor State have an obligation of result.[222] In his Fifth Report, ILC Special Rapporteur Šturma indicated that "even if the wording may appear rather weak, one should recall the concept of *pactum de negotiando* in international law", i.e. that the obligation "to negotiate with a view to concluding an agreement—must be fulfilled in good faith, in accordance with the fundamental principle *pacta sunt servanda*".[223] While this is true, it remains that the wording is indeed very "weak". The formulation used leaves wide open the possibility that the parties never reach an agreement. There are basically no negative consequences under the Guidelines if they do not. As pointed out by the US in its statement to the Sixth Committee, the language "appears to be binding, but it is unclear what that legal obligation entails in practice"; it is more an "exhortation to cooperate" than anything else.[224] As such, Guideline 10 offers limited guidance to the States concerned.[225]

Second, what is worse is that if the States concerned do not "agree on how to address the injury", the injured State would be left with no debtor against whom it could file a claim for reparation. This outcome would result in a wrong remaining unpunished. This is precisely the outcome that ILC Special Rapporteur Šturma described as a solution "hardly compatible with the objectives of international law".[226] The language of Draft Article 10(1) (obligations "pass to the successor State") would have prevented such an unfair outcome.

Third, a strongly worded provision, like Draft Article 10(1), would have still allowed the parties concerned to reach whatever agreement they wish to enter into on the matter. One of the basic principles at the heart of the work of the ILC is the subsidiary nature of the solutions put forward in the Guidelines.[227] This is indeed what earlier Draft Article 10(3) provided for ("unless the States concerned, including an injured State, otherwise agreed").

Fourth, the Chair explained that the provision "is intended to encourage States to seek a solution to questions of international responsibility in

222 Ibid.

223 ILC Special Rapporteur Šturma, Fifth Report, 2022, para 18.

224 US, letter sent to the UN GA Sixth Committee, rep. 72nd sess. 2021, adding "What is the legal consequence of a breach of this obligation? If one party proposes a means to address an injury to which the other party does not agree, does the failure to agree constitute an internationally wrongful act? Despite the inclusion of seemingly binding language, these draft articles appear to be exhortations to cooperate that seem more appropriately located in guidelines".

225 Czech Rep., ibid, rep. 77th sess. 2 Nov. 2022.

226 ILC Special Rapporteur Šturma, Second Report, 2018, para 147.

227 Guideline 1(1).

situations of a merger between States".[228] States are of course always free to reach an agreement. They don't need any "encouragement" under Guideline 10 to do so. In that sense, the provision is rather useless.

3.2 *State Practice Supports the Principle of Succession*

I have found only one relevant example of State practice where the question of succession to obligations arose in the context of unification. It involves the successor State *agreeing* to take over liabilities of the predecessor States. I have not found any example of State practice where the successor State refused the transfer of such obligations. I have also not found any example where a judicial body, or any other authority, *imposed* the solution of succession to a reluctant successor State.

The creation of the United Arab Republic was the result of the unification of Egypt and Syria in 1958. This example, further examined below, supports the principle of succession to responsibility.[229] It should be added that ILC Special Rapporteur Šturma refers to another relevant example in the context of the merger of South and North Viet Nam to create a new State in 1976.[230] In 1995, Viet Nam and the US concluded a lump-sum agreement under which the former would provide US$ 208 million in compensation to US nationals whose properties had been expropriated at the end of the war.[231] The example also supports the principle of succession.[232]

---

228 ILC, Statement, Galvão Teles, 2021, 5. See also, ILC, Commentaries, 2022, para 89, Art. 10, sub-para 4.

229 Agreeing: ILC Special Rapporteur Šturma, Second Report, 2018, para 153; Šturma, State Succession, 661. *Contra*: ILC, "Provisional Summary Record of the 3434th Meeting", 70th sess., 20 July 2018, A/CN.4/SR.3434, statement by ILC Member Huang (China).

230 ILC Special Rapporteur Šturma, Second Report, 2018, paras 154–155, referring mistakenly to compensation of US$ 240 million.

231 *Agreement between the Government of the United States of America and the Government of the Socialist Republic of Viet Nam concerning the settlement of certain property claims*, 28 January 1995, 2420 *UNTS* No. 43661. See, T.J. Lang, "Satisfaction of Claims Against Vietnam for the Expropriation of U.S. Citizens' Property in South Vietnam in 1975", 28 *Cornell ILJ* 1995, 266–268.

232 A letter sent by the delegation of Vietnam to the UNGA Sixth Committee at its 73rd sess. "put in record its reservations" about the paragraphs of the Second Report mentioning the agreement and stated that the interpretation given of the agreement "was incorrect and did not reflect the common understanding of both State parties". This passage probably refers to the Report's mention (at para 155) that under the agreement Vietnam was "accepting full responsibility for wrongful acts of expropriation committed by its predecessor State". The agreement does not refer to any such acceptance of responsibility. One ILC member went further, ILC, "Provisional Summary Record of the 3434th Meeting", 70th sess., 20 July 2018, A/CN.4/SR.3434, statement by ILC Member Huang (China) indicating that the agreement was "essentially a political agreement between the two States, and

3.2.1 United Arab Republic (1958)

The creation of the United Arab Republic was the result of the unification of Egypt and Syria in 1958.[233] This unification lasted for only three years.[234] There are at least three examples where the United Arab Republic (the successor State) decided to take over the responsibility for obligations arising from internationally wrongful acts committed by the predecessor States and to provide compensation to injured third States.[235] All cases involved actions taken by Egypt against Western properties in the context of the nationalisation of the Suez Canal in 1956 and the "Egyptianisation" of foreign-owned properties.[236] In none of these cases, which will now be examined, did the United Arab

was irrelevant to the issue of succession of State responsibility; much less could it be seen as exemplifying *opinio juris* on rules of State succession". While it is true that the agreement may have had an undeniable political dimension and that it does not show any *opinio juris* from the parties, it remains, in my view, that this example is very much relevant to the issue of succession to responsibility.

233 The "United Arab Republic" should not be confused with the "United Arab States" which was a Confederation established between the United Arab Republic (i.e. Egypt and Syria) and North Yemen. This Confederation existed from 1958 to 1961.

234 The Proclamation of 1 February 1958 makes it clear that this is not merely a "union of States"; it expressly mentioned that the two States were uniting "into one State". However, Cotran, 349–350, believes that this case is not one of State succession but rather a case of "amalgamation", whereby the legal personality of the two predecessor States is not extinguished. This point of view has been (rightly) qualified as a "problem of semantics" by Karl Zemanek, "State Succession after Decolonization", *Rec. des cours*, v. 116, 1965–III, 212. For O'Connell, State Succession, v. II, 74, it is difficult to place this *sui generis* case within any of the traditional categories.

235 For the same conclusion: ILC Special Rapporteur Šturma, First Report, 2017, para 42; Ibid Second Report, 2018, para 153. For Reyes Gajardo, 76, this example "rejects the idea of an automatic succession" to responsibility and shows the "importance of the consent of the successor State that is willing to assume the obligations and responsibility from a wrongful act of the extinct predecessor State". *Contra*: Cotran, 366, examining these examples but concluding just a few pages later (368) that no claim for alleged internationally wrongful acts committed by the predecessor States was filed by a third State. He believes that had such claim been filed, the rule should have been that the new State is not bound by internationally wrongful acts committed by the predecessor States. However, as mentioned above, he interprets the creation of the United Arab Republic as a case of "amalgamation". He concludes that "there is no authority for saying that in such case [of "amalgamation"] any pre-existing liability of the parts does not rest in newly created whole".

236 No case was found concerning wrongful acts committed by Syria before the unification. In an article dealing with the dissolution of the United Arab Republic in September 1961 (further examined below in Chapter 2, Section 4.3.1). C. Rousseau, "Chronique des faits internationaux", *RGDIP* 1962, 414, seems to be suggesting that the United Arab Republic could not be responsible for any obligations arising from wrongful acts committed by Syria before the unification.

Republic argue that, as a matter of principle, it could not succeed as a new State to the obligations arising from internationally wrongful acts committed by its predecessors.[237]

The first example deals with the nationalisation of the *Société Financière de Suez* by Egypt in July 1956.[238] An agreement was entered into on 13 July 1958 between the United Arab Republic and the private corporation under which the former undertook, *inter alia*, to pay some EGY£ 28.3 million to the shareholders of the latter.[239] This is clearly an example of a new State being held liable for the obligations arising from internationally wrongful acts committed by the predecessor State.[240]

The second example involves an agreement signed on 22 August 1958 between the United Arab Republic and France resuming cultural, economic and financial relations between the two States, which had been broken off as a result of the military actions taken by France in 1956 at the time of the nationalisation of the Suez Canal ("les événements d'octobre et de novembre 1956" as referred to in the agreement).[241] The agreement provided (Articles 3 and 4) that the United Arab Republic, as the successor State, would restore the goods and property of French nationals which had been taken by Egypt and that compensation would be paid for those goods and property not returned.[242] This is an

237 Cotran, 367: "It does not appear that any question was raised during the negotiations leading to these Agreements as to the nature and effect of the change, if any, in the personality of Egypt".

238 See, Cotran, 366; L. Focsaneanu, "L'accord ayant pour objet l'indemnisation de la compagnie de Suez nationalisée par l'Egypte", *AFDI* 1959, 161–204.

239 UN Doc. A/3898, S/4089, 23 September 1958.

240 This is also the position of L. Focsaneanu, "L'accord ayant pour objet l'indemnisation de la compagnie de Suez nationalisée par l'Egypte", *AFDI* 1959, 196, who refers to the United Arab Republic as the acting successor to the Egyptian government.

241 *Accord général entre le gouvernement de la République française et le gouvernement de la République arabe unie*, in : *La documentation française*, 18 October 1958, no. 2473; *RGDIP* 1958, 738ff. The Agreement was followed by the adoption by the United Arab Republic of Decree no. 36, 18 September 1958. See, Cotran, 366; C. Rousseau, "Chronique des faits internationaux", *RGDIP* 1958, 681.

242 The French government also undertook to stop any measures it had taken relating to Egyptian interests. Under Art. 7, the Agreement is considered by the Parties to be a final settlement of the reciprocal claims of the two States arising from the Suez Canal Crisis. It should be noted that the question of the implementation of this Agreement was finally settled a few years later (after the dissolution of the United Arab Republic in 1961). The first agreement was entered into on 5 November 1964 between France and the United Arab Republic on the question of the settlement of claims arising out of the Egyptian sequestrations which occurred after 1956. See, *JORF* 1964, 11149, also mentioned in: Burns H. Weston & Richard B. Lillich, *International Claims: Their Settlement by Lump Sum Agreements* (UP Virginia 1975) (hereinafter "Weston & Lillich"), 371. Another

example of succession to obligations arising from the commission of internationally wrongful acts.[243]

Contrary to what has been stated in scholarship,[244] a similar agreement was also signed on 28 February 1959 by the United Arab Republic and the UK.[245] The preamble to the agreement expressly provided that it was entered into by the United Arab Republic "as successor of the Government of the Republic of Egypt, and acting so far only as concerns the territory of the Republic of Egypt". Under this agreement, the United Arab Republic undertook to terminate all sequestration measures taken against British property.[246] The agreement also provided for a lump sum of UK£ 27.5 million to be paid by the United Arab Republic as compensation "in full and final settlement" of British claims.[247]

---

agreement was entered into by the two States on 28 July 1966 (in force on 1 September 1967): *Agreement between the Government of the French Republic and the Government of the United Arab Republic Concerning the Settlement of Problems Relating to Estates of French Nationals Situated on the Territory of the United Arab Republic*, *JORF* 1967, 9939; *RGDIP* 1968, 289; Weston et al., 324. This last agreement dealt with the implementation of the two previous ones. Thus, it provides (at Art. 2) for the "property, rights and interests for which French owners have demanded restoration" in accordance with the first 1958 Agreement to be "remitted to the claimants within 6 months". It also dealt with compensation to be paid to French nationals whose properties have been confiscated by Egypt.

243 This is also the position of Habib Guerari, "Quelques observations sur les Etats éphémères", *AFDI* 1994, 424, for whom this agreement shows that the United Arab Republic "a pris la suite de l'Egypte en matière de responsabilité internationale".

244 For instance, Czaplinski, 342.

245 *Agreement between the Government of the United Kingdom of Great Britain and Northern Ireland and the Government of the United Arab Republic Concerning Financial and Commercial Relations and British Property in Egypt*, in *UKTS* 1959, no. 35 (Cmd. 723); 343 *UNTS* 159. See, Cotran, 366.

246 Art. 3(a) of the Agreement indicates that the United Arab Republic shall "terminate the application of all measures of sequestration taken by the United Arab Republic against British property between October 30, 1956, and the date of the signature of the present Agreement, and all restrictive measures taken against UK nationals during the same period". According to Art. 3(b), the United Arab Republic shall "return all British property (or the proceeds of any such property sold between October 30, 1956, and the date of the signature of the present Agreement) to the owners thereof". Art. 3(e) deals with the "full payment and transfer of Egyptian Government pensions to UK nationals". The question of the termination of the sequestration measures is further explained in: X, "Sequestration of Enemy Property in Egypt. A Note on Current Development & Procuration no. 5 on Trade Relations with British and French Nationals and Measures Applying to their Properties", 14 *Rev. égyptienne d.i.* 1958, 137ff.

247 Art. 4(1) b) of the Agreement refers to "all claims in respect of injury or damage to property suffered" from sequestration and restrictive measures "taken by the United Arab Republic against British property between October 30, 1956, and the date of the signature of the present Agreement".

4 Dissolution of State

State practice and international and municipal case law regarding the question of succession to international responsibility in the context of dissolution is not uniform. There are examples in favour of both the principles of succession and non-succession.

There are, nevertheless, certain tendencies in State practice and case law that may be identified:

- Older examples of State practice and municipal courts cases generally support the principle that the successor States are not responsible for the obligations arising from internationally wrongful acts committed by the predecessor State (Section 4.2);
- There are several recent examples of State practice where the successor State has accepted to take over the obligations arising from internationally wrongful acts committed by the predecessor State (Section 4.3).

I will first examine the position adopted by the Institute and the ILC and explain what my view is (Section 4.1).

4.1 *The Position Adopted in This Study and That of the Institute and the ILC*

My position is that in cases of dissolution of State the possibility to transfer the obligation to repair to the successor States *should not be rejected as a matter of principle.* This proposition is in accordance with some trends observed in modern State practice (examined in Section 4.3, below). This is illustrated by the 2001 *Agreement on Succession Issues* entered into among all the successor States to the former SFRY[248] and by the position taken by the ICJ in the *Gabčíkovo-Nagymaros* case.[249] After having examined several examples of State practice in the context of dissolution, Crawford noted that "it is significant that in each of the cases identified, the successor state voluntarily accepted liability with respect to the unlawful acts of its predecessor".[250] This is an important point. The examples of modern practice (examined below in Section 4.3) involve the new State *accepting* to take over responsibilities. I have not found any example where the solution of succession was *imposed* on a reluctant new State by a court or by any other authority.

248 *Agreement on Succession Issues*, 29 June 2001, 41 *ILM* 2002, 3.
249 *Gabčíkovo-Nagymaros* case, para 151.
250 Crawford, State Responsibility, 455.

A *strict and automatic* application of the principle of non-succession in the context of dissolution would be in complete contradiction with the very idea of justice. The injured third State would be left with no debtor to provide compensation for the damage it suffered as a result of the commission of the internationally wrongful act.

The unfairness which would result from the application of such a strict and automatic principle of non-succession in cases of dissolution has been acknowledged by the Arbitral Tribunal in the *Lighthouse Arbitration* case.[251] The same position is supported by some writers[252] (but rejected by others[253])

251 *Lighthouse Arbitration* case, 23 *ILR* 1956, 93: "What justice, or even what juridical logic, would there be, for example, in the hypothesis of an international wrong committed against another Power by a State which subsequently splits up into two new independent States, in regarding the later as being free from an international obligation to make compensation which would without any doubt have lain on the former, predecessor, State which had committed the wrong?".

252 According to Verzijl, 219–220, in the situation where a "State responsible for such a wrong splits into two before the reparation due is adjusted", "it would really be absurd to assume that the successor State can nevertheless take shelter behind the argument put forward by the dominant doctrine, according to which the offences of its predecessor(s) do not regard it". For Georg Schwarzenberger, *International Law as Applied by International Courts and Tribunals*, v. I (3rd edn, Steven & Sons 1957) (hereinafter "Schwarzenberger") 175–176, whenever a State "split into two States" after the commission of an "international tort", the successor States should be held responsible for that act "based on ground of estoppel" and "on the rules governing the principle of good faith". See also, Reyes Gajardo, 81–2 ("the mere extinction of an obligation to repair an internationally wrongful act goes against the very nature of international law"). For Pajnkihar, 341, "given that the predecessor State was the holder of rights and obligations pertaining to an injury arising from its internationally wrongful act at the date of succession, it can be concluded by applying the rules applicable to all other matters of succession that those rights and obligations pass to the successor State. This is all the truer considering that, as an objectively existing fact, the injury continues to exist in an identical form after the date of succession, unaffected by the succession, which is a legal phenomenon".

253 Jenning & Watts, 222. See also, the argument developed by Atlam, 283, for whom "[L]e passif de la responsabilité internationale de l'Etat démembré ne pourrait, d'après nous, que s'éteindre à la suite de la dislocation de son propre titulaire. En d'autres termes, aucune succession de l'un ou de l'autre des Etats issus du démembrement d'Etats ne nous paraît ici admise". For him (see 284), this solution of non-succession is in accordance with principles of State succession, whereby (in his opinion) the absence of continuity of the international legal personality between the predecessor State and its successors calls for the application of the principle of *tabula rasa* with respect to responsibility. He also believes (285) that this solution of non-succession is in line with principles of State responsibility, whereby a State is only responsible for the acts it has committed and not for those committed by others.

and by Judge Cançado Trindade in the *Croatia Genocide Convention* case.[254] The same position was adopted by the ILC Special Rapporteur.[255] It has been argued that it is precisely because of the unjust nature of the consequences of the application of such a strict "rule" of non-succession that States tend to provide *ex gratia* reparation to injured States.[256] The adoption of a strict principle of non-succession would be particularly unfair whenever the dissolution is the result of an *agreement* between the different successor States.[257] In such a case, the concept of good faith would call for the right of the injured State for compensation to be respected by the successor States.[258]

My position that the *strict and automatic* application of the principle of non-succession should be rejected in cases of dissolution should, however, not be understood as an endorsement of the opposite radical solution of the *automatic transfer* of the obligation to repair to the new States.[259] Whether the obligations arising from the commission of internationally wrongful acts may be transferred to the successor States (which is accepted in the present book as a matter of principle) will ultimately depend on the *particular circumstances* of each case; it should not be applied automatically and mechanically. Thus, not *all* new successor States should *always* be held accountable for the obligations arising from internationally wrongful acts committed by the predecessor State

254 *Croatia Genocide Convention* case, Diss. op. Judge Cançado Trindade, para 31: "After all, the consequences of the commission of grave violations of international law will, in most cases, continue to affect and victimize certain human groups even after the date of succession, and even more so when surrounded by violence. In such circumstance, it would be unjust for the victims if no responsibility could be vindicated for the commission of internationally wrongful acts and their consequences extended in time. To argue that responsibility would vanish with the dissolution of the State concerned would render the Genocide Convention irrelevant. An internationally wrongful act and its continuing consequences cannot remain unpunished and without reparation for damages".

255 ILC Special Rapporteur Šturma, Second Report, 2018, para 147.

256 For Rousseau, v. III, 505, the principle of non-succession to responsibility applies to cases of dissolution. He concedes, however, that this situation is "évidemment injuste" and that therefore "la pratique a admis à diverses reprises la possibilité d'une réparation *ex gratia* fondée sur l'équité et qui ne correspond à aucun degré à l'exécution d'une obligation antérieure".

257 Crawford, Brownlie's, 442, indicating that his general position of non-succession to responsibility is "less cogent" for "voluntary" dissolution. See also, Sastry, 209.

258 Peterschmitt, 33.

259 Reyes Gajardo, 81, refers to the "existence of a general, though not absolute rule of non-automatic succession to State responsibility" for cases of dissolution, but adding that this is "not absolute" because "rules and principles of international law in other areas" than State succession (including unjust enrichment) will offer "solutions" and exceptions to this rule when the predecessor State ceases to exist.

before the date of succession. Such a mechanical application of a principle of succession would undoubtedly be unfair in certain cases. For instance, in the case of a successor State which had nothing to do with the commission of the internationally wrongful act. I will examine in detail in a subsequent chapter,[260] that the actual involvement, behaviour and participation of the authorities of the successor States (when they were still part of the predecessor State) in the commission of the wrongful act should be taken into account. Another relevant aspect (further discussed below[261]) is the existence of a link between the territory of one (or more) of the new States and the consequences of the wrongful act.[262] Pajnkihar refers to those circumstances as "special rules".[263] ILC Special Rapporteur Šturma refers to several examples where the ECHR used the territoriality[264] and organs[265] principles to settle claims dealing with property issues. The unjust enrichment of one successor State as a result of the commission of wrongful acts should also be examined.[266] Chapter 3 examines the different factors and circumstances that may be relevant to determine which successor States should be held accountable for obligations arising from internationally wrongful acts committed by the predecessor State.[267] It has been argued by one writer that even in situations "involving no specific link between the individual successor States and the matter of succession", there should be succession by the new States to the consequences of responsibility "in equitable shares" by them.[268]

260 The question is discussed in detail in Chapter 3, Sections 5 and 7.

261 See, Chapter 3, Section 10.1.

262 Pajnkihar, 338, 341 ("In the presence of a specific link, the first special rule would already apply, according to which the successor State fully succeeds to all secondary rights and obligations arising from its specific link to the matter of succession").

263 Pajnkihar, 338ff, 341 ("A successor State that has a special link to the matter of succession (i.e., injury) shall fully succeed to the secondary rights and obligations of reparations relating to that matter, followed by conditional succession to other secondary rights and obligations").

264 ILC Special Rapporteur Šturma, Fifth Report, 2021, paras 47–49, referring to *Ališić et al v. Bosnia and Herzegovina, Croatia, Serbia, Slovenia and the former Yugoslav Republic of Macedonia* [GC], appli. no. 60642/08, ECHR 2014, v. IV. See, concurring Op. of Judge Ziemele, paras 1–3.

265 Ibid para 50, referring to *Zaklan v. Croatia*, appli. no. 57239/13, ECHR, judgment, 16 December 2021.

266 The question is discussed in detail in Chapter 3, Section 8.

267 For Schwarzenberger, 175–176, the "share of the liability" between the successor States for internationally wrongful acts committed by the predecessor State before the date of succession "can be determined only by equitable considerations".

268 Pajnkihar, 340, adding that "in the absence of a specific link between the successor State and the matter of succession, only succession in proportional shares is possible under the *principle of equity*" (emphasis in the original).

The same general approach was followed under Article 15(1) of the Institute's Resolution: the obligations arising from the commission of a wrongful act by the predecessor State "pass" to "one, several or all the successor States" depending on the circumstances mentioned in Article 15(2)(3).[269] It was also adopted by ILC Special Rapporteur Šturma in Draft Article 11(1).[270] In his Report, he explained that the application of the general rule of non-succession for dissolution "would mean that no State incurs obligations arising from internationally wrongful acts". He added that such a "solution would be hardly compatible with the objectives of international law, which include equitable and reasonable settlement of disputes".[271] This is why he said that "the general rule of non-succession should be replaced rather by a presumption of succession in respect of obligations arising from State responsibility".[272] He added that "this is not an unqualified or absolute succession, because the presumption of such transfer of obligations may be confirmed, rebutted or modified by agreements, including agreements on distribution (sharing) of such obligations, where appropriate".[273] Later, he mentioned that "while accepting the presumption of the transfer of obligations from the predecessor State to the successor State or States, [the Articles] underlines the role of agreements".[274] Thus, under Draft Article 11(1), any such transfer of obligations was "subject to an agreement" between the concerned States. In other words, there must be an agreement for any such transfer of obligations to occur.[275] Article 15(1) of the Institute's Resolution does not contain such a caveat.[276]

Article 15(3) of the Institute's Resolution indicates that "in order to determine which of the successor States becomes bearer of the obligations" to repair, there are two "relevant factors".[277] Importantly, succession is not automatic

269 See, Kohen & Dumberry, 118ff.

270 ILC Special Rapporteur Šturma, Second Report, 2018, paras 147, 167, 185.

271 Ibid para 147.

272 Ibid para 148. For a critical analysis of any such "presumption", see: Reyes Gajardo, 80–1.

273 Ibid para 148.

274 Ibid para 187. For a critical assessment: Kaplane, 36, indicating that the provision "appears to be the vaguest" of all clauses and that "transfer of responsibility is left for the states to regulate", adding that it would have seem instead "natural to concentrate on this type of succession and provide more comprehensive legal guidance, considering the complexity" of dissolution cases.

275 Ibid para 187, indicating that he "takes a slightly more cautious approach" than the one adopted in the Institute's Resolution. Yet, elsewhere (para 189) he indicated that he "wishes to make it clear that a transfer of obligations may take place according to or in the absence of an agreement".

276 See, IIL, Final Report, Kohen, para 49; Kohen & Dumberry, 120.

277 It should be added that under Art. 7 ("Plurality of successor States") whenever it is not possible to identify a single successor, all successor States will assume the obligations in

under Article 15(3); these are just "relevant factors" to be considered for the distribution of obligations among the successor States. The first relevant factor is the existence of a "direct link" between the consequences of an internationally wrongful act committed by the predecessor State and the territory or the population of one of the successor States.[278] ILC Draft Article 11(2) also referred to the importance of this "direct link".[279] The second factor mentioned in Article 15(3) of the Institute's Resolution is to consider whether the author of the internationally wrongful act was an organ of the predecessor State that later became an organ of the successor State. While ILC Draft Article 11(2) did not refer specifically to this "organ" factor,[280] it remains that the "organ" factor is certainly one of those "other relevant factors" (mentioned in Draft Article 11(2)) that would have to be considered.[281]

The ILC provisionally adopted Guideline 11 at its seventy-third session, in 2022, after it had been provisionally adopted by the Drafting Committee at the same session.[282] The provision (which was never formally adopted by the ILC) is substantially different compared to both Article 15 of the Institute's Resolution and the draft article put forward by ILC Special Rapporteur Šturma. Guideline 11 no longer contains the clear and affirmative language found in Draft Article 11(2) (obligations "pass, subject to an agreement" to one or several successor State(s)). It merely indicates that "the

---

an equitable manner. Art. 7(2) establishes what criteria must be taken into consideration to determine an equitable apportionment of obligations among the successor States.

278 Art. 15(2) deals with the "direct link" factor concerning the situation of a wrongful act committed *against* the predecessor State (succession to *rights*). Yet, the use of the words "in addition to that mentioned in paragraph 2" in Art. 15(3) indicates that this factor is also relevant in the context of succession to *obligations*.

279 The provision indicates that the "Successor States should negotiate in good faith with the injured State and among themselves in order to settle the consequences of the internationally wrongful act of the predecessor State". The provision further adds that in this context, "they should take into consideration a territorial link, an equitable proportion and other relevant factors". This provision does not refer to "population", but only to the "territorial" link. See, comment by the Netherlands, letter sent to the UN GA Sixth Committee, rep. 74th sess. 5 Nov. 2019, recognising the "relevance of a link in such situations", but adding that the concept should be clarified.

280 But ILC Special Rapporteur Šturma, Second Report, 2018, para 188, does refer to this factor in the context of dissolution.

281 This is also clear from this passage in ILC, ibid para 188: "When it comes to the factors to be considered in determining the holder of obligations, the analysis of State practice also supports considering both the factor of a territorial link and of the devolution of an organ of the predecessor State into the organ of one of the successor States". The criteria are also mentioned in ibid, Fifth Report, 2022, paras 50–52.

282 ILC, "Text of Draft Guidelines 6, 7 bis, 10, 10 bis, 11, 12, 13, 13 bis, 14, 15 and 15 bis", provisionally adopted, Drafting Committee, 73rd sess., 12 July 2022, A/CN.4/L.970.

injured State and the relevant successor State or States should agree on how to address the injury".[283]

In the next paragraphs, I will make a few observations regarding this modification.

First, Special Rapporteur Šturma explained that the solution under Guideline 11 was "a middle-ground approach" adopted "to overcome the dichotomy between the clean slate rule and automatic succession".[284] The same observation is also found in the Commentary.[285] Some ILC members remarked that the earlier draft provision "espoused a general presumption of succession to responsibility that was inconsistent with the general rule of non-succession in respect to State responsibility identified in draft article 6".[286] They argue that "there was not sufficient State practice in support of such a presumption of succession, which found support only in some academic writings and in the work of the Institute of International Law".[287] For these members, "in the absence of consent, it was simply not possible to deduce any assumption of obligations by the successor State".[288] It is interesting to note in this respect the completely opposite positions adopted by the Netherlands[289] and Austria[290]

283 It should be added that when it was decided in 2022 to adopt Guidelines rather than draft articles, the Drafting Committee replaced the word "shall" by "should".

284 ILC Special Rapporteur Šturma, Fifth Report, 2022, para 6. See also, ILC, Statement, Galvão Teles, 2021, 9.

285 ILC, Commentaries, 2022, para 89, Art. 11, sub-para 3.

286 ILC Report, 70th sess., 2018, para 249 (examining comments regarding both situations of unification and dissolution).

287 Ibid.

288 Ibid, adding that for some members "the policy rationale underlying such a reversal of the general rule of non-succession may in fact lead to inequitable or unjust results".

289 Netherlands, letter sent to the UN GA Sixth Committee, rep. 72nd sess. 1st Nov. 2021: "My Government would reiterate its position, as previously expressed, that the point of departure should be the principle that no legal vacuum in terms of State responsibility should emerge. This applies both to situations of dissolution or unification, where the original State has disappeared, and to situations of secession, where the predecessor State remains. Whether rights or obligations be transferred in specific situations should be assessed on a case-by-case basis and be addressed in a succession agreement. If such agreement cannot be reached, the legal vacuum should be avoided by transferring rights and obligations to the successor State or States".

290 Austria, ibid, rep. 73rd sess, 30 Oct. 2018: "Draft Article 10 (2) on incorporation and Draft Article 11 on dissolution are obviously prompted by the claim for justice according to which no unlawful act should remain without responsibility. However, state practice does not warrant the solution contained in these provisions. The practice as characterised by the report of the Special Rapporteur is not very convincing, since most of the cases concern succession into treaties or debts, or explicit acknowledgements of the responsibility by the successor state".

on this issue in comments made to the UN GA Sixth Committee. As such, the approach finally adopted by the ILC is radically different from the one followed by the Institute in Article 15.

Second, the Commentary to Guideline 11 indicates that the provision "recognizes the existence of an *obligation* among the concerned States to seek to agree on how to address the injury".[291] In fact, this is merely an "obligation" *to negotiate*. There is obviously no "obligation" to actually reach any agreement. This is clear from the fact that elsewhere the Commentary mentions that the phrase "is to be understood in the same manner as in draft guidelines 10 and 10 bis, including the obligation to negotiate in good faith".[292] As mentioned above,[293] there is clearly no obligation imposed on the concerned States to reach any agreement under Guidelines 10 and 10 *bis*. My comments above about the consequences of adopting such weak language equally applies to Guideline 11. I would simply add that ILC Special Rapporteur Šturma explained in his Second Report that "modern State practice" in the context of dissolution "allows for a rejection of a strict and automatic application of the principle of non-succession"[294] which "would be in complete contradiction with the very idea of justice".[295] However, the weak language used in Guideline 11 does not in any manner hinder the concerned States from failing to reach an agreement on the allocation of obligations. If they do not, there would simply be no transfer of obligations to the successor State(s). This would result in a wrongful act remaining unpunished. Such an outcome would undoubtedly be "in complete contradiction with the very idea of justice".[296]

Third, another important point is that the expression "the injured State and the relevant successor State or States should agree on how to address the injury", used in Guideline 11, only concerns the relationship between the successor State(s) and the injured State.[297] The provision does not cover an agreement between the successor States themselves.[298] What if the successor States

291 ILC, Commentaries, 2022, para 89, Art. 11, sub-para 4, emphasis added.

292 Ibid sub-para 6.

293 See, Chapter 2, Sections 2.2 and 3.1.

294 ILC Special Rapporteur Šturma, Second Report, 2018, para 167.

295 Ibid, quoting my 2007 book, 104.

296 Ibid.

297 ILC, Commentaries, 2022, para 89, Art. 11, sub-para 4.

298 ILC, Statement, Galvão Teles, 2021, 10: "Regarding the scope ratione personae of the provision, it was noted that the dissolution of a State might give rise to different kinds of legal relations: the inter se relations between the successor States, and the relations between the successor State or States and the injured State and the successor State or States. Draft article 11 only covers the latter kind of legal relations".

decide that none of them should be responsible for the wrongful acts committed by the predecessor State? This situation is not covered by Guideline 11.[299] No solution is provided. In contrast, under the Institute's Resolution, the injured State would necessarily have to consent to such an annihilation of its right to reparation.[300]

Fourth, it should be recalled that Article 15(3) of the Institute's Resolution refers to two factors ("organ" and "direct link") that are relevant to determine which of the successor States becomes the bearer of the obligations to repair. These factors therefore play a major role. They are used to determine which of the successor States should inherit the obligation to repair. Guideline 11 also refers to a non-exhaustive list of factors. For example, the second line of ILC Guideline 11 indicates that the injured State and the "relevant successor State or States" "should take into account any territorial link, any benefit derived, any equitable apportionment, and all other relevant circumstances".[301] This is a non-exhaustive list[302] of factors that the injured State and the successor State(s) "may take into account in determining how best to address the injury" suffered by the former.[303] These factors therefore play a much more modest role under Guideline 11. They are only relevant to help the injured State assess with whom it should enter negotiations to address the suffered injury. In other words, they "serve as a guide for the determination of which successor State or States are to be considered 'relevant' for purposes of draft guideline 11".[304] Only the "relevant" successor State(s) (i.e. those which have "a closer connection with the injury than others"[305]) should be concerned with such

---

299 The point was highlighted by Slovenia, letter sent to the UN GA Sixth Committee, rep. 69th sess. 31 Oct. 2017: "Before the date of succession, the injured state may invoke the responsibility of the responsible (predecessor) state, whereas, in the case of invocation after the date, rules regulating the extent (and modality) of the succeeded responsibility and rules for different categories of succession are needed in order to evaluate how 'succession agreements' influence the injured state. For example, does agreement between successor states not recognising their joint and several responsibility diminish the invocation entitlement of the injured state?".

300 As noted by IIL, Final Report, Kohen, para 26, a devolution agreement "cannot by itself relieve the State author of the internationally wrongful act of its obligation to repair".

301 ILC, Commentaries, 2022, para 89, Art. 11, sub-para 8, adding that "relevant circumstances include those that establish a link between the successor State or States and the internationally wrongful act or the injury, such as the continuity of organs (i.e. a personal link), or unjust enrichment".

302 Ibid para 89, Art. 11, sub-para 8.

303 Ibid sub-para 7.

304 Ibid sub-para 7.

305 ILC, Statement, Galvão Teles, 2021, 10. See also: ILC, Commentaries, 2022, para 89, Art. 11, sub-para 4; ILC Special Rapporteur Šturma, Fifth Report, 2022, para 43, noting that "the

negotiations.[306] At the end of the day, the importance of these factors has been significantly downgraded under Guideline 11 when compared to the previous draft article.[307] They are no longer "factors to be considered in determining the holder of obligations" as initially envisaged by the ILC Special Rapporteur.[308]

In sum, Guideline 11 (which was never formally adopted by the ILC) is a much weaker clause than Article 15 of the Institute's Resolution. This is obviously the result of some members' strong opposition to the very idea of succession to obligations. I nevertheless believe that a more appropriate solution would have been to follow these two logical steps: (1) staunchly affirm the principle of succession, i.e. that the obligation to repair "pass" to the successor State(s) and then (2) provide guidance as to which factors should be taken into account to determine which successor State should be the bearer of this obligation after the date of succession. In contrast, Guideline 11 provides limited guidance to States on what to do beyond encouraging them to "agree on how to address the injury". If they do not, a wrong will remain unpunished. Ultimately, the solution I support is based on justice, equity and fairness for all parties concerned.

4.2 *Ancient State Practice Generally Supports the Principle of Non-succession*

Two older examples of State practice have adopted the doctrine of non-succession to responsibility. It was clearly applied in the context of the dissolution of the Kingdom of Westphalia in 1813, where the Treaty expressly excluded the passing of delictual debts from the predecessor State to the successor States. Similarly, in the context of the dissolution of Austria-Hungary after the First World War, several Austrian municipal court decisions supported the principle that a new State (as Austria was considered in these decisions) should not be held responsible for obligations arising from internationally wrongful acts committed before the date of succession. On the other hand, the

---

injured State may not know, at least a priori, which of the successor States is relevant" and "may therefore request reparation from one, several or all successor States".

306 In fact, the expression "relevant" successor State(s) was adopted to reflect the idea that "the obligation to agree how to address the injury might not be relevant to all successor States to an equal extent". See, ILC, Statement, Galvão Teles, 2021, 10. Other successor States "that do not have an interest in addressing the injury" should "not necessarily be involved in negotiations on the question" (ILC, Commentaries, 2022, para 89, Art. 11, sub-para 5).

307 See, comment by Croatia, letter sent to the UN GA Sixth Committee, Rep. 73rd sess., 31 Oct. 2018, supporting the inclusion of both factors and indicating (using the wording "it is our strong opinion") that they "should be explicitly included in the draft Article 11".

308 ILC Special Rapporteur Šturma, Second Report, 2018, para 188.

practice in the context of the dissolution of Colombia supports the principle of succession.

4.2.1 Kingdom of Westphalia (1813)

Authors often refer to an old example of State practice: the Treaty of Westphalia of 1842 between Prussia, Hanover, Hesse, Lüneburg and Brunswick regulating the dissolution of the Kingdom of Westphalia in 1813.[309] In this Treaty (Article 13), the successor States decided to share the debts of the Kingdom but expressly excluded delictual debts, which had not been recognised by the predecessor State (the Kingdom of Westphalia).[310]

This example has been analysed by most scholars as an illustration of the principle of non-succession to responsibility.[311] This seems to be the proper interpretation to be given to this example.[312]

4.2.2 Austria-Hungary Dual Monarchy (1918)

A much more controversial case of dissolution is the break-up of the Austria-Hungary Dual Monarchy after the First World War. The case is controversial to the extent that it is not so clear whether it must be understood as the dissolution of a State or instead as a case of the secession of Poland, Czechoslovakia and Yugoslavia (with both Austria and Hungary being considered the continuing States). The majority of writers believe that the case of Austria-Hungary is one of dissolution.[313] The question whether the case of the Austria-Hungary Dual Monarchy was indeed one of dissolution is in fact directly linked to the issue of State succession to international responsibility.

---

309 *Vertrag di Regulierung der Central-Schuldverhältnisse des vormaligen Königreichs Westphallen betreffend*, 29 July 1842, G.F. De Martens, *Nouveau recueil général de traités*, v. III, 410.

310 See, analysis in: Feilchenfeld, 156–162; Monnier, 73–74; Rousseau, v. III, 505; O'Connell, State Succession, v. I, 486.

311 Monnier, 73–74; Rousseau, v. III, 505; Atlam, 205.

312 Others have concluded, on the contrary, that the fact that the parties have explicitly excluded the delictual debts from the Treaty shows that they wanted to avoid the application of a general principle of succession to responsibility. For Volkovitsch, 2176, this example "is probably viewed as an exception to the general rule [of succession of States to international responsibility] rather than its confirmation". This argument is explicitly rejected by Monnier, 74, for whom "on peut conclure dès lors qu'en soustrayant les demandes d'indemnités des dettes réparties entres elles, les Puissances signataires du Traité de Berlin n'avaient pas l'intention d'exclure des obligations qui, à défaut, auraient pesé sur elles".

313 For an overview of the legal arguments advanced by both sides: Oskar Lehner, "The Identity of Austria 1918/19 as a Problem of State Succession", 44 *ÖZöRV* 1992, 63–84, 81.

The "Allied and Associated Powers" (the British Empire, France, Italy, Japan, the United States, etc.) held that this was not a case of dissolution. They viewed post-War Austria and Hungary as *identical* with the now extinct Dual Monarchy.[314] The Allies insisted on both States being considered the continuing States in order to make sure that they would be held responsible for the internationally wrongful acts committed by the Dual Monarchy during the War.[315] They feared that if the break-up of Austria-Hungary was interpreted as a case of dissolution, the "rule" of non-succession would apply.

The Peace Treaty of St. Germain (entered into by the Allied Powers and Austria) thus contained a clause providing for Austria's responsibility for the War (Article 177).[316] This was also the position adopted by the US, which concluded a separate peace treaty with Austria in 1921.[317] That Treaty contained an important provision specifying that all property of the Imperial Austro-Hungarian Government would be retained by the US until suitable provision would be set up by Austria to compensate nationals of the US who had suffered "loss, damage, or injury to their persons or property, directly or indirectly" or "in consequence of hostilities or of any operations of war" for acts committed during the War by Austria-Hungary.[318] The US also considered Hungary the

314 See, discussion in: Marek, 220ff.

315 Verzijl, 126.

316 *Treaty of Peace between the Allied and Associated Powers and Austria; Protocol, Declaration and Special Declaration*, 10 September 1919, in force on 16 July 1920, *UKTS* 1919 No. 11 (Cmd. 400). Art. 177 reads as follows: "The Allied and Associated Governments affirm and Austria accepts the responsibility of Austria and her Allies for causing the loss and damage to which the Allied and Associated Governments and their nationals have been subjected as a consequence of the war imposed upon them by the aggression of Austria-Hungary and her Allies".

317 *Treaty between the United States and Austria to establish Securely Friendly Relations between the two Nations*, 24 August 1921, 16 *AJIL* 1922, Suppl., 13–16. The 1919 Peace *Treaty of St. Germain-en-Laye* entered into by Austria and the other European Powers was not ratified by the US. This is essentially the reason why the US signed a separate peace treaty with Austria.

318 Hyde, 438. Art. 1 of the Treaty mentioned that "Austria undertakes to accord to the US and the US shall have and enjoy all the rights, privileges, indemnities, reparations or advantages" which are specified in the Joint Resolution passed by the US Congress and approved by the President on 2 July 1921. The relevant part of the Joint Resolution dealing with Austria reads as follows: "all property, of the Imperial and Royal Austro-Hungarian Government, or its successor or successors, and of all Austro-Hungarian nationals which was on December 7, 1917, in or has since that date come into the possession or under control of, or has been the subject of a demand by the US or any of its officers, agents, or employees from any source or by any agency whatsoever, shall be retained by the US and no disposition thereof made, except as shall have been heretofore or specifically hereafter shall be provided by law until such time as (…) the Imperial and Royal Austro-Hungarian

continuing State of Austria-Hungary and signed with it a separate peace treaty in 1921 which contains the exact same clause as that in the above-mentioned treaty with Austria.[319]

The US ratified a treaty in 1924 with Hungary and Austria dealing with the "determination of the amounts to be paid" by these two States as a result of the previous treaties it had entered into with them in 1921.[320] The Commission set up under this treaty decided that compensation for damage suffered by US nationals during the War would be borne by Austria in the percentage of 63.6% and by Hungary for 36.4%.[321] The Commission specifically indicated that the other States (i.e. Poland, Czechoslovakia and Yugoslavia) should bear no responsibility for such damage.[322] The same position was taken by Polish municipal courts, which held that Austria was the "continuator" of the Dual Monarchy and that, accordingly, it should be held accountable for the illegal acts committed by Austria-Hungary before that date.[323]

Austria took the position that it was a *new* State in 1918. The break-up of Austria-Hungary was interpreted by Austria as a case of dissolution in order

---

Government, or their successor or successors, shall have respectively made suitable provision for the satisfaction of all claims against said Governments respectively, of all persons, whosesoever domiciled, who owe permanent allegiance to the US and who have suffered, through the acts of the (…) Imperial and Royal Austro-Hungarian Government or its agents since July 31, 1914, loss, damage, or injury to their persons or property, directly or indirectly, whether through the ownership of shares of stock in (…) Austro-Hungarian, American, or other corporations, or in consequence of hostilities or of any operations of war, or otherwise and also shall have granted to persons owing permanent allegiance to the US most-favoured-nation treatment whether the same be national or otherwise, in all matters affecting residence, business, profession, trade, navigation, commerce, and industrial property rights and until the (…) Imperial and Royal Austro-Hungarian Government or its successor or successors shall have respectively confirmed to the US all fines, forfeitures, penalties, and seizures imposed or made by the US during the war, whether in respect to the property of the … Imperial and Royal Austro-Hungarian Government or Austro-Hungarian nationals, and shall have waived any and all pecuniary claims against the US".

319 *Treaty Establishing Friendly Relations between the United States of America and Hungary*, 29 August 1921, *USTS* no. 660; 16 *AJIL* 1922, Suppl., 13–16.

320 The Agreement of 26 November 1924 can be found in: *LNTS* v. 48, 70; *UNRIAA* v. VI, 199.

321 *Administrative Decision no. 1*, 25 May 1927, Tripartite Claims Commission, *UNRIAA* v. VI, 203, 207.

322 Ibid 210: "All of the Successor States other than Austria and Hungary are classed as 'Allied or Associated Powers' and under the Treaties it is entirely clear that none of them is held liable for any damage suffered by American nationals resulting from acts of the Austro-Hungarian Government or its agents during either the period of American neutrality or American belligerency".

323 These Polish municipal law cases are further discussed in Chapter 2, Section 6.2.2.

precisely not to have to assume any obligations arising out of the War.[324] This claim of non-continuity was approved by the Austrian Constitutional Court in several cases dealing with issues of State succession. In these cases, it was decided that Austria was not responsible for the obligations of Austria-Hungary and for the claims against it, with the exception of those for which the new State had expressly decided to take over.[325] Thus, the new State of Austria would be bound to take over an appropriate part of the liabilities of Austria-Hungary only based on a statute or an international treaty.[326]

The break-up of the Austria-Hungary Dual Monarchy is an illustration of the principle of non-succession to international responsibility. Thus, the position of all parties on the controversial question of Austria's and Hungary's continuity with the Dual Monarchy was dictated by their own perception that in a case of dissolution, a new State could not be bound by wrongful acts committed before the date of succession.

4.2.3 Union of Colombia (1829–1831)

Reference is often made[327] to the dismemberment of the Union of Colombia (*Gran Colombia*), which took place from 1829 to 1831.[328] A few years later,

324 Marek, 199, see also 218–219.

325 *Military Pensions (Austria) Case*, Austria, Constitutional Court, 7 May 1919, case no. 126, *VfSlg*, v. I (1919), no. 9, 17, *AD* 1919–1922, 66. See also, another case decided by the Constitutional Court on 20 October 1919, case no. 253–254, *VfSlg*, v. I (1919), no. 18–19, 36–37, *AD* 1919–1922, 67. The same conclusion was also reached in the *Austrian Empire (Succession) Case*, Constitutional Court, 11 March 1919, case no. 18, *VfSlg*, v. I (1919), no. 2, 5, *AD* 1919–1922, 67.

326 *Case Relating to the Revalorization of Annuity Awarded against Austrian Railways before World War I (1923)*, Austria, Supreme Court, *Entsheidungen des Obersten Gerichtshofs in rechtssachen*, v. 5 1923, no. 271, 666, *AD* 1923–1924, case 34. In this case, by a judgment given in 1909 the plaintiff was awarded an annuity as damages for a railway accident for which the Austrian State Railways had been held responsible. The Court confirmed the judgment of the lower Court of Innsbruck dismissing the action for valorisation of the annuity (following a currency depreciation) on the ground that the Austrian Republic could not be regarded as the successor to the Treasury of the Dual Monarchy.

327 See, comments by: Rousseau, v. III, 506; Monnier, 75–76; Czaplinski, 341; Atlam, 206; Volkovitsch, 2175–2176. For general backgound to the case, see: Feilchenfeld, 296–299.

328 In 1830, both Venezuela and Ecuador left the Union of Colombia. What remained of the Union of Colombia was New Grenada (composed of present-day Colombia and Panama). New Grenada later changed its name to the "United States of Colombia" in 1863. It was re-organised in 1886 under the name of "Republic of Colombia". On these historical developments, see: Frida Armas Pfirter & Silvina González Napolitano, "Secession and International Law: Latin American Practice", in: Marcelo G. Kohen (ed), *Secession: International Law Perspectives* (CUP 2006) 374–415.

the US submitted a claim for the seizure in 1827 of a US ship by the Union of Colombia, which was then still a unified State. The US claimed that all three successor States (Venezuela, Ecuador and New Grenada) had a "joint and several" obligation to provide compensation.[329]

The three successor States agreed to recognise and share among themselves the compensation related to the damage alleged by the US. Venezuela (in 1852), Colombia (in 1857) and Ecuador (in 1862) all signed separate treaties with the US whereby they apparently agreed to divide the responsibility among themselves in proportion to the division of the national debt of the Union of Colombia as established in 1834 soon after the dissolution of the Union (i.e. New Granada 50%, Ecuador 21.5% and Venezuela 28.5%[330]).[331]

Some authors have interpreted this example as supporting the principle of the transfer of the obligation to repair from the predecessor State to the successor States.[332] Indeed, none of the parties involved (the three successor States and the injured State) seem to have doubted the application of the principle of succession in the present case. It should be added that some other writers have attenuated the importance that should be given to this example by making reference to the fact that apparently the US did not obtain full compensation and that the amount recovered in the three agreements did not cover the total

329 See, letter of 12 February 1839 by US Secretary of State, Mr Forsyth, to Mr Semple, Chargé d'affaires to New Grenada, in: Moore, Digest, v. V, 342: "Upon the dissolution of that Confederacy (that of Colombia) its members became, and have been informed that we hold them, jointly and severely liable for our claims".

330 O'Connell, The Law of State Succession, 1956, 158.

331 *Protocol between the United States of America and Venezuela*, 1 May 1852, in: William M. Malloy, *Treaties, Conventions, International Acts, Protocols and Agreements between the United States of America and other Powers, 1776–1909*, v. II (GPO 1910–1938) (hereinafter "Malloy") 1842. Both treaties signed by the US with Ecuador and New Grenada are found in: ibid, v. I, 319, 432. According to Volkovitsch, footnote no. 56 (quoting documents taken from: John Bassett Moore, *History and Digest of the International Arbitrations to which the United States has been a Party*, v. II (GPO 1898) (hereinafter "Moore, History"), 1576, 1384–1396, 1415–1420), the agreements with Ecuador and New Grenada only provided for the creation of international commissions which would have to adjudicate the claims. He indicates that the Ecuadorian Commission applied the same system of proportionate liability provided for in the US-Venezuela Treaty. As for the New Grenada Commission, he notes that available records are not clear on the conclusion it reached. For Volkovitsch, what is more relevant is the fact that the records of the work of these commissions show no general rejection of the principle of succession to responsibility.

332 Volkovitsch, 2175–2176; Mikulka, State Succession, 292. Monnier, 76, and Atlam, 216, analyse this case as one rare exception to the general rule of non-succession, in the sense that absent this explicit recognition by the successor States, no such succession could have occurred. See also, ILC Special Rapporteur Šturma, Second Report, 2018, paras 167–8.

amount claimed.[333] It has also been suggested that the position of succession adopted by the three successor States could be explained based on the overwhelming power of the US in the region at that time and that the solution arrived at could have simply been imposed upon them.[334]

4.3 *Modern State Practice Supports the Principle of Succession*

I have found two examples of State practice where the successor States have accepted to take over the obligations arising from internationally wrongful acts committed by the predecessor State before the date of succession. The most recent case is the 2001 *Agreement on Succession Issues* entered into among all the successor States to the former SFRY.[335] The dissolution of the United Arab Republic in 1961 is also a clear example of State practice whereby one of the two successor States (Egypt) took over responsibility for wrongful acts committed by the predecessor State before the date of succession.

The principle of succession to responsibility was recognised in the *Compromis* entered into between Slovakia and Hungary to refer a dispute to the ICJ. The validity of the principle was also recognised (at least implicitly) by the ICJ in the *Gabčíkovo-Nagymaros* case, in which it stated that the successor State (Slovakia) "may be liable to pay compensation not only for its own wrongful conduct but also for that of Czechoslovakia" (i.e. the predecessor State).[336] However, it should be noted that the Court's finding was solely based on the specific language contained in the *Compromis* between the Parties. The Court did not endorse any *general* principle of succession to responsibility. At the most, it can be argued that the Court did not reject the validity of the possibility of the transfer of the obligation to repair from the predecessor State to the successor State. The same is true regarding the ICJ *Croatia Genocide Convention* case.[337]

Importantly, the examples examined in this section involve the new State *accepting* to take over responsibilities. I have not found any example where the solution of succession was *imposed* on a reluctant successor State by a judicial authority.

333 Czaplinski, 341–342. On this point, Volkovitsch, 2176, indicates that this assertion is not supported by any evidence.

334 Atlam, 216; Monnier, 76.

335 *Agreement on Succession Issues*, 29 June 2001, 41 *ILM* 2002, 3.

336 *Gabčíkovo-Nagymaros* case, para 151.

337 *Croatia Genocide Convention* case.

4.3.1 United Arab Republic (1961)

As previously observed, the United Arab Republic was created in 1958 by the unification of Egypt and Syria into a single State.[338] The marriage was short-lived, as on 28 September 1961, following a coup in Damascus, Syria left the United Arab Republic.

The United Nations considered Syria not as a new State but as an "old" State which was simply readmitted to the organisation and reinstalled in its seat as if its membership had simply been "suspended" during the three years during which it had merged with Egypt to form the United Arab Republic.[339] The procedure adopted by the United Nations and the international community in general has been criticised as contrary to rules of succession of States.[340] In 1961, Syria was clearly *a new State*. This is the prevailing view[341] and the one adopted by at least one municipal court decision.[342] The events of September 1961 in Damascus led to the *dissolution* of the United Arab Republic as both Syria and Egypt went their own ways. After that date, Egypt nevertheless continued to use the name "United Arab Republic" until September 1971, at which time it became known as the "Arab Republic of Egypt".

After the dissolution, Egypt (as one of the two successor States) entered into several agreements with other States whereby it provided compensation to

338 The circumstances of the unification have already been explained above: Chapter 2, Section 3.2.1.

339 Syria requested its "readmission" to the UN in a letter dated 8 October 1961 (A/4914, 9 October 1961). On 13 October 1961, the President of the UN GA called the content of the letter to the attention of the member States during a plenary meeting. Since no objection was raised against Syria being given a seat "as a member of the United Nations", Syria was duly seated in the same day: UN GA, Provisional Verbatim Record of the 1035th Meeting, A/P.V. 1035, 13 Oct. 1961, 2–3; ibid, 1036th Meeting, A/P.V. 1036, 13 Oct. 1961, 21–22.

340 Strong criticisms can be found in: Charles Rousseau, "Chronique des faits internationaux", *RGDIP* 1962, 413–417; Lucius Caflisch, "Les Nations Unies et le respect du droit international, le retour de la Syrie à l'O.N.U., une procédure critiquable", *Tribune de Genève*, 21 October 1961.

341 Rousseau, ibid; Habib Guerari, "Quelques observations sur les Etats éphémères", *AFDI* 1994, 426–429. *Contra*: Richard Young, "The State of Syria: Old or New?", 56 *AJIL* 1962, 482–488, for whom post-September 1961 Syria was the same State as pre-1958 Syria. It may be true that these "two Syria" have, indeed, the same territory and other similar characteristics. However, from a legal standpoint, it is not the same entity because it had ceased to exist for some three years. As so rightly pointed out by Marek, 6, "there is no legal resurrection in international law. Once a State has become extinct, it cannot resume a continued existence".

342 *Arab Republic of Syria v. Arab Republic of Egypt*, Supreme Court of Brazil (Plenary Sess.), case no. 298–DF, 14 April 1982, *RTJ*, v. 104, 1983, 889, 91 *ILR* 288. See, position of Judge Alves in his concurring opinion (at 311–313).

foreign nationals whose properties had been nationalised by the United Arab Republic (the predecessor State) before the date of succession (i.e. during the period 1958–1961). The decision of Egypt to provide compensation to injured States is most likely based on the ground that the acts of nationalisation were actually committed *in the territory of Egypt itself* and not in Syria.[343] This situation suggests that the parties to these agreements may have considered that there was a "direct link" between the consequences of the internationally wrongful act committed by the United Arab Republic and the territory of Egypt.[344] This example is an illustration of the "direct link" element mentioned in Article 15(2) of the Institute's Resolution.[345] The principle of unjust enrichment may have also played a role in the outcome of these cases.[346]

A lump sum agreement in the amount of EGY£ 2 million was concluded between Italy and the United Arab Republic (the name Egypt continued to use at the time) in 1965.[347] The agreement covered Italian properties, rights and interests which were affected by measures taken by the United Arab Republic before and after the dissolution of State in 1961.[348] Another example is the Agreement of 13 September 1971 between the Arab Republic of Egypt and Great Britain with respect to compensation for British properties, rights and interests affected by the measures of nationalisation taken by the predecessor State.[349]

343 ILC Special Rapporteur Šturma, Second Report, 2018, para 170.

344 This question is further examined below, Chapter 3, Section 10.1.

345 Kohen & Dumberry, 126.

346 The concept of unjust enrichment is examined below: Chapter 3, Section 8.

347 *Agreement Between Italy and the United Arab Republic Relative to the Indemnisation of Italian Interests in Egypt with Protocol for the Application of the Exchange of Notes*, 23 March 1965, in force on 5 September 1966, *Gaz. Off.*, No. 215, 1 April 1966; 7 *Dir. Intern.* 1966, Pt. II, 231; Weston et al., 139. An exchange of notes dated 20 August 1968 extended the Agreement (10 *Dir. Intern.* 1969, Pt. II, 254). See, Andrea Giardina, "International Claims: Contemporary Italian Practice", in: Weston & Lillich, 110.

348 Art. 2 of the Agreement.

349 *Agreement between the Government of the United Kingdom of Great Britain and Northern Ireland and the Government of the Arab Republic of Egypt Regarding Compensation for British Property, Rights and Interests Affected by Arab Republic of Egypt Measures of Nationalisation and other Matters Concerning British Property in the Arab Republic of Egypt*, in force on 28 March 1972, *UKTS* 1972, no. 62 (Cmd. 4995); 858 *UNTS* 3; Weston et al., 179. Under the Agreement (Art. 2), Egypt agreed to pay the amount of GB£ 2.1 million in "settlement of claims for compensation in respect of British properties, rights and interests nationalised". Such payments were final and covered all British claims against the Arab Republic of Egypt (Art. 2(5)). It is true that the title of the Agreement refers to the nationalisation acts committed by the *Arab Republic of Egypt* and not those of the United Arab Republic. However, in Art. 1 the expression "relevant Arab Republic of Egypt measures" is designed to include all nationalisation laws promulgated by the Government of

A similar agreement was also signed in 1971 between the Arab Republic of Egypt and Sweden "concerning the compensation of Swedish interests affected by the measures of nationalisation and other restrictive measures enacted in the Arab Republic of Egypt".[350] An agreement was entered into between the Arab Republic of Egypt and the US on 1 May 1976 for a claim settlement in the amount of US$ 10 million "in full settlement and discharge of all the claims of nationals of the US against the Egyptian Government".[351] Other different types of agreements[352] were also entered into by the United Arab Republic with Switzerland (1964),[353] Lebanon (1964),[354] Denmark (1965),[355] Greece

---

Egypt *between 1960 and 1964*, therefore including those nationalisation acts committed by the United Arab Republic *before* the dissolution in 1961.

350 *Agreement between the Kingdom of Sweden and the Arab Republic of Egypt Concerning the Compensation of Swedish Interests*, 10 November 1971, in force on 7 August 1972, 969 *UNTS* 317; Weston et al., 185. Here again, the mention in the Agreement of acts committed by the "Arab Republic of Egypt" should not disguise the fact that some of the items covered were concerning measures of nationalisation which took place before the dissolution (see Art. 2).

351 *Agreement between the Government of the United States of America and the Government of the Arab Republic of Egypt Concerning Claims of United States Nationals*, in force on 27 October 1976, 4 *UST* 1976, 4214; *TIAS* no. 8446; Weston et al., 235. The scope of the Agreement is as follows: "Property, rights and interests in Egypt affected by Egyptian measures of land reform, sequestration, nationalisation, expropriation, confiscation, and other restrictive measures against such property rights and interests, as well as financial and fiscal matters decreed *by the Arab Republic of Egypt*, which occurred *since January 1, 1952*, and before the entry into force of this Agreement" (emphasis added). The Agreement therefore covers nationalisation acts committed by the United Arab Republic from 1958 to 1961. Pursuant to Art. 4, the US Foreign Claims Settlement Commission adjudicated claims against Egypt. The legislation (US Public Law 455, 81st Cong.) codified as 22 USC no. 1623(a) led to the enactment of "Subchapter I: Claims Against Egypt" of the "International Claims Settlement Act" of 1949. 85 claims were filed to the Commission which awarded US$ 5.2 million in compensation (US Foreign Claims Settlement Commission, "Annual Report, 2001"). One example is *Claim no. E8* (in: *Digest of United States Practice in the International Law 1977* (GPO) 693).

352 The agreements gave the possibility for nationals to recover compensation for 65% of what they would be entitled to under the laws of the United Arab Republic.

353 *Accord entre la Suisse et la République Arabe Unie concernant l'indemnisation des intérêts suisses*, 20 June 1964, in force on 16 June 1965, *Rec. Off. lois fédérales*, 1965, 502; *RGDIP* 1964, 731. The text is quoted in: Message of the Swiss government (*Conseil fédéral*), 9 October 1964, *Feuille fédérale* 1964 II, 941ff. See, P. Guggenheim, "La pratique suisse, 1964", *ASDI* 1965, 175. The Agreement (Art. II) covers acts of nationalisation committed before September 1961.

354 Agreement, 18 November 1964, in: H. Abou-Fadel, J. Malha & I. Kraidy, *Lebanon, its Treaties and Agreements*, v. 3, 89. See, Weston & Lillich, 371.

355 Agreement, 12 June 1965, *Lovtidende* C, 1966, 208; See, ibid 372.

(1966)[356] and the Netherlands (1971).[357]

4.3.2 The *Gabčíkovo-Nagymaros* Case (1997) in the Context of the Dissolution of Czechoslovakia (1992)

A more recent example of dissolution of State is the break-up of Czechoslovakia on 1 January 1993.[358] Two new States emerged as successor States to Czechoslovakia: the Czech Republic and the Republic of Slovakia.[359] There is almost no controversy on the question whether the break-up of Czechoslovakia is a case of a dissolution of a State.[360] The Czech Republic officially declared (in its Constitutional Law,[361] its "Proclamation to all Parliaments and Nations of the World",[362] and in a letter sent to the UN Secretary-General[363]) that it would respect all obligations arising from Czechoslovakia's multilateral and bilateral treaties. The same types of declarations were made by Slovakia.[364] As one of the two successor States, the Czech Republic stated its willingness to take over "rights and obligations" deriving from the predecessor State

356 Agreement, 26 September 1966, *Greek Gov. Gaz.* 1967, 474. See, ibid.

357 Agreement, 25 February 1971, *Trb.* 1971, 96. See, ibid. The Agreement is slightly different from the others because it provides Dutch nationals the possibility to recover compensation at 50% (and not 65%) of an award under the laws of the United Arab Republic.

358 On 25 November 1992, the Czechoslovak Federal Assembly voted the Constitutional Act no. 542/1992 (which came into force on 8 December 1992) indicating that the Federation would cease to exist on 31 December 1992.

359 On the question of State succession, the legislative bodies of the two constituent Republics enacted the relevant acts prior to the dissolution. On 17 July 1992, the Slovak National Council adopted the *Declaration on the Sovereignty of the Slovak Republic*, which was shortly followed by the proclamation of the Constitution of the Slovak Republic on 3 September 1992 (which came into force on 1 October 1992). Both Republic's National Council adopted "proclamations" aiming at giving the international community assurances as to the stability of treaty relations after the dissolution of Czechoslovakia (Slovakia, 3 December 1992; Czech Republic, 17 December 1992). See also: Letter of the Permanent Representative of Czechoslovakia to the UN to the UN Secretary-General, 31 December 1992, A/47/848.

360 On the contrary, Jiri Malenovsky, "Problèmes juridiques liés à la partition de la Tchécoslovaquie", 39 *AFDI* 1993, 317, believes that Slovakia seceded from Czechoslovakia.

361 *Constitutional Law No. 4/1993*, proclaimed by the Czech Republic's National Council, 15 December 1992, see Art. 5.

362 *Proclamation of the National Council of the Czech Republic to all Parliaments and Nations of the World*, 17 December 1992.

363 Letter of 16 February 1993, received by the UN Secretary-General on 22 February 1993.

364 *Declaration on the Sovereignty of the Slovak Republic*, adopted by the Slovak National Council, 17 July 1992; Constitution of the Slovak Republic, adopted on 3 September 1992, Art. 153; *Proclamation of the National Council of the Slovak Republic to Parliaments and Peoples of the World*, 3 December 1992.

(Czechoslovakia) to the extent that they were committed in the territory of the former Czech Federal Republic.[365] It has been argued that the language used is not wide enough to cover obligations arising from internationally wrongful acts committed by the predecessor State.[366]

Reference to the issue of State succession to responsibility in the context of the dissolution of Czechoslovakia can be found in the *Gabčíkovo-Nagymaros* case.[367] This case concerned a 1977 Treaty between Czechoslovakia and Hungary envisaging a joint investment for the construction and joint operation of a large, integrated and indivisible complex of structures and installations for a barrage system on specific parts of the territories of the two parties along the Danube.

The question of State succession that the ICJ had to decide was whether Slovakia had become a Party to the 1977 Treaty between Czechoslovakia and Hungary as a successor State to one of the original Parties to the Treaty.[368] Hungary contended that the 1977 Treaty, being simply a joint investment, had ceased to be in force as of 31 December 1992 as a result of the disappearance of one of the Parties as a subject of international law.[369] According to Slovakia, the 1977 Treaty remained in force between itself, as successor State, and Hungary

365 Art. 5, *Constitutional Law No. 4/1993*: "The Czech Republic takes over rights and obligations (...) deriving from [Czechoslovakia] on the date of its extinction from international law, except those (...) relating to the territory which was under [Czechoslovakia's] sovereignty but is not under the sovereignty of the Czech Republic".

366 This is the position of Vaclav Mikulka, "The Dissolution of Czechoslovakia and Succession in Respect to Treaties" in: Mojmir Mrak (ed), *Succession of States* (Martinus Nijhoff 1999) 110, for whom "this formulation covers the rights and obligations deriving from both customary international law and international treaties". Similarly, for Jiri Malenovsky, "Problèmes juridiques liés à la partition de la Tchécoslovaquie", 39 *AFDI* 1993, 334–335, the principle remains that the new States are not bound by Czechoslovakia's internationally wrongful acts. The only exception is in the context of the *European Convention for the Protection of Human Rights and Fundamental Freedom* (213 UNTS 222), where the new States made declarations to that effect. This is discussed in the Czech Republic's National Report on "State Succession in Respect of Treaties" submitted to the Council of Europe, in: Jan Klappers (ed), *State Practice Regarding State Succession and Issues of Recognition* (Kluwer 1999) 402.

367 *Gabčíkovo-Nagymaros* case, at paras 116–124.

368 Ibid para 117.

369 According to Hungary (ibid para 118), "there is no rule of international law which provides for automatic succession to bilateral treaties on the disappearance of a Party". Hungary contended that it never accepted Slovakia as successor to the 1977 Treaty. Furthermore, Hungary argued that it was not a Party to the 1978 *Vienna Convention* and that the so-called rule of automatic succession to treaties contained in Art. 34 of the Convention was not a statement of general international law.

since it could not have been terminated through the disappearance of one of the original Parties.[370]

The Court did not tackle the many interesting arguments put forward by both sides on State succession.[371] Instead, it focused its analysis on the particular nature and character of the 1977 Treaty, which was found to be of a "territorial character".[372] It concluded that the 1977 Treaty became binding upon Slovakia (as successor State) on 1 January 1993.[373]

The Court determined that before the date of succession, Czechoslovakia (the predecessor State) had committed an internationally wrongful act[374] and that it was under the obligation to pay compensation to Hungary (the injured State).[375] The Court *did not address* the question of transfer of obligations arising from such acts to Slovakia (the successor State). The Court simply made reference to the second paragraph of the Preamble to the Special Agreement (*Compromis*) of 2 July 1993 entered into between Slovakia and Hungary, which indicates that:

> *Bearing in mind* that the Slovak Republic is one of the two successor states of the Czech and Slovak Federal Republic and the sole successor state in respect of rights and obligations relating to the Gabčíkovo-Nagymaros Project.

This is therefore a situation where both parties agreed that there should be a "devolution under international law of secondary obligations or rights deriving from a breach of an international obligation from the predecessor to the successor State".[376] Both parties agreed that Slovakia (and not the Czech Republic,

---

370 Slovakia argued that the "general rule of continuity" would apply in cases of dissolution as provided by Art. 34 of the 1978 *Vienna Convention*. It argued that the principle of automatic succession was a statement of customary international law and that State practice in cases of dissolution tends to support continuity.

371 These issues are discussed in: Jan Klabbers, "Cat on a Hot Tin Roof: The World Court, State Succession, and the Gabčíkovo-Nagymaros Case", 11 *Leiden JIL* 1998, 345–355.

372 Thus, according to the Court, the Treaty had established the navigational regime for the Danube and created a situation where the interests of other users of the Danube were affected. Therefore, the Treaty being of a "territorial character", the rights and obligations which were "attached" to part of the Danube were unaffected by the succession of States. The Court therefore followed Slovakia's position on this point.

373 *Gabčíkovo-Nagymaros* case, para 123.

374 Ibid paras 82, 87, 88.

375 Ibid para 152. The Court also concluded that before the date of succession Hungary had committed an internationally wrongful act and that it was under the obligation to pay compensation to Czechoslovakia (paras 108–110).

376 Mikulka, State Succession, 296.

the other successor State to the former Czechoslovakia) should be the holder of such rights and obligations. This is certainly because of the existence of a "direct link" between the wrongful acts and the territory and the population of *that* successor State.[377] On the Czechoslovakian side, the project was indeed located in the territory of Slovakia. This example is an illustration of the "direct link" element mentioned in Article 15(2) of the Institute's Resolution.

The Court interpreted the Preamble to the Special Agreement to mean that Slovakia was the successor to Czechoslovakia's responsibility:

> According to the Preamble to the Special Agreement, the Parties agreed that Slovakia is the sole successor State of Czechoslovakia in respect of rights and obligations relating to the Gabčíkovo-Nagymaros Project. Slovakia thus may be liable to pay compensation not only for its own wrongful conduct but also for that of Czechoslovakia, and it is entitled to be compensated for the damage sustained by Czechoslovakia as well as by itself as a result of the wrongful conduct of Hungary.[378]

What is clear is that the Court's conclusion as to the responsibility of Slovakia for internationally wrongful acts committed by Czechoslovakia was admitted solely on the ground that the Parties to the Special Agreement had already agreed that Slovakia was "the sole successor State of Czechoslovakia in respect of rights and obligations relating to the Gabčíkovo-Nagymaros Project".[379] The Court did not make any determination on the question of the transfer of the obligation to repair from one State to another.[380] This conclusion is all the more obvious when considering that both Parties in their Memorials, as well as during the oral proceedings, explicitly rejected the existence of any such *general* principle of succession to international responsibility. This point is further examined in the next paragraphs.

The argument advanced by Hungary was that "the Special Agreement draws a distinction between the 1977 Treaty as such … and the Gabčíkovo-Nagymaros Project" for the reason that Slovakia was never part of the 1977 Treaty and that

---

377 Kohen & Dumberry, 124. See also: ILC Special Rapporteur Šturma, Second Report, 2018, para 175, indicating that "the close link between the internationally wrongful act or its consequences and the territory is another important factor" which explain the decision of the Court. See also, at para 188.

378 *Gabčíkovo-Nagymaros* case, para 151.

379 Ibid. See also: Reyes Gajardo, 77; Kaplane, 19; Pajnkihar, 309.

380 This is also the position of Russia, letter sent to the UN GA Sixth Committee, Rep. 72nd sess, 24 Oct. 2017; ibid rep. 73rd sess. 31 October 2018. See also: Malaysia, ibid Rep. 73rd sess. 31 Oct. 2018.

"breaches of that Treaty committed by the Czech and Slovak Federal Republic were not attributable to [Slovakia]".[381] For Hungary, Slovakia's responsibility must be based on the rule of attribution under State responsibility: "Slovakia's responsibility towards Hungary *depends on the attribution of Czechoslovakia's wrongful conduct* in the implementation of the Original Project and of Variant C *to Slovakia*".[382] Hungary's contention was that Slovakia (as successor State) remained bound by "the obligation to repair the damage caused by the wrongful acts" in violation of the 1977 Treaty as well as in breach of other international obligations contained in other treaties and in customary international law.[383] In other words, the "secondary obligations" resulting from the violation of the 1977 Treaty committed by Czechoslovakia would simply not vanish with the break-up of Czechoslovakia (and the termination of the 1977 Treaty).

A closer look at the arguments put forward by Hungary, however, shows that it did not base its conclusion regarding the responsibility of Slovakia on a *general* principle of succession to international responsibility. In its pleadings, Hungary refers to the "well-established principle that there is in general no succession to international responsibility".[384] However, to this negative principle would remain an "exception": "the key exception is where a successor State, by its *own* conduct, has acted in such a way as to assume the breaches of the law committed by its predecessor".[385] The principle and the exception were described as follows at the oral proceedings by Dupuy, Counsel for Hungary:

> La Slovaquie prétend constamment qu'à l'égard du traité de 1977, elle a succédé à la Tchécoslovaquie et qu'elle est donc à son tour partie à ce traité. Si l'on suivait le raisonnement slovaque, il y aurait bien entendu là un fondement suffisant pour établir sa responsabilité, si toutefois on évitait d'appliquer le *principe général selon lequel il n'y a pas succession à la responsabilité*.

---

381 "Memorial", Hungary, v. 1, 2 May 1994, para 6.06. See also, paras 8.02, 10.108, 10.109.

382 Ibid para 8.01 (emphasis added).

383 Ibid para 8.03: "The first legal consequence is that Slovakia cannot be deemed responsible for breaches of treaty obligations attributable only to Czechoslovakia, which no longer exists. Nevertheless, Czechoslovakia's breaches of the 1977 Treaty, other bilateral treaties, various multilateral conventions and customary international law created a series of secondary obligations; namely, the obligation to repair the damage caused by the wrongful acts. These secondary obligations were neither extinguished by the termination of the 1977 Treaty nor by the disappearance of Czechoslovakia".

384 "Reply", Hungary, v. 1, 20 June 1995, para 3.163.

385 Ibid, emphasis in the original.

> *A ce dernier principe, il est toutefois une exception.* Celle qui se trouve réalisée lorsqu'un Etat revendique et poursuit les faits illicites de son prédécesseur. Or, c'est bien sur ce second fondement que la Slovaquie est responsable des manquements au droit accomplis par la Tchécoslovaquie.[386] (emphases added)

The reasoning of Hungary thus indicates that it was of the view that there should be a transfer of the obligation to repair to the new State *only* because the new State had *endorsed and continued* the internationally wrongful act (i.e. the derivation of the Variant C project) originally committed by the predecessor State before the date of succession.[387] Thus, by endorsing and continuing the internationally wrongful act initially committed by Czechoslovakia, Slovakia was not only responsible for the damage resulting from its *own illicit act* committed after its creation in January 1993, but also for the internationally wrongful act committed by *the predecessor State* before January 1993.[388]

The argument put forward by Hungary indicates that although it does not support any *general* principle of succession to responsibility, it has in fact endorsed the soundness of such solution in *one circumstance*. Thus, Hungary's position is that the successor State (Slovakia) should be held responsible for

386 Oral Pleadings, 7 March 1997, para 6 of Pierre-Marie Dupuy's transcript of his pleadings.

387 "Memorial", Hungary, v. 1, 2 May 1994, para 8.04: "Slovakia continues to be responsible for these secondary obligations because Variant C continued to exist and to be operated after 1 January 1993. Indeed it was further developed under the control and responsibility of Slovakia and within its exclusive territorial jurisdiction. From the first day of its existence as a sovereign State, Slovakia uninterruptedly continued the operation of Variant C, as earlier implemented by Czechoslovakia. From 1 January 1993, Slovakia's actions have effectively endorsed its international responsibility for Variant C". A similar explanation is given at ibid para 8.05: "The second preambular paragraph of the Special Agreement therefore simply reflects a known fact. It is an explicit way of delineating a legal relationship that was already in existence. In short, this preambular paragraph is nothing but a declaratory statement, showing that, from its beginning, Slovakia assumed the obligations, as operator of variant C, to repair damage caused by present and prior breaches of international law. Further, Slovakia immediately accepted this heritage, first by its action, then by its statement in preambular paragraph 2 of the Special Agreement".

388 "Memorial", Hungary, v. 1, 2 May 1994, para 8.06: "Slovakia is therefore responsible for damage and loss caused by Czechoslovakia in relation to the implementation of Variant C until the disappearance of Czechoslovakia on 31 December 1992. This responsibility extends to damage caused by any part of the material of the Original Project that was wrongfully converted or taken over for use in Variant C. From 1 January 1993 onwards, Slovakia is of course responsible, as a successor, for damage created by its own conduct". This aspect is also dealt with in: "Reply", Hungary, v. 1, 20 June 1995, para 3.164, and in: Oral Pleadings, 7 March 1997, paras 6 to 8 of Pierre-Marie Dupuy's transcript of his pleadings.

wrongful acts committed *before* its creation as an independent State. The issue of succession to continuous internationally wrongful acts will be further discussed below.[389]

Slovakia mostly focused its attention on rules of State succession to treaties. It nevertheless briefly dealt with the question of whether there exists any rule of State succession to responsibility. Slovakia thus referred to the "widely accepted thesis of non-succession to delictual responsibility",[390] quoting the work of Monnier to "recall" "the practically unanimous view of the doctrine" on this question.[391] Slovakia did not further explore the argument submitted by Hungary on this point,[392] nor did it discuss Hungary's argument on its responsibility for continuous internationally wrongful acts.[393]

In conclusion, the Court's brief mention of the issue cannot be analysed as a clear endorsement of the principle of State succession to responsibility. The Court's conclusion was based on the Special Agreement where the parties had already agreed that Slovakia was "the sole successor State of Czechoslovakia" with respect to responsibility.[394] At the most, it can be argued that the Court did not reject the validity of the possibility of the transfer of the obligation to repair from the predecessor State to the successor State.[395] ILC Special Rapporteur Šturma has taken the position that in this case the Court has *endorsed* the principle of succession.[396] For him, this case may be the "most

389 See, Chapter 3, Section 5.

390 "Counter-Memorial", Slovakia, v. 1, 5 December 1994, para 3.59.

391 Ibid para 3.60. Logically, Slovakia admitted (ibid para 3.60, again quoting the work of Monnier) that as a new State it does not take up the *rights* belonging to the predecessor State as a result of any internationally wrongful acts committed before the date of succession. Thus, Slovakia's right to obtain compensation from Hungary in the context of the Gabčíkovo-Nagymaros Project "is not based on succession to Czechoslovakia *per se*, it is based on the [1977] Treaty" (ibid para 3.61). This question is further examined in Part 3, Chapter 5, Section 3.2.2.

392 Ibid para 3.69. Slovakia concluded that there was "no need to rebut the Hungarian thesis for *ipso iure* succession to the secondary obligations deriving from an internationally wrongful act" because Slovakia had committed "no breach of the 1977 Treaty or other international obligations [of] Czechoslovakia".

393 The argument is simply mentioned in: ibid para 3.59.

394 Crawford, State Responsibility, 446–7.

395 Kohen & Dumberry, 124. This point is discussed by the following authors: Stern, Responsabilité, 346–347; Sir Arthur Watts, "State Succession: Some Recent Practical Legal Problems" in: Volkmar Götz, Peter Selmer & Rüdiger Wolfrum (ed), *Liber amicorum Günther Jaenicke* (Springer 1999) 405; Eisemann, Emprunts russes, 61; Crawford, State Responsibility, 446–7.

396 ILC Special Rapporteur Šturma, First Report, 2017, para 50 ("Notwithstanding the special agreement between Hungary and Slovakia, the Court thus seems to recognize the succession in respect of secondary (responsibility) obligations and secondary rights resulting

important judicial decision in favour of the transfer of responsibility".[397] While he also explained that he was not in any way denying the importance of the Special Agreement, he nevertheless argued that "the role of the presumed consent (in the Special Agreement) should not be overestimated".[398] For him, there were also "other relevant circumstances" which explained the findings of the Court: the 1977 treaty establishing a territorial regime, the "close link" between the wrongful act and the territory of the new State, and the actions of the authorities of one of the republics of the Czechoslovak federation before the date of succession.[399] This is a valid point. But it remains that, in essence, the Court simply confirmed what was already recognised by international case law and accepted by scholars, namely that nothing prevents the successor State from freely deciding to take over the consequences of internationally wrongful acts committed by the predecessor State.[400] The (limited) reasoning of the Court does not provide any guidance as to the solution that should be adopted in the absence of such consent by the successor State.

4.3.3 Socialist Federal Republic of Yugoslavia (1991–1992)

4.3.3.1 *This Is a Case of a Dissolution of State*

Issues of State succession arising from the collapse of the Socialist Federal Republic of Yugoslavia (SFRY) are both complex in their formulation and tragic in their consequences.[401] The process of dissolution took place over a

---

from wrongful acts"); ibid, para 59 ("Slovakia did not incur responsibility on the basis of continuing the breach of Czechoslovakia after the date of succession (1 January 1993). Its responsibility, held by the International Court of Justice, thus can only be explained as a matter of succession to certain obligations arising from the wrongful act committed by Czechoslovakia", see also, para 102). He adopted the same position elsewhere: Šturma, State Succession, 664 ("The ICJ thus recognized succession with respect to secondary responsibility obligations and secondary rights resulting from wrongful acts").

397 Ibid, Second Report, 2018, paras 172–3, 175. See also, Lena Raxter, "Responsibility After Succession: The Work of the International Law Commission and Its Application for Seeking Redress After the Breach of Investor-State Agreements", 88(3) *Int. J. Arb. Med. & Disp. Man.*, 2022, 372, citing this case and concluding that "the jurisprudence of the ICJ supports both the concept of succession of obligations and the adoption of the obligations of a predecessor state".

398 Ibid, Second Report, 2018, paras 172–3, 175.

399 Ibid para 175. See also: Brockman-Hawe, 866.

400 Dupuy & Kerbrat, 84–5. This point is further discussed in detail in Chapter 3, Section 4.

401 Snezana Trifunovka, *Yugoslavia Through Documents-From its Creation to its Dissolution* (Martinus Nijhoff 1994); Snezana Trifunovka, *Former Yugoslavia Throught Documents-From Its Dissolution to the Peace Settlement* (Martinus Nijhoff 1999); Brigitte Stern (ed), *Le statut des Etats issus de l'ex-Yougoslavie à l'ONU: Documents* (Montchrestien 1996); B.G. Ramcharan (ed), *The International Conference on the Former Yugoslavia: Official Papers*, 2 vols. (Kluwer 1997).

period of several months as each Republic proclaimed its independence one after the other.[402] In its "Opinion no. 1" (29 November 1991), the Arbitration Commission (the Badinter Commission) declared that the SFRY was in a "process of dissolution",[403] and by 4 July 1992, in its "Opinion no. 8", that this process was now completed and that the SFRY no longer existed.[404] It should be noted that by that time (on 27 April 1992), the former Republics of Montenegro and Serbia had established the Federal Republic of Yugoslavia (FRY) with a new constitution proclaiming it to be the "continuator" of the former SFRY.[405] Other former Republics strongly opposed such pretension by the FRY.[406] The same position was also adopted by the majority of States.[407] The UN Security Council and the UN General Assembly,[408] as well as the Badinter

402 See: Rahim Kherad, "La reconnaissance des États issus de la dissolution de la R.S.F.Y. par les membres de l'Union Européenne", 101 *RGDIP* 1997, 663–693; Michael C. Wood, "Participation of the Former Yugoslav States in the United Nations and in Multilateral Treaties", 1 *Max Planck Yrbk. UNL* 1997, 231–258.

403 "Opinion no. 1", 29 November 1991, 92 *ILR* 1993, 166. The European Community Peace Conference on Yugoslavia established an Arbitration Commission for the settlement of disputes (Joint Statement, 28 August 1991, *EC Bull.* No. 7/8, 115 (1991)). The Commission was made up of five presidents of five European Union's constitutional courts; it was chaired by Judge Badinter. The Commission delivered 15 (non-binding) "opinions". For an assessment of the work of the Commission, see the series of articles by Alain Pellet in: 37 *AFDI* 1991, 329–348; 38 *AFDI* 1992, 220–238; 39 *AFDI* 1993, 286–303. See also: Matthew C.R. Craven, "The European Community Arbitration Commission in Yugoslavia", 66 *British YIL* 1995, 333–413.

404 "Opinion no. 8", 4 July 1992, 92 *ILR* 1993, 202. See also, "Opinion no. 9", 4 July 1992, 92 *ILR* 1993, 203, and "Opinion no. 10", 4 July 1992, 92 *ILR* 1993, 206.

405 *Declaration on the Formation of the Federal Republic of Yugoslavia*, joint session of Yugoslavia Assembly, the National Assembly of the Republic of Serbia and the Assembly of the Republic of Montenegro, 27 April 1992, annexed to Letter of 27 April 1992 from the Chargé d'affaires of the Permanent Mission of Yugoslavia to the UN addressed to the President of the SC (1992) S/23877 (1992). See also: Letter of the interim Chargé d'Affaires at the Permanent Mission of Yugoslavia at the UN to the UN Secretary-General, 6 May 1992, A/46/915.

406 Letter of the Minister of Foreign Affairs of the Republic of Slovenia to the UN Secretary-General, 27 May 1992, A/47/234, S/24028; Letter of the Permanent Representatives of Bosnia-Herzegovina and Croatia to the UN to the UN Secretary-General, 25 September 1992, A/47/474; Letter of the Interim Chargé d'Affaires at the Permanent Mission of Croatia to the United Nations to the UN Secretary-General, 2 August 1995, A/50/333. It should be noted that subsequently the former Republics all formally recognised each other as independent States: *Agreement on Normalisation between the Federal Republic of Yugoslavia and Republic of Croatia*, 23 August 1996, A/51/318-S/1996/706, 35 *ILM* 1996, 1219.

407 This is, for instance, the case of the European Union: *Déclaration du Conseil Européen concernant l'ancienne Yougoslavie*, 28 May 1992, UN. Doc. A/47/234, S/24028.

408 UN SC Res. 777 (1992), 19 September 1992, which was followed by UN GA Res. 47/1 (1992), 22 September 1992.

Commission,[409] refused to recognise the FRY as the "continuator" of the former SFRY.[410] The FRY, however, adopted a different position after the political changes which occurred in 2000 and no longer pretends to be the "continuator" of the former SFRY.[411] The break-up of the former SFRY should therefore be analysed as a case of dissolution.

In the following sections, I will examine several examples of State practice and case law.[412]

4.3.3.2 *The 2001* Agreement on Succession Issues *among the Successor States*

After the dissolution of the former SFRY, the Badinter Arbitral Commission,[413] the UN Security Council[414] and the "United Nations/European Communities

---

409 "Opinion no. 10", 4 July 1992, 92 *ILR* 1993, 206.

410 For an analysis, see: Juan Miguel Ortega Terol, "The Bursting of Yugoslavia: An Approach to Practice Regarding State Succession", in: Eisemann & Koskenniemi, 892–900.

411 The FRY was officially admitted (as a new State) to the UN on 1 November 2000: UN GA Res. 55/12. See also, the position adopted by the FRY in: *Application for Revision of the Judgement of 11 July 1996 in the Case Concerning the Application of the Convention on the Prevention and Punishment of the Crime of Genocide* (*Bosnia and Herzegovina v. Yugoslavia*), *Preliminary Objections* (Yugoslavia v. Bosnia-Herzegovina), Judgment, 3 February 2003, ICJ Rep. 2003, 6. In this case, the Court observed (at para 70) that the FRY's claim of continuity had not been "generally accepted". In the *Agreement on Succession Issues*, 29 June 2001, 41 *ILM* 2002 (further examined in the next section) entered into among all former Republics, the preamble refers to all new States (including the FRY) as "being in sovereign equality the five successor States to the former Yugoslavia".

412 Reference should also be made to another case involving nationals of a successor State claiming reparation to that State for wrongful acts committed by another State decades before independence: *Applicants v. Slovenia*, II Ips 449/2007, ILDC 3348 (SI 2008), 10th January 2008, Slovenia; Supreme Court. The case dealt with the claim of children who had been forcibly removed from their families by Germany during WWII when it occupied Yugoslavia. According to the facts summary: "They sought compensation from Slovenia, claiming that Slovenia was responsible for their damage because it was the legal successor of the SFRY, which they accused of unlawfully failing to recover compensation for the damage caused to them by the Third Reich, or unlawful conduct, which consisted of recovering compensation but not paying it to them as victims". (Oxford Rep. IL in Domestic Courts, F2). The Court denied the claim for several reasons unrelated to State succession matters. It also made this comment, which seems to be an *obiter dictum*, about the question of the "transferability or non-transferability of obligations from the predecessor state to the successor state regarding unlawful acts": "According to international jurisprudence, the rights and obligations arising from international obligations were closely connected with the State as a legal entity and ceased together with it" (Id., H7, para 18 of the decision).

413 "Opinion no. 9", 4 July 1992, 92 *ILR* 1993, 203.

414 UN SC Res. 1022 (1995), 22 November 1995.

International Conference on the Former Yugoslavia"[415] all came to the conclusion that the successor States to the former SFRY had to resolve by agreement all questions relating to succession of States. The FRY has also concluded several bilateral agreements with the former Republics whereby this principle is recognised.[416] After some 10 years of negotiations, a final settlement was eventually reached among the successor States.[417]

On 29 June 2001 was entered into among all the successor States (including the FRY) an *Agreement on Succession Issues*.[418] The preamble indicates that the Agreement was reached after discussions and negotiations "with a view to identifying and determining the equitable distribution among themselves of rights, obligations, assets and liabilities" of the former SFRY. Article 7 indicates

---

415 See, *Statement on Principles* of 26 August 1992, whereby as a requirement for a final settlement of all questions of succession to the former SFRY, the International Conference stressed that all parties should "share the duties and responsibilities of successor states" (Principles ix), 31 *ILM* 1992, 1527.

416 *Agreement on Normalisation between the Federal Republic of Yugoslavia and Republic of Croatia*, 23 August 1996, A/51/318-S/1996/706 35 *ILM* 1996, 1219; *Agreement on the Regulation of Relations and Promotion of Cooperation between the Republic of Macedonia and the Federal Republic of Yugoslavia*, 8 April 1996, S/1996/291 35 *ILM* 1996, 1246; Joint Statement of President Milosevic and President Izetbegovic, 3 October 1996, A/51/461-S/1996/830.

417 In 1991 was set up the "European Community Conference on Yugoslavia" (31 *ILM* 1992, 1421ff) which was shortly after replaced by the United Nations/European Communities "International Conference on Former Yugoslavia" (31 *ILM* 1992, 1527ff). This Conference established various Working Groups, including a "Succession Issues Working Group" which issued on 23 August 1994 a *Draft Treaty Concerning Succession to the Former SFRY*. After the signing of the *Dayton Peace Agreement* (35 *ILM* 1996, 75), the High Representative of the international community in Bosnia and Herzegovina (Mr Carl Bildt) ended the work of the Conference and replaced it with a "Peace Implementation Council". The working group on State succession issues nevertheless continued its work. In March 1996, the High Representative appointed a "Special Negotiator for Succession Issues" (Sir Arthur Watts). After very limited progress in the first few years and an interruption during the Kosovo War (1999), the negotiations finally resumed with the change of regime in Belgrade (2000) and the abandonment by the FRY of its position as the legal "continuator" of the SFRY.

418 41 *ILM* 2002, 1–39. The Agreement was ratified by Croatia on 3 May 2004. It was the fifth (and last) instrument deposited to the UN Secretary General acting as depositary of the Treaty. In accordance with Art. 12(1) of the Agreement, it entered into force on 12 June 2004. See: Castren Stahn, "The Agreement on Succession Issues of the Former Socialist Federal Republic of Yugoslavia", 96(2) *AJIL* 2002, 379–397; Jenny Stavridi & Alexandros Kolliopoulos, "L'Accord du 29 juin 2001 portant sur des questions de succession entre les Etats issus de la dissolution de l'ex-Yougoslavie", *AFDI* 2002, 163–184; Ryszard Piotrowicz, "Status of Yugoslavia: Agreement at Last", 77 *Australian LJ* 2001, 95–99.

that this Agreement "finally settles the mutual rights and obligations of the successor States in respect of succession issues covered by this Agreement".

Article 2 of Annex F of the Agreement (entitled "Other rights, interests and liabilities")[419] specifically deals with the issue of internationally wrongful acts committed by the SFRY against third States before the date of succession. It reads as follows:

> All *claims against the SFRY* which are not otherwise covered by this Agreement shall be considered by the Standing Joint Committee established under Article 4 of this Agreement. The successor States shall inform one another of all such claims against the SFRY[420] (emphasis added)

The fact that "[a]ll claims against the SFRY" will be "considered" by the Standing Joint Committee indicates clearly that the obligations of the predecessor State toward third States do not simply disappear as a result of the dissolution of the SFRY. This is an example of the application of the principle of the transfer of the obligation to repair from the predecessor State to the successor States.[421] This is indeed the position which was adopted by Serbia in its pleadings in the *Croatia Genocide Convention* case.[422] This position is admittedly controversial ever among those who negotiated the agreement.[423]

---

419 According to Art. 6, annexes are an integral part of the Agreement.

420 Annex F also contains a provision (Art. 1) in favour of the transfer of the *right to reparation* from the predecessor State to the successor States. This point is discussed in Part 3, Chapter 5, Section 3.2.4.

421 Kohen & Dumberry, 122; ILC Special Rapporteur Šturma, Second Report, 2018, paras 178, 183; Šturma, State Succession, 665; Crawford, State Responsibility, 451–2 (for whom Annex F "suggests that issues arising from the international responsibility of the SFRY were not treated as simply disappearing, with the precise division of liability between them being determined by the Committee").

422 *Croatia Genocide Convention* case, Verbatim Record, Andreas Zimmermann (Serbia), 27 March 2014, paras 52–53, indicating that Art. 4 "according to the former Special Negotiator, the late Sir Arthur Watts, *governs claims arising out of succession to international responsibility directed against the SFRY*. It precludes the submission of the claim in the current proceedings, or, at the very least, presupposes that prior to bringing the matter before the Court, Croatia ought to have seized the Committee set up by the Agreement. Yet, Croatia has so far never done so". Emphasis added.

423 Thus, conflicting doctrinal opinions on the interpretation to be given to this provision have been advanced in private letters (on file with the author) exchanged between the present author and two legal scholars who were involved in the drafting of the Agreement. Compare the position adopted by Sir Arthur Watts, who was the "Special Negotiator for Succession Issues" and under whose supervision the Agreement was signed, with that of Professor Vladimir-Djuro Degan, a representative of Croatia during the negotiations which led to the Agreement. In a letter dated 13 November 2002, Sir Arthur Watts

One interesting feature of the Agreement is the establishment of a mechanism for settlement of disputes whereby a Standing Joint Committee, consisting of senior representatives of each successor State,[424] would not only do the "monitoring of the effective implementation of the Agreement"[425] but also settle any "differences" among the successor States arising over the "interpretation and application" of the Agreement.[426] The role of the Standing Joint Committee in dealing with claims against the SFRY was explained as follows by Sir Arthur Watts in a letter sent to the present author:

> In respect of any given claim against the SFRY the Committee might decide that it was now a matter solely for one or other of the successor States, or that it was a matter for two or more of them jointly, or that it [has] nothing to do with any of them—i.e. in the last case their position would be that the claim died with the SFRY.[427]

indicated that "it was understood by all concerned (at least, if it wasn't, it should have been!) that Articles 1 and 2 of Annex F included within their scope such items of international responsibility as might exists, whether involving outstanding claims by the SFRY against other States (Article 1) or outstanding claims by other States against the SFRY (Article 2)". A completely different view is adopted by Professor Vladimir-Djuro Degan (letter dated 21 October 2002). He believes that Annex F to the Agreement does not deal with any issue of succession of States to international responsibility: "During the negotiations on succession issues since 1992 nobody raised question of any possible claim by a third State as a consequence of [the SFRY's] internationally wrongful acts. And vice versa, no party raised any possible claim on the same legal ground on behalf of the former SFRY against any third State. Because in ten years that elapsed since its demise there were no actual allegations on this basis, it is reasonable to assume that no such serious legally grounded claims exist at all". Therefore, according to Degan, the Agreement does not deal with such issues "simply because there were no such claims against the predecessor State (SFRY), or on its behalf". I was given permission to refer to the content of both letters in the context of the present study.

424 Art. 4(1).

425 Art. 4(2). The other task of the Committee is to serve "as a forum in which issues arising in the course of [the implementation of the Agreement] may be discussed" (Art. 4(2)).

426 Under Art. 5, differences should be first settled through "discussions" among the States. If such discussions fail, the matter may be referred to either "an independent person of their choice" or to the Standing Joint Committee for resolution. However, any other agreement among the successor States providing for another mechanism for the settlement of disputes may prevail over the one indicated in Art. 5.

427 Letter dated 13 November 2002 by Sir Arthur Watts to the present author (on file with the author).

The powers of the Committee are, however, limited insofar as it may only make "appropriate recommendations to the Governments of the successor States".[428] The Committee does not act as a court or an arbitral tribunal. This apparent lack of power of the Committee should nevertheless be read in conjunction with Article 9, which indicates that this Agreement "shall be implemented by the successor States in good faith in conformity with the Charter of the United Nations and in accordance with international law". Article 8 is also relevant, as it imposes an obligation on the successor States to implement the Agreement in their national legal orders.[429] The Committee has apparently never considered any claims.[430]

4.3.3.3 *The* Tokic v. Government of Yugoslavia *Case*

The case arose out of an incident which took place in 1988 outside the premises of the Yugoslav Consulate in Sidney, Australia, during which an Australian national (Mr Tokic) was shot and wounded by an unidentified person firing from within the Consulate's premises.[431] On 28 August 1990, Mr Tokic submitted a claim for damage against the Government of Yugoslavia before the Supreme Court of New South Wales. On 12 December 1991, Mr Justice McInerney of the Supreme Court of New South Wales found that the person who had fired the shot was an employee of the Consulate and that the defendant was not immune for its action. The claimant was awarded the sum of AU$ 46,854 in damages against the State of Yugoslavia.

In 1992, Australia notified the International Conference on the Former Yugoslavia of "the existence of a debt owed by the former SFRY to an Australian national" arising out of an "unsatisfied judgement of an Australian Court of Competent Jurisdiction against the 'Government of Yugoslavia'".[432] The letter

428 Art. 4(2).

429 Art. 8 reads as follows: "Each successor State, on the basis of reciprocity, shall take the necessary measures in accordance with its internal law to ensure that the provisions of this Agreement are recognised and effective in its courts, administrative tribunals and agencies, and that the other successor States and their nationals have access to those courts, tribunals and agencies to secure the implementation of this Agreement".

430 Slovenia, comments from the Permanent Mission to the UN, doc no. 848/21, 22 Dec. 2021.

431 For background information, 12 *Australian YIL* 455–463; 13 *Australian YIL* 258. This case is referred to in: Andreas Zimmermann, *Staatennachfolge in völkerrechtliche Verträge: Zugleich ein Beitrag zu den Möglichkeiten und Grenzen völkerrechtlicher Kodifikation* (Springer 2000) 68.

432 Letter of Australia's Permanent Representative to the UN in Geneva, Mr Ronald Walker, to the Co-Chairmen of the Steering Committee for the International Conference on the Former Yugoslavia, Lord Owen and Mr Cyrus Vance, 15 September 1992, in: P. Hewitson, "Australian Practice of International Law", 14 *Australian YIL* 417–418.

further explains that "neither the Government of the SFRY before its dissolution nor any of its successor States have paid the assessed damages and costs in accordance with the judgement".

This case is clearly one where the injured State (Australia, in the person of one of its nationals) requested that the new successor States take over the obligations arising from the internationally wrongful act committed by the predecessor State. The outcome of this dispute is, however, not known, and no information was found as to whether any of the successor States did provide compensation to the injured State.[433]

4.3.3.4 *The Return of Cultural Properties Taken from Vukovar*

In his book, Jakubowski refers to the "partial destruction of cultural treasures" which took place in 1991 in the city of Vukovar on the Serbo–Croatian border.[434] Following Croatia's declaration of independence (June 1991), the city was invaded by the Yugoslav forces and during the siege, between August and November 1991, many items from the city's museums were taken and evacuated to the city of Novi Sad, in what would soon become FRY's territory.[435] According to the Yugoslav authorities, this was done for their protection. Unfortunately and contrary to their claim, the property was not cared for properly and some items were stolen. In December 2001, a protocol on the return of the cultural treasures was signed between the FRY and Croatia.[436] A Joint Commission for the Return of Cultural Property was soon established and, apparently since then "a great majority of the items from Vukovar have been returned" in 2001.[437] At the time the Protocol was signed, the FRY no longer argued that it was the continuator of the former Yugoslavia; it had been admitted to the United Nations as a new State a year earlier. For Jakubowski,

433 The present author sent several letters to the relevant Australian authorities to enquire about the outcome of this case. All letters have remained unanswered.

434 Jakubowski, State Succession, 230ff, referring to Branka Šulc, "The Protection of Croatia's Cultural Heritage During the War 1991–95", in Robert Layton et al. (eds), *Destruction and Conservation of Cultural Property* (Routledge 2001) 157, 162.

435 Jakubowski, State Succession, 230.

436 *Protocol on the Transport of Objects of Art, Cultural Assets and Other Exhibits from the Museum of Vojvodina and the Novi Sad City Museum (in Yugoslavia) to the Vukovar City Museum*, 7 December 2001, in: *Yb. of Int. Hum. L* 2001, 482.

437 Jakubowski, State Succession, 230ff. He also mentions that in 2012, Serbia and Croatia concluded a protocol on the restitution of Croatian cultural assets from Serbia to Croatia and that more "than 1000 works of art taken during the 1990s would be returned from Serbia to Croatia". See, Andrzej Jakubowski, "Cultural Heritage and State Succession", in F. Francioni & A.F. Vrdoljak (ed), *The Oxford Handbook of International Cultural Heritage Law* (OUP 2020) 602.

this is an example where "Serbia assumed responsibility for violations of the rules governing war conduct, under the 1954 Hague Convention, in relation to cultural heritage crimes committed by the Federal Republic of Yugoslavia (FRY) during the war with Croatia".[438] In fact, the incident (the removal of items followed by a lack of proper care) took place both before and after the creation of the FRY in 1992. Although this is a case of war damages involving two successor States,[439] it is noteworthy as an instance where a new State (FRY) took over the consequences of wrongful acts which had been committed, at least partially, by the predecessor State (SFRY)[440] and provided reparation to the injured State.

4.3.3.5 *The ICJ 2015* Croatia Genocide Convention *Case*

In 1999, Croatia filed an application to the ICJ against the FRY "for violations of the Convention on the Prevention and Punishment of the Crime of Genocide". Ultimately, the Court found that no acts of genocide or other violations of the Convention had been proven.

To establish the Court's jurisdiction, Croatia invoked Article IX of that Convention to which both Croatia and Yugoslavia were parties. In its 2008 Judgment, the Court found that it had jurisdiction over events which had taken place *after* 27 April 1992, i.e. the date when the FRY came into existence and when it became party, by way of succession, to the Genocide Convention. For the purpose of this book, the relevant question was whether any acts which occurred *before* 27 April 1992 fell within the scope of jurisdiction under Article IX of the Convention.

Croatia's arguments. Croatia advanced "two alternative grounds" to show that the Court had jurisdiction over these acts.[441] The first argument is based on Article 10(2) of the ILC *Articles on State Responsibility* and the second one "upon the law of State succession".[442] The Court summarised the first argument as follows:

---

438 Jakubowski, ibid 602.

439 I have explained above (Part 1, Section 4.6) why I consider these examples to be less relevant in the context of this study focusing on wrongs affecting or being committed by third States.

440 Thus, at the time when the property was taken from Croatia, in August-November 1991, the SFRY was still considered to be a State. It was only later that the SFRY would be considered in a "process of dissolution" (Badinter Commission, "Opinion 1", 29 Nov. 1991) which was completed within a year ("Opinion 8", 4 July 1992).

441 *Croatia Genocide Convention* case, para 101.

442 Ibid.

> Croatia maintains that, although the FRY was not proclaimed as a State until 27 April 1992, that proclamation merely formalized a situation that was already established in fact. During the course of 1991, according to Croatia, the leadership of the Republic of Serbia and other supporters of what Croatia describes as a "Greater Serbia" movement took control of the JNA and other institutions of the SFRY, while also controlling their own territorial armed forces and various militias and paramilitary groups. This movement was eventually successful in creating a separate State, the FRY Croatia contends that its claim in relation to events prior to 27 April 1992 is based upon acts by the JNA and those other armed forces and groups, as well as the Serb political authorities, which were attributable to that movement and thus, by operation of the principle stated in Article 10 (2), to the FRY.[443]

I have examined elsewhere in some detail the parties' arguments and the Court's reasoning on this point.[444] The Court explained that "the FRY was not bound by the obligations contained in the Genocide Convention until it became party to that Convention", i.e. on 27 April 1992.[445] Hence, the Court concluded that even if any acts alleged by Croatia that took place before that date, could be attributable to a "movement", "they cannot have involved a violation of the provisions of the Genocide Convention but, at most, only of the customary international law prohibition of genocide".[446] Therefore, the Court did not take position on whether the acts committed prior to 27 April 1992 "were attributable to a 'movement', within the meaning of Article 10 (2) of the ILC Articles".[447] Nor did it examine whether these acts "became attributable to the FRY by operation of the principle" set out in Article 10(2).[448] Ultimately, the Court's decision does not provide much insight as to the nature and scope of application of Article 10(2).

The Court then turned to Croatia's "alternative argument that the FRY succeeded to the responsibility of the SFRY".[449] The argument was put forward late in the proceedings.[450] It was only mentioned and developed at the oral

443 Ibid para 102.

444 Dumberry, Rebellions, 349ff.

445 *Croatia Genocide Convention* case, paras 104–105.

446 Ibid para 105.

447 Ibid.

448 Ibid.

449 Ibid para 106.

450 The argument was not raised when Serbia filed its Counter-Memorial. This is clear from this passage: "it is important to note what Croatia does *not* say. Neither in its Memorial nor its Written Statement does it suggest that Serbia had succeeded to the international

pleadings.[451] According to the Court, Croatia had in fact put forward "two separate grounds on which it claims the FRY succeeded to the responsibility of the SFRY".[452]

First, it relied on the "application of the principles of general international law regarding State succession".[453] I will further examine this point in the next paragraph. The second argument was that when the FRY notified its intention to succeed to the Convention, it was not only "succeeding to the treaty obligations of the SFRY, but also that it succeeded to the responsibility incurred by the SFRY for the violation of those treaty obligations".[454] Serbia rejected this argument: the 27 April 1992 declaration "was concerned only with succession to the treaties themselves and not with succession to responsibility".[455] This question is further examined below.[456]

Before examining the Court's reasoning regarding the first argument, Croatia's position should be briefly explained. It is closely linked to Croatia's principal argument about the application of Article 10(2) of the ILC Articles, mentioned above. Under this argument, Croatia submitted that "the SFRY simply was not functioning as a State" and, consequently, "to hold that only the SFRY could have been responsible for conduct by the JNA would be a legal fiction".[457] For Croatia, at the time, "the JNA was by now plainly an organ of the nascent Serbian State". Croatia's "alternative" argument was submitted only "[I]f the Court were to find that the SFRY, and only the SFRY, was responsible for conduct by the JNA during the relevant period". If that were to be the case, Croatia added that "a further finding of succession to responsibility is called for".[458] Yet, Croatia said very little about this last-minute argument. It cited the *Lighthouse Arbitration* case and carefully laid out the point as follows: "We say

responsibility that was incurred prior to its coming into existence as a State. This is telling because—as Judge Tomka observed in his separate opinion appended to the judgment of 18 November 2008—the mechanism of State succession might have been a possible argument of attempting to attribute responsibility to a State that came into being by way of succession" (Serbia, "Counter-Memorial", December 2009, para 278, emphasis in the original).

451 *Croatia Genocide Convention* case, Verbatim Record, 21 March 2014, CR 2014/21, 21, Crawford (Croatia), paras 20ff. See, at para 39.

452 *Croatia Genocide Convention* case, para 107.

453 Ibid para 107.

454 Ibid.

455 Ibid para 108.

456 See, Chapter 3, Section 11.

457 *Croatia Genocide Convention* case, Verbatim Record, 21 March 2014, CR 2014/21, 21, Crawford (Croatia), para 39.

458 Ibid para 39.

the rule of succession can occur in particular circumstances if it is justified. There is no general rule of succession to responsibility but there is no general rule against it either".[459]

Importantly, the argument was *not* based on the general idea of succession to responsibility whereby the new State (FRY) should be held responsible for the wrongful acts *committed by the predecessor State* (SFRY).[460] It was rather based on the application of a specific circumstance calling for succession. As summarised by the Court, the FRY "largely controlled the armed forces of the SFRY during the last year of the latter's formal existence".[461] This situation, in turn, "justify the succession of the FRY to the responsibility incurred by the SFRY for the acts of armed forces that subsequently became organs of the FRY".[462] In other words, according to Croatia, there should be succession to responsibility due to the continuity between the organs (the JNA) of an autonomous entity ("the nascent Serbian State") which later became the organs (the army) of a new State (FRY).[463]

While the argument may have been technically different from Article 10(2) of the ILC Articles, which (as further examined later[464]) does not deal with State succession per se, it was undoubtedly closely related. This is clear when one looks at Croatia's principal argument. Croatia considered that in the period between the start of the break-up of the SFRY and the official proclamation of the FRY as a State, the FRY emerged as a State *in statu nascendi*. It argued that the acts carried out by the officials and organs of the emerging State of the FRY (taking place *before* 27 April 1992) should be attributable to the FRY.[465] For Croatia, "the principle that a state *in statu nascendi* is responsible for conduct carried out by its officials and organs or otherwise under its direction and

459 Ibid para 42.

460 *Croatia Genocide Convention* case. On the contrary, Decla. Judge Xue, para 8, seems to consider the argument as one of *continuity* between the SFRY and the FRY: "Croatia's two arguments are built on two different political premises, which are mutually exclusive in the context of the present case. In other words, Serbia should be treated either as a successor or as a continuator of the SFRY, but cannot be both at the same time. (…) Croatia's alternative argument, however, is presumably based on the continuity between the SFRY and the FRY".

461 *Croatia Genocide Convention* case, para 107.

462 Ibid.

463 This principle is further examined below: Chapter 3, Section 7.

464 See, Chapter 3, Section 6.

465 Croatia, "Memorial", 1 March 2001, para 8.40, stating that the fact that the FRY "only formally proclaimed itself on 27 April 1992 does not mean that acts occurring prior to that date cannot be attributed to it".

control is well-established, and is recognised in Article 10(2)".[466] In Croatia's view, the proclamation of April 1992 formally creating the FRY "did not create a State out of thin air", it only "formalised a set of social, economic and political arrangement which were, at that time, already largely in place".[467] Thus, the proclamation simply "formalised a preexistent situation"[468] "which had arisen with the dissolution of the SFRY, namely the emergence of FRY (comprising the Republics of Serbia and Montenegro) as a State *in statu nascendi*, under the control of President Milošević and the rest of the Serbian leadership".[469] Croatia emphasised the existence of "sufficient continuity in terms of personnel and organization between the movement itself and the subsequent government".[470] It referred to the existence of a "factual connection between the movement and the subsequent formation of a new State".[471]

While here Croatia referred to a "movement", elsewhere it focused on the link between the *organs* of an entity which later became the organs of an independent State. For Croatia, "international responsibility could be engaged and attributable to the FRY" before 27 April 1992, starting from the "moment at which the organs of what was later become the FRY had cemented their separate existence from the rest of the SFRY".[472] Croatia explained that "from October 1991, the relevant organs of government and other federal authorities of the SFRY ceased to function as such and became *de facto* organs and authorities of the emerging FRY acting under the direct control of the Serbian leadership, embodied in particular in the President of Serbia but extending

466 Ibid para 8.42, referring to I. Brownlie, *Principles of Public International Law* (5th edn, Clarendon 1998) 77–78. In its "Written Statement", 29 April 2003, 18, point (i), Croatia further explained that it is "well established that a State may be responsible for conduct prior to the establishment of the State" and explained the rationale behind this principle (para 3.24).

467 Croatia, "Written Statement", 29 April 2003, para 3.25.

468 Ibid para 3.25.

469 Croatia, "Memorial", 1 March 2001, para 8.40.

470 Croatia, "Written Statement", 29 April 2003, paras 3.36, 3.37.

471 Ibid para 3.38. See also, para 3.40, referring to the "considerable *de facto* continuity in personnel and policies between a number of significant organs of the SFRY once they had fallen into the hands of the Serbian leadership and those of the FRY following its formal creation in April 1992". See also: Croatia, "Memorial", 1 March 2001, para 8.45: "[m]oreover, by virtue of its insistence (at the time and until the year 2000) on its constitutional and political continuity with the former SFRY, the FRY explicitly recognised the links between the former SFRY's state administration and officials of the Socialist Republic of Serbia and Socialist Republic of Montenegro. These were the same people, carrying out the same policies, policies which, it has been shown, were genocidal in character".

472 Croatia, "Written Statement", 29 April 2003, para 3.25.

also to relevant officials in Ministries of Defence and Interior".[473] Specifically, "the JNA ceased to be the army of the SFRY and became, initially, a *de facto* organ of the emerging FRY".[474] Croatia thus argued that there was a "structural and organic continuity between the Serbian military and political leadership and the FRY".[475] At the oral hearings, it was argued that this "structural" and "organic" continuity between the two "was complete".[476]

In sum, Croatia used the same argument based on Article 10(2) of the ILC Articles, but applied it more broadly outside the specific context of a civil war or an insurrection. It used it in relation to the organs of an autonomous entity rather than to an insurrectional "movement". Croatia's argument is therefore an illustration of the "organ" element mentioned in Article 15 of the Institute's Resolution.[477] A principle further discussed below.[478]

Serbia's argument was straightforward: "there is no principle of succession to responsibility in general international law".[479] It also argued that all matters of succession to responsibility were in fact governed by the 2001 *Agreement on Succession Issues* entered into by the successor States.[480]

The Court's reasoning. The Court mentioned that in order to determine "whether Serbia is responsible for violations of the Convention", it would have to address the following three questions:

> (1) whether the acts relied on by Croatia took place; and, if they did, whether they were contrary to the Convention;
> (2) if so, whether those acts were attributable to the SFRY at the time that they occurred and engaged its responsibility; and
> (3) if the responsibility of the SFRY had been engaged, whether the FRY succeeded to that responsibility.[481]

When assessing its jurisdiction under Article IX of the Genocide Convention, the Court noted that this clause "speaks generally of the responsibility of a

473 Ibid para 8.40.
474 Ibid para 8.40.
475 *Croatia Genocide Convention* case, Verbatim Record, 21 March 2014, CR 2014/21, 21, Crawford (Croatia), para 28.
476 Ibid.
477 Kohen & Dumberry, 127–8.
478 See, Chapter 3, Section 7.
479 *Croatia Genocide Convention* case, para 108. See, Verbatim Record, CR 2014/22, 27 March 2014, Zimmermann (Serbia), para 54 ("the better arguments suggest that new States do not succeed to responsibility").
480 Ibid paras 52–53.
481 *Croatia Genocide Convention* case, para 112.

State and contains no limitation regarding the manner in which that responsibility might be engaged".[482] In other words, responsibility may be incurred by way of succession. It therefore held that it had jurisdiction, under Article IX of the Genocide Convention, over acts which took place *before* 27 April 1992.[483] While this conclusion was endorsed by the majority of judges,[484] it was rejected by others.[485] Interestingly, the incurred responsibility had been denied by Judge Tomka in his separate opinion in the Preliminary Objections phase of the proceedings (2008).[486] Regardless, the Court mentioned that at this stage it was "not necessary to decide whether the FRY, and therefore Serbia, actually succeeded to any responsibility that might have been incurred by the SFRY".[487] Thus, the question of succession to responsibility "would require a decision only if the Court finds that the acts relied upon by Croatia were contrary to the Convention and were attributable to the SFRY at the time of their commission".[488] Ultimately, the Court did not find those acts to be contrary to the Convention. As a result, the question of succession to responsibility did not arise. The way the Court dealt with the argument has been criticised by some judges[489] and writers.[490] The "problem" with the Court's reasoning was identified by Judge Skotnikov as follows:

482 Ibid para 114.

483 Ibid para 117.

484 Ibid, Diss. op. Judge Cançado Trindade, paras 12ff, stating that it is "generally accepted that certain types of treaties—such as human rights treaties—remain in force by reason of their special nature" and that the Genocide Convention applied to events taking place before 27 April 1992.

485 Ibid, Sep. op. Judge Tomka, paras 7ff; Sep. op. Judge Owada, paras 17ff; Sep. op. Judge Sebutinde, paras 6ff.

486 *Croatia Genocide Convention* case, Preliminary Objections, ICJ Rep. 2008, Sep. op. Judge Tomka, 412, 520, para 13, indicating that the issue of State succession to responsibility did not "fall within the jurisdiction of the Court under Article IX of the Genocide Convention" because "that jurisdiction covers 'disputes between the Contracting Parties relating to the interpretation, application or fulfilment of the … Convention' by its Contracting Parties" and that "the FRY, now continuing as Serbia, became a Contracting Party on 27 April 1992". On this point, see: Kaplane, 25–6.

487 *Croatia Genocide Convention* case, Judgment, 2015, para 117.

488 Ibid para 114.

489 Ibid, Sep. op. Judge Owada, para 20; Decla. Judge Xue, para 17.

490 Lorenzo Palestini, "The Relevant Time for Assessing Jurisdiction and the *Ratione Temporis* Objection in the *Genocide* (*Croatia v. Serbia*) Case", in: K. Polackova Van der Ploeg et al. (eds), *International Law and Time* (Springer 2022) 258 ("The Court's reasoning is unsettling. (…) I believe that by finding jurisdiction and examining the events preceding the FRY's proclamation, the ICJ put the cart before the horse. The ICJ should have first ruled on the existence of State succession to responsibility under general international law. Had the Court found in favor of its existence, it could have then examined the events prior

> However, identifying the law which would have been applicable if the Court had jurisdiction is no substitute for establishing that the Court has jurisdiction under Article IX of the Genocide Convention. The task before the Court in the present Judgment was either to identify the legal mechanism by which the FRY assumed obligations under the Genocide Convention before it came into existence, or to determine that no such legal mechanism existed. Ultimately, the Court does neither. It merely suggests that obligations under the Genocide Convention might be applicable to the FRY before 27 April 1992 by virtue, as Croatia argues, of succession to responsibility. Then it transforms this preliminary issue into a question for the merits (see Judgment, para. 117), and goes on to consider whether acts contrary to the Genocide Convention took place prior to 27 April 1992. After answering this question in the negative, the Court does not return to the issue of succession to responsibility.[491]

The Court therefore did not address the argument developed by Croatia on State succession to responsibility. But many judges in their individual opinions had a lot to say on the matter. In his Separate Opinion, Judge Owada noted that while "the Judgment tries to disassociate itself from any position that might look like an endorsement of this doctrine" of succession to responsibility, it remains that the question "lies crucially at the heart of the logic of the Judgment".[492] Tomka also noted the fundamental importance the issue of succession to responsibility had in the decision compared to the 2008 judgement.[493] He also mentioned that "it is only on the basis of Croatia's 'alternative

---

to 27 April 1992, provided, however, that such events would fall within the scope *ratione materiae* of Article IX of the Genocide Convention"); Surabhi Ranganathan, "The 2015 Judicial Activity of the International Court of Justice", 110(3) *AJIL* 2016, 508 (the Court "based its jurisdiction on a doctrine of dubious status, which it ultimately failed to clarify"); Hemi Mistry, "The International Court of Justice's Judgment in the Final Balkans Genocide Convention Case", 16 *Human Rights LR* 2016, 366–7 ("Given the willingness of only two judges out of 17 to express support for the only mode of Serb responsibility speculatively proposed by the Court, this is a significant flaw in the legal reasoning of the Court, as indicated by Judge Owada").

491 *Croatia Genocide Convention* case, Sep. op. Judge Skotnikov, paras 2–3.

492 Ibid, Sep. op. Judge Owada, para 17.

493 Ibid, Sep. op. Judge Tomka, para 5: "I cannot fail to mention that what in the 2008 Judgment was for the Court 'a question of the applicability of the obligations under the Genocide Convention to the FRY before 27 April 1992' (...) has now become for the Court the question of whether 'the responsibility of the SFRY had been engaged' and, if so, 'whether the FRY succeeded to that responsibility' (...). I also note that while in the 2008 Judgment the Court indicated that it would have to deal, in the context of the admissibility of the claim in relation to facts prior to 27 April 1992, with 'the consequences to be drawn with

argument' that Serbia's responsibility results from succession to the responsibility of the SFRY that the Court concludes that its jurisdiction extends to acts prior to 27 April 1992".[494] In fact, in their individual opinions, a number of judges adopted the view that the Court had actually based its analysis on a "presumption" that any such succession to responsibility was indeed possible.[495] This was, for instance, the position adopted by Judge Xue.[496] In his Separate Opinion, Judge Skotnikov indicated that "the fact that the Court limits itself to answering only the first question does not render this 'three-step solution' any more tenable".[497] Thus, the very fact that the Court asked the third question and mentioned the words "whether the FRY succeeded to that responsibility" presupposes that any such succession is, at least theoretically, *possible*. For Judge Skotnikov, it would have been an "impossible task" for the Court "to establish that the doctrine of succession to responsibility was part of general international law at the time of Serbia's succession to the Genocide Convention" because there is "no jurisprudence or State practice to support this hypothesis".[498] He expressly rejected the possibility of any such succession to responsibility.[499]

Judge *ad hoc* Kreća also adopted this position.[500] He started his analysis by noting that "the impression is that the Court qualified succession to

---

regard to the responsibility of the FRY for those same facts under the general rules of State responsibility' (…), in the present Judgment the issue of whether the FRY is responsible is to be determined by the rules of general international law on State succession (…) 'if the responsibility of the SFRY had been engaged'" (citations omitted).

494 Ibid, Sep. op. Judge Tomka, para 7.

495 Ibid, Sep. op. Judge Sebutinde, paras 13: "That construction in effect presupposes that the Court has jurisdiction to deal with issues of State succession to obligations of the SFRY which may have arisen as a consequence of breaches of the Convention when the SFRY was still in existence; which issues may have been relevant if the Court had in 2008 deemed Serbia to be a continuator of the SFRY rather than a successor State".

496 Ibid, Decla. Judge Xue, para 22: "When the Court sets out to determine whether the alleged acts of genocide relied on by Croatia against Serbia were attributable to the SFRY and thus engaged its responsibility, its consideration, regardless of the ultimate finding, is necessarily based on the presumption in favour of succession to responsibility and the presumption that Serbia may succeed to the responsibility of the SFRY for the latter's violation of the obligations under the Convention. Thus, the Convention is actually applied retroactively to Serbia". For Judge Xue, "when a State ceases to exist, it does not necessarily mean that all its rights and obligations simultaneously cease to exist" (para 25). See also, Sep. op. Judge Owada, para 17.

497 Ibid, Sep. op. Judge Skotnikov, para 5.

498 Ibid para 4.

499 Ibid para 5.

500 Ibid, Sep. op. Judge Kreća, paras 60ff.

responsibility as a rule of general international law with amazing ease,"[501] adding that the Court "gives no indication of any source of international law that would vindicate the qualification that the rules of succession of States to responsibility pertain to the *corpus* of rules of general international law".[502] For him, there are only "a few isolated decisions" on the issue which "seemingly (…) stand on diametrically opposed positions".[503] Judge Kreća argued that "the opinions expressed in that regard are a doctrinal plea for the formulation of a comprehensive doctrine of succession to responsibility rather than an all-embracing and comprehensive doctrine *per se*".[504] For him, "the only possible form of succession to responsibility in the circumstances surrounding the case could be succession to the responsibility of SFRY *ex consenso*".[505] Judge Sebutinde also said that "the notion that the FRY (Serbia) could conceivably assume responsibility for the wrongful acts of its predecessor State (SFRY), seems untenable".[506]

In sum, it could be argued that while the Court did not formally take position on the issue, at the same time it also "*did not reject* the possibility for a new successor State to be held responsible for obligations arising from the commission of wrongful acts by the predecessor State before the date of succession".[507] ILC Special Rapporteur Šturma agrees.[508] The decision does seem to be based on the idea that such a succession is possible.[509] As Judge *ad hoc* Kreća noted, the Court adopted this approach "with amazing ease".[510] The Court provided almost no explanation, apart from citing the *Lighthouse Arbitration* case.[511] Yet, this lack of reasoning can probably be explained by

501 Ibid para 60.

502 Ibid para 61.

503 Ibid para 62, referring to the *Lighthouse Arbitration* case as the "paradigm of succession to responsibility" and the *R.E. Brown* case as the "paradigm of non-succession to responsibility". He is specifically critical of the Court's reliance only on the *Lighthouse Arbitration* case (para 61), adding that the "qualification of the decision as the expression of the acceptance of succession to responsibility is exaggerated" (para 64).

504 Ibid para 65.1.

505 Ibid para 79, referring to the *Agreement on Succession Issues* between the successor States to the SFRY.

506 Ibid, Sep. op. Judge Sebutinde, para 9.

507 Kohen & Dumberry, 11, emphasis added.

508 ILC Special Rapporteur Šturma, First Report, 2017, para 58 ("It is worth mentioning that the Court did not refuse and thus accepted the alternative argument of Croatia as to its jurisdiction over acts prior to 27 April 1992"). See also, Ibid, Second Report, 2018, paras 179, 182.

509 See also, Kaplane, 24.

510 *Croatia Genocide Convention* case, Sep. op. Judge Kreća, para 60.

511 Kaplane, 26–7.

the fact that it knew it would not have to resort to the doctrine anyways. In any event, for ILC Special Rapporteur Šturma the decision is the "most recent pronouncement in favour of the argument that the responsibility of a State might be engaged by way of succession".[512] In a letter sent subsequently to the UN GA Sixth Committee, Croatia considered that the "organ" factor had been recognised by the Court: "the Court, by accepting the jurisdiction in this case, obviously opened the possibility for succession of state responsibility on the basis of the devolution of organs, but never really tackled this issue because of a negative response to the first question in its jurisdictional construct".[513] One question left opened, but mentioned by Judge Tomka,[514] is whether the other successor States could have potentially also been held responsible for any wrongful acts committed before the dissolution.[515]

5 Cession and Transfer of Territory

The analysis of State practice and international and municipal case law in the context of cession and transfer of territory clearly shows the existence of a

512 ILC Special Rapporteur Šturma, First Report, 2017, para 54. See also: Šturma, State Succession, 666; Kaplane, 25 ("this judgment is still of utmost importance, since the Court for the first time expressly—not implicitly, as in the first [Bosnia] Genocide case—acknowledged the possibility of incurring responsibility by succession"). *Contra*, ILC, "Provisional Summary Record of the 3434th Meeting", 70th sess., 20 July 2018, A/CN.4/SR.3434, statement by ILC Member Huang (China), for whom the case "could hardly vindicate the Special Rapporteur's views" since the ICJ had "offered no guidance on the succession of State responsibility".

513 Croatia, letter sent to the UN GA Sixth Committee, Rep. 73rd sess., 31 Oct. 2018, agreeing with the position of the ILC Special Rapporteur that this factor "seems also to be recognized by the International Court of Justice as a part of its 'jurisdiction construct'" in this case. See also: "In short, the Court's jurisdictional construct can be paraphrased in the following manner: the Genocide Convention did not apply to Serbia retroactively, but—although at the relevant time Serbia was not a party to the Genocide Convention—on the basis of the supposed violation thereof, the attributability of such violation to SFRY, which was a party to the Genocide Convention, and the responsibility for the violation that FRY "inherited" from the SFRY due to the devolution of the organs of the SFRY into the organs of the FRY, (which responsibility) Serbia took over from the FRY—Serbia is potentially responsible for the violations of the Genocide Convention".

514 *Croatia Genocide Convention* case, Sep. op. Peter Tomka, para 32: "Serbia is only one of five equal successor States to the SFRY. A decision as to the international responsibility of the SFRY may well have implications for several, if not each, of those successor States, depending on what view is taken on the question of the allocation of any such responsibility as between them".

515 Kaplane, 25–6.

general principle. It also indicates the existence of one important *exception* to this general principle. In the following sections, I will examine these two aspects:

- The *general principle* is that the continuing State remains responsible for the commission of *its own* internationally wrongful acts before the date of succession. The obligations arising from the commission of such acts should therefore not be transferred to the successor State (Section 5.2);
- There is one *exception* to this principle. In cases where the internationally wrongful act is committed by a local administration having a substantial autonomy from the predecessor State prior to the date of succession, the successor State should take over the obligations arising from the commission of such act (Section 5.3).

I will first refer to the position adopted by the Institute and the ILC and explain my own view on this issue (Section 5.1).

5.1 *The Position Adopted in This Study and That of the Institute and the ILC*

The principle that clearly emerges from the analysis of State practice (further examined in Section 5.2, below) is that when the predecessor State continues to exist after the cession of part of its territory to another State (the successor State), it should remain responsible for *its own* internationally wrongful acts committed before the date of succession. Thus, as a matter of principle, the continuing State should continue its previous responsibility for these acts notwithstanding the transformation affecting its territory. This principle is supported by scholars.[516] In fact, this solution is based on the application of basic principles of State responsibility rather than State succession.[517]

516 Jenning & Watts, 227; Philippe Drakidis, "Succession d'Etats et enrichissements sans cause des biens publics du Dodécanèse", 24 *RHDI* 1971, 72–123; Sastry, 209. It should be noted, however, that scholars usually analyse this issue in the light of their findings with respect to similar cases of separation (where the predecessor State also does not cease to exist as a result of the changes affecting its territory). See, long list of writers (Chapter 2, Section 6.1) who made similar statements in the context of separation.

517 Pajnkihar, 317: "International responsibility in this respect was established by virtue of the State's legal identity with the predecessor State or its continued legal personality. However, the continuator State did not *succeed* to international responsibility (or the rights and obligations that accompany it) as the acts were attributed to it and it was bound by the primary rule at the time of the act. The continuator State is therefore internationally responsible according to the rules of State responsibility", emphasis in the original.

The same principle was adopted by the Institute. The Resolution includes a general clause (Article 4) providing the general framework of analysis regarding matters involving succession to obligations in the specific situation where the predecessor State continues to exist after the date of succession. Article 4(1) expresses the basic principle that only the State, which has actually committed an internationally wrongful act, should have its responsibility engaged. Article 4(2) explains that, in general, the predecessor State should remain responsible for its own internationally wrongful acts, including those committed before the date of succession. Finally, Article 4(3) explains that there are specific circumstances where the injured State can request reparation from the successor State, or from both the predecessor State *and* the successor State. In the context of cession, the basic principle under Article 11(1) of the Institute's Resolution follows the same pattern: the obligations arising from an internationally wrongful act committed by the predecessor State do not pass to the successor State. This is because the predecessor State continues to exist and should therefore remain the holder of obligations arising from wrongful acts which took place before the date of succession.

The same principle of non-succession was initially followed by ILC Special Rapporteur Šturma in his draft Articles attached to his 2018 Second Report (Draft Article 9(1)):[518] the obligations "do not pass" to the successor State. The clause was later grouped with two other provisions (dealing with separation and Newly Independent States), and a new proposal for a single clause was submitted by Special Rapporteur Šturma.[519] At its seventy-second session, in 2021, the ILC provisionally adopted, *inter alia*, this new clause (Draft Article 9), which had been provisionally adopted by the Drafting Committee at the seventy-first session in 2019.[520] In 2022, the provision would become Guideline 9. It follows a different approach. It indicates that "an injured State continues to be entitled to invoke the responsibility of the predecessor State even after the date of succession".

518 ILC Special Rapporteur Šturma, First Report, 2017, para 17; ibid, Second Report, 2018, para 139.

519 The three provisions were merged into a single provision because of their "common denominator" (the fact that they involve a predecessor State continuing to exist) and to avoid "unnecessary repetition". See, ILC Special Rapporteur Šturma, Third Report, 2019, para 65; ILC, Succession of States in respect of State responsibility, "Statement, Chair of the Drafting Committee, Claudio Grossman Guiloff", 31 July 2019 (hereinafter "ILC, Statement, Grossman Guiloff, 2019") 6.

520 ILC, "Text of Draft Articles 7, 8 and 9", provisionally adopted, Drafting Committee, 71st sess., 24 July 2019, A/CN.4/L.939/Add.1. The language is similar to Art. 4(2) of the Institute's Resolution.

State practice (examined in Section 5.3, below) shows the existence of one exception to this general principle of non-succession. It concerns internationally wrongful acts committed by a local administration having a substantial autonomy from the predecessor State prior to the date of succession. In such cases, the successor State should be held responsible for the obligations arising from the commission of such acts. I will further examine this principle below.

The same solution was adopted in Article 11(3) of the Institute's Resolution providing for one possible exception to the general principle of non-succession.[521] This is the situation when the author of a wrongful act was an "organ of the territorial unit of the predecessor State", such as an autonomous government, "that has later become an organ of the successor State". For example, an act of expropriation committed by a province, a canton, or any kind of a State-unit with significant autonomy, against a foreign investor before independence. After that entity is integrated into the successor State, the obligations arising from the wrongful act may pass to the successor State "if particular circumstances so require". For example, a successor State benefiting from expropriated assets without having compensated the owner.

The solution adopted in Article 11(3) of the Institute's Resolution was initially followed by ILC Special Rapporteur Šturma in Draft Article 9(2).[522] It should be noted that the ILC's earlier work contained a second exception to the general principle of non-succession.[523] ILC Draft Article 9(3) indicated that: "If particular circumstances so require, the obligations arising from an internationally wrongful act of the predecessor State, where there is a direct link between the act or its consequences and the territory of the successor State or States, are assumed by the predecessor and the successor State".[524] There is some support for this linkage in the context of cession.[525] One of the most intriguing features of Guideline 9 (which was never formally adopted by the ILC) is that it no longer contains any explicit reference to the "organ" and "direct link" exceptions. This provision will be critically assessed in the next section dealing with separation.[526]

---

521 See, Kohen & Dumberry, 78ff.

522 ILC Special Rapporteur Šturma, Second Report, 2018, paras 138ff.

523 The Institute's Resolution does not contain this exception in the context of succession to *obligations* regarding cession. On this question, see Kohen & Dumberry, 85–86.

524 ILC Special Rapporteur Šturma, Second Report, 2018, paras 98ff.

525 Shaw, 877; Pajnkihar, 338.

526 See, Chapter 2, Section 6.1.

5.2 *The Continuing State Remains Responsible for Internationally Wrongful Acts Committed before the Date of Succession*

The principle of non-succession was accepted and applied by *municipal courts* of the *successor State* to which the ceded territory was now attached. For instance, in the cases of *Mordcovici v.* P.T.T.,[527] *Sechter*[528] and *Vozneac*,[529] all decided by the Court of Cassation of Romania, and in the cases of *Alsace-Lorraine Railway v. Ducreux Es-qualité*[530] and *Kern v. Chemin de fer d'Alsace-Lorraine*, decided by French courts.[531] The principle was also adopted by one municipal court of a *continuing* State (from which the ceded territory was detached): the case of *Kalmar v. Hungarian Treasury* before the Supreme Court of Hungary.[532] These cases are examined in Sections 5.2.1, 5.2.2 and 5.2.3. A different solution was adopted in only one significant case (examined below under Section 5.2.6).

One important observation should be made. These municipal law cases do *not* involve questions of succession to *international* responsibility. They deal with wrongful acts which were committed by the predecessor State not against another State (or a national of another State) but against *its own nationals* which became nationals of the successor State after the date of succession (with one exception[533]).[534] The fact that these cases dealt with claims by nationals for past wrongful acts may in fact explain the verdict reached by some municipal courts. It is therefore with a great level of prudence that any extrapolation can be made as to how municipal courts would have reacted in the different circumstances of an internationally wrongful act committed against another State (or a national of another State).

527 *Mordcovici v.* P.T.T., Romania, Court of Cassation, 29 October 1929, *Buletinul deciziunilor Inaltei Curti de Casatie*, LXVI 1929, Part 2, 150, *AD* 1929–1930, 62.

528 *Sechter v. Ministry of the Interior*, Romania, Court of Cassation, 1929, *Jurisprudenta Română a Inaltei Curti de Casatie si Justitie*, XVII(4) 1930, 58, *AD* 1929–1930, case no. 37.

529 *Vozneac v. Autonomous Administration of Posts and Telegraphs*, Romania, Court of Cassation, 22 June 1931, ibid, 1932, 36–38, *AD* 1931–1932, case no. 30.

530 *Alsace-Lorraine Railway v. Ducreux Es-qualité*, French Court of Cassation, Ch. Civ. 30 March 1927, 55 *JDI* 1928, 1034; *Sirey*, 1928, Part. 1, 300; *AD* 1927–1928, 85.

531 *Kern v. Chemin de fer d'Alsace-Lorraine*, Cour de Colmar (Première Ch, civile), 16 May 1927, 56 *JDI* 1929, 446ff.

532 *Kalmar v. Hungarian Treasury*, Hungary, Supreme Court, 24 March 1929, P.VI.5473/1928, *Maganjog Tara*, X, no. 75, *AD* 1929–1930, 61.

533 The only exception is the case of *Kalmar v. Hungarian Treasury*, ibid, where the injured individual opted for the nationality of the continuing State at the date of succession.

534 The reasons for treating these types of cases differently have been explained above: Part 1, Section 4.7.

The *Lighthouse Arbitration* case, decided by an *international* arbitral tribunal, is a good illustration of the principle that the continuing State should remain responsible for *its own* internationally wrongful acts committed before the date of succession (the case is examined in Section 5.2.5).[535] This is expressed by the Arbitral Tribunal in its reasoning concerning Claim no. 12–a, whereby France sought compensation against Greece (the successor State) for acts committed directly by the authorities of the Ottoman Empire (the predecessor State). The Arbitral Tribunal ruled that no internationally wrongful act had been committed in the present case but added that had the Ottoman Empire actually committed that act, Greece could not be held liable for it and that it should be for Turkey (the "continuator" of the Ottoman Empire) to compensate the injured French company for its "own" acts committed before the loss of a portion of its territory.

Finally, the rule that the continuing State should remain, in principle, responsible for *its own* internationally wrongful acts committed before the date of succession was also affirmed by the French-German MAT in a series of awards, including the case of *Levy v. German State*.[536] It has also been applied in *State practice*, for instance, in the *Paris Peace Treaty* of 1947.[537] These examples are examined in Sections 5.2.2 and 5.2.4.

5.2.1 Romanian Court Cases in the Context of the Transfer of Bessarabia to Romania (1918)

Three cases were decided by Romanian courts in the context of the transfer of the territory of Bessarabia from Soviet Russia to Romania in April 1918.[538] Russia was not a party to the Treaty providing for the transfer of territory imposed by the "Allied and Associated Powers" (the British Empire, France,

535 *Lighthouse Arbitration* case, 23 *ILR* 1956, 81. This case is also an illustration of the existence of one *exception* to that principle, see Chapter 2, Section 5.3.1.

536 *Levy v. German State*, French-German MAT, 10 July 1924, *RDTAM* v. IV, 726, *AD* 1923–1924, case no. 27. Verzijl, 223, mentions that the same reasoning was applied in several other cases decided by the French-German MAT.

537 *Paris Peace Treaty*, 10 February 1947, in force on 15 September 1947, 49 *UNTS* 126; *UKTS* 1948, no. 50 (Cmd. 7481).

538 After the Russian Revolution, the territory of Bessarabia declared its independence as the "Moldavian Democratic Republic" on 24 January 1918. Soon after (in April 1918), the Bessarabian legislature voted in favour of unification with Romania. The union was confirmed by Romania's Western allies in the *Treaty between the Principal Allied Powers and Romania respecting Bessarabia*, 28 October 1920, *UKTS* 1922, No. 15 (Cmd. 1747). Given that the "independence" of this entity lasted for merely three months, this is an example of a transfer of territory (from Russia to Romania) rather than a case of an incorporation of State.

Italy, Japan, US, etc.).[539] In all three cases, it was held that the continuing State (in the present case, Russia) should remain responsible for the wrongful acts it committed in the territory of Bessarabia before the transfer of territory.[540]

In the case of *Mordcovici v. P.T.T.*, the Court of Cassation of Romania stated that the transfer of Bessarabia to Romania did not result in a succession of Romania to the obligations of Soviet Russia in respect of Bessarabia since there was no convention between the two States to that effect and no declaration of Romania recognising such obligations.[541] The same Court rendered a similar decision in the case of *Sechter v. Ministry of the Interior*.[542] Similarly, in the *Vozneac* case, it was held that according to scholarship and State practice the

539 Art. 9 of the Treaty states: "The High Contracting Parties will invite Russia to adhere to the present Treaty as soon as a Russian Government recognised by them shall be in existence". Russia and subsequently the USSR never recognised the transfer of territory. During WWII (in June 1940), the USSR annexed the territory of Bessarabia. This annexation was later recognised by the Allies: Art. 1, *Treaty of Peace Concluded between the Allied and Associated Powers and Romania*, 10 February 1947, in force on 15 September 1947, *UKTS* 1948, No. 55 (Cmd. 7486); *UNTS* 42, 3.

540 This is also the conclusion reached by Czaplinski, 350. On the contrary, Atlam, 221, interprets these cases as supporting, more broadly, the principle of non-succession to obligations.

541 *Mordcovici v. P.T.T.*, Romania, Court of Cassation, 29 October 1929, *Buletinul deciziunilor Inaltei Curti de Casatie*, LXVI(2) 1929, 150, *AD* 1929–1930, 62. This case dealt with events which took place in January 1918, when parts of Bessarabia (at the time still formally a Russian territory) were occupied by Romanian Troops. The plaintiff had paid at the post office in Chisinau (Bessarabia) the sum of 2,784 Russian roubles to be transferred to an addressee in another part of Bessarabia. The transfer was not made and the money was lost. After Bessarabia became part of Romania, the plaintiff started legal proceedings against the Romanian Administration of Posts and Telegraphs. He maintained that his transaction constituted a contract between him and the Russian Administration and that the contract had passed unaltered to the Romanian postal administration after the transfer of the territory of Bessarabia to Romania in April 1918.

542 *Sechter v. Ministry of the Interior*, Romania, Court of Cassation, 1929, *Jurisprudenta Română a Inaltei Curti de Casatie si Justitie*, V. XVII(4) 1930, 58, *AD* 1929–1930, case no. 37. In this case, the plaintiff had been commissioned by the governing authorities of Bessarabia (then part of Russia) to print the voting papers for the election of the Russian Constituent Assembly in 1917. Having not being paid, the plaintiff submitted his claim to Romanian courts after the territory of Bessarabia was transferred to Romania. The Court of Cassation dismissed the plaintiff's claim. It stated that the principle of universal succession to rights and obligations applied only in cases of total annexation. In cases of partial annexation (such as here), the Court stated that questions of succession to debts should be settled by means of a direct arrangement between the States concerned. In the absence of an arrangement between Romania and Russia, the Court concluded that the claim could therefore not be admitted before Romanian courts.

responsibility for debts to individuals was the concern of the continuing State (Russia).[543]

5.2.2 French Court Cases and French-German Mixed Arbitral Tribunal Cases in the Context of the Cession of Alsace-Lorraine to France (1919)

The cession of Alsace-Lorraine by Germany to France after the First World War is also the source of some interesting decisions by municipal courts.[544] The issues dealt with by the courts were all concerning railway-related incidents. The solution adopted by the courts was no doubt the result of the application of Article 67 of the *Versailles Treaty*, which indicated that France was taking over railways in Alsace-Lorraine but not the responsibility for any payments.[545]

In the case of *Alsace-Lorraine Railway v. Ducreux Es-qualité*, the French Court of Cassation held that France (the successor State) was not bound by pre-succession obligations based on the general principle of international law that a State is not responsible for acts which it has not committed.[546] The same conclusion was also reached by another French court in the case of *Kern v. Chemin de fer d'Alsace-Lorraine*.[547] Finally, this solution of non-succession was also adopted by a series of decisions by the French-German MAT, such as in the case of *Levy v. Germany*.[548]

---

543 *Vozneac v. Autonomous Administration of Posts and Telegraphs*, Romania, Court of Cassation, 22 June 1931, ibid, 1932, 36–38, *AD* 1931–1932, case no. 30. This case was also dealing with an amount of money which was paid by the plaintiff at the post office in a city situated in Bessarabia (then part of Russia) and which was subsequently lost.

544 In accordance with Art. 51 of the *Versailles Treaty*, 28 June 1919, in force on 10 January 1920, *UKTS* 1919, No. 8 (Cmd. 223) (hereinafter "*Versailles Treaty*"), the territories of Alsace-Lorraine which were "ceded" by France to Germany in accordance with the Preliminaries of Peace and the *Treaty of Frankfurt* (1871) were "restored to French sovereignty as from the date of the Armistice of November 11, 1918".

545 Art. 67, *Versailles Treaty*: "The French Government is substituted in all the rights of the German Empire over all the railways which were administered by the Imperial railway administration and which are actually working or under construction … This substitution shall not entail any payment on the part of the French State".

546 *Alsace-Lorraine Railway v. Ducreux Es-qualité*, French Court of Cassation, Ch. Civ. 30 March 1927, 55 *JDI* 1928, 1034; *Sirey*, 1928, Part. 1, 300; *AD* 1927–1928, 85. The Court held that France was not bound to respect and to provide compensation for a private contract entered by the plaintiff with the former German railway administration in the territories of Alsace-Lorraine when it was still part of the territory of Germany.

547 *Kern v. Chemin de fer d'Alsace-Lorraine*, Cour de Colmar (Première Ch, civile), 16 May 1927, 56 *JDI* 1929, 446ff. This case dealt with the non-payment for construction work undertaken by the plaintiff before the War.

548 *Levy v. German State*, Franco-German MAT, 10 July 1924, *RDTAM* v. IV, 726, *AD* 1923–1924, case no. 27.

5.2.3 A Hungarian Court Case in the Context of the Cession of Transylvania to Romania (1920)

The *Kalmar* case was decided by the Supreme Court of Hungary.[549] It dealt with an act committed in 1914 by policemen against an ethnic Hungarian in the territory of Transylvania, which at the time was still part of the Austria-Hungary Dual Monarchy. Before the end of the First World War, the local courts had ordered the Treasury of Austria-Hungary to pay a life annuity to the plaintiff. At the end of the War, and as a result of the break-up of the Dual Monarchy, the territory of Transylvania was ceded to Romania pursuant to the *Treaty of Trianon* of 1920.[550] The plaintiff retained his Hungarian nationality and moved to Hungary after the cession of territory. He brought his claim against the Hungarian Treasury. The Court held that Hungary should continue the previous responsibility undertaken at the time of Austria-Hungary notwithstanding the transformation affecting the territory ceded:

> There is no rule according to which the Successor State [Romania] is liable to pay life-annuities in favour of Hungarian citizens living in the present territory of Hungary in the case where the damage originated in the territory detached by the Peace Treaty … The objection raised by the defendant [Hungary] that the administrative liabilities of the ceded territories *ipso facto* fall on the Successor State is unfounded.[551]

---

549 *Kalmar v. Hungarian Treasury*, Hungary, Supreme Court, 24 March 1929, P.VI.5473/1928, *Maganjog Tara*, X, no. 75, *AD* 1929–1930, 61.

550 *Treaty of Peace between the Allied and Associated Powers, and Hungary, Protocol and Declaration*, (*Treaty of Trianon*), 4 June 1920, *LNTS* v. 6, 187; *UKTS* 1920, No. 10 (Cmd. 896). In fact, the *Versailles Treaty* had already recognised in 1919 the sovereignty of Romania over Transylvania.

551 *Kalmar* case, *AD* 1929–1930, 61. In defence, the Hungarian Treasury maintained that, *inter alia*, the injury had been done by the authorities of the ceded territory and that it occurred in a territory now part of Romania. Consequently, the liability should rest with the successor State to that territory (Romania). It should be noted that the Supreme Court of Hungary was of the view that Hungary was a *new State* in 1918 as a result of the break-up of the Austria-Hungary Dual Monarchy (and was not the continuing State of Austria-Hungary). As mentioned above (Chapter 2, Section 4.2.2), this position was, however, rejected by other States. The Court therefore held that as a new State Hungary took over the obligations arising from internationally wrongful acts which took place before 1918. This case could have therefore been examined in the section dealing with separation (Section 6, below). In any event, it should be noted that the Court must have been strongly influenced by the fact that the plaintiff was a "Hungarian citizens living in the present territory of Hungary". Another feature, which must have also had an impact on the verdict reached by the Court, was the nature of the claim and the fact that it was an "administrative debt".

5.2.4 The 1947 *Paris Peace Treaty* in the Context of the Cession of the Dodecanesian Islands to Greece (1947)

Pursuant to Article 14 of the 1947 *Paris Peace Treaty* signed by, *inter alia*, Greece and Italy, the Dodecanesian Islands were ceded by Italy to Greece.[552] During the period of Italian occupation and sovereignty over the Islands, several properties belonging to local Greek nationals were expropriated without any compensation.[553] In accordance with Article 38 of the Peace Treaty, Italy (the continuing State) was under the obligation to financially compensate the victims of expropriations committed during the period of occupation and sovereignty over the Dodecanesian Islands.[554]

5.2.5 Claims Nos. 11 and 12–a Decided by the Arbitral Tribunal in the *Lighthouse Arbitration* Case (1956) in the Context of the Cession of Crete to Greece (1913)

The *Lighthouse Arbitration* case was decided in 1956 by the French-Greek Arbitral Tribunal, which had been set up under the rules of the PCA in The Hague.[555] It should be noted at this juncture that two connected aspects of this French claim against Greece had previously been decided by the Permanent Court of International Justice in two different cases:[556]

552 *Paris Peace Treaty*, 10 February 1947, in force on 15 September 1947, 49 *UNTS* 126; *UKTS* 1948, no. 50 (Cmd. 7481). The Dodecanesian Islands were under Ottoman Empire sovereignty until 1912, when they became under Italian military occupation (from 1912 to 1924). In 1924, the Islands were ceded to Italy. In 1947, the Islands were ceded to Greece.

553 This question is examined in great detail by Philippe Drakidis, "Succession d'Etats et enrichissements sans cause des biens publics du Dodécanèse", 24 *RHDI* 1971, 109–110.

554 The issue was the object of at least one case before Greek courts (after the cession of 1947) dealing with the fate of a concession granted to locals ethnic Greeks in 1908 by the Ottoman Empire to exploit a sulphur mine on the Island of Nissyros which had been in effect expropriated by an Italian Decree of 1933. The Greek State Council decided in the *Nissyros Mines* case (case no. 1848, 1952, *Justice nouvelle*, 1952, 706; *Archives de jurisprudence*, 1953, 39–43; *ILR* 1952, 135; *RHDI* 1954, 274) that the Decree was invalid, as it did not respect the acquitted rights of the Greek nationals. See, O'Connell, State Succession, v. I, 325.

555 *Sentence arbitrale en date des 24/27 juillet 1956 rendue par le Tribunal d'arbitrage constitué en vertu du Compromis signé à Paris le 15 juillet 1932 entre la France et la Grèce*, UNRIAA v. 12, 155. The Award (in French) is found in 9 *RHDI* 1956, 176. This case is better known as the *Lighthouse Arbitration* case. An unofficial English version of the Award is reported in 23 *ILR* 1956, 81. See, Charles Rousseau, "L'Affaire franco-hellénique des Phares et la sentence arbitrale du 24 juillet 1956", 63 *RGDIP* 1959, 248–292.

556 *Lighthouse Case between France and Greece*, Judgment, 17 March 1934, PCIJ *Series A/B*, no. 62. See, J.H.W. Verzijl, *The Jurisprudence of the World Court: A Case by Case Commentary*, v. I (A.W. Sijthoff 1965) (hereinafter "Verzijl, Jurisprudence") 370–382.

the *Lighthouse* case of 1934 and the *Lighthouse in Crete and Samos* case of 1937.[557]

The present case before the French-Greek Arbitral Tribunal, the *Lighthouse Arbitration* case, involved concession rights obtained in 1860 by a French company from the Ottoman Empire for maintaining lighthouses in Crete, a Greek territory then under Ottoman sovereignty.[558] Several claims (contractual and delictual) against Greece were brought by the French owner of the concession (*la Société Collas et Michel*) after Greece gained sovereignty over the territory (in 1913) and decided to expropriate the concession during the First World War. France had no less than 27 claims and Greece 10 counterclaims. Only three of these claims are relevant for this study. There is an important distinction to be made about these three claims. One claim was submitted by France for acts allegedly entirely committed by the Ottoman Empire (Claim no. 12–a). The other two claims were for acts for which the Cretan autonomous authorities were allegedly partially responsible (Claim no. 11) and entirely responsible (Claim no. 4).[559]

Claim no. 12–a. In this claim, France was seeking compensation against Greece (the successor State) for acts committed by the *authorities of the Ottoman Empire* (the predecessor State).[560] The alleged internationally wrongful act was the unauthorised removal by the Ottoman Empire of a buoy belonging to the French company. The Arbitral Tribunal ruled that the Ottoman

557 *Lighthouses in Crete and Samos*, Judgment, 8 October 1937, PCIJ *Series A/B*, no. 71. See, Verzijl, ibid 483–495.

558 A few words should be said about the history of the Greek-speaking region of Crete which was under Ottoman occupation since the 17th Century. A series of revolts against the Turks in the 19th Century reached its climax in the insurrection of 1896–1897 that led to war (in 1897) between Greece and the Ottoman Empire. The European Powers intervened in the war, forcing the Ottoman Empire to evacuate Crete in 1898. An autonomous Cretan State was formed under nominal Ottoman rule but in fact governed by a high commission of the occupying powers (England, France, Russia and Italy). Crete was in favour of union with Greece, but the occupying powers rejected its demand. The Young Turks revolution of 1908, however, enabled the Cretans to proclaim their union with Greece and in 1909 foreign occupation troops were withdrawn. In 1913, as a result of the Balkan Wars, Crete was officially incorporated into Greece: Art. 4, *Treaty of London*, 17–30 May 1913, in: G.F. De Martens, *Nouveau recueil général de traités*, Gr. VII, v. 8, 16. On the question of the legal status of Crete under international law, see: G. Streit, "La question crétoise au point du vue du droit international", *RGDIP* 1897, 61–104, 446–483; *RGDIP* 1900, 5–52, 301–369; *RGDIP* 1903, 222–282, 345–418; H. Couturier, *La situation de la Crète au point du vue international*, thesis, Fac droit Paris, 1900; J. Dutkowski, *Une expérience d'administration internationale d'un territoire, l'occupation de la Crète (1897–1909)* (Pedone 1953).

559 Claim no. 4 is examined in Section 5.3.1.

560 *Lighthouse Arbitration* case, 23 *ILR* 1956, 106.

authorities had not committed any internationally wrongful act and that the acts were legitimate for reasons of security.

In an *obiter dictum*, the Arbitral Tribunal nevertheless indicated that even if the Ottoman Empire had indeed committed an internationally wrongful act, Greece could not be held liable for it. It is Turkey (the continuing State of the Ottoman Empire[561]) which would be liable for its "own" acts committed before the loss of a substantial portion of its territory. This was in accordance with Article 9 of Protocol XII of the *Lausanne Peace Treaty* of 24 July 1923.[562] For the Arbitral Tribunal, the "critical date" to determine which State should be responsible for which internationally wrongful acts was the date at which the Peace Treaty established that the territory lost by the Ottoman Empire would be transferred to the different successor States.[563] The Arbitral Tribunal added that this solution was not only dictated by the terms of the *Lausanne Peace Treaty* but also that it was in conformity with rules of State succession:

561 On the question whether or not Turkey should be considered as the same State as the Ottoman Empire under international law, see, *inter alia*: P. Dumberry, "Is Turkey the 'Continuing' State of the Ottoman Empire under International Law?", 59(2) *Netherlands ILR* 2012, 235–262; P. Dumberry, "Turkey's International Responsibility for Internationally Wrongful Acts Committed by the Ottoman Empire", 42 *Revue générale de droit* 2012, 562–589; Vahagn Avedian, "State Identity, Continuity, and Responsibility: The Ottoman, the Republic of Turkey and the Armenian Genocide", 23(3) *EJIL* 2012, 797–820; E. Öktem, "Turkey: Successor or Continuing State of the Ottoman Empire?" 24(3) *Leiden JIL* 2011, 561–583; P. Tacar & M. Gauin, "State Identity, Continuity, and Responsibility: The Ottoman Empire, the Republic of Turkey and the Armenian Genocide: A Reply to Vahagn Avedian," 23(3) *EJIL* 2012, 821–835; E. Zamuner, "Le Rapport entre Empire ottoman et République turque face au droit international". 6(2) *J. Hist. IL* 2004.

562 *Treaty of Peace of Lausanne*, 24 July 1923, *UKTS* 1923, No. 16 (Cmd. 1929), *LNTS* v. 28, 11; 18 *AJIL* 1924, Supp., 4. Art. 9 reads as follows: "In territories detached from Turkey under the Treaty of Peace signed this day, the State which acquires the territory is fully subrogated as regards the rights and obligations of Turkey towards the nationals of the other Contracting Powers, and companies in which the capital of the nationals of the said Powers is preponderant, who are beneficiaries under concessionary contracts entered into before the 29th October, 1914, with the Ottoman Government or any local Ottoman authority. The same provision will apply in regards concessionary contracts entered into with the Ottoman Government or any Ottoman local authority before the coming into force of the Treaty providing for the transfer of the territory. This subrogation will have effect as from the coming into force of the treaty by which the transfer of territory was effected except as regards territories detached by the Treaty of Peace signed this day, in respect of which the subrogation will have effect as from the 30th October, 1918".

563 *Lighthouse Arbitration* case, 23 *ILR* 1956, 108: "The critical date evidently serves as the termination of Turkish responsibility and the commencement of Greek responsibility in the sense that everything which happened before the critical date and which can have given rise to charges against the concessionary firm continues to involve the responsibility of the Turkish State".

> One can only admit that within the scope of this conventional sharing of responsibilities according to time, some other autonomous and complementary principle, borrowed from the general doctrines of State succession, may be invoked to upset the juridical effects of the said sharing of responsibilities according to the Protocol.[564]

The reasoning of the Tribunal has been interpreted by some as supporting the principle that the successor State should not take over the obligations arising from internationally wrongful acts committed by the predecessor State.[565] In fact, the Arbitral Tribunal's *obiter dictum* supports *another* rule: in cases of cession of territory, the continuing State should remain responsible for *its own* internationally wrongful acts committed before the date of succession.[566] This is indeed how the claims has been analysed by the Institute[567] and by ILC Special Rapporteur Šturma.[568]

Claim no. 11. This claim concerned compensation sought by France against Greece (the successor State) relating to expenditures incurred by the French owner of the concession in the course of the construction of two new lighthouses from 1903 to 1908.[569] The Arbitral Tribunal found that the responsibility for the damage suffered by the French concessionaire was divided between the French company itself and both the Cretan authorities and the Ottoman Empire. It decided that Greece should not be held accountable for the commission of these internationally wrongful acts. The reasoning of the Arbitral Tribunal is as follows:

> [T]he Tribunal sees no real reason to saddle, after the event, Greece, who had absolutely nothing to do with the dealings between those parties, with this responsibility, in whole or in part. Not even the part of the general responsibility for the events of 1903 to 1908 to be imputed to the autonomous State of Crete can be regarded as having devolved upon Greece. Such a transmission of responsibility is not justified in the present case either from the particular point of view of the final succession of Greece to the rights and obligations of the concession in 1923/1924—if

564 Ibid.

565 C. Rousseau, "L'Affaire franco-hellénique des Phares et la sentence arbitrale du 24 juillet 1956", 63 *RGDIP* 1959, 274.

566 Atlam, 242.

567 Kohen & Dumberry, 81.

568 ILC Special Rapporteur Šturma, Second Report, 2018, paras 142ff.

569 *Lighthouse Arbitration* case, 23 *ILR* 1956, 81.

> only for the reason that the said events took place outside the scope of the concession—or from the more general point of view of its succession in 1913 to the territorial sovereignty over Crete.[570]

The Arbitral Tribunal decided that Greece should not be held accountable for the portion of responsibility related to acts committed *directly by the Ottoman Empire*. It also came to the same conclusion with respect to the portion of these acts for which the *autonomous Government of Crete* was responsible. The reasoning was apparently based on the specific facts of the case. Thus, the Tribunal indicated that the territorial succession of Greece to the Island in 1913 and the acts committed by the local Cretan authorities from 1903 to 1908 were "too remote to justify a decision which would fix Greece and Greece alone with the general responsibility for the acts and omissions of others who were complete strangers to her".[571] The Arbitral Tribunal's finding was also grounded on principles of succession of States.[572]

It has been suggested that the Arbitral Tribunal's handling of Claim no. 11 was based on the application of the principle of non-succession to obligations arising from wrongful acts committed by the predecessor State.[573] The outcome can probably be understood as an application of the other rule that the continuing State (Turkey) should continue its previous responsibility for internationally wrongful acts committed before the transformation affecting its territory. To this principle, the Arbitral Tribunal's reasoning in dealing with Claim no. 11 suggests that there could be a possible exception to the principle of non-succession when the acts are committed by an autonomous entity. Yet, the Arbitral Tribunal did not apply this exception in that case. In fact, the Arbitral Tribunal's decision with respect to another claim (Claim no. 4, which is analysed below[574]), shows that in other circumstances the exception should be applied.

---

570 Ibid 89.

571 Ibid.

572 This seems to be the reasoning of the Arbitral Tribunal, since it used the words "ni au point de vue plus générale de sa succession à la souveraineté territoriale sur Crète en 1913".

573 C. Rousseau, "L'Affaire franco-hellénique des Phares et la sentence arbitrale du 24 juillet 1956", 63 *RGDIP* 1959, 274; Atlam, 249; Monnier, 82–83.

574 See, Section 5.3.1.

5.2.6 A German Court Case in the Context of the Transfer of Upper Silesia to Poland (1951)

I have found only one significant case decided by a municipal court where the principle that the continuing State should remain responsible for the commission of *its own* wrongful acts before the date of succession was *not applied.*

The *Personal Injuries* (*Upper Silesia*) case was decided by the Court of Appeal of Cologne in 1951.[575] The Court held that the Federal Republic of Germany (FRG) was not liable to pay compensation to the plaintiff for the reason that "the alleged liability of the Reich Postal Administration vis-à-vis the plaintiff arose wholly outside that territory and has no connection whatsoever with the latter, [and that] any liability of the Federal Postal Administration is out of the question".[576] The Court also stated that the identity of the Reich with the FRG was limited to the territory of what was now the Federal Republic. The Court concluded by stating that "the practical result of holding the Federal Republic liable for all debts of the German Reich—regardless of when and where such debts arose—would indeed be untenable".[577] The outcome of this case may be surprising at first. It would have been perfectly normal after all for a German court to order Germany to provide reparation to a German national for a wrong which had been committed on the territory of Germany. Yet, any such finding would have had much wider repercussions given the vast territories transferred to Poland after the War.

It was thus held that the FRG (the continuing State) could not be held liable to compensate the plaintiff for wrongful acts committed before the territory of Upper Silesia became part of Poland. Since Poland was not a party to the proceedings, the Court did not, however, indicate that it should be for the

---

575 *Personal Injuries* (*Upper Silesia*) *Case*, Court of Appeal of Cologne, 10 December 1951, *NJW*, 5 (1952), 1300, *ILR* 1951, 67ff. In this case, the plaintiff had sustained personal injuries in 1943 after a collision with a motor vehicle owned by the Postal Administration of the German Reich in the territory of Upper Silesia which at that time was part of the territory of the Reich. The territory of Upper Silesia became part of Poland after WWII. After the War, the plaintiff brought an action for damages against the FRG and alleged that his injuries were caused by the Postal Administration of the Reich. The plaintiff was most probably an "ethnic German" and had left the territory of Upper Silesia after the transfer of territory in 1945; he was now living in Germany. He argued that the FRG was liable for all acts of negligence committed by servants of the Reich in any part of the latter's territory, notwithstanding the fact that the territory was subsequently severed from the Reich. The FRG contended that in the absence of special legislation to that effect, it was not liable for internationally wrongful acts committed in parts of the former Reich which were no longer part of its territory.

576 Ibid 68.

577 Ibid.

successor State (Poland) to take over the obligations arising from the commission of the internationally wrongful act. There is no indication that the plaintiff filed a claim before Polish courts.

5.2.7 Other Less Significant Examples

One very old example is usually mentioned in the literature: the cession of territory in a 1343 treaty between King Philippe of France and Humbert, whereby upon the death of the latter, his territory (the *Dauphiné*) was to pass to the second son of the King of France. According to Article 8 of the Treaty, the successor to Humbert was to pay all debts and would be responsible for all liabilities arising out of "torts" committed by Humbert as "a son is bound by the obligations of his father".[578] Some view this example as relevant to the issue of succession to obligations arising from the commission of wrongful acts.[579] A better interpretation is probably that this old treaty ultimately reflects an era when the territory of a State was seen as the private patrimony of the monarch and when a territory could be exchanged between sovereigns in contracts or as part of a succession.[580] This example seems irrelevant in contemporary international law.

It should finally be mentioned that Hurst makes reference to several cases which were decided by Italian courts in the context of the cession of Lombardy by Austria to the Kingdom of Sardinia (Italy) in 1859.[581] Article 8 of the *Treaty of Zurich* (10 November 1859) stated that the Italian government (the successor State) undertook to consider compensation for the losses caused by requisitions made by the Austrians in Lombardy as a charge on the Italian State.[582]

578 This provision, reproduced in: Feilchenfeld, 20, provides in its original (old) French version that the succcessor "soit tenu d'amander les torts faicts de nous & de nos Predecesseurs, ainsy que le filz est tenu pour le pere".

579 Feilchenfeld, 20, described this case as an illustration that there is "no general custom exempting tort obligations from the rules of succession". For Volkovitsch, 2176, this example "expressly provides for the transfer of liabilities for international delicts from the predecessor to the successor".

580 Czaplinski, 341. See also, Volkovitsch, 2176, for whom this example needs to be view as an expression of the diplomatic practice of that time. On this period, see Verzijl, 298ff.

581 The defeats of Austria at the battles of Solférino and Magenta against the combined forces of France and Sardinia led to the loss of the territories of Lombardy and Tuscany to the Kingdom of Sardinia. These cases are discussed in: Hurst, 174ff. Other cases are discussed in: "Brief", US, *Hawaiian Claims* case, in: Nielsen, 113ff.

582 The provision reads as follows: "The Government of His Majesty, the King of Italy, succeeds to the rights and obligations resulting from contracts regularly stipulated by the Austrian administration of objects of public interest concerning specially the ceded country".

The Italian Minister of Interior issued a circular to that effect on 16 August 1860.[583] Based on this treaty provision, Italian municipal courts have held that the successor State should take over the obligations arising from the commission of wrongful acts committed by the predecessor State.[584]

5.3 *A Special Case: Acts Committed by Autonomous Entities*

As previously examined (Section 5.2), the principle that clearly emerges from State practice in the context of cession and transfer of territory is that the continuing State should remain responsible for *its own* wrongful acts committed before the date of succession. I have found one exception to this general principle: whenever the internationally wrongful act is committed by a local administration having a significant autonomy from the predecessor State prior to the date of succession. In such case, it should be for the successor State to be held responsible for the obligations arising from the commission of such act. I will further examine this principle below.[585] This exception is illustrated by the decision of the Arbitral Tribunal in the *Lighthouse Arbitration* case concerning Claim no. 4,[586] as well as by the decision of the Court of the Aegean Islands (Greece) in the *Samos (Liability for Torts) case*.[587] Both cases are examined in the following sections.

Importantly, these two cases do *not* involve the successor State formally *agreeing* to take over liabilities of the predecessor State in relation to the ceded territory. These are not examples of voluntary transfer of obligations. The solution of succession was decided by a tribunal based on the specific circumstances prevailing in each case.

583 The circular is found in: Keith, 74–75: "The King's Government assumes the responsibility for and has decided in the Council of Ministers to consider at the cost of the state the compensation for the losses arising out of the requisitions regularly made by the Austrians in Lombardy".

584 *Minister of Finance v. Siro Corbella*, 1877, Civil Court of Cassation of Turin, *Giurisprudenza Italiana*, v. 29, Part 1, Section 1, column 996, referred in "Brief", US, *Hawaiian Claims* case, in: Nielsen, 117. In the case of *Finzi v. Minister of the Treasury*, Court of Cassation (in: Hurst, 174ff), it was held, on the contrary, that no definitive liability had ever been established against the Austrian government (the predecessor State) and that Italy (as the successor State) could therefore not be responsible for those unsettled claims.

585 See, Chapter 3, Section 7.

586 *Lighthouse Arbitration* case, 23 *ILR* 1956, 81.

587 *Samos (Liability for Torts) Case*, Greece, Court of the Aegean Islands, 1924, N° 27, *Thémis*, v. 35, 294, *AD* 1923–1924, 70 (hereinafter "*Samos* case").

5.3.1 Claim No. 4 Decided by the Arbitral Tribunal in the *Lighthouse Arbitration* Case (1956) in the Context of the Cession of Crete to Greece (1913)

As previously observed, the French-Greek Arbitral Tribunal in the *Lighthouse Arbitration* case came to the conclusion in dealing with Claims nos. 12-a and 11 that the continuing State (Turkey) should remain responsible for *its own* internationally wrongful acts committed before the cession of the territory of Crete to Greece in 1913.[588] In Claim no. 4, also known as the *Haghios Nicolaos* case, the Arbitral Tribunal came to a different conclusion.[589]

Claim no. 4 dealt with tax exemptions granted to a Greek shipping company and its ship (the Haghios Nicolaos) by a law proclaimed by the local authorities of Crete in 1908. After 1913, when the Island became officially part of Greece, the law remained in place. This tax exemption was alleged by the French company to be in violation of its existing concession rights. France therefore sought reparation from Greece.

Right from the outset, the Arbitral Tribunal indicated that the liability of Greece should not be based on the above-mentioned provision of the *Lausanne Peace Treaty* of 1923 which dealt with the rights and obligations of Turkey and not Crete. The Arbitral Tribunal held that such liability:

> [C]ould result only from a transmission of responsibility in accordance with the rules of customary law or the general principles of law regulating the succession of States in general.[590]

The Arbitral Tribunal concluded that the acts were violations of a *contractual* obligation which had been committed by Crete. Crete was described has an "autonomous island State the population of which had for decades passionately aspired to be united, by force of arms if necessary, with Greece, which was regarded as the mother country".[591] The Arbitral Tribunal added that this violation by the Cretan authorities was made in favour of a Greek company and that the Greek authorities maintained the situation after 1913. The Arbitral Tribunal thus concluded on this point that:

> [T]he Tribunal can only come to the conclusion that Greece, having adopted the illegal conduct of Crete in its recent past as autonomous

588 *Lighthouse Arbitration* case, 23 *ILR* 81. These two claims were examined above: Section 5.2.5.
589 Ibid 81.
590 Ibid 90.
591 Ibid 92.

> State, is bound, as successor State, to take upon its charge the financial consequences of the breach of the concession contract. Otherwise, the avowed violation of a contract committed by one of the two States, linked by a common past and a common destiny, with the assent of the other, would, in the event of their merger, have the thoroughly unjust consequence of cancelling a definite financial responsibility and of sacrificing the undoubted rights of a private firm holding a concession to a so-called general principle of non-transmission of debts in cases of territorial succession, which in reality does not exist as a general and absolute principle.[592]

The analysis of the Arbitral Tribunal was so far based on *contractual* obligations by Crete and Greece. However, the Arbitral Tribunal was quick to point out that the solution would have been the same even if the obligation had been regarded as *delictual* and not contractual.[593] The Arbitral Tribunal clearly distanced itself from the two precedents of the *R.E. Brown*[594] and *Hawaiian Claims* cases[595] by stating that "the Tribunal does not attach a decisive importance to the rare and disparate precedents of international or municipal courts".[596] The Arbitral Tribunal finally came to the conclusion that:

> The thesis, one of theory rather than of practice, that there can never be a question of transmission … is not, in general, well founded.[597]

The Arbitral Tribunal awarded reparation to France in an amount of 7,830,424 French francs. The Arbitral Tribunal therefore found Greece responsible for the illegal acts committed against the French company in Crete. The important question, which will now be examined, is for which internationally wrongful acts exactly was Greece held liable.

There is no doubt that Greece was held responsible for its *own* internationally wrongful acts (delict of omission) committed *after* 1913 when Crete was officially ceded to Greece. Thus, Greece was responsible for maintaining

592 Ibid.

593 Ibid. According to Stern, Responsabilité, 339, the Tribunal has therefore clearly rejected the distinction, from a succession of States point of view, between contractual and delictual debts.

594 *R.E. Brown* case, 129. See, analysis in Part 2, Chapter 2, Section 2.1.4.2.

595 *Hawaiian Claims* case, 157. See, analysis in Part 2, Chapter 2, Section 2.1.5.

596 *Lighthouse Arbitration* case, 23 *ILR* 1956, 91.

597 Ibid 92.

in place the discriminatory practice *after* it had undeniable sovereignty over the Island.[598] This is therefore an example of the successor State being held responsible for *continuing* (after the date of succession) a wrongful act.

The question remains whether Greece was also held accountable, as the successor State, for acts committed by Crete *before* 1913. This is a difficult question, as there are arguments in favour of both positions. On the one hand, the plain language of the following quote from the decision of the Arbitral Tribunal seems to suggest that Greece was *not* found responsible for Crete's internationally wrongful acts committed *before* 1913:

> [T]he Tribunal can only come to the conclusion that Greece, *having adopted the illegal conduct of Crete in its recent past as autonomous State*, is bound, as successor State, to take upon its charge the financial consequences of the breach of the concession contract.[599] (emphasis added)

This interpretation also seems to be supported by the fact that in its pleadings, Rousseau (Counsel for France) observed that scholars and case law did not admit the transfer of the obligation to repair from the predecessor State to the successor State.[600]

On the other hand, however, the Award's repeated critical assessment of the doctrine of non-succession and its conclusion that there is no such general and absolute principle[601] seems to suggest that the Arbitral Tribunal actually found Greece to be responsible for Crete's internationally wrongful acts committed *before* 1913. This is also supported by the subsequent writings of Verzijl, who acted as President of the Arbitral Tribunal in the *Lighthouse Arbitration* case. He maintains that not only did the Arbitral Tribunal held Greece responsible for its own internationally wrongful act but that "the circumstances equally justified admitting her responsibility as a successor to the autonomous state of Crete over the preceding period".[602] For him, the special circumstances of

598 ILC Special Rapporteur Šturma, Second Report, 2018, para 145.

599 *Lighthouse Arbitration* case, 23 *ILR* 1956, 92.

600 *Différend au sujet de diverses réclamations et contre-réclamations relatives à la concession des phares de l'Empire ottoman*, pleadings of Rousseau, 29 (in: Monnier, 81). However, even though France admitted the existence of a general principle of non-succession to responsibility it nevertheless indicated that this was inoperant for cases of concessions (such as in the present case), where the new State needs to respect the acquired rights of the company.

601 *Lighthouse Arbitration* case, 23 *ILR* 1956, 92.

602 Verzijl, 223. See also: Volkovitsch, 2190–2191.

this case "justified the admission of the transmission of liability for torts from Crete to Greece".[603]

Not surprisingly, writers also have conflicting views on this question. Some authors have taken the position that Greece was found liable for its own acts committed *after* the cession of territory of Crete as well as for those committed *before* such cession (as successor State).[604] This is also the view held by ILC Special Rapporteur Crawford.[605] Other writers believe that Greece was only found responsible for its own acts committed *after* the annexation of 1913:

> [L]e tribunal a dégagé la responsabilité de la Grèce, comme successeur de l'Etat autonome de Crète, du fait qu'elle avait connu, puis endossé, comme si elle était régulière, l'infraction au contrat de concession, réalisée au profit d'un de ses ressortissants, alors que, d'après le tribunal, l'étroitesse de ses liens avec la Crète lui faisait un devoir d'intervenir pour mettre fin à l'infraction. C'est, en d'autres termes, pour avoir 'fait sienne la conduite illégale de la Crète' que la Grèce voit sa responsabilité engagée. Il s'agit là, en quelques sorte, d'une responsabilité par omission … Il n'y a pas à proprement parler, de succession d'Etats, puisque la responsabilité de l'Etat successeur n'est pas une responsabilité 'héritée' sans conditions, la transmission de la responsabilité de l'Etat prédécesseur n'étant rendue possible que par l'existence d'une responsabilité concomitante à la charge de l'Etat successeur.[606]

---

603 Verzijl, 223. It should be recalled that he is a strong opponent of the strict application of the rule of non-succession.

604 Volkovitsch, 2190. See also, comment by W. Wengler, in: 51 *Annuaire IDI* 1965, 168–169: "dans l'affaire des phares en Crète, on a admis la responsabilité de la Grèce pour des dommages causés à une époque où la Crète ne faisait pas partie de la Grèce".

605 ILC, "First Report on State Responsibility (*addendum* no. 5)", Special Rapporteur James Crawford, 22 July 1998, A/CN.4/490/Add.5., para 282: "In the *Lighthouses* arbitration, a tribunal held Greece liable for the breach of a concession agreement initiated by Crete at a period when the latter was an autonomous territory of the Ottoman Empire, *partly on the basis that the breach had been 'endorsed by* [*Greece*]*'*" (emphasis added).

606 Monnier, 84–85. This seems to be also the position of Czaplinski, 345–346, who indicates that the Tribunal accepted the principle of succession to responsibility in the context of Claim no. 4 but acknowledges that in this case "there was no difficulty in attributing the acts to the successor State as it had itself committed the same delict". Later he specifies (356) that the principle of acceptance of succession to responsibility was "in a certain sense special as the successor State was equally responsible for its own acts". Similarly, Crawford, Brownlie's, 442, indicating that Greece had adopted the wrong and recognised responsibility. See also: A. Verdross, *Völkerrech* (4th edn, Springler 1959) 198; A. Verdross & B. Simma, *Universelles Völkerrecht, Theorie und Praxis* (Dunker & Humblot 1984) 633–634; Natalino Ronzitti, *La successione internazionale tra stati* (Giuffrè 1970) 218.

This is also the position taken by Judge Kreća, for whom it "appears that the qualification of the decision as the expression of the acceptance of succession to responsibility is exaggerated" given that there are some indications in the award that Greece had a "direct responsibility for tort of her own".[607]

A more nuanced position is adopted by Stern indicating that the Arbitral Tribunal in its evaluation of Claim no. 4 did indeed admit the legal soundness and validity of the principle of succession of States to responsibility.[608] She nevertheless believes that this case is not a strong precedent in support of the principle of succession to the obligation to repair, because "il s'agit d'une responsabilité plus ou moins partagé, au moment où elle est née, par la Grèce en tant que mère-patrie".[609] A similar opinion was expressed by Rousseau, for whom:

> L'on ne saurait déduire, d'une solution exclusivement dictée par des considérations propres à l'espèce, un acquiescement quelconque à un prétendu principe général de succession aux actes illicites.[610]

This is undoubtedly true. The *special circumstances* of the case, referred to in the subsequent writing of Verzijl (who acted as President of the Arbitral Tribunal),[611] did indeed dictate the findings of the Tribunal. These circumstances are the fact that the acts were committed by an autonomous government with very strong links to Greece. This case, therefore, is an illustration that in the context of cession of territory there is an exception to the principle that the continuing State should always be responsible for the acts committed in the ceded territory before the date of succession.[612] The exception is when the internationally wrongful acts were committed by a largely autonomous government. At the time of the events, Crete had indeed a largely autonomous government.[613] In such cases, the successor State (i.e. the State to

607 *Croatia Genocide Convention* case, sep. op. Judge Kreća, para 64, quoting Verzijl, 223.

608 Stern, Responsabilité, 338. See also, Atlam, 248.

609 Ibid 339.

610 C. Rousseau, "L'Affaire franco-hellénique des Phares et la sentence arbitrale du 24 juillet 1956", 63 *RGDIP* 1959, 275. See also, Jacques Barde, *La notion de droit acquis en droit international public* (Publ. univ. Paris, 1981) (hereinafter "Barde") 182–183; Atlam, 245.

611 Verzijl, 223.

612 ILC Special Rapporteur Šturma, Second Report, 2018, para 144.

613 *Lighthouse Arbitration* case, *UNRIAA* v. 12, 181. The Arbitral Tribunal indicated about Crete that "son émancipation comme entité autonome a déja commencé en 1868 … [d]epuis lors, l'île de Crète a vécu une vie politique séparée … et mené l'existence d'un Etat autonome, investi de pouvoir très larges, mais sous la suzeraineté de l'Empire Ottoman". The cession of territory in 1913 by the Ottoman Empire is described by the Arbitral Tribunal as

which the territory is ceded) should be held responsible for obligations arising from internationally wrongful acts committed before the date of succession.[614] The Institute considered that this case is an illustration of Article 11(3) of the Resolution.[615] The same position was followed by ILC Special Rapporteur Šturma[616] and other writers.[617] He also noted that the decision could be explained based on the continuing character of the act and that another relevant aspect may have been the existence of a "direct link between the consequences of this act and the territory transferred".[618]

It should be added that in a letter sent to the UN GA Sixth Commission, Turkey recently rejected any such interpretation and refused to give any importance to this precedent. It stated that the award was an "individual and partial interpretation over the Lausanne Treaty and status of Turkey respectively", a "one sided deduction" and, "consequently it should be neither reflected as a general principle, nor should it be used to formulate a principle as a ground as if corresponded to a general recognition".[619] It also noted that the ILC Special Rapporteur had referred to Turkey as the "continuing State of the Ottoman Empire" and explained, rather ambiguously, that there were "different opinions with regards to the case of the Ottoman Empire".[620]

5.3.2 The *Samos* Case in the Context of the Cession of the Aegean Islands to Greece (1913)

The *Samos* (*Liability for Torts*) case, which was decided by the Court of the Aegean Islands (Greece), concerned an action for compensation brought against the Greek State after the cession of the Aegean Islands to Greece in 1913.[621] It concerned damage allegedly caused by customs officials of the Island

---

"sa renonciation finale à un résidu de droits de suzeraineté qu'il avait encore retenus après avoir érigé l'île en Etat autonome".

614 This point is further discussed in Chapter 3, Section 7.

615 See, Kohen & Dumberry, 88–90.

616 ILC Special Rapporteur Šturma, Second Report, 2018, para 145: "there are also other particular circumstances that may justify the transfer of obligations arising from the wrongful acts of the predecessor State (continuing) to the successor State. Here, the award underlines the autonomous status of a territory under the Ottoman Empire".

617 Brockman-Hawe, 866.

618 ILC Special Rapporteur Šturma, Second Report, 2018, para 145.

619 Turkey, letter sent to the UN GA Sixth Committee, Rep. 73rd sess. 31 Oct. 2018. See also: "one arbitral tribunal award in the sense of legal ground does not suffice at all to identify or to formulate a rule by itself about the topic".

620 Turkey, ibid, Rep. 76th sess. Oct–Nov. 2021.

621 *Samos* case, 70.

of Samos at the time it was still under Ottoman rule.[622] The Court held that the Greek State was substituted to the former Principality of Samos and that it must be deemed to be responsible for the injurious acts complained about before the cession of territory. In other words, it held that as the successor State, Greece should be held accountable for wrongful acts committed before the date of succession.

In scholarship, the solution found in this case has been explained by the autonomous status which the Island enjoyed prior to its cession to Greece in 1913 and the fact that "its absorption in Greece did not involve a total abolition of the local administration".[623] This is indeed a case supporting the principle that whenever an internationally wrongful act is committed by a largely autonomous government before the date of succession, it should be for the successor State (and not the continuing State) to be held responsible for the obligations arising from such act.[624] The Institute considered that this case is an illustration of Article 11(3) of the Resolution.[625] Other writers agree.[626]

6 Separation

The analysis of State practice and case law in the context of secession shows the existence of a *general principle*: the continuing State should remain responsible for *its own* internationally wrongful acts committed before the date of succession.[627] Thus, the obligations arising from the commission of such acts

622 The Aegean Islands (Samos, Chio, etc.) were a former autonomous province of the Ottoman Empire which was ceded to Greece in May 1913 pursuant to the *Treaty of London*, 17–30 May 1913, in: G.F. De Martens, *Nouveau recueil général de traités*, Gr. VII, v. 8, 16. The alleged damage arose in the present case from the fact that the customs officials disregarded the provisions of Samos law by declining to issue to the plaintiffs exportation permits in regard to a quantity of timber.

623 O'Connell, State Succession, v. I, 492. See also, Barde, 179.

624 This point is further discussed in Chapter 3, Section 7. Other writers believe that this case has limited value: Barde: "sa valeur est très relative et elle est dépourvue de portée quant à l'existence de la règle de non transmission de la responsabilité interne". In the *Lighthouse Arbitration* case, 23 *ILR* 1956, 91 the Tribunal indicated specifically that this precedent (as well as others) was not conclusive: "the Tribunal does not attach a decisive importance to the rare and disparate precedents of international or municipal courts".

625 See, Kohen & Dumberry, 88.

626 Brockman-Hawe, 866.

627 See also, Patrick Dumberry, "Is a New State Responsible for Obligations arising from Internationally Wrongful Acts Committed before its Independence in the Context of Secession?", 43 *Canadian YIL* 2005, 419–453.

should not, in general, be transferred to the successor State (the point is examined at Section 6.2). A different solution was adopted in a single significant State practice case (examined at Section 6.3). I will first refer to the position adopted by the Institute and the ILC and explain my own view on the matter (Section 6.1).

6.1 *The Position Adopted in This Study and That of the Institute and the ILC*

The analysis of State practice (examined in Section 6.2, below) shows that when the predecessor State continues to exist after the creation of the new State, it should remain, as a matter of principle, responsible for the consequence of *its own* internationally wrongful acts committed before the date of succession. The "continuing" State should therefore continue its previous responsibility for these acts notwithstanding the transformation affecting its territory. This is the prevailing view among writers[628] and it is certainly the correct basic position

628 Stern, Responsabilité, 335–336 ("[e]n vertu des principes très clairs gouvernant l'imputation de l'acte illicite à un Etat … on peut affirmer que l'Etat continuateur continue bien entendu à être responsable des actes qu'il a commis, même s'il subit certaines transformations"); Czaplinski, 357; Wesley L. Gould, *An Introduction to International Law* (Harpers & Bros 1957) 428; Monnier, 67 (for whom the continuing State "reste par conséquent titulaire des droits et des obligations engendrées par l'acte illicite"); Marek, 11; Volkovitsch, 2200; Peterschmitt, 54; Shaw, 877; C. Rousseau, "Jurisprudence française en matière de droit international public", *RGDIP* 1976, 969 (commenting on the *Société E. & B. Vidal* case, Conseil d'Etat, 20 June 1975, *Gaz. Palais*, 12–13 March 1976, 76, and concluding that it "confirme le principe général suivant lequel en cas de mutation territoriale ou d'accession d'un Etat nouveau à l'indépendance les obligations nées d'actes illicites commis antérieurement au changement de souveraineté incombent exclusivement à l'Etat prédécesseur"); Atlam, 258 ("l'Etat prédécesseur conservant intacte sa personnalité internationale, c'est lui et lui seul—qui serait tenu de répondre, le cas échéant, des faits internationalement illicites commis, à la veille de la réalisation de la succession d'Etats, par ses propres organes"); Jenning & Watts, 224 ("since the parent State still exists, there is no occasion for the new State to succeed to … claim for damages against it; but there would be justification for it to be … liable on those claims, having a local character attaching to the territory of the new State and which the parent State is therefore in no position to fulfil or meet"); Hans Kelsen, "Théorie générale du droit international public. Problèmes choisis", *Rec. des cours*, v. 42, 1932–IV, 327, 333–334 ("lorsqu'une partie seulement du territoire d'un Etat devient territoire d'un autre Etat, le prédécesseur demeure bien, en principe, le sujet des droits et des obligations qui lui appartenaient jusque-là"); Jakubowski, State Succession, 195–6, 267; Pajnkihar, 315–7, 338; Crawford, State Responsibility, 455; Vahagn Avedian, "State Identity, Continuity, and Responsibility: The Ottoman, the Republic of Turkey and the Armenian Genocide", 23(3) *EJIL* 2012, 804; Mikulka, State Succession, 292. See also, *Croatia Genocide Convention* case, Decla. Judge Xue, para 12 *a contrario* ("Under international law, the implication of the new political premise is arguably threefold for the FRY. First of all, the FRY, being one of the successor States rather than the sole continuator of

to be adopted. As mentioned above, this solution is based on the application of basic principles of State responsibility rather than State succession.[629]

That principle was followed in Article 12(1) of the Institute's Resolution: the obligations arising from an internationally wrongful act committed by the predecessor State *do not pass* to the successor State.[630] The same principle of non-succession was initially followed by ILC Special Rapporteur Šturma in the draft Articles attached to his 2018 Second Report regarding separation (Draft Article 7(1)).[631] As mentioned above, three provisions were later grouped, and a new proposal for a single clause was submitted by Special Rapporteur Šturma.[632] At its seventy-second session, in 2021, the ILC provisionally adopted, *inter alia*, Draft Article 9, which had been provisionally adopted by the Drafting Committee at the seventy-first session in 2019.[633] In 2022, the provision would become Guideline 9 (never adopted). It followed a different approach. It indicates that "an injured State continues to be entitled to invoke the responsibility of the predecessor State even after the date of succession".

In my view, the wording used in Guideline 9(1) is not the most efficient. In his Second Report, ILC Special Rapporteur Šturma had clearly adopted (as recognised by the Chair of the Drafting Committee[634]) the principle of non-succession in the context of separation[635] *precisely because* the predecessor State remains responsible for its own wrongful act.[636] He also explained that

---

the SFRY, does not enjoy all the rights of its predecessor, nor does it continue to assume all of the SFRY's international obligations and responsibility as the same international personality").

629 Pajnkihar, 317.

630 Kohen & Dumberry, 92ff.

631 ILC Special Rapporteur Šturma, First Report, 2017, para 17; ibid, Second Report, 2018, paras 46, 77, 80.

632 Ibid, Third Report, 2019, para 65; ILC, Statement, Grossman Guiloff, 2019, 6.

633 ILC, "Text of Draft Articles 7, 8 and 9", provisionally adopted, Drafting Committee, 71st sess., 24 July 2019, A/CN.4/L.939/Add.1. The language is similar to Art. 4(2) of the Institute's Resolution.

634 ILC, Statement, Grossman Guiloff, 2019, 6, noting that the three provisions "expressed the general rule that obligations arising from an internationally wrongful act of the predecessor State *did not pass* to the successor State and then identified exceptions that applied in particular circumstances", emphasis added.

635 The same rule also applied to Newly Independent States (ILC Special Rapporteur Šturma, Second Report, 2018, para 124) and transfer of territory (ibid, para 139, indicating that transfer of territory was "a clear case in which the general principle of non-succession to State responsibility applies. The responsibility rests with the predecessor State").

636 This is clear from this passage, ibid, para 46: "It seems to be generally acceptable that the main (or default) rule governing the issue of succession to obligations arising from an internationally wrongful act of the predecessor State committed before the date of succession in the context of separation of parts of a State is the principle of non-succession.

this "general rule of non-succession" was supported by State practice.[637] This proposition is not controversial. It is indeed supported by scholars and established by numerous examples of State practice.[638] It may have been preferable for Guideline 9(1) to simply affirm the uncontested proposition that, as a matter of principle,[639] the obligation to repair "does not pass" to the successor State and that the predecessor State *remains* responsible for *its own* wrongful acts.[640] In fact, the point is already covered by Guideline 6.[641] Such language would have been more effective than merely stating the (rather obvious) fact that the injured State "continues to be entitled to invoke the responsibility of the predecessor State" after the date of succession.[642] While this language may not be optimal, it is far better than some of the other propositions that were discussed at the Commission.[643]

Nevertheless, the question remains whether the principle mentioned in the previous paragraphs should apply *uniformly in all cases* and whether there

Since the predecessor State continues to exist, 'the continuing State should remain responsible for its own internationally wrongful acts committed before the date of succession'".

637 Ibid, para 80, examining many examples (paras 81ff).

638 See, analysis in Kohen & Dumberry, 92ff. These examples are examined in Section 6.2.

639 With a few possible exceptions, further discussed below.

640 Pajnkihar, 338: "General rule: The rights and obligations arising from international responsibility remain with the internationally responsible State after the date of succession if it continues to exist, unless they are succeeded to by a successor State in accordance with special rules. Thus, as a general rule, succession does not affect the secondary rights and obligations of the internationally responsible State".

641 The provision indicates that State succession "has no effect upon the attribution to [the 'continuing State'] of an internationally wrongful act committed by that State before the date of succession". For a critical assessment of an earlier version of that provision, see: Kaplane, 29–31.

642 See also, this interesting observation by the Czech Rep., letter sent to the UN GA Sixth Committee, rep. 71th sess. 6 Nov. 2019: "In our view, by shifting the focus from the question of reparation of injury (proposed by the Special Rapporteur) to that of invocation of responsibility, this provision does not capture satisfactorily the fact that this article applies also to situations when the injured State invoked responsibility of the predecessor State already before the date of succession of States, but the predecessor State did not make full reparation for the injury before that date (i. e. made no reparation at all or made only a partial reparation). These situations may be, in fact, the most frequent in practice".

643 Thus, the Drafting Committee "considered that a proposal indicating that the injured State 'may request' reparation was not appropriate since this expression was not sufficiently normative". See, ILC, Statement, Grossman Guiloff, 2019, 7–8, indicating that "referring to an entitlement to 'invoke the responsibility of the predecessor State' was more appropriate than referring to an entitlement to 'reparation', since the responsibility of the predecessor State was comprehensive before the succession of States".

should not be some circumstances where the new successor State could be held accountable for internationally wrongful acts committed before the date of succession. Examples where the principle of succession was applied are mentioned in Section 6.3, below. The position adopted in the present study is that, as a matter of principle, the continuing State should *not always* be responsible for internationally wrongful acts committed before the date of succession. There are several circumstances where, on the contrary, it should be for the successor State to be held responsible for obligations arising from wrongful acts committed before its independence.[644] These circumstances (or "special rules"[645]) are examined later in Chapter 3. One such circumstance is whenever the new State has unjustly enriched itself as a result of such act.[646] Another circumstance is when the internationally wrongful act had been committed by an autonomous political entity (before separation) with which the secessionist State has a structural continuity.[647] The *Bijelić* case in the context of the separation of Montenegro supports the existence of this exception.[648] One example of State practice discussed in Section 6.3 (the separation of Belgium in 1830) supports, to some extent, the existence of a another possible exception when there is a territorial link between the wrong and the new State. In my view, these exceptions should apply based on basic principles of equity, justice and fairness.

644 This is, for instance, the position of Stern, Responsabilité, 335–336, who first affirms that "puisque l'Etat reste le même, il n'y a aucune raison de ne pas admettre la continuité de la responsabilité". However, she adds that the question remains open as to whether in some circumstances the new successor State should not be held responsible for the illegal acts committed at the time it was still part of the predecessor State. She gives the example of a wrongful nationalisation of a gold mine, which would now be situated in the territory of the new successor State and ask the question whether in this situation it should still be for the continuing State to provide compensation to the injured third State. See also, Pajnkihar, 338.

645 Pajnkihar, 338ff. See, at 341: "The rights and obligations arising from international responsibility remain with the internationally responsible State after the date of succession if it continues to exist, unless they are succeeded to by a successor State *in accordance with special rules*. A successor State that has a special link to the matter of succession (i.e., injury) shall fully succeed to the secondary rights and obligations of reparations relating to that matter, followed by conditional succession to other secondary rights and obligations", emphasis added.

646 See, Chapter 3, Section 8.

647 See, Chapter 3, Section 7.

648 *Bijelić v. Montenegro and Ser*bia, ECHR, Appl no 11890/05, judgment, 11 June 2009 (hereinafter "*Bijelić* case"). The case is further examined below, see, Chapter 3, Section 7.

Article 12(3) of the Institute's Resolution provides for one possible exception to the general principle of non-succession mentioned in Article 12(1).[649] This provision covers the situation where the author of a wrongful act committed before independence was an "organ of the territorial unit of the predecessor State", such as an autonomous government, "that has later become an organ of the successor State".

The same solution was initially followed by ILC Special Rapporteur Šturma, referring to "circumstances justifying deviation from the general rule"[650] including the "organ" exception in Draft Article 7(2).[651] He stated that "acts committed by an autonomous entity of the predecessor State should be accepted as one of the elements in support of the succession to responsibility".[652] The earlier work of the ILC contained a second "direct link" exception to the general principle of non-succession.[653] ILC Draft Article 7(3) indicated that: "If particular circumstances so require, the obligations arising from an internationally wrongful act of the predecessor State, where there is a direct link between the act or its consequences and the territory of the successor State or States, are assumed by the predecessor and the successor State or States".[654] Some writers also support this territorial link element.[655] In his Report, the Special Rapporteur indicated that, in the context of separation, the successor

649 Kohen & Dumberry, 98ff.

650 ILC Special Rapporteur Šturma, Second Report, 2018, para 92, see title of the section.

651 Ibid, paras 94ff. See also, ILC Report, 70th sess., 2018, para 264, indicating that the term "an organ of a territorial unit" refers to "situations where such organs had a substantive degree of autonomy, such as in the case of federal States".

652 ILC Special Rapporteur Šturma, Second Report, 2018, para 97.

653 It should be added that the Institute's Resolution does not contain this exception in the context of succession to *obligations* regarding separation. Art. 12(2) only concerns the existence of a "direct link" between the consequences of an internationally wrongful act committed *against* the predecessor State before the date of succession and the territory or the population of the successor State(s). It does not address the reverse situation of a wrongful act committed *by* the predecessor State. For an analysis, see Kohen & Dumberry, 98–101.

654 ILC Special Rapporteur Šturma, Second Report, 2018, paras 98ff.

655 Shaw, 877 ("Where the predecessor state continues, in principle that state should still be responsible for its unlawful acts, unless there is a clear, direct and intrinsic link between the consequences of the act and the territory and population of the part of the state which either separates and becomes independent or merges with a third state"); Pajnkihar, 338 ("First special rule: A successor State that has a special link to the matter of succession (i.e., injury) shall fully succeed to the secondary rights and obligations of reparations relating to that matter, followed by conditional succession to other secondary rights and obligations. This rule refers to the special part of the succession matter and applies to all types of succession and independently of the existence of a continuator State").

State was "not *automatically* responsible" for such obligations "solely based on the fact that such acts took place on what is now its territory", adding that "the linkage of the acts to the territory is only *one relevant element* that needs to be taken into account".[656] Both exceptions ("organ" and "direct link") applied only "if particular circumstances so require".[657]

One of the most intriguing features of Guideline 9 (which was never formally adopted by the ILC) is that it no longer contains any explicit reference to the "organ" and "direct link" exceptions. This outcome is surprising considering the importance given to them by ILC Special Rapporteur Šturma. He stated in his Second Report that "despite non-succession being a general principle in this context" (i.e. separation) "it might not be of an absolute character".[658] He spoke of the "need to draft an article (…) in which the general principle of non-succession is complemented by a number of exceptions".[659] He referred to the "direct link" and "organ" exceptions as "situations that would justify a different approach" than the principle of non-succession.[660] In contrast, Guideline 9(2) simply indicates that "in particular circumstances, the injured State and the successor State should endeavour to reach an agreement for addressing the injury".[661]

In the following paragraphs, I will make three observations about the new language contained in Guideline 9.

First, in his 2019 Statement, the Chair of the Drafting Committee explained that the "purpose" of Guideline Article 9(2) was to "address exceptional situations where there is a direct link between the act or its consequences and the territory of the successor State or States" and that "in such circumstances, the predecessor State may not be in a position to address the injury alone and may need the cooperation with the successor State to do so".[662] The same observation is contained in the Commentary to Guideline 9.[663] The Chair also added

656 ILC Special Rapporteur Šturma, Second Report, 2018, para 103, emphasis in the original.

657 On the vagueness of this expression, Kaplane, 33.

658 ILC Special Rapporteur Šturma, Second Report, 2018, para 92.

659 Ibid para 122.

660 Ibid para 92. See also, his conclusion in paras 97, 103.

661 ILC, Statement, Grossman Guiloff, 2019, 8. As a result of the decision in 2022 to adopt guidelines rather than draft articles, the expression "shall endeavour" was changed to "should endeavour". It should be added that Guideline 9(3) states that "Paragraphs 1 and 2 are without prejudice to any apportionment or other agreement between the predecessor State and the successor State when implementing paragraphs 1 and 2". This provision simply reiterates the subsidiary nature of the articles (Guideline 1(2)). See, ILC, Commentaries, 2021, para 165, Art. 9, sub-para 6.

662 ILC, Statement, Grossman Guiloff, 2019, 8.

663 ILC, Commentaries, 2021, para 165, Art. 9, sub-para 4.

that "the term 'in particular circumstances' covers diverse situations where a successor State may be addressing the injury, which will be described in the commentary".[664] In the Commentary to Guideline 9,[665] reference is made to both the "organ" and "direct link" exceptions,[666] as well as in situations involving restitution of property,[667] or unjust enrichment.[668] These clarifications in the Commentary are very useful. Yet, it shows that both the Special Rapporteur and the Drafting Committee always had in mind the "organ" and "direct link" exceptions as "particular circumstances" which could require a different solution than non-succession. In my view, a better approach would have been to explicitly mention these two exceptions (and possibly others) in Guideline 9(2) text, just as it was done in Draft Article 7.

Second, Guideline 9 is fundamentally different from Draft Article 7 put forward by ILC Special Rapporteur Šturma. Draft Article 7(3) indicated that in cases where there is a "direct link" between the consequences of a wrongful act and one successor State's territory, the obligation to repair would be ("if particular circumstances so require") "assumed" by *both* the predecessor State and the successor State.[669] Similarly, in the context of the "organ" exception under Draft Article 7(2), the obligation to repair is ("if particular circumstances so require") "transferred" to the successor State. Guideline 9(2) is vastly different. The successor State no longer has to "assume" (or be "transferred") *any obligation*. This is a significant and deliberate change, not a minor drafting anomaly. For Slovakia, the use of "soft language" is "entirely appropriate" given that the use of other terms, such "transfer", "assume" or "pass", "presupposes the existence of an existing legal basis for such automatic devolution".[670] The Drafting Committee Chair explained that the purpose of paragraph 2 was "not to create obligations entailing the automatic transfer of obligations to the successor State, but instead is to signal the possibility for the successor State to reach an agreement with the injured State for addressing the injury".[671] The same observation is contained in the Commentary to Guideline 9.[672]

664 ILC, Statement, Grossman Guiloff, 2019, 8.
665 ILC, Commentaries, 2021, para 165, Art. 9, sub-para 5.
666 Ibid: "the successor State may be relevant in a situation where (…) there is a link between the territory or an organ of the successor State and the internationally wrongful act".
667 Ibid.
668 Ibid.
669 See, also Art. 9(3) in the context of transfer of territory.
670 Slovakia, letter sent to the UN GA Sixth Committee, Rep. 73rd sess. 30 Oct. 2018.
671 ILC, Statement, Grossman Guiloff, 2019, 8.
672 ILC, Commentaries, 2021, para 165, Art. 9, sub-para 4.

In my view, Guideline 9 is a good example of a provision that was initially meant to impose some obligations on the successor State, but was later completely diluted of its "binding" content. The successor State no longer has any obligation ("if particular circumstances so require") to actually repair the damage done. While the language had been significantly weakened, it seems that it was still too strong for Austria: "the purported rule seems to be based on the erroneous assumption of a transfer of responsibility between the predecessor and the successor state", adding that "the rule is vague and imprecise and fails to indicate elements that may help ascertain such particular circumstances".[673] In any event, under Guideline 9 the injured State merely has the possibility to reach an agreement with the successor State on the matter. While the parties concerned may very well reach such an agreement, they are certainly under no obligation to do so. If they do not, a wrongful act could remain unpunished.[674]

Third, the modification completely changes the very nature of both exceptions. Under Draft Article 7, the "organ" and the "direct link" exceptions were relevant to determine whether or not there could be a transfer of the obligation to repair to the successor State.[675] This is no longer the case. Now, the two exceptions are only useful in the context of a potential agreement reached between the concerned States.[676] This stems from the fact that when there is a direct link between a wrongful act (and its consequences) and the territory of

673 Austria, letter sent to the UN GA Sixth Committee, rep. 72nd sess. 2 Nov. 2021.

674 In fact, the continuing State is likely to reject any claim by the injured State precisely on the ground that there is a "direct link" between the consequences of the wrongful act and the territory of the successor State. It will argue that it is for the successor State to provide reparation to the injured State. If the injured State and the successor State do not reach an agreement on the matter, the wrongful act will remain unpunished.

675 Interestingly, Austria (letter sent to the UN GA Sixth Committee, rep. 72nd sess. 2 Nov. 2021) does not consider that these exceptions have anything to do with the question of transfer of obligations per se: "The examples of such particular circumstances given in paragraph 5 of the commentary, such as when an expropriated factory is situated in the territory of a successor state or when a successor state would be unjustly enriched, demonstrate that the resulting 'exceptional situation' is not at all a transfer of responsibility from the predecessor to the successor state. Rather, it may be a justified consequence of the rule calling for the avoidance of unjust enrichment". See also, letter sent to the UN GA Sixth Committee, rep. 70th sess. 30 Oct. 2018: "In our view, only in cases where a successor state acknowledges and adopts the unlawful acts of a predecessor state as its own, in line with Article 11 of the State Responsibility Articles, or is unjustly enriched as a consequence of such an act, the obligations arising from the internationally wrongful act of the predecessor state would be transferred to the successor state. However, it is doubtful whether this transfer of obligations is the consequence of a succession of states at all. Rather, it seems to be based on other rules of international law".

676 ILC, Commentaries, 2021, para 165, Art. 9, sub-para 4.

the successor State, the "predecessor State may not be in a position to address the injury alone and cooperation with the successor State may be necessary".[677] In other words, in these circumstances the injured State may want to address its claim to the successor State rather than the continuing State. Thus, the role and importance of both exceptions has been significantly downgraded.[678] They are now only useful to the injured State in assessing whether the "successor State may be relevant for addressing the injury".[679]

In sum, the overall impression is that Guideline 9(2) is much less efficient than Draft Article 7 in protecting the interests of injured States. The Chair of the Drafting Committee nevertheless explained that "the purpose of paragraph 2 is also to signal that the consequences of the internationally wrongful act do not disappear simply because of the succession of States".[680] That signal was indeed clear under the earlier draft Articles. They explicitly referred to the possibility of obligations being "assumed" or "transferred" to the successor State when there is a "direct link" or when the act was committed by an "organ" of a territorial unit. However, the wording used in Guideline 9(2) no longer "signals" any possible accountability. As a result of the modification, the real "purpose" of Guideline 9(2) is merely to express "the possibility of an agreement between the successor State and the injured State" regarding the consequences of wrongful acts committed before independence.[681]

Yet, as noted by one ILC member, "the fact that a successor State might have the possibility to 'raise the issue of reparation' did not mean that the predecessor State no longer had that possibility".[682] What was the "rule" in such a case? Who was entitled to reparation? He rightly noted that "there was a risk that that question would be overlooked as a result of the shift of focus from a substantive rule of succession to the procedural possibility of seeking reparation".[683] Thus instead of focusing on this procedural aspect (the "possibility" of raising a claim), the emphasis should be on "identifying a general

677 Ibid.

678 But for some States, even this soft language was still suspicious. Thus, Austria, letter sent to the UN GA Sixth Committee, Rep. 72nd sess. 2021, had "serious concerns" about this provision and indicated that the "purported rule seemed to be based on the erreneous assumption of a transfer of responsibility between the predecessor and the successor State".

679 ILC, Commentaries, 2021, para 165, Art. 9, sub-para 5.

680 ILC, Statement, Grossman Guiloff, 2019, 8.

681 ILC, Commentaries, 2021, para 165, Art. 9, sub-para 1.

682 ILC, "Provisional Summary Record of the 3477th Meeting", 73rd sess., 10 July 2019, A/CN.4/SR.3477, statement by ILC Member Georg Nolte (Germany).

683 Ibid.

rule or specific rules of succession in respect of the substance of the claims in question".[684] This is indeed what should have been done. At the end of the day, what is striking is that Guideline 9(2) does not show the existence of any "rule" imposing any binding obligations on anyone. Moreover, as the Czech Republic noted in a statement to the Sixth Committee, it seems to suggest that both States have "an equal obligation" to try to reach an agreement, which seems unfair from the perspective of the injured State, the victim of a wrong.[685] The Czech Republic also stated that "It would be wrong to suggest that, in such situations, talks between the injured State and the successor State should start from a 'clean slate'", adding that "Paragraph 2 was thus disappointing and should be revisited, to strengthen and protect the position of the injured State".[686]

684 Ibid. See also: "It was unclear what purpose was served by recognizing a procedural position of successor States instead of identifying a general rule or specific rules of succession in respect of the substance of the claims in question. If there was no connection between the procedural position and the substance of the claim, different claimants would be able to seek reparation and the difficulty of determining entitlement would remain. However, if there was a connection between them, it should be clearly set out, particularly for the purpose of determining which State among several was entitled to reparation. The Special Rapporteur referred at times to the 'possibility' of raising a claim and, at other times, as in paragraph 60, to States' being 'entitled to reparation'. (…) Instead of evading the question of who was entitled to reparation in a case of State succession by recognizing only procedural 'possibilities to claim', the Commission should, in his view, more openly make proposals aimed at progressively developing the law on succession of States in respect of State responsibility".

685 Czech Rep., letter sent to the UN GA Sixth Committee, Rep. 71st sess., 6 Nov. 2019: "The injured State, let us not forget, is a victim of an internationally wrongful act of the predecessor State. The Successor State, even if having international legal personality distinct from that of the predecessor State, is not entirely 'out of the hook' as far as the material consequences of the said internationally wrongful act are concerned (…). In addition, the successor State cannot pretend that the problem is somehow 'res inter alios acta'. It would be wrong to suggest, that, in similar situation, the talks between the injured State and the successor State start around a 'tabula rasa' or from a 'clean slate'. Suggesting that both of these States have an equal obligation to simply [and I quote] 'endeavor to reach an agreement for addressing the injury' gives precisely this impression. The proposed paragraph 2 is disappointing and should be revisited. The position of the injured State must be strengthened and guaranteed much better".

686 ILC Special Rapporteur Šturma, Fourth Report, 2020, para 10, referring to a statement made by the Czech Rep., GA Sixth Committee, 74th sess., 32nd meeting, A/C.6/74/SR.32, para 101.

6.2 *The Continuing State Remains Responsible for Internationally Wrongful Acts Committed before the Date of Succession*

The principle that the continuing State continues its previous responsibility is well established by decisions of municipal courts.[687] It was adopted by municipal courts of the *new successor State*, for instance, in the *Dzierzbicki* case decided by the Supreme Court of Poland.[688] This was also the solution reached by the Supreme Court of Poland in two other decisions concluding that Austria was not a new State in 1917 and that, accordingly, it should be held accountable for the illegal acts committed by Austria-Hungary before that date.[689] The principle was also applied by one municipal court of the *continuing* State: the case of *Baron A. v. Prussian Treasury* decided by the German *Reichsgericht*.[690] These cases are examined in Section 6.2.2. It should be noted that these municipal law cases do *not* involve questions of succession to *international* responsibility. The wrongful acts were committed by the predecessor State not against another State (or a national of another State) but against *its own nationals* (which became nationals of the successor State after the date of succession).[691]

The review of State practice shows a clear tendency in support of the principle that whenever the predecessor State continues to exist after the separation of part of its territory, it should remain responsible for the commission of its own internationally wrongful acts. There are several examples supporting this principle. One is in the context of the break-up of the USSR (Section 6.2.4). In one treaty entered into with Germany in 1992, Russia (the continuing State) continued its responsibility for internationally wrongful acts committed by the USSR during and after the Second World War, namely the pillage of works of art and cultural property in Germany.[692] In another treaty signed with France in 1997, Russia continued its responsibility for measures of expropriation of

687 The same examples are also examined in: ILC Special Rapporteur Šturma, Second Report, 2018, paras 81ff; Kohen & Dumberry, 92ff.

688 *Dzierzbicki v. District Electric Association of Czestochowa*, Supreme Court, 1st Div. 21 Dec. 1933, *OSP*, 1934, no. 288, *AD* 1933–1934, 89.

689 *Niemiec & Niemiec v. Bialobrodziec and Polish State Treasury*, Supreme Court, 3rd Div., 20 February 1923, 2 *AD* case no. 33; *Olpinski v. Polish Treasury (Railway Division)*, Supreme Court, 3rd Div., 16 April 1921, *OSP*, I, no. 15, *AD* 1919–1922, 63.

690 *Baron A. v. Prussian Treasury*, Reichsgericht in Civil Matters, 19 December 1923, *ERZ*, v. 107, 382, *AD* 1923–1924, 60.

691 The reasons for treating these types of cases differently have been explained above: Part 1, Section 4.7.

692 Jakubowski, State Succession, 195–6, 267, recognising that this example is an illustration of this basic principle.

bonds issued in France which were taken by newly Soviet Russia after the 1917 Revolution. This principle is also supported by the official position taken by the authorities of the GDR, which held that it was not responsible for obligations arising from internationally wrongful acts committed before and during the Second World War (Section 6.2.3). The position taken by the "Allied and Associated Powers" in the context of the break-up of the Austria-Hungary Dual Monarchy (in 1918) also supports the principle of non-succession (Section 6.2.1). I will also examine a special case in the context of the separation of the Kingdom of the Netherlands from the French Empire in 1815 (Section 6.2.5). The separation of Montenegro in 2006 will be examined in Section 6.2.6.

6.2.1 The Position Taken by the Allies in the Context of the Break-up of the Austria-Hungary Dual Monarchy (1918)

The break-up of the Austria-Hungary Dual Monarchy after the First World War was considered by Austria a case of *dissolution* with itself being a new State.[693] On the contrary, the Allies (the "Allied and Associated Powers" or the "Entente Powers", i.e. the British Empire, France, Italy, Japan, US, etc.) held that this was not a case of dissolution, but one involving the *secession* of Poland, Czechoslovakia and Yugoslavia, with both Austria and Hungary being considered the continuing States of the Dual Monarchy. The Allies considered that post-War Austria and Hungary were both *identical* with the former Dual Monarchy.[694] Both States were therefore considered responsible for the internationally wrongful acts which had been committed during the War. This is clear from the *Peace Treaty of St. Germain* (entered into by the European Powers and Austria)[695] and from the separate peace treaties entered into in 1921 by the US with Austria[696] and with Hungary.[697] A Commission set up under a 1924 treaty[698] entered into by the US with Hungary and Austria specifically indicated that the other secessionist States (i.e. Poland, Czechoslovakia

693 This point was already discussed in Chapter 2, Section 4.2.2.

694 Marek, 220ff.

695 *Treaty of Peace between the Allied and Associated Powers and Austria; Protocol, Declaration and Special Declaration*, 10 September 1919, in force on 16 July 1920, *UKTS* 1919 No. 11 (Cmd. 400), see Art. 177.

696 *Treaty between the United States and Austria to establish Securely Friendly Relations between the two Nations, 24 August 1921*, 16 *AJIL* 1922, Suppl., 13–16.

697 *Treaty Establishing Friendly Relations between the United States of America and Hungary*, 29 August 1921, *USTS* n. 660; 16 *AJIL* 1922, Suppl., 13–16.

698 Agreement, 26 Nov. 1924, in *LNTS* v. 48, 70; *UNRIAA* v. VI, 199.

and Yugoslavia) should bear no responsibility for internationally wrongful acts committed during the War.[699]

This example shows (at least from the perspective of the Allies) that a continuing State continues its responsibility for its own acts which took place before the date of succession.

6.2.2 Polish and German Court Cases in the Context of the Secession of Poland (1918)

After Poland became an independent State in 1918,[700] a few cases decided by the courts of the new State dealt with issues of State succession to responsibility. These cases support the principle that the continuing State remains responsible for the commission of its own internationally wrongful acts on the territory that has since then seceded.[701] Some writers have, however, analysed these cases as an illustration that the successor State is not bound by the obligations arising from internationally wrongful acts committed by the predecessor State except when it has expressly recognised them.[702]

In the *Dzierzbicki* case, the Supreme Court of Poland dealt with a claim arising from an accident caused by the Russian railway authorities in a territory which was at the time still part of the Russian Empire.[703] The Court concluded that the new State of Poland should not bear any responsibility for the internationally wrongful acts committed by the predecessor State (Russia) against a Polish national:

> In accordance with the views of the contemporary science of international law, the new State is not the legal successor of the previous State

699 *Administrative Decision no. 1*, 25 May 1927, Tripartite Claims Commission, *UNRIAA* v. VI, 203, 210.

700 See, A. Wyrozumska, "The Role of Polish Courts in the Development of International Law after Regaining Independence by Poland in 1918", 9(1) *Polish Rev. Int. & Eur. L* 2020, 73–97, examining domestic court cases where Poland was considered instead as the same State as the one existing before its partition in the 18th Century.

701 Ibid 81–2.

702 This is the position of Czaplinski, 349, analysing the *Dzierzbicki case*. The *Niemiec* case is interpreted by O'Connell, Recent Problems, 163, as showing that after its independence "Poland did not become liable for the wrongs of its predecessor". See also: O'Connell, State Succession, v. I, 493. For Barde, 188, this last case confirms his position that there is no succession to responsibility if the obligation to repair is not liquidated before the date of succession.

703 *Dzierzbicki v. District Electric Association of Czestochowa*, Supreme Court, 1st Div. 21 Dec. 1933, *OSP*, 1934, no. 288, *AD* 1933–1934, 89. A sum was awarded by a Russian Court in Warsaw in April 1914.

> from which it took over part of the territory, and is responsible for the charges and debts only insofar as it has expressly assumed them. There is no reason for not applying this principle to the obligations of the partitioning power arising from the responsibility for damage and losses caused in the course of running railways.[704]

In several other cases, the Supreme Court of Poland frequently held that the Polish State Treasury was not bound to pay damages on account of accidents involving State railways which, at the time of the incident, belonged to Austria-Hungary. It held that Austria was not a new State and that it was the "continuator" of the Dual Monarchy's previous responsibility. This principle was applied in the case of *Niemiec and Niemiec v. Bialobrodziec and Polish State Treasury*.[705] The same solution was also reached by the Supreme Court of Poland in the *Olpinski* case.[706]

Finally, the same principle was also applied by a German court in the context of a delict that took place in 1913 in a territory which was then part of Germany and later became Polish.[707] The German *Reichsgericht* found that Poland was

704 Ibid. The Court also stated: "The Polish State is entirely free of obligations which were incumbent upon any of the partitioning powers with the exception of such obligations as the Polish State had itself assumed". The Court noted that under the peace treaty of Riga entered into by Russia and Poland the new Polish State did not accept responsibility for such obligations.

705 *Niemiec and Niemiec v. Bialobrodziec and Polish State Treasury*, Supreme Court, 3rd Div. 20 February 1923, 2 *AD* 1923–1924, case no. 33, 64. In this case, an incident took place in 1917 in a territory then part of Austria-Hungary where the plaintiffs' building was destroyed by a fire which had allegedly been caused by sparks from the engine of a passing train belonging to Austria's State railways.

706 *Olpinski v. Polish Treasury (Railway Division)*, Supreme Court, 3rd Div., 16 April 1921, *OSP*, I, no. 15, *AD* 1919–1922, 63. In this case, an individual had suffered damage in August 1918 caused by the conductor of a train in a territory that was still under Austria-Hungary rule. After the independence of Poland, the plaintiff sued the Polish Treasury on the ground that the Polish State took over Austria-Hungary's State railways on its territory. The Court of First Instance and the Court of Appeal gave judgments in favour of the plaintiff based, *inter alia*, on the principle of legal continuity, according to which the new State takes over obligations localised in territories which it acquired. The two lower courts also rendered their decisions based on the ground that a new State cannot take over assets without taking over liabilities. The Supreme Court of Poland rejected the claim and decided that the plaintiff would have to file suit against the Austrian railway since this State continued to exist after 1918.

707 *Baron A. v. Prussian Treasury*, Reichsgericht in Civil Matters, 19 Dec. 1923, *ERZ*, v. 107, 382, *AD* 1923–1924, 60. This case involved an action introduced in 1913 by the legal predecessor of the plaintiff (the owner of some landed property) against the Prussian State for damage caused to him in consequence of some irrigation works undertaken by Prussia. The

not responsible for the sum awarded by a German court for internationally wrongful acts committed by the authorities of Prussia when the territory was still part of Germany.[708]

6.2.3 German Democratic Republic (1949)

As previously observed,[709] questions of State succession to obligations arising from internationally wrongful acts committed before 1949 do not arise in the context of the Federal Republic of Germany, as it is considered the legal "continuator" of the German Reich. The issue only arises with respect to the German Democratic Republic (GDR). The official position of the GDR concerning its legal status is confused, as it was modified several times.[710] Its final position was adopted in 1956. The GDR was of the view that there were two different *new* States in Germany and that both States were *successor States* to the German Reich, which had disappeared.[711] The GDR therefore believed that this was a case of a dissolution of a State. The prevailing view, however, was that in 1949 the GDR was a new State which had in effect "seceded" from the German Reich.[712] While this position is adopted in the present study, it is also clear that the example of the GDR is very complex and that many other interpretations

case was decided in favour of the plaintiff by the District Court of Danzig (May 1913) and by the Court of Marienwerder (Prussia, June 1920).

708 Prussia contended that, *inter alia*, as the land in question was now situated in Poland, the latter should be held responsible for the amount claimed by the plaintiff and that German courts could not assume jurisdiction in an action that was in fact against a foreign State. The German Court indicated that in accordance with Art. 256 of the *Versailles Treaty* Poland acquired all the property of Germany and of the German State in the ceded territories. However, it also indicated that Poland, in the absence of a special agreement, was not responsible for the payment of the sum claimed by the plaintiff.

709 This point is discussed in: Chapter 2, Section 2.3.1.

710 The official position, case law and scholarship are discussed in: B. Guerin, *L'évolution du statut juridique de l'Allemagne de 1945 au traité fundamental* (Droste 1978) 97–105. During a first period (1949–1951), the GDR considered itself to be *identical* with the German Reich. At the time, the GDR viewed itself as representing Germany as a whole. This position was radically changed by decisions of the District Court of Appeal ("*Oberlandesgericht*"), on 18 June 1951 (*NJ* 1951, 468ff) and 31 October 1951 (*NJ* 1952, 222ff), where it was held that the German Reich had disappeared as a result of the War by *debellatio*. According to this new position, the GDR was a different State and, most importantly, it was *not a successor State*. This position prevailed until 1956.

711 Guerin, ibid, 109ff, provides many examples illustrating this new position of the GDR.

712 Oeter, 350–351, explains that the dominant interpretation in scholarship is that the GDR had in fact seceded but that the secession was "provisional" and not "final" since no final settlement on the status of Germany had been reached. He quotes many writers supporting this view. This is also the position of K. Heilbronner, "Legal Aspects of the Unification of the Two German States", 2 *EJIL* 1991, 21, indicating that "the process of German division

are possible. It could even be argued that this is not a case of State succession at all.

One question which arose at the time was whether the GDR (as a new successor State) should be held responsible for the obligations arising from internationally wrongful acts committed by Nazi Germany.[713] The official position taken by the authorities of the GDR was that it was a new State "ideologically" totally different from the predecessor State and that, consequently, it could not be held responsible for obligations arising from internationally wrongful acts committed by the German Reich. One illustration is the position adopted by the GDR with respect to the claim submitted by Libya for compensation for damages arising from the presence of remnants of the Second World War on its territory. The GDR refused to cooperate with Libya on the ground that it could not be held accountable for the acts committed by the Third Reich.[714] The FRG was responsible for these acts. Two other examples will be examined below which may be interpreted as exceptions to the official position taken by the GDR.[715]

6.2.4 Union of Soviet Socialist Republics (199)

6.2.4.1 *Introduction*

The break-up of the USSR was officially completed at the end of 1991 with the establishment of the "Commonwealth of Independent States" (CIS).[716] It was agreed among the former Republics (with the exception of the three Baltic States) that Russia would be considered the "continuator" of the international legal personality of the USSR in international organizations, including the United Nations.[717] The legal qualification of the dismemberment of the USSR

---

and secession of the GDR remained provisional until a final settlement on Germany as a whole could be achieved with the Four Powers".

713 See, Bert-Wolfgang Eichhorn, *Reparation als völkerrechtliche Deliktshaftung: Rechtliche und praktische Probleme unter besonderer Berücksichtigung Deutschlands (1918–1990)* (Nomos 1992).

714 Ali Dawi, *Les problèmes juridiques internationaux posés par les restes matériels des guerres, notamment en Libye*, doctoral thesis, Université d'Orléans (France), 1994, 105.

715 These examples are discussed below: Chapter 2, Sections 6.3.3 and 6.3.4.

716 The CIS was first formed by Russia, Belarus and Ukraine on the basis of the *Minsk* agreement: *The Agreement Establishing the Commonwealth of Independent States*, 13 December 1991, A/46/771, 31 *ILM* 1992, 138. As a result of the *Declaration of Alma Ata*, 21 December 1991, A/47/60, 31 *ILM* 1992, 147, the CIS was expanded to other former Republics (except for the Baltic States), with Georgia joining in October 1993.

717 *Declaration of Alma Ata*, ibid. See also: *Decision by the Council of Heads of State of the Commonwealth of Independent States*, 21 December 1991, 31 *ILM* 1992, 151; Letter of Russia's President Yeltsin to the UN Secretary-General, 24 December 1991, 1991/RUSSIA (24 December 1991), Appendix, 31 *ILM* 1992, 138.

in 1991 is controversial.[718] It has been suggested by many writers that because Russia is the continuing State of the USSR, all other former Republics (with the exception of the Baltic States) seceded from the Union.[719] The affirmation that Russia is the continuing State of the USSR is clearly based on a legal fiction.[720] Thus, the USSR did, in fact, cease to exist in 1991 as a result of both the Declaration of Alma Ata and the Minsk Agreement.[721] Logically, Russia could not continue the existence of a State which had ceased to exist;[722] there is no "resurrection" of State in international law.[723] It could therefore be argued that the break-up of the USSR is a case of dissolution.[724] Yet, it may be that these statements were merely *political* and not meant to result in the actual dissolution of the USSR.[725] In any event, the fact remains that all States concerned (including Russia itself) have viewed Russia as the *continuing State* of the USSR. Thus, in their *actual practice*, States have considered the break-up of the USSR as a series of "secessions" by the former Soviet Republics (but not the three Baltic States). This is indeed the position adopted by most writers[726] and the one reached by the ILC[727] and the Institute.[728] Several domestic

---

718 This question is examined in detail in: I. Ziemele, "Is the Distinction between State Continuity and State Succession Reality or Fiction? The Russian Federation, the Federal Republic of Yugoslavia and Germany", 1 *Baltic YIL* 2001, 194.

719 W. Czaplinski, "La continuité, l'identité et la succession d'États-évaluation de cas récents", 26 *RBDI* 1993, 388; Photini Pazartzis, *La succession d'Etats aux traités multilatéraux à la lumière des mutations territoriales récentes* (Pedone 2002) 55–56.

720 Pierre Michel Eisemann, "Rapport du Directeur de la section de langue française du Centre", in Eisemann & Koskenniemi, 40; Eric Wyler, "Le droit de la succession d'États à l'épreuve de la fiction juridique", in G. Distephano, G. Gaggioli & A. Heche (eds), *La Convention de Vienne de 1978 sur la succession d'États en matière de traités : Commentaire article par article et études thématiques* (Bruylant 2015) 1632.

721 The preamble to the *Minsk Agreement* clearly states that the USSR "as a subject of international law and geopolitical reality no longer exists". The *Declaration of Alma Ata* also mentions that "with the establishment of the CIS, the USSR ceases to exist".

722 For this reason, some writers have argued that Russia is *not* the "continuator" of the USSR but a new State: R. Rich, "Recognition of States: The Collapse of Yugoslavia and the Soviet Union", 4(1) *EJIL* 1993, 45; Y.Z. Blum, "Russia Takes over the Soviet Union's Seat at the United Nations", 3(2) *EJIL* 1992, 357–359.

723 Marek, 6.

724 Stern, Succession, 220–222.

725 M. Shaw, "State Succession Revisited", 5 *Finnish YIL* 1994, 49–50; J. Crawford, *The Creation of States in International Law* (2nd ed. OUP 2006) 677–678.

726 See, Anne Østrup, "The Dissolution of the USSR", in: Jure Vidmar, Sarah McGibbon & Lea Raible (eds), *Research Handbook on Secession* (Elgar 2022) 237ff.

727 ILC Special Rapporteur Šturma, Second Report, 2018, paras 86–88.

728 Kohen & Dumberry, 92.

court decisions have also considered Russia as the continuing State of the USSR.[729]

The first two relevant examples of State practice are treaties entered into by Russia with, on the one hand, Germany, and, on the other hand, France, whereby it (as the continuing State of the USSR) continued its responsibility for the internationally wrongful acts committed by the USSR during and after the Second World War and by Russia after the 1917 Revolution. The third example deals with a Lithuanian law requesting compensation from Russia, as the continuing State, for damage resulting from its annexation and occupation by the USSR (1940–1990). These three examples illustrate the principle that whenever a State does not cease to exist as a result of territorial transformations, it should remain responsible for wrongful acts it committed in the past.[730]

6.2.4.2 *The Pillage of Works of Art and Cultural Property in Germany during and after the Second World War*

During the Second World War, German troops seized numerous works of art in each of the occupied territories and brought them to Germany. The pillage, as well as the destruction, was particularly important in the territory of the USSR. The victory of the Red Army in 1945 was also followed by the pillage of works of art and cultural property in Germany. It is thus estimated that more than 2.5 million works of art were transferred from Germany to the Soviet Union at the time.[731] Some of these works of art were returned to the German

729 See, Guido Acquaviva, "Russia as the State Continuing the Legal Personality of the USSR: An Inquiry into State Identity or Succession", 23 *J. Hist. IL* 2021, 315ff.

730 It should be added that ILC Special Rapporteur Šturma, Fifth Report, 2021, para 45, refers to a decision of the Supreme Court of Justice of Austria, 1Ob149/02x, 30 September 2002. The case is also mentioned in a letter (dated February 2022) sent by Austria in reply to a request by the ILC for relevant documentation. The case dealt with a claim filed by an Austrian citizen for compensation from Austria because of a "(quasi) expropriation" act (his arrest by the Soviet occupying forces in 1952 and subsequent detention at a Soviet military prison). According to the translation contained in the letter, the Court "held that according to the rules of international law there was no legal succession into personal rights and duties in the area of state responsibility. When a sovereign state ceased to exist, its responsibility under international law for the internationally wrongful act committed by this state was also extinguished". While this passage is clearly in favor of non-succession, it is very much an *obiter dictum* considering that the Court was dealing with a situation of legal continuity between the USSR and Russia. At the end of the day, the relevance of this case is limited given that the Court rendered its decision without examining any relevant State succession issue.

731 An official 1958 statement by the Central Committee of the Communist Party of the Soviet Union refers to some "2,614,874 objects of art and culture located in the USSR". During the 1994 negotiations between Russia and Germany, the latter listed some two

Democratic Republic in the 1950s and 1960s.[732] Up until recently, the content and the location of these treasures remained largely unknown.

Before the break-up of the USSR, two treaties were entered into on 9 November 1990 between the USSR and the Federal Republic of Germany.[733] The substance of Article 16 of the *1990 German-Soviet Union Good-Neighbourliness Treaty*[734] was later reaffirmed in a *Cultural Agreement* entered into in 1992 (i.e. after the break-up of the Soviet Union) between Germany and Russia, where the parties committed to the restitution of cultural property which was "lost" or "unlawfully brought into the territory" of Russia.[735] This provision contains the commitment by Russia (as the continuing State of the USSR) to provide reparation to Germany (in the form of the restitution of German cultural property) as a result of internationally wrongful acts committed by the Soviet Union (i.e. the cultural property "unlawfully brought" into its territory).[736] A dispute arose between the two States concerning the interpretation of the 1992 Treaty. In 1997, a Russian law was passed stating that all cultural properties brought to

---

hundred thousand works of art, two million books as well as three kilometres of archives to be restituted to museums, libraries, archives and collections in Germany (see para 4 of the Bonn Protocol of 30 June 1994). See, Wilfried Fiedler, "Legal Issues Bearing on the Restitution of German Cultural Property in Russia", in: E. Simpson (ed), *The Spoils of War-World War II and its Aftermath: the Loss, Reappearance, and Recovery of Cultural Property* (Harry N. Abrams 1997) 175–180.

732 This aspect is discussed in Section 6.3.3.

733 *Treaty between the Federal Republic of Germany and the Union of Soviet Socialist Republics on Good-Neighbourliness Partnership and Cooperation*, 9 Nov. 1990, 30 *ILM* 1991, 505; *RGDIP* 1991, 214. *Treaty on the Development of Comprehensive Cooperation in the Field of Trade, Industry, Science and Technology*, 9 Nov. 1990, *BGBl.* 1991, v. II, 700.

734 Art. 16 of the Treaty reads as follows: "The FRG and the USSR will seek to ensure the preservation of cultural treasures of the other side in their territory. They agree that missing or unlawfully removed art treasures which are located in their territory will be returned to the owners or their legal successors".

735 *Abkommen Zwischen der Regierung der Bundesrepublik Deutschland und der Regierung der Russischen Föderation über kulturelle Zusammenarbeit*, 16 Dec. 1992, *BGBl.*, 1993, v. II, 1256, see Art. 15.

736 Crawford, State Responsibility, 453. More generally, see: Wilfried Fiedler, "Legal Issues Bearing on the Restitution of German Cultural Property in Russia", in: E. Simpson (ed), *The Spoils of War-World War II and its Aftermath: the Loss, Reappearance, and Recovery of Cultural Property* (Harry N. Abrams 1997) 175–180; A. Hiller, "The German-Russian Negotiation over the Content of the Russian Repositories", in: Simpson, ibid; A. Gattini, "Restitution by Russia of Works of Art Removed from German Territory at the End of the Second World War", 7(1) *EJIL* 1996, 66–88; Stephan Wilske, "International Law and the Spoils of War: To the Victor the Right of Spoils?: The Claims for Repatriation of Art Removed from Germany by the Soviet Army During or as a Result of World War II", 3 *UCLA JILFA* 1998, 223.

Russia as a result of the Second World War were now properties of the Russian Federation and that, consequently, no restitution (with some exceptions) would be made to Germany.[737] Apparently, some restitution were made, but only on an *ex gratia* basis.[738]

I have found another example involving pillage which shows that the continuing State remains responsible for wrongful acts it committed before the date of succession. The case involves archives religious documents belonging to the Lubavitch Chasidim Jewish community.[739] They were originally located in the Russian Empire before the First World War and subsequently moved to Poland before the Second World War. Later during the War, they were taken by German troops from occupied Poland to Germany. Finally, after the War they were illegally relocated to the USSR as war booty. As the Court noted, "Soviet Army's 1945 seizure and appropriation of the Archive from its Nazi captors as spoils of war" was a "taking in violation of international law".[740] After fruitless efforts with the Russian authorities in the 1990s to recover the documents, and also books, the claimant filed a claim in 2004 before US courts against, *inter alia*, Russia. The judicial saga involves complicated aspects of US law applicable to matters of sovereign immunity that are beyond the scope of this book. Suffice it to note that the Court entered a default judgment against Russia in 2010, ordering it to return the materials. What is relevant for the present purpose is the fact that the Court never questioned that Russia was the proper respondent in these proceedings and that it was responsible for wrongful acts committed by the Soviet Union decades ago (well before the break-up of that country) and for not returning the documents. The judgment simply noted

---

737 *Federal Law on Cultural Values Removed to the USSR as a Result of World War II and Located in the Territory of the Russian Federation*, 5 February 1997, in: *Spoils of War, International Newsletter*, no. 4, August 1997, 10–19. See, Pierre D'Argent, "La loi russe sur les biens culturels transférés: Beutekunst, agression, réparations et contre-mesures", *AFDI* 1998, 114–143; Gattini, ibid. The constitutionality of the law was upheld by the Russian Constitutional Court in its Decision of 20 July 1999. See, Alexander Blankenagel, "Eyes Wide Shut: Displaced Cultural Objects in Russian Law and Adjudication", 8(4) *East Eur. Const. Rev.* 1999, 75–80.

738 Jakubowski, State Succession, 196. See, W. Eichwede, "Trophy Art as Ambassadors: Reflections Beyond Diplomatic Deadlock in the German-Russian Dialogue", 17 *Int. J. Cult. Prop.* 2010, 387–412; P. Grimsted, "Russian Legal Instruments Relating to Cultural Valuables Displaced as a Result of the Second World War, 1990–2009", 17 *Int. J. Cult. Prop.* 2010.

739 *Agudas Chasidei Chabad v. Russian Federation*, US Dist. Court DC, 466 F. Supp. 2d 6, 10–12 (DDC 2006), discussed in: Irina Tarsis & Elizabeth Varner, "Reviewing the Agudas Chasidei Chabad v. Russian Federation, et al. Dispute", 18(8) *ASIL Insight*, 19 March 2014.

740 Ibid.

that "The Soviet Union dissolved on December 25, 1991, and was replaced by the Russian Federation".

Similarly, another case before US courts involved a claim by the plaintiffs' relatives who were Polish Army officers who had been executed in the Katyn Forest by the Soviet Union army during World War II.[741] While the Court dismissed the claim against Russia because it was entitled to immunity under the Foreign Sovereign Immunities Act ("FSIA"), no one disputed the fact that, as the continuing State, it could be held responsible for such wrongful acts. In fact, the judgement simply noted that "Plaintiffs now bring claims against the Russian Federation, as successor to the Soviet Union", adding that the "parties do not contest the Russian Federation's status as a successor to the Soviet Union". In the context of this case, the term "successor" was clearly a reference to Russia being the "continuator" State.

6.2.4.3 *Measures of Expropriation of French Bonds after the 1917 Revolution*

Private and public pre-revolutionary Russian bonds issued in France were nationalised as a result of the Russian Revolution of 1917. Since then, the USSR had always refused to compensate the hundreds of thousands of private owners of bonds on the ground that the revolutionary Soviet government was not bound by the debts contracted by the previous Tsarist government.

The 1917 Revolution led not only to a radical change of form of government but also to some important losses of territory. The changes have traditionally been analysed from the angle of a *succession of government*, whereby the new revolutionary government was held to be bound by the international obligations undertaken by the previous monarchist government.[742] These

741 *Kozorowski et al. v. The Russian Federation et al.*, 19 September 1997, No. 93–16388.

742 The firm position of Western States on this question is well-illustrated by this 1921 official communication from the British government to Mr Krassin, the agent of the Soviet Union in London: "The first [question] is that of the acceptance by the Soviet Government of the obligations which had been entered into and were binding upon previous Government in Russia. The accepted rule among civilized States is that contracts made by and debts incurred by a Government are to be regarded as the obligations of the nation it represented and not as the personal engagements of the ruler. Although the form of Government may change, the people remain bound" (in: Lord McNair, *International Law Opinions*, v. I (CUP 1956) 9). The same position is also clearly expressed in the British-French joint declaration of 28 March 1918: "Aucun principe n'est mieux établi que celui d'après lequel une nation est responsable des actes de son gouvernement sans qu'un changement d'autorité affecte les obligations encourues: ces engagements ne peuvent être répudiés par aucune autorité, quelle qu'elle soit, sans quoi la base même du droit international se trouverait ébranlée" (in: Paul Fauchille, *Traité de droit international public*, v. I (8th edn, A. Rousseau 1922) 342). See, Marek, 34ff.

transformations can also be viewed as a problem of *succession of States*. Thus, the USSR (which was officially created in 1922) did not have the same territory as the Russian Empire just before the Revolution.[743] At any rate, from 1922 on the USSR should certainly be viewed as the *continuing State* of the Russian State which emerged from the 1917 Revolution. Consequently, it should be held responsible for the acts committed in Russia between 1917 and 1922 (including any measures of expropriation).

A final settlement of reciprocal financial and property demands was signed by the Federation of Russia and France on 27 May 1997.[744] The agreement provided that Russia pay France US$ 400 million in exchange for both signatories giving up financial and property claims (which arose before May 1945) on their own behalf or on behalf of their nationals (corporations and individuals).[745] Even if the measures of expropriation taken by the Soviet authorities against French property, rights and assets without any compensation were undoubtedly internationally wrongful acts,[746] the settlement reached between the Parties is, however, clearly *ex gratia* in the sense that Russia does not recognise

743 In 1922, the Soviet Union was comprised of four Soviet Republics: Russia, Ukraine, Byelorussia and the "Transcaucasian Soviet Federated Socialist Republic" (which existed from 1922 to 1936 and included Georgia, Armenia and Azerbaijan). It no longer included Bessarabia which had been transferred to Romania. Also, new States were created on what used to be the territory of the Empire (Poland, the Baltic States, Finland, etc.).

744 *Accord du 27 mai 1997 entre le Gouvernement de la République française et le Gouvernement de la Fédération de Russie sur le règlement définitif des créances réciproques financières et réelles apparues antérieurement au 9 mai 1945*. The Agreement and the Memorandum of 26 November 1996 for mutual understanding were approved by the French National Assembly on 19 December 1997 (Bill No. 97–1160, *JORF* 15 May 1998). See, Sandra Szurek, "Épilogue d'un contentieux historique. L'accord sur le règlement des créances réciproques entre la France et la Russie", 44 *AFDI* 1998, 144–166; P. Juillard & B. Stern (eds), *Les emprunts russes et le règlement du contentieux financier franco-russe* (Cahiers internationaux n°16 2002) and, in particular, Eisemann, Emprunts russes, 53–78.

745 The Agreement covers the following type of claims: all loans and bonds issued/guaranteed to the French government or French individuals (including corporations) by the Government of the Russian Empire before 7 November 1917; claims concerning interests and assets based in territories ruled by the Government of the Russian Empire and subsequent governments to which the French government or private and legal persons were deprived of property or ownership rights. A French Commission was set up to deal with the compensation procedure.

746 On this question, Payam Shahrjerdi, "L'indemnisation à raison des mesures soviétiques de nationalisation ou d'expropriation à l'encontre de biens français", in: P. Juillard & B. Stern (eds), *Les emprunts russes et le règlement du contentieux financier franco-russe* (Cahiers internationaux n°16 2002) 89–120. This is also the position of Eisemann, Emprunts russes, 53–78.

any legal responsibility for the acts committed after the 1917 Revolution.[747] In this agreement, Russia is therefore viewed as the continuing State of the Soviet Union,[748] which was itself the "continuator" of the Russian State existing between 1917 and 1922.[749]

6.2.4.4 *The Lithuanian* Law on Compensation of Damage Resulting from the Occupation by the USSR

As a result of the unlawful Soviet occupation which started in 1940 and last until independence, the *de jure* statehood of the three Baltic States remained in place and, accordingly, they are not considered to be "successor" States.[750] This is indeed the position which was put forward by Judge Ziemele in her dissenting opinion in *Andrejeva v. Latvia*,[751] and which has since then been endorsed by the ECHR.[752]

Lithuania passed in June 2000 a *Law on Compensation of Damage Resulting from the Occupation by the USSR*.[753] The Law provides that Lithuania will submit

747 Art. 7 of the Agreement of 27 May 1997 reads as follows: "Le versement de la somme mentionnée à l'article 3 du présent Accord n'est pas réputé valoir reconnaissance par l'une ou l'autre Partie de l'existence d'une responsabilité lui incombant au titre de quelque créance que ce soit réglée par le présent Accord, ni valoir confirmation de la réalité juridique de l'une quelconque desdites créances". See, Sandra Szurek, "Epilogue d'un contentieux historique. L'accord sur le règlement des créances réciproques entre la France et la Russie", 44 *AFDI* 1998, 157.

748 Crawford, State Responsibility, 452–3.

749 Eisemann, Emprunts russes, 76–77, refers to the automatic transmission to the Russian Federation of all international responsibility of the USSR because it is its "continuator". He also notes that even if Russia was not considered to be the continuing State of the USSR, the international responsibility of that State (including the consequences for the commission of internationally wrongful acts) would pass in equitable proportion to the new States (including Russia).

750 L. Mälksoo, *Illegal Annexation and State Continuity: The Case of the Incorporation of the Baltic States by the USSR* (Martinus Nijhoff 2003) 255–256.

751 *Andrejeva v. Latvia*, ECHR, Appli. 55707/00, judgment, 18 February 2009, diss. op. Judge Ziemele.

752 See, *Case of Savickis and Others v. Latvia*, App. 49270/11, Judgment, 9 June 2022, at paras 104–106.

753 *Valstybės žinios*, 2000 No. 52–1486, Law VIII–1727, 13 June 2000, in: *Foreign Power, Excerpts from Lithuanian Laws on Communism, Occupation, Resistance*, paper of the Seimas (Parliament) of the Republic of Lithuania, 2000, 32. See, Dainius Zalimas, "Commentary on the Law of the Republic of Lithuania on Compensation of Damage Resulting from the Occupation of the USSR", 3 *Baltic YIL* 2003, 97–163. More generally, see: L. Mälksoo, *Illegal Annexation and State Continuity: The Case of the Incorporation of the Baltic States by the USSR* (Martinus Nijhoff 2003) 258–263; Rytis Satkauskas, "A Bill for the Occupants or an Issue to negotiate?: the Claims of Reparations for Soviet Occupation", 3 *Baltic YIL* 2003, 77–96; Lauri Maelksoo, "State Responsibility and the Challenge of the Realist

an estimate of damages inflicted by the Soviet occupation and start negotiations with Russia for compensation. Whether or not Russia ends up paying,[754] what matters for the present purpose is that Lithuania considers Russia as the continuing State of the USSR and therefore that it remains responsible for its wrongful acts committed during the period 1940–1990.[755]

6.2.5 Kingdom of the Netherlands (1815)

The Kingdom of Holland, an independent State, was formally annexed by the French Empire in 1810 (it had already been under French domination for quite some time).[756] Holland regained its independence in 1815 with the creation of the Kingdom of the Netherlands (consisting of modern day Netherlands, Belgium and Luxembourg).

After the independence of the Kingdom of the Netherlands, the US brought several claims against the Netherlands (as the successor State) for damage suffered by US ships as a result of their seizure in Dutch ports in 1809 and 1810.[757] It is important to note that these internationally wrongful acts were committed *before* the date of the Kingdom of Holland's formal annexation by France in July 1810 but, at any rate, at the time of strong French domination.[758]

Paradigm: the Demand of Baltic Victims of Soviet Mass Repressions for Compensation from Russia", 3 *Baltic YIL* 2003, 57–76; Ineta Ziemele, "State Continuity, Succession and Responsibility: Reparations to the Baltic States and their Peoples" 3 *Baltic YIL* 2003, 165–189; Nika Bruskina, "Compensation for Damages Sustained by Natural Persons during World War II on Account of Acts of Nazi Germany: Practice of Lithuanian Courts in Light of International Law and European Union Law", 11 *Baltic YIL* 2011, 113–134.

754 A. Avdeev, "Russian-Lithuanian Relations: An Overview", 2(6) *Lithuanian Foreign Pol. Rev.* 2000, 27–33, 29.

755 The preamble to the Law indicates that "according to international law, the Russian Federation is the state continuing the rights and obligations of the USSR".

756 Prior to this formal annexation, the region was already under strong French influence since 1795 as an aftermath of the French Revolution. After that date, Holland remained nonetheless an independent State known as the Batavian Republic. In 1806 Napoleon Bonaparte compelled the Batavian Republic to "request" Louis Napoleon Bonaparte (Napoleon Bonaparte's brother) to accept the crown of the newly founded Kingdom of Holland. This period of direct French domination lasted for four years until Louis Napoleon Bonaparte abdicated on 1 July 1810. The Kingdom of Holland was formally annexed into France by a Royal Decree of 9 July 1810.

757 For discussion: Monnier, 74–75; O'Connell, State Succession, v. I, 486; Rousseau, v. III, 506; Atlam, 205; Volkovitsch, 2178, 2181. For a complete history of the events that led to the claim (as well as the negotiations which followed): Letter of US Secretary of State, Mr Fish, to Mr de Westenberg, 9 April 1873, in: Francis Wharton, *A Digest of the International Law of the United States*, v. II (1888) 50ff. See also, Moore, History, v. V, 4473–4476.

758 The fact that the events took place before July 1810 is clear from this passage of the letter dated 9 April 1873, ibid: "During these frequent changes, and *mainly during the last*

A series of correspondence followed between representatives of the US and the Kingdom of the Netherlands. The US took the view that the new State was responsible for obligations arising from the internationally wrongful acts.[759] In response, the Kingdom of the Netherlands indicated that at the time of the commission of the acts, "Holland had ceased for a long time to form an independent State" and that it was in effect under a foreign State's occupation. In its view, the Kingdom of the Netherlands could not be held responsible for acts which had been, in fact, committed by the French authorities.[760] Faced with this firm denial of responsibility from the Kingdom of the Netherlands, the US finally decided to drop the claims a few years later.[761]

Subsequently, the owners of the ships that had been seized took their case before a US internal commission which had been established by the Convention of 4 July 1831 between France and the US.[762] In 1831, the commission ruled in favour of the claimants and held France responsible for damages.[763]

This case has been interpreted by some as an example supporting the view that a new State should not be held responsible for obligations arising from internationally wrongful acts committed by the predecessor State and that the continuing State should remain responsible for such acts.[764] The particular

---

two years of the reign of Louis Bonaparte, several vessels of the US and their cargoes were seized and condemned or confiscated in the port which had before then formed the territorial domain of their High Mightiness the States-General" (emphasis added).

759 Letter of US Secretary of State John Quincy Adams dated 10 August 1818, quoted in: Letter dated 9 April 1873, ibid 53: "The rights and obligations of a nation in regard to the other States are independent of its internal revolution of government (...) [A]nd when the King of the Netherlands came to the sovereignty of the country he assumed with it the obligation of repairing the injustices against other nations which had been committed by his predecessor, however free from all participation in them he had been himself".

760 Letter of Baron de Nazel dated 14 June 1819, quoted in: Letter dated 9 April 1873, ibid 51: "The principle that the present Government of the Netherlands is responsible for all the acts of the predeceding Governments from 1795 to 1813, is one which the King cannot admit without restriction. If it might be admitted in regard to a succession of legitimate Governments, it could not be in regard to a Government established by violence, and which was not itself responsible for the acts to which it was forced by a foreign usurper; that the political nullity of this Government has long been a matter of public notoriety".

761 Thus, US Secretary of State Fish explained in a letter written many years after the events (and dealing with another matter) that the US finally accepted the view held by the Kingdom of the Netherlands that it was, indeed, a new State and that it had no continuity with the previous State: Letter dated 9 April 1873, ibid 51.

762 The history and the functioning of this commission can be found in: Moore, History, v. v, 4447ff, see at 4460.

763 This case is discussed in: Moore, ibid 4473–4476.

764 This is the position held by Monnier, 74–75; Keith, 74–75. *Contra*: Volkovitsch, 2181.

feature of this case is, however, that the acts had not been committed (at least formally) by the predecessor State (France) but by the Kingdom of Holland (which was formally annexed by France after the events).

There is another possible interpretation of this example. It is an illustration of the principle that France (the continuing State) should remain responsible for the internationally wrongful acts committed *before* its formal annexation of the Kingdom of Holland. This is because France directed and controlled that State at the time the acts were committed. Under Article 17 of the ILC *Articles on State Responsibility*, a State which "directs and controls another State in the commission of an internationally wrongful act" is held internationally responsible for such act.[765] This principle was (at least in the early 20th Century) recognised by tribunals[766] and scholars.[767] Interestingly enough, the Kingdom of the Netherlands emphasised this point insofar as it stated that it could not be held responsible for the acts of the Kingdom of Holland "to which it was forced by a foreign usurper".[768] The decision of the Commission in 1831 was also based on the fact that at the time of the commission of the wrongful acts, it was France that was in command in the territory of the Kingdom of Holland. Thus, after having clearly established that during the relevant period of 1809–1810 Holland was "tributary to all the project of France", the commission concluded:

> The brief account which has been given of the political condition of Holland for the year 1809 till it was formally merged in the French empire, sufficiently explains the reason for allowing [the claims]. Holland was already a dependent Kingdom, and Louis [Bonaparte] a merely nominal sovereign. The Treaty [of 16 March 1810 between France and the Kingdom of Holland] was a form; in substance it was an imperial decree.[769]

765 ILC's *Articles on State Responsibility*, 2001.

766 *Affaire des biens britanniques au Maroc Espagnol* (Great-Britain v. Spain), Award of Umpire Huber, 23 October 1924, *UNRIAA* v. II, 639, 648–649.

767 Guggenheim, v. II, 27 ("[l]'Etat protecteur est responsable indirectement pour l'Etat protégé, s'il conduit lui-même la politique étrangère de ce dernier"); Paul Reuter, *Droit international public* (PUF 1958) 154 ("est internationalement responsable celui qui assure la représentation internationale d'un Etat ou d'un territoire"); Bardonnet, 304, 306–307.

768 Letter of Baron de Nazel, 14 June 1819, quoted in: Letter of US Secretary of State, Mr Fish, to Mr de Westenberg, 9 April 1873, in: F. Wharton, *A Digest of the International Law of the United States*, v. II (1888), 49, 53.

769 The relevant passage from the decision of the commission can be found in: Moore, History, v. V, 4473–4474.

One likely explanation of the outcome of this case may be found in the application of principles of State responsibility rather than on any "rule" of State succession to responsibility. This example is therefore only of limited relevance.

6.2.6 Montenegro (2006)

Following a referendum, the National Assembly of Montenegro made a formal declaration of independence in 2006.[770] The independence of the new State was soon recognised by several members of the international community (including Serbia) and on 28 June 2006 Montenegro was admitted to the United Nations.[771] The accession of Montenegro to independence must be considered in legal terms as a case of separation. Following Montenegro's declaration of independence, the National Assembly of Serbia declared that Serbia was the "successor State" to the State Union of Serbia-Montenegro.[772] In the context of this declaration, the word "successor" was clearly meant to proclaim Serbia as the "continuator".[773]

Montenegro's independence had some important consequences in the context of the then on-going *Genocide Convention Case* brought by Bosnia and Herzegovina against Serbia-Montenegro before the ICJ.[774] Bosnia and Herzegovina argued that Serbia *and* Montenegro should both remain respondents in this case.[775] Montenegro rejected this

770 Art. 60(4) of the Constitution of the State Union of Serbia and Montenegro expressly envisaged the "secession of the state of Montenegro from the State Union of Serbia and Montenegro". See also, Art. 60(5).

771 UN GA Res. A/60/264, 12 July 2006.

772 "Decision on Obligations of Public Authorities of the Republic of Serbia in Assuming Powers of the Republic of Serbia as Successor State to the State Union of Serbia and Montenegro", 12 June 2006.

773 This is clear from the letter of 3 June 2006 from the President of Serbia to the UN Secretary-General (referred to in *Application of the Convention on the Prevention and Punishment of the Crime of Genocide* (*Bosnia and Herzegovina* v. *Serbia and Montenegro*), Judgment, 26 February 2007, ICJ Rep. 2007, 43, at para 67).

774 By letters dated 19 July 2006, the Court Registrar requested the Agent of Bosnia and Herzegovina, the Agent of Serbia and Montenegro and the Foreign Minister of Montenegro to communicate to the Court the views of their governments on the consequences to be attached to the developments in the context of the case.

775 Bosnia first acknowledged that Serbia's position as the continuator of Serbia-Montenegro had been accepted by both Montenegro and the international community. It nevertheless added that "at the time when genocide was committed and at the time of the initiation of this case, Serbia and Montenegro constituted a single state" and that therefore both States "jointly and severally, are responsible for the unlawful conduct that constitute the cause of action in this case" (Letter to the Registrar, 16 October 2006, by the Agent of Bosnia and Herzegovina, in *Application of the Convention on the Prevention and Punishment of*

position.[776] Serbia simply took the view that this question should be decided by the Court.[777] In its final judgment, the Court first noted that "the facts and events on which the final submissions of Bosnia and Herzegovina are based occurred at a period of time when Serbia and Montenegro constituted a single State".[778] The Court also noted Serbia's position of continuity and its commitment to be bound by international treaties concluded by Serbia and Montenegro.[779] For the Court, "the Republic of Montenegro does not continue the legal personality of Serbia and Montenegro; it cannot therefore have acquired, on that basis, the status of Respondent in the present case".[780] Since Montenegro had not given its consent to the jurisdiction of the Court over this case,[781] the Court concluded that the Republic of Serbia would remain the only respondent in the case.[782]

It could be argued that in doing so, the Court "managed to avoid this issue by holding that regardless of whether Montenegro succeeded to the whole or part of the FRY's responsibility it did not succeed to the ongoing litigation before the Court, that is, it did not provide its consent to have proceedings brought before it".[783] Thus, the Court did not say anything on State succession to responsibility. It only went so far as to make this rather vague observation: "it has to be borne in mind that any responsibility for past events determined in the present Judgment involved at the relevant time the State of Serbia and Montenegro".[784] Some authors consider this remark as supporting the possibility of succession to responsibility.[785] In my view, the Court did not address the possibility of joint and several responsibility by Serbia and Montenegro,

the Crime of Genocide (*Bosnia and Herzegovina v. Serbia and Montenegro*), Judgment, 26 February 2007, ICJ Rep. 2007, 43, at para 71).

776 Letter dated 29 November 2006 by the Chief State Prosecutor of Montenegro, in: ibid at para 72.

777 Ibid para 73.

778 Ibid para 74.

779 Ibid para 75. In a letter of 26 July 2006 (ibid, at para 70), the Agent of Serbia and Montenegro took the view that "there [was] continuity between Serbia and Montenegro and the Republic of Serbia".

780 Ibid para 76.

781 Ibid.

782 Ibid para 77.

783 Marko Milanovic, "The Spatial Dimension: Treaties and Territory", in: C.J. Tams et al. (eds), *Research Handbook on the Law of Treaties* (Cheltenham 2014) 219.

784 *Application of the Convention on the Prevention and Punishment of the Crime of Genocide* (*Bosnia and Herzegovina v. Serbia and Montenegro*), Judgment, 26 February 2007, ICJ Rep. 2007, para 78.

785 Kaplane, 21.

let alone any kind of obligation incumbent on Montenegro for the internationally wrongful act committed by the predecessor State.

Yet, as noted in Kohen's Final Report, "what is beyond doubt in the Court's reasoning is that the continuator State has to assume the obligations of internationally wrongful acts committed before the date of State succession as a result of the separation of part of its population and territory in order to constitute a new State".[786] ILC Special Rapporteur agreed with this comment.[787] He also considered that this case "supports the continuing legal personality and responsibility of the continuing State".[788] The same conclusion about Serbia's continuing responsibility was (at least implicitly) reached by the arbitral tribunal in the case of *Mytilineos Holdings SA v. The State Union of Serbia & Montenegro and Republic of Serbia* involving a Greek claimant starting arbitration proceedings in 2004 under the 1997 Greece-FRY bilateral investment treaty.[789] The ECHR has stated in many cases that after the separation of Montenegro in 2006, Serbia was the sole respondent in proceedings started before the date of succession.[790]

I will further examine below[791] the *Bijelić v. Montenegro* case decided by the ECHR as one specific example dealing with the "organs" exception where the general principle of non-succession should *not* apply because of the structural continuity between an autonomous government and the new State.[792]

6.3 *Examples Where the Principle of Succession Was Applied*

In Sections 6.1 and 6.2, I have examined the *general principle* whereby the continuing State should remain responsible for *its own* internationally wrongful acts committed before the date of succession. Thus, as a matter of principle, the obligations arising from the commission of such acts should *not* be

786 IIL, Final Report, Kohen, para 79.

787 ILC Special Rapporteur Šturma, Second Report, 2018, para 91. See also, Pajnkihar, 316–7.

788 Ibid para 90.

789 *Mytilineos Holdings SA v. State Union of Serbia & Montenegro and Republic of Serbia*, UNCITRAL, Partial Award on Jurisdiction, 8 Sept. 2006, where the Tribunal noted that since the claim had been filed, Montenegro had declared its independence, adding that "while the Tribunal has not been requested to rule on any ensuing State succession issues, it takes note that it appears uncontroversial that the Republic of Serbia will continue the legal identity of the State Union of Serbia and Montenegro on the international level" (para 158).

790 Pajnkihar, 315, citing several cases.

791 See, Chapter 3, Section 7.2.

792 *Bijelić v. Montenegro and Serbia*, ECHR, Appl no 11890/05, judgment, 11 June 2009.

transferred to the successor State. I have also explained that there are circumstances where there should be an exception to this general principle.

Apart from the *Bijelić* case (further examined below[793]), I have found only one *significant* example of State practice where the principle that the continuing State should remain responsible for its own internationally wrongful acts committed before the date of succession was *not* applied. This example arose in the context of the separation of Belgium (1830) (examined in Section 6.3.1).

Three other less significant examples of State practice where the solution of succession was adopted will also be briefly discussed below: the 1926 Treaty between the US and Panama; the war reparation paid by the GDR to the USSR for acts committed by the German Reich during the Second World War; and the offer made by the GDR to Jewish groups to provide compensation for crimes committed by the Third Reich (Sections 6.3.2, 6.3.3, and 6.3.4).

6.3.1 Belgium (1830)

Problems of State succession arose in the context of the struggle for independence of the Belgian provinces which finally ended with their separation from the Kingdom of the Netherlands in November 1830. During the armed revolt, the city of Antwerp (situated in the Belgian provinces) was bombarded in October 1830 by the Dutch forces. During the bombardment, a public warehouse was destroyed in which were stored the goods of several foreigners. Some years later, Austria, Brazil, France, Great Britain, Prussia and the US submitted claims for compensation for the damage suffered by their nationals.[794]

Great Britain took the view that the Kingdom of the Netherlands (the predecessor and continuing State) "was not liable for the disasters occasioned by the bombardment" of October 1830.[795] Apparently, Austria, Brazil, France and Prussia also adopted the same position.[796] There is also some indication in the diplomatic correspondence of the time that France, Great Britain, Prussia and the US made a joint application to Belgium (the successor State) requesting compensation for the damage "solely [based] upon the ground that the

793 Ibid. See, Chapter 3, Section 7.2.

794 Moore, Digest, v. VI, 942.

795 This is apparently what the Attorney General of England concluded following a request made by the British Minister of Foreign Affairs. This information is found in: Letter of US Secretary of State, Mr Marcy, to French Minister Count Sartiges concerning the claims of French subjects as a result of the US bombardment of Greytown in 1854, 26 February 1857, in: MS. Notes to French Leg. VI. 301; S. Ex. Doc. 9, 35 Cong. 1 sess. 3, in: Moore, ibid 929.

796 This is the conclusion reached by US Secretary of State, Mr Marcy in a letter dated 26 February 1857, ibid.

obligation to indemnify for such losses rested upon the country within which the injury was inflicted".[797]

More information is available with respect to the claims filed by the US against *both* Belgium and the Kingdom of the Netherlands in the hope that they would come up with a satisfactory and voluntary arrangement as to the proportion of responsibility that each one would bear for the damage suffered by US nationals as a result of the bombardment of October 1830.[798] Accordingly, the US submitted its claim against the Kingdom of the Netherlands as the actual perpetrator of the act. Apparently, the Dutch government excused its bombardment of the city on the ground of a breach by the Belgian insurgents of a suspension of hostilities which had been agreed upon for the protection of the city.[799] It is not clear from the information available whether or not the Kingdom of the Netherlands ended up paying any compensation to the US.

The position adopted by the US towards Belgium is, however, clear: it requested a prompt and speedy settlement of the dispute:

> Policy as well as justice prescribes to Belgium the course she ought to pursue, and the forbearance of the US in pressing these claims, notwithstanding their urgency and the sufferings of our citizens interested, furnishes a powerful reason for their speedy settlement by the Belgian Government, and imposes additional obligation upon the President [of the US] who greatly regrets the circumstances which have heretofore occasioned such unexpected delay, to adopt the most prompt and efficient measures for

---

797 Ibid.

798 Message of US President Jackson, 5 December 1836, in: *Messages and Papers of the Presidents*, v. 3, 237, in: Moore, Digest, v. VI, 947ff. The issue is also mentioned in this internal US diplomatic communication: Letter of US Secretary of State, Mr Forsyth, to Mr Davezac, US Chargé d'Affaires to the Netherlands, 10 September 1836, *MS. Inst. Netherlands*, XIV. 24, in: Moore, ibid 943: "Had the contest, in the course of which this bombardment took place, terminated favourably to the Netherlands, no doubt is entertained that US would have had a just claim upon the Government of that country to the indemnification of [US] citizens for the loss which they had sustained. The fact that the conflict had a different termination can not impair the right of this [US] Government or its citizens to indemnification; but from which of the countries, or in what proportion from both, the satisfaction is to come it would have been most gratifying to the President [of the US] to have had determined by themselves. He has accordingly for a long time forborne, notwithstanding the importunity of the sufferers, to urge their claims which appeared to him so just, in the hope that some mutual and voluntary arrangement for their liquidation would have been made ere this between the Governments of Belgium and the Netherlands".

799 Moore, ibid 947.

> their satisfactory adjustment. It is the [US] President's wish therefore that you should ascertain whether any measures have been taken by Belgium towards the accomplishment of an object deemed by him of the greatest consequence in the preservation and promotion of those feelings of amity which subsist between the two nations, and to urge upon that government such speedy action on the subject as the equity of the claims, and the length of time which has elapsed since the injuries were sustained clearly demand.[800]

For the US, there was no doubt about the responsibility of the new State of Belgium for the internationally wrongful act committed by the Netherlands against the Belgian city. One of the legal grounds invoked by the US for Belgium to be held responsible for the action concerned the territorial link between the internationally wrongful act and the tortfeaser, as illustrated by this other internal diplomatic correspondence:

> The governments of the respective merchants whose property was destroyed by the bombardment claimed indemnity for these losses from the Kingdom of Belgium. The ground of the claims was, that the injury was inflicted on a territory which, at the time the reclamation was made, had become a part of Belgium; but Belgium attempted to evade it by alleging that the Dutch government received the property, had it in possession, and destroyed it; and from Holland, and not Belgium, indemnity must be sought.[801]

In other words, since the acts took place in the territory of what would later become Belgium, the US took the view that the new State should therefore be held responsible for it. Another legal argument invoked by the US was that Belgium should be held responsible based on the well-recognised principle of international law[802] according to which a new government is responsible for the acts committed by the previous government.[803] The position adopted by

800 Letter of US Secretary of State, Mr Forsyth, to Mr Marcy, US Chargé d'affaires to Belgium, 12 June 1837, *MS. Inst. Belgium*, I. 24, in: Moore, ibid 945.

801 This assessment of the position taken by the US concerning the Antwerp bombardment is found in: Letter of US Secretary of State, Mr Marcy, to French Minister Count Sartiges, 26 February 1857, in: Moore, ibid 929–930.

802 See, Dumberry, Rebellions, 35ff.

803 Letter of US Secretary of State, Mr Webster, to Mr Marcy, US Chargé d'Affaires to Belgium, 26 February 1842, in: *MS. Inst. Belgium*, I. 34, in: Moore, Digest v. VI, 945–947: "There is no doubt that the duty or obligation of indemnity, whatever it is, for the losses at Antwerp,

the US seems to be based on a fundamental mischaracterisation of the events of November 1830. These events should not be analysed as mere *change of government* but, rather, as the emergence of a *new State*.

In any event, Belgium initially denied its responsibility on the obvious ground that the acts were committed by the Dutch forces and that, therefore, only the Dutch government should be responsible for them.[804] Belgium apparently subsequently changed its initial position and finally agreed to pay compensation to the owners of merchandise which had been destroyed during the incident.[805]

Verzijl described this example as a "clear case of asserted responsibility of a territorial successor to injuries inflicted by its predecessor".[806] This is the only clear example of State practice in the context of separation where the continuing State did not remain responsible for internationally wrongful acts *it committed* before the date of succession.[807] The outcome of this case is very surprising. It is also contrary to one principle applicable in the context of State succession (which is further examined below):[808] in cases where the insurgents are successful at establishing a new State, the latter should not be held accountable for internationally wrongful acts committed *by the predecessor State* against third States in its efforts to block the rebels' struggle for independence.[809] This case is also an illustration of the well-established principle that a new State is always free to take over responsibility for wrongs committed

falls upon Belgium. The Belgians, as a civilized people, must be considered at all times under some form of civil government, and however often they may see fit to change this form, these changes cannot affect their just responsibility to any foreign state, its citizens or subjects. Succeeding governments necessarily take upon themselves, so far at least as foreign nations are concerned, the obligations of the governments which preceded them, whether those obligations were created by treaty or by the general principles of national law. It is on this ground that the restored governments of Europe have made indemnities to foreign states for excesses committed on the property of citizens or subjects of these states by the revolutionary governments (…). The Belgians saw fit to change their government which, so far as foreign nations are concerned, they had a right to do. But in doing this they shook off no national responsibility. The moment the authority of the King of the Netherlands ceased over the Belgians, that moment every one of his obligations towards foreign nations, so far as that part of his Kingdom was concerned, devolved on the new government that succeeded him".

804 Moore, ibid 947. Belgium also argued that the injuries suffered were due to an unavoidable incident of war.

805 This is, for instance, the conclusion reached by Verzijl, 226–227.

806 Ibid.

807 Another example of succession is the *Bijelić* case. See, Chapter 3, Section 7.2.

808 See, Chapter 3, Section 6.

809 See, Dumberry, Rebellions, 365ff.

by the predecessor State.[810] The surprising fact that the new successor State was forced to pay compensation for acts for which it had simply nothing to do, and of which it was in fact the victim, may be based on *political* reasons. Thus, at the time of its independence, Belgium was probably not in a position to refuse to provide reparation to the much more powerful claimant States. In other words, the solution adopted in this case can hardly be considered to be the foundation of any *general* principle in favour of succession in the context where the predecessor State continues its existence. In fact, this case matters more as an illustration of the importance to be given to the existence of a *direct territorial link* between a wrongful act committed by the predecessor and the new State.[811] Under Article 12(4) of the Institute's Resolution, in such a situation, the obligations arising from such an act can be assumed by *both* the predecessor State and the successor State.[812] The same solution was initially put forward by ILC Special Rapporteur Šturma, but ultimately not kept in the Guidelines.[813]

6.3.2 Panama (1903)

In 1903, Panama seceded from Colombia. Many years before (in 1855), a fire broke out in the city of Colon, situated in the Department of Panama, which was then part of the territory of Colombia.[814] The fire caused damage to US nationals. After Panama's separation, the US submitted a claim against the new State for the acts committed on its territory while it was still part of Colombia. Panama refused to be held responsible. On 28 July 1926, the US and Panama signed a treaty concerning reciprocal claims which arose *after* 1903.[815] The treaty also envisaged *future* arbitration proceedings with respect to the consequences of the 1855 fire in the city of Colon.[816] The two questions that Panama

810 This principle is further discussed below, Chapter 3, Section 4.

811 Kohen & Dumberry, 101. See also ILC Special Rapporteur Šturma, Second Report, 2018, para 101.

812 Kohen & Dumberry, 101.

813 ILC Draft Article 7(3); ILC Special Rapporteur Šturma, Second Report, 2018, para 103.

814 The facts are explained in: Feilchenfeld, 351–352; Verzijl, 222.

815 *Claims Convention between the United States and Panama*, 28 July 1926, ratified on 3 October 1931, *LNTS* v. 138, 120–126; *UNRIAA* v. VI, 301. Under the Treaty, both Parties agreed to submit to an arbitral tribunal all claims of their nationals against the other State arising out of events which took place *after* Panama became an independent State in 1903. However, claims for compensation for damage caused in connexion with the construction of the Panama Canal were excluded as they were to be dealt with by the Joint Land Commission under the Panama Canal Convention of 18 November 1903.

816 Art. I(2) of the Treaty reads as follows: "Panama agrees in principle to the arbitration of such claims under a Convention to which the Republic of Colombia shall be invited

and the US agreed should be put to a future arbitral tribunal, upon a new convention being entered into, were as follows:

> First, whether the Republic of Colombia incurred any liability for losses sustained by American citizens on account of the fire that took place in the city of Colon on 31 March 1885; and, second, in case there should be determined in the arbitration that there is an original liability on the part of Colombia, to what extent, if any, the Republic of Panama has succeeded Colombia in such liability on account of her separation from Colombia on November 3, 1903.

No subsequent convention was entered into by Panama and the US on this issue and no arbitration ever took place. This example of State practice is therefore less significant, as it remains theoretical. It is nevertheless interesting to note that both the injured State (the US) and the new State (Panama), had, at least theoretically (or "implicitly"[817]), recognised that the successor State could be held liable for the internationally wrongful act committed by the predecessor State (Colombia) before the date of succession.[818]

6.3.3 War Reparation Paid by the GDR to the USSR

The official position of non-succession adopted by the GDR, as described above,[819] did not prevent the USSR and Poland from requesting war reparation to the GDR for damage resulting from internationally wrongful acts committed during the Second World War by the predecessor State (the German Reich). In accordance with the *Potsdam Agreement*, Germany was to pay war reparation to the USSR in the form of direct taking and seizure of industrial equipment situated in the German territories occupied by the Soviet Red Army (and in other parts of Eastern Europe).[820] The *Potsdam Agreement* also indicated that

to become a party and which shall provide for the creation or selection of an arbitral tribunal".

817 ILC Special Rapporteur Šturma, First Report, 2017, para 44; Šturma, State Succession, 662.

818 Thus, Panama "agreed in principle to the arbitration of such claims" and for the establishment of an arbitral tribunal to decide "to what extent, if any" it had succeeded to the original liability of the predecessor State.

819 See, Section 6.2.3.

820 Sect. IV, Potsdam Agreements, 2 August 1945 (*Tripartite Agreement by the United States, the United Kingdom and Soviet Russia*, following the Berlin-Potsdam Conference held in 1945, 68 *UNTS* 190): "1. Reparation claims of the USSR shall be met by removals from the zone of Germany occupied by the USSR, and from appropriate German external assets". The Treaty also provides (at point 4) that "in addition to the reparations to be taken by the USSR from its own zone of occupation, the USSR shall receive additionally from the

"the USSR undertakes to settle the reparation claims of Poland from its own share of reparations".[821] A treaty between Poland and the USSR subsequently dealt with the allocation between the two States of compensation resulting from war reparation paid by Germany.[822] This reparation regime was essentially enforced during the period of Soviet occupation (1945–1949). It continued for a few years after the official creation of the GDR in 1949. Therefore, after 1949, the reparation regime established under the *Potsdam Agreement* was imposed upon the GDR. In a declaration made on 22 August 1953, the USSR declared that it no longer requested the payment of any war reparation by the GDR.[823] On 23 August 1953, Poland also renounced reparation payments from the GDR.[824]

This example is not entirely significant. Thus, its outcome was dictated by an agreement between the victorious powers after the Second World War and

---

Western Zones" a certain percentage of the industrial capital equipments specified in the Treaty. Finally, in the Treaty (at point 8) the USSR "renounces all claims in respect of reparations to shares of German enterprises which are located in the Western Zones of Germany as well as to German foreign assets in all countries" (with the exception of those assets situated in Bulgaria, Finland, Hungary, Romania and Eastern Austria). Similarly (at point 9), the UK and the US "renounce all claims in respect of reparations to shares of German enterprises which are located in the Eastern Zone of occupation in Germany, as well as to German foreign assets in Bulgaria, Finland, Hungary, Romania and Eastern Austria".

821 Sect. IV, Potsdam Agreements, at point 2.

822 *Agreement between the USSR and the Provisional Government of National Unity of Poland Concerning the Reparation of Damage caused by the German Occupation*, 16 August 1945, in: *British and Foreign State Papers*, v. 145, 1943–1945, 1168–1170. See, D'Argent, 208ff.

823 *Protocol Concerning the Discontinuance of German Reparations Payments and Other Measures to Alleviate the Financial and Economic Obligations of the German Democratic Republic Arising in Consequence of the War*, 22 August 1953, 221 *UNTS* 129; 8 *Europa-Archiv*, 1953, 597. In May 1950, the USSR had already decided to reduce the total amount in reparation due by the GDR, having seized property in an amount of US$ 3.6 billion.

824 "Declaration of the Polish People's Republic", 9 *Zbior Documentow*, 1953, no. 9, 1830, quoted in: 49 *BVerfG* 169. The relevant quote from the binding declaration reads as follows: "In consideration of the fact that Germany has already complied to a significant extent with its obligation to pay reparations and the fact that the improvements of the economic situation of Germany lies in the interests of its peaceful development, the government of the People's Republic of Poland has resolved, effective January 1, 1954, to waive the reparation payments to Poland, in order to thereby make a further contribution to the resolution of the German question in the spirit of democracy and peace in accordance with the interests of the Polish and all peace-loving people" (quoted in: Rudolf Dolzer, "The Settlement of War-Related Claims: Does International Law Recognize a Victim's Private Right of Action? Lessons After 1945", 20 *Berkeley JIL* 2002, 296, 322). See, W. Czaplinski, "Property Questions in Relations Between Poland and the Federal Republic of Germany", 29(1–2) *La Pologne et les affaires occidentales* 1988, 122–123.

Germany, which was not a party to the *Potsdam Agreement*. After the GDR became an independent State (1949), it was part of the Socialist bloc and was not in a position to reject any Soviet claims for compensation. This is therefore ultimately an example driven by Cold War *realpolitik* rather than by the application of any legal principles.

6.3.4 Offer of Compensation Made by the GDR to Jewish Groups

Notwithstanding its official position of non-succession, the GDR recognised in February 1990 the responsibility of "all Germans" for past crimes committed by the Third Reich against the Jewish people before and during the Second World War.[825] This change of policy was made after the fall of Mr Honecker as General-Secretary of the Socialist Unity Party and as head of the government (October 1989) and after the fall of the Berlin Wall (November 1989). A few months later (in April 1990), the GDR reiterated its acceptance of responsibility for these crimes and pledged to pay DM 6.2 million in compensation in the following years.[826] This marked a radical change from the previous attitude adopted by the GDR, which had always rejected any international responsibility for the atrocities committed by the Third Reich against the Jewish people.[827]

However, due to the integration of the GDR into the Federal Republic of Germany, no compensation was actually paid. This is therefore not a significant example of succession to responsibility.

825 The Declaration was attached to a letter dated 1 February 1990 signed by the GDR's Prime Minister, Mr Modrow, addressed to the President of the World Jewish Congress, Mr Edgard Bronfman. At that time the question of the amount of reparation was still not settled. See, Gareth Winrow, "East Germany, Israel and the Reparations Issue", 20(1) *Soviet Jewish Affairs*, 1990, 37ff; J. Charpentier, "Pratique française du droit international", 35 *AFDI* 1990, 986; C. Rousseau, "Chronique des faits internationaux", *RGDIP* 1990, 764–765; G. Schuster, "Volkerrechtliche Praxis der Bundesrepublik Deutschland im Jahre 1990", 52 *ZaöRV* 1992, 1026; D'Argent, 217.

826 This declaration was made before the GDR's parliament (*Volkskammer*) by its newly elected Prime Minister, Mr Lothar de Maizière.

827 The GDR never responded to a demand made by the Government of Israel in March 1951 requesting compensation in the amount of US$ 500 million. A little-known fact is that in November 1976, the GDR offered to a Jewish organisation (the Claims Conference) the amount of US$ 1 million in reparation to former German nationals of Jewish origin now living in the US. The Claims Conference rejected the proposal; it requested instead in 1979 the payment of some US$ 100 million in compensation. The GDR refused to pay compensation. See, Gareth Winrow, "East Germany, Israel and the Reparations Issue", 20(1) *Soviet Jewish Affairs*, 1990, 32–33.

7 Newly Independent States

In this section, I will first refer to the position adopted by the Institute and the ILC and explain my own view on the situation which should prevail for Newly Independent States (Section 7.1). This analysis will be followed by an assessment of State practice and case law (Sections 7.2 and 7.3).

7.1 *The Position Adopted in This Study and That of the Institute and the ILC*

Writers generally support the principle of non-succession in the context of the creation of Newly Independent States. The colonial power, which continues its existence, should therefore provide reparation for the consequences of its own internationally wrongful acts committed before the date of succession.[828] According to Bedjaoui, "en droit … il ne saurait y avoir de succession à l'ordre colonial, en dehors de l'œuvre volontaire du nouveau successeur".[829] Similarly, for Makonnen, "any attempt to carry over the predecessor State's rights and duties to the successor State without the consent of the latter would put the successor in an inferior position and thus might violate the principle of sovereign equality of States".[830] Volkovitsch is in favour of a principle of non-succession for public policy reasons: it would "manifestly be unfair to hold the State emerging from the yoke of tyranny responsible for the acts of its

828 Volkovitsch, 2201; D.P. O'Connell, "Independence and Problems of State Succession", in: W. O'Brien (ed), *The New Nations in International Law and Diplomacy* (Stevens & Sons 1965) 31; Stern, Succession, 246 ("il serait paradoxal d'obliger un Etat illégalement occupé à assumer les obligations de l'Etat qui l'a agressé"); M. Shaw, "State Succession Revisited", 5 *Finnish YIL* 1994, 58; Atlam, 258; F. Okoye, *International Law and the New African States* (Sweet & Maxwell 1973) 178ff; Jenning & Watts, 233–234. See also, Zyade Motala, "Under International Law, Does the New Order in South Africa Assume the Obligations and Responsibilities of Apartheid Order? An Argument for Realism over Formalism", 30 *Comp. & ILJ S. Afr.* 1997, 291, for whom "international law recognizes that [Newly Independent States] start with a clean slate with regard to wrong committed and treaties concluded on their behalf by the former colonial power". He believes (at 303) that South Africa after its first free election of 1994 was a "new" State which could rely on this doctrine of non-succession.

829 Bedjaoui, 520.

830 Y. Makonnen, *International Law and the New States of Africa* (UNESCO 1983) 202. See also, Yilma Makonnen, "State Succession in Africa: Selected Problems", *Rec. des cours*, v. 200, 1986–V, 126. The author adopted this approach in the context of State succession to treaties, but believes that it should also apply to other questions of State succession (at 134).

master".[831] For him, "a clear line of practice and precedent demonstrates that primary responsibility in such cases remains with the predecessor State and that former colonies and victims of occupation will only be held responsible for their predecessor's delictual liability if they have expressly agreed to assume it".[832] Many States have expressed the view that a special regime should prevail for Newly Independent States and that they should never be held responsible for wrongful acts committed by the predecessor State.[833]

The basic principle under Article 16(1) of the Institute's Resolution is that the obligations arising from an internationally wrongful act committed by the predecessor State *do not pass* to the Newly Independent State. The predecessor State should remain the holder of obligations arising from wrongful acts which took place before the date of succession. The same non-succession principle was initially followed by ILC Special Rapporteur Šturma in Draft Article 8(1).[834] As mentioned above, three provisions were later grouped, and a new proposal for a single clause was submitted by Special Rapporteur Šturma.[835] Guideline 9 (which was never formally adopted by the ILC) follows a different approach. It indicates that "an injured State continues to be entitled to invoke the responsibility of the predecessor State even after the date of succession". I have explained above why this language is not optimal.[836]

Another question is whether this principle of non-succession should apply uniformly in all cases. As mentioned above,[837] in situations of separation and cession/transfer of territory, I believe that the continuing State should *not always* be responsible for wrongful acts committed before the date of succession. There are circumstances (further discussed below[838]) where, on the contrary, the successor State should be held responsible for the obligations

831 Volkovitsch, 2201. For him, in cases of colonisation and occupation, there should exist an exception to his proposition of a rebutable presumption of succession to obligations arising from the commission of internationally wrongful acts.

832 Ibid. Same conclusion: Natalino Ronzitti, *La successione internazionale tra stati* (Giuffrè 1970) 216–217; Buser, 438 ("there is an 'overwhelming tendency' that denies succession of newly independent States to reparatory obligations of the former colonial power before the date of independence and instead supports the responsibility of the continuing State for its own internationally wrongful acts"); Ruy & Baecke, 16.

833 See, discussion held at the GA Sixth Committee in 1975, 30th sess. See, comments made by Czechoslovakia ("1546th meeting, 22 October 1975", A/C. 6/SR. 1546, 103, para 3) and Liberia ("1539th meeting, 17 October 1975", A/C. 6/SR. 1542, 86, para 22).

834 ILC Special Rapporteur Šturma, Second Report, 2018, paras 124, 130.

835 The clause also deals with separation and cession of territory. See, ibid, Third Report, 2019, para 65; ILC, Statement, Grossman Guiloff, 2019, 6.

836 See, Section 6.1.

837 See, Sections 5.1 and 6.1.

838 See, Chapter 3.

arising from wrongful acts committed before the date of succession. It could be argued that the same principle should also apply to Newly Independent States.

There is some support for the proposition that the principle of succession should apply to situations where an internationally wrongful act was committed not by the colonial State but, rather, by the local authorities of a non-independent colonial entity while still part of the predecessor State.[839] Others disagree.[840] As mentioned above, Article 12(3) of the Institute's Resolution provides for the same "organ" exception to the general principle of non-succession in the context of separation.[841] Importantly, the Institute's Resolution does *not* apply this "organ" exception in the context of Newly Independent States.[842] The commentary to the resolution explained that applying this exception in this context "may undermine the very reason for distinguishing between Newly independent States and cases of separation" and that "even if the Newly independent State could be considered as having enjoyed some substantial autonomy in some areas, it remains that what characterizes this category is the *dependent* nature of its relationship with the predecessor State".[843] There are undoubtedly good reasons not to apply the "organ" exception to Newly Independent States.

ILC Special Rapporteur Šturma initially adopted a slightly different position on the matter. Thus, Draft Article 8(2) provided for an exception to the non-succession principle (set out at Article 8(1)) whereby two "particular circumstances" "may be taken into consideration": (1) the existence of a "direct link" between the act or its consequences and the territory of the new State,[844]

839 For Czaplinski, 356–357, the principle of non-succession should not apply in instances where the colony possessed a distinct personality under the municipal law of the former metropolitan power. In such case, the wrongful act could be attributed directly to the local authorities and not to the colonial power. Verzijl, 219–220, gives the following example where "a colony which enjoy a very developed autonomy commits acts coming within those autonomous powers, but which are illegal and obnoxious to a third State; before the colony itself or the State internationally responsible for its conduct has given satisfaction to the injured State, the colony attains independence". Verzijl believes that in such cases "it would really be absurd to assume that the successor State can nevertheless take shelter behind the argument put forward by the dominant doctrine, according to which the offences of its predecessor(s) do not regard it". This seems also to be the position of Peterschmitt, 62–63.

840 Ruy & Baecke, 16; Buser, 437.

841 It concerns the situation when the author of a wrongful act committed before independence was an "organ of the territorial unit of the predecessor State", such as an autonomous government, "that has later become an organ of the successor State".

842 On this point, see Kohen & Dumberry, 131.

843 Ibid 132, emphasis in the original.

844 See also, agreeing: Pajnkihar, 338, indicating that the "special rule" that "a successor State that has a special link to the matter of succession (i.e., injury) shall fully succeed to the

and (2) "where the former dependent territory had substantive autonomy". The language that was ultimately used suggested that these two "particular circumstances" were in fact envisaged only as potential exception to the non-succession principle. Article 8(2) makes this clear as it outlines that the Newly Independent States would have to "agree" to any such transfer. ILC Special Rapporteur Šturma also mentioned that the "limited State practice seems to confirm" the conclusion reached by Bedjaoui that there should be no succession "without the consent of the successor State".[845] The text of Guideline 9 (which was never formally adopted by the ILC) no longer contains any explicit reference to the "organ" and "direct link" exceptions.

In any event, there is no doubt that the principle of succession should prevail in the specific situation where insurgents have committed internationally wrongful acts in their successful attempt to create a new State.[846] I have explained elsewhere that the principle under Article 10 of the ILC *Articles on State Responsibility* applies to Newly Independent States.[847] Therefore, the continuing colonial State should *not* be responsible for wrongful acts committed by successful rebels in their efforts to establish a new State in the context of decolonisation. The same position was adopted by the Institute under Article 16(3): the conduct of a national liberation movement, representing a people entitled to self-determination, which succeeds in establishing a Newly Independent State will be considered an act of that State under international law.[848] The same solution was also adopted by ILC Special Rapporteur Šturma[849] and in ILC Guideline 8. It is also supported by writers.[850] As further

secondary rights and obligations of reparations relating to that matter" "applies to all types of succession and independently of the existence of a continuator State").

845 ILC Special Rapporteur Šturma, Second Report, 2018, para 133, referring to the practice of Namibia.

846 This principle is examined in Chapter 3, Section 6. For a detailed analysis, see Dumberry, Rebellions, 299. It should be noted, however, that this situation does not deal *per se* with issues of State succession.

847 Ibid 339. See also, ILC Special Rapporteur Šturma, Second Report, 2018, para 131.

848 IIL, Resolution 2015, Art. 16(3) reads as follows: "[t]he conduct, prior to the date of succession of States, of a national liberation movement which succeeds in establishing a newly independent State shall be considered the act of the new State under international law". On this question, see: Kohen & Dumberry, 138.

849 ILC Special Rapporteur Šturma, Second Report, 2018, paras 108, 115, 131. See, Draft Article 8(3).

850 Jakubowski, State Succession, 267; Andrzej Jakubowski, "Cultural Heritage and State Succession", in F. Francioni & A.F. Vrdoljak (ed), *The Oxford Handbook of International Cultural Heritage Law* (OUP 2020) 602 ("the responsibility for internationally wrongful acts against cultural heritage committed by such a national liberation movement shall, in principle, pass to the successor State").

discussed below, French courts have consistently held that the new State of Algeria should, as a matter of principle, provide compensation to French nationals who were victims of internationally wrongful acts committed by the FLN in its war efforts to achieve independence.

The survey of relevant State practice and municipal case law in the next sections shows that the principle of non-succession has surprisingly only been applied in some instances. Contrary to the view held by some writers, there is no "clear line of practice and precedent"[851] in support of this principle. State practice is not consistent. In Section 7.3, I will examine several examples of State practice and municipal courts' decisions where the opposite principle of succession was applied. This is a surprising result. The special status of Newly Independent States does not seem to have any impact on the way the question of succession to responsibility is being dealt with in State practice and before municipal courts.[852] What is even more striking is the fact that the principle of succession was even applied in cases where internationally wrongful acts were committed *by the predecessor State* in its effort to defeat the insurgent movements.[853] These examples are contrary to the well-established principle that a new State is generally not responsible for the acts committed by the predecessor State when fighting rebels during an insurgency.[854]

In the following sections, I will examine examples of State practice and municipal courts cases where:

- The continuing State remained responsible for internationally wrongful acts committed before the creation of the new State (Section 7.2); and
- The new State took over the obligations arising from wrongful acts committed before the date of succession (Section 7.3).

---

851 Volkovitsch, 2201.

852 Jenning & Watts, 233–234, believe that, in general, cases of separation and Newly Independent States should be treated in the same way and that no special regime should prevail for the latter. It should be noted that their assessment, however, does not deal specifically with the question of State succession to responsibility.

853 For instance, *Van der Have v. State of the Netherlands*, Dist. Court of The Hague, 12 January 1953, *NJ* 1953, no. 133, *ILR* 1953, 80. See also, *Minister of Defence, Namibia v. Mwandinghi*, Supreme Court, 25 October 1991, 1992 (2) *SA* 355 (NmS), 365, 91 *ILR* 358 (hereinafter "*Mwandinghi* case, Namibia, Supreme Court"). However, it should be noted that a rule of non-succession was consistently applied by French courts in the similar context of internationally wrongful acts committed by the colonial authorities against French nationals in fighting the FLN in Algeria (see, below Section 7.2.3).

854 See, Dumberry, Rebellions, 365ff.

7.2 *Examples Where the Continuing State Remained Responsible for Internationally Wrongful Acts Committed before the Date of Succession*

I have found examples of decisions of *municipal courts* supporting the principle that the continuing State remains responsible for internationally wrongful acts committed before the creation of the new State. This principle has been applied by decisions of municipal courts of Belgium in the context of the independence of Congo,[855] by the French *Conseil d'Etat* in the context of the independence of Vanuatu,[856] and by Indian courts in the context of the partition of India (Sections 7.2.1, 7.2.2, and 7.2.4). In the context of the independence of Algeria, State practice (and in particular an interpretation given by the French Ministry of Foreign Affairs) as well as several decisions of French municipal courts support the existence of one exception to the general principle of succession established in Article 18 of the *Déclaration de principes relative à la ooperation économique et financière* entered into between France and Algeria: the continuing State (France) remains responsible for the internationally wrongful acts it committed against *French nationals* in fighting the rebels of the FLN (Section 7.2.3). Yet, there are also cases in the context of Algeria's independence where the new State was considered responsible for obligations arising from wrongful acts committed before the date of succession.[857] I will also examine the *Mutua* case decided by the UK's High Court in the context of Kenya's independence (Section 7.2.7).[858] However, it is important to note that all these municipal law cases only dealt with wrongful acts committed by the colonial predecessor State against its *own nationals* and not against another State (or a national of another State).[859]

I have also found two other much less significant examples of *State practice* where the principle of non-succession was applied: the 1958 peace treaty

855 Belgian courts made statements in support of this principle in two cases: *Crépet v. Etat belge et Société des forces hydro-électriques de la colonie*, Civil Tribunal of Brussels, 30 January 1962, *J. trib.* 1962, 242; *Pittacos v. Etat Belge*, Brussels Court of Appeal (2nd Ch.), 1 December 1964, ibid, 1965, 7, 9; *Pasicrisie Belge*, 1965, II, 263, 45 *ILR* 24.

856 *Russet*, Conseil d'Etat, 5 October 1984, case no. 51543, *Rec. Lebon*, *RGDIP* 1986, 249, 89 *ILR* 15.

857 These examples are further discussed below, Section 7.3.3.

858 *Mutua et al. v. The Foreign and Commonwealth Office*, 21 July 2011, High Court of Justice, Judgments of Justice McCombe, [2011] EWHC 1913 (QB) and of 5 October 2012, [2012] EWHC 2678 (QB).

859 The reasons for treating these types of cases differently have been explained in Part 1, Section 4.7. Another limitation to the relevance of some of these cases is the fact that they can be interpreted as involving issues of war damage between the predecessor State and the successor State.

between Indonesia and Japan and another one in the context of the independence of Ghana (Sections 7.2.5 and 7.2.6).

7.2.1 The Partition of India (1947)

India and Pakistan both became independent States on 15 August 1947 pursuant to the *Indian Independence Act (1947)* voted by Great Britain's House of Commons.[860] India has generally been considered the *continuing State* of the British Dominion of India,[861] while Pakistan has been viewed as having seceded from India in 1947.[862] The relevant legislation dealing with issues of succession of States is the *1947 Indian Independence (Rights, Property and Liabilities) Order* of 14 August 1947.[863] Section 10 of the Order provides for the transfer of "liabilities for actionable wrong other than breach of contract" from the predecessor State (British Dominion of India) to the independent States of India and Pakistan, depending on which part of the territory the "cause of action arose".[864] The term "actionable wrong" has been interpreted to include both contractual and tortious claims.[865] Many decisions of Indian courts have interpreted Section 10 of the Order.[866] Courts came to the conclusion that

860 *Indian Independence Act (1947)*, 10 and 11 Geo. VI, c. 30; *L.R. Statues* 1947.

861 This is stated in: *Indian Independence (International Arrangements) Order*, Gaz. India Extra, 14 August 1947, 911. The same opinion was also expressed by the UN Legal Department: UN Press Release, PM/473, 12 August 1947. This question is examined in: Sastry, 77ff.

862 The qualification is rather superficial given that both India and Pakistan have become independent States at the same time following the adoption of the *Indian Independence Act (1947)*, 10 & 11 Geo. VI, c. 30, by the British parliament. On this point see: O'Connell, State Succession. v. I, 8. See also, ILC Special Rapporteur Šturma, Fifth Report, 2021, para 35, referring to this case as an example of a "plurality of successor States" in the case of the "separation of parts of a State, where more than one new State [India and Pakistan] separates from a predecessor State [UK] which continues to exist".

863 *1947 Indian Independence (Rights, Property and Liabilities) Order*, Gaz. India Extra, 14 August 1947, 910, Art. 10, in: M.M. Whiteman, *Digest of International Law*, v. II (Dept. of State 1973) 873. See, S.D.K. Sen, "The Partition of India and Succession in International Law", *Indian LR* 1947 190; Hari Om Agarwal, *State Succession: A Study of Indian Cases* (Allahbad Law Agency 1980); Hari Om Agarwal, "State Succession: A Study of Indian Cases", 5(9) *Int. Law Rep.* 156–177; Sastry.

864 *Indian Independence (Rights, Property and Liabilities) Order*, Gaz. India Extra, 14 August 1947, 913, Art. 10.

865 S.K. Agrawala, "Law of Nations as Interpreted and Applied by Indian Courts and Legislature", 2 *Indian JIL* 1962, 431, 442.

866 See, decisions cited in O'Connell, State Succession, v. I, 493; S.K. Agrawala, ibid. It should be noted that many decisions deal with cases of merger of different Indian entities (called "States") before and after the independence of India. For instance, see the case of *Kishangarh Electric Supply Co. Ltd v. United States of Rajasthan*, High Court of Rajasthan,

India, the continuing State of the British Dominion, remains responsible for internationally wrongful acts committed before the date of succession.

7.2.2 Belgian Court Cases in the Context of the Independence of Congo (1960)

Congo became an independent State on 30 June 1960.[867] Belgium's *Conseil d'Etat* and other courts have rendered many decisions dealing with several different problems of State succession.[868] In some cases, the *Conseil d'Etat* decided that Belgium should be responsible for the wrongful acts committed by the Belgian military in Congo even *after* its independence.[869] Some other cases concerned administrative actions and "delicts" committed by the colonial power before the independence of Congo.[870] In two cases, Belgian

5 May 1959, *All Indian Rep* 1960 Rajasthan 49, 40 *ILR* 365; 54 *AJIL* 1960, 900–901. In this case, the Court held that the successor "State" (Rajasthan) was not liable for the tortious acts (i.e. the taken of property without any compensation in return) of the former "State" (Kishangarh) committed against the plaintiff. For this reason, ILC Member Rajput (India) (ILC, "Provisional Summary Record of the 3379th Meeting", 69th sess., 16 Aug. 2017, A/CN.4/SR.3379) considers that these cases involving "provinces" within India are not relevant regarding the question of succession to responsibility.

867 Paul De Visscher, "Le problème de la succession d'Etats envisagé dans l'histoire diplomatique du Congo", 11 *Comunicazioni e studi*, 1960–1962, 53–83; Suzanne Bastid, "La succession du Congo belge aux obligations de l'Etat indépendant du Congo", *RJPUF* 1957, 356ff.

868 For an analysis of these cases: Paul De Visscher, ibid 75–85; Jean-Victor Louis, "L'accession du Congo belge à l'indépendance, problèmes de succession d'Etats dans la jurisprudence belge", *AFDI* 1966, 731–756; Jean-Pierre De Brandt, "De quelques problèmes de succession d'Etats à la suite de l'accession à l'indépendance de la République du Congo (Léopoldville)", *RBDI* 1965, 497–523; M. Waelbroeck, "Arrêt no. 8160 du Conseil d'Etat Belge, note d'observations", *RJDA* 1961, 34ff; L.F. Ganshof, "Les dettes de l'ex-colonie du Congo belge", *Rev. Juri. Congo*, 1964, 9 (ibib, 1965, 13); M. Rougevin-Baville, "Le sort des droits et obligations de l'ancienne 'Colonie du Congo belge' d'après la jurisprudence des juridictions de Belgique", 2(1) *Rev. Juri. Congo*, 1963, 1; A Durieux, "Le problème juridique des dettes du Congo et de l'Etat du Congo", *Aca. Roy. Sciences d'Outre-Mer*, Mémoire, t. 28, fasc. 3, 1961; Mulumba Lukoji, *Succession d'États aux droits patrimoniaux: le cas de l'ex-Congo belge (Zaïre): la dette publique coloniale* (PU Zaire 1979) 188ff.

869 These cases are mentioned in: Louis, ibid 742.

870 See, for instance, *Meert*, Opinion ("Avis") no. 8166, Conseil d'Etat, 21 October 1960, *J. Trib.* 1960, 738, *RJDA* 1961, 28; *Brasseries indigènes du Congo*, Opinion ("Avis") no. 9921, Conseil d'Etat, 8 March 1963, *RAACE* 1963, 217. Other cases are discussed in: Jean-Pierre De Brandt, "De quelques problèmes de succession d'Etats à la suite de l'accession à l'indépendance de la République du Congo (Léopoldville)", *RBDI* 1965–2, 505–509. On the question of the jurisdiction of Belgian courts over problems dealing with wrongful acts which took place in the territory of the new State of Congo, see: Jean-Victor Louis, "L'accession du Congo belge à l'indépendance, problèmes de succession d'Etats dans la jurisprudence belge", *AFDI* 1966, 734–744. This jurisdiction ended with the enactment of the Constitutional Law

courts made some interesting comments on the issue of State succession to responsibility.

The first case is *Crépet v. Etat belge et Société des forces hydro-électriques de la colonie* decided by the Civil Tribunal of Brussels,[871] without the appearance of Congo. The Court refused to hold Congo responsible for obligations arising from wrongful acts on the ground that, as a matter of principle, these acts do not pass automatically to the new State without any specific agreement to that effect between the predecessor State and the successor State.[872] Some writers have concluded that the Tribunal applied the principle of non-succession to responsibility.[873] This case is also an illustration of the principle that the continuing State (Belgium) remains responsible for wrongful acts it has committed in the colony before the independence of the new State.[874]

The second case is *Pittacos v. Etat Belge*, which was decided by the Appeal Court of Brussels.[875] The Court first confirmed the reasoning of the lower court

of Congo of 18 July 1963. See, Jean-Pierre De Brandt, "Jurisprudence belge relative au droit international public", *RBDI* 1966, 546–547.

871 *Crépet v. Etat belge et Société des forces hydro-électriques de la colonie*, Civil Tribunal of Brussels, 30 January 1962, *J. Trib.* 1962, 242. See, De Brandt, ibid 514–516. In 1958 (i.e. before the independence of Congo), the plaintiff filed a suit against the colonial Belgian Congo and a company for non-payment of public work he had performed. After the independence of Congo, the action was subsequently filed against the new State of Congo before a Belgian Court.

872 Ibid 244. This is relevant quote from the decision of the Tribunal: "Attendu, au contraire, que le second chef de demande se fonde sur un quasidélit, qu'aurait commis l'Etat prédécesseur et a trait à des dettes qui, en l'absence de convention internationale, ne se transmettent pas, en principe, à l'Etat successeur; Attendu qu'aucun traité relatif au passif de l'ancienne colonie du Congo belge n'a été conclu jusqu'ores entre la Belgique et le République du Congo et qu'aucune loi belge n'a été promulguée en la matière". It should be noted that the Civil Tribunal of Brussels also declared the action valid with respect to the *contractual debt* because it involved a "local debt" which was transmissible to the successor State (Congo). A similar statement was also made by the Civil Tribunal of Brussels in the case of *Société Forces de l'Est v. Etat belge*, 22 May 1962, *J. Trib.* 1962, 440–441.

873 O'Connell, Recent Problems, 164–165, for whom "the logical correlative of this [case] was that delictual claims arising against the Belgian Congo did not pass to the Republic of the Congo". See also, O'Connell, State Succession, v. 1, 483; Volkovitsch, 2201.

874 Jean-Pierre De Brandt, "De quelques problèmes de succession d'Etats à la suite de l'accession à l'indépendance de la République du Congo (Leopoldville)", *RBDI* 1965–2, 517, for whom "une dette basée sur un quasidélit ne se transmet pas automatiquement à l'Etat successeur *mais reste à charge de l'Etat démembré*" (emphasis added). Supporting the position adopted by the court: Michel Waelbroeck, "Arrêt no. 8160 du Conseil d'Etat Belge, note d'observations", 1 *RJDA* 1961, 34, 40.

875 *Pittacos v. Etat Belge*, Brussels Court of Appeal (2nd Ch.), 1 December 1964, *J. Trib.* 1965, 7, 9; *Pasicrisie Belge*, 1965, II, 263, 45 *ILR* 24. See, De Brandt, ibid 517–520; Verzijl, 227–228. This case dealt with damage arising out of the destruction in 1952 of the coffee

on the distinct legal personality of the colonial Belgian Congo and the legal consequences which followed.[876] The repeal of the "Colonial Charter" after the independence of Congo did not change the situation, as it was still not for Belgium to take over any of the assets and liabilities of the former colony.[877] The Appeal Court of Brussels nevertheless affirmed, based on equity grounds, the "principles of international law" whereby quasi-delictual debts arising before the independence of Congo remain those of the continuing State (Belgium):

> Attendu, certes que l'origine donnée par le sieur Pittacos à l'obligation qu'il impute à l'intimé de lui verser des indemnités complémentaires est quasi-délictuelle; que, par ailleurs, c'est sur l'équité que se fonde le principe de droit international public selon lequel *les dettes quasi-délictuelles nées avant le démembrement d'un Etat restent à la charge de l'Etat démembré* (*lequel serait, en l'occurrence, la Belgique*).[878] (emphasis added)

However, the Court concluded that the measures taken by the local colonial authorities may have been illegal, but they were certainly not inappropriate in the special circumstances of the case, as such measures greatly benefited the

plantations of the plaintiff by the authorities of the colonial Belgian Congo which had ordered its destruction to combat the progression of a disease in the region. The plaintiff had first brought his claim before the Court of First Instance of Stanleyville (in the colonial Belgian Congo) requesting some 40 million of Belgian Francs in compensation. In a judgment of 26 March 1960, the Court granted him compensation in the amount of some 15 million Belgian Francs. After the independence of the Republic of Congo, the plaintiff filed a claim *against Belgium* before the 2nd Ch. of the Court of First Instance of Brussels for compensation in an amount of some 5 million Belgian Francs.

876 In *Pittacos v. Etat Belge*, Court of First Instance of Brussels Tribunal (2nd Ch.), 14 January 1963, *J. Trib.* 1963, 64ff, the Court decided that an action for internationally wrongful acts committed during the colonial period was not receivable against Belgium itself but that, in accordance with the "Colonial Charter", it had to be filed against another entity, the colonial Belgian Congo. It should be noted that under the Colonial Charter ("*Charte coloniale*") of 18 October 1908, the "*Congo belge*" had a distinct legal personality from Belgium: *Loi sur le gouvernement du Congo belge*, 18 October 1908, *Pasicrisie belge*, 1908, no. 265. See, Paul De Visscher, "Le problème de la succession d'Etats envisagé dans l'histoire diplomatique du Congo", 11 *Comunicazioni e studi* 1960–1962, 67–74.

877 The Court of First Instance of Brussels (*Pittacos v. Etat Belge*, ibid) had decided that with respect to events which arose before the independence of the Congo, the existence of colonial Belgian Congo as a distinct legal entity was unaffected by the creation of the new State in 1960. A similar statement was also made by the Court of Appeal of Brussels in *Met Den Ancxt v. Belgium* (*Minister of Finance*), 9 January 1968, 69 *ILR* 28. This argument is criticised by De Visscher, ibid 82.

878 *Pittacos v. Etat Belge*, Brussels Court of Appeal (2nd Ch.), 1 December 1964, *J. Trib.* 1965, 7, 9; *Pasicrisie Belge*, 1965, II, 263, 45 *ILR* 24.

colony as a whole. The Court therefore decided, also *based on the principle of equity*, that under these specific circumstances, the delictual debts should not be borne by the continuing State (Belgium).[879] The decision of the Brussels Court of Appeal was confirmed by the Court of Cassation.[880] It should be noted that the new State of Congo was not a party to the proceedings and that the Court did not state that Congo should be held responsible for obligations arising from the wrongful acts.[881]

One issue which has recently been examined by scholars is Belgium's possible responsibility for crimes committed in Congo during the period of colonisation.[882]

7.2.3 State Practice of France and French Court Cases Supporting the Principle of Non-succession in the Context of the Independence of Algeria (1962)

The former French colony of Algeria became an independent State in July 1962 after a national liberation war which lasted for eight years. Many issues of succession of States have arisen in the years that followed independence.[883] Article 18 of the *Déclaration de principes relative à la coopération économique et financière* (dated 19 March 1962), which is part of the *Evian Accords* that ended the war, indicates that Algeria (the successor State) took over the obligations arising from internationally wrongful acts committed before the date

879 Ibid: "Attendu, qu'il se déduit de ces considérations que l'équité ne commanderait point que la dette d'indemnité pouvant résulter de la destruction dont litige soit à la charge de l'Etat démembrée".

880 *Pittacos v. Etat Belge*, Court of Cassation, 26 May 1966, *Pasicrisie Belge*, 1966, Part 1, 1221, 48 *ILR* 20ff. The Court once again confirmed that under the Colonial Charter, the Belgian Congo constituted an entity distinct from Metropolitan Belgium and that the assets and liabilities of Belgium and the colony were to be separated. Thus, the intention of the legislators was to prevent Belgium from being bound by the colony's obligations. The Court also indicated that the independence of Congo had repealed the Charter but that this in no way implied a merger of the assets and liabilities of the colony with those of Metropolitan Belgium ("a merger that would be irreconcilable with the sovereignty of the new independent State": 48 *ILR* 22).

881 On the contrary, Atlam, 218, interprets the *Pittacos* case as one example where the Court decided that the successor State (Congo) should take over the liabilities of the predecessor State.

882 Ruy & Baecke.

883 See, M. Flory et al., *La succession d'Etats en Afrique du Nord* (Coll. Etu. Ann. Afrique du Nord, CNRS, 1968) 104 p; Ch. Rousseau, "Chronique des faits internationaux", *RGDIP* 1963, 118–131.

of succession.[884] This point is discussed in detail below.[885] The new State of Algeria did not fully implement its obligations under Article 18 of the *Déclaration*.[886] Faced with such refusal by the Algerian authorities, France decided to compensate *French nationals* which had suffered damage during the national liberation war.[887] The new position taken by France was explained by the French Minister of Foreign Affairs in response to a question asked at the National Assembly:

> La réparation des dommages matériels consécutifs aux événements survenus en Algérie depuis le 1er novembre 1954 est une obligation de l'Etat algérien découlant ... de l'Article [sic] 19 de la Déclaration de principes relative à la coopération économique et financière des accords d'Evian (19 mars 1962). Les autorités algériennes qui avaient rempli cette obligation jusqu'au 31 décembre 1962, en ont interrompu l'exécution dès le début de l'année 1963. A la suite de cette interruption, le Gouvernement français, conscient de la situation dans laquelle se trouvaient certains de nos compatriotes victimes de dommages matériels, a décidé de leur accorder, au lieu et place de l'Algérie défaillante, un dédommagement dont le caractère social a été tout particulièrement marqué par l'exclusion des sociétés commerciales et la limitation à 100 000 francs de l'indemnité total susceptible d'être allouée à chacun d'eux pour l'ensemble de leurs sinistrés.[888]

However, such compensation was limited to those debts which were liquidated: "la créance dont le règlement est demandé doit être certaine, liquide et exigible".[889] One important limitation to the new French policy was that *it excluded foreigners* (as well as companies) from receiving any compensation

884 *JORF* 20 March 1962, 3019–3032. Art. 18 reads as follows: "Algeria shall assume the obligations and enjoy the rights contracted on behalf of itself or of Algerian public establishments by the competent French authorities".

885 See, Section 7.3.3.

886 This is the conclusion reached by J. Charpentier, "Pratique française du droit international", *AFDI* 1963, 1015–1016, 1021–1023.

887 Art. 13, *Loi de finances rectificative*, 31 July 1963, Decree no. 64–505, 5 June 1964. See also, the Decision of 20 April 1966. These developments are discussed in: J. Charpentier, "Pratique française du droit international", *AFDI* 1970, 942–943. The cases were handled by a special Commission ("*Commission interministérielle des dommages matériels*"). The procedure of the Commission is explained in: Charpentier, ibid *AFDI* 1969, 882.

888 *JORF Assemblée nationale*, no. 9458, 7 March 1970, 540, in: Charpentier, ibid *AFDI* 1970, 942–943.

889 This is the position adopted by the French government as illustrated by the response given by the State Secretary for Algerian Affairs to a question asked at the National

for damage suffered during the war.[890] This is an important point that somewhat limits the relevance of this example. Thus, it is not at all surprising that France provided compensation to individuals which were its nationals at the time the events took place and which had remained its nationals after the independence of Algeria.[891] Further, it seems that all plaintiffs had left Algeria since independence and were now living in France. In other words, this example does not deal with any issue of *international* responsibility.

The above-mentioned new position taken by France was subsequently further explained in an official statement by the State Secretary for Algerian Affairs indicating that compensation for acts of expropriation committed by France should be dealt with by Algeria only to the extent that these acts were done "in the name" of Algeria.[892] Faced with such an official statement, French Courts requested from the Ministry of Foreign Affairs of France an official interpretation of Article 18 of the *Déclaration*.[893] The official position of the Ministry, which was delivered to the *Conseil d'Etat* in letters dated 13 February 1963 and 30 July 1963, starts with a general assessment of the practice of State succession, which is described as a "collection de pratiques disparates plutôt qu'un corps de règles coherent", and the indication that such practice is of no great help to solve the issue in the context of the independence of Algeria.[894] The

Assembly: *JORF Assemblée nationale*, no. 3814, 28 September 1963, 4919, in: Charpentier, ibid *AFDI* 1963, 1021. See also: Barde, 186.

890 Charpentier, ibid *AFDI* 1968, 880; M. Flory et al., *La succession d'Etats en Afrique du Nord* (Coll. Etu. Ann. Afrique du Nord, CNRS 1968) 97.

891 Thus, the above-mentioned statement of the French Minister of Foreign Affairs, which was made in 1970 (i.e. almost 10 years after the independence of Algeria), makes reference to "nos compatriotes victimes de dommages matériels". This is a clear reference to the fact that the victims were French nationals at the time when compensation was provided.

892 Statement of the French State Secretary for Algerian Affairs, *JORF Assemblée nationale*, no. 3814, 28 September 1963, 4919, in: Jean Charpentier, "Pratique française du droit international", *AFDI* 1963, 1021: "Les créances résultant de décisions des autorités françaises sont donc désormais à la charge de l'Algérie si ces décisions peuvent être considérées comme ayant été prises au nom de cette dernière ou d'un établissement public algérien (…) Ces dispositions sont notamment applicables aux indemnités d'expropriation pour cause d'utilité publique".

893 This request was made in *Union régionale d'Algérie de la C.F.T.C.*, Conseil d'État, 5 March 1965, in: Ch. Rousseau, "Jurisprudence française en matière de droit international public", *RGDIP* 1965, 846–847; 44 *ILR* 43; *JDI* 1967–2 387.

894 "Conclusions de M. le Commissaire du Gouvernement Fournier", extracts in *JDI* 1967–2, 387: "Il est de fait qu'en ce domaine les certitudes sont rares et que les exemples que l'on peut tirer de certains précédents internationaux, souvent fort anciens, sont difficilement applicables aux problèmes, à bien des égards nouveaux, que pose au XXème siècle l'accession à l'indépendance d'un grand nombre de pays jusqu'alors colonisés. Ni la succession des Etats-Unis d'Amérique à la fin du XVIIIème siècle, ni l'émancipation des colonies

Ministry took the view that Algeria should not be responsible for the acts and measures taken by France that were *specifically directed against the rebellion of the FLN*. France should therefore remain responsible for the consequences of such measures. This is the reasoning of the Ministry:

> Tout d'abord, l'accession à l'indépendance de ce pays [l'Algérie] a été précédée d'un conflit prolongé au cours duquel un certain nombre de mesures ont été prises par le Gouvernement français en vue, précisément, d'empêcher cette accession à l'indépendance. On ne pouvait guère envisager, quelle que fussent les perspectives de relations futures entre les deux pays, de voir les autorités algériennes accepter de prendre en charge les obligations contractées à ce titre par l'Etat français. Il est donc normal de considérer que le contentieux de ces mesures, prises en vue de faire échec aux mouvements insurrectionnels, n'intéresse pas l'Etat algérien au sens du protocole. On ne fait ici que rejoindre une distinction faite depuis longtemps par les théoriciens du droit international qui, s'ils admettent que l'Etat successeur doit prendre une part du passif de son prédécesseur, en excluent toujours les dettes dites de guerre ou de régime, c'est-à-dire celles qui ont été contractées en vue d'empêcher l'annexion ou de s'opposer à l'émancipation.[895]

This principle has been consistently applied by French municipal courts.[896] The position of the Ministry seems to be in accordance with the principle,

---

espagnoles d'Amérique latine au début du XIXème siècle, ni l'apparition plus récente d'Etats européens nouveaux issus du démantèlement de l'Autriche-Hongrie ne peuvent ici être d'un grand secours, quant à la détermination des règles applicables, tant sont différentes les circonstances de temps et de lieu".

895 Ibid 389.

896 *Union régionale d'Algérie de la C.F.T.C.*, Conseil d'Etat, 5 March 1965, 44 *ILR* 43; *Etat français v. Consorts Caldumbide*, Cass. Civ. 3e, 7 November 1969, *Jurisclasseur périodique* (*la Semaine juridique*), 1970, no. 16248 (in: Jean-François Lachaume, "Jurisprudence française relative au droit international public (1969)", *AFDI* 1970, 904, in: D.R. "Chronique de Jurisprudence française", *JDI* 1970, 718); *Bounouala*, Conseil d'Etat, 25 May 1970, *Rec. Déc. Conseil d'Etat*, 1970, 350, 72 *ILR* 56; *Kaddour*, Conseil d'Etat, case no. 04642, 10 May 1968, *Rec. Lebon; Veuve Haffiade Messaoud*, Conseil d'Etat, case no. 51458, 10 May 1968, *Rec. Lebon; Saiah*, Cour de Cassation, Ch. Civile 1, case no. 76–14704, 12 December 1977, *Bull. arrêts Cour de Cassation*, Ch. Civ. 1 N. 470, 373; *Consorts Deguy-Charon-Gerst*, Cour de Cassation, Ch. Civile 1, case no. 69–11738, 29 May 1973, *Bulletin*, ibid 1 N. 183, 163; *Consorts Richard*, Cour de Cassation, Ch. Civ. 3, case no. 69–70143, 19 March 1970, *Bulletin*, ibid 3 N. 222, 163; *Veuve Chaurand v. Agent judiciaire du trésor public*, Tribunal de grande instance of Riom, 2 October 1963, *Gaz. palais*, 1964, 1, 155 (in: Ch. Rousseau, "Jurisprudence française en matière de droit international public", *RGDIP* 1964, 750, *AFDI* 1964, 871, 44 *ILR* 39).

which is examined below,[897] that whenever damage is inflicted by the *actions of the predecessor State* (i.e. the French colonial authorities) in fighting secessionist "rebels" (which later become an independent State), the consequences of these wrongful acts should not be supported by the new State upon its independence. In such instances, the continuing State should remain responsible for the wrongful acts *it committed* before the date of succession. French courts have applied a different solution when wrongful acts were committed *by the FLN*.[898]

This exception to the principle of succession established in Article 18 of the *Déclaration* was thus limited to measures taken by France that were specifically directed *against the rebellion of the FLN* and provided compensation only for *French nationals*. Therefore, Algeria was responsible for all other types of obligations arising from wrongful acts committed before the date of succession as well as for those committed against *foreign nationals* and other States. I have found one case of State practice involving the commission of a wrongful act against a *foreign national* where France nevertheless decided to provide reparation.

This case involves damage to property suffered in May 1961 by a Swiss national, Mr Gehrig, a trader who was also the Consular Agent of Switzerland in Oran.[899] The internationally wrongful acts were not committed by the French colonial authorities but by the OAS (*Organisation armée secrète*), a para-military organisation of French nationals in Algeria opposed to its independence. Switzerland negotiated directly with the French government to settle these claims.[900] France (as the continuing State) recognised its responsibility for the wrongful act probably based on the ground that the perpetrators were French nationals opposed to the independence of Algeria and that it would have been contrary to equity for the new State of Algeria to be held accountable for such act.

897 This principle is discussed in Chapter 3, Section 6. See, Dumberry, Rebellions, 365.

898 For an analysis, see ibid 299.

899 This case is mentioned in: *Rap. Conseil fédéral*, 1965, 28, in: Paul Guggenheim, "La pratique suisse 1965", 23 *ASDI* 1966, 87. See, Ch. Rousseau, "Chronique des faits internationaux", *RGDIP* 1966, 995–996; Rousseau, ibid, *RGDIP* 1961, 602–603; Natalino Ronzitti, *La successione internazionale tra stati* (Giuffrè 1970) 217.

900 The Swiss government (ibid) refers to the unresolved issue of compensation for 50 Swiss nationals which suffered damage before the independence of Algeria (with the exception of the claim of Mr Gehrig discussed here).

7.2.4 A French Court Case in the Context of the Independence of Vanuatu (1980)

In the *Russet* case, the French *Conseil d'Etat* ordered France to pay to Mr Russet an amount equivalent to the compensation originally awarded by the judgment of the Court of Appeal of Nouméa before the independence of the Republic of Vanuatu.[901] It held that the continuing State (France) should pay compensation for wrongful acts *it committed* against a French national before the independence of Vanuatu.[902] The *Conseil d'Etat* also indicated that France should in turn ask the UK and the Republic of Vanuatu for payment of this sum of compensation.

It has been suggested that the decision is an illustration of the fact that the new State should not take over the consequences of internationally wrongful acts committed before its independence.[903] In fact, the reasoning of the *Conseil d'Etat* shows that the continuing State continues its responsibility for

901 *Russet*, Conseil d'Etat, 5 October 1984, case no. 51543, *Rec. Lebon*, in: Ch. Rousseau, "Jurisprudence française en matière de droit international public", *RGDIP* 1986, 249; 89 *ILR* 15. This case arose from the necessity to improve security at the airport of Port-Vila and a 1971 joint decision issued by the "Resident Commissioner" for France and the UK on the New Hebrides Island formally requiring Mr Russet, a French national who owned land adjoining the airport, to cut down a certain number of coconut palms and remove certain buildings. Mr Russet refused and the question was finally decided by the (French) Court of Appeal of Nouméa in 1974 awarding him substantial damages. Mr Russet tried unsuccessfully to obtain the execution of the judgment. Following the accession of the territory to independence as the Republic of Vanuatu on 30 July 1980, Mr Russet instituted proceedings against France (the continuing State) before French administrative courts requesting an order for the payment of the compensation which had been awarded by the courts before the independence of Vanuatu. In a judgment of the administrative Tribunal of Paris, 24 November 1982, the application was rejected. Mr Russet filed an appeal to the *Conseil d'Etat*.

902 This is the relevant quote from the decision: "In order to refuse to execute the judicial award, the State based itself on the ground that the accession of the New Hebrides to internal autonomy pursuant to a diplomatic exchange of letters of 15 September 1977, and subsequently independence on 30 July 1980, had deprived Mr Russet of all means of action against the debtor in order to obtain payment of the compensation award. In these circumstances, the French State, by refusing to ensure the execution of the order made against it in 1974 [by the Court of Appeal of Nouméa], committed a fault such as to engage its responsibility".

903 Jean-François Lachaume, "Jurisprudence française relative au droit international (année 1985)", *AFDI* 1986, 931: "A s'en tenir aux principes les plus classiques du droit international public, il s'avérait difficile de mettre en cause la responsabilité de Vanuatu; l'acte reproché à la France, dans la mesure où il aurait été constitutif d'une faute, ne saurait engager la responsabilité de l'Etat successeur; ce dernier pouvait faire valoir que l'occupation du domaine, étant liée au processus de succession d'Etats, il y aurait là une dette odieuse qu'il n'était pas tenu d'honorer".

pre-succession damage and that this applies *a fortiori* when dealing with the obligation to honour the administrative debts which were its own before the date of succession.[904] It should be noted, however, that in another case in the context of the independence of Vanuatu the Court came up with a different solution.[905]

7.2.5 The 1958 Peace Treaty between Indonesia and Japan

Indonesia became an independent State a few years after the Second World War.[906] On 20 January 1958, Indonesia entered into a peace treaty with Japan terminating the state of war between the two countries.[907] The treaty provided for Japan to pay reparation arising out of the internationally wrongful acts it committed during the Second World War at the time Indonesia was still a Dutch colony.[908] Under Article 5 of the treaty, Japan waived its claims against the Republic of Indonesia for any internationally wrongful acts which may have been committed by the predecessor State (the former Netherlands East Indies) before the creation of Indonesia as an independent State.[909]

904 Charles Rousseau, "Jurisprudence française en matière de droit international public", *RGDIP* 1986, 252.

905 S.A. *Ballande Vanuatu* case, Conseil d'Etat, 27 September 1985, *Rec. Lebon*, 1985, 680; *RFDA* 1986, 273, in: Jean-François Lachaume, "Jurisprudence française relative au droit international (année 1985)", *AFDI* 1986, 930. This case dealt with damage caused to property of a company whose premises were illegally occupied in 1978–1979. The Resident Commissioner for France had failed to take action to remove the occupiers by force. The Conseil d'Etat concluded that although the company had obtained a judicial order in May 1980, there had been insufficient time for the French authorities to decide what action to take prior to the accession of the territory to independence in July 1980 and that from that date the French authorities were no longer responsible for the enforcement of the order.

906 During WWII, the Dutch colony of Indonesia was occupied by Japan. The Republic of Indonesia was officially created on 17 August 1945 when its independence was proclaimed just days after Japan surrendered to the Allies during WWII. This declaration of independence was not recognised by the Netherlands, the former colonial power, which made several military offensives between 1945 and 1949 to reoccupy Indonesia. Finally, in November 1949, the Netherlands recognised the sovereignty of the Republic of Indonesia. On 27 December 1949 the Dutch East Indies ceased to exist. On 28 September 1950, Indonesia became a UN member. Between 1949 and 1956, Indonesia entered into a real union with the Netherlands.

907 *Treaty of Peace between Japan and the Republic of Indonesia*, in force on 15 April 1958, 324 *UNTS* 227, 3 *Jap. AIL*, 1959, 158; Weston & Lillich, 158.

908 Aspects of the treaty dealing with Indonesia's right to reparation are analysed below: Part 3, Chapter 5, Section 3.4.2.

909 Art. 5: "(1). Japan waives all claims of Japan and its nationals against the Republic of Indonesia and its nationals arising out of the War or out of actions taken because of the existence of a state of war. (2). The foregoing waiver includes any claims arising out of actions taken by the former Netherlands East Indies or the Republic of Indonesia with

This provision may be interpreted as the acknowledgement by Japan that the new State of Indonesia could not be held responsible for the acts committed by a State (the Netherlands) whose continuity was not affected by the birth of the new State. Another interpretation is more simply that Japan only waived its claims against Indonesia in reciprocity for a similar waiver made by Indonesia in the treaty.[910]

7.2.6 Ghana (1957)

Ghana became an independent State on 6 March 1957. Almost ten years before, riots had erupted in the then British colony of Gold Coast; it involved natives demonstrating against British rule in the colony. During the trouble, a Swiss company suffered damage to its property.[911] After the events, Switzerland and the UK entered into diplomatic discussions which eventually led to the recognition by the latter of its responsibility under international law for the acts committed by rioters against foreign properties. It is important to note that this agreement took place in 1957, just *before* the independence of Ghana. The effective payment by the UK to the Swiss government for the damage suffered was, however, made in August 1957, i.e. *after* Ghana had become an independent State.

One possible interpretation of this example is that it supports the view that the continuing State (the UK) should remain responsible for internationally wrongful acts committed before the creation of the new State. Another more likely interpretation is that the UK made payment *after* the independence of Ghana simply based on good faith and the fact that it had already agreed to it before the date of succession.

7.2.7 The *Mutua* Case in the Context of the Independence of Kenya (1963)

The case involves allegations of "torts of assault and battery and negligence" committed by the Colonial British Government in Kenya during the so-called

---

respect to Japanese ships between September 1, 1939, and September 2, 1945, as well as any claims and debts arising in respect to Japanese prisoners of war and civilians internees in the hands of the former Netherlands East Indies or the Republic of Indonesia, but does not include Japanese claims specifically recognized in the laws of the Republic of Indonesia enacted since September 2, 1945".

910 Art. 4(2): "Indonesia waives all reparations claims of the Republic of Indonesia and all other claims of the Republic of Indonesia and its nationals arising out of any actions taken by Japan and its nationals in the course of the prosecution of the War".

911 These events are referred to in: *Rap. Conseil fédéral*, 1957, 152, in: Paul Guggenheim, "La pratique suisse, 1957", 15 *ASDI* 1958, 257.

"Mau-Mau" uprising in the 1950s. The revolt against British colonial rule in Kenya led to the proclamation of a formal state of emergency (which lasted from 1952 until 1960).[912] The claim was filed by five Claimants who were veterans of the Mau Mau movement.[913] The claim was filed before an English Court on the grounds that the defendant (the UK) was liable for acts committed by the colonial authority, or, alternatively, owed a duty of care which it negligently failed to discharge.[914] The defendant argued that no claim could be brought against the UK government, since the Colonial Administration had acted on its own. It filed an application for orders to strike out the claims and/or for summary judgment dismissing it.[915] This case involves a wrongful act committed by the predecessor State (the British colonial authorities) *against the local population* of Kenya during the insurrection period before independence. The important difference (already discussed above[916]) between this type of case and others involving third States was highlighted by the Judge.[917]

The position of the UK Foreign Office was summarised as follows by Justice McCombre:

> The FCO [Foreign and Commonwealth Office] has brought applications to strike out the claims and for summary judgment in its favour, in advance of a full trial, on the grounds that the claims disclose no cause of action in law and have no real prospect of success against the

912 *Mutua et al. v. The Foreign and Commonwealth Office*, High Court of Justice (Justice McCombe), judgments of 21 July 2011, [2011] EWHC 1913 (QB) and of 5 October 2012, [2012] EWHC 2678 (QB).

913 Ibid Judgment, 21 July 2011, para 1.

914 Ibid Summary of Judgment, para 5.

915 Ibid para 3.

916 See, Part 1, Section 4.7.

917 *Mutua*, Judgment, 21 July 2011, paras 88–99, referring to material submitted by the claimants (two Vienna Conventions on State succession and the *R.E. Brown* and the *Hawaiian Claim* cases) and stating: "I accept the defendant's submission that it really takes the matter nowhere as it clearly deals with the succession of states in respect of obligations assumed to other states. It has nothing to do with liability of a newly independent state under municipal law for torts of a previous government committed on private individuals. Equally, the second category is unhelpful as it deals with claims between the *governments/states* of the US and the UK respectively on the international plane. We are concerned with claims by private individuals, against one or more governments, on one or more domestic planes". He also noted that "decisions in the French, German and Dutch courts arising out of the pre-independence actions of the pre-existing colonial governments in Algeria, Tanganyika (Tanzania) and Indonesia" were "more promising from the claimants' point of view" because they are "decisions of domestic courts on claims made by private individuals or entities against former colonial powers".

> UK Government. The FCO's case (in very broad outline) is that any claim that the claimants might have had could only have been brought against the direct perpetrators of the alleged assaults and/or their employer at the time, the Colonial Government in Kenya, and not against the British government.[918]

The Claimants' arguments were summarised as follows:

> The claimants have argued in contrast that the British government are at least arguably liable to them for their injuries on five different legal bases. First, they say that the liabilities of the old Colonial Government (which ceased to exist in 1963) devolved upon the U.K. Government on independence, under the common law incorporating general principles of public international law. Secondly and thirdly, it is said that the U.K. Government was and is directly liable to the claimants for having instigated and procured, through (a) the Army and (b) the Colonial Office, a system of torture and ill-treatment of detainees as part of a common design shared with the Colonial Government in Kenya. Fourthly, the claimants argue that in July 1957 the British government expressly instructed, authorised or approved a policy of mistreatment of detainees, as shown by a series of exchanges between the Governor of the colony and the Colonial Office in London. (Copies of the most important documents on this issue, as presently available, are annexed to the judgment.) Fifthly, it is said that the UK Government, as paramount colonial power, owed a duty of care in law to the claimants to prevent abuses, which it knew were being committed and which it had the power to prevent; it is alleged that the UK Government is liable to the claimants for breach of that duty.[919]

Justice McCombe of the High Court considered that "the liability for present claims (in so far as available against the Colonial Government) would have passed to/remained with the new independent monarchy in December 1963" (i.e. when Kenya became an independent State).[920] Justice McCombe added that "it was for Kenya, as an independent State, to decide whether or not it was willing to assume the liabilities of the British Colonial Administration".[921]

918 Ibid Summary of Judgment, para 3.

919 Ibid Summary of Judgment, para 5.

920 Ibid Judgment, 21 July 2011, para 79.

921 Ibid para 79. See also, para 83: "[i]n this case, there was no express transfer of rights and liabilities to the new Kenyan state by the Independence Act. However, the mechanism of the Act and related instruments was to leave the rights and liabilities of the old Kenyan

Yet, as mentioned by the Claimants, "neither the Kenya Independence Act 1963, nor any other UK statute or instrument, addresses the question of the succession of liabilities of the Colonial Administration for assaults against the Claimants".[922] Therefore, for the Judge, the matter had to be "resolved under the Common Law", adding that "one source of the common law is customary international law, including principles on state succession".[923] It is in this context that the High Court examined issues of State succession to responsibility.

The Claimants argued that under a principle of "customary international law", after the independence of a former colony, the predecessor State remains responsible for its own wrongful acts committed against the population of that colony.[924] Specifically, the Claimants stated (referring to French cases mentioned above in the context of the independence of Algeria[925]) that "in the context of decolonisation it has been accepted by predecessor states that liabilities for tortious acts of their colonial administrations in respect of the suppression of an insurrectional movement should be opposable to the predecessor state upon independence".[926] Justice McCombe was however not persuaded by that position: "I agree with the defendant, however, that the Claimants have not been able to establish with any clarity a sufficiently 'extensive and virtually uniform' rule of customary international law to constitute it as the basis of a claim under the common law of England".[927] As a result, the High Court was hesitant to recognise the principle of non-succession which had been adopted by France in the context of the independence of Algeria.[928]

administration with the new Kenyan administration. As I have said, it was for the independent Kenya to determine the extent to which it wished to exclude its government from such liabilities before its own courts for the future".

922 Ibid para 81(a).

923 Ibid para 81(a)(b).

924 Ibid para 81(d): "In accordance with the principles of customary international law relating to the creation of a new state in the context of decolonisation (the successor state), a liability of the colonial administration of the predecessor state in respect of tortious acts committed against the native population devolves to the predecessor state upon independence. Therefore, under the common law, the liability to compensate the Claimants for injuries inflicted by the Colonial Administration of the Crown in right of Kenya devolved to the Crown in right of the UK upon the independence of Kenya".

925 See, Section 7.2.3.

926 *Mutua*, Judgment, 21 July 2011, para 90.

927 Ibid para 95.

928 Ibid para 93: "[a]gain, however, I think that there is force in the defendant's submission that the French cases (to which I was not taken individually or in any detail) seem to have turned upon the agreements known as the Evian Accords and Protocols and were, in effect, decisions on specific treaties made on the creation of the independent Algeria. It is

Nevertheless, the High Court rejected the Defendant's request to dismiss the case before it would come to a trial. This first judgment then opened the way for an examination of the responsibility of the British Government for the alleged acts at the merits stage of the trial. A settlement was eventually reached between the Claimants and the UK in 2013 for the "payment of a settlement sum in respect of 5,228 claimants, as well as a gross costs sum, to the total value of £19.9 million".[929] In his declaration to the House of Commons, Foreign Secretary Hague stated that while the UK "continue[s] to deny liability (…) for the actions of the colonial administration in respect of the claims" and that "the courts have made no finding of liability against the Government in this case", it nevertheless "recognises that Kenyans were subject to torture and other forms of ill treatment at the hands of the colonial administration" and "sincerely regrets that these abuses took place, and that they marred Kenya's progress towards independence".[930]

At the end of the day, while the judgement did not endorse the principle of non-succession, Justice McCombe also rejected the proposition that Kenya was, as a matter of principle, *responsible* for obligations arising from wrongful acts committed by the British colonial authorities (the predecessor State). Thus, he made it clear that, upon independence in 1963, "it was a matter for the Kenyan parliament to decide whether it wished to exclude such claims by separate legislation".[931] The Kenyan parliament was free "to enact legislation to prevent the Kenyan government being sued in the Kenyan courts in respect of such pre-December 1963 government liabilities as it chose", adding that "the remedy lay in the hands of an independent Kenya—a result which is hardly repugnant to the concept of a free and independent state".[932] Interestingly, the UK mentioned this case in a letter following a request by the ILC for relevant documents related to State succession to responsibility and indicated that the judge "found that the Claimant had not established a rule of succession to international responsibility under customary international law".[933] Yet, as noted by Crawford, this case was not really about international responsibility, but rather about municipal torts committed by the colonial administration.[934]

---

argued that this series of cases cannot, therefore, simply be transposed onto the circumstances of the Mau Mau uprising and the subsequent independence of Kenya".

929 "Statement to Parliament on settlement of Mau Mau claims", Foreign & Commonwealth Office, 6 June 2013.

930 Ibid.

931 *Mutua*, Judgment, 21 July 2011, para 79.

932 Ibid para 78.

933 UK, letter to the ILC, Dec. 2018.

934 Crawford, State Responsibility, 436.

In any event, the Judge recognised the basic principle whereby a new State is always free to accept responsibility for wrongs committed before the date of succession.[935]

7.3 *Examples Where the Successor State Took Over the Obligations Arising from the Commission of Internationally Wrongful Acts*

I have just examined several examples of State practice and municipal court cases where the continuing State remained responsible for wrongful acts committed before the creation of the new State. I have also found other examples where, on the contrary, the new successor State took over the obligations arising from wrongful acts committed before the date of succession. This is, for instance, the case of Dutch courts' decisions which held that the new State of Indonesia took over the obligations arising from wrongful acts committed by the Netherlands during the Second World War (Section 7.3.1).[936] It should be noted that these municipal law cases do *not* involve questions of succession to *international* responsibility, as the wrongful acts were committed by the predecessor State not against another State (or a national of another State) but against individuals who were at the time *its own nationals*.[937]

I have found some treaties involving Newly Independent States where the parties agreed that the new State would, after its independence, take over all existing liabilities and obligations for which the predecessor colonial State was responsible before the date of succession:[938]

- Treaty on the creation of the Republic of Cyprus, signed by the UK, Greece, Turkey and Cyprus;[939]
- Agreement between the US and the Philippines; [940]

935 This principle is discussed in: Chapter 3, Section 4.

936 *Poldermans v. State of the Netherlands*, Court of Appeal of The Hague (First Ch.), 8 December 1955, *NJ* 1959, no. 7, *ILR* 1957, 69; *Poldermans v. State of the Netherlands*, Supreme Court, 15 June 1956, ibid. *Van der Have v. State of the Netherlands*, District Court of The Hague, 12 January 1953, *NJ* 1953, no. 133, *ILR* 1953, 80.

937 The reasons for treating these types of cases differently have been explained in Part 1, Section 4.7.

938 See, ILC, "Succession of States in respect of State responsibility, Information on treaties which may be of relevance to the future work of the Commission on the topic", Memorandum by the Secretariat, A/CN.4/730*, 20 March 2019.

939 *Treaty concerning the Establishment of the Republic of Cyprus*, 16 August 1960, 382 *UNTS*, no. 5476, 8, Art. 8(1): "All international obligations and responsibilities of the Government of the UK shall henceforth, in so far as they may be held to have application to the Republic of Cyprus, be assumed by the Government of the Republic of Cyprus".

940 *The Treaty of General Relations and Protocol between the United States of America and the Philippines*, 4 July 1946, in force on 22 October 1946, 7 *UNTS*, no. 88, 3, Art. 4: "The Republic of the Philippines agrees to assume, and does hereby assume, all the debts and liabilities

- Agreement between the Netherlands and Indonesia;[941]
- Agreement between Italy and Libya; [942]
- Agreement between France and Morocco;[943]
- Agreement between France and Algeria;[944] and
- Agreement between Malaysia and Singapore.[945]

---

of the Philippine Islands, its provinces, cities, municipalities and instrumentalities, which shall be valid and subsisting on the date hereof".

941 *Draft Agreement on Transitional Measures*, part of the *Round-Table Conference Agreement* entered into by the Kingdom of the Netherlands and the Republic of Indonesia, 2 November 1949, 69 *UNTS*, no. 894, 200, 267, Art. 4(1): "The Kingdom of the Netherlands and the Republic of the United States of Indonesia recognize and accept that all rights and obligations of Indonesia, under private and public law, are ipso jure transferred to the Republic of the United States of Indonesia, unless otherwise provided for in the special agreements included in the Union Statute".

942 *Agreement on Economic Cooperation and Settlement of Issues Arising from Resolution 388 (V) of 15 December 1950*, 2 October 1956, in force on 7 December 1957, 2328 *UNTS*, no. 41716, 149. Art. 5: "The Libyan Government, as the successor to the Italian State in the property rights referred to in the preceding article, declares that it recognizes the property rights of third parties, who consequently may not bring any claim against the Italian State in respect of those rights. The Libyan Government shall exercise the rights previously held by the Italian State vis-à-vis third parties". By an exchange of notes dated 2 October 1956 (2328 *UNTS*, no. 41716, 149, notes I (A) and II (A)), the parties further confirmed certain understandings, including with reference to Art. 5 of the Agreement, whereby the "Libyan Government declares that it assumes responsibility for any compensation still owed to Libyan nationals as a result of expropriations carried out by the Italian Government and the former Italian administration in Libya. The Italian Government shall see to the payment of such compensation still owed to Italian nationals".

943 *Treaty between France and Morocco*, 28 May 1956, in: UN, *Materials on Succession of States*, 1967, ST/LEG/SER.B/14, 169, Art. 11: "Le Maroc assume les obligations résultant des traités internationaux passés par la France au nom du Maroc, ainsi que celles qui résultent des actes internationaux relatifs au Maroc qui n'ont pas donné lieu à des observations de sa part" (translation: "Morocco assumes the obligations resulting from international treaties entered into by France on behalf of Morocco, as well as those resulting from international acts relating to Morocco which have not given rise to observations by Morocco").

944 Art. 18, *Déclaration de principes relative à la coopération économique et financière* entered into between France and Algeria as part of the *Evian Accords* providing that the new State of Algeria will make reparation for all wrongful acts committed before the date of succession. This treaty is further examined in Section 7.3.3.

945 *Agreement Relating to the Separation of Singapore from Malaysia as an Independent and Sovereign State*, 7 August 1965, 563 *UNTS*, no. 8206, 89. The Agreement provides that "Singapore shall cease to be a State of Malaysia on the 9th day of August, 1965" (called "Singapore Day") "and shall become an independent and sovereign state". See, Annex B, Art. 9 (entitled "Transfer of property and succession to rights, liabilities and obligations"): "All property, movable and immovable, and rights, liabilities and obligations which before Malaysia Day belonged to or were the responsibility of the Government of Singapore and which on that day or after became the property of or the responsibility of

In his First Report, the ILC Special Rapporteur mentioned that "many devolution agreements concluded by the former dependent territories of the UK (...) also provide for the continuity of delictual responsibility of the new States".[946] In fact, these treaties only provide for the transfer of obligations to the new State *in relation to treaties* that the UK was party to before independence. One typical example is the treaty between the UK and Ghana.[947] Agreements entered into by the UK with former colonies very rarely mentioned anything about succession to obligations, liabilities or torts. I have found only one example:[948] the above-mentioned 1960 treaty concerning Cyprus.[949]

As further explained below, the principle of succession is well-illustrated by the Constitution of Namibia, which indicates that, as a matter of principle, the new State is responsible for the obligations arising from internationally wrongful acts committed by South Africa (but also that Namibia may repudiate such acts). The transfer of the obligation to repair to the successor State has been applied by the Supreme Court of Namibia in the case of *Minister of Defence, Namibia v. Mwandinghi*[950] (Section 7.3.4). Another relevant example, further examined below (Section 7.3.2), illustrating the principle of succession is the Constitution of the Federation of Malaya. Finally, the principle of succession is also supported by Article 18 of the *Déclaration de principes relative à la coopération économique et financière* entered into between France and Algeria and by official statements made by the French government which clearly indicate that

---

the Government of Malaysia shall on Singapore Day revert to and vest in or devolve upon and become once again the property of or the responsibility of Singapore".

946 ILC Special Rapporteur Šturma, First Report, 2017, para 40.

947 *Exchange of Letters Constituting an Agreement Relative to the Inheritance of International Rights and Obligations by the Government of Ghana*, 25 November 1957, 287 *UNTS*, no. 4189, 233. See, Art. (i) indicating that "all obligations and responsibilities of the Government of the UK which arise from any valid international instrument shall henceforth, in so far as such instrument may be held to have application to Ghana, be assumed by the Government of Ghana". Art. (ii) indicates that "the rights and benefits heretofore enjoyed by the Government of the UK in virtue of the application of any such international instrument to the Gold Coast shall henceforth be enjoyed by the Government of Ghana".

948 I have examined: UN, *Materials on Succession of States*, 1967, ST/LEG/SER.B/14; ILC, "Succession of States in respect of State responsibility, Information on treaties which may be of relevance to the future work of the Commission on the topic", Memorandum by the Secretariat, A/CN.4/730*, 20 March 2019.

949 The treaty is mentioned in: ILC Special Rapporteur Šturma, First Report, 2017, para 98.

950 *Mwandinghi* case, Namibia, Supreme Court, 358. See also, the previous decision of the High Court: *Mwandinghi v. Minister of Defence, Namibia*, 14 December 1990, 1991 (1) *SA* 851 (Nm), 91 *ILR* 343 (hereinafter "*Mwandinghi* case, Namibia, High Court").

Algeria should be liable for *all* internationally wrongful acts committed before the date of succession (Section 7.3.3).[951]

It is important to note that although several examples have been found where the successor State was held responsible for pre-succession damage, some of these cases are not entirely convincing and can hardly support any general principle in favour of succession in the context of Newly Independent States. Thus, it seems that the outcome of several of these cases was ultimately *politically motivated* and driven by special circumstances. This aspect is further discussed below.

7.3.1 Dutch Court Cases in the Context of the Independence of Indonesia (1949)

There are at least two decisions of Dutch courts which held that it was for the new State of Indonesia to take over the consequences of a wrongful act committed by the Netherlands during the Second World War.

The first case was decided by the District Court of The Hague in the *Van der Have* case.[952] The Netherlands argued that according to Article 4 of the 1949 *Draft Agreement on Transitional Measures* entered into between the Kingdom of the Netherlands and the Republic of Indonesia, liabilities for the "Asian part" of the Kingdom of the Netherlands were transferred to the new Republic of Indonesia.[953] The Court held that it was, as a matter of principle,

---

951 An exception to this rule of succession has already been examined (Section 7.2.3): the continuing State (France) should remain responsible for the wrongful acts it committed against *French nationals* in fighting the rebels of the FLN.

952 *Van der Have v. State of the Netherlands*, District Court of The Hague, 12 January 1953, *NJ* 1953, no. 133, *ILR* 1953, 80. This case concerned the death of an Indonesian native who was killed unlawfully by a soldier of the Royal Netherlands Indies Army in the context of the repression by the Dutch Army of the rebellions of native Indonesian secessionist groups in Java (these events are known as the "second military action" of 18 December 1948). After WWII, the widow sought to recover compensation before Dutch Courts for the loss she had suffered from the death of her husband.

953 *Draft Agreement on Transitional Measures*, part of the *Round-Table Conference Agreement between the Kingdom of the Netherlands and the Government of the Republic of Indonesia*, 2 November 1949, 69 *UNTS* 200, 267. Art. 4 reads as follows: "The Kingdom of the Netherlands and the Republic of the United States of Indonesia recognize and accept that all rights and obligations of Indonesia, under private and public law, are *ipso jure* transferred to the Republic of the United States of Indonesia, unless otherwise provided for in the special agreements included in the Union Statute". The Netherlands stated that it was only the "European part" of the Kingdom of the Netherlands and that the military forces which operated during the second military action on Java were in fact doing so in the service of the other "Asian part" of the Kingdom. The State of the Netherlands therefore contended that liability for internationally wrongful acts committed by soldiers rested on the "Asian part" of the Kingdom.

the Republic of Indonesia (the successor State) which should be responsible for the unlawful acts committed by the Dutch Army during its military campaign combating secessionist rebel groups. The Court further indicated that this did not, however, exclude the possible responsibility of the Netherlands for the internationally wrongful acts. The outcome of the case is, in fact, not clear and writers disagree on the actual findings of the Court.[954]

The second case decided by a Dutch court is that of *Poldermans v. State of the Netherlands*, which arose from the internment by the Japanese occupation authorities of a Dutch civil servant (from 1942 to 1945).[955] The Supreme Court rejected the claim based on the application of Article 4 of the *Draft Agreement on Transitional Measures* between the Netherlands and Indonesia. For the Court, this provision reflected:

> [T]he accepted rules of international law, that the Republic [of Indonesia]—which succeeded to all the rights of the former Netherlands Indies—should also have to bear all its obligations. Since no specification of those obligations was given at the time, the provision must be construed as covering all debts which at the time of the transfer of sovereignty existed according to the Indonesian law then in force.[956]

---

954 Some writers have indicated that the Court finally decided that the Netherlands should *also* compensate the plaintiff based on internal constitutional grounds. See, analysis by H. Lauterpacht, *ILR* 1953, 80. This is also the position of Volkovitsch, 2182, 2201, who concludes that both Indonesia and the Netherlands were held responsible by the Court. For him, the Court "strongly urged the recognition of a principle of joint liability by which the former power would not escape responsibility". Others have concluded that only Indonesia was found liable by the Court. For instance, Verzijl, 226, who simply concludes that in this case the Court decided, entirely wrongly in his view, that it was solely for the Republic of Indonesia, as the successor State, to be held responsible for the unlawful acts committed by the Dutch Army.

955 *Poldermans v. State of the Netherlands*, Court of Appeal of The Hague (First Ch.), 8 December 1955, *NJ* 1959, no. 7, *ILR* 1957, 69; *Poldermans v. State of the Netherlands*, Supreme Court, 15 June 1956, ibid. During this period of internment, the plaintiff received no salary while at the same time his contract of service had not been terminated or cancelled. After the War, he sued the Netherlands for payment of that salary.

956 *ILR* 1957, 72. The Court also dismissed the plaintiff's argument that the debt under consideration could not be regarded as coming within the definition of Art. 4 because it was a "debt arising from tort—the kind of debt which, owing to its so-called 'odious' character, cannot be held to come under that provision". The Court refused to discuss the value of this theory and instead simply added that it was not warranted in the present action. The Court concluded that "the debt, if it exists at all, has therefore, as the Court of Appeal decided, passed to the Indonesian Republic".

The findings of these two Dutch courts that the new State of Indonesia should be held accountable for the wrongful acts committed by the predecessor State was criticized by writers.[957] The findings seem to be contrary to the principle (which is examined below)[958] that a new State should not be responsible for obligations arising from internationally wrongful acts committed by the predecessor State during the armed struggle led by "insurrectional movements" to establish that new State.[959] The findings of both courts may, however, be explained by the existence of an express provision contained in a treaty between Indonesia and the Netherlands, whereby the new State was held responsible for the acts committed by the Netherlands before the date of succession.[960] These cases are also an illustration of the well-established principle that a new State is always free to decide to take over responsibility for wrongs committed by the predecessor State.[961]

7.3.2 The Constitution of Malaya (1957)

In 1957, the Federation of Malaya became an independent country.[962] It later became known as Malaysia. Article 167(1) of the Federal Constitution (entitled "Rights, liabilities and obligations") provided that "all rights, liabilities and obligations of … Her Majesty in respect of the government of the Federation … shall on and after [Independence] Day be the rights, liabilities and obligations of the Federation". In other words, all liabilities and obligations of the predecessor State, the UK, were transferred to the new State.

While the language of the provision is rather straightforward, its meaning was recently debated in the *Keyu* case before the UK Supreme Court.[963] The case arises from events which took place when the UK was the colonial power in Malaya. The UK government sent troops there in 1948 in response

957 For instance, Verzijl, 226, concluded that the Court in the *Van der Have* case was entirely wrong to hold Indonesia responsible for the unlawful acts committed by the Dutch Army. Similarly, H. Lauterpach, *ILR* 1953, 80, stated that "from the perspective of international law the judgment seems to depart drastically from the accepted practice in respect of the liability of the successor State for torts".

958 This principle is further discussed in Chapter 3, Section 6.

959 See, Dumberry, Rebellions, 365ff.

960 This is the view of Czaplinski, 348, for whom the findings of the Court were solely based on the treaty and did not express any rule of international law.

961 See, Chapter 3, Section 4.

962 See, *Federation of Malaya Independence Act 1957*. The *Federation of Malaya Independence Order in Council No 1933* of 1957 gave effect as from 31 August 1957 to a new Federal Constitution.

963 *Keyu and others (Appellants) v. Secretary of State for Foreign and Commonwealth Affairs and another (Respondents)* [2015] UKSC 69, on appeal from [2014] EWCA Civ 312.

to an insurgency and a patrol of Scots Guards killed 23 unarmed civilians. The Appellants in this case are relatives of the victims. They applied for judicial review following the respondent's refusal to hold a public inquiry into the events many years after independence. The appeal was rejected. What is relevant, for the present purposes, is that the Court examined one argument by the Respondent denying jurisdiction on the ground that the UK could not be held responsible for refusing to hold an inquiry because "any liabilities or obligations which the UK may have had prior to 1957 passed that year to the newly independent Federation by virtue of article 167(1) of the Federal Constitution".[964] The Court rejected this argument.

Lord Mance, writing for the majority, first noted that he was "not persuaded by the respondents' submission that the grant of full independence in 1957 relieved the UK of any potential obligation, otherwise arising towards alleged victims of alleged pre-1957 misconduct by the UK army, to hold an inquiry into such misconduct".[965] He had "considerable doubt" that "any potential liability or obligation to hold an inquiry into the deaths in December 1948" could be said to be "in respect of the government of the Federation".[966] He also had "difficulty" considering that the army was "acting 'in respect of the government of the Federation'" "even though it was there to protect" Malaya "from external hostile attacks or for similar purposes".[967] He then referred to Brownlie's book indicating that "preponderance of authority is in favour of a rule that responsibility for an international delict is extinguished when the responsible state ceases to exist", but also noted that there was an exception when "a successor state accepts the existence of succession".[968] He referred to the *Mwandinghi* case (further discussed below) as an example of such an acceptance by the new State in its Constitution. He indicated that if the conduct of the British army could be regarded as being "in respect of the government of the Federation", it "might be said to have been adopted by the Federation by article 167(1) of the 1957 Constitution".[969] Yet, any such adoption by the new State should not "at the same time release the UK in domestic, or even international, law vis-à-vis the victims of such conduct".[970] He stated that:

964 Ibid para 154.
965 Ibid para 192.
966 Ibid.
967 Ibid.
968 Ibid paras 194–196, quoting Crawford, Brownlie's, 442.
969 Ibid para 197.
970 Ibid.

> Apart from adoption, the general rule which appears is that state liability for a death remains with the state responsible for the deaths, so long as that state exists, and does not pass to a successor state which takes over the relevant territory or activities. Different arrangements made as between the UK and the Federation should not on any view affect the rights which victims otherwise have against the UK domestically, whether such domestic rights arise by reference to the Convention rights, international law or pure common law principles. Assuming that the deaths in December 1948 were and remain the UK's responsibility domestically, responsibility for any inquiry now called for into them must prima facie also remain with the UK.[971]

The Judge therefore rejected this jurisdictional argument against holding an inquiry. It is true that the Court seems to distinguish between the issue of responsibility for wrongful acts committed by the army, on the one hand, and the other question of the existence of any obligation to hold an inquiry, on the other hand. Yet, the Judge seems rather reluctant to conclude that Article 167 of the Constitution covered wrongs committed by the UK before independence. The reasoning is rather surprising insofar as the goal of such provision is precisely to transfer the consequences of any such wrong to the successor State.

The example seems to confirm that acceptance of responsibility is very much an exception to the basic principle that the continuing State remains, as a matter of principle, responsible for its own wrongful acts committed before the date of succession.

7.3.3 State Practice of France and French Court Cases Supporting the Principle of Succession in the Context of the Independence of Algeria (1962)

When Algeria was still a French colony, the Algerian Assembly had established a compensation regime for victims of "terrorist" acts committed during the national liberation war (i.e. those committed by the FLN, the insurgent group fighting for independence).[972] The question of compensation was also on the agenda during the negotiations between France and the FLN which led to the independence of Algeria. It was specifically addressed in Article 18 of the *Déclaration de principes relative à la coopération économique et financière*

971 Ibid paras 197–8.

972 Decision no. 55–032 of 10 June 1955.

(dated 19 March 1962), which is part of the *Evian Accords* that ended the national liberation war.[973] This clause provided that:

> Algeria shall assume the obligations and enjoy the rights contracted on behalf of itself or of Algerian public establishments by the competent French authorities.[974]

This provision has been interpreted as meaning that it was for the new State of Algeria (and not for France, the continuing State) to compensate victims of wrongful acts committed between 1 November 1954 and 9 July 1962 (the period of the national liberation war). The obligation of the new State to provide compensation applied for French nationals and foreigners alike. This is clear from statements made by the French Minister of Foreign Affairs[975] and the French State Secretary for Algerian Affairs.[976]

---

973 *JORF* 20 March 1962, 3019–3032. Negotiations between France and the FLN led to a cease-fire signed on 18 March 1962, at Evian, France. The *Evian accords* also provided for continuing economic, financial, technical and cultural relations between the two States. It also installed an interim administrative arrangement until a referendum on self-determination could be held. The referendum was finally held in Algeria on 1 July 1962. Algeria became an independent State in July 1962. Previously, the *Evian Accords* had also been approved by referendum in France on 8 April 1962.

974 The original French version reads as follows: "L'Algérie assume les obligations et bénéficie des droits contractés en son nom ou en celui des établissements publics algériens par les autorités françaises compétentes".

975 This is the response given by the Minister of Foreign Affairs to a question asked at the French National Assembly: "La réparation des dommages matériels subis en Algérie *par des nationaux ou par des résidents étrangers* au cours de troubles de l'ordre public pose un problème de droit interne algérien" (emphasis added). See, *JORF Assemblée nationale*, no. 7496, 17 January 1970, 104, in: Jean Charpentier, "Pratique française du droit international", *AFDI* 1970, 942–943.

976 This is an extract of the debate at the French National Assembly and the statement made by the State Secretary for Algerian Affairs (*JORF Assemblée nationale*, no. 82, 16 March 1970, 2408, in: Charpentier, ibid, *AFDI* 1963, 1022): "La décision no. 55–032 de l'Assemblée algérienne a posé le principe de la responsabilité de l'Algérie en ce qui concerne la réparation des dommages causées aux personnes et aux biens à l'occasion des événements qui se sont déroulés sur ce territoire depuis le 1er novembre 1954. Les difficultés qu'a connues l'Algérie en 1962 ont profondément perturbé les procédures normales d'attributions des indemnités et les retards dans l'étude des droits des intéressés sont très importants. Il n'en demeure pas moins que, aux termes des accords d'Evian et spécialement de l'article 18 de la déclaration de principes relative à la coopération économique et financière, l'Algérie reste tenue d'assumer les obligations de l'espèce contractées en son nom par les autorités françaises compétentes". Another statement by the State Secretary for Algerian Affairs is worth quoting (*JORF Assemblée nationale*, no. 3298, 28 September 1963, 4919, quoted in: Charpentier, ibid 1022–1023): "Il appartient donc en droit aux autorités algériennes de

The French Minister of Foreign Affairs expressed the view that Article 18 of the *Déclaration*, under which Algeria was held responsible for obligations arising from wrongful acts committed before the date of succession, was "l'application des règles du droit international relative à la succession d'États".[977] The same assessment was made by French courts.[978] It has been argued that the solution adopted by Article 18 was, on the contrary, not in accordance with principles of State succession.[979]

As previously observed above,[980] to this principle of succession existed an exception. French municipal courts consistently held that France should remain responsible for the wrongful acts committed by France which were *specifically directed against the rebellion of the FLN* and the victims were *French nationals*. French courts have, however, applied a different solution when the acts were committed *by the FLN*. They have applied the specific principle, which is examined in detail below,[981] that whenever wrongful acts are *committed by rebels* in their struggle to achieve independence, the responsibility for such acts should be transferred to the new State upon its independence.[982] This principle has been consistently applied by French courts.[983] Its application has been viewed favourably by scholars.[984]

---

liquider et de régler les indemnités afférentes aux dommages corporels et matériels subis du fait d'événements d'Algérie, que ces évènements aient eu lieu avant ou après l'indépendance algérienne et de quelque manière que ce soit".

977 Statements in response to a question asked at the National Assembly, *JORF Assemblée nationale*, no. 4275, 20 January 1968, 145.

978 In particular, the decision of the Court of Appeal of Paris of 17 May 1969 in *Agent judiciaire du trésor public v. Labeunie*, where the Court indicated that "l'article 18 (…) doit s'interpréter selon la règle du Droit des Gens dite de succession des Etats, comme posant le principe fondamental selon lequel l'Algérie assume toutes les obligations et bénéficie de l'ensemble des droits contractés par les autorités françaises dans l'exercice des compétences transférées lors de l'indépendance au nouvel Etat algérien" (quoted in the decision of the Cour de Cassation, Ch. Civ. 1, case no. 69–13387, 15 June 1971, *Bull. arrêts Cour de Cassation*, Ch. Civ. 1 N. 195, 164; *JDI* 1972, 812; 72 *ILR* 53). However, in this case, the Court decided that France (and not Algeria) should pay compensation to the plaintiff.

979 M. Charpentier, "Pratique française du droit international", *AFDI* 1968, 881; Barde, 186.

980 See, Section 7.2.3.

981 This principle is discussed in Chapter 3, Section 6.

982 See, Dumberry, Rebellions, 303ff.

983 *Perriquet*, Conseil d'Etat, case no. 119737, 15 March 1995, *Rec. Lebon*; *Hespel*, Conseil d'Etat, 2/6 SSR, case no. 11092, 5 December 1980, *Rec. Lebon*; Conseil d'Etat, 2/4 SSR, case no. 5059, 25 May 1970, *Tables du Rec. Lebon; Etablissements Henri Maschat*, Conseil d'Etat, case no. 04878, 10 May 1968, *Rec. Lebon*; *Consorts Hovelacque*, Conseil d'Etat, 2/6 SSR, case no. 35028, 13 January 1984, *Rec. Lebon*.

984 Jean-François Lachaume, "Jurisprudence française relative au droit international public (1970)", *AFDI* 1971, 1004, for whom this solution, however correct it may be from a legal

The outcome of these decisions by French courts can hardly be considered to be firm precedents in the establishment of any principle of succession to international responsibility in the context of Newly Independent States. Thus, it seems that the courts simply applied a *special rule* which prevails in the *specific context* of wrongful acts committed by an insurrectional movement in its struggle for independence during a civil war. Moreover, Algeria was not a party in any of the proceedings before these French courts. Consequently, these court decisions did not formally hold Algeria responsible for the commission of the internationally wrongful acts of the FLN. These decisions simply held that France could not be responsible for such acts which only "concerned" ("*intéressent*") Algeria. These decisions therefore had only limited concrete implication outside of France.

7.3.4 Namibia (1991)

In March 1990, Namibia became an independent State after a period of German colonisation (1884–1915), British occupation (1915–1920) and South African Mandate (1920–1966), which was followed by a period of continuous illegal presence by South Africa.[985]

7.3.4.1 *The United Nations Council of Namibia as the Predecessor State of Namibia*

Prior to its independence, Namibia was represented in its international relations by the United Nations Council of Namibia.[986] The Council represented Namibia in several international conferences, including the 1978 UN Conference on State succession to treaties and the 1983 UN Conference on succession to State property, archives and debts.[987] In the context of these two Conferences, two resolutions were passed and annexed to the Final Act. The resolutions (both entitled "Resolution Concerning Namibia") indicated that in the case of

standpoint, is nevertheless difficult to implement in practice as the Algerian authorities would probably not provide any such compensation to the victims.

985 See, more generally on Namibia: Raymond Goy, "L'indépendance de la Namibie" 37 *AFDI* 1991, 387; M. Kamto, "L'accession de la Namibie à l'indépendance" 94 *RGDIP* 1990, 577; Georges Abi-Saab, "Namibia and International Law: An Overview", 1 *African YIL* 1993, 3–11; Yilma Makonnen, "Namibia: Its International Status and the Issues of Succession of States", 3 *Lesotho LJ* 1987, 183–221. The United Nations Institute for Namibia also published in 1984 a book entitled "Independent Namibia: Succession to Treaty Rights and Obligations Incorporating Namibian Treaty Calendar" (154 p).

986 The legislative history of the Council is discussed below in Part 3, Chapter 5, Section 3.4.5.

987 The United Nations invited the Council to participate in the 1978 Conference (A/AC.131/61, 4 April 1967).

Namibia, the articles of the Convention should be "interpreted … in conformity with United Nations resolutions on the question of Namibia". One such resolution specifically states that "South Africa is not the predecessor State of the future independent State of Namibia".[988] Accordingly, it was decided that the United Nations Council of Namibia should be regarded as the "predecessor State".[989] According to one representative of the Council, Namibia would be a *sui generis* case of succession, with the United Nations itself (in fact the United Nations Council of Namibia) as the predecessor State.[990]

This position received some support in scholarship at the time.[991] It should be noted that *in practice* South Africa was nevertheless deemed to be the "predecessor State" of Namibia. Thus, in the case of *Mwandinghi v. Minister of Defence, Namibia* before the High Court, which will be examined below, specific reference is made to South Africa as being the "predecessor State".[992]

7.3.4.2 *Article 140(3) of the Namibian Constitution*

Prior to the independence of Namibia, questions of State succession had been the object of some comments by scholars. It was largely agreed that the rule of *tabula rasa* should apply to the new State of Namibia, including with respect to any internationally wrongful acts committed by South Africa.[993] The

988 UN, "Conference on Succession of States in Respect to Treaties", A/CONF.80/16/add.1, v. III, 177. This point is further discussed in: Yilma Makonnen, "Namibia: Its International Status and the Issues of Succession of States", 3 *Lesotho LJ* 1987, 201–203.

989 This was also the position adopted by the representatives of SWAPO (the insurgent movement fighting for independence): UN, ibid v. I, 96, para 66.

990 Ibid 44, para 55.

991 See, for instance, Yilma Makonnen, "State Succession in Africa: Selected Problems", *Rec. des cours*, v. 200, 1986–V, 173; Yilma Makonnen, "Namibia: Its International Status and the Issues of Succession of States", 3 *Lesotho LJ* 1987, 202.

992 *Mwandinghi* case, Namibia, High Court, 352–353.

993 See, Yilma Makonnen, "Namibia: Its International Status and the Issues of Succession of States", 3 *Lesotho LJ* 1987, 210ff, indicating that all dealings of South Africa with Namibia were illegal. His analysis dealt more generally with "economic and financial rights and obligations" but can also be applied to the issue of succession to responsibility. The *tabula rasa* rule he adopted (210) is based on the ground that "the essence of colonization [in Namibia] was economic domination and exploitation of the colonized peoples and territories" and that "Namibia's entire wealth, their resources as well as their economic activities [were] in the hands of South Africans and other aliens" (213). He concludes (213) that "the effect of succession of States on [these] alien economic interests will in fact be the most important single factor which will determine the degree of independence of the future state of Namibia" and that future Namibia would be "guided by the principle of self-determination and decolonization with the objective of eradicating alien exploitation and domination of all forms and manifestations" (217). Also supporting the

position finally adopted by Namibia upon its independence sharply contrasts with these previous assessments. Article 140(3) of the Namibian Constitution provides that the acts of the South African government should be deemed as those of the new Namibian State.[994] Importantly, this provision also reserves the right for the new State to repudiate (by an act of legislation) the internationally wrongful acts committed by South Africa.[995] This is the text of the provision entitled "The Law in Force at the Date of Independence":

> (1) Subject to the provisions of this Constitution, all laws which were in force immediately before the date of Independence shall remain in force until repealed or amended by Act of Parliament or until they are declared unconstitutional by a competent Court.
> (2) Any powers vested by such laws in the Government, or in a Minister or other official of the Republic of South Africa shall be deemed to vest in the Government of the Republic of Namibia or in a corresponding Minister or official of the Government of the Republic of Namibia, and all powers, duties and functions which so vested in the Government Service Commission, shall vest in the Public Service Commission referred to in Article 112 hereof.
> (3) Anything done under such laws prior to the date of Independence by the Government, or by a Minister or other official of the Republic of South Africa shall be deemed to have been done by the Government of the Republic of Namibia or by a corresponding Minister or official of the Government of the Republic of Namibia, unless such action is subsequently repudiated by an Act of Parliament, and anything so done by the Government Service Commission shall be deemed to have been done by the Public Service Commission referred to in Article 112 hereof, unless it is determined otherwise by an Act of Parliament.

There is no doubt that the adoption of this provision of the Namibian Constitution was largely influenced by the *political context* in which the independence of Namibia occurred. When Namibia became an independent

clean slate rule: Booysen, 207; Paul C. Szasz, "Succession to Treaties under the Namibian Constitution", 15 *South African YIL* 1989–1990, 65–80 (in the field of succession to treaties).

994 *Constitution of Namibia*, adopted by the Constituent Assembly of Namibia on 9 February 1990, in force on 21 March 1991, S/20967/Add.2.

995 This aspect of the Constitution is discussed in: *Government of the Republic of Namibia and Another v. Cultura 2000 and Another*, Supreme Court, 15 October 1993, 1993, 3 *LRC* 175, 103 *ILR* 104, 111–112.

State and the Constitution was drafted (March 1990), South Africa's President F.W. de Klerk had announced (in February 1990) the lifting of a 30-year ban on the ANC (African National Congress) and other anti-apartheid organisations as well as the release of some political prisoners, including Mr Nelson Mandela, the historical leader of the ANC. This period was therefore marked by the end of the apartheid regime in South Africa.

Article 140(3) of the Namibian Constitution has been the object of many comments by scholars.[996] It has been rightly suggested that this provision illustrates the principle that a successor State is always free to agree to accept the obligations arising from internationally wrongful acts committed by the predecessor State.[997] It has also been considered contrary to the view generally held by many that the successor State is not bound by internationally wrongful acts committed by the predecessor State.[998]

The scope and content of this provision was analysed in two decisions rendered by Namibian courts.

7.3.4.3 *The Case of* Minister of Defence, Namibia v. Mwandinghi

The case of *Mwandinghi v. Minister of Defence, Namibia*[999] before the High Court of Namibia and that of *Minister of Defence, Namibia v. Mwandinghi*[1000] before the Supreme Court of Namibia involved damages arising out of the shooting of Mr Mwandinghi, a Namibian national, by forces operating for the South African Defence Forces in 1987.[1001] Before independence, the plaintiff submitted a claim for damages against the Minister of Defence of South Africa. Upon independence, he sought to substitute the Minister of Defence of Namibia as defendant based on Article 140(3) of the new Namibian Constitution. He applied to the High Court with a notice of motion for an order to allow the substitution.

---

996 See, for instance: H.A. Strydom, "Namibian Independence and the Question of the Contractual and Delictual Liability of the Predecessor and Successor Governments", 15 *South African* YIL 1989–90, 111–121.

997 John Dugard, *International Law; a South African Perspective* (2nd edn, Juta 2000) 232–233. This principle is further explained in Chapter 3, Section 4.

998 Booysen, 207–208. He is favour of the application of a rule of non-succession to responsibility based on principles of private law (see 209–210).

999 *Mwandinghi* case, Namibia, High Court, 343.

1000 Ibid, Supreme Court, 358.

1001 These two decisions are examined in: Neville Botha, "To Pay or Not to Pay?: Namibian Liability for South African Delicts", 16 *South African* YIL 1990–91, 156–162; Neville Botha, "Succession to Delictual Liability: Confirmation", 17 *South African* YIL 1991–92, 177–179; Booysen, 204–214; Crawford, State Responsibility, 454–5.

The Minister of Defence of Namibia opposed the motion on the ground that the Namibian Constitution did not make the new State responsible for obligations arising from wrongful acts committed by the predecessor State. The argument was based on the fact that, on the one hand, Article 140(3) would not cover "delicts" (i.e. internationally wrongful acts) and, on the other hand, that Article 145 of the Constitution contains a disclaimer according to which an obligation may be accepted by Namibia only to the extent that it is recognised as binding under international law. Article 145 of the Namibian Constitution reads as follows:

> (1) Nothing contained in this Constitution shall be construed as imposing upon the Government of Namibia:
> (a) any obligations to any other State which would not otherwise have existed under international law;
> (b) any obligations to any person arising out of the acts or contracts of prior Administrations which would not otherwise have been recognised by international law as binding upon the Republic of Namibia.
>
> (2) Nothing contained in this Constitution shall be construed as recognising in any way the validity of the Administration of Namibia by the Government of the Republic of South Africa or by the Administrator-General appointed by the Government of the Republic of South Africa to administer Namibia.

In its judgment, the sitting Judge of the High Court indicated that Article 140 of the Constitution was an "acceptance by the new government of all that was previously done under those laws in the exercising of the powers conferred thereby" but added that this provision contains "no express reference to delicts or wrongs committed by the previous government".[1002] The sitting Judge went on to state that the words "anything done under such laws" of Article 140(3) should be given their wide and ordinary meanings and should not be limited to lawful acts performed by the previous government. The sitting Judge concluded that it was wide enough to cover the claim of the plaintiff for "delicts" committed by the South African Defence Forces.

Similarly, the words "any obligations to any persons arising out of the acts or contracts of prior Administrations" of Article 145(1)b should also not be construed so as to include only lawful obligations and acts. This provision was

1002 *Mwandinghi* case, Namibia, High Court, 346.

described by the Judge as "a disclaimer clause by the new State of the Republic of Namibia in respect of obligations incurred by its predecessor, the Republic of South Africa", under which the question is whether the obligation to the plaintiff for acts of the predecessor State "is recognised by international law as one which is binding on the successor State".[1003] The Minister of Defence of Namibia submitted that under international law "a new State does not succeed to delicts committed by its predecessor and consequently, applying art. 145(1)(b), the Minister of Defence of Namibia is not liable and cannot be substituted for the wrong committed by the Minister of Defence of the Republic of South Africa".[1004] The sitting Judge seems to have accepted this argument, as a matter of principle, and stated:

> [F]or the purpose of this case, I shall accept that in international law a new State is not liable for the delicts committed by its predecessor.[1005]

However, in the concrete situation of the present case, he had already concluded that Article 140(3) expressed the acceptance by the new State of the internationally wrongful acts committed by the predecessor. Therefore, he stated:

> The question whether in international law delicts committed by a predecessor State become the delicts of a successor Sate or not is no longer relevant. By its acceptance of such debts, in this case in terms of the Constitution, the debt became that of the new State in terms of the municipal law of the State and is according to municipal law principles justiciable in the courts of the land.
>
> When art 145(1)(b) refers to 'acts or contracts ... which would not otherwise have been recognised by international law as binding upon the Republic of Namibia', it can therefore not mean to refer to the recognition in international law of non-liability of a new State for delicts committed by its predecessor. This mater is now dealt with, according to our Constitution, in terms of the municipal law, and if the new State of Namibia wishes to repudiate such liability, provision is specifically made therefore at art 140(3).[1006]

1003 Ibid 352–353.

1004 Ibid 353. In support of its position, the defendant referred to the *R.E. Brown* case, 129, and the *Hawaiian Claims* case, 157. They have been discussed above: Chapter 2, Sections 2.1.4.2 and 2.1.5.

1005 Ibid.

1006 Ibid 354.

In other words, the sitting Judge concluded that it made little difference whether or not the rules of State succession *under international law* called for Namibia to take over responsibility for wrongful acts committed by South Africa because the Namibian Constitution specifically provided for such acceptance of liability *under its own municipal law*. The Judge thus stated that "in the present case the new State chose to accept liability, subject to its right to repudiate, and is therefore liable".[1007] He further maintained that "I know of no principle whereby international law can step in and undo such an acceptance by a State".[1008] The Judge therefore decided that the Minister of Defence of Namibia was substituted as the defendant in the present case to the Minister of Defence of the Republic of South Africa. The Minister of Defence of Namibia appealed this decision before the Supreme Court.

The Supreme Court dismissed the appeal and confirmed the decision of the lower court. The Court started its analysis by making this (rather controversial) remark:

> There can be no doubt that when delict was committed, the respondent acquired a private right to compensation for damages against the administration then in control of the country. Such private rights do not cease on a change of sovereignty.[1009]

It seems that the Court here confused the right to start procedure (which is not contested) and the "acquired right" to "compensation for damages", which is undoubtedly quite another thing. For the Court, Article 140(3) of the Constitution "cannot be said to have amended the position of international law pertaining to private rights".[1010] It also seems that the Court analysed Article 140(3) of the Constitution as a question of attribution to the new *government* of internationally wrongful acts committed by the previous *government*, rather than a question of succession of *States*. This is clear from this extract from the decision:

> [W]hat art 140 succeeds in doing is to confirm in no uncertain terms that the successor Government would inherit liability for anything done by the predecessor Government under laws existing prior to independence

1007 Ibid 355.
1008 Ibid 354–355.
1009 *Mwandinghi* case, Namibia, Supreme Court, 358, see 359–360.
1010 Ibid 361.

> unless such laws were repealed by the successor government by means of an Act of Parliament.[1011]

The Court's confusion between the two distinct concepts of succession of "governments" and succession of "States" is also evident from the fact that in support of its finding it relied on Article 15(1) (which later became Article 10(1) in the final version) of the ILC *Articles on State Responsibility*, which only deals with succession of *governments*.[1012] The Court interpreted this provision as:

> attribut[ing] to the State which has a new government after the insurrection, not only the acts of the organs of the insurrectional movement, but also those committed by the State before the insurrection has ceased.[1013]

This is another controversial statement by the Court that is misleading. Firstly, the Court should have referred to Article 10(2) of the ILC Articles dealing with succession of States and not to Article 10(1) concerning changes of governments. Secondly, the Court's affirmation of the principle of succession to responsibility is correct insofar as it deals with acts committed by an *insurrectional movement* during its armed struggle for independence.[1014] However, the solution is different for those acts committed *by the predecessor State* in combating the secessionist rebellion. Thus, under Article 10 of the ILC's Articles, as a matter of principle, the new State (Namibia) which emerged as a result of the struggle of a national liberation movement (SWAPO, South West Africa People's Organisation) *should not* be held responsible for the acts committed by the predecessor State (South Africa) during that period of trouble.[1015] The Court is therefore wrong in stating that the work of the ILC means that "when a

---

1011 Ibid 360–361. The Court also quoted the work of Hazem M. Atlam, "National Liberation Movements and International Responsibility", in: M. Spinedi & B. Simma (eds), *United Nations Codification of State Responsibility* (Oceana 1987) 51–52, in support its proposition. However, this reference is misleading. Thus, for Atlam the solution adopted by the ILC, whereby the new government is responsible for the acts committed by the previous government, is an "unacceptable solution" in the context of racist regimes overthrown. The case of Namibia would certainly fit the criteria of a racist regime overthrown. It has been rightly pointed out that by subscribing to the work of Atlam, the Court was in effect endorsing an "unacceptable solution": Neville Botha, "Succession to Delictual Liability: Confirmation", 17 *South African YIL* 1991–1992, 178.

1012 ILC's *Articles on State Responsibility*, 2001.

1013 *Mwandinghi* case, Namibia, Supreme Court, 358, at 360. Here again, in support of this proposition, the Court quoted the above-mentioned work of Atlam.

1014 This principle is further examined in Chapter 3, Section 6.

1015 Ibid.

national liberation movement becomes the new government of a State, as was the case in Namibia, the new State will be attributed with the conduct which would have been previously considered an act of the pre-existing state, that is, the new government inherits responsibility for the acts committed by the previous organs of the State".[1016] This misinterpretation of the work of the ILC by the Court has not passed unnoticed. ILC Special Rapporteur Crawford noted:

> Namibia, as a new State created as the result, *inter alia*, of the actions of the South West Africa People's Organization, a recognized national liberation movement, was not responsible for the conduct of South Africa in respect of its territory. That it assumed such a responsibility attests to its concern for individual rights, but it was not required by the principles of article 15 [now Article 10].[1017]

This being said, nothing prevents a new State to decide, such as in the present case, based on policy grounds, to take over the liability for acts committed by the predecessor State.[1018] The flaw in the reasoning of the Court is to say that there is a legal requirement for the new State to do so under Article 10 of the ILC's Articles. In other words, the Court should have concluded in favour of the transfer of obligations based on the clear provision of the Namibian Constitution. The Court was wrong in trying to validate its conclusion based on the work of the ILC.

The Court, as the sitting Judge before it, interpreted the words "anything done under such laws" of Article 140(3) as to include unlawful acts performed by the previous State. The Court then indicated that Namibia did not repudiate any such acts with the use of Article 140(3). It concluded:

> The necessary consequence which therefore follows is that [Namibia] is saddled in law with the liability to compensate the plaintiff for the damage which he alleges he has suffered from the delictual acts of the official of the predecessor Government. International law does not preclude any such liability and, even if it did, the Namibian State was free to elect, as it did, on a proper construction of art 140(3) to accept such liability.[1019]

1016 *Mwandinghi* case, Namibia, Supreme Court, 358, at 361.

1017 ILC, "First Report on State Responsibility (*addendum* no. 5)", Special Rapporteur James Crawford, 22 July 1998, A/CN.4/490/Add.5., at para 277.

1018 This principle is further explained in Chapter 3, Section 4.

1019 *Mwandinghi* case, Namibia, Supreme Court, 358, at 365–366.

The Court then examined the relevance of Article 145 of the Constitution and whether there was a rule of international law, as submitted by the Minister of Defence of Namibia, according to which the successor State would not take over the liabilities of the predecessor State. The Court did not really answer the point. It seems to have agreed with the argument submitted by the Respondent according to which the disclaimer clause of Article 145 would only refer to apartheid law, and that the delict in question here would not fall within the categories described in Article 145. At any rate, the Court relied instead on the fact that international law must recognise the liabilities accepted by Namibia under its own municipal law.

The Court therefore dismissed the appeal. The Minister of Defence of Namibia was therefore substituted as the defendant in the present case to the Minister of Defence of the Republic of South Africa.

The logical construction of the two judgments is therefore different. The High Court accepted, as a matter of principle, the proposition submitted by the Ministry of Defence of Namibia according to which "in international law a new State is not liable for the delicts committed by its predecessor".[1020] The Supreme Court seems to have been much more open to the possibility of the transfer of the obligation to repair from one State to another, as it indicated that "international law does not preclude" such transfer.[1021] In both cases, however, this mattered little since the courts concluded that Namibia chose to accept liability in its Constitution.

This aspect of the decisions has been received with great scepticism by some commentators, for whom it was contrary to both the Namibian Constitution and principles of international law whereby "a new State does not succeed to the delicts of its predecessor".[1022] Thus, it has been argued that the Court interpreted too widely Article 140(3) and that it should have instead excluded internationally wrongful acts of South Africa from the scope of this provision.[1023] The same writer also points out that if this provision is read together with Article 145, "it is extremely doubtful whether there is any clear intention on the

1020 *Mwandinghi* case, Namibia, High Court, 353.

1021 *Mwandinghi* case, Namibia, Supreme Court, 365–366. For John Dugard, *International Law; a South African Perspective* (2nd edn, Juta 2000) 233, the Court "expressed doubt as to whether there [was] a general rule of international law extinguishing delictual responsibility when the wrongdoer State ceases to exist".

1022 Neville Botha, "To Pay or Not to Pay?: Namibian Liability for South African Delicts", 16 *South African YIL* 1990–91, 162. See also, Booysen, 210–211.

1023 Booysen, ibid 210.

part of the new State to deviate from the international law rule that there is no succession to delictual liability".[1024]

The Supreme Court was right in deciding that in accordance with Article 140 of the Constitution, Namibia took over the obligations arising from internationally wrongful acts committed by the predecessor State before the date of succession. This is all the more so since Namibia had the opportunity to repudiate the wrongful acts by an Act of parliament and it failed to do so. The outcome is nevertheless unexpected given that Namibia greatly suffered under many years of illegal South African occupation and that its struggle for independence was long and laborious. The fact that Namibia should pay for wrongful acts that were in fact committed by the racist regime of South Africa in its deliberate efforts to suppress the legitimate struggle of the Namibian people for freedom and independence is (to say the least) surprising. Yet, the example does not challenge the soundness of the general applicable rule of non-succession set out in Article 16(1) of the Institute's Resolution. It simply shows that a Newly independent State, like any other State, can decide on its own to take over the burden of reparation of internationally wrongful acts committed by the predecessor State.[1025] In fact, ILC Special Rapporteur Šturma initially included a provision specifically dealing with this situation where a Newly independent State agrees to such transfer of obligations.[1026]

In any event, the outcome of the case may be partially explained by the fact that at the time Namibia became an independent State, South Africa was undergoing major political changes marked by the end of the apartheid regime. A certain brotherhood now existed between Namibia and post-apartheid South Africa.

The fact that this case involved the undeniable suffering of a Namibian national as a result of violent acts attributed to South Africa may also have had some impact on its outcome. The courts indeed rendered their judgments barely one year after the end of the liberation struggle of the Namibian people. Thus, the reasoning of the courts may have been influenced by the fact that fairness would certainly call for proper compensation to be provided to Mr

1024 Ibid 210–211. He argues (212–213) that South Africa can no longer be sued before Namibian courts for *its* wrongful acts committed against Namibian nationals before independence.

1025 Kohen & Dumberry, 135. See, analysis of unilateral acts by successor States under Art. 6(3) of the Institute's Resolution.

1026 ILC Special Rapporteur Šturma, Second Report, 2018, para 136. See, Draft Article 8(2): "If the newly independent States agrees, the obligations arising from an internationally wrongful act of the predecessor State may transfer to the successor State".

Mwandinghi for the damage he suffered.[1027] In the present case, both courts, however, only decided to grant the application by Mr Mwandinghi to have the Minister of Defence of Namibia substituted to the Minister of Defence of the Republic of South Africa. The courts did not award any damages as a result of the internationally wrongful act committed against Mr Mwandinghi.

It is not clear whether the High Court and the Supreme Court would have adopted the same reasoning had the internationally wrongful act been committed by South Africa not against a Namibian national taking part in the armed struggle for freedom but against a third State (or a national of a third State). It can only be supposed that the courts would have probably been more inclined to make use of Article 145(1) of the Namibian Constitution and to develop the argument that any succession to obligations arising from the commission of internationally wrongful acts would impose upon Namibia an obligation "not otherwise … recognised by international law as binding upon the Republic of Namibia". They may also have considered that if Namibia were to take over the obligations arising from internationally wrongful acts committed by South Africa during the time of the illegal occupation, this would in effect recognise "the validity of the Administration of Namibia by the Government of the Republic of South Africa", in clear violation of Article 145(2) of the Namibian Constitution. In other words, Namibian courts would have been probably less keen to apply the principle of succession if faced with a claim submitted by a national of *another* State. Ultimately, the outcome of the *Mwandinghi* cases was driven by internal considerations.

1027 In fact, in *Mwandinghi* case, Namibia, High Court, the Judge does mention that Art. 140 of the Constitution should be interpreted in a "liberal manner" to protect human rights: "Although [Art.] 140 is not part of [chapter] 3 of the Constitution, [i.e.] that part which sets out the Fundamental Human Rights and Freedoms, the article concerns in particular the continuance, *inter alia*, of vested rights of individuals and should therefore be interpreted in the same purposive and liberal manner for the preservation of such rights, as would be the case with [chapter] 3" (350). The same liberal approach to the Namibian Constitution was also adopted by the Supreme Court in another case: *Government of the Republic of Namibia and Another v. Cultura 2000 and Another*, Supreme Court, 15 October 1993, 1993, 3 *LRC* 175; 103 *ILR* 104, 116: "A constitution is an organic instrument. Although it is enacted in the form of a statute it is *sui generis*. It must be interpreted broadly, liberally and purposively so as to avoid the 'austerity of tabulated legalism' and so as to enable it to continue to play a creative and dynamic role in the expression and the achievement of the ideals and aspirations of the nation in the articulation of the values bonding its people and in disciplining its government".

8 Conclusion to Chapter 2

The analysis of State practice and case law indicates that there is no uniform and standard solution to deal with the question of whether the successor State takes over the consequences of an internationally wrongful act committed by the predecessor State. The fundamental assumption made at the outset of the present study is thus confirmed: the solution adopted in State practice and international and municipal case law essentially depends on the *different types* of mechanisms of State succession involved.

The first noticeable point which emerges from this investigation of State practice and case law is that there are many examples where successor States have accepted to take over the responsibility for internationally wrongful acts committed before the date of succession. It can therefore no longer be said that such a possibility is rare or exceptional. This point is further discussed below.[1028] The following paragraphs summarise the findings for each different type of succession.

The examination of State practice in the context of incorporation shows that older cases (considered to be "annexation" of States) support the principle that the successor State is not responsible for the obligations arising from internationally wrongful acts committed by the predecessor State. This principle of non-succession has been applied in State practice,[1029] by one decision of a municipal court[1030] and by two awards of an international Arbitral Tribunal.[1031] The analysis of three examples in the context of the incorporation of the German Democratic Republic into the Federal Republic of Germany (1990) shows that *modern* practice supports the principle that the successor State is responsible for the obligations arising from internationally wrongful acts committed by the predecessor State. The principle of succession is also endorsed by the Institute's Resolution.[1032] I have not found any example of modern State practice where the successor State refused the transfer of obligations.

1028 See, Chapter 3, Section 4.

1029 In the context of the unity of Italy (1860–1861), the annexations of Burma by Great Britain (1886), of Madagascar by France (1896) and of the Boer Republic of South Africa by Great Britain (1902).

1030 *West Rand Central Gold Mining Company Ltd. v. The King*, 1 June 1905, LR 1905, 2 KB 391.

1031 The US-Great Britain Arbitral Commission in the *R.E. Brown* case, 129 and in the *Hawaiian Claims* case, 157.

1032 Art. 14, IIL, Resolution, 2015. See, Kohen & Dumberry, 114.

Two examples of State practice were found in the context of unification of States.[1033] In both cases, the successor States decided to take over the responsibility for obligations. I have not found any example of State practice where the successor State refused the transfer of obligations. The transfer of the obligation to repair to the successor State is also supported by scholars. The principle of succession is also endorsed by the Institute's Resolution.[1034]

The conclusion seems less straightforward in the context of dissolution. Thus, on the one hand, I have found two rather old examples of State practice where States have adopted the doctrine of non-succession to responsibility.[1035] This position was also adopted by the municipal courts of one State.[1036] State practice also shows that *injured States* have submitted claims to the successor States notwithstanding the existence of the so-called "rule" of non-succession supported by many.[1037] There are also examples where the *successor States* have agreed to take over obligations arising from internationally wrongful acts committed by the predecessor State. In several cases, the agreement was reached between the injured State and the successor State(s).[1038] In other cases, an accord was concluded among the successor States themselves.[1039] State practice is therefore not uniform in the context of dissolution. At the very least, one can agree with ILC Special Rapporteur Šturma's comment that "modern State practice, though not very frequently occurring (some agreements and cases), allows for a rejection of a strict and automatic application of the principle of

1033 The unifications of the United Arab Republic (1958) and Vietnam (1976).

1034 Art. 13, IIL, Resolution, 2015. See, Kohen & Dumberry, 111.

1035 These examples are in the context of the dissolutions of the Kingdom of Westphalia (1813) and the Austria-Hungary Dual Monarchy (1918).

1036 Decisions of Austrian courts in the context of the dissolution of Austria-Hungary (1918).

1037 This is, for instance, the position of Australia in the *Tokic* case in the context of the dissolution of the former Yugoslavia (1991–1992). See also, the position of the US in the context of the dissolution of the Union of Colombia (1829–1831).

1038 In the context of the dissolution of the Union of Colombia (1829–1831), the three successor States entered into separate agreements with the injured State (US). In the context of the dissolution of the United Arab Republic in 1961, one of the two successor States (Egypt) entered into several agreements with other States (Italy, Switzerland, Lebanon, Denmark, Greece, Netherlands, UK, Sweden and the US) under which compensation was provided to foreign nationals whose properties had been nationalised during, *inter alia*, the period of the existence of the United Arab Republic (the predecessor State, 1958–1961). A *Compromis* to refer a dispute to the ICJ (*Gabčíkovo-Nagymaros* case) was signed between Hungary and Slovakia, whereby both States agreed that Slovakia was the successor State to Czechoslovakia in the context of the construction of a barrage. However, as mentioned above, both Hungary and Slovakia rejected in their pleadings the existence of any rule of State succession to responsibility.

1039 2001 *Agreement on Succession Issues* among the successor States to the former Yugoslavia.

non-succession".[1040] While the ICJ in the *Croatia Genocide Convention* case did not take position on the issue, several judges in their individual opinions believe that the Court actually adopted a presumption of succession to responsibility.[1041] In both this case and the *Gabčíkovo-Nagymaros* case, the ICJ did *not* reject the possibility of succession to responsibility. Yet, it should be also added that in both cases the respondent States rejected during the proceedings the existence of any general principle in favour of State succession to responsibility. Scholars supports the position that the successor States should, in some circumstances, take over the obligations arising from the commission of internationally wrongful acts. The principle of succession has been endorsed by the Institute's Resolution.[1042] Under Article 15 of the Institute's Resolution, there are two "relevant factors" (further discussed in the next chapter) to determine which of the successor States should become the bearer of the obligations to repair.

Therefore, it can be concluded that in the context where the predecessor State *ceases to exist* as a result of the events affecting its territorial integrity (integration, unification and dissolution), the modern practice is clearly leaning towards succession to the obligation to repair. Yet, all these examples of modern practice involve the successor State *accepting* to take over responsibilities. I have not found any example where the solution of succession was *imposed* on a reluctant successor State by a court or by any other authority.

One rule that seems to be clearly established is that in cases of cession and transfer of territory (when the predecessor State continues to exist) the continuing State (not the successor State) should remain, as a matter of principle, responsible for the commission of *its own* wrongful acts before the date of succession. This principle has been applied in State practice on at least one occasion.[1043] The rule was also adopted and applied by municipal courts of a successor State,[1044] by one municipal court of a continuing State,[1045] by an international MAT,[1046] and by another international arbitral tribunal.[1047] Only

1040 ILC Special Rapporteur Šturma, Second Report, 2018, para 167.

1041 *Croatia Genocide Convention* case.

1042 Art. 15, IIL, Resolution, 2015. See Kohen & Dumberry, 118ff, 128.

1043 *Paris Peace Treaty*, 10 February 1947, in force on 15 September 1947, 49 *UNTS* 126; *UKTS* 1948, no. 50 (Cmd. 7481).

1044 For instance, three cases (*Mordcovici, Sechter, Vozneac*) decided by Romanian Courts. See, Chapter 2, Section 5.2.1. See also, two cases decided by French courts. See, Chapter 2, Section 5.2.2.

1045 *Kalmar v. Hungarian Treasury*. See, Chapter 2, Section 5.2.3.

1046 *Levy v. German State*. See, Chapter 2, Section 5.2.2.

1047 *Lighthouse Arbitration* case, 23 *ILR* 1956, dealing with Claim no. 11 and in an *obiter dictum* dealing with Claim no. 12-a.

one municipal court decision was found where it was decided, on the contrary, that the continuing State could not be held responsible for the wrongful acts which were committed before the date of succession.[1048] Two other decisions, one by a municipal court[1049] and the other by an international Arbitral Tribunal,[1050] support the existence of one exception to this principle that the continuing State continues to be responsible (after the date of succession) for its pre-succession wrongful acts. Thus, whenever the wrongful act was committed by a local administration having a substantial autonomy before the date of succession, the successor State should be held responsible for such act.

In cases of separation, it is also established that the continuing State should remain responsible for the commission of *its own* internationally wrongful acts before the date of succession. This principle has been applied by municipal courts of the new successor State[1051] as well as by courts of the continuing State.[1052] The review of State practice shows a clear tendency in support of this principle[1053] (with only one relevant exception[1054]). Some scholarships support the view that in some circumstances the opposite rule of succession should apply. Article 12(3) of the Institute's Resolution provides for one possible exception to the general principle of non-succession: when the author of the internationally wrongful act was an organ of the predecessor State that later became an organ of the successor State.[1055] This principle (further discussed below[1056]) was applied in *Bijelić v. Montenegro* decided by the ECHR.[1057]

1048 *Personal Injuries (Upper Silesia) Case*. See, Chapter 2, Section 5.2.6. It should be noted that since Poland was not a party to the proceedings, the Court did not indicate that it should be for the successor State (Poland) to take over the obligations arising from the commission of the internationally wrongful act.

1049 *Samos* case, 70.

1050 *Lighthouse Arbitration* case, 23 *ILR* 1956, dealing with Claim no. 4.

1051 *Dzierzbicki*, *Niemiec* and *Olpinski* cases. See, Chapter 2, Section 6.2.2.

1052 *Baron A.* case. See, Chapter 2, Section 6.2.2.

1053 In the context of the break-up of the USSR, Russia entered into agreements with both Germany and France, whereby it remained responsible for the internationally wrongful acts committed by the USSR during and after WWII (the pillage of works of art and cultural property in Germany) and for measures of expropriation committed by Soviet Russia after the 1917 Revolution. The official position taken by the authorities of the GDR was that it could not be responsible for internationally wrongful acts committed by the German Reich before and during WWII. Finally, the Allies took the view in the context of the break-up of the Austria-Hungary Dual Monarchy that Austria and Hungary were both the "continuator" States of the Monarchy and should, consequently, remain responsible for internationally wrongful acts it committed during WWI.

1054 Claims in the context of the separation of Belgium (1830).

1055 See, Kohen & Dumberry, 118ff, 102.

1056 See, Chapter 3, Section 6.

1057 *Bijelić* case.

It is difficult to draw a definitive conclusion from the analysis of State practice and decisions of municipal courts in the context of Newly Independent States. There seems to be equal support for both the principles of succession and non-succession. There are examples of municipal court decisions that follow the principle that the continuing colonial State should remain responsible for the internationally wrongful acts committed before the creation of the new State.[1058] The opposite principle that the new State should take over obligations arising from the commission of internationally wrongful acts has been applied by other municipal court decisions.[1059] This principle of succession was also stated in the Namibian Constitution[1060] and applied by the courts of that country.[1061] Finally, State practice and decisions of French municipal courts rendered in the context of the independence of Algeria support both solutions of succession and non-succession to international responsibility.[1062] While State practice is divided, there are good reasons for supporting the proposition that, as a matter of principle, the rule of non-succession should apply to Newly Independent States (except for acts committed by insurrectional movements).

It can therefore be concluded that in the context where the predecessor State *continues to exist* as a result of the events affecting its territorial integrity (cession/transfer of territory, separation and Newly Independent States), there is a clear tendency toward non-succession to the obligation to repair. As a matter of principle (with some exceptions examined in the next chapter), the

1058 This principle was applied by Belgian municipal courts in the context of the independence of Congo. See, Chapter 2, Section 7.2.2. It was also applied by Indian municipal courts in the context of the partition of India (1947) and by a decision of a French municipal court in the context of the independence of Vanuatu (1980). See also, *Mutua et al. v. The Foreign and Commonwealth Office*, UK, 21 July 2011, [2011] EWHC 1913 (QB) and of 5 October 2012, [2012] EWHC 2678 (QB).

1059 This principle was applied by Dutch courts in the context of the independence of Indonesia. See, Chapter 2, Section 7.3.1.

1060 *Constitution of Namibia*, in force on 21 March 1991, S/20967/Add.2.

1061 *Mwandinghi* case, Namibia, Supreme Court, 358.

1062 Thus, Art. 18 of the *Déclaration de principes relative à la coopération économique et financière* entered into by France and Algeria as well as official statements made by the French government clearly indicate that Algeria should be liable for all internationally wrongful acts committed before the date of succession. However, French courts have consistently held that the continuing State (France) should remain responsible for the tortious acts committed by the colonial authorities against *French nationals* in fighting the rebels of the FLN. French Courts have also held, on the contrary, that whenever the wrongful acts were committed by the FLN against French nationals in its struggle to achieve independence, the new State of Algeria should be responsible to provide compensation to victims of such acts.

continuing State remains responsible for *its own* internationally wrongful acts committed before the date of succession.

Finally, the review of State practice and case law has shown that the solution to the issue of State succession to responsibility depends, not only on the different *types* of succession involved, but also on some other *factors, criteria and circumstances*. The next chapter examines the different factors and circumstances under which *specific problems* of State succession to responsibility require *specific solutions*.

CHAPTER 3

Analysis of Specific Issues

1 Introduction

The previous chapter examined State practice and decisions of both municipal and international judicial bodies. Some conclusions can be reached as to which of the principles of succession or non-succession should apply depending on the different *types* of succession.[1] For instance, in the context of cession/transfer of territory, the rule of non-succession should be applied. However, I have found some examples of case law also showing that whenever the internationally wrongful act was in fact committed by a local administration having a substantial autonomy from the predecessor State, it is the successor State that should be held responsible for the act committed before the date of succession.[2] This is one specific circumstance which calls for a specific treatment. The aim of the present chapter is to determine what are the other relevant *factors and circumstances*. In other words, which *specific problems* of State succession to responsibility require *specific solutions*. Similarly, the Institute's Resolution also considered several different factors and circumstances (including the "organ" and "direct link" elements, further discussed below) to determine whether there should be succession to obligations and rights. While ILC Special Rapporteur Šturma initially took the same general approach in his reports[3] and in the draft articles he put forward, the Drafting Committee subsequently took a drastically different direction.

The method of analysis used here is not novel. It corresponds to the methodology which was adopted by the Arbitral Tribunal in the *Lighthouse Arbitration* case. Not only did it recognise that the solution to problems of State succession to responsibility may vary depending on the different types of State succession involved, but also that specific factors and circumstances need to be taken into account.[4] This is also the position of O'Connell:

1 The same approach was adopted by the Institute's Resolution and the work of the ILC: ILC Special Rapporteur Šturma, First Report, 2017, paras 83–84; ibid Second Report, 2018, para 16.

2 *Lighthouse Arbitration* case, 23 *ILR* 1956, 81 (dealing with Claim no. 4); *Samos* case, 70.

3 ILC Special Rapporteur Šturma, Fourth Report, 2020, para 57.

4 *Lighthouse Arbitration* case, 23 *ILR* 1956, 91, where the Arbitral Tribunal asked this question: "Is it a matter of contractual or delictual obligations? Of private or of public law?—recognized or disputed?—liquidated or unliquidated?" In its evaluation of Claim no. 4 the Tribunal further developed its reasoning. It explained that the nature of the obligations is

 | DOI:10.1163/9789004703810_006

> It is exasperating not to be able to propose a synthetic structure of State succession doctrine which can accommodate the problem of torts, but the truth is that the matter cannot be brought to any finer focus than in Verzijl's conclusion in the *Lighthouse case* that *many concrete factors*, including the continuing nature of the wrong, and its liquidated or unliquidated character, are to be taken into account, and the factors may require different evaluation in different types of successions of States.[5] (emphases added)

I believe that there are at least five different groups of factors and circumstances under which State practice and case law call for specific solutions to problems of State succession to responsibility.

A first group of relevant factors and circumstances is related to the position taken *by the predecessor State* with respect to the internationally wrongful act it committed before the date of succession. Thus, whenever the predecessor State has recognised its own responsibility, the successor State should have the obligation to provide reparation to the injured State (Section 2). The same solution should prevail whenever the liability of the successor State has been determined (before the date of succession) by a judicial body (Section 3).

A second group of relevant factors and circumstances is related to the position taken *by the successor State* and its actual behaviour in dealing with internationally wrongful acts committed before the date of succession. State practice shows many examples where successor States have accepted to take over the consequences of internationally wrongful acts. This is a situation where the rule of succession must apply (Section 4). Another relevant circumstance is whenever the successor State *continues* an internationally wrongful act which was initially committed by the predecessor State (Section 5). In this case, the successor State is responsible for its own internationally wrongful act committed *after* the date of succession. I will address the question as to whether the successor State should also be responsible for obligations arising from the wrongful act committed by the predecessor State *before* that date.

A third group of relevant factors and circumstances is related to the identification of the entity which has *actually committed* the internationally wrongful act. It is well recognised in State practice, case law and scholarship that the successor State should take over the obligations arising from internationally wrongful acts committed by an *insurrectional movement* during an armed

different depending on whether it is a violation of international law directly made against a State, or whether it is made against one of its nationals.

5 O'Connell, Recent Problems, 164.

struggle which eventually led to the creation of the new State.[6] This is, however, not a case of succession of States *per se*. On the contrary, the successor State should not be responsible for obligations arising from internationally wrongful acts committed by the *predecessor State* during the armed struggle led by an insurrectional movement to establish that new State (Section 6).[7] There is also some support in State practice for the more general principle that the successor State should, in some circumstances, be responsible for obligations arising from internationally wrongful acts committed by an *autonomous government* (while still part of the predecessor State) with which it has an "organic and structural continuity" (Section 7). Several provisions of the Institute's Resolution (as well as some of the earlier draft articles put forward by ILC Special Rapporteur Šturma) recognises this principle.

A fourth group of relevant factors and circumstances is related to the practical consequences that the application of the solution of succession or non-succession would have on the States involved. In my view, general principles of law, such as the principle of unjust enrichment and the principles of equity and justice, are indeed relevant to determine which of the continuing State or the successor State (and in case of dissolution, which one among the successor States) should be responsible for obligations arising from the commission of internationally wrongful acts. The following two principles will be discussed. The first principle is that the State (whether "continuator" or successor) that has unjustly enriched itself as a result of an internationally wrongful act committed before the date of succession should provide reparation to the injured State (Section 8). The second principle is that the outcome of the allocation of liability between the continuing State and the successor State (and in case of a dissolution of State, among the successor States themselves) should be fair and equitable (Section 9).

A fifth group of relevant factors and circumstances is related to the *nature*, the *origin* and the *character* of the obligation breached by the predecessor State. My review of relevant State practice and case law shows that there is no support for the general proposition that the successor State is *automatically* responsible for obligations arising from internationally wrongful acts committed by the predecessor State *solely based* on the fact that such acts took place prior to its independence on what is now its territory. Yet, the work of the Institute and the draft articles put forward by ILC Special Rapporteur Šturma both recognise that one relevant factor is the existence of a "direct link"

---

6 See, Dumberry, Rebellions, 303ff.

7 Ibid 365ff.

between the consequences of an internationally wrongful act committed by the predecessor State and the territory or the population of the successor State. I will also show that there is support for the principle that the successor State does take over the consequences of violations of *territorial regimes* obligations committed by the predecessor State (Section 10). The review of State practice and case law will also show that there is no support for the general proposition that the responsibility resulting from the violation of a treaty by the predecessor State before the date of succession is automatically transferred to the successor State when it becomes party to that treaty by way of succession (Section 11). Finally, it is submitted that there is no special rule for violations of *jus cogens* norms or other "odious" acts committed by the predecessor State and that such breaches should not be treated any differently than other "ordinary" violations of international law (Section 12).

2 The Predecessor State Recognises Its Liability for an Internationally Wrongful Act

When an internationally wrongful act is committed by the predecessor State and when, before the date of succession, it recognises its responsibility for the commission of the act, the question arises as to whether the successor State is bound by such recognition. The question is only relevant insofar as such recognition did not lead to any (or only partial) compensation to the injured State before the date of succession. The issue also only concerns cases where the predecessor State *ceases to exist* as a result of the events affecting its territorial integrity (such as, for instance, cases of dissolution of State).[8]

The first point that should be highlighted is that the solution to the issue of succession to the obligation to repair exists quite *independently* of the question whether or not the predecessor State has recognised any liability. In other words, the solution to the problem does not depend *only* on the recognition of liability by the predecessor State. There will be cases (examined in the next sections) where succession to the obligation to repair will prevail *even if* the predecessor State did not recognise any liability. But when the predecessor State *does* recognise such responsibility, the solution of succession should prevail.

Whenever the predecessor State recognises its responsibility for the commission of the internationally wrongful act, the injured third State has some

8 The issue simply does not arise in the context where the predecessor State *continues* to exist. Thus, in cases of separation the continuing State is bound by *its own* recognition of responsibility before the date of succession.

sort of an "acquired right" to reparation in the sense that such right is "liquidated" and certain; it is not a mere expectation.[9] There is support in scholarship for the proposition that in such case the successor State is bound to respect the "acquired right" of the injured State and, accordingly, to provide reparation.[10] Ultimately, the principle that the successor State is responsible for obligations arising from the commission of internationally wrongful acts for which the predecessor State has recognised its liability is based on good faith. This principle may also be applied, in some circumstances, based on the other principle of *estoppel*.[11] The only support found in State practice in favour of this proposition are a few cases decided by Italian municipal courts in the context of the unity of Italy.[12]

3 A Judicial Body Finds the Predecessor State Responsible for an Internationally Wrongful Act

The question whether or not a successor State takes over the consequences of obligations arising from the commission of internationally wrongful acts does not depend *per se* on any determination of liability by a judicial body. In

9 This is the position of Barde, 184.

10 Barde, 177 ("Le nouvel Etat n'est pas responsable des délits (actes illicites) de son prédécesseur à moins que celui-ci ait reconnu sa dette avant de disparaître"); Jenning & Watts, 218 (in the context of merger of States: "where, however, [the extinct State] had acknowledged its liability and compensation had been agreed, a debt has arisen which, it is suggested, ought to survive the extinction of personality and be discharged by the absorbing State"); Ivan A. Shearer, *Starke's International Law* (11th edn, Butterworths 1994) 303 ("The successor State is not bound to respect an unliquidated claim for damage in tort. If, however, the amount of the claim has become liquidated by agreement of the parties or through a judgment or award of a tribunal, then in the absence of any suggestion of injustice or unreasonableness, the successor State may be bound to settle the amount of this liquidated claim"); Georg Dahm, *Völkerrecht*, v. 1 (W. Kohlhammer 1958) 121; Atlam, 216–217; Monnier, 67; Hurst, 177; Jacques Brossard & Daniel Turp, *L'accession à la souveraineté et le cas du Québec* (2nd edn, PU. Montréal, 1995) 693–4.

11 In the case of *Land, Island and Maritime Frontier Dispute* (El Salvador v. Honduras), *Application to Intervene*, Judgment, 13 September 1990, ICJ Rep. 1990, 92, paras 118–119, the ICJ defined the concept of estoppel as "a statement or representation made by one party to another and reliance upon it by that other party to his detriment or to the advantage of the party making it".

12 *Orcesi v. The Ministry of War*, Court of Cassation of Florence, 21 December 1881, in: Hurst, 177; *Verlengo v. Finance Department*, 1878, Court of Cassation of Florence, *Giurisprudenza Italiana*, 3rd Ser. v. 30, Pt. 1, Sec. 1, col. 1206, in: "Brief", US, *Hawaiian Claims* case, in: Nielsen, 119–120.

other words, the solution of succession may very well prevail *without* any such finding by a judicial body. Nevertheless, whenever a judicial body has determined (before the date of succession) that the predecessor State was responsible for the commission of an internationally wrongful act, the successor State should take over the obligations arising from the commission of such act.[13] Thus, in a case where a judicial body made a determination on the veracity of the facts surrounding an alleged internationally wrongful act and the quantum of the damage suffered, the claim should be deemed "liquidated". The question is then one of succession to "administrative debts" of the predecessor State. There is support in scholarship for the proposition that the successor State is responsible for such "administrative debts".[14] The issue only concerns cases where the predecessor State *ceases to exist* as a result of the events affecting its territorial integrity (such as, for instance, cases of dissolution of State).[15]

It should be added, importantly, that from the mere fact that a claim is *not* "liquidated" at the time of the date of succession, one should not automatically conclude that obligations arising from an internationally wrongful act committed by the predecessor State cannot be transferred to the successor State. Yet, there is some support in international case law for the principle of *non-succession* for "unliquidated" claims. In the *R.E. Brown* case, one of the reasons why the US-Great Britain Arbitral Commission rejected the claim of Mr Brown was because it "was simply a pending claim for damages against

13 This is also the position of these writers: Ivan A. Shearer, *Starke's International Law* (11th edn, Butterworths 1994) 303; Volkovitsch, footnote 235; Sastry, 209.

14 O'Connell, State Succession, v. I, 448: "There has never been any doubt that a successor State is under an obligation to respect those debts incurred in the ordinary routine of governmental administration in the territory acquired by it". Similarly, for Volkovitsch, 2191, "there is a genuine question as to whether a completely liquidated claim should be treated as a delictual obligation at all, or whether it is better viewed as an administrative debt of the predecessor State for a fixed sum of damage". See also, Pajnkihar, 304: "As pointed out by Special Rapporteur Šturma, for succession to international responsibility to be established, the wrongful act must take place before the date of succession, whereas the confirmation of its legal consequences must occur only after the date of succession. If the confirmation of the legal consequences took place before the date of succession, these consequences would be defined as a debt of the predecessor State, which would be succeeded to by the successor State in accordance with the rules on succession to debts". The author uses the expression "confirmation of its legal consequences" to refer to the situation where a court has decided the issue of responsibility arising from the commission of a wrongful act (305).

15 The issue simply does not arise in the context where the predecessor State *continues* to exist. Thus, in cases of separation the continuing State is bound by a finding made by a judicial body before the date of succession.

certain officials and had never become a liquidated debt of the former State".[16] Similarly, in the *Lighthouse Arbitration* case, the Arbitral Tribunal rejected Claim no. 11 but added in the form of an *obiter dictum* that "[i]n any event, the claim was not admitted by either of those States, nor was it liquidated or easily ascertainable".[17] The same Arbitral Tribunal accepted Claim no. 4 and added that this was so, moreover, based on the fact that the claim was susceptible of being easily liquidated.[18]

It has been argued by some scholars that "unliquidated" claims cannot be protected by international law in the context of State succession and therefore become extinct at the date of succession.[19] Other writers believe, on the contrary, that this distinction between "liquidated" and "unliquidated" debts is "inapplicable to inter-State relations and lack[s] sufficient justification in that

16 *R.E. Brown* case, 129. See, O'Connell, State Succession, v. 1, 488.

17 *Lighthouse Arbitration* case, 23 *ILR* 1956, 83.

18 Ibid 89.

19 Sir Jenning & Watts, 218 (noting that there is "good authority" for the rule of non-succession to unliquidated damages); Louis Henkin et al., *International Law, Cases and Materials* (3rd edn, West 1993) 293 ("if the claim has not been reduced to a money judgment, which may be considered a debt, or an interest on the part of the claimant in assets of fixed value, there is no acquired right in the claimant, and no obligation to which the successor State has succeeded"); S.K. Agrawala, "Law of Nations as Interpreted and Applied by Indian Courts and Legislature", 2 *Indian JIL* 1962, 431, 442 ("a claim for unliquidated damages is not protected by international law"); Barde, 183–184 ("il est frappant de constater qu'une condition est toujours exigée pour que le transfert soit possible aussi bien, en matière de responsabilité internationale que de responsabilité interne: pour être imputable à l'Etat successeur et constituer un droit acquis, le droit à réparation doit être liquide c'est-à-dire bien arrêté, certain et donc définitivement entré dans le patrimoine de la victime avant le changement de souveraineté. L'unanimité de la doctrine, la pratique gouvernementale, la jurisprudence internationale et la jurisprudence interne concordent sur ce point: le droit à réparation n'est pas un droit acquis tant qu'il n'est pas liquide") and 185 ("le caractère liquide de la dette est une condition toujours nécessaire mais pas suffisante dans tous les cas d'illicéité pour que le droit à réparation soit un droit acquis"); Shaw, 872 ("claims to unliquidated damages will not continue beyond the succession"); Feilchenfeld, 728–729 ("[t]here is, moreover, another reason which speaks against the classification of most unawarded or unrecognised diplomatic tort claims as debts … As long as it is not certain that the State against which the claim is directed will have to pay money, the doubt concerns not merely the point that the amount of the debt is undefined, but the more fundamental question whether or not a debt will be created at all. Unless it is clear that money is owed, it is not established that a debt exists which may subsequently be protected in case of State succession"); Nkambo Mugerwa, "Subject of International Law", in: Max Sorensen, *Manual of Public International Law* (Macmillan 1968) 292; John O'Brien, *International Law* (Cavendish 2001) 604; Charles Rousseau, *Les transformations territoriales des Etats et leurs conséquences juridiques* (Les cours de droit 1964–1965) 142; Atlam, 216–217; T. Sastry, 210.

field".[20] For Crawford, "the liquidated or unliquidated character of the claim is irrelevant to the transmission of responsibility, merely that it will not be determinative".[21] As rightly observed by Stern, it would be rather illogical to determine the sake of the transmission of the obligation to repair to the successor State solely based on the moment in time when such right is invoked or determined by a judicial body.[22] This distinction would be particularly inequitable in cases where the internationally wrongful act itself would arise from the State's denial of justice and refusal to give the opportunity to the individual to liquidate its claim.[23]

At any rate, the "unliquidated" nature of a claim should not prevent the injured State from exercising its right to *bring an action* before a judicial body *after the date of succession* for the damage it has suffered from an internationally wrongful act committed by the predecessor State before the date of succession.[24] This right of the injured State is, of course, not tantamount to any automatic "acquired right" to compensation from the successor State.[25] As suggested by O'Connell, it is only a right to bring an action which may eventually lead to a judgment awarding reparation.[26]

---

20 Verzijl, 220, for whom this theory is "too rigid and too unduly influenced by Anglo-Saxon doctrine concerning the non-transferability of non-liquidated debts in the field of private law". O'Connell, State Succession, v. 1, 485, adopts a more prudent position in so far as he believes, on the one hand, that any attempt to maintain the difference between "liquidated" and "unliquidated" debts is "apt to torture the problem rather than resolve it", but also, on the other hand, that such criterion is not "altogether irrelevant, either singly or in association with other factors, in distinguishing claims which devolve upon a successor State from those which do not" (See also, his comments in: O'Connell, Recent Problems, 164). Sastry, 210, 212, indicates that Indian municipal courts in the context of the partition have not treated "liquidated" and "unliquidated" damages differently.

21 Crawford, State Responsibility, 441–2.

22 Stern, Responsabilité, 337. See also, Peterschmitt, 22.

23 Stern, ibid. This is also the position of Volkovitsch, 2190–2191.

24 Stern, ibid. See also: S.K. Agrawala, "Law of Nations as Interpreted and Applied by Indian Courts and Legislature", 2 *Indian JIL* 1962, 431, 442: "In case of unliquidated claims, the claimant has no more than the capacity to appear before a court which thereupon may or may not create a debt against the offending State".

25 Thus, for Volkovitsch, 2205, the "acquired right" of the injured State is *not* the right to "automatic compensation but rather the right to bring an action that will be adjudicated". For him, the doctrine of acquired rights "guarantees the existence of a claim and a defendant, but not a valid claim and a defendant able to pay".

26 O'Connell, State Succession, v. 1, 485: "It has been argued that a tort committed by the agents of a State merely gives rise to a right of action for unliquidated damages of a penal or compensatory character. It does not create an interest in assets of a fixed or determinable value. The claimant has no more than the capacity to appear before a court, which

4 The Successor State Accepts to Take Over the Responsibility for an Internationally Wrongful Act

One of the most fundamental underlying principles in the Institute's Resolution is the subsidiary character of the rules contained in the Resolution (Article 3).[27] ILC Guideline 1(2) also indicates that "the present draft articles apply in the absence of any different solution agreed upon by the states concerned". As further discussed below, the "solutions" are agreements and unilateral declarations.[28] In other words, both institutions recognised the priority of agreement between the concerned States[29] over any other solutions contained in the documents.[30] As such, ILC Special Rapporteur Šturma envisaged the Draft Articles as serving two purposes: "First, they can present a useful model that may be used and also modified by the States concerned. Second, in cases of lack of agreement, they can present a default rule to be applied in case of dispute".[31]

It has long been recognised that nothing in international law prevents a successor State from deciding to succeed to an internationally wrongful act committed by the predecessor State.[32] There is unanimity on that point.[33] This is a rule of State responsibility rather than a principle applicable only to issues of State succession.[34] The basic principle that nothing prevents a successor State from deciding to succeed to an internationally wrongful act committed by the predecessor State has been confirmed by the ICJ in the *Gabčíkovo-Nagymaros* case.[35] In this case, the *Compromis* between the parties had recognised that the Slovak Republic, as one of the two successor States to Czechoslovakia,

---

thereupon may or may not create in his favour a debt against the offending State. Until such a debt is created, however, the claimant's interest is not an acquired right".

27 See, Kohen & Dumberry, 29ff; IIL, Final Report, Kohen, paras 44ff.

28 ILC, "Statement of the Chairperson of the Drafting Committee", Charles Chernor Jalloh, 3 August 2018, 3.

29 See Kohen & Dumberry, 30.

30 ILC Special Rapporteur Šturma, Third Report, 2019, para 17; ibid, First Report, 2017, para 87ff.

31 Ibid, First Report, 2017, para 86.

32 Stern, Responsabilité, 350.

33 Udina, 768; Stern, ibid; H. Lauterpacht, *Oppenheim's International Law*, v. 1 (Longmans Green 1955) 162; Jenning & Watts, 218; John O'Brien, *International Law* (Cavendish 2001) 605; Dupuy & Kerbrat, 84–5; W. Schönborn, *Staatensuccession, Handbuch des Völkerrechts*, v. 2 (1913) 49; Monnier, 67, 90; Volkovitsch, 2199–2200; Natalino Ronzitti, *La successione internazionale tra stati* (Giuffrè 1970) 221; John Dugard, *International Law; a South African Perspective* (2nd edn, Juta, 2000) 232–233; Booysen, 207; Sastry, 209; Ruy & Baecke, 24; Pajnkihar, 308, 321.

34 Pajnkihar, 321.

35 *Gabčíkovo-Nagymaros* case.

was the "sole successor state in respect of rights and obligations relating to the Gabčíkovo-Nagymaros Project". The Court did not question whether the Slovak Republic could freely decide to be held solely liable for the internationally wrongful act committed by the predecessor State; it simply accepted this position as a fact.[36] Similarly, in interpreting Article 140(3) of the Namibian Constitution, the sitting Judge of the Namibian High Court in the case of *Mwandinghi v. Minister of Defence, Namibia* stated that "in the present case the new State chose to accept liability, subject to its right to repudiate, and is therefore liable".[37] He added: "I know of no principle whereby international law can step in and undo such an acceptance by a State".[38]

The review of State practice and case law in the previous chapter has shown that successor States have accepted to take over the consequences of international responsibility of the predecessor State in two ways.

First, acceptance can be found in an agreement. I have found many examples of treaties entered into by the successor State and the injured State.[39] In his First Report, ILC Special Rapporteur Šturma refers to such agreements as "claims agreements".[40] Another possibility is an agreement between the successor States themselves.[41] Another common scenario is a treaty between the predecessor and the successor States.[42] I have mentioned above[43] several examples of agreements where the parties agreed that the Newly Independent State would, after its independence, take over all existing liabilities and obligations for which the predecessor colonial State was responsible before the date

36 Ibid para 151.

37 *Mwandinghi* case, Namibia, High Court, 355.

38 Ibid 354–355. It has been suggested by Booysen, 213–214, that third States may object to the decision by Namibia to take over internationally wrongful acts committed by South Africa during its racist and oppressive rule over the colony.

39 Two treaties were entered into by the successor State with injured States in the context of the unification of the United Arab Republic (1958). See, Chapter 2, Section 3.2.1. One international agreement was entered into by the successor State in the context of the integration of the GDR into West Germany (1990) (Chapter 2, Section 2.3.1.3. In the context of the dissolution of the Union of Colombia (1829–1831), the three successor States entered into separate agreements with the injured State (Chapter 2, Section 4.2.3). See also, the agreement between the US and Vietnam. Another (rather theoretical and less significant) example is in the context of the separation of Panama (1903).

40 ILC Special Rapporteur Šturma, First Report, 2017, paras 100ff.

41 *Agreement on Succession Issues*, 29 June 2001, 41 *ILM* 2002, 3, among the successor States to the former Yugoslavia.

42 One example is Art. 38, *Paris Peace Treaty*, 10 February 1947, in force on 15 September 1947, 49 *UNTS* 126; *UKTS* 1948, no. 50 (Cmd. 7481), dealing with the cession of the Dodecanesian Islands.

43 See, Chapter 2, Section 7.1.

of succession. Some of these agreements were signed before the date of succession by the predecessor State with an autonomous government,[44] or with insurgents.[45] I have also found States' acceptance to obligations arising from the commission of a wrongful act in agreements with private foreign companies[46] as well as in a *compromis* between two States to refer a dispute to the ICJ.[47] Other types of agreements are also possible.[48]

Article 6 of the Institute's Resolution contains a very detailed clause on "devolution agreements".[49] It is beyond the scope of this book to examine the question of who are the different parties to these agreements which can be concluded between different actors both before and after the date of succession.[50] The same is true regarding the detailed analysis done by ILC Special Rapporteur Šturma, distinguishing between three types of agreements and providing numerous examples of State practice involving them.[51] The ILC Secretariat also published a comprehensive and very useful survey of such agreements.[52]

It is sufficient here to note how Article 6 of the Institute's Resolution deals with the effect and the consequences of such an agreement on a *third* party. A devolution agreement is only binding on the parties to this instrument.[53] It is not binding on the injured State, who is not a party to the agreement. Article 6 focuses on the need to protect the interests of the injured State, i.e. the *victim* of an internationally wrongful act.[54] The injured State needs to consent to the transfer of the obligation to repair from the predecessor State to the successor State.[55] While ILC Special Rapporteur Šturma first took a rather ambiguous

44 *Agreement relating to the Separation of Singapore from Malaysia as an Independent and Sovereign State*, 7 August 1965, 563 *UNTS* 89, No. 8206.

45 Art. 18, *Déclaration de principes relative à la coopération économique et financière*, 19 March 1962, part of the *Evian Accords* (*JORF*, 20 March 1962, 3019–3032) entered into by France and the FLN to end the national liberation war in Algeria.

46 One such agreement was entered into by the successor State in the context of the unification of the United Arab Republic (1958): Agreement of 13 July 1958 between the United Arab Republic and the *Société Financière de Suez*.

47 *Compromis* between Hungary and Slovakia in the context of the *Gabčíkovo-Nagymaros* case.

48 For a detailed analysis, see Kohen & Dumberry, 30–2, 36ff.

49 See, ibid, 36ff.

50 See, ibid, 38ff.

51 ILC Special Rapporteur Šturma, First Report, 2017, paras 83ff.

52 ILC, "Succession of States in respect of State responsibility, Information on treaties which may be of relevance to the future work of the Commission on the topic", Memorandum by the Secretariat, A/CN.4/730*, 20 March 2019.

53 Art. 34, *Vienna Convention on the Law of Treaties*, 1155 *UNTS* 331.

54 Kohen & Dumberry, 41–46.

55 Ibid, 46. See, comment by Greece, letter sent to the UN GA Sixth Committee, Rep. 68th sess., 25 Oct. 2017. See also, Vergara Lamadrid, 132–3, 226.

position on the matter,[56] which was criticized by some States[57] and in the commentary to the Institute's Resolution,[58] he seems to have later changed his mind.[59] In any event, what is clear is that the parties to an agreement cannot decide on the *extinction* of obligations arising from the commission of a wrongful act without the consent of the injured State.[60]

While the work of the ILC initially contained a clause dealing with agreements (Article 3(2) of the ILC draft), it was later deleted.[61] This absence is somewhat surprising given that Special Rapporteur Šturma had highlighted the paramount importance of agreements in the context of State succession.[62] It should be recalled that Guideline 1(2) indicates that the solutions put forward only apply in the "absence of any different solutions agreed upon by the States concerned". Yet, as a result of this modification, no provision explains what these "solutions" are; a reference is found in the Commentary.[63]

---

56 ILC Special Rapporteur Šturma, First Report, 2017, para 99: "When it comes to rights of third States, *their assent may be presumed*. A transfer of obligations from State responsibility to the successor State may be viewed so as to accord rights to the third injured State. However, it is also possible that succession will bring some obligations for third States. Then it is required that the third State expressly accepts such obligations" (emphasis added).

57 See, comment by Greece, letter sent to the UN GA Sixth Committee, Rep. 68th sess., 25 Oct. 2017: "in case the predecessor State continues to exist, third States affected by the internationally wrongful act of the predecessor State might not be always in favor of the devolution of the relevant obligations to the successor State by means either of a devolution agreement or of a unilateral declaration. For this reason, we consider that the relevant assent of third States should not be taken for granted as implied, in relation to devolution agreements, in paragraph 99 of the Special Rapporteur's report. Likewise, the assumption in draft article 4 that, in case of a unilateral declaration of succession to responsibility made in clear and specific terms that the relevant obligations devolve to the successor State, should be tested against the scenario that the third State who has suffered the damage does not concede to such a transfer of obligations".

58 Kohen & Dumberry, 45–46. See also, Vergara Lamadrid, 132–3, 226.

59 ILC Special Rapporteur Šturma, Fifth Report, 2022, para 69: "The principle of relative effects of agreements (the *pacta tertiis* principle) excludes agreements between predecessor and successor States alone (devolution agreements) as the sole legal basis for a possible transfer of rights and obligations arising from internationally wrongful acts".

60 IIL, Final Report, Kohen, paras 26, 49.

61 See, ILC Special Rapporteur Šturma, Fifth Report, 2022, paras 71ff, explaining the reasons for deleting this provision, including (at the end of para 73) taking into account some critical comments made by Kohen & Dumberry, 43.

62 ILC Special Rapporteur Šturma, First Report, 2017, para 87, 111; ibid, Second Report, 2018, para 14; ibid, Fourth Report, 2020, para 22.

63 ILC, Commentaries, 2019, para 118, Art. 1, sub-para 7–8: "Such solutions may be expressed in a variety of forms, which could include, for example, international agreements, unilateral declarations, or a combination thereof. In this regard, the words 'agreed upon' are

There is also a second form of States' acceptance of international responsibility. It can be found in national constitutions,[64] in national laws[65] as well as in unilateral declarations.[66] Article 6 of the Institute's Resolution contains a very detailed clause on "unilateral declarations".[67] Under that clause, a unilateral act alone is not sufficient for the successor State to automatically take over any obligations toward the injured State. According to the Final Report, acceptance by the successor State "does not automatically produce the effect desired by" that State.[68] A unilateral undertaking by that State "will not be enough for succession to apply with respect to that tort".[69] The injured party must be given the possibility to accept or reject the solution unilaterally adopted by the successor State regarding the devolution of obligations.[70] The goal is to protect the right of the injured State to receive adequate reparation for the damage suffered. ILC Draft Article 4(2), put forward in Special Rapporteur Šturma's First Report, contained a similar clause (but with this additional sentence at the end:[71] "unless its

to be understood in a broad sense and do not refer only to the consent to be bound by a treaty". See also: ILC, "Statement of the Chairperson of the Drafting Committee", Charles Chernor Jalloh, 3 August 2018, 3.

64 *Constitution of Namibia*, in force on 21 March 1991, S/20967/Add.2. See also: *Treaty on the Establishment of German Unity*, 31 August 1990, 30 *ILM* 1991, 457.

65 For instance, in the context of the integration of the GDR into the FRG (1990). See also: *Indian Independence (Rights, Property and Liabilities) Order*, Gaz. India Extra., 14 August 1947, 913, Art. 10.

66 One example of a unilateral declaration is that of Slovenia informing the UN Human Rights Committee that victims of human rights violations committed by the former Yugoslavia remained entitled to remedy from the successor State: UN Human Rights Committee, *Concluding Observations of the Human Rights Committee: Slovenia*, 21 September 1994, CCPR/C/79/Add.40; A/49/40, paras 334–353 (1994), para 6. See also, similar statements: ibid Ukraine, 26 July 1995, CCPR/C/79/Add.52 (1995), para 3; ibid Slovakia, 4 August 1997, CCPR/C/79/Add.79 (1997), para 7; ibid Azerbaijan, 3 August 1994, CCPR/C/79/Add.38; A/49/40, paras 291–311 (1994), para 3.

67 See, Kohen & Dumberry, 36, 47ff.

68 IIL, Final Report, Kohen, para 68.

69 Ibid.

70 Ibid, 50ff. *Contra*: Ruy & Baecke, 24 ("Contrary to what the Institut appears to suggest in its Tallinn resolution, there is indeed no reason whatsoever why a successor State cannot unilaterally accept—in a legally binding manner—the obligations resulting from the internationally wrongful acts of the predecessor through such a declaration").

71 ILC Special Rapporteur Šturma, First Report, 2017, paras 113, 132. For a critical analysis, see Kohen & Dumberry, 51–2. ILC Special Rapporteur acknowledged this point in ibid, Fifth Report, 2022, para 75. This question is examined by Vergara Lamadrid, 134.

unilateral declaration is stated in clear and specific terms"). The clause was later deleted.[72]

Interestingly enough, examples of State practice whereby the new State accepted to be bound by the consequences arising from the internationally wrongful acts of the predecessor State were found in the context of different types of State succession. Thus, such an acceptance of the transfer of the obligation to repair has been observed in the context of unification and integration of State,[73] dissolution,[74] separation[75] and the creation of Newly Independent States.[76] No such acceptance was found, however, in the context of cession and transfer of territory.

These cases of clear and positive acceptance of responsibility must be distinguished from the other situation where a State agrees to pay compensation to another injured State on an *ex gratia* basis without any acceptance of the principle of responsibility for the acts.[77] Many (old) examples of *ex gratia* compensation were found in the context of cession and transfer of territory.[78]

5 The Successor State Continues an Internationally Wrongful Act Committed by the Predecessor State

This section deals with the continuation by the successor State of an internationally wrongful act initially committed by the predecessor State before the date of succession. There are *two different* internationally wrongful acts. The first is committed by the predecessor State and ends at the time of the creation of the new State. The second commences at this very moment and the successor State is responsible for it.[79] These two categories are dealt with separately in this section.

---

72 See, ibid, Fifth Report, 2022, para 75, explaining the reasons for deleting this provision, including (at the end of para 75) taking into account some critical comments made by Kohen & Dumberry, 51.

73 Several examples were found in the context of the unification of the United Arab Republic (1958) and the integration of the GDR into West Germany (1990).

74 In the context of the dissolutions of the Union of Colombia (1829–1831), Yugoslavia and Czechoslovakia.

75 In the context of the separation of Belgium from the Kingdom of the Netherlands (1830).

76 In the context of the independence of Namibia.

77 Stern, Responsabilité, 350.

78 For instance, in the context of the annexations of Burma by Great Britain (1886), of the Boer Republic by Great Britain (1902) and of Madagascar by France (1896).

79 Agreeing: Czech Rep., letter sent to the UN GA Sixth Committee, rep. 76th sess. 2 Nov. 2021.

It should be added that Article 9 of the Institute's Resolution distinguishes between acts having a *continuing* and a *composite* character. The first paragraph of Article 9 of the Institute's Resolution refers to the situation where a successor State "continues the breach of an international obligation constituted by an act of the predecessor State having a continuing character". This situation is covered by ILC Guideline 7.[80] The second paragraph of Article 9 of the Institute's Resolution addresses the different situation when a successor State "completes a series of actions or omissions" after the date of succession which were "initiated by the predecessor State" before that date. Examples of such composite acts include genocide, crime of apartheid or crimes against humanity.[81] This situation is covered by ILC Guideline 7 *bis*.[82] While I fully support the distinction between these two types of acts, this section will only address "continuing" acts.[83]

80 The question was initially dealt with in Draft Article 6(3), attached to ILC Special Rapporteur Šturma, Second Report, 2018. For reasons explained in ILC, Statement, Grossman Guiloff, 2019, 2–3, ILC Special Rapporteur later proposed a new Article 5. It was later renumbered as Guideline 7. See, ILC, Succession of States in respect of State responsibility, "Statement of the Chair of the Drafting Committee Mr Ki Gab Park", 14 July 2022, annex (hereinafter "ILC, Statement, Park, 2022").

81 Kohen & Dumberry, 60, 63ff.

82 ILC, Statement, Park, 2022.

83 A few words should nevertheless be said about composite acts. Under Art. 9(2) of the Institute's Resolution, when a successor State completes a series of actions or omissions initiated by the predecessor State, and the composite wrongful act is considered having been performed, it bears international responsibility for the *entire* period, including for what happened *before* the date of succession. See, IIL, Final Report, Kohen, para 114; Kohen & Dumberry, 63–4. The question is examined in detail in: ILC Special Rapporteur Šturma, Second Report, 2018, paras 63–76. ILC Draft Articles 6(1) (first sentence) and 6(2), which were put forward in the Second Report, were to the same effect. In ibid, Fourth Report, 2020, paras 109ff, he further examined the topic and put forward a separate provision dealing only with composite acts: Article 7 *bis*. In 2022, the Drafting Committee completely redrafted the provision (Guideline 7 *bis*). Guideline 7 *bis* (3) concerns the situation where a "composite act is started by the predecessor State before the date of succession of States and continued and completed by the successor State afterwards" (ILC, Statement, Park, 2022, 6). The Drafting Committee concluded that the "available State practice, in light of its inconsistency, did not allow [it] to draw a firm conclusion as to the content of the law" and that, accordingly, it "decided to present the paragraph in the form of a without prejudice clause" (ibid 7). As a result, the Drafting Committee decided to "leave[] open the question of whether the responsibility of a successor State for a such a composite act is possible under international law" (ibid 7). Ultimately, the third paragraph says nothing on what happens to composite acts that occurs across the date of succession. For this reason, the Czech Rep., letter sent to the UN GA Sixth Committee, rep. 77th sess. 2 Nov. 2022, rightly questioned whether this provision was really needed at all.

5.1 *Acts Committed by the Successor State after the Date of Succession*

The fact that the new successor State is responsible for the acts it has committed *after* its independence is uncontroversial and is widely recognised in scholarship.[84] This is in fact not a problem of succession of States,[85] since there is no "transfer" of an obligation from one State to another. Rather, it involves the creation of a *new obligation* for the successor State. This principle is clearly expressed by Monnier as follows:

> La responsabilité qui incombe dans des cas de ce genre à l'Etat successeur n'est pas une responsabilité 'héritée' de l'Etat prédécesseur, mais une responsabilité nouvelle. L'Etat successeur ne reprend pas, ce faisant, des obligations délictuelles de l'Etat antérieur. Il n'y a donc pas *stricto sensu*, succession d'États.[86]

According to Article 9(1) of the Institute's Resolution, the successor State bears responsibility for its actions from the date of succession onwards, as well as for the entire duration in which the act remains in violation of the relevant international obligation. The same solution has been adopted by ILC Special Rapporteur Šturma[87] and supported by States.[88]

Another question is whether the predecessor State or the successor State should bear the responsibility for the damage caused by acts that occurred *before* the date of succession.[89] This point is examined in the next section.

---

84 Volkovitsch, 2199; Udina, 768; Erik Castren, "Aspects récents de la succession d'Etats", *Rec. des cours*, v. 78, 1951–I, 391; Volinka Reina, "Iraq's Delictual and Contractual Liabilities: Would Politics or International Law Provide for Better Resolution of Successor State Responsibility?", 22 *Berkeley JIL* 2004, 583, 590; A. Verdross & B. Simma, *Universelles Völkerrecht, Theorie und Praxis* (Dunker & Humblot 1984) 633–634; Max Huber, *Die Staatensuccession: völkerrechtliche und staatsrechtliche Praxis im XIX. Jahrhundert* (Duncker & Humblot 1898) 65–66; Pajnkihar, 327.

85 Pajnkihar, 327.

86 Monnier, 89. See also, Stern, Responsabilité, 349: "Il existe un cas de figure dans lequel il peut sembler qu'il y a une transmission de responsabilité de l'Etat prédécesseur à l'Etat successeur, mais ... en réalité la responsabilité de l'Etat successeur naît de sa propre violation d'une obligation continue qui avait antérieurement été violée par l'Etat prédécesseur".

87 ILC Special Rapporteur Šturma, Second Report, 2018, para 59. See Draft Article 5 (later changed to 7) (first sentence).

88 Czech Rep., letter sent to the UN GA Sixth Committee, Rep. 74th sess. 6 Nov. 2019; Czech Rep., ibid Rep. 76th sess. 2 Nov. 2021; Austria, ibid Rep. 74th sess. 2 Nov. 2021.

89 Pajnkihar, 327, describing the issue as follows: "From the date of succession onwards, the successor State would succeed to the primary rule (i.e., replace the predecessor State in respect of that rule) and, at the same time, continue to engage in an identical breach of

5.2 *Acts Committed by the Predecessor State before the Date of Succession*

In my view, there are good reasons to support the proposition that when the new State continues the original internationally wrongful act committed by the predecessor State, that new State should be held accountable not only for *its own* act committed after the date of succession *but also* for the damage which was caused by the predecessor State *before* that date. In other words, the new State should take over obligations arising from internationally wrongful acts committed by the predecessor State *before* its independence *because* of its continuation of the original internationally wrongful act.[90] Some States have taken the same position.[91] The Czech Republic noted that even in such cases, "these would still be two independent acts of two different States"; "They would not become one continuing wrongful act, as the Interim report of the Drafting committee suggests".[92]

Some of the comments made by ILC Special Rapporteur Crawford suggest that he was also of the opinion that the successor State should be responsible for the acts committed before its independence whenever it continues such acts after the date of succession. In his "First Report on State Responsibility (*addendum* no. 5)", he indicated that the subsequent adoption of an illegal

---

said rule (i.e., replace the predecessor State in conduct)". He also examines (at 327–8) the question as to whether the successor State can be considered to succeed to the secondary obligation of cessation.

90 I have found a rather unique example where the same solution was applied to wrongs which were *not* committed by the predecessor State. It concerns the Foreign Claims Settlement Commission in the context of the US 1976 "Claim Program" which was set up to deal with outstanding property claims in the GDR. The Commission held that the GDR should be responsible for the illegal taking of property committed *by the Soviet Union* during its military occupation of East Germany (1945–1949) since the Soviet expropriations "were subsequently ratified by [the] GDR after its establishment in 1949". See, *Earl N. Reinsel* case, Claim no. G–0433, Decision no. G–2674, *Index-Digest of Decisions*, v. III (1976–1986), 22. See also, the *Anna Low Bollinger* case, Decision no. G–2055, ibid: "The fact that the GDR was not officially established until October 1949 *did not preclude* a finding that actions by prior governmental authorities before October of 1949 in the territory administered by the Soviet military authorities after World War II constituted a taking for which the Government of the GDR was responsible" (emphasis added).

91 Czech Rep., letter sent to the UN GA Sixth Committee, Rep. 76th sess. 2 Nov. 2021: "We support the main gist of the second sentence of article 7, namely that, in certain circumstances, the successor States shall assume secondary obligations resulting from its predecessor's wrongful conduct before the date of State succession". See also, Czech Rep., letter sent to the UN GA Sixth Committee, Rep. 74th sess. 6 Nov. 2019. *Contra*: Austria, ibid Rep. 74th sess. 2 Nov. 2021.

92 Czech Rep., letter sent to the UN GA Sixth Committee, rep. 74th sess. 6 Nov. 2019.

conduct by a State (dealt with in Article 11 of the ILC's Articles)[93] was also applicable in the more specific context of succession of States:

> All the bases for attribution covered in chapter II (with the exception of the conduct of insurrectional movements under article 15) assume that the status of the person or body as a State organ, or its mandate to act on behalf of the State, are established at the time of the allegedly wrongful conduct. But that is not a necessary prerequisite to responsibility. *A State might subsequently adopt or ratify conduct not otherwise attributable to it; if so, there is no reason why it should not be treated as responsible for the conduct.*[94] (emphasis added)

In the 2001 Commentaries to the Articles, Special Rapporteur Crawford also specifically referred to questions of State succession and to the *Lighthouse Arbitration* case, where Greece had endorsed and continued a breach committed by Crete before the date of succession.[95] Special Rapporteur Crawford expressed the view that:

> In the context of State succession, it is unclear whether a new State succeeds to any State responsibility of the predecessor State with respect to its territory. However, if the successor State, faced with a continuing wrongful act on its territory, endorses and continues that situation, the inference may readily be drawn that it has *assumed responsibility for it.*[96] (emphasis added)

In reference to the "retroactive effects" of State responsibility as applied in the *Lighthouse Arbitration* case, the Special Rapporteur concluded in the ILC's "First Report on State Responsibility (*addendum* no. 5)" that:

93 ILC's *Articles on State Responsibility*, 2001. The provision reads as follows: "Conduct which is not attributable to a State under the preceding articles shall nevertheless be considered an act of that State under international law if and to the extent that the State acknowledges and adopts the conduct in question as its own".

94 ILC, "First Report on State Responsibility (*addendum* no. 5)", Special Rapporteur James Crawford, 22 July 1998, A/CN.4/490/Add.5., para 281.

95 *Lighthouse Arbitration* case, 23 *ILR* 1956, 81.

96 ILC, Commentaries, State Responsibility, 2001, 121, para 3. See also, ILC, "First Report on State Responsibility (*addendum* no. 5)", Special Rapporteur James Crawford, 22 July 1998, A/CN.4/490/Add.5., para 282.

> This has the desirable consequence of allowing the injured State to obtain reparation in respect *of the whole transaction or event*. It is also consistent with the position established by Article 15 for insurrectional movements.[97] (emphasis added)

One important point to highlight is that there is no "yes" or "no" answer to the question as to whether the successor State should bear the responsibility for the damage which was caused by acts that occurred *before* the date of succession. The solution depends on whether the predecessor State continues its existence or not as a result of the events affecting its territorial integrity.

The same approach was adopted by the Institute. Article 9(1) does not provide for any general solution with respect to the question of succession to obligations for the portion of the continuing act which took place *before* the date of succession.[98] The Final Report indicates that "the specific rules for each category" of Part 3 of the Resolution should apply.[99] The Commentary explains how Article 9(1) is concretely applied in each type of succession.[100] The same general approach seems to have been adopted by ILC Special Rapporteur Šturma in his Second Report.[101] However, Guideline 7 (which was never formally adopted by the ILC) is different. It simply indicates that when the successor State "acknowledges and adopts the act" of the predecessor State, it is responsible for the consequences of the continuing act committed *before* the date of succession.[102] The language is based on Article 11 of the ILC *Articles on State responsibility*.[103] It has been criticised by some States.[104]

97 ILC, First Report, ibid, para 283. Similar remarks were made in: ILC, Commentaries, ibid 122, para 4, where it is further indicated that the "retroactive effect of responsibility" is what the *Lighthouse* award did and that this "avoids gaps in the extent of responsibility for what is, in effect, the same continuing act".

98 Kohen & Dumberry, 61.

99 IIL, Final Report, Kohen, para 112.

100 For a detailed analysis, see Kohen & Dumberry, 61–63.

101 ILC Special Rapporteur Šturma, Second Report, 2018, para 59, explaining that "The breach of an international obligation having a continuing character entails the responsibility of a successor State, if such State continues in the act commenced before the date of succession", but adding that "Yet the question remains whether it is the sole responsibility of the successor State or a shared responsibility with the predecessor State". According to him, the answer to that question "is contingent on several factors to be addressed in special draft articles" (para 73).

102 See, ILC, Statement, Grossman Guiloff, 2019, 4.

103 Ibid.

104 Czech Rep., letter sent to the UN GA Sixth Committee, Rep. 76th sess. 2 Nov. 2021, supporting the second sentence of article 7, but adding: "We however doubt whether such rule could rely on the concept of the 'acknowledgement' and 'adoption' of predecessor's

In the next sections, I will separately examine situations where the predecessor State ceases to exist and those where it does not.

5.2.1 The Predecessor State Ceases to Exist

The above-mentioned principle that the new State takes over the obligations arising from internationally wrongful acts committed by the predecessor State *before* its independence when, after its independence, it continues such acts should be applied in situations where the predecessor State becomes extinct (such as in cases of dissolution and unification of States).[105] This is a sound and equitable principle which prevents an internationally wrongful act from simply disappearing along with its perpetrator.[106] The different solution of non-succession would result in an internationally wrongful act remaining unpunished. The commentary explains the reasons why, under Article 9 of the Institute's Resolution, the successor State in the context of dissolution is responsible for the portion of the wrongful act it continues after that date.[107] Ultimately, what matters is not so much the "continuing" character of the act, but rather to provide reparation to the injured State.[108]

---

conduct by the successor State, borrowed from Article 11 of the Articles on Responsibility of States for Internationally Wrongful Acts and significantly altered". Thus, this provision "deals solely with the conduct of private actors (subjects)"; it "does not deal with the attribution to a State of the conduct of another State". It concluded that "it seems that the premise of 'acknowledgment' or 'adoption' laid down in draft article 7 does not have support" in the ILC Articles. See also: Czech Republic, ibid, Rep. 73rd sess., 30 Oct. 2018, stating that Article 11 has nothing do with matters of State succession and that it is not relevant in this context. See also, Czech Rep., ibid, Rep. 74th sess. 6 Nov. 2019; Slovakia, ibid Rep. 76th sess., 3 Nov. 2021 ("The wording of draft article 7 focuses primarily on the situation of an internationally wrongful act of successor State after the date of succession, which is entirely governed by the articles on the responsibility of States, and not relevant for the present topic. In our opinion, the article could rather contain a clear rule on whether a successor State succeeds in the responsibility for an internationally wrongful act of a continuous character of a predecessor State that commenced prior to the date of succession or whether there are any specificities of succession regime resulting from the continuous character of the internationally wrongful act"). See also, Malaysia, ibid, Rep. 77th sess., 2 Nov. 2022.

105 This is also the position of Peterschmitt, 64.

106 Agreeing: Ruy & Baecke, 28: "certainly in situations where the predecessor State ceases to exist, the fact that the successor State continues the wrongful conduct (coupled with the desire to avoid a legal vacuum for injured parties), counts as an important factor indicating that it would be 'reasonable' for the successor State to succeed in the obligations resulting from the wrongful conduct of the predecessor State".

107 Kohen & Dumberry, 62–3.

108 Czech Rep., letter sent to the UN GA Sixth Committee, rep. 76th sess. 2 Nov. 2021: "It seems therefore that the issue at stake is not the continuing character of the wrongful act, but

The position that the new State should be responsible for internationally wrongful acts committed by the predecessor State when it continues the acts after the date of succession was endorsed by Hungary in its pleading in the *Gabčíkovo-Nagymaros* case, involving a case of dissolution.[109] Thus, to the "well-established principle that there is in general no succession to international responsibility",[110] Hungary maintained that there remains one "key exception": when "a successor State, by its *own* conduct, has acted in such a way as to assume the breaches of the law committed by its predecessor".[111] The argument developed by Hungary in its Memorial clearly indicates that by endorsing and continuing the internationally wrongful act (i.e. the unilateral derivation of the Variant C project), Slovakia was not only responsible for the damage resulting from its own illicit act committed upon its creation in January 1993 but also for the act committed by the predecessor State. It mentioned that Slovakia must "assume the obligations, as operator of variant C, to repair damage caused by *present and prior breaches of international law*".[112] This position is also clear in this passage:

> Slovakia is therefore responsible for damage and loss caused *by Czechoslovakia* in relation to the implementation of Variant C *until the disappearance of Czechoslovakia* on 31 December 1992. This responsibility extends to damage caused by any part of the material of the Original Project that was wrongfully converted or taken over for use in Variant C. From 1 January 1993 onwards, Slovakia is of course responsible, as a successor, for damage created by its own conduct.[113] (emphases added)

Dupuy, Counsel for Hungary, also indicated that "lorsqu'un Etat revendique et poursuit les faits illicites de son prédécesseur" this new State (Slovakia) "est responsable des manquements au droit accomplis par la Tchécoslovaquie".[114] He further explained his view as follows:

rather lasting consequences of predecessor's wrongful act and the ability of the successor State to contribute to the elimination of these consequences (e.g., by the restitution of the status quo ante)".

109 *Gabčíkovo-Nagymaros* case.

110 "Reply", Hungary, v. I, 20 June 1995, para 3.163.

111 Ibid, emphasis in the original text. See also, Oral Pleadings, 7 March 1997, para 6 of Dupuy's transcript of his pleadings.

112 "Memorial", Hungary, v. I, 2 May 1994, para 8.05, emphasis added.

113 Ibid para 8.06. This aspect is also dealt with in "Reply", Hungary, v. I, 20 June 1995, para 3.164.

114 Oral Pleadings, 7 March 1997, see at para 6 of Dupuy's transcript of his pleadings.

En réalité, *la raison pour laquelle la Slovaquie est responsable des agissements tchécoslovaques constitue bien un fait de succession.* Mais c'est de la succession à un comportement illicite qu'il s'agit, non de la succession à l'acte juridique que constitue le traité. En réalité, la dérivation unilatérale du Danube dans le cadre du projet qu'elle appelle 'Variante C' constitue un ensemble de faits illicites dont tous sont 'continus' selon la terminologie que le professeur Ago fit adopter à la Commission du droit international. Cette continuité, loin d'avoir été interrompue, comme il aurait convenu qu'elle le fût a été poursuivie et consolidée par le nouvel Etat.

Dès l'instant de sa naissance, la Slovaquie, prolongeant sans aucune interruption une action dont elle avait d'ailleurs été l'inspiratrice en tant qu'Etat fédéré, perpétua cet ensemble de faits, *les reprenant ainsi intégralement à son compte* ...

Par une action persistant dans l'illicite, elle a au contraire endossé la responsabilité de la Tchécoslovaquie évanouie parce qu'elle a fait survivre, puis croître et aggraver un comportement de fait attentatoire aux droits de la Hongrie, dont elle a immédiatement et intégralement revendiqué la paternité.

Par le fait même, elle devenait responsable de la série des agissements tchécoslovaques antérieurs. Ceux qui, s'échelonnant du 13 mai 1989 à la disparition de la Tchécoslovaquie, avaient constitué les phases successives devant inexorablement mener à la dérivation unilatérale de ce fleuve international.[115] (emphases in the original)

But, as explained by the ILC Special Rapporteur, the issue of continuing violation "was not relevant" in this case. The diversion of the Danube (the operation of "Variant C" in October 1992) was an instantaneous act committed by Czechoslovakia, not a continuing act. For the ILC Special Rapporteur, "Slovakia did not incur responsibility on the basis of continuing the breach of Czechoslovakia after the date of succession", but "as a matter of succession to certain obligations arising from the wrongful act committed by Czechoslovakia".[116]

It should be added that two writers have recently used the concept of continuing act to examine how the rules of succession to responsibility could potentially be used regarding crimes committed by Belgium during the period of its colonisation of Congo.[117]

115 Ibid at paras 6–7.

116 ILC Special Rapporteur Šturma, Second Report, 2018, paras 58, 60.

117 Ruy & Baecke, 27–32.

5.2.2 The Predecessor State Continues Its Existence

The question arises as to whether the solution of succession should also apply in situations where the predecessor State continues to exist (such as in cases of separation).

As observed Chapter 2, in cases where the predecessor State does continue its existence, the analysis of State practice and case law has clearly shown that, in principle, the continuing State remains liable for internationally wrongful acts it has committed *before* the date of succession.[118] There is no reason why a different solution should apply in situations where the successor State continues and endorses such acts (after the date of succession).[119] In other words, the fact that the successor State subsequently endorses such acts should not, logically, result in the continuing State no longer having any responsibility for the act it initially committed. In such a case, there would in fact be two different internationally wrongful acts committed by two different States. Each State should bear its own responsibility for the commission of its own wrongful act.

The same solution is adopted by the Institute. Under Article 4(2) when the predecessor State continues to exist after the changes affecting its former territory have occurred, that State should remain *responsible* for *its own* wrongful act committed *before* the date of succession.[120] As mentioned in the commentary, "as a matter of principle, that solution should prevail *even if* the act is subsequently continued by the successor State after the date of succession".[121]

The commentary to the Institute's Resolution also mentions one exception to this principle. This is the situation where the author of the wrongful act was an organ of a territorial unit of the predecessor State that has later become an organ of the successor State. Thus, "whenever the successor State is continuing such a wrongful act, it should be accountable for the consequences arising from the portion of the act which was initially committed by that organ *before* the date of succession".[122] This is indeed a logical solution. It does not prevent

118 However, this is not so clear in the context of Newly Independent States where State practice is not uniform.

119 *Contra*: Peterschmitt, 64.

120 This basic rule applies to three types of succession: transfer of territory (Art. 11 (1)), separation (Art. 12 (1)) and Newly Independent States (Art. 16 (1)).

121 Kohen & Dumberry, 61, emphasis in the original.

122 Ibid, emphasis in the original, adding that "the successor State would be accountable for the *consequences* arising from the commission of the pre-succession portion of the act" and that "in contrast, the successor State would be *responsible* for the continuation of the illegal act occurring *after* the date of succession" (emphasis in the original).

the predecessor State from also bearing some form of responsibility for actions taking place before the date of succession.[123]

It could be argued that the reasoning of the *Lighthouse Arbitration* case[124] (in the context of a cession of territory) dealing with Claim no. 4 supports this proposition. This is indeed the position adopted by ILC Special Rapporteur Crawford[125] and, more recently, in the ILC Commentary to Guideline 7.[126] The Arbitral Tribunal concluded that Greece should be held responsible for its own internationally wrongful acts (delicts of omission) committed *after* 1913 (the date of the cession of territory of Crete) and for the financial consequences of the illegal acts committed by the autonomous Government of Crete *before* the date of succession. The Tribunal held that: "[T]he Tribunal can only come to the conclusion that Greece, having adopted the illegal conduct of Crete in its recent past as autonomous State, is bound, as successor State, to take upon its charge the financial consequences of the breach of the concession contract".[127] The Tribunal's conclusion was certainly influenced by the fact that the actual perpetrator of the wrongful act was not the predecessor State (the Ottoman Empire), but an autonomous entity (Crete), which was, at the time, struggling for its integration into Greece.

123 Thus, Art. 9(3) indicates that this solution is "without prejudice to any *responsibility* incurred by the predecessor State if it continues to exist". Kohen & Dumberry, 62, explain that the fact that "the successor State may be accountable for the *consequences* arising from the commission of the *pre*-succession portion of a wrongful act committed by an organ does not prevent the predecessor State from being *responsible* for the same portion of the act" (emphasis in the original).

124 For a detailed analysis of this case, see, Chapter 2, Section 5.3.1.

125 As mentioned above, for the ILC Special Rapporteur this case stands for the proposition that "if the successor State, faced with a continuing wrongful act on its territory, endorses and continues that situation, the inference may readily be drawn that it has *assumed responsibility for it*" (ILC, Commentaries, State Responsibility, 2001, 119, para 3, emphasis added). See also, ibid, para 4, speaking of the "retroactive effect of responsibility" which was done by the *Lighthouse* tribunal and that it "avoids gaps in the extent of responsibility for what is, in effect, the same continuing act".

126 ILC, Commentaries, 2021, para 165, Art. 7, sub-para 4, indicating that in this case Greece was "liable for breach of a concession agreement initiated by Crete at a period when the latter was an autonomous territory of the Ottoman Empire, partly on the basis that the breach had been endorsed and eventually continued by Greece, even after the acquisition of territorial sovereignty over the island. Even if the claim was originally based on a breach of a concession agreement, if the successor State, faced with a continuing breach on its territory, endorses and continues that situation, the inference may be drawn that it has assumed responsibility for it".

127 *Lighthouse Arbitration* case, 23 *ILR* 1956, 92.

6 An Insurrectional Movement Commits an Internationally Wrongful Act during Its Struggle to Establish a New State

Under Article 10(2) of the ILC *Articles on State Responsibility*, whenever a "movement, insurrectional or other" succeeds in establishing a new State, its pre-succession conducts and its wrongful acts committed against a third State or a foreign investor "shall be considered an act of the new State under international law" once it comes to power. The same principle has since then been adopted by the Institute's Resolution in the context of separation.[128] ILC Guideline 8(1) is to the same effect.[129] The rule is based on the existence of a structural and organisational "continuity" between the rebels and the new State:[130] "The structure of the organisation of the insurrectional movement then becomes those of the organisation of the new State".[131] Thus, as explained by the ILC:

> The attribution to the new state of the acts of the organs of the insurrectional movement which preceded it, and of such acts only, is then justified by virtue of the continuity between the organisation of the insurrectional movement and the organisation of the state to which it has given rise. From being only an embryo State, the insurrectional movement has become a State proper, without any break in the continuity between the two. It is in fact the same entity which previously had the characteristics of an insurrectional movement and which now has those of a State proper.[132]

It is important to mention that the principle discussed here is solely based on the mechanisms of State responsibility, and *not* on any rule of State

128 Art. 12(6)). Similarly, Art. 16(3) is concerned with acts committed by national liberation movements in the context of decolonisation.

129 ILC Special Rapporteur Šturma, Second Report, 2018, paras 107ff.

130 On this question, see: Dumberry, Rebellions, 312ff; P. Dumberry, "Why are Wrongful Acts Committed by Rebels during a Civil War Attributable to the State when they are Successful? A Critical Analysis of Theory and Practice", 6 *Euro. Invest. L. & Arb. Rev.* 2021, 189–213.

131 ILC, "Fourth Report on State Responsibility", Special Rapporteur Roberto Ago, 24th sess., 1972, A/CN.4/264 and Add.1, ILC Report, A/8710/Rev.1 (A/27/10), 1972, chp. IV(B), paras 72–73, in: *Yearbook ILC* II, 1972, 71 (hereinafter "ILC, Ago Report, 1972"), 150, paras 159, 194.

132 ILC Report, 27th sess., 1975, A/10010/Rev.l, *ILC Yearbook II*, 1975 (hereinafter "ILC, Report, 1975") 101, para 6. Very similar wording is used in ILC, Commentaries, State Responsibility, 2001, 59ff, para 6. See also, ILC, Ago Report, 1972, 131, paras 159, 194.

succession.[133] Thus, as noted by the ILC, "Article 10 deals with the *special case of attribution*".[134] This is a matter of attribution of conduct, rather than attribution of responsibility.[135] Article 10(2) refers to the conduct of an entity *other* than that of the new State, which shall nevertheless be "considered an act of the new State". These wrongful acts are "attributable" to the new State, because that State *cannot* be held "responsible", per se, for acts that it did not commit. *A fortiori,* this is the case when that State *did not exist* when the acts were committed.

I have decided not to address this question in detail in the second edition of this book because I have recently published another book examining the scope and content of Article 10 of the ILC Articles. It analyses all relevant questions of State responsibility and attribution arising from the conduct of "insurrectional movements" (or other rebels groups) or that of the government in power in the context of a rebellion or a civil war, which ultimately results in either the establishment of a new government or the creation of a new State.[136] The book contains an entire chapter (some 100 pages) dealing with the issue of what happens with the wrongs committed by rebels during an insurgency when the struggle to create a new State is successful.[137] While some of the examples of State practice I have found are clearly not the strongest precedents, they generally support the basic principle underlying Article 10(2) of the ILC Articles.[138] As mentioned above,[139] one such example is the practice of France and decisions by French courts in the context of the independence of Algeria (1962). In the *Croatia Genocide Convention* case, Croatia's principal argument dealt with the application of Article 10(2).[140] The Court did not take position on the status of this provision.[141] In his separate opinion, Judge Kreća indicated that there was limited case law supporting the provision.[142] The book also examines in detail whether the rule is applicable in situations others than separation.[143]

133 ILC, Report, 1975, 101, para 8. See also, ILC, Ago Report, 1972, 131, para 159.

134 ILC, Commentaries, 2001, 51, para 1, emphasis added.

135 Pajnkihar, 235–242, 317–318. On this question, see: Dumberry, Rebellions, 27–30.

136 Dumberry, Rebellions.

137 Ibid 303.

138 Ibid 324ff.

139 See, Chapter 2, Section 7.3.3.

140 *Croatia Genocide Convention* case, para 102. See, Chapter 2, Section 4.3.3.5.

141 I have examined elsewhere the arguments of the parties and the reasoning of the Court: Dumberry, Rebellions, 349ff.

142 *Croatia Genocide Convention* case, sep. op. Judge Kreća, paras 66ff.

143 Dumberry, Rebellions, 329ff. On this question: P. Dumberry, "State Responsibility of New States for Wrongful Acts Committed by Rebels in the Context of Civil Wars: Does the Rule Apply to Cases Other than Secession?", in: Jorge Viñuales, Andrew Clapham, Laurence

My conclusion is that, while there is no doubt that the principle should find application in the context of Newly Independent States and dissolution, this is not the case regarding transfer of territory, incorporation and unification of States.

In my book, I also explained that when a rebel group is successful in creating a new State, that State is *not* responsible for acts committed by the predecessor State while fighting the rebels during the insurgency.[144] Thus, after the date of succession, the predecessor State (if it continues to exist) remains responsible for its own wrongs. I examined several examples of State practice and case law supporting this principle. Yet, the rule is problematic in situations where the predecessor State ceases to exist, such as dissolution.

Finally, the book also addresses what happens when the rebels are *not successful* in their attempt to create a new State.[145] Two rules apply. On the one hand, the acts committed by the rebels during the insurgency are not attributable to the State; and, on the other hand, the State is responsible for its own failure to exercise its due diligence obligation to protect foreigners and third States. I examined several cases and examples of State practice supporting both principles.

7 An Autonomous Government Commits an Internationally Wrongful Act

Under international law, the acts of a federated entity or any other political subdivisions are regarded as those of the State.[146] Accordingly, a State would have to compensate another State for the acts committed by any of its political subdivisions.[147] This is, at least, the situation prevailing *before* this political

Boisson de Chazournes & Mamadou Hébié (eds), *The International Legal Order in the XXIst Century; Essays in Honour of Professor Marcelo Gustavo Kohen* (Brill 2023), 556–570.

144 Ibid 365ff.

145 Ibid 384ff.

146 Art. 4, ILC *Articles on State Responsibility*: "The conduct of any State organ acting in that capacity shall be considered an act of that State under international law … whatever its character as an organ of the central government or of a territorial unit of the State".

147 According to the ILC, Commentaries, State Responsibility, 2001, 90, para 10, there would be one exception to that rule. There are cases where provinces (or other entities) of a federation can enter into international agreements on their own account and where other States may agree to limit themselves to recourse against such entities in the event of a breach. In such cases, the matter will solely involve the responsibility of such entities and not the federal State. It should be noted that this is a limited exception to the general rule

entity itself becomes an independent State. The situation is different when a political entity, which had previously committed an internationally wrongful act when still part of the predecessor State, becomes an independent State. The question then arises as to whether the consequences of the commission of the act should be borne by the predecessor State (provided, of course, that it continues to exist) or the new State.

The principle (mentioned in the previous section) established in Article 10(2) of the ILC Articles in relation to acts committed by insurrectional movements in their armed struggle for independence may be used, by analogy, in the *different context* where independence is achieved as a result of a process where no rebel group is involved. It is true that this provision *does not* involve any question of succession of States. Yet, the logic behind this provision may nevertheless be applied in the context of succession to responsibility.[148] I have explained elsewhere that it is the *continuity of the structure* between the organisation of the insurrectional movement and that of the new State which is relevant in determining whether the latter should be liable for the acts committed by the former.[149] This approach has been endorsed by the ILC in the context of a rebellion leading to the establishment of a new State.[150] The same theory can certainly apply to cases beyond the scope of Article 10(2) where there is also a structural continuity between the new State and *an autonomous political entity* which committed an internationally wrongful act before independence. This approach, which I have put forward in

---

of State responsibility in so far as it is applicable only between the parties to a treaty for matters covered by the treaty.

148 Agreeing: ILC Special Rapporteur Šturma, Second Report, 2018, paras 94–5; Reyes Gajardo, 84.

149 Dumberry, Rebellions, 318. See also, agreeing: Gérard Cahin, "Attribution of Conduct to the State: Insurrectional Movements", in James Crawford, Alain Pellet, Simon Olleson and Kate Parlett (eds), *The Law of International Responsibility* (OUP 2010), 279; Atlam, 476, 479; Crawford, State Responsibility, 178–9.

150 ILC, Report, 1975, 101, para 6: "The attribution to the new state of the acts of the organs of the insurrectional movement which preceded it, and of such acts only, is then justified by virtue of the continuity between the organisation of the insurrectional movement and the organisation of the state to which it has given rise. From being only an embryo State, the insurrectional movement has become a State proper, without any break in the continuity between the two. It is in fact the same entity which previously had the characteristics of an insurrectional movement and which now has those of a State proper". Very similar wording is used in ILC, Commentaries, 2001, 59ff, para 6. See also, in ILC, Ago Report, 1972, 131, paras 159, 194.

the first edition of this book, has since been endorsed by the Institute,[151] the ILC[152] and others.[153]

In my view, the successor State should be held responsible for obligations arising from internationally wrongful acts committed before its independence whenever the acts were committed by an autonomous government (or by any other clearly identifiable political entity) with which the new State has an *organic and structural continuity*. There should be a transfer of the obligation to repair to the successor State whenever the following four basic requirements are met:

(1) An autonomous government was in place in the predecessor State at the time of the commission of the internationally wrongful act;[154]
(2) the organs of this autonomous government committed the internationally wrongful act;[155]
(3) there is an organic and structural continuity between the organs of this autonomous government and the organs of the new State;[156] and
(4) There are particular circumstances calling for the transfer of the obligation to repair to the successor State.

151 Kohen & Dumberry, 88; IIL, Final Report, Kohen, paras 63ff.

152 ILC Special Rapporteur Šturma, Second Report, 2018, para 112: "The very same argument could be used also for State organs of the predecessor that evolved into State organs of the successor, especially if they consist of the same personnel, which is the case in many situations".

153 European Commission for Democracy through Law (Venice Commission), *amicus* brief in the *Bijelić* case, opinion no. 495/2008, CDL-AD(2008)021, 20 Oct. 2008, paras 33, 41ff; Reyes Gajardo, 84.

154 IIL, Final Report, Kohen, para 64, referring to an entity that "enjoyed a great amount of autonomy within the predecessor State". This would certainly be the case of political entities forming a federation. See, ILC Report, 70th sess., 2018, para 264, indicating that the term "an organ of a territorial unit" refers to situations where such organs "had a substantive degree of autonomy, such as in the case of federal States". It could also be the case for some centralised States which, nevertheless, have some sort of asymmetrical decentralisation, for instance, the autonomous regions of Catalonia, Galicia and the Basque Country in Spain, or the relative autonomy of Scotland and Wales in the UK. On this question, see, M. Bracke, *The Rules of State Succession Applied to a Hypothetical Flemish Independence*, Ghent Univ., Master thesis, 2019–2020, 49, 54.

155 IIL, Final Report, Kohen, para 64, indicating that the "central organs did not play a role in the decision or execution of the internationally wrongful act".

156 Peterschmitt, 63, speaks of a "continuité organisationnelle" between this autonomous entity and the successor State. See also, Pajnkihar, 325, speaking of a "structural continuity between the organs of the territorial unit of the predecessor and the organs (government) of the successor State", and adding that "this continuity is the basis for the identification of the special matter of Succession". For him, "the structural continuity of the organs is relevant because of their link to the international responsibility of the predecessor State". For a detailed analysis of this continuity requirement, in the different context of "insurgents". See Dumberry, Rebellions, 312ff.

While there was limited support for this proposition back in 2007,[157] the approach put forward in the first edition of my book has been generally adopted since then by many, including in the Institute's work discussed in the next section.[158] It should be added that this is a rule of State responsibility, rather than a rule of State succession per se.[159]

7.1 *The Position Adopted by the Institute and the* ILC

The same basic principle was adopted by the Institute. In the context where the predecessor State continues to exist, the Institute's Resolution provides for one possible exception to the general principle of non-succession.[160] It concerns the situation when the author of a wrongful act committed before independence was an "organ of the territorial unit of the predecessor State", such as an autonomous government, "that has later become an organ of the successor State". After that entity becomes an independent State, the obligations arising from the wrongful act *may pass* to the successor State "if particular circumstances so require".[161] This is just a possibility; it is not automatic. This is a sound proposition. There are indeed situations where there are "particular circumstances" calling for the transfer of the obligation to repair to the successor State. One such circumstance mentioned in the Final Report is the "existence of some benefit derived from the internationally wrongful act".[162]

157 Peterschmitt, 62–63. See also: Michel Waelbroeck, "Arrêt no. 8160 du Conseil d'Etat Belge, note d'observations", *RJDA* 1961, no. 1, 36 ("lorsqu'il existe une relation d'affinité étroite entre l'ancien souverain et l'Etat successeur, on pourra parfois considérer qu'il y a transmission de responsabilité"). This seems also to be the view of Udina, 769.

158 European Commission for Democracy through Law (Venice Commission), *amicus* brief in the *Bijelić* case, opinion no. 495/2008, CDL-AD(2008)021, 20 Oct. 2008, paras 33, 41ff; Kohen, Succession of States, 169; M. Bracke, *The Rules of State Succession Applied to a Hypothetical Flemish Independence*, Ghent Univ., Master thesis, 2019–2020, 49, 54; Reyes Gajardo, 84. See also, Pajnkihar, 338 ("First special rule: A successor State that has a special link to the matter of succession (i.e., injury) shall fully succeed to the secondary rights and obligations of reparations relating to that matter, followed by conditional succession to other secondary rights and obligations. This rule refers to the special part of the succession matter and applies to all types of succession and independently of the existence of a continuator State") 339 (indicating that one such "special link" is "the structural continuity between the organs of the predecessor State and those of the successor State").

159 Reyes Gajardo, 84. A different position seems to have been taken by Pajnkihar, 323–4, referring to this situation as one of "real" succession to responsibility where rules of State succession apply. Yet, he also examined the *Bijelić* case (317–321) as an example of the application of a rule of State responsibility.

160 See, Art. 12(3) in the context of separation and Art. 11(3) for transfer of territory.

161 IIL, Final Report, Kohen, para 63.

162 Ibid, para 65.

One example would be a new State benefiting from assets expropriated by an autonomous government prior to independence without having compensated the owner of the property. Basic fairness and the principle of unjust enrichment (further examined below[163]) would require that the new State take over the obligation to repair. Another example is a new State benefiting from not fulfilling contractual obligations entered into by an autonomous government with a foreign investor.

The same solution was initially followed by ILC Special Rapporteur Šturma in Draft Article 7(2) dealing with separation: "If particular circumstances so require, the obligations arising from an internationally wrongful act of the predecessor State will transfer to the successor State when the act was carried out by an organ of a territorial unit of the predecessor that has later become an organ of the successor State".[164] He spoke of the "need to draft an article (…) in which the general principle of non-succession is complemented by a number of exceptions".[165] He referred to the "organ" (and the "direct link") exceptions as "situations that would justify a different approach" than the principle of non-succession.[166] He clearly stated that "acts committed by an autonomous entity of the predecessor State should be accepted as one of the elements in support of the succession to responsibility".[167]

In contrast, Guideline 9(2) (which was never formally adopted by the ILC) simply indicates that "in particular circumstances, the injured State and the successor State should endeavour to reach an agreement for addressing the injury".[168] The Chair of the Drafting Committee explained that "the term 'in particular circumstances' covers diverse situations where a successor State may be addressing the injury, which will be described in the commentary".[169] In the Commentary to Guideline 9,[170] reference is made to both

163 See, Section 7.

164 ILC Special Rapporteur Šturma, Second Report, 2018, paras 94ff. The same solution is found in Art. 9(2) (transfer): ibid, Second Report, paras 139, 144–145. See, however the different approach taken in Draft Art. 8 in the context of Newly Independent States. It indicates that "If the newly independent States agrees, the obligations arising from an internationally wrongful act of the predecessor State may transfer to the successor State" and that one of the "particular circumstances" which "may be taken into consideration" is "where the former dependent territory had substantive autonomy". For a critical analysis of this provision, see Kohen & Dumberry, 131–132.

165 Ibid, Second Report, 2018, para 122.

166 Ibid para 92. See also, his conclusion in paras 97, 103.

167 Ibid para 97.

168 ILC, Statement, Grossman Guiloff, 2019, 8.

169 Ibid.

170 ILC, Commentaries, 2021, para 165, Art. 9, sub-para 5.

the "organ" and "direct link" exceptions,[171] but also to situations involving restitution of property,[172] or unjust enrichment.[173] I have already explained above, the reasons why this new clause is not the most effective to protect the interests of injured States.[174] Suffice it to mention here that Guideline 9 no longer contains a direct reference to the "organ" exception and that its potential role and importance has been significantly downgraded.

In the context of dissolution, Article 15(1) of the Institute's Resolution establishes the solution of succession: the obligations arising from the commission of a wrongful act by the predecessor State "pass" to "one, several or all the successor States" depending on the circumstances mentioned in Article 15(2) and (3). Under Article 15(3), "in order to determine which of the successor States becomes bearer of the obligations" to repair, there are two "relevant factors".[175] Importantly, succession is not automatic under Article 15(3); these are just "relevant factors" to be considered for the distribution of obligations among the successor States. One such factor is when the author of the internationally wrongful act was an organ of the predecessor State that later became an organ of the successor State.

The same general approach was adopted by ILC Special Rapporteur Šturma in Draft Article 11(1) dealing with dissolution.[176] While ILC Draft Article 11(2) did not refer specifically to this "organ" factor,[177] it remains that it is certainly one of those "other relevant factors" (mentioned in Draft Article 11(2)) that would have to be considered.[178] In his Second Report, he refers to the organ element as one of the two "factors to be considered in determining the holder of obligations".[179] Guideline 11 (never formally adopted by the ILC), no longer contains the clear and affirmative language found in Draft Article 11 (obligations "pass, subject to an agreement" to one or several successor State(s)).

171 Ibid: "the successor State may be relevant in a situation where (...) there is a link between the territory or an organ of the successor State and the internationally wrongful act".

172 Ibid.

173 Ibid.

174 See, analysis in the section on separation: Chapter 2, Section 6.1.

175 It should be added that under Art. 7 ("Plurality of successor States") whenever it is not possible to identify a single successor, all successor States will assume the obligations emerging from the responsibility relationship, in an equitable manner. Art. 7(2) establishes what criteria must be taken into consideration in order to determine an equitable apportionment of obligations among the successor States.

176 ILC Special Rapporteur Šturma, Second Report, 2018, paras 147, 167, 185.

177 Ibid para 188, mentioning this factor in the context of dissolution.

178 The criteria are mentioned in ILC Special Rapporteur Šturma, Fifth Report, 2022, paras 50–52.

179 Ibid, Second Report, 2018, para 188.

It merely indicates that "the injured State and the relevant successor State or States should agree on how to address the injury". The second line of Guideline 11 indicates that the injured State and the "relevant successor State or States" "should take into account any territorial link, any benefit derived, any equitable apportionment, and all other relevant circumstances". One such "circumstance" mentioned in the Commentary is the "continuity of organs".[180] This is a non-exhaustive list[181] of factors that the injured State and the successor State(s) "may take into account in determining how best to address the injury" suffered by the former.[182] I have already explained above[183] that the importance of these "factors" has been significantly downgraded under Guideline 11 in comparison to the previous draft article.

7.2 *The Application of This Principle to Different Types of Succession*

The principle of succession was applied by one international tribunal as well as by a municipal court in the context of cession of territory. They both held that the successor State should be responsible for obligations arising from internationally wrongful acts committed by a local administration having a substantial autonomy from the predecessor State. In the *Samos* (*Liability for Torts*) case, a Greek Court decided that the successor State (Greece) was responsible for the damage caused by the Island of Samos' customs officials when it was still under Ottoman rule.[184] The Court's findings has been explained on the ground that the Island of Samos had an autonomous status when it was part of the Ottoman Empire prior to its cession to Greece in 1913.[185] The same interpretation was adopted by the Institute.[186] The French-Greek Arbitral Tribunal in the 1956 *Lighthouse Arbitration* case reached the same solution.[187] In its evaluation of Claim no. 4, the Arbitral Tribunal decided that Greece should be responsible for its own acts of omission committed after the date of succession (1913) as well as for those committed by the *de facto* autonomous Government of Crete before that date.[188] One reason why the Court held that Greece was responsible is because the acts were committed by the largely autonomous

180 ILC, Commentaries, 2022, at para 89, Art. 11, sub-para 8.
181 Ibid.
182 Ibid sub-para 7.
183 See, Chapter 2, Section 4.1.
184 *Samos* case, 70. See, analysis in Chapter 2, Section 5.3.2.
185 O'Connell, State Succession, v. I, 492; Barde, 179.
186 Kohen & Dumberry, 88.
187 *Lighthouse Arbitration* case, 23 *ILR* 1956, 81. This case was examined in Chapter 2, Section 5.3.1.
188 Kohen & Dumberry, 196–200.

government of Crete before the date of succession. The same interpretation was adopted by the Institute,[189] the ILC[190] and others.[191] Yet, it should be added that in both cases there was no structural continuity between the autonomous government and the successor State.

In my view, there are no valid reasons not to apply a similar solution in the context of separation. As mentioned above, this is the position adopted by the Institute (Article 12(3)).[192] In circumstances where there is an organic and structural continuity between the organs of the autonomous government (which committed the wrongful act while still part of the predecessor State) and the organs of the new State, the latter should be held responsible for the acts committed by the former against third States.[193]

This solution was recently applied in the *Bijelić v. Montenegro* case decided by the ECHR.[194] The case involved three Serbians nationals. Proceedings began in 2005–2006 against Serbia-Montenegro in relation to the non-execution of a final decision which had been rendered by a court of first instance on 26 January 1994 ordering the eviction of a person from a property.[195] The applicants alleged that the non-execution by the authorities constituted a continuing violation of Articles 6(1) and 8 of the Convention as well as of Article 1 of Protocol No. 1. It should be noted that this action was taken before Montenegro became an independent country in June 2006. The Court asked the question: "Which State, Montenegro or Serbia, could be held responsible for the impugned inaction of the authorities between 2 March 2004 and 5 June 2006?"[196] Serbia took the position that it could not be held responsible for the acts since they took place in the territory in Montenegro which was at the time an autonomous entity having the obligation to protect human rights in its own territory:

189 Ibid 90.

190 ILC Special Rapporteur Šturma, Second Report, 2018, para 145, indicating that the award "can be interpreted in various ways" and that "in addition to the continuing act" "there are also other particular circumstances that may justify the transfer of obligations arising from the wrongful acts of the predecessor State (continuing) to the successor State".

191 Brockman-Hawe, 866.

192 See, Kohen & Dumberry, 102.

193 The same argument is developed in: European Commission for Democracy through Law (Venice Commission), *amicus* brief in the *Bijelić* case, opinion no. 495/2008, CDL-AD(2008)021, 20 Oct. 2008, paras 33, 41ff.

194 The case is examined in Kohen & Dumberry, 103–4.

195 *Bijelić* case.

196 Ibid para 61.

> The Serbian Government firstly noted that each constituent republic of the State Union of Serbia and Montenegro had the obligation to protect human rights in its own territory (see paragraph 37, Article 9 above). Secondly, the impugned enforcement proceedings were themselves solely conducted by the competent Montenegrin authorities. Thirdly, although the sole successor of the State Union of Serbia and Montenegro (see paragraph 37, Article 60 above), Serbia cannot be deemed responsible for any violations of the Convention which might have occurred in Montenegro prior to its declaration of independence. Lastly, Serbia could not, within the meaning of Article 46 of the Convention, realistically be expected to implement any individual and/or general measures in the territory of another State. In view of the above, the Serbian Government concluded that the application as regards Serbia was incompatible ratione personae and maintained that, to hold otherwise, would be contrary to the universal principles of international law.[197]

In response to a question asked by the Court, Montenegro made the following statement: "[it] 'support[ed] the remarks presented to the Court' by the Serbian Government 'relating to the issue of … [succession as regards] … the enforcement of the judgment … [in question]'".[198] Montenegro also mentioned Article 5 of the Constitutional Law on the Implementation of the Constitution of Montenegro that provided that "Provisions of international treaties on human rights and freedoms, to which Montenegro acceded before 3 June 2006, shall be applied to legal relations which have arisen after their signature".[199]

When it became an independent State, Montenegro indicated to the Council of Europe its willingness to succeed to several treaties, which had been originally ratified by Serbia-Montenegro.[200] One year later, the Council of Europe decided that Montenegro was to be regarded as a party to the Convention and related Protocols with a retroactive effect from 6 June 2006 (the date of succession).[201] There was therefore no doubt that the new State was bound by the Convention in June 2006. But what about before that date? The Court considered that Montenegro had accepted succession to human rights treaties to

197 Ibid para 62.

198 Ibid para 63.

199 Ibid para 42.

200 Letters of 6 and 12 June 2006 from Mr Miodrag Vlahovic, Minister of Foreign Affairs of Montenegro, to Mr Terry Davis, Secretary General of the Council of Europe.

201 Council of Europe Committee of Ministers, Resolution CM/Res (2007)7, 9 May 2007, 994bis meeting of the Ministers' Deputies.

which the State Union of Serbia and Montenegro were parties with retroactive effect.[202] Montenegro was therefore bound by the Convention from 3 March 2004, i.e. the date of entry into force of the Convention for the State Union.[203] The Court considered that Montenegro had consented to be responsible for acts which took place on its territory *before* it became an independent State.[204] The Court held that Montenegro was indeed responsible for violations of the Convention.[205]

While some have considered this decision to be the recognition of the principle of automatic succession to the Convention,[206] it was actually based, as some States have noted,[207] on the fact that Montenegro had *agreed* during the proceedings to take over any responsibility arising from wrongful acts which had been committed *before* the date of succession.[208] The decision supports the proposition that a new successor State should be held responsible for obligations arising from internationally wrongful acts committed before its independence insofar as the acts were committed by an autonomous government with which the new State has an organic and structural continuity. This is indeed the position which was taken by the Venice Commission in an *amicus* brief in the context of the proceedings.[209] Many authorities have

202 *Bijelić* case, para 68(i): "the only reasonable interpretation of Article 5 of the Constitutional Act on the Implementation of the Constitution of the Republic of Montenegro (see paragraph 42 above), the wording of Article 44 of the Montenegrin Right to a Trial within a Reasonable Time Act (see paragraphs 46–48 above), and indeed the Montenegrin Government's own observations, would all suggest that Montenegro should be considered bound by the Convention, as well as the Protocols thereto, as of 3 March 2004, that being the date when these instruments had entered into force in respect of the State Union of Serbia and Montenegro".

203 Ibid para 69.

204 This point is highlighted by Pajnkihar, 320–1.

205 *Bijelić* case, paras 70, 85, 92–99.

206 Brockman-Hawe, 853–854; Marcel Szabó, "State Succession and the Jurisprudence of the European Court of Human Rights", in: Christina Binder & Konrad Lachmayer (eds), *The European Court of Human Rights and Public International Law Fragmentation or Unity?* (Nomos 2014) 128–9. See also, the comments made in: ILC Special Rapporteur Šturma, Second Report, 2018, paras 120–121. On this point, see Kohen & Dumberry, 104.

207 Russia, letter sent to the UN GA Sixth Committee, rep. 73rd sess. 31 October 2018.

208 P. Dumberry, "La succession d'Etats en matière de responsabilité internationale et ses liens avec la responsabilité des Etats en matière de traités", in: G. Distephano, G. Gaggioli & A. Hêche (eds), *La Convention de Vienne de 1978 sur la succession d'État en matière de traités : Commentaire article par article et études thématiques* (Bruylant 2015) 1601ff, paras 33–35.

209 European Commission for Democracy through Law (Venice Commission), *amicus* brief, opinion no. 495/2008, CDL-AD(2008)021, 20 Oct. 2008, paras 38ff, para 41ff, at para 43: "it is undoubtedly reasonable to hold the newly-independent state of Montenegro responsible

since then considered the decision as supporting the "organ" exception to the principle of non-succession, including the Institute,[210] ILC Special Rapporteur Šturma[211] and many scholars[212] (but this position has been rejected by a few

for all the alleged breaches of the ECHR which occurred in Montenegro between 3 March 2004 and 6 June 2006. Conversely, it would be unreasonable to hold Serbia, as the 'continuing state' of the former State Union, responsible for these alleged breaches. As already explained (paragraph 9 above), the relevant public services within Montenegro were under the full control of the Montenegrin authorities. There is full continuity between these authorities and the authorities of the present state of Montenegro. If, in different factual circumstances, the European Court of Human Rights were to be satisfied beyond reasonable doubt that an alleged *specific* breach of the ECHR in Montenegrin territory was wholly due to the action, or inaction, of the *Union* authorities, the Court would be justified in holding that this responsibility would not *wholly* devolve to the Montenegrin authorities".

210 Kohen & Dumberry, 104–5.

211 ILC Special Rapporteur Šturma, Second Report, 2018, para 121.

212 See, Brockman-Hawe, 864: "the Court explicitly held that the transfer from predecessor to successor was justified because (i) the predecessor State was comprised of at least one largely autonomous sub-unit (ii) to which the impugned acts could be attributed and (iii) the formerly largely autonomous region evolved to become new State to which responsibility could attach. In other words, Bijelić is the first decision of the ECHR to confirm the importance of attributing the impugned situations to a (previously) sub-national authority that shares an identity with a successor respondent state". See also, his conclusion: "it is probable that the reasoning and interpretive analysis of the Court in Bijelić will take on increased importance as an authority supportive of a trend in general international law to take into account the relative autonomy of sub- State government units in existence before a succession event to which impugned conduct may be attributed". See also: Marko Milanovic, "The Spatial Dimension: Treaties and Territory", in: C.J. Tams et al (eds), *Research Handbook on the Law of Treaties* (Cheltenham 2014) 220 ("[the Court] applied a functional approach whereby it allocated responsibility to that (new) State which organically continued the part of the old joint State whose conduct was the object of the case. Thus, if it were Montenegrin courts that were alleged to have breached the applicant's right to a fair trial before Montenegro's independence, it would be the State of Montenegro and not Serbia that would be responsible for that act post-independence"); Marcel Szabó, "State Succession and the Jurisprudence of the European Court of Human Rights", in: Christina Binder & Konrad Lachmayer (eds), *The European Court of Human Rights and Public International Law Fragmentation or Unity?* (Nomos 2014) 143 ("the responsibility of Montenegro was based on the fact that even at the time of the federation, issues related to execution belonged in the exclusive competence of Montenegrin authorities, therefore, Serbia was relieved of any responsibility in this respect"); M. Bracke, *The Rules of State Succession Applied to a Hypothetical Flemish Independence*, Ghent Univ., Master thesis, 2019–2020, 57; Pajnkihar, 319 (not taking position on the existence of a rule of succession, but noting that "the Commission based the above on the 'full continuity' between the authorities of Montenegro as a federal unit and the authorities of Montenegro as an independent State and on the high degree of autonomy of the federal republics within the State Union of Serbia and Montenegro").

others[213]). In fact, according to ILC Special Rapporteur Šturma, "following the *Bijelić* case, the ECHR accepted as a rule that, in case of a wrongful act committed by organs of Montenegro in time of the State Union of Serbia and Montenegro, responsibility is succeeded by Montenegro".[214] For him, the Court "seems to combine the test of institutional continuity with the territoriality principle".[215]

The "organ" exception to the principle of non-succession is perfectly applicable in the context of dissolution as envisaged under Article 15(3) of the Institute's Resolution.[216] As mentioned above,[217] in the *Croatia Genocide Convention* case, Croatia invoked the argument regarding acts committed by the organs of an autonomous entity that later became organs of the FRY. The Court did not take position on the matter. Yet, as mentioned above, some judges in their individual opinions, believe that the Court had based its analysis on a "presumption" that any such succession to responsibility was possible. It should be added that although Judge Tomka rejected the Court's jurisdiction over the events that took place before 27 April 1992, he nevertheless recognised that nothing should prevent the Court from taking these acts into consideration, adding that "there was undoubtedly a certain factual continuation and identity between those who were actors in the period of armed conflict which raged in Croatia both before and after 27 April 1992".[218] In fact, he seems to have

213 See, ILC Report, 70th sess., 2018, para 234. See, for instance, ILC, "Provisional Summary Record of the 3434th Meeting", 70th sess., 20 July 2018, A/CN.4/SR.3434, statement by ILC Member Huang (China), for whom the case deals with the "transfer of State civil liability to a private individual rather than the succession of State responsibility".

214 ILC Special Rapporteur Šturma, Second Report, 2018, para 121, referring to several cases. See, *O. Lakićević and Others v. Montenegro and Serbia*, Nos. 27458/06 and 3 others, 13 December 2011, para 22, 41, indicating that under Article 9(1) of the Constitutional Charter of the State Union of Serbia and Montenegro, each member State of the Union "was responsible for the protection of human rights in its own territory" and that the "entire proceedings have been conducted solely within the competence of the Montenegrin authorities, which also had the exclusive competence to deal with the subject matter". See also, *Milić v. Montenegro and Serbia*, No. 28359/05, 11 December 2012; *Mandić v. Montenegro, Serbia and Bosnia and Herzegovina*, No. 32557/05, Decision (Fourth Sect.) of 12 June 2012, para 40.

215 ILC Special Rapporteur Šturma, Fifth Report, 2021, para 54.

216 See, Kohen & Dumberry, 126ff.

217 See, analysis in Chapter 2, Section 4.3.3.5.

218 *Croatia Genocide Convention* case, Sep. op. Judge Tomka, para 26. Same conclusion: diss. op., Judge Cançado Trindade, paras 24–25.

recognised the soundness of the "organ" argument in his separate opinion in the Preliminary Objections phase of the proceedings (2008).[219]

In the *Gabčíkovo-Nagymaros* case, the ICJ referred to the important role played by the then federative State of Slovakia in the commission of the breach of international law by Czechoslovakia (the implementation of Variant C). The Court decided not to infer any legal consequences from the crucial role played by Slovakia (while still part of the predecessor State) since it had already determined that the 1977 Treaty was of a territorial character and that as such it was binding upon Slovakia on 1 January 1993.[220] It has been suggested that the Court was in fact inclined to find Slovakia (the successor State) responsible for obligations arising from the internationally wrongful act committed by the predecessor State due to the importance of the role played by the federal entity of Slovakia before it became an independent State.[221] ILC Special Rapporteur Šturma also mentions this case as an example supporting the "organ" exception.[222] On the contrary, Judge Tomka in his separate opinion in the Preliminary Objections phase of the proceedings in the *Croatia Genocide Convention* case indicated that the case did not support the "organ" argument.[223]

219 *Croatia Genocide Convention* case, Preliminary Objections, ICJ Rep. 2008, Sep. Op. Judge Tomka, 412, 520, para 13: "When that State ceases to exist, as was the case of the SFRY (...) the *issue of succession to responsibility may arise*. Similarly, when *a territorial unit* of a predecessor State succeeds in its effort to secede and establishes itself as a separate State, the issue of the responsibility of the separate State for acts which were committed *by the organs of that entity* before it established itself as a State with international legal personality may arise", emphasis added. Yet, and importantly, he further added that "But clearly, regarding these two issues, neither that of succession into responsibility of the predecessor State nor that of the responsibility of an entity for acts committed before it became a State—and thus could have become a party to the Genocide Convention—fall within the jurisdiction of the Court under Article IX of the Genocide Convention. That jurisdiction covers 'disputes between the Contracting Parties relating to the interpretation, application or fulfilment of the ... Convention' by its Contracting Parties. The FRY, now continuing as Serbia, became a Contracting Party on 27 April 1992".

220 *Gabčíkovo-Nagymaros* case, para 124.

221 This is the position of Philippe Weckel, "Convergence du droit des traités et du droit de la responsabilité internationale: à la lumière de l'Arrêt du 25 septembre 1997 de la Cour Internationale de Justice relatif au projet Gabčíkovo-Nagymaros (Hongrie/Slovaquie)", 102 *RGDIP* 1998, 672–673. See also, Peterschmitt, 70; Brockman-Hawe, 866.

222 ILC Special Rapporteur Šturma, Second Report, 2018, para 175. See also, at para 188.

223 *Croatia Genocide Convention* case, Preliminary Objections, ICJ Rep. 2008, Sep. Op. Judge Tomka, 412, 520, para 14: "It is to be noted that the acts, despite in reality being performed on the ground by Slovak authorities, were always considered by the Court as those of Czechoslovakia (...) and, in relation to them, the Court refers to Czechoslovakia and not to Slovakia in the operative clause".

Finally, I have already explained the reasons why the "organ" exception should not apply to Newly Independent States.[224]

8 The Use of the Principle of Unjust Enrichment to Resolve Issues of Succession to Responsibility

This section discusses the use of the principle of unjust enrichment (*enrichissement sans cause*) to resolve problems of State succession to responsibility. I believe that this principle is indeed a very useful tool to determine which of the predecessor State or the successor State should be held accountable for the consequences of internationally wrongful acts committed before the date of succession.

8.1 *The Principle of Unjust Enrichment*

The concept of unjust enrichment is intrinsically ambiguous and imprecise. However, this is not a reason to refrain from making use of it. Thus, as explained by O'Connell, "the concept of unjust enrichment may not be notably articulate in practice, but once one perceives that practice corresponds roughly to its fundamental requirements, that, with a consideration of the relevant social and ethical factors, suffices".[225] Because of its ambiguous nature, one needs to "take into account all the circumstances of each specific situation" to determine whether a situation of unjust enrichment occurred.[226] Importantly, a situation of unjust enrichment derives from a *state of fact*, which may be caused by a legal or an illegal act. The concept has often been used in instances involving the infringement of property rights of foreigners in cases where the acts did *not* amount to an internationally wrongful act.[227] A situation of unjust enrichment arises when (i) one party has enriched itself, (ii) such enrichment is "unjust" and (iii) is detrimental to another party. These different requirements (which

224 See, discussion in Chapter 2, Section 7.1. The "organ" exception is not mentioned in the Institute's Resolution regarding Newly Independent States (Art. 16). On this point, Kohen & Dumberry, 131.

225 O'Connell, The Law of State Succession, 1956, 274.

226 This is specifically mentioned *in Sea-Land Service, Inc. v. Iran, et al*, Award No. 115-33-1, 22 June 1984, in 6 *Iran-US CTR* 149, at 168–169; *Schlegel Corp. v. National Iranian Copper Industries Co.*, Award No. 295-834-2, 27 March 1987, in 14 *Iran-US CTR* 176, at 181–183.

227 Christoph H. Schreuer, "Unjustified Enrichment", in Bernhardt, 382. See, *Sea-Land Service*, ibid, 169.

I have examined in detail elsewhere[228]) were expressed as follows by the Iran-US Claims Tribunal in the *Sea-Land Service* case:

> There are several instances of recourse to the principle of unjust enrichment before international tribunals. There must have been an enrichment of one party to the detriment of the other, and both must arise as a consequence of the same act or event. There must be no justification for the enrichment, and no contractual or other remedy available to the injured party whereby he might seek compensation from the party enriched.[229]

8.2 *The Principle Has Been Mentioned by Courts Dealing with Issues of State Succession*

The principle of unjust enrichment was mentioned by two international tribunals and two national court decisions deciding issues involving questions of State succession.

In the *Emeric Koranyi* case, the Hungary-Romania MAT first determined that the outstanding debt was of an administrative character.[230] The Tribunal used the concept of unjust enrichment to decide the question of the successor State's responsibility. Thus, the Tribunal indicated that for the successor State (Romania) to be held liable for the outstanding debt, it would need to have been contracted in the "interest" of the territory subsequently transferred and the money received or to be received, would allow that territory "to obtain some improvement or benefit". However, the Tribunal came to the conclusion that this sum of money deposited was for the exclusive use of the plaintiffs

228 See, P. Dumberry, *A Guide to General Principles of Law in International Investment Law* (OUP 2020) 234ff.

229 *Sea-Land Service, Inc. v. Iran, et al.*, Award No. 115-33-1, 22 June 1984, in 6 *Iran-US CTR* 149, 168–169.

230 *Emeric Koranyi & Mme. Ernest Dengcjel (née Koranyi) v. Romanian State*, Hungary-Romania MAT, Award, 27 February 1929, *RDTAM* v. 8, 980, *AD* 1929–1930, 64. In this case, the plaintiffs (apparently Hungarian nationals) had deposited in 1918–1919 a sum of money (8,000 Hungarian crowns) in a tax-collector office of the city of Maromarossziget, which was then part of the Austria-Hungary Dual Monarchy. By a decision of the Hungarian District Court of Maromarossziget the tax-collector office was ordered to return the money (with interests) to the plaintiffs. In the meantime, and before the office could make the payment, the territory of Transylvania (where the city of Maromarossziget was located) was ceded to Romania after the break-up of the Dual Monarchy pursuant to the *Trianon Treaty*. The Romanian office which took over the assets of the plaintiff refused to return the money on the ground that the deposit had been made before the territory was ceded to Romania.

and Romania, therefore, had not "profited" from it. Accordingly, the Tribunal decided that Romania should not be held responsible for the reimbursement of the sum of money deposited.

As mentioned above,[231] the *Lighthouse Arbitration* case, which was decided by the French-Greek Arbitral Tribunal,[232] involved several French claims and Greek counterclaims. Two of them concerned the concept of unjust enrichment. In Claim no. 13, France requested the reimbursement for some work conducted by a French Company, which occurred prior to the cession of the territory of Crete (at the time a territory formally under the control of the Ottoman Empire) to Greece in 1913. France based its claim on the grounds that Greece (as the successor State) had enriched itself by the increase in value of the property resulting from the repair of a light by the French Company. The Tribunal found that the repair work undertaken by the French Company was within the normal scope of contractual obligations of the concessionaire.[233] It therefore rejected the claim without pronouncing itself on the validity of the concept of unjust enrichment. In its analysis of Greece's Counter-claim no. 9, the Tribunal was called to decide on the costs of a port beacon which had been erected by the French concessionaire during the military occupation and had been subsequently maintained by Greece. The Tribunal decided that there had been no enrichment. Interestingly, the Tribunal used the words "supposed principle" suggesting that it was not convinced that the concept should be considered a general principle of law.[234]

In the *Zilberszpic* case, a private contractor had concluded an agreement with the Russian Orthodox Charitable Society of Kielce, which was at the time located in Polish territory under Russian ruling.[235] The agreement for the construction of an apartment house for the Society was partially performed by the contractor. But, as a result of World War I, the money due to him remained unpaid. Under Article XII of the Peace Treaty of Riga of 18 March 1921, Poland was recognised as the owner of all former Russian State property in its territory. This included property rights that had been given up by the former Russian Tsars, such as the property of the Society. The Supreme Court of Poland concluded that the building had never been a Russian State property before the date of succession. In the absence of any contractual relationship between the

---

231 See, Chapter 2, Sections 5.2.2 and 5.3.1.

232 *Lighthouse Arbitration* case.

233 Ibid 209.

234 Ibid 241 (referring to "prétendu principe général de droit").

235 *Zilberszpic v. (Polish) Treasury*, Supreme Court of Poland, First Div., 14 December 1928, *Zb. OSN* 1928, no. 190, 4 *AD* 1927–1928, 82.

plaintiff and Poland regarding the building of the apartment, the Court concluded that the plaintiff could claim part of his expenditures for the increase in value of the land resulting from its investment (with the deduction of the sum already paid for this construction). The Court specifically made reference to the notion of unjust enrichment. However, it did so solely on the ground that this concept existed under Polish municipal law, without any discussion as to whether it was also embodied in international law.

Finally, the *Niedzielskie* case involved a contract signed by the authorities of the Austria-Hungary Dual Monarchy for work done on certain government buildings before the outbreak of the First World War.[236] In dealing with the property at stake, the Supreme Court of Poland referred to the concept of unjust enrichment, but concluded that in the present case, no such enrichment occurred.[237]

In sum, the analysis of these decisions illustrates that even though courts have referred to the principle of unjust enrichment, the concept was actually never used to decide any of these cases on the merits.[238]

8.3 *Analysis of Scholarship and the Position Adopted in This Study*

One of the most vocal advocates of the use of the principle of unjust enrichment to deal with questions of State succession is O'Connell.[239] For him, the principle is in fact central to the whole question of succession, noting that it has a "special significance in the solution of problems of State succession when one of the party to a legal relationship has disappeared".[240] In his view, "the juridical justification for the obligation to pay compensation is to be found in the concept of unjustified enrichment".[241]

236 After the end of the War, the territory where the buildings were situated was ceded to Poland, and the buildings taken over by the latter.

237 *Niedzielskie v. (Polish) Treasury*, Poland, Supreme Court, 13 October 1926, in *Rw. III, 1485/* 26/I; 3 *AD*, 1925–26, 75: "It is true that Poland took over all the immovable property of the Austrian State, but no question of unjustified enrichment arises seeing that, apart from school buildings, hospitals, and state forests, Poland had to pay for the properties taken over by a contribution to the cost of war to be paid to the Allied Powers".

238 See also, ILC Special Rapporteur Šturma, Second Report, 2018, para 106, indicating that these cases "are not directly relevant, because they mostly concern succession in respect of debts".

239 O'Connell, State Succession, v. I, 266–7, 348–9, 352; O'Connell, Recent Problems, 140.

240 Ibid 34, see also: 266–7, 348–9, 352.

241 O'Connell, The Law of State Succession, 1956, 273. He also mentions that this principle "is the norm behind the doctrine of respect for acquired rights in the law of State succession".

Writers are generally favourable to the use of the principle of unjust enrichment to solve problems of State succession.[242] In fact, some of the writers who reject the possibility of any succession to responsibility make an exception for the special situation when such acts result in the unjust enrichment of the successor State. In this context, they believe that the successor State should provide reparation for the acts that took place before the date of succession.[243] One example is the work of Drakidis, who applied this principle specifically in the context of the cession of the Dodecanesian Islands to Greece in 1947.[244] Two other writers have recently referred to the concept to examine how the rules of State succession to responsibility could potentially be used regarding crimes committed by Belgium during its colonisation of Congo.[245] The Institute's Resolution on "State Succession in Matters of Property and Debts" refers to the principle of unjust enrichment.[246] Thus, Article 8 of the Resolution indicates that the result of the apportionment of property and debts should be equitable and that "unjust enrichment shall be avoided".[247]

Other scholars have been more prudent in their appraisal of the application of this principle in the context of State succession to responsibility.[248] Some have clearly rejected the proposition that the concept could be helpful to solve problems of State succession. This is the position of Judge Kreća in his separate

---

242 See, analysis in: P. Dumberry, "The Use of the Concept of Unjust Enrichment to Resolve Issues of State Succession to International Responsibility "39(2) *RBDI*, 2006, 506–528.

243 Udina, 769–770; Oscar Schachter, "State Succession: the Once and Future Law" 33(2) *Va. JIL* 1993, 256; Ivan A. Shearer, *Starke's International Law* (11th edn. Butterworths 1994) 303; A. Verdross, *Völkerrecht* (4th edn Springler 1959) 198; A. Verdross & B. Simma, *Universelles Völkerrecht, Theorie und Praxis* (Dunker & Humblot 1984) 633–634; *Restatement of the Law Third: the Foreign Relations Law of the United States*, vol 1, (American Law Inst. 1987), 209(g), 105, Rep. notes no. 7, at 107; Lynn Berat, "Genocide: The Namibian Case Against Germany", *Pace Int'l LR* 1993, 193. This is also the position of Natalino Ronzitti, *La successione internazionale tra stati* (Giuffrè 1970) 220–221, who, however, is of the view that the obligation of the new successor State is a *new obligation*, which does not arise from the previous obligations of the predecessor State.

244 Philippe Drakidis, "Succession d'Etats et enrichissements sans cause des biens publics du Dodécanèse" 24 *RHDI* 1971, 109–110. He is of the view that, as a matter of principle, in the context of a cession of territory it should be for the continuing State (Italy) to compensate the victim of expropriation acts. Yet, whenever the successor State (Greece) has unjustly enriched itself as a result of the acts, it should be for that State to compensate its nationals.

245 Ruy & Baecke, 28–32.

246 IIL, State Succession in Matters of Property, 2001, 713ff.

247 Ibid, see also, Arts. 11 and 13.

248 Monnier, 89–90; Louis Henkin et al., *International Law, Cases and Materials* (3rd edn, West 1993) 293.

opinion in the *Croatia Genocide Convention case.*[249] For Bedjaoui, the principle should not find application in the context of decolonization.[250] He rejects the existence of any obligation for Newly Independent States to provide compensation to Western companies resulting from acts of nationalization.[251] For him, it would be "difficult, if not impossible" to prove that the successor State has been enriched, that the enrichment took place at the expense of the claimant, and that the enrichment is unjustified.[252] He believes that the principle should not apply in a case of nationalization because the property is simply returned to its original owner whose goods had been *illicitly* taken by the Colonial power in the first place.[253] Thus, for him, the theory of unjustified enrichment "is completely inapplicable because enrichment can be considered legitimate in the case of decolonization; it is not unjustified, since it constitutes compensation for the exploitation of the territory during the preceding decades".[254] In fact, if the principle of unjust enrichment were to apply, it should be *against the foreign company*, rather than against the new State.[255] This is especially the case when rights were given to a foreign company by the colonial power during the "suspicious period", i.e. just before the proclamation of independence.[256]

249 *Croatia Genocide Convention* case, sep. op. Judge Kreća, paras 65.1, 65.2, indicating that the principle of unjust enrichment is by its "nature, unsuitable to uphold the idea of responsibility *in personam*, such as responsibility for violation of the Genocide Convention".

250 Bedjaoui, 554ff.

251 Ibid 550 ("[l]es raisons morales de l'indemnisation en droit international général comme en matière de succession d'Etats, ont pris chaque fois le pas d'autant plus aisément que le fondement juridique de l'indemnisation restait encore à trouver"); ILC, Second Report Bedjaoui, 1969, 9 ("It has been pointed out that the acquired right to compensation is very fragile, since a solid foundation has still not been found for it. It was believed that the duty to pay compensation could be justified by the doctrine of unjustified enrichment. This doctrine, which has been carried over from municipal private law, is open to methodological objections based on the principle of such transposition. Above all, however, it is largely inapplicable in the case of succession resulting from decolonization").

252 ILC, Second Report Bedjaoui, 1969, 95.

253 Bedjaoui, 550: "il n'y a pas lieu de consentir à une indemnisation lorsque survient l'indépendance, car la colonisation a enrichi la métropole et a rempli une fonction historique considérable dans l'industrialisation, la puissance et la prospérité de l'Etat conquérant". See also (at 551): "On s'aperçoit donc pas comment l'équité ou le principe de l'enrichissement sans cause pourraient recevoir application dans le cas de ces biens qui font tout simplement retour, par la décolonisation, à leur propriétaire d'origine qui en avait été dépossédé".

254 ILC, Second Report Bedjaoui, 1969, 96.

255 Bedjaoui, 556.

256 Ibid 557: "Comment enfin indemniser des 'droits acquis' pendant la 'période suspecte', c'est-à-dire des droits certes régulièrement acquis conformément à la législation de l'État

Needless to say that his position has been rejected by other writers.[257]

In a recent book,[258] I developed the idea that the principle of unjust enrichment should play a role in investment arbitration when solving issues of State succession involving *State contracts*. This would be applicable when, for example, a contract is performed by an investor *specifically in one part* of predecessor State's territory, which later becomes an independent State (such as in cases of secession and dissolution) or is ceded from one State to another. The fact that the contract is executed in one specific part of the country is important insofar as it provides benefits to that territory and its population.[259] One clear example of such a situation is when the contract involves the construction of infrastructures, such as roads, bridges, airports, etc. These infrastructures stay in their original place within the given territory following the date of succession. Problems may arise if certain obligations under the contract have not been completely fulfilled on the date of succession. One especially complicated situation is when the State has not fulfilled all its payment obligations under the contract on that date. The event of succession may result in some confusion regarding the fate of the contract under which these infrastructures were built. The most problematic situation arises in the context of a dissolution, where the State party to the contract ceases to exist as an independent State. What happens to the contract in this situation? Should any of the new successor States continue to execute the contract (and, if so, which one?)? There is also confusion in the context of secession. Should the new State or the continuing State continue to execute the contract? These are situations where the principle of unjust enrichment becomes useful. If a new State has benefited, after its independence, from such a situation, it should be considered bound by the

prédécesseur, mais obtenus à la hâte à la veille de l'indépendance grâce à une réglementation de circonstance et dans le but manifeste de diminuer ou *d'appauvrir* le patrimoine de l'État successeur. Si la théorie de l'enrichissement sans cause devait s'appliquer, elle serait dans ce cas opposable non pas à l'État successeur mais à l'État prédécesseur qui a tenté d'appauvrir le premier. Un cas typique de droits acquis pendant la 'période suspecte' est celui de l'Union minière du Haut-Katanga [in the context of the independence of Congo, 1960]" (emphasis in the original). Elsewhere he also explained that "If the theory of unjustified enrichment were to be applied, it would in this case be applicable not to the successor State but to the predecessor State, which had tried to impoverish its successor" (ILC, Second Report Bedjaoui, 1969, 96).

257 See, for instance, Gruber, 108–9.

258 P. Dumberry, *A Guide to State Succession in International Investment Law* (Elgar 2018) 393ff. See also, P. Dumberry, "State Succession to State Contracts: A New Framework of Analysis for an Unexplored Question", 19 *J. World Invest. & Trade* 2018, 595–627.

259 O'Connell, State Succession, v. 1, 367 ("the more locally identified is the contract the greater is the presumption that it has benefited the absorbed territory").

obligations arising from the original contract (even though it was signed prior to the date of succession by another State; the predecessor State). The new State should accordingly provide payment for the work performed.

I believe that the principle of unjust enrichment should also be used to resolve questions of State succession to responsibility.[260] The principle is generally used as a subsidiary tool to redress the undesirable effect of a situation when it is not covered by other areas of law, such as contract law and torts law.[261] It is, in other words, a remedy used in judicial practice to "reverse accretions of wealth under circumstances in which contractual or delictual principles would have been unable to reach this result".[262] As O'Connell puts it, the function of the principle of unjust enrichment "is to mitigate the hardship which would result in certain cases from an application of strict law by applying principles of justice and equity".[263] The principle therefore plays a "mediating role between the categories of justice and of law"[264] and is "on the borderland of law and ethics".[265] It has been rightly argued that the usefulness of this concept is that it "entirely sidesteps the question of whether international law includes a specific 'legal' rule as a 'general principle' imposing a fiscal obligation upon successor states in cases of state succession".[266] In other words, when using this concept the question can deviate from whether there is a *positive legal rule* indicating that in one situation or another the successor State should take over obligations arising from the commission of internationally wrongful acts committed before the date of succession. Instead, one should focus on the evaluation of a *factual situation*: whether one State has unjustly enriched itself as a result of an act committed before the date of succession.

The importance of the principle of unjust enrichment to resolve issues of State succession to responsibility has been recognised by the Institute. The concept is mentioned in Article 7 concerning situations where there is a "plurality" of successor States,[267] like in the context of

260 Agreeing: Ruy & Baecke, 28; Reyes Gajardo, 82–3.

261 Christoph H. Schreuer, "Unjustified Enrichment", in: Bernhardt, 381.

262 Christoph H. Schreuer, "Unjustified Enrichment in International Law" 22 *Am.J.Comp. L.* 1974, 289. See also: *Sea-Land Service, Inc. v. Iran, et al*, Award No. 115-33-1, 22 June 1984, in 6 *Iran-US CTR*, 169.

263 D.P. O'Connell, "Unjustified Enrichment", 5 *Am.J.Comp.L.* 1956, 16.

264 O'Connell, State Succession, v. I, 34. See also, O'Connell, The Law of State Succession, 1956, 273.

265 D.P. O'Connell, "Unjustified Enrichment", 5 *Am.J.Comp.L.* 1956, 4.

266 M.H. Hoeflich, "Through a Glass Darkly: Reflections Upon the History of the International Law of Public Debt in Connection with State Succession", *U.Ill.L.Rev.* 1982, 39, 46.

267 Kohen & Dumberry, 53: The provision "applies when the application of the provisions of the Resolution does not result in identifying specifically the State that should be the

dissolution.[268] Article 7(2) lists the "criteria that may be taken into consideration" to determine an "equitable" apportionment of obligations among the concerned States, including, *inter alia*, the "need to avoid unjust enrichment". The same reference is mentioned in Article 12(5) regarding separation.

The work of the ILC also refers to this concept. Special Rapporteur Šturma did not however consider the principle "as an independent basis for succession to responsibility", but rather as "one of criteria and circumstances relevant to the case" that "should be taken into consideration".[269] Guideline 11, dealing with dissolution, indicates that the injured State and the "relevant successor State or States" "shall agree on how to address the injury" and that they "should take into account any territorial link, any benefit derived, any equitable apportionment, and all other relevant circumstances". One circumstance mentioned in the Commentary is unjust enrichment.[270] Guideline 9(2), applicable in the context of separation and transfer of territory, indicates that "in particular circumstances, the injured State and the successor State should endeavour to reach an agreement for addressing the injury". The Commentary explains that one such circumstance is unjust enrichment and provides this illustration: "cases where an expropriated factory belonging to foreign investors or an object of art belonging to another State is retained on the territory of the successor State".[271] Interestingly, Austria commented on this passage and this example; it considered that it had nothing to do with any question of transfer of obligations per se, but was simply an application of the unjust enrichment principle.[272]

---

holder of the rights or obligations arising from an internationally wrongful act which occurred before the date of succession".

268 Ibid 53ff.

269 ILC Special Rapporteur Šturma, Second Report, 2018, para 106. See also, this comment, in: ILC Report, 72th sess., 2021, A/76/10, chap. VII, at para 154: "Regarding the principle of unjust enrichment, the Special Rapporteur again stated that such principle was relevant as one of the special elements or circumstances that supported the exceptional transfer of obligations arising from State responsibility to a successor State or States. However, he clarified that he had deliberately not expressly mentioned the principle in the proposed draft articles, as he did not accept it as the only ground for the responsibility of successor States for several reasons. The principle was considered to be ambiguous and imprecise, and was often linked to the concept of 'acquired rights', which was considered outdated and not in conformity with modern international law".

270 ILC, Commentaries, 2022, at para 89, Art. 11, sub-para 8.

271 Ibid sub-para 5.

272 See, Austria, letter sent to the UN GA Sixth Committee, rep. 72nd sess., 2021: "The examples of such particular circumstances given in paragraph 5 of the commentary, such as when an expropriated factory is situated in the territory of a successor state or when a successor state would be unjustly enriched, demonstrate that the resulting 'exceptional

Ultimately, it does not truly matter whether unjust enrichment is treated "as an independent basis for succession to responsibility" or just as one relevant criterion among others. It is also not significant that the principle does not come from the realm of State succession.[273] What matters is that unjust enrichment is a general principle of law. This is indeed the position adopted by many scholars and several tribunals.[274] As such, it should be applied by international tribunals and used by States in their practice in all fields of international law, including when dealing with matters of State succession to responsibility.

8.4 *Application of the Principle to Different Types of Succession of States*

As recognised by the Institute and the ILC,[275] the principle should apply in the context where the predecessor State *does not* cease to exist as a result of the events affecting its territorial integrity, such as cases of separation. The relevant question is: Who has enriched itself as a result of an unlawful act committed before the date of succession, the continuing State or the successor State?[276] It would be unjust for the continuing State to be held liable for the commission of internationally wrongful acts for which it did not receive any benefit/advantage. The continuing State should not pay reparation to the injured State when the successor State benefitted. The same is true in opposite circumstances: the successor State should not be held responsible for the consequences of wrongful acts when only the continuing State was enriched. In certain situations, both the continuing State and the successor State may have enriched themselves. In such cases, they should both be held accountable in proportion to the actual benefits/advantage they derived from the commission of the internationally wrongful act. As explained above, when there is a history

situation' is not at all a transfer of responsibility from the predecessor to the successor state. Rather, it may be a justified consequence of the rule calling for the avoidance of unjust enrichment". See also, ibid, 70th ses., 2018: "In our view, only in cases where a successor state acknowledges and adopts the unlawful acts of a predecessor state as its own, in line with Art. 11 of the State Responsibility Articles, or is unjustly enriched as a consequence of such an act, the obligations arising from the internationally wrongful act of the predecessor state would be transferred to the successor state. However, it is doubtful whether this transfer of obligations is the consequence of a succession of states at all. Rather, it seems to be based on other rules of international law".

273 Reyes Gajardo, 82–3, noting that "the principle of unjust enrichment corrects a situation that, though legal, is considered against the nature of international law. But this solution does not stem from the topic of State succession to international responsibility".

274 For a detailed analysis on this point, see: P. Dumberry, *A Guide to General Principles of Law in International Investment Law* (OUP 2020) 237ff.

275 See, Art. 12(5), IIL, Resolution, 2015; ILC Guideline 9(2).

276 See, Stern, Responsabilité, 336, who refers to the issue. See also, Peterschmitt, 57–61.

of colonialization, determining if the principle should be applied for Newly Independent States should be carefully analysed. The Institute's Resolution does not apply the principle in this specific context.[277]

In the context of dissolution, it is essential that an internationally wrongful act does not remain unpunished as a result of the disappearance of its perpetrator. The relevant question is which of the successor States (if any) has benefited from the commission of the internationally wrongful act. Here again, there may be cases where several successor States will have benefited from the act. The solution put forward in Article 7 of the Institute's Resolution should apply. As mentioned above,[278] in the context of the dissolution of the United Arab Republic in 1961, one of the two successor States (Egypt) entered into several agreements with other States (Italy, Switzerland, Lebanon, Denmark, Greece, the Netherlands, Great Britain, Sweden, and the US) under which compensation was provided to foreign nationals whose properties had been nationalised during, *inter alia*, the existence of the United Arab Republic (the predecessor State, 1958–1961). The successor State (Egypt) provided compensation because the properties expropriated were located in the territory of Egypt, and not in Syria. The principle of unjust enrichment was certainly relevant in this case.[279]

Finally, the case of *Compagnie d'Enterprises* CFE SA *v. Yemen*, illustrates how the principle should be used in the context of a unification of States. The decision of the Supreme Court of Cyprus considered the principle of unjust enrichment to determine the issue of succession to State contracts:

> Acquired rights remain in force, regardless of the prevailing legal situation in the successor state. Such rights are transferred to the new state, insofar as the (original) contracting state continued to exist or, at least, retained sovereignty over the geographical area wherein the contractual right was granted or pertained and wherein the (original) contracting state has already benefited from the performance of the contract, especially when works have been done in its territory that remain in the same geographical area; this is so even if the political situation has changed or the government or the (original contracting) state was transformed into a new entity in international law. (…) If the new state has benefited from

277 Compare Art. 12(5), in the context of separation, referring to the concept but not in Art. 16 dealing with Newly Independent States.

278 Chapter 2, Section 4.3.1.

279 See also, Reyes Gajardo, 82–3.

> the works of the predecessor state, then it has to bear responsibility for them.[280]

The Supreme Court held that the new State of Yemen was bound by an arbitration clause in a State contract signed by one of the predecessor States. The court found it particularly important that the contract had been performed on the territory of one of the predecessor States, which had since then become the territory of the new successor State as a result of the unification. Thus, the Court refers to the fact that the new State had *benefited* from the performance of the contract for the construction and maintenance of a harbour on what is now its territory and should, accordingly, be responsible for the obligations arising from that contract.

9 The Use of the Principle of Equity to Resolve Issues of Succession to Responsibility

The concept of equity has been described as "the key … to the entire problem of State succession".[281] According to the *1983 Vienna Convention*, in cases of dissolution, separation and the cession/transfer of territory, the debts of the predecessor State "pass to the successor State[s] in an equitable proportion, taking into account, in particular, the property, rights and interests which pass to the successor State[s] in relation to that State debt".[282] The Institute's Resolution on "State Succession in Matters of Property and Debts" indicates in Article 8 that "the result of the apportionment of property and debts must be equitable".[283] Stern speaks of a "customary international rule requiring the equitable distribution of the national debts" of the predecessor State.[284] In

280 *Yemen v. Compagnie d'Enterprises CFE SA*, Cyprus, Supreme Court, Appeal judgment, No 10717, ILDC 630 (CY 2002), 28 June 2002, See, analysis in: Oxford Rep IL [H1 to H3], referring to [12–14] of the decision.

281 O'Connell, The Law of State Succession, 1956, 268.

282 See Art. 37, 40 and 41, 1983 *Vienna Convention*. According to Stefan Oeter, "State Succession and Struggle over Equity: Some Observations on the Laws of State Succession with Respect to State Property and Debts in Cases of Separation and Dissolution of States", 38 *German YIL* 1995, 101–102 (See also, 90–92), in the context of separation and dissolution the adoption of liability *pro rata* is the only viable solution because it "promises to bridge the gap between the legitimate expectations of creditors and the legitimate aspirations of successor States".

283 IIL, Resolution 2015.

284 Stern, Concluding Remarks, 204. See also, Stern, Succession, 171.

that context, the notion of equity is used for the establishment of "equitable criteria of repartition" of rights and obligations between the different States involved.[285] There is no doubt that the rules of State succession applicable in relation to debts, property, etc, are also relevant to solve matters of succession to responsibility.[286]

The concepts of equity and fairness can also be used for the allocation of *liability* between the predecessor State and the successor State (and in case of dissolution, among the different successor States).[287] This is in accordance with the findings of the Badinter Arbitration Commission in its "Opinion no. 1": "the outcome of succession should be equitable, the States concerned being free to settle terms and conditions by agreement".[288]

The principle of equity should also find application in the context of State succession to responsibility.[289] Some writers (and tribunals[290]) have made use of the concepts of justice and equity as the cornerstone of their analysis of the

285 Vladimir D. Degan, "Equity in Matters of State Succession", in: Ronald St. John Macdonald (ed), *Essays in Honour of Wang Tieya* (Martinus Nijhoff 1993) 207. See also, Sandrine Maljean-Dubois, "Le rôle de l'équité dans le droit de la succession d'Etats", in: Eisemann & Koskenniemi, 145, 149.

286 Pajnkihar, 6, indicating that his book is based on the assumption that "The rights and obligations stemming from internationally wrongful acts are therefore juxtaposed with rights and obligations related to other succession matters to form a coherent whole". His conclusion is that: "Based on a comprehensive presentation of the field of State succession and the resulting rules that apply to all established areas of succession, it is not reasonable to interpret succession to international responsibility differently from other matters. It is therefore appropriate to apply the rules applicable to succession in general to succession to the rights and obligations arising from international responsibility" (341).

287 This is also the opinion of W. Czaplinski, "Equity and Equitable Principles in the Law of State Succession", in: Mojmir Mrak (ed), *Succession of States* (Martinus Nijhoff 1999) 72, for whom "the notion of 'equitable principles' within the law of State succession refers to the equitable global result of division of assets and liabilities rather than to equitable (balanced) criteria applied to the division of specific kinds of sorts of property".

288 "Opinion no. 1", 29 November 1991, 92 *ILR* 1993, 166 (under letter 1) e). For a critical analysis of this statement, see: P.M. Eisemann, "Rapport du Directeur de la section de langue française du Centre", in: Eisemann & Koskenniemi, 28.

289 Vladimir D. Degan, "Equity in Matters of State Succession", in: Ronald St. John Macdonald (ed), *Essays in Honour of Wang Tieya* (Martinus Nijhoff 1993) 207, believes that "one should reach an equitable solution in *any* specific problems arising from State succession" (emphasis added).

290 *Pittacos v. Etat Belge*, Court of Appeal (2nd Ch.), 1 December 1964, in: *J. Trib.* 1965, 7, 9. This case is discussed in detail in Chapter 2, Section 7.2.2. The Court held that: "c'est sur l'équité que se fonde le principe de droit international public selon lequel les dettes quasi-délictuelles nées avant le démembrement d'un Etat restent à la charge de l'Etat démembré (lequel serait, en l'occurrence, la Belgique)".

issue.[291] More specifically, the allocation of liability between the continuing State and the successor State (or among the different successor States in the context of dissolution) should be fair and equitable.[292] It should be fair from the perspective of the interests of both the continuing State and the successor State(s). But also from the point of view of the *injured State*. In other words, the outcome needs to respect the injured State's right to have its damage redressed.[293] The injured third State is not bound by any agreement entered

291 This is the position of Volkovitsch, 2172, who summarises this issue as the confrontation of two inherently antagonistic equitable principles in international law: "Is it more important that every victim of an international wrong be allowed a remedy? Or should States only be held liable for those acts that they can be truly said to have caused?" He concludes (2200) that "the balance of the compelling equitable considerations of providing compensation to the victim and attributing responsibility to a somewhat distant party tips strongly in favour of the former". Thus, for the author (see 2211–2212), it is fairer to compensate the victims and to impose liability on a State even though traditional notions of State responsibility would not call for such liability to be imposed on that State. He believes that the same phenomenon also exists under municipal law where he observed "a shift from a system centered on the punishment of tortfeasors to one that focuses on the compensation of victims and the avoidance of incidents". For him, the situation prevailing under municipal law with respect to torts is relevant in deciding issues of State succession to responsibility. Thus, "the competing equities in both cases are the same, that of compensation for the victim as opposed to the imposition of liability on a party whose 'fault' would not have been sufficient to engender liability under traditional notions of torts, and the answer reached in one case can illuminate the decision in the other". See also, Jakubowski, State Succession, 270, indicating that in the context of succession to cultural property a "pragmatic approach" "based on fairness and equity" may be preferable to the "zeal of standardization" adopted by the Institute which, he considers, "appears superfituous and doctrinally formalistic in detecting customary rule". *Contra*: Georg Dahm, *Völkerrecht*, v. 1 (W. Kohlhammer 1958) 121, for whom there is no general principle of succession to responsibility even based on the concept of equity. See also; European Commission for Democracy through Law (Venice Commission), *amicus* brief in the *Bijelić* case, opinion no. 495/2008, CDL-AD(2008)021, 20 Oct. 2008, para 41.

292 ILC Special Rapporteur Šturma, Fourth Report, 2020, para 18 ("The concept of equity, equitable proportion or distribution of rights and obligations seems to be important"); ibid, Fifth Report, 2021, para 17. For Schwarzenberger, 175–176, in the context of dissolution, the "share of the liability" among the successor States for the wrongful act committed by the predecessor State before the date of succession "can be determined only by equitable considerations". See also, Pajnkihar, 340: "In the event of the dissolution of the predecessor State, the secondary rights and obligations involving no specific link between the individual successor States and the matter of succession (i.e., the general part of the matter) shall be succeeded to in equitable shares by all successor States. In the absence of a specific link between the successor State and the matter of succession, only succession in proportional shares is possible under the principle of equity".

293 In the context of the division of debts, see: Art. 36, 1983 *Vienna Convention*. See also, Art. 24(1), IIL, State Succession in Matters of Property, 2001: "A succession of States should not affect the rights and obligations of private creditors and debtors".

into between the predecessor State and the successor State(s) deciding the allocation of liability between them.[294] As mentioned above,[295] under Article 6 of the Institute's Resolution, the injured State needs to consent to the transfer of the obligation to repair from the predecessor State to the successor State.[296]

The strict and automatic application of a principle of *non-succession* to responsibility could lead, in some circumstances, to unjust and unfair results. This is recognised by writers.[297] This is even admitted by those who support the principle of non-succession but who nevertheless accept the transmission of the consequences of internationally wrongful acts to the successor State on grounds of equity.[298] The concept of equity is central to the work of the Institute and its rejection of any general rule in favour of non-succession:

> The sort of 'clean slate' rule applicable to all cases of State succession in the field of international responsibility, which is supported by some writers, would result in numerous situations where the consequences of illegality would simply be erased and unaccounted for. Such an outcome flies in the face of the requirement for stability in international relations as well as the very idea of equity and justice. Such an outcome would also be contrary to the interests of all States affected by an event of State succession, i.e. both the successor and predecessor States as well as third States. It would crucially affect the interest of the holder of a right to reparation following the commission of the wrongful act. In sum, the application of a strict non-succession rule would result in the victim no longer having any possibility of obtaining reparation if the wrongdoer State ceased to exist. Not only would such an outcome constitute a rather unusual way to end a relationship of responsibility, it would also be, most importantly, fundamentally contrary to the principles of justice and equity governing international relations.[299]

294 Art. 34, *Vienna Convention on the Law of Treaties*, 1155 UNTS 331.

295 See, Chapter 3, Section 4.

296 Kohen & Dumberry, 46. See also, ILC Special Rapporteur Šturma, Fifth Report, 2022, para 69.

297 Thus, for Stern, Responsabilité, 336, the application of a strict doctrine of non-transferability would go against the idea of justice: "Une absence systématique de succession en matière de responsabilité choque cependant l'esprit de justice". See also, Verzijl, 220; Peterschmitt, 33.

298 Monnier, 90, admits that, in some circumstances, "la transmission des obligations nées de l'acte illicite (…) répondrait à des considérations de justice et d'équité".

299 Kohen & Dumberry, 10.

The same idea was at the heart of the work of ILC Special Rapporteur Šturma: "the specific rules and exceptions to be drafted in that regard had to be worded in such a way as to prevent unjust and inequitable results".[300]

I have examined above several situations, for instance in the context of unification and dissolution, where the application of a strict and automatic principle of non-succession would be unfair for the injured State which would be left with no debtor. The unfairness of such an outcome is recognised by writers[301] and (in the form of an *obiter dictum*) by the Arbitral Tribunal in the *Lighthouse Arbitration* case.[302] The role of equity, and the application of the different rules examined in Chapter 3, is to ensure that an internationally wrongful act does not remain unpunished. Similarly, in the context of separation, these rules and the principle of equity will help to determine whether the continuing State or the new State should be responsible for the wrongful act.

The Institute's Resolution and the ILC also recognised the importance of equity.[303] Under Article 7(1), applicable in situations of dissolution, in cases where "it is not possible to determine a single successor State, all the successor States will enjoy the rights or assume the obligations arising from the commission of an internationally wrongful act in an equitable manner", unless otherwise agreed by the concerned States.[304] Paragraph 2 establishes the criteria which may be taken into consideration to determine an "equitable apportionment" of obligations among the successor States:

– Whether there exists "any special connections" between one or more successor States "with the act giving rise to international responsibility";

300 ILC Report, 70th sess., 2018, A/73/10, chap. X, paras 219–266, para 259.

301 Stern, Responsabilité, 336: "Il nous paraît (…) particulièrement préoccupant qu'une responsabilité délictuelle encourue par un Etat disparaisse purement et simplement dans toutes les hypothèses où ne subsiste, à l'issue d'un processus successoral, aucun Etat continuateur". See also, Schwarzenberger, 175–176; Peterschmitt, 33, 72.

302 *Lighthouse Arbitration* case, 23 *ILR* 1956, 93: "What justice, or even what juridical logic, would there be, for example, in the hypothesis of an international wrong committed against another Power by a State which subsequently splits up into two new independent States, in regarding the later as being free from an international obligation to make compensation which would without any doubt have lain on the former, predecessor, State which had committed the wrong?".

303 See, this reference in the preamble of the Institute's Resolution: "Considering that law and equity require the identification of the States or other subjects of international law to which, after the date of succession of States, pertain the rights and obligations arising from internationally wrongful acts committed by the predecessor State or injuring it".

304 The same solution is followed by Pajnkihar, 340.

- "The size of the territory and of the population";
- "The respective contributions to the gross domestic product of the States concerned at the date of succession";
- The "need to avoid unjust enrichment".[305]

One example of a fair and equitable allocation of liabilities among the different successor States in the context of dissolution is the dismemberment of the Union of Colombia (from 1829 to 1831).[306] Apparently, the allocation of liability among the three successor States was in proportion to Colombia's national debt as agreed among them at the time of the dissolution. Another example of a fair and equitable way to decide questions of allocation of liabilities among the different successor States is the establishment of a settlement of disputes mechanism such as the one included in the 2001 *Agreement on Succession Issues* entered into by all successor States in the context of the dissolution of Yugoslavia.[307] The preamble to the Agreement indicates that the Agreement was reached after discussions and negotiations "with a view to identifying and determining the equitable distribution among themselves of rights, obligations, assets and liabilities of the former Socialist Federal Republic of Yugoslavia". It should be added that the financial assets of Yugoslavia were divided among the successor States in proportion[308] which "generally reflect the size of the territory and population of the States concerned and their respective contributions to the GDP of the predecessor State".[309] In particular, Article 2 of Annex F to the Agreement deals with the principle of the transfer of the "obligation to repair" from the predecessor State to the successor States and indicates that "all claims against the SFRY" shall be "considered" by the Standing Joint Committee, which will settle any "differences" among the successor States arising over the "interpretation and application" of the Agreement.[310]

305 The same reference to the "equitable apportionment" of obligations is found in ILC Guideline 11 and in Art. 12(5) (separation) of the Institute's Resolution.

306 See, Chapter 2, Section 4.2.3.

307 41 *ILM* 2002, 1–39. See, Chapter 2, Section 4.3.3.2.

308 See, Art. 5 of Annex C to the Agreement: Bosnia and Herzegovina—15.5 %; Croatia—23 %; Macedonia—7.5 %; Slovenia—16 %; and Serbia and Montenegro (later Serbia)—38 %.

309 ILC Special Rapporteur Šturma, Fifth Report, 2021, para 39.

310 Under Art. 5, these differences should be first settled through "discussions" among the States. The matter may be referred to either "an independent person of their choice" or to the Standing Joint Committee which may make "appropriate recommendations to the Governments of the successor States" (Art. 4(2)).

10 The Relevance of the Territorial Factor to Resolve Issues of Succession to Responsibility

As previously observed, the modern theory of territory in international law is the *Kompetenztheorie*, whereby the territory of a State is defined as the "territorial sphere of validity of the national legal order called a State".[311] The correlative aspect of the sovereignty of a State over its territory is, logically, that, in principle, it is responsible for internationally wrongful acts committed within its territory.[312] There is no doubt that the territorial element is, generally speaking, of great importance to determine any issue of State succession.[313] This importance is recognised by writers.[314]

This section addresses the question of the relationship between the territory of a State and a wrongful act in the context of State succession to responsibility. More specifically, I will examine (in Section 10.1) whether there is a general rule whereby the successor State is automatically responsible for obligations arising from internationally wrongful acts committed by the predecessor State before the date of succession solely based on the fact that such acts took place on what is now its territory. This section also addresses (in Section 10.2) whether a rule of transfer of the obligation to repair exists with respect to violations of territorial regime obligations.

10.1 *The Existence of a "Direct Link" between the Consequences of a Wrongful Act and a Territory*

Some writers have emphasised the importance of the location where an internationally wrongful act was actually committed to determine which of the continuing State or the successor State should bear the responsibility for

311 Hans Kelsen, *Principles of International Law* (2nd edn, Holt, Rienhart & Winston 1966) 307.

312 See, Malcolm N. Shaw, "Territory in International Law", 13 *Netherlands YIL* 1982, 73. See also, *Case of the S.S. "Lotus"*, Judgment, 7 September 1927, PCIJ *Serie A*, no. 10, Diss. Op. Judge Moore, 68.

313 Thus, both Vienna Conventions include provisions specifically related to the element of territory. See, for instance, Art 11 and 12 of the 1978 *Vienna Convention*.

314 Udina, 690, admits that, in principle: "La transmissibilité des droits et obligations internationaux résulte du fait qu'ils trouvent un point de rattachement, plutôt que dans leur titulaire, dans des choses matérielles, *dans des lieux ou territoires déterminés* … qui peuvent passer indifféremment d'un sujet à l'autre" (emphasis added). However, for Udina this reasoning applies only to cases where no *intuitu personae* rights and obligations exist. For him (see 767), internationally wrongful acts committed by the predecessor State against third States are so "strictly personal" to the former that they cannot be transferred to the successor State. Therefore, Udina expressly excludes the relevance of the element of territory with respect to internationally wrongful acts.

it.[315] One example is the work of Hyde.[316] The opposite position was taken by Hurst.[317] Monnier has convincingly shown the limits of Hurst's theory.[318] He is also critical of Hyde's position:

> La thèse opposée, qui veut rattacher l'acte illicite au territoire, 'dépersonnalise' en quelque sorte l'obligation qu'il engendre. S'il n'est pas contestable que la souveraineté territoriale forme l'assise des pouvoirs de l'Etat, cette constatation ne saurait pour autant justifier une construction liant au sol l'obligation délictuelle au même titre que les obligations de nature réelle contenues par exemple dans un traité concernant la fixation d'une frontière ou l'exploitation d'un cours d'eau. Cette théorie, qui ne trouve

---

315 Peterschmitt, 28.

316 Hyde, 437–438. According to the author, internationally wrongful acts committed by a State cannot be separated from the territory: all international tortious acts committed by a State have a territorial basis, even the one committed outside of the territory of that State. He is particularly critical (see 437) of the "prevailing theory that seemingly disassociates State responsibility from the territory that undergoes a complete change of sovereignty" which he concluded "leaves something to be desired". He is in favour of a principle under which there would be a "connection between the territory as such and certain forms of conducts committed thereon as to cause [the new State] to afford under some conditions a means of redress regardless of a change of sovereignty that marks the extinction of the tort feasor" (see 437–438). Hyde believes that "the particular territory concerned, despite the extinction of the former sovereign, should, at least under certain conditions, be made to bear the burden of requiting wrongs due to, and growing out of, the assertion of supremacy therein" (438). Hyde concludes his analysis by stating that his proposition, according to which "the territory should be made the means of redressing wrongs necessarily attributable to the exercise of sovereignty within it", is "worthy of the faithful consideration of the international society" (ibid).

317 Hurst, 178: "What the conqueror annexes is the territory of the former State, not the State itself, still less its Government. When once this principle is realized, it will be seen that in sound theory it is impossible to hold the conqueror liable for the torts of the Government which he has displaced, because the torts were the torts of the Government and not the torts of the territory".

318 Monnier, 87–88: "Le phénomène que le droit international qualifie de succession d'Etats ne consiste pas seulement dans l'acquisition par un Etat du territoire appartenant à un autre Etat. Il s'analyse, ainsi que nous l'avons montré au début de cette étude, dans la substitution d'un ordre juridique étatique à un autre sur un territoire déterminé. L'extension territoriale de l'Etat nouveau n'est que la cause de la substitution. Mais cette théorie soulève encore une objection d'un autre ordre en tant qu'elle sert de légitimation et d'encouragement à une politique d'intervention dont les grandes Puissances ont usé en maintes circonstances détestables au cours du 19e siècle et jusque dans la première moitié du siècle actuel".

> d'ailleurs aucun appui dans la pratique diplomatique ou arbitrale, est trop artificielle pour être retenue.[319]

Other writers deny that any emphasis should be placed on the territorial element when deciding questions of State succession to responsibility.[320]

In my view, there exists no principle whereby the successor State is *automatically* responsible for obligations arising from internationally wrongful acts committed by the predecessor State before the date of succession *solely based* on the fact that those acts took place on what is now its territory. In any event, the application of such a general theory could lead, in certain circumstances, to unfair results. This is the case whenever an internationally wrongful act is committed before the date of succession in the territory of a new State but with which that new State had nothing to do and for which it received no benefit or advantage. In such circumstances, it would seem unfair to transfer the obligation to repair to the new State. The fact that a wrongful act took place on the territory of the new State before its independence should not, *in itself*, be the reason for finding this State responsible for such act.[321] It is only one relevant element among many that need to be taken into account to determine which State should be responsible for the consequences of an act.

As explained in the commentary to the Institute's Resolution, "what matters (apart from the special case of territorial regimes) is not *where* the wrongful act took place, but rather to identify the *consequences* arising from the act".[322] The Final Report also explained that what matters is the "existence of a direct link between the *consequences* of the internationally wrongful act and the territory or the population that becomes part of the territory or the population of the successor State.'"[323]

In the context of dissolution, Article 15(1) of the Institute's Resolution establishes the solution of succession. Article 15(2)(3) indicates that "in order to determine which of the successor States becomes bearer of the obligations" to repair, there are two "relevant factors" to be considered. One such factor is the existence of a "direct link" between the consequences of an internationally wrongful act committed by the predecessor State and the territory or the population of one of the successor States.[324] This approach has been endorsed

319 Ibid 88–89.
320 Udina, 690, 767.
321 IIL, Final Report, Kohen, paras 57–58.
322 Kohen & Dumberry, 84, emphasis in the original.
323 IIL, Final Report, Kohen, para 60, emphasis added.
324 See, analysis in Kohen & Dumberry, 126.

by writers.[325] One example, already mentioned above, is an act of expropriation, without any compensation, committed by the predecessor State against a foreign investor on the territory which later becomes an independent State. In such a case, there is clearly a link between, on the one hand, the territory of the new State, where the property or the assets are located, and, on the other hand, the consequences of a wrong committed before independence, i.e. the new State benefiting from this property for "free". Whenever there exists such a link, the presumption is that this new State has benefited from the wrong, and, consequently, that it should provide proper reparation to the injured party. As mentioned above, this is a situation where the concepts of unjust enrichment and continuous violation are also relevant.

The same general approach was adopted by ILC Special Rapporteur Šturma in Draft Article 11.[326] In contrast, Guideline 11 merely indicates that "the injured State and the relevant successor State or States should agree on how to address the injury" and that they "should take into account any territorial link, any benefit derived, any equitable apportionment, and all other relevant circumstances".[327] I have already provided a critical assessment of this modification.[328]

In the context of separation, Draft Article 7(3) put forward by ILC Special Rapporteur Šturma contained one exception to the general principle of non-succession: "If particular circumstances so require, the obligations arising from an internationally wrongful act of the predecessor State, where there is a direct link between the act or its consequences and the territory of the successor State or States, are assumed by the predecessor and the successor State or States".[329] That position is also supported by writers.[330] In his Report, the

325 Jakubowski, State Succession, 266, 269–271.

326 ILC Special Rapporteur Šturma, Second Report, 2018, paras 147, 167, 185.

327 ILC, Commentaries, 2022, para 89, Art. 11, sub-para 8, adding that "Relevant circumstances include those that establish a link between the successor State or States and the internationally wrongful act or the injury, such as the continuity of organs (i.e. a personal link), or unjust enrichment".

328 See, in the section on dissolution: Chapter 2, Section 4.1.

329 See, ILC Special Rapporteur Šturma, Second Report, 2018, paras 98ff. A similar exception was also mentioned in the context of transfer of territory (Draft Article 9(3)). See also, Draft Article 8(2) in the context of Newly Independent States using different language.

330 Shaw, 877, referring to a "clear, direct and intrinsic link between the consequences of the act and the territory and population'" of the new State. See also, Kaplane, 37; Pajnkihar, 338 ("First special rule: A successor State that has a special link to the matter of succession (i.e., injury) shall fully succeed to the secondary rights and obligations of reparations relating to that matter, followed by conditional succession to other secondary rights and obligations. This rule refers to the special part of the succession matter and applies to all types of succession and independently of the existence of a continuator State") 339

Special Rapporteur indicated that, in the context of separation, the successor State was "not *automatically* responsible" for such obligations "solely based on the fact that such acts took place on what is now its territory", adding that "the linkage of the acts to the territory is only *one relevant element* that needs to be taken into account".[331] In contrast, Guideline 9(2) (which was never formally adopted by the ILC) no longer contains any explicit reference to the "direct link" exception; it is only mentioned in the Commentary.[332] I have already provided above a critical assessment of this modification.[333]

The Institute's Resolution does not contain this territorial link exception in the context of separation.[334] Yet, the commentary nevertheless recognises the possibility of the existence of such a territorial link.[335] It refers to the example (mentioned above) of an act of expropriation, without any compensation, committed by the predecessor State against a foreign investor on the territory which later becomes an independent State. In my view, if the successor State does not provide compensation/restitution after the date of succession, it could be considered that it has benefited from the act and should, therefore, provide proper reparation to the injured party. In such a case, restitution by the continuing State is not possible given that the property is now located in the new State's territory.[336] In these cases, the concepts of continuing wrongful act and unjust enrichment are important.[337]

There is limited case law on the application of this territorial link element. One relevant example is an incident which arose in the context of the separation of Belgium from the Kingdom of the Netherlands in 1830.[338] France, Great

---

(speaking of the existence of a "specific link to a constitutive element of one of the successor States" which therefore "belongs to it in its entirety" and to the "link between the injury and the territory or population of the successor State").

331 ILC Special Rapporteur Šturma, Second Report, 2018, para 103, emphasis in the original, citing the first edition of my book, 287.

332 ILC, Commentaries, 2021, para 165, Art. 9, sub-para 5.

333 See, in the section on separation: Chapter 2, Section 6.1.

334 Art. 12(2) only concerns the existence of a "direct link" between the consequences of an internationally wrongful act committed *against* the predecessor State before the date of succession and the territory or the population of the successor State(s). It does not address the reverse situation of a wrongful act committed *by* the predecessor State. See, Kohen & Dumberry, 98–101.

335 Kohen & Dumberry, 85, discussing the point in the context of transfer of territory, but the reasoning equally applies to instances of separation. See, 100–101, explaining that this is a situation where Art. 12(4) could find application whereby both the predecessor State and the successor State would have to assume responsibility.

336 ILC Special Rapporteur Šturma, Fourth Report, 2020, para 41; Kohen & Dumberry, 86.

337 Ibid, Fourth Report, 2020, para 63. See, Sections 4 and 8 above.

338 This example was discussed in Chapter 2, Section 6.3.1.

Britain, Prussia and the US made a joint application to Belgium (the new successor State), requesting compensation "solely upon the ground that the obligation to indemnify for such losses rested upon the country within which the injury was inflicted".[339] One of the legal grounds invoked by the US for holding Belgium responsible for the damage specifically referred to the territorial link between the "tort" and the tortfeasor:

> The governments of the respective merchants whose property was destroyed by the bombardment claimed indemnity for these losses from the Kingdom of Belgium. The ground of the claims was, that the injury was inflicted on a territory which, at the time the reclamation was made, had become a part of Belgium; but Belgium attempted to evade it by alleging that the Dutch government received the property, had it in possession, and destroyed it; and from Holland, and not Belgium, indemnity must be sought.[340]

In other words, since the acts took place in the territory of what would later become Belgium, the US took the view that the new State should therefore be held responsible for it. Belgium agreed to pay compensation to the owners.[341] The example has been considered by both the Institute and ILC Special Rapporteur Šturma an illustration of the existence of a direct territorial link between the consequences of a wrongful act committed by the predecessor State and the new State.[342]

Another example mentioned above[343] is in the context of the dissolution of the United Arab Republic. After the dissolution, Egypt (as one of the two successor States) entered into several agreements with other States whereby it provided compensation to foreign nationals whose properties had been nationalised by the United Arab Republic (the predecessor State) before the date of succession. Egypt's decision to provide compensation was certainly based on the ground that the acts of nationalisation were committed *in the territory of Egypt itself,* and not in Syria. Both the Institute and ILC Special Rapporteur

339 Letter dated 26 February 1857 by US Secretary of State, Mr Marcy, to French Minister Count Sartiges, MS. Notes to French Leg. VI. 301; S. Ex. Doc. 9, 35 Cong. 1 sess. 3, Moore, Digest, v. VI, 929.

340 Ibid.

341 Verzijl, v. 7, 226–227.

342 Kohen & Dumberry, 101–102; ILC Special Rapporteur Šturma, Second Report, 2018, para 101.

343 See, Chapter 2, Section 4.3.1.

Šturma consider this example an illustration of a "direct link" between the consequences of the internationally wrongful act committed by the United Arab Republic and the territory of Egypt.[344]

Another relevant example is the *Gabčíkovo-Nagymaros* case, where the *Special Agreement* entered into by the parties to refer a dispute to the ICJ indicates that "the Slovak Republic is one of the two successor States of the Czech and Slovak Federal Republic and the sole successor State in respect to rights and obligations relating to the Gabčíkovo-Nagymaros Project".[345] On the Czechoslovakian side, the project was located in the territory of Slovakia. There is no doubt that Slovakia (and not the Czech Republic, the other successor State to the former Czechoslovakia) was considered the holder of such rights and obligations because of the existence of a "direct link" between the alleged wrongful acts and its territory.[346] ILC Special Rapporteur Šturma also mentions this case as an example supporting the territorial link exception.[347] Another essential element was the fact that the 1977 treaty established a territorial regime (a question further examined in the next section).

10.2 *Violation of Territorial Regime Obligations*

One well-recognised principle favouring the stability in international relations is that successor States are bound to respect pre-existing international borders and international boundary treaties established by the predecessor State.[348] Similarly, a successor State cannot denounce an "objective" situation created by

344 Kohen & Dumberry, 126; ILC Special Rapporteur Šturma, Second Report, 2018, para 170.

345 *Gabčíkovo-Nagymaros* case, para 2. See, Chapter 2, Section 4.3.2.

346 Kohen & Dumberry, 124.

347 See, ILC Special Rapporteur Šturma, Second Report, 2018, para 102, being rather prudent: "What remains disputable is whether the *Gabčíkovo-Nagymaros Project* case cannot be considered directly relevant in this regard". He is more affirmative later (para 175) indicating that "the close link between the internationally wrongful act or its consequences and the territory is another important factor" which explain the decision of the Court. See also, at para 188.

348 *Frontier Dispute Case* (Burkina Faso v. Mali), Judgment, 22 Dec. 1986, ICJ Rep. 1986, 554; *Case Concerning the Determination of the Maritime Boundary between Guinea and Guinea-Bissau*, Arbitral Tribunal, Award of 14 February 1985, *UNRIAA* v. 19, 149, para 40. On this point, see: Maria del Carmen Marquez Carrasco, "Régimes de frontières et autres régimes territoriaux face à la succession d'États", in: Eisemann & Koskenniemi, 493–577; Photini Pazartzis, *La succession d'Etats aux traités multilatéraux à la lumière des mutations territoriales récentes* (Pedone 2002) 164–169; Stern, Succession, 255–262; Mohamed S. Helal, "Inheriting International Rivers: State Succession to Territorial Obligations, South Sudan, and the 1959 Nile Waters Agreement", 27 *Emory ILR* 2013 907.

a treaty regarding territory, such as "servitudes" or other territorial regimes.[349] This is the solution provided for in Article 12 of the 1978 *Vienna Convention*.[350] In the *Gabčíkovo-Nagymaros* case, the Court considered that "Article 12 reflects a rule of customary international law".[351]

To the extent that a successor State inherits territorial regimes obligations from the predecessor State, it should also take over the *consequences* of the violation of such obligations committed by the predecessor State prior to the date of succession. There is support for this proposition,[352] including in the work of the Institute.[353] Thus, the high degree of importance that the international community accords to the respect of those rights and obligations specifically linked to the territory of a State should also be reflected in the way violations of such obligations are dealt with. An internationally wrongful act committed by the predecessor State related to a territorial regime should not go unpunished. Logically, only the State(s) having in fact inherited rights and obligations from servitudes and other territorial regimes as a result of the mechanisms of succession of States should bear the responsibility for any violation related to such obligations committed prior to the date of succession.

---

349 O'Connell, State Succession, v. II, 17ff, providing a long list of examples of "active" servitudes (such as the right of way by a State over the territory of another, rights respecting the maintenance of river banks and international railways and rights to navigate in national waterways) as well as examples of "negative" servitudes (such as the neutralisation or demilitarisation of a territory).

350 1978 *Vienna Convention*.

351 *Gabčíkovo-Nagymaros* case, para 123. See also, Stern, Succession, 165.

352 Jenning & Watts, 224 (when the predecessor State does not cease to exist, it is nevertheless the new successor State which should be held liable for "those claims, having a local character attaching to the territory of the new State"); Monnier, 88–89 ("[s]'il n'est pas contestable que la souveraineté territoriale forme l'assise des pouvoirs de l'Etat, cette constatation ne saurait pour autant justifier une construction liant au sol l'obligation délictuelle au même titre que les obligations de nature réelle contenues par exemple dans un traité concernant la fixation d'une frontière ou l'exploitation d'un cours d'eau"); Ivan A. Shearer, *Starke's International Law* (11th edn, Butterworths 1994) 303 ("where a tort relates to territory, as where there has been a wrongful diversion of water … it may in some circumstances be reasonable to bind the successor State to respect the unliquidated claim against its predecessor"); Volkovitsch, 2207–2208 (for whom the principle of servitude "does provide further support for a presumption of succession to responsibility for those delicts that have a clear territorial element"); Peterschmitt, 28–29.

353 IIL, Final Report, Kohen, para 58: "Wrongful acts whose core element is territory, such as in the case of violations of obligations stemming from territorial regimes or in relation to acts that must essentially be accomplished within a given territory, for its benefit or as a burden to it (for example, works benefitting a specific area, rights of passage on a given territory, fishing rights in a given waterway), deserve an exceptional treatment" (at para 61). See, analysis in Kohen & Dumberry, 83–84.

One relevant example[354] is the *Gabčíkovo-Nagymaros* case[355] where a new State (Slovakia) decided to specifically take over consequences arising from the internationally wrongful act of the predecessor State (Czechoslovakia) concerning the violation of obligations stipulated in a territorial regime (a series of dams along the Danube).[356] According to the Court, the 1977 Treaty had established the navigational regime for the Danube and created a situation where the interests of other users of the Danube were affected. Given that the Treaty was of a "territorial character", the rights and obligations which were "attached" to part of the Danube were considered unaffected by the succession of States. For that reason, Slovakia was bound by the Treaty.[357]

11 The Relevance of Treaty Succession to Resolve Issues of Succession to Responsibility

I recently published a book dealing with State succession issues arising in the context of investor-State arbitration.[358] One of the questions examined is whether a successor State in the context of separation or dissolution is bound by the bilateral investment treaties (BITS) to which the predecessor State was a party.[359] In other words, the question is whether or not *one State* (the successor State) is bound to respect the obligations contained in a treaty which was originally concluded by *another State* (the predecessor State). I explained that while there is no automatic succession to BITS, in many instances the parties (i.e. the successor State and the "other State party") have *expressly* agreed that a BIT should remain in force between them. There are also situations where there is a *tacit* agreement between these States for the continued application of a specific BIT. Whenever this is the case, the successor State will obviously be responsible *for its own* breach of the treaty regarding facts having occurred *after* its independence.

This section examines another question involving breaches of treaty obligations committed by the predecessor State *before* the date of succession. It

354 See, analysis in Kohen & Dumberry, 84; ILC Special Rapporteur Šturma, Second Report, 2018, paras 102, 188.

355 See, analysis in Chapter 2, Section 4.3.2.

356 *Gabčíkovo-Nagymaros* case, para 123.

357 Ibid.

358 P. Dumberry, *A Guide to State Succession in International Investment Law* (Elgar 2018).

359 On this question, see, ibid 33ff; P. Dumberry, "State Succession to Bilateral Treaties: A Few Observations on the Incoherent and Unjustifiable Solution Adopted for Secession and Dissolution of States under the 1978 Vienna Convention", 28 *Leiden JIL* 2015, 13–30.

involves the situation where a successor State has agreed (expressly or tacitly) to be bound by the obligations contained in a treaty concluded by the predecessor State with another State. What happens to breaches of that treaty which were committed by the predecessor State *before* the date of succession? Should the successor State bear the consequences of a treaty breach committed by the predecessor State before independence? To take a simple illustration, if there is evidence that both Croatia and France have (expressly or tacitly) agreed that the France-SFRY BIT is in force between them, does it follow that Croatia should bear the consequences of any treaty breach committed *by SFRY before* its breakup against a French investor?

Both the Institute and the ILC have decided not to examine this question in their works.[360] Interestingly, one of the arguments put forward by Croatia in the *Croatia Genocide Convention* case was based on this proposition: "Croatia argues that the FRY, by the declaration of 27 April 1992 already discussed, indicated not only that it was succeeding to the treaty obligations of the SFRY, but also that it succeeded to the responsibility incurred by the SFRY for the violation of those treaty obligations".[361] Serbia rejected this argument: the declaration of 27 April 1992 "was concerned only with succession to the treaties themselves and not with succession to responsibility".[362] While the Court did not address the argument, one Judge supported it.[363]

It has been argued by Stern that whenever a successor State becomes party to a treaty by way of succession, there is an automatic transmission of the international obligations arising from prior treaty violations committed by the predecessor State before the date of succession.[364] The same position has

360 Kohen & Dumberry, 20; ILC Special Rapporteur Šturma, First Report, 2017, para 73. See, this comment by Greece, letter sent to the UN GA Sixth Committee, Rep. 68th sess., 25 Oct. 2017: "Another matter deserving consideration is whether there should be a link between succession to a treaty and succession to the obligations arising from the breach of such a treaty. In this regard, the principal question seems to be whether a successor State which does not concede to succession to a treaty of the predecessor State could be held liable, by way of a default rule, to any breaches of such a treaty committed by the predecessor State".

361 *Croatia Genocide Convention* case, para 107.

362 Ibid para 108.

363 Ibid, Diss. Op. Judge ad hoc Vukas, para 2, interpreting the declaration made by the FRY on 27 April 1992 as meaning that "the FRY succeeded also as to the responsibility for acts committed by the SFRY (…) for the alleged violations of the Genocide Convention before 27 April 1992".

364 Stern, Responsabilité, 344–348, referring to the existence of a "principle de transmission en même temps que le traité de la responsabilité née de la violation de ce traité".

been supported by one State.[365] There is however no State practice or case law supporting such a principle.[366] In fact, I have only found one very old case that could possibly be read as supporting this principle.

This is the *Mechanic* case involving a US schooner, the Mechanic, being captured in May 1824 by another ship licensed by the Republic of Colombia, which was at the time engaged in a war of independence with Spain.[367] The seizure by Colombia was contrary to Article 15 of the 1795 *Treaty of Friendship, Boundaries, Commerce and Navigation* between the US and Spain.[368] Ecuador was still part of Colombia at the time of the incident; it later became an independent State (in 1830) upon the dissolution of the Union of Colombia. Based on an 1862 arbitration agreement between the US and Ecuador for the settlement of outstanding claims,[369] the US brought a claim against Ecuador (now an independent State) on behalf of the insurers for the seizure of the ship. The argument developed by the US was that Colombia was bound by the 1795 Treaty between the US and Spain, whether as part of Spain at the time of the

365 Cameroon, letter sent to the UN GA Sixth Committee, rep. 77th sess., 2022): "ma délégation fait observer que lorsqu'un État devient partie à un traité par voie de succession, il en découle une transmission automatique de la responsabilité internationale qui résulte d'une violation du traité ayant été commise par l'État prédécesseur avant la date de la succession. En d'autres termes, pour ma délégation, il y a une succession automatique à la responsabilité internationale du seul fait que l'État successeur est désormais partie à un traité dont l'une des dispositions a été violée par l'État prédécesseur. Pour ma délégation, il s'agit de la transmission en même temps que le traité, de la responsabilité. Ma délégation estime logique que la succession à un traité de la part d'un État implique aussi la succession de ce même État à la responsabilité internationale découlant de la violation de ce traité. Ceci est indéniablement le cas dans les situations où il y a une succession automatique à un traité. Ma délégation estime qu'il s'agit en la matière de préserver le maintien des relations conventionnelles par rapport à un territoire donné et d'assurer la sécurité juridique dans les relations internationales. Ma délégation estime que la nécessité d'une continuité des rapports juridiques qui est au cœur même de l'idée d'une succession automatique milite certainement en faveur d'un transfert à un État successeur des conséquences de la responsabilité internationale qui découle de toute violation conventionnelle".

366 On this question, see: P. Dumberry, "La succession d'Etats en matière de responsabilité internationale et ses liens avec la responsabilité des Etats en matière de traités", in: G. Distefano, G. Gaggioli & A. Hêche (eds), *La Convention de Vienne de 1978 sur la succession d'États en matière de traités: Commentaire article par article et études thématiques* v. II (Bruylant 2015) 1601ff.

367 See, Moore, Digest, v. V, 342–343; Moore, History, v. III, 3221–3227; A. de Lapradelle, & A. Politis, *Recueil des arbitrages internationaux*, v. II, 1856–1872 (Pedone 1923) 433; Lord McNair, *The Law of Treaties* (Clarendon 1961) 611.

368 The Treaty can be found in: Malloy v. II, 1795.

369 The Agreement can be found in: Malloy, v. I, 432.

events or by way of succession to treaties upon its independence.[370] At any rate, it was argued that upon its independence from Colombia, Ecuador was equally bound by the 1795 Treaty through the mechanisms of State succession to treaties.

A commission decided in 1865 that Ecuador should be condemned for the internationally wrongful act committed in 1824 by the authorities of the predecessor State (Colombia).[371] The commission held that Colombia was bound by Spain's treaties and also that Ecuador, in turn, had succeeded to Colombia's treaties. It has been suggested by scholars that the commissioners "may have intended to say that Ecuador has succeeded to the responsibility of [the predecessor State] rather than to the continuing obligations of the treaty under which responsibility arose".[372] Thus, one possible way to analyse the decision of the Commission is that Ecuador (the successor State) was bound by the 1795 Treaty and, consequently, it was found responsible for obligations arising from the initial violation of that Treaty by Colombia (the predecessor State).[373]

Stern refers to the *Gabčíkovo-Nagymaros* case, arguing that the ICJ adopted the principle of succession to responsibility arising from of a treaty violation.[374] The same interpretation has recently been adopted by Slovakia.[375]

---

370 The position of the US is expressed in: Letter of US Secretary of State, Mr Adams, to Mr Anderson, US Minister appointed to Colombia, 27 May 1823, *British & Foreign State Papers*, v. 13, 459, 480–481, in: Moore, History, v. III, 3224. The same affirmation of continuity of the Treaty is also mentioned in: Letter of US Secretary of State, Mr Forsyth, to Mr Semple, the Chargé d'affaires to New Grenada, 12 February 1839, in: Moore, Digest, v. V, 342.

371 Opinion delivered by Commissioner Hassaurek in the name of the Commission in the case of *Atlantic & Hope Insurance Co. v. Ecuador*, Moore, Digest, v. V, 342–343. In fact, Ecuador paid only 21.5% of the original amount claimed. This was the proportion of the old Colombian debts for which the new State of Ecuador was held liable after the dissolution of Colombia.

372 O'Connell, State Succession, v. II, 94.

373 However, it has been observed by O'Connell, ibid 93, that the decision is obscurely reasoned and that the role which the Treaty of 1795 played in the decision of the Commission is not clear at all.

374 Stern, Responsabilité, 344, stating that "le principe de la succession pour la responsabilité résultant de la violation d'un traité a été appliqué [by the Court], pour ainsi dire sans le moindre débat".

375 Slovakia, letter sent to the UN GA Sixth Committee, Rep. 73rd sess. 30 Oct. 2018: "An internationally wrongful act may consist in a breach of an international obligation deriving from customary international law, but it may also consist in a breach of a treaty obligation. The treaty in question may contain provisions on responsibility in case of its breach. If such a treaty, by rules governing succession of States in respect of treaties, remained in force, its provisions on responsibility would eventually also be relevant for the successor State and other Parties to this treaty. The *Gabčíkovo-Nagymaros* case provides an example of such situations".

However, the Court found Slovakia liable to pay compensation to Hungary for the wrongful conduct of Czechoslovakia solely based on the *Compromis* between the parties whereby Slovakia affirmed that it was the sole successor State of Czechoslovakia regarding rights and obligations relating to the Gabčíkovo-Nagymaros Project.[376] The Court did not discuss the question whether any obligation to repair arising from the treaty violation committed by Czechoslovakia should be transmitted to Slovakia because it became party to the 1977 Treaty.[377] In fact, none of the Parties invoked this argument in their pleadings. Slovakia maintained that Czechoslovakia had not breached the 1977 Treaty.[378] Hungary only went so far as to state that secondary obligations resulting from the violation of the Treaty committed by Czechoslovakia would not simply vanish with the break-up of the country.[379] Ultimately, Hungary's position was that the 1977 Treaty had ceased to be in force as of 31 December 1992 (the date of the dissolution of Czechoslovakia) and that, consequently, Slovakia had never been party to the Treaty.[380] Moreover, both Parties, in fact, denied the existence of any "rule" of succession to obligations arising from the commission of an internationally wrongful act.[381]

376 Dupuy & Kerbrat, 84–5.

377 *Gabčíkovo-Nagymaros* case, para 123. The Court determined that the 1977 treaty entered into by Hungary and Czechoslovakia was of a "territorial character" and that, consequently, it became binding upon Slovakia (as successor State) on 1 January 1993.

378 "Counter-Memorial", Slovakia, 5 December 1994, para 3.69. Therefore, the question whether in becoming Party to the 1977 treaty it also became responsible for any eventual treaty violations committed by the predecessor States simply did not arise.

379 "Memorial", Hungary, v. 1, 2 May 1994, para 8.03: "The first legal consequence is that Slovakia cannot be deemed responsible for breaches of treaty obligations attributable only to Czechoslovakia, which no longer exists. Nevertheless, Czechoslovakia's breaches of the 1977 Treaty, other bilateral treaties, various multilateral conventions and customary international law created a series of secondary obligations; namely, the obligation to repair the damage caused by the internationally wrongful acts. These secondary obligations were neither extinguished by the termination of the 1977 Treaty nor by the disappearance of Czechoslovakia".

380 Ibid para 6.05: "Although the Slovak Republic sought Hungarian agreement to its succession to the 1977 Treaty, the Republic of Hungary declined to agree to this". See also, para 6.06, where Hungary states that the 1977 treaty "has *never* been in force between the parties to the present case", emphasis in the original.

381 "Reply", Hungary, v. 1, 20 June 1995, para 3.163; "Counter-Memorial", Slovakia, v. 1, 5 December 1994, para 3.59. The argument developed by Hungary was that Slovakia should be responsible for internationally wrongful acts committed by the predecessor State because when becoming a State (on 1 January 1994) Slovakia continued and maintained the acts initially committed by Czechoslovakia (see, para 8.03 of its "Memorial", 2 May 1994).

Another potentially relevant case is *Bijelić,* decided by the ECHR, which held that the European Convention of Human Rights remained in force over the territory of Montenegro at all times as of the date of independence.[382] As mentioned above, some writers have argued that the decision supports the existence of a principle of automatic succession to human rights treaties and to responsibility for their breaches.[383] Yet, the conclusion reached by the Court can be explained by the fact that Montenegro had *agreed* during the proceedings to take over any responsibility arising from wrongful acts which had been committed *before* the date of succession.

Similarly, the ECHR concluded that it had jurisdiction over the internationally wrongful acts which had been committed by Czechoslovakia (the predecessor State) against its nationals from the date of ratification of the Convention by Czechoslovakia (18 March 1992) to the date of the disintegration of the Federation (31 December 1992). In *Brezny,* the Court found Slovakia responsible for acts committed before its independence based on its consent to take over liability expressed during the proceedings.[384] The Court came to the same conclusion based on the tacit consent of the Czech Republic in the *Kuchar* case.[385] In other words, although the Court concluded that both successor States were responsible for acts which were committed before their independence, it is only based on the explicit or implicit consent of these States.

In my view, the origin of the breached obligation (whether it is a treaty breach or a violation of a customary rule) is not, in itself, significant.[386] There is no reason why a different and specific regime should exist only for *treaty* violation. Therefore, I agree with the view that succession to treaty "does not necessarily imply that a successor State would also succeed in the international responsibility of the predecessor State for past violations of these treaties".[387] This is because "the continued application of the treaty and the succession in the obligations resulting from past breaches are indeed separate issues".[388] In an article I co-authored with Kohen, I argued that the solutions set out in the Institute's Resolution for different types of succession should apply to this

382 *Bijelić* case, para 69. See, Section 7.2.

383 Brockman-Hawe, 853–854.

384 *Brezny & Brezny v. Slovakia,* ECHR, case no. 23131/1993, judgement, 4 March 1996, DR 85-A. 65.

385 *Jiri Kuchar & Petr Stis v. Czech Rep.* ECHR, case no. 37527/97, 23 May 2000, para 70.

386 Kohen & Dumberry, 20.

387 Ruy & Baecke, 19.

388 Ibid.

issue.[389] The same approach has been adopted by ILC Special Rapporteur Šturma.[390]

12 Internationally Wrongful Acts Having a Special Character

The question addressed in this section is whether the *character* of the internationally wrongful act committed by the predecessor State before the date of succession does in any way influence the issue of State succession to the obligation to repair. So-called "odious" acts and violations of *jus cogens* norms will be examined.

12.1 *Commission of "Odious" Acts*

There is support for the principle that "odious debts" are non-transmissible from the predecessor State to the successor State as a matter of customary international law.[391] The so-called "odious debts" include war debts contracted by the predecessor State in its war efforts against the successor State.[392]

389 M. Kohen & P. Dumberry, "State Succession and State Responsibility in the context of Invest or-State Dispute Settlement', 37(1–2) *ICSID Rev.* 2022, 85–100.

390 ILC Special Rapporteur Šturma, First Report, 2017, para 73: "the application of rules governing succession of States in one area does not prejudge or condition the applicability of rules governing succession of States in respect of another category of relations. In other words, while it may be a presumption that a successor State that succeeded to a treaty of the predecessor State could also succeed to obligations arising from the violation of the treaty, it should not be taken as granted. The two areas of succession of States are independent and governed by special rules. The question whether or not the successor State has certain obligations or rights arising from the responsibility of the predecessor State is a separate question from the succession in respect of primary obligations (under the given treaty)".

391 Stern, Responsabilité, 341. See also, ILC, "Ninth Report on Succession of States in Respect of Matters Other than Treaties", M. Bedjaoui, Special Rapporteur, 28th sess., 1977, A/CN.4/301 and Add.1, ILC Report, A/32/10, 1977, chp. III(A)(1), para 49, *Yearbook ILC*, 1977, v. II, 45, 67 (hereinafter "ILC, Ninth Report Bedjaoui, 1977"), paras 115ff, see, para 173, Art. D ("Non-transferability of odious debts"), providing that "odious debts contracted by the predecessor State are not transferable to the successor State". See also, ILA, "Economic Aspects of State Succession", Final Report 2006 ("there is general agreement in practice, confirmed unanimously by international legal writing, that so-called odious debts (ie debts of the State which do not relate to any interest of the population of the territory, or incurred in pursuit of illegal aims, like war) are not subject to succession").

392 Stern, 341, providing numerous examples. On this concept, see, C. Paulus, "The Evolution of the "Concept of Odious Debts"?", 68 *ZaöRV* 2008, 391; A. Reinisch, "A History of the Doctrine of Odious Debts: Serving Individual/Bilateral or Community Interests?", in

Another variation of such "odious debts" are the so-called "subjugation" debts (or "hostile debts") which have been defined as those "contracted by a State with a view to attempting to repress an insurrectionary movement or war of liberation in a territory that it dominates or seeks to dominate, or to strengthen its economic colonization of that territory".[393] A similar language has been used by the Iran-US Claims Tribunal.[394]

In case of "odious debts", it is argued that it would be illogical if these debts were to pass to the successor State since they were in fact incurred with the very aim of defeating the successor State's struggle for independence.[395] There would indeed be "ethical, moral and political reasons" for such debts not to bind the successor State, since such transmission would "constitute a serious impairment of (a successor's) interests".[396] The ILC took the position that "if the debt was contracted by a State for the purpose of committing a wrongful act against another State, the position is clear: the other State, if it becomes a successor State, will not acknowledge the debts".[397] This solution of non-succession to odious war debts was applied in the case of *S. Th. v. German Treasury* decided by a German Court: "in no case would there be any liability on the successor State in regard to the debts arising out of the conduct of war or otherwise connected with the war".[398]

Ulrich Fastenrath et al. (eds), *From Bilateralism to Community Interest: Essays in Honour of Bruno Simma* (OUP 2011).

393 ILC, Ninth Report Bedjaoui, 1977, 67, para 118.

394 *United States v. Iran (Case B-36)*, Award No. 574–B36–2, 3 Dec. 1996, 32 *Iran-US CTR* 162. Iran argued that a 1948 contract between the US and pre-revolution Iran was imposed by the former on the latter. The Tribunal rejected this argument and indicated (at para 51) that "[t]he Tribunal is of the opinion that the debt under the 1948 Contract cannot be classified under the notion of 'odious debts' as understood in international law. They were not contracted with a view to attaining objectives contrary to the legitimate interests of Iran nor were they contracted with an aim and for a purpose not in conformity with international law". It should be noted that the Tribunal also indicated (at para 49) that there was no evidence that these were "subjugation debts", since the debts had not been "incurred by Iran for the purpose of suppressing any such war or revolution".

395 Paul Fauchille, *Traité de droit international public*, v. I (8th edn, Rousseau 1922) 352: "il paraît en effet difficile d'obliger l'Etat acquéreur à supporter les dettes que l'Etat cédant avait contractée pour le combattre et amener sa défaite".

396 P.K. Menon, *The Succession of States in Respect to Treaties, State Property, Archives, and Debts* (Mellen 1991) 161–162.

397 ILC, Ninth Report Bedjaoui, 1977, 68–69, para 130.

398 *S. Th. v. German Treasury*, German Reichsgericht in Civil Matters, 3 June 1924, *ERZ* v. 108, 298, *AD* 1923–1924, 59–60. In this case, the personal debt of a plaintiff living in the German colony of "German East Africa" was (partially) contracted as part of a war effort to assist the conduct of German military operations during WWI against the UK and other allies.

This was, however, not a case of succession of States *per se*.[399]

This is no doubt a sound approach, as it involves claims *between* the predecessor State and its successor for acts committed *against each other*. However, it has been already observed at the outset of the present study that "odious debts" would not be analysed precisely because they deal with claims *between* these two States.[400] This study focuses on succession to obligations arising from internationally wrongful acts committed by the predecessor State *against a third State*.[401]

Some authors have used the notion of "odious debts" to make reference, more generally, to "odious acts" of States.[402] The proposition that obligations arising from "odious" acts committed by a predecessor State should, in principle, not pass to its successor is supported by limited case law. In the *Lighthouse Arbitration* case, the Tribunal indicated that Claim no. 4 should be admitted, adding that this was so moreover because such claim "had nothing odious" for Greece.[403] This reference, in the form of an *obiter dictum*, seems to suggest that had the claim been related to an "odious" act committed by the predecessor State, the Tribunal would have been more reluctant to find the successor State responsible for it. The language used sometimes by courts seems to refer to the odious character of acts, which in fact may be broader than "debts" as it speaks of obligations and liabilities. The argument was, for instance, raised by the claimant in the case of *West Rand Central Gold Mining Company Ltd. v. The King* before the High Court of Justice of England:

> [B]y international law, where one civilized State after conquest annexes another civilized State, the conquering State, in the absence of stipulations to the contrary, takes over and becomes bound by all the contractual

399 This case arose in the context of the cession of all German colonial territories after WWI pursuant to Art. 119, *Versailles Treaty*. The territory known as Tanganyika (and later Tanzania) became a British Mandate under the League of Nations in 1920. The UK was therefore not a "successor State" to the territory of "German East Africa".

400 See, Part 1, Section 4.6.

401 The other question of the regime applicable for internationally wrongful acts committed by a third State *against the predecessor State* is examined in Part 3.

402 Thus, O'Connell, Recent Problems, 165, is using the term "odious debts" and affirms the "repugnancy of the suggestion that successor States should be responsible for *reprehensive actions* of their predecessor" (emphasis added). Similarly, Joe Verhoeven, *Droit international public* (Larcier 2000) 189, indicates that "les dettes directement liées à des *comportements infamants* paraissent difficilement transmissibles" (emphasis added).

403 *Lighthouse Arbitration* case, UNRIAA v. 12, 199.

> obligations of the conquered State, *except liabilities incurred for the purpose of or in the course of the particular war.*[404] (emphasis added)

Similarly, the question was dealt with in an opinion presented by British Crown Counsel to the British Colonial Office on 30 November 1900 concerning the possible repudiation by Great Britain of war bonds as well as other loans floated by the Boer South African Republic to finance its military operations against Great Britain during the Boer War:

> We think that obligations incurred during the war, or in contemplation of the war, stand upon a different footing, and we do not know of any principle in international law which would oblige Her Majesty's Government to recognise such obligations.[405]

The first problem with the proposition that the consequences of the commission of "odious" acts by the predecessor State should not pass to the successor State is that there is no clear definition of what does indeed constitute an "odious" act. No attempt has ever been made to define such a loose concept, and it would arguably be impossible to come up with any satisfactory definition.

A second problem with the proposition is the fact that there is no theoretical reason justifying the conclusion that such "odious" acts should be treated differently than other "ordinary" violations of international law. On the contrary, justice and fairness would, in some circumstances, militate in favour of the application of the principle of succession. Thus, non-succession in the context of dissolution and unification of States would lead to the unsatisfactory result that grave breaches of international law, or "odious" acts, would simply go unpunished.[406] Such a situation would certainly be unfair for the injured State. From the perspective of the injured State, it does not matter much whether the obligation breached was "odious" or not; what is relevant is that it suffered a damage for which no reparation is available. In fact, the concepts of fairness and equity (which have been referred to above[407]) calling for the rejection of an automatic "rule" of non-succession with respect to "ordinary" violations of international law should apply *a fortiori* when "odious" acts are committed. In that sense, the situation for "odious" acts is not any different from that of any

404 *West Rand Central Gold Mining Company Ltd. v. The King*, 1 June 1905, LR 1905, 2 KB 391.
405 Referred to in: ILC, Ninth Report Bedjaoui, 1977, 70, para 143.
406 Agreeing: Jakubowski, State Succession, 269.
407 See, Section 9.

other breach of international law. The same position has been adopted by the Institute.[408]

12.2 *Breach of* jus cogens *Norms*

It has been suggested that in cases when the predecessor State breaches a peremptory (*jus cogens*) norm of international law, the successor State(s) should automatically be held responsible for the consequences of such grave acts.[409] Other authors have doubted that such principle, however convenient it may be, does actually exist in international law.[410] Stern believes that State practice does not support the principle of the automatic transferability of the obligation to repair in case of violations of *jus cogens* norms.[411] She is right. The same position has been adopted by the Institute.[412] As a matter of principle, the situation of the consequences of violations of *jus cogens* norms should not be treated differently from other "ordinary" norms of international law.

408 Kohen & Dumberry, 19–20: "the successor State inherits, or not, the rights or obligations stemming from the commission of an internationally wrongful act, no matter the *nature* of the obligation breached", emphasis in the original. See also, Jakubowski, State Succession, 269.

409 This is the position of Volkovitsch, 2200, for whom: "each successor state is bound by such norms as an implicit condition of its entry into international society, and accepts with them the obligation to enforce them and provide remedies for their violation. The maintenance of such norms is essential to the health of the international system and cannot depend on the vagaries of history that sometimes determine the circumstances of state succession. Nor can international law allow a State to avoid such liability by splitting itself into two purportedly 'new' entities otherwise committing 'State suicide'". See also, Jakubowski, State Succession, 270–71.

410 Stern, Responsabilité, 349; Peterschmitt, 38.

411 Stern, ibid, giving the example of the *Socony Vaccum Oil Company* case, *ILR* 1954, 55, where Yugoslavia apparently refused to succeed to the responsibility arising from acts of genocide committed by the Nazi puppet "independent" State of Croatia during WWII. However, this case (examined in: Dumberry, Rebellions, 393) does not seem to support this proposition insofar as it did not deal with acts of genocide but only with unlawful nationalisations. On this point, see Peterschmitt, 39.

412 Kohen & Dumberry, 19–20.

CHAPTER 4

General Conclusion to Part 2

The question addressed in this Part was: Should the continuing State or the successor State be held responsible for obligations arising from internationally wrongful acts committed by the predecessor State against a third State before the date of succession?

The response of the "traditional" doctrine of non-succession to this question is that the successor State is not bound by internationally wrongful acts committed by the predecessor State before the date of succession. I demonstrated that the "traditional" doctrine suffers from many flaws. The arguments brought forth by authors supporting this approach are generally unconvincing (a point also recognised by scholars in recent years). At any rate, the issue addressed in this study is not the transfer of *responsibility* for internationally wrongful acts, but rather the succession to the *consequences* of international responsibility *arising from* the commission of such acts. Scholars are increasingly accepting that, as a matter of principle, the solution to the issue of State succession to the obligation to repair depends on the circumstances of each case. Since the publication of the first edition of this book, many have rejected the strict and automatic "rule" of non-succession. Yet, it is important to note that this "traditional" doctrine of non-succession is still supported by many States and their positions explain why the ILC Draft Articles initially put forward by ILC Special Rapporteur Šturma would later be transformed into mere "guidelines" with their content significantly diluted (a question further examined in Part 4). In the *Croatia Genocide Convention* case, several ICJ judges expressly endorsed this doctrine.

The review of State practice and case law confirms the basic assumption adopted in this study that there are different solutions to the issue of State succession to responsibility depending on the types of State succession involved. The practice also supports another assumption: different problems of State succession to the obligation to repair deserve specific solutions. There are several examples of contemporary practice which do not support the application of a strict and automatic "rule" of non-succession. I have found several examples where the obligation to repair has been transferred to the successor State depending on specific factors and circumstances. They include when the successor State has accepted to take over such obligations; when a wrong was committed by the insurrectional movement during the struggle which eventually led to the creation of the new State; and when the successor State

 | DOI:10.1163/9789004703810_007

continues after its independence the internationally wrongful act which was initially committed by the predecessor State before the date of succession. There is also some support in State practice and case law (as well as in scholarships) for the proposition that, depending on the specific circumstances of each case, the obligation to repair may pass to the successor State when there is a "direct link" between the consequences of an internationally wrongful act committed by the predecessor State and the territory or the population of the successor State. The same is true when the author of the internationally wrongful act was an organ of the predecessor State that later became an organ of the successor State.

Finally, several *factors* (the principles of unjust enrichment, equity, fairness and justice) need to be taken into account to determine whether the continuing State or the successor State (and in the context of dissolution, which of the successor States) should be held responsible for obligations arising from internationally wrongful acts committed before the date of succession.

PART 3

Succession of States to the Right to Reparation

General Introduction of Part 3

This Part explores the issue of State succession to the *right to reparation*. The issue analysed in the present Part arises from the commission of an internationally wrongful act *by a third State against the predecessor State*. Before the date of succession, the predecessor State is the *creditor* of the *right to reparation* against the third State that has committed the internationally wrongful act. The question addressed in this Part is what happens to this right in the context of a succession of States. In other words, after the date of succession, who from the continuing State or the successor State should have the right to reparation as a consequence of the internationally wrongful act committed by a third State against the predecessor State.

The present Part is divided into two chapters. The first chapter (Chapter 5) examines the situation where the internationally wrongful act committed by a third State *directly* affected the predecessor State. The second chapter (Chapter 6) focuses on the other situations where the internationally wrongful act committed by a third State affected a *national* of the predecessor State. This distinction, which is not often observed in scholarship, is nevertheless necessary.[1] This is so because situations where the victim of the wrongful act is a national of the predecessor State (and not the State itself) involve complex issues of diplomatic protection which need to be examined separately.

1 This distinction is made by O'Connell, State Succession, v. 1, 538: "A distinction might be urged between cases where action is brought by the State in its own right, as a signatory, and cases where it is brought to recover damages on behalf of the injured individual". See also, Stern, Responsabilité, 354; Peterschmitt, 39; Atlam, 24–25. The distinction is also made by the Arbitral Tribunal in the *Lighthouse Arbitration* case, 23 *ILR* 1956, 91.

 | DOI:10.1163/9789004703810_008

CHAPTER 5

The Commission of an Internationally Wrongful Act Directly Affecting the Predecessor State

1 Introduction

This chapter examines the situation where an internationally wrongful act committed by a third State directly affected the predecessor State.

The first section (Section 2) explores the theoretical dimension of the question whether the transfer of the right to reparation from the predecessor State to the successor State is accepted in international law. It examines in detail (Section 2.1) the legal arguments advanced by the doctrine of non-succession, which deny any such transfer of rights to the successor State. This section also examines some criticisms of these arguments (Section 2.2). Finally, Section 3 assesses State practice and case law where questions of State succession to the right to reparation arose.

2 Analysis of Scholarship

2.1 *The Doctrine of Non-succession*

The question of the transfer of the right to reparation is rarely addressed by writers.[1] The issue is divided into two different situations which must be clearly distinguished. The first scenario is when the predecessor State continues to exist as a result of territorial modifications. The second scenario is when the predecessor State ceases to exist.

The first scenario is when the predecessor State *continues to exist* (such as in cases of separation, cession/transfer of territory, and the creation of Newly Independent States). In this context, the continuing State, i.e. the victim of an internationally wrongful act, should, in principle, remain entitled to submit a claim for reparation against the third State responsible for the act. In fact, the existence of the State responsible for the act *and* that of the State that has suffered from it is not jeopardised. The continuing State may therefore submit

1 One notable exception: V. Mikulka, "Succession of States in Respect of Rights of an Injured State", in: J. Crawford, A. Pellet & S. Olleson (eds), *The Law of International Responsibility* (OUP 2010) 965–967.

 | DOI:10.1163/9789004703810_009

a claim for reparation to the responsible third State based on the application of principles of State responsibility. This principle is largely accepted by scholars,[2] and recognised in Article 5 of the Institute's Resolution. The other question, which is not generally extensively dealt with, is whether this rule should apply *in all circumstances* and whether there should not be cases where the successor State would instead be allowed to claim reparation from the third State responsible for the internationally wrongful act. This issue, which is covered by Article 5 of the Institute's Resolution will be examined in this study when addressing examples of separation and Newly Independent States (Sections 5.3.3 and 5.3.4).

The second scenario is when the predecessor State, which has been the victim of an internationally wrongful act committed by a third State before the date of succession, *ceases to exist* as a result of territorial modifications (e.g., unification and dissolution). Very few authors have examined this issue. It has been suggested that there is simply no example of State practice or case law on this subject.[3] This is not accurate. In fact, I have found several examples of State practice and case law where the question did arise. They are examined in Section 3 below.

The conclusion reached by most authors is that in situations where the predecessor State *ceases to exist* there can be no transfer of the right to reparation to the successor State.[4] Some writers even believe that there is a *general* customary rule of international law *against* any such succession.[5] Scholars argue

---

2 Ibid 966; Stern, Responsabilité, 354; Monnier, 67; Peterschmitt, 40; Atlam, 31.

3 This is, for instance, the assessment made by these writers: Monnier, 71–72, 86; Atlam, 30, 104; Cotran, 368–369 ("in the law of succession [of States] there is no authority on the question whether a successor State is entitled to recover damages for a wrong committed against the predecessor State").

4 Monnier, 86 ("l'Etat nouveau ne reprend pas les droits appartenant à l'Etat antérieur du fait d'un acte illicite dont il a été la victime"); Peter Malanczuk, *Akehurst's Modern Introduction to International Law* (7th edn, Routledge 1997) 169 ("no succession occurs to the rights of the claimant State or to the obligations of the defendant State"); Louis Delbez, *Principes généraux du droit international public* (3rd edn, LGDJ 1964) 275 ("il n'existe pas de succession au droit à réparation de l'Etat prédécesseur"); Suzanne Bastid, *Droit international public, Principes généraux*, Fasc. II (Univ. Paris les Cours de droit, 1966–1967) 730 ("si l'acte illicite a atteint l'Etat [prédécesseur] directement ... l'Etat successeur n'est pas en droit d'agir"); A. Verdross, *Völkerrecht* (4th edn, Springler 1959) 198; A. Verdross & B. Simma, *Universelles Völkerrecht, Theorie und Praxis* (Dunker & Humblot 1984) 633–634.

5 Lauri Mälksoo, *Illegal Annexation and State Continuity: The Case of the Incorporation of the Baltic States by the USSR* (Martinus Nijhoff 2003) 257. *Contra*: Volkovitsch, 2198 (See also, 2172–2173), for whom the doctrine of non-succession "lacks the necessary foundation in practice and theory to be accepted as a customary norm of international law. Both the provisions of international agreements and the history of diplomatic practice

that the right to reparation "belongs" only to the predecessor State.[6] For these authors, this is a "personal" right of the predecessor State.[7] This is Cavaglieri's position:

> Qu'il s'agisse de l'observance des principes de droit international commun, qui lie les Etats dès le moment de leur reconnaissance mutuelle comme sujet de droit … le rapport est toujours si personnel, si étroitement lié avec son sujet que leur sort ne peut être que le même. Il est absurde de penser qu'un Etat … puisse hériter les droits fondamentaux que l'Etat disparu tenait de sa qualité de membre de la communauté internationale.[8]

These scholars believe that, in principle, only the "injured State" is entitled to invoke the international responsibility of another State.[9] The ILC's work on State responsibility defines the "injured State" as the State "whose individual right has been denied or impaired by the internationally wrongful act or which has otherwise been particularly affected by that act".[10] The argument is that a new State, which did not exist at the time the internationally wrongful act was committed, cannot be considered to have been injured. Consequently, it should not be entitled to seek redress against the responsible State. In other

---

on the subject are inconsistent and have been frequently misunderstood. Nor do the varied decisions of international tribunals or municipal courts provide sufficient support for a theory of nonsuccession. Moreover, the various theoretical bases proposed for such a principle are each plagued by fundamental flaws". See also, Feilchenfeld, 20, indicating that there is "no general custom exempting tort obligations from the rules of succession".

6 This is the position of Rousseau, v. III, 142, for whom the right to claim reparation is "propres à l'Etat au profit duquel elles sont née et elles dépendent de la continuation d'une relation légale qui ne survit pas au changement de souveraineté".

7 Atlam, 118: "les droits de réclamations sont de par leur nature même tellement attachés à la personne de leur sujet actif que toute tentative visant à envisager une succession juridique à leur égard ne serait qu'hasardeuse". He, however, supports the rule of succession to the right to reparation in the context of unification of States because he (wrongly, in my view) maintains that in such cases the legal personality of the predecessor States remains unaltered.

8 Cavaglieri, Effets, 190.

9 Atlam, 119.

10 ILC, Commentaries, State Responsibility, 2001, 293, para 2. The Draft Articles adopted in 1996 (ILC, Commentaries, State Responsibility, 1996) contained a distinct provision (Art. 40) defining the concept: "For the purposes of the present articles, 'injured State' means any State a right of which is infringed by the act of another State, if that act constitutes, in accordance with Part One, an internationally wrongful act of that State".

words, the new State is considered to be a "third State" and does not have the right to reparation.[11]

2.2 *Challenges and Criticisms of the Doctrine of Non-succession*

There is an important difference between the question of succession to the *right to reparation* and the other question of succession to the *obligation to repair* (examined in Part 2). As noted by ILC Special Rapporteur Šturma,[12] in the former case, the State responsible for the internationally wrongful act remains the same and is not affected in any way by territorial modifications. Thus, the difficult question of the "imputation" of an internationally wrongful act to a State does not arise.[13] In other words, before and after the date of succession, the liability of the State responsible for the act cannot be doubted.[14] The fact that the injured predecessor State may have ceased to exist does not alter in any way the undeniable reality that the wrongdoer's responsibility remains intact.[15] The only question that arises is whether or not such a right to reparation, for which the predecessor State was the creditor before the date of succession, should simply vanish at the same time that the predecessor State ceases to exist.

One way to prevent that an internationally wrongful act remains unpunished as a result of an event of succession is to allow the transfer of the right to reparation to the successor State. There is some support in scholarship for allowing such transfer.[16] This solution is sound and logical. Thus, as a matter of principle, the possibility of a transfer of the right to reparation to the successor State should be accepted as valid under international law. As further explained below, this approach has been followed by the Institute in its Resolution and by the work of ILC Special Rapporteur Šturma. This should certainly be the case *a fortiori* when the State responsible for an internationally wrongful act

11 Atlam, 119, for whom any other solution would be against the principle of the equality of States under international law.

12 ILC Special Rapporteur Šturma, Third Report, 2019, para 42: "this State (and its wrongful act) remains the same and *not affected* by territorial modifications giving rise to the succession of States", emphasis in the original.

13 Stern, Responsabilité, 353.

14 The same position is taken by the Czech Rep., letter sent to the UN GA Sixth Committee, Rep. 76th sess. 2 Nov. 2021.

15 Peterschmitt, 43.

16 Thus, according to Stern, Responsabilité, 354, the non-continuity of the existence of the predecessor State "[n]e devrait avoir aucune conséquence sur l'imputabilité continue de l'acte illicite à l'Etat tiers et la transmission du droit à réparation correspondant; L'Etat prédécesseur a en effet une réclamation directe, une créance à l'égard de l'Etat tiers, qui peut être transmise à l'Etat successeur". See also, Peterschmitt, 43.

recognises, *before the date of succession,* its own responsibility for the act.[17] This solution should also apply when the State responsible for such act explicitly or implicitly accepts a transfer *after* the date of succession.[18] I will examine below several examples of this situation in State practice and international case law.[19] The same solution should also apply when the wrongful act is of a "continuing" character.[20]

It would be illogical to accept (in some circumstances examined in Part 2, Chapter 3) that the *obligations* arising from the commission of internationally wrongful acts can be transferred to the successor State but the *right* to seek redress for the consequences arising from such acts could not.

The possibility of a transfer of the right to reparation should be accepted even if (at least formally) the new successor State cannot be deemed to have been "directly" and "individually" injured at the time when the internationally wrongful act was committed by the responsible State. It would be wrong to

17 It has also been suggested that the successor State should have the right to continue the claim already submitted by the predecessor State against the responsible third State. Peterschmitt, 33, argues that in such cases the principle of transferability of the right to reparation would be based on the concept of good faith.

18 Monnier, 86, for whom "*en l'absence de convention contraire,* l'Etat nouveau ne reprend pas les droits appartenant à l'Etat antérieur du fait d'un acte illicite dont il a été la victime", emphasis added.

19 This is, for instance, the case of the restitution of cultural properties by the USSR to the GDR (see, Chapter 5, Section 3.3.4). This is also the case of the peace treaties entered into by Japan with Indonesia, Malaysia, and Singapore after WWII (see, Chapter 5, Section 3.4.2).

20 Czech Rep., letter sent to the UN GA Sixth Committee, Rep. 76th sess., 2 Nov. 2021: "the Commission did not analyse a reverse situation, namely that of internationally wrongful acts of continuing character committed by a State against the predecessor State which were followed, after the date of State succession, by the same kind of wrongdoing against the successor State. In this scenario, [the wrongdoing State is the same both before and after the date of State succession, however the victims of its continuing wrongful acts are two different States—namely the predecessor State and the successor State. At the same time,] the real impact of the wrongful conduct, both before and after the date of State succession, may be felt by the same population or may affect the same property, even if they passed from the jurisdiction of the predecessor State under the jurisdiction of the successor State. The successor State should be entitled to reparation of injury which accumulated both in the period after the date of State succession, but also in the period before that date. This would be consistent with what the Commission proposes in the second sentence of draft article 7". The letter also adds: "It seems that for this purpose it also is not important whether the wrongful act consisted of a single act or was of continuing character. The focus should be rather on consequences of an international wrongful act committed by the predecessor State or against it from the perspective of lasting adverse effects of such act and their desired elimination, in accordance with requirements of fairness and restoration of justice".

deny the possibility of the transfer of the right to seek reparation based on the ground that the new successor State is a "third" State regarding the internationally wrongful act which was committed before the date of succession. In fact, in many instances, the successor State should be considered an injured State. There is often an undeniable connection between that State and the act. For instance, there will be cases where the internationally wrongful act will have affected the *territory* which became part of the new State after the date of succession. In other instances, it will be the *population* of that successor State which will have been the victim of the internationally wrongful act.[21] Judge Cançado Trindade acknowledged this point in his dissenting opinion in the *Croatia Genocide Convention* case.[22] Even if the injured predecessor State ceases to exist, the *consequences* of the internationally wrongful act will *continue after* the date of succession.[23] The only difference being that after the date of succession the State suffering damage from the commission of such an act will no longer be the predecessor State but the successor State. Whenever the circumstances demonstrate that the successor State is in fact the "injured" State after the date of succession, it should be allowed to submit a claim for reparation to the State responsible for the internationally wrongful act.[24]

21 This also seems to be the position taken by ILC Special Rapporteur in his Third Report, 2019, para 22: "the invocation of responsibility (secondary obligations or rights of the predecessor State against a successor State or by a successor State) may depend on particular circumstances, such as the existence of a territorial or personal nexus (link of the wrongful act or its consequences to the territory or population of the State); or other considerations, such as the existence of unjust enrichment resulting from an internationally wrongful act; or the determination of an equitable proportion when it comes to distribution of losses and reparation among several States". See also: M. Bracke, *The Rules of State Succession Applied to a Hypothetical Flemish Independence*, Ghent Univ. Master thesis, 2019–2020, 54.

22 *Croatia Genocide Convention* case, Diss. Op. Judge Cançado Trindade, para 31, explaining that "the consequences of the commission of grave violations of international law will, in most cases, continue to affect and victimize certain human groups even after the date of succession, and even more so when surrounded by violence". He believes that "in such circumstance, it would be unjust for the victims if no responsibility could be vindicated for the commission of internationally wrongful acts and their consequences extended in time", adding that "an internationally wrongful act and its continuing consequences cannot remain unpunished and without reparation for damages".

23 Czech Rep., letter sent to the UN GA Sixth Committee, Rep. 76th sess. 2 Nov. 2021, indicating that "the real impact of the wrongful conduct, both before and after the date of State succession, may be felt by the same population or may affect the same property, even if they passed from the jurisdiction of the predecessor State under the jurisdiction of the successor State".

24 This solution should apply to *continuous* internationally wrongful acts as well.

This principle should apply in cases where the predecessor State *ceases to exist* (such as in instances of dissolution). In such cases, the question of which successor State inherits the right to reparation should be determined by examining which of these States is now (i.e. after the date of succession) specifically injured as a consequence of the internationally wrongful act committed before the date of succession.[25] The injured State(s) should be allowed to claim reparation. This approach has been adopted by the Institute in its Resolution (Art. 15(2)). The next section examines some examples of State practice supporting this principle.[26] Interestingly, ILC Special Rapporteur Šturma first noted that, in the context where the predecessor State ceases to exist, "the prevailing opinion in doctrine is that there is no devolution of the right to reparation from the predecessor State to the successor State", and that "according to this view, the successor State or States cannot claim reparation for injury from an internationally wrongful act committed against the predecessor State before the date of succession".[27] Yet, later in his report, after having examined several examples of State practice, he is more supportive of the principle of succession.[28]

The same principle should also apply in the context where the predecessor State *continues to exist* (such as separation).[29] This approach has been adopted by the Institute (Art. 12(2)) and by ILC Special Rapporteur Šturma in his Third Report.[30] My analysis of State practice and international case law in the next section (Section 3) shows that there are several examples where such a transfer of the right to reparation from the predecessor State to the successor State did indeed occur based on the ground that the latter was considered the injured State.[31] I have also found examples where *both* the continuing State and the

25 Peterschmitt, 44.

26 See, Sections 5.3.1 and 5.3.2, examining examples in the context of the unification of the United Arab Republic, and the dissolutions of both Czechoslovakia and Yugoslavia.

27 ILC Special Rapporteur Šturma, Third Report, 2019, para 46, referring to the work of Monnier.

28 Ibid para 81: "All the above examples seem to support the possibility for the successor States to submit claims to reparation even for damage caused by internationally wrongful acts committed before the date of succession, while stressing the primary role of agreements".

29 This seems to be the position of V. Mikulka, "Succession of States in Respect of Rights of an Injured State", in: J. Crawford, A. Pellet & S. Olleson (eds), *The Law of International Responsibility* (OUP 2010) 966. Peterschmitt, 41 (see also, 45), is of the same view. However, she argues that the continuing State should *also* simultaneously have the right to claim reparation, since it was initially its right which was infringed.

30 ILC Special Rapporteur Šturma, Third Report, 2019, para 45.

31 See, Sections 5.3.3 and 5.3.4, examining examples in the context of the "secession" of the GDR, the creation of Vanuatu and several treaties entered into by Japan with the Newly Independent States of Indonesia, Malaysia and Singapore.

successor State were considered to be the injured States.[32] In such cases, nothing should prevent both States from making reparation claims for the portion of damage they have suffered.

3 Analysis of State Practice and Case Law

The present section analyses the relevant State practice and case law, taking into account the different types of succession involved.[33] For each type, I will first provide a summary of findings at the beginning of the section. I will also examine the position of scholars, of the Institute and of the ILC regarding which principle of succession or non-succession should apply.[34]

3.1 *Unification and Incorporation of States*

3.1.1 The Position Adopted in This Study and That of the Institute and the ILC

There is support in scholarship for the proposition that in cases of unification of States (and incorporation of State) the transfer of the right to reparation to the successor State should be allowed.[35] This is indeed a sound and logical approach. In Part 2, I came to the conclusion that in cases of unification and incorporation of States, the successor State should be held responsible for obligations arising from internationally wrongful acts committed by the predecessor State before the date of succession.[36] Since international rights

---

32 One illustration is Pakistan's succession to the *Agreement on Reparation from Germany, on the Establishment of an Inter-Allied Reparation Agency and on the Restitution of Monetary Gold*. See, Section 5.3.3.3, below.

33 Atlam, 32, 37, 104, and in particular 39: "Il est tout à fait impossible de chercher à formuler dans l'abstrait une solution a priori quant au sort des droits de réclamations de l'Etat prédécesseur lors d'une succession d'Etats. Et c'est précisément cette impossibilité-là qui a échappé à l'esprit de la doctrine classique lors de son examen de cette question".

34 I have not found any example of State practice in the context of transfer of territory. Art. 11 of the Institute's Resolution covers this situation.

35 Stern, Responsabilité, 354; Peterschmitt, 43; Pajnkihar, 340 ("In the case of incorporation and unification, the successor State succeeds to all the secondary rights and obligations arising from the international responsibility of the predecessor State(s)"). The same position is also taken by Atlam, 78, 119–123, but based (at 67–79) on the (questionable) assumption that in cases of unification of States, the predecessor States keep their own international legal personalities intact and that there is in fact no creation of a new State. His position (see 120–122) on the question of the transfer of the right to reparation in the context of unification of States is therefore based on the application of rules of State responsibility, not rules of State succession.

36 See, Part 2, Chapter 2, Sections 2 and 3.

and obligations are two sides of the same token, it seems only logical that the new State should be entitled to exercise the rights which were those of the predecessor State before the date of succession, including the right to claim reparation against other States responsible for internationally wrongful acts.

The same solution was adopted by the Institute in Articles 13 and 14: the right "pass to the successor State".[37] In contrast, both ILC Guidelines 13 (unification) and 13 *bis* (incorporation), which was never formally adopted by the ILC, do not contain the same positive and affirmative language (i.e. "pass"). They merely indicate that the successor State (or the "incorporating State"[38]) "may invoke the responsibility" of the wrongdoing State.[39] The language is slightly different from that used regarding separation, further examined below.[40] It should be added that Guideline 13 *bis* (2) contains a specific clause whereby when a wrongful act is committed, before the date of succession, against the "incorporating State" (i.e. the State existing prior to incorporating another State), that State "continues to be entitled to invoke the responsibility of the wrongdoing State". This additional clause was not necessary. Thus, given that the status of the incorporating State is not affected by an event of succession, there is no doubt that it continues to be the holder of the right to reparation after the date of succession.

I have found only one relevant example of State practice in the context of unification.

37 Kohen & Dumberry, 112, 115.

38 ILC, Statement, Park, 2022, 13, explaining that "it was considered clearer and more intuitive to use phrasing" such as the "incorporating State" in the context of incorporation and that it has the same meaning as "successor State". See also, ILC, Commentaries, 2022, at para 89, Art. 13 *bis*, sub-para 1.

39 ILC Draft Article 13 (unification) put forward by the Special Rapporteur in his Third Report stated that the successor State "may request reparation from the responsible State". See also, ILC Special Rapporteur Šturma, Third Report, 2019, para 69.

40 ILC, Statement, Park, 2022, 12, explaining that this expression was chosen (rather than the phrase "may be entitled to invoke" used in Guideline 12, dealing with separation) because "in the context of unification where there is only one successor State, the challenge of determining which State might be entitled to invoke responsibility did not arise". He also noted that "in draft guideline 12, the notion of 'entitled to invoke' was linked to the idea of continuation in paragraph 1 and to the idea of 'particular circumstances' in paragraph 2., neither of which were relevant to draft guideline 13". The same comment is made in: ILC, Commentaries, 2022, para 89, Art. 13, sub-para 4 (see also, Art. 13 *bis*, sub-para 2).

3.1.2 Agreements between the United Arab Republic and Other States in the Context of the Suez Crisis (1956)

The creation of the United Arab Republic was the result of the merger of Egypt and Syria in 1958.[41] The new State submitted claims requesting "adequate compensation" from the UK and France for actions committed during the 1956 Suez Canal crisis by these two States against Egypt (one of the two predecessor States).[42] The damages claimed by the United Arab Republic from the two States were in the amount of UK£ 78 million.[43] The United Arab Republic apparently also claimed reparation from Israel.

Both the UK and Israel refused to admit any responsibility and to pay any compensation to the United Arab Republic.[44] The question of the claim submitted by the United Arab Republic to the UK was dealt with in an exchange of notes leading to the conclusion of an Agreement between the two States on 28 February 1959.[45] The exchange of notes provided for both parties to waive their respective claims "arising out of the events of October–November 1956" (i.e. the Suez Canal crisis).[46] The United Arab Republic waived all its claims for war damage against the UK in return for the UK's waiver of its claims for compensation arising out of Egypt's seizure of the Suez Canal.[47] The exchange of notes mentions that both parties "do not admit liability in respect of any of these claims".

Similarly, the Agreement of 22 August 1958 between the United Arab Republic and France does not refer to any payment for war damage having been paid by France.[48] It has been suggested that France did pay some

41 The relevant circumstances of this case have already been examined in Part 2, Chapter 2, Section 3.2.1.

42 Cotran, 368–369; Ian Brownlie, *International Law and the Use of Force by States* (Clarendon 1963) 145; D'Argent, 299–301.

43 Ch. Rousseau, "Chronique des faits internationaux", *RGDIP* 1958, 681.

44 See, documents in: Ian Brownlie, *International Law and the Use of Force by States* (Clarendon 1963) 145.

45 *Agreement between the Government of the United Kingdom of Great Britain and Northern Ireland and the Government of the United Arab Republic Concerning Financial and Commercial Relations and British Property in Egypt*, in: *UKTS* 1959, no. 35 (Cmd. 723); 343 *UNTS* 159; 14 *Rev. égyptienne d.i.*, 1958, 364; 54 *AJIL* 1960, 511–519; Weston & Lillich, 57ff.

46 54 *AJIL* 1960, 511–519; M.M. Whiteman, *Digest of International Law*, v. 11 (Dept. of State 1973) 875.

47 Thus, the UK waived its claims "in respect of United Kingdom Government property situated in the Suez Canal Base … and in respect of the costs incurred by the Government of the United Kingdom for clearance of the Suez Canal".

48 *Accord général entre le gouvernement de la République française et le gouvernement de la République arabe unie*, in: *La documentation française*, 18 October 1958, no. 2473; *RGDIP* 1958, 738ff. Thus, Art. 7 indicates: "Les deux gouvernements considèrent que le présent

compensation to the new State.[49] However, France always denied having paid any such compensation.[50]

This example is obviously not the most solid and persuasive precedent given that the two States responsible for the damage ultimately denied the claim for reparation submitted by the new State. In fact, it has been suggested that the United Arab Republic implicitly renounced in these agreements to claims for reparation against the two countries.[51] What is relevant for the purpose of the present discussion is not so much that no compensation was paid (although this remains rather unclear in the case of France). What matters is the fact that there is no indication from the available documentation that either France or the UK ever objected, as a matter of principle, to the right of the new State (the United Arab Republic) to seek reparation for internationally wrongful acts committed by them against one of the predecessor States (Egypt) before the date of succession.[52] As a matter of fact, the UK explicitly accepted that such claim for reparation by the new State be part of the negotiations leading to the 1959 Agreement.[53]

Accord et ses annexes ainsi que les autres accords et leurs annexes signés ce jour constituent un règlement final de leurs réclamations nées des événements d'octobre et de novembre 1956".

49 This is, for instance, the assessment made by Cotran, 369, referring to an article published in *The Times* (14 July 1958) apparently indicating that France had paid the sum of UK£ 20 million to the United Arab Republic for damage done in Egypt in 1956. This is also the position of Peterschmitt, 43.

50 Ch. Rousseau, "Chronique des faits internationaux", *RGDIP* 1958, 681, refers to such rumours of compensation having been paid by France to the United Arab Republic prior to the signature of the 1958 Agreement between the two States. He indicates that France denied having provided any compensation.

51 Rousseau, ibid; Ian Brownlie, *International Law and the Use of Force by States* (Clarendon 1963) 145–146.

52 ILC Special Rapporteur Šturma, Third Report, 2019, para 73; Peterschmitt, 43. Cotran, 368–369, raises the question whether the UK and France may be liable to pay compensation to the new State despite the fact that the internationally wrongful acts were committed against one of the predecessor State. He believes that there is no authority in international law on this point. However, Cotran interprets the creation of the United Arab Republic not as a case of succession of States but as one of "amalgamation", whereby the legal personality of the two predecessor States are not extinguished but have "fused" into the new State. In light of this (controversial) interpretation, he concludes that: "[T]here is no reason why the United Arab Republic should be deprived of the right to recover damages for torts committed against Egypt or Syria before the Union. If the United Arab Republic has taken over the obligations of Egypt and Syria, then it is only reasonable and natural that it should take over the corresponding rights, whether they are rights in property, contract or delict".

53 Thus, in the Agreement the United Arab Republic waived its claims against the UK for "damage to Government and private property, and damage to public utilities including

3.2 *Dissolution of State*

3.2.1 The Position Adopted in This Study and That of the Institute and the ILC

Scholarship is divided on whether the successor States in the context of dissolution should be allowed to claim reparation for internationally wrongful acts committed before the date of succession. Some have argued that because there is a break in the chain of the continuous international legal personality between the predecessor State and the new successor States, the rule of *tabula rasa* should apply. The right to claim reparation would belong only to the predecessor State before the date of succession.[54] In my view, the fact that the new States have a different legal personality than the predecessor State should not, in itself, prevent the former to claim reparation for internationally wrongful acts committed against the latter. Thus, the right to reparation, for which the predecessor State was the creditor, should not simply vanish as a result of the dissolution.[55] My position is that the right to reparation should be transferred to one (or more) successor State(s), if that State can still (after the date of succession) be considered injured as a result of an internationally wrongful act committed before the dissolution.[56] To determine if a successor State is still "injured" one needs to examine whether the consequences of a wrongful act continue to be felt in *its* territory or by *its* population after the date of succession.[57] These criteria, which have been elaborated by the Institute in its Resolution, are further discussed in the next paragraphs.

Article 15(1) of the Institute's Resolution establishes the solution of succession: the rights arising from the commission of an internationally wrongful act against the predecessor State "pass" to "one, several or all the successor States"

loss of revenue, damage to the Suez Canal including loss of revenue to the Suez Canal Authority and other damage to the Egyptian economy".

54 Atlam, 107–109, and 117–118: "[L]a rupture dans la personnalité internationale entre l'Etat prédécesseur démembré et les Etats successeurs issue de son démembrement constitue ici le prélude à l'application de la règle de la table rase à l'égard des droits de réclamations du premier ... Les Etats successeurs y exercent dans ce cas leur propre souveraineté naissante et originale et non pas une souveraineté qui leur aura été transmise de l'Etat prédécesseur à la suite de la mutation territoriale. Dans une telle situation, il serait sans doute inacceptable d'opter pour une dévolution des droits de réclamations de l'Etat prédécesseur démembré à l'un ou l'autre des Etats successeurs nés de la dislocation". Atlam also indicates (118) that when all new States voluntarily and freely decide to dissolute a State they should not be able to take over the right to reparation of the predecessor State with which they have decided to break-up definitively.

55 Peterschmitt, 44.

56 This is also the conclusion reached by Peterschmitt, 44.

57 Kohen & Dumberry, 85.

depending on the circumstances mentioned in Article 15(2).[58] This provision indicates that "in order to determine which of the successor States becomes bearer" of the right to reparation, one "relevant factor" will be the existence of a "direct link" between the consequences of an internationally wrongful act committed against the predecessor State and the territory or the population of the successor State(s).[59] The commentary further explains this concept of "direct link":

> There are many possible examples illustrating the existence of such territorial direct link. For instance, this should be the case whenever the act is affecting *one* territory specifically, such as in the context of pollution and other form of environmental damages. One could also think of the destruction of property located in the territory transferred to the successor State. Another example would be illegal fishing and other violations of the law of the sea committed within the territorial sea or the internal waters of the territory transferred. What matters is that the consequences of these wrongful acts are felt in the territory of *that* successor State (not in that of others) or, in the context of Article 11 (2), in *that* territory transferred. Regarding the existence of a direct link between the consequences of a wrongful act and a population concerned, the Final Report indicates that 'if the population directly concerned by the wrongful act becomes the population of the successor State, the situation also deserves to constitute an exception to the non-succession rule in cases in which the predecessor State continues to exist.' One illustration of this principle would be, for instance, any wrongful acts targeting the population in one specific area of the predecessor State which later becomes the territory of the successor State.[60]

As noted in the commentary, "the existence of such a link militates in favour of transferring this right to reparation to that specific successor State".[61] But this is just one of the "factors" which may be relevant to the analysis.[62] The

58 See, ibid 120–2.

59 See, ibid 123ff.

60 Ibid 83, emphasis in the original, citing IIL, Final Report, Kohen, para 62. This observation is made in the context of transfer of territory, but it is also applicable in situations of dissolution.

61 Kohen & Dumberry, 123.

62 Ibid 123–4. Art. 7 of the Institute's Resolution further explains that whenever it is not possible to identify a single successor, all successor States will assume the right to reparation in an "equitable" manner taking into account the criteria mentioned in Art. 7(2).

"direct link" approach adopted by the Resolution in the context of dissolution has since then been endorsed by writers.[63]

Draft Article 16(1) put forward by ILC Special Rapporteur Šturma did not contain the same affirmative language as the Institute's Resolution. It merely stated that "one or more successor States may request reparation from the responsible State".[64] Guideline 14(1), adopted by the Drafting Committee in 2022, uses a different wording: the State(s) "may, in particular circumstances, be entitled to invoke the responsibility of the wrongdoing State". Surprisingly, despite the language specifically used in that provision (which was never formally adopted by the ILC), some passages in the Commentary seem to be suggesting that the right to reparation *does* in fact "pass" to one of the successor States.[65] This is the main concern Austria had

---

63 Jakubowski, State Succession, 269–271, 331 ("In regard to the problem of state succession in rights arising from internationally wrongful acts against cultural heritage committed prior to the date of succession, the principle of 'intrinsically direct link' is also correct as it departs from the narrow notion of injured state towards a more equitable human solution. Indeed, wrongful acts committed against cultural heritage primarily affect collective cultural rights of human communities in a given territory. Thus, the secondary obligations shall be owed by the successor state if the wrongful act has consequences in respect of its population, and in cases of grave violations of international law such obligations shall also be owned by the international community as a whole"); Pajnkihar, 338 ("First special rule: A successor State that has a special link to the matter of succession (i.e., injury) shall fully succeed to the secondary rights and obligations of reparations relating to that matter, followed by conditional succession to other secondary rights and obligations. This rule refers to the special part of the succession matter and applies to all types of succession and independently of the existence of a continuator State") 339 (speaking of the existence of a "specific link to a constitutive element of one of the successor States: which therefore "belongs to it in its entirety" and to the "link between the injury and the territory or population of the successor State").

64 See also, ILC Special Rapporteur Šturma, Third Report, 2019, para 81: "All the above examples seem to support the possibility for the successor States to submit claims to reparation even for damage caused by internationally wrongful acts committed before the date of succession, while stressing the primary role of agreements".

65 ILC, Commentaries, 2022, at para 89, Art. 14, sub-para 3, explaining that the language used in Guideline 14(1) was chosen "to reflect the idea that, while not all successor States *will necessarily be* entitled to invoke responsibility, one or more *will*" (emphasis added). The passage seems to be suggesting that at least one successor State *will be entitled* to invoke responsibility. See also, this passage: "The phrase 'in particular circumstances' reflects the fact that the identification of the successor State or States that *are* entitled to invoke responsibility in respect of the injury to the predecessor may depend on a number of factors and that it will not necessarily be all successor States who are so entitled" (emphasis added). Again, this wording suggests that at least one successor State *is indeed entitled* to invoke responsibility. The same comments were made in ILC, Statement, Park, 2022, 14; see at 15, speaking of the "identification of which successor State or States *is entitled* to invoke responsibility" (emphasis added).

with this language. It noted the "ambiguity" resulting from the wording that successor States "may request reparation", but added that it "would have no problem" if it was "understood as permitting successor states to ask for reparation which may be granted by the injuring states ex gratia", but that it would nevertheless "question the added value of such a provision".[66] But for Austria, "seen in the context of the other rules, it is likely to be understood as a veritable rule of automatic succession into the claims of the predecessor state by the successor state", which "does not find a basis in international law and should also not be included among the de lege ferenda provisions".[67] In the end, according to Austria, "the Special Rapporteur would in fact replace the principle of non-succession by a principle of succession".[68]

In any event, these "particular circumstances" are mentioned in Guideline 14(2): "The wrongdoing State and the relevant successor State or States should endeavour to reach agreement for addressing the injury" and "they should take into account any territorial link, any loss or benefit derived for nationals of the successor State, any equitable proportion and all other relevant circumstances". The Commentary further explains that the phrase "particular circumstances" refers to a "territorial or personal link between an internationally wrongful act or its consequences and one or more of the successor States".[69] It added that "the most obvious link seems to be in situations where the injurious consequences of an internationally wrongful act affect only the territory of one successor State", mentioning the *Gabčíkovo-Nagymaros* Case (further discussed below) as an illustration.[70] In his Fifth Report, the Special Rapporteur added that in a situation where it is not possible (based on the territorial or personal link) "to determine a single successor State, each injured successor State may separately invoke that responsibility".[71]

While the Chair of the Drafting Committee explained that "paragraph 2 emphasizes the importance of agreement between the wrongdoing State and the relevant successor State or States in the context of a dissolution",[72] it

66 Austria, letter sent to the UN GA Sixth Committee, Rep. 71st sess. 5 Nov. 2019.

67 Ibid.

68 Ibid.

69 ILC, Commentaries, 2022, para 89, Art. 14, sub-para 4. See also, ILC Special Rapporteur Šturma, Third Report, 2019, para 22; ibid, Fifth Report, 2022, para 36.

70 ILC, Commentaries, 2022, at para 89, Art. 14, sub-para 4.

71 ILC Special Rapporteur Šturma, Fifth Report, 2021, para 36, adding that "this should be done in an equitable manner so as to ensure that any injured State does not recover more than the damage it has suffered".

72 ILC, Statement, Park, 2022, 14. The same comment is made in: ILC, "Text of the Draft Guidelines and Commentaries", provisionally adopted, 72nd sess., in ILC Report, 73rd sess., 2022, A/77/10, chap. VII, at para 89, Art. 14, sub-para 2.

remains that they do not have any obligation to reach such an agreement. If they don't, there will simply be no transfer of the right to reparation to any of the successor States. I believe that it would have been preferable to follow the logical steps set out in Article 15 of the Institute's Resolution: (1) firmly affirm the principle of succession and then (2) provide guidance as to which factors should be taken into account to determine which successor State(s) should be the holder of the right to reparation after the date of succession.

I have found a few relevant examples of State practice. The *Agreement on Succession Issues*, reached in the context of the dissolution of Yugoslavia, is an example where the successor States accepted the transfer of the right to claim reparation from the predecessor State to the successor States.[73] Two other decisions by international judicial bodies in the context of the dissolution of Czechoslovakia are less clear regarding the right for the successor State to claim compensation for internationally wrongful acts committed before the date of succession. It seems that in both cases, the tribunals simply endorsed prior agreements reached between the parties. At most, it can be argued that both judicial bodies did not reject the possibility of the transfer of such right to reparation to the new States. Overall, one can agree with ILC Special Rapporteur Šturma, for whom these examples "seem to support the possibility for the successor States to submit claims to reparation even for damage caused by internationally wrongful acts committed before the date of succession".[74]

3.2.2 The *Gabčíkovo-Nagymaros* Case (1997) in the Context of the Dissolution of Czechoslovakia (1992)

In the *Gabčíkovo-Nagymaros* case, the ICJ determined that before the date of succession Hungary had committed an internationally wrongful act and that it was under the obligation to pay compensation to Czechoslovakia (the predecessor State).[75] The Court however *did not* address the question whether this right to reparation, for which Czechoslovakia was the creditor before the date of succession, had vanished as a result of the dissolution of the federal State or whether such right could be transferred to the new State of Slovakia. The Court simply made reference to the Special Agreement entered into by Slovakia and Hungary which expressly stated that Slovakia, one of the two successor States, was "the sole successor State in respect of rights and obligations relating to the Gabčíkovo-Nagymaros Project".[76] As mentioned above, this is because of the

73 Agreement on Succession Issues, 41 *ILM* 2002, 1–39.

74 ILC Special Rapporteur Šturma, Third Report, 2019, para 81.

75 *Gabčíkovo-Nagymaros* case, paras 108–110, 152.

76 Ibid para 2.

existence of a "direct link" between the wrongful acts and the territory and the population of *that* successor State.[77] The Court interpreted the Preamble to the Special Agreement to mean that Slovakia was "entitled to be compensated for the damage sustained *by Czechoslovakia* as well as by itself as a result of the wrongful conduct of Hungary" with respect to the Gabčíkovo-Nagymaros Project.[78] The Court thus acknowledged that the new State of Slovakia was entitled to seek redress from Hungary for the internationally wrongful act committed by the latter against the predecessor State (Czechoslovakia) before the date of succession.

However, it must be emphasised that the Court seems to have accepted the transfer of the right to reparation solely based on the wording of the Special Agreement.[79] In fact, Slovakia in its pleadings explicitly rejected the existence of any principle of succession to the right to reparation.[80] This position adopted by Slovakia was certainly coherent with its rejection of the principle of succession to *obligations*.[81] The ground invoked by Slovakia for finding Hungary responsible was that the latter had committed an internationally wrongful act "of a continuing character which extended beyond the date of the dissolution of Czechoslovakia".[82] Slovakia argued that it was "entitled to all remedies available to the injured State by the rules of international law governing *State responsibility*".[83] In fact, Slovakia claimed reparation only for the portion of the

77 Kohen & Dumberry, 123–4. See also, ILC, Commentaries, 2022, para 89, Art. 14, sub-para 4.

78 Ibid para 151, emphasis added.

79 This is clear from this passage, *Gabčíkovo-Nagymaros* case, para 151: "*According to the Preamble to the Special Agreement, the Parties agreed* that Slovakia is the sole successor State of Czechoslovakia in respect of rights and obligations relating to the Gabčíkovo-Nagymaros Project. Slovakia *thus* may be liable to pay compensation not only for its own wrongful conduct but also for that of Czechoslovakia, and it is entitled to be compensated for the damage sustained by Czechoslovakia as well as by itself as a result of the wrongful conduct of Hungary" (emphasis added).

80 In its "Counter-Memorial", v. 1, 5 December 1994, para 3.60, Slovakia mentioned (quoting the work of Monnier) that as a new State it did not take over the rights belonging to the predecessor State as a result of any internationally wrongful act committed before the date of succession. Thus, Slovakia argued that its right to obtain compensation from Hungary in the context of the Gabčíkovo-Nagymaros Project was "not based on succession to Czechoslovakia *per se*" but that it was instead "based on the [1977] Treaty" (at para 3.61).

81 Thus, Slovakia's ultimate aim was to avoid any responsibility for the internationally wrongful acts committed by Czechoslovakia before its dissolution. Having rejected the existence of any principle of succession to the obligation to repair, Slovakia, quite logically, also rejected the existence of any rule in favour of succession to the right to reparation.

82 "Counter-Memorial", Slovakia, v. 1, 5 December 1994, para 3.63.

83 Ibid, emphasis added.

internationally wrongful act committed by Hungary *after* the date of succession. Slovakia thus considered that it could not claim reparation from Hungary for damage which occurred *before* the break-up of Czechoslovakia.[84]

This example is therefore not entirely conclusive. At most, it can be argued that the Court did not reject the possibility for the successor State to claim compensation for internationally wrongful acts committed before the date of succession.[85]

3.2.3 Claim Submitted by the Czech Republic before the UNCC for Damage to the Czechoslovak Embassy Caused by Iraq

The UNCC was set up to deal with claims arising from the invasion and occupation of Kuwait by Iraq in 1990–1991.[86] After the dissolution of Czechoslovakia (1 January 1993), the Czech Republic filed a claim in the amount of US$ 11,208 for damage caused by Iraq to the *Czechoslovak* Embassy in Baghdad during the Gulf War (i.e. before the dissolution of the Federation).

In its Report and Recommendations, the Panel of Commissioners recommended an award in the amount of US$ 4,733.[87] The Panel acknowledged that the Czech Republic (the successor State) was not the injured State at the time of the commission of the internationally wrongful act to the Embassy. The Panel concluded that the Czech Republic should nevertheless be deemed the "proper and sole claimant in respect of these losses" based on the agreement which had been entered into between the two successor States to the Czechoslovak Federation "at the time of the separation" whereby the

84 Ibid para 3.60.

85 Kohen & Dumberry, 125.

86 One category of claims (the "F4" claims) dealt with claims by governments "for losses related to departure and evacuation costs of their nationals or damage to physical property". The nature of the UNCC is further examined in detail in Chapter 6, Section 3.1.4.

87 *Report and Recommendations made by the Panel of Commissioners Concerning the Second Instalment of "F1" Claims*, UNCC Governing Council, S/AC.26/1998/12, 2 October 1998, see at footnote no. 3 of the Report. This is the relevant quote from the Report: "The Czech Republic's claim includes a statement explaining that the Czech and Slovak Federal Republic ceased to exist on 31 December 1992 and was succeeded by the Czech Republic and the Slovak Republics on 1 January 1993. Based on agreements concluded at the time of the separation, the Czechoslovak Embassy and Embassy residence in Baghdad became the property of the Czech Republic. Accordingly, although it had been the Federal Republic [of Czechoslovakia] that had suffered the losses in respect of which compensation is claimed, the Czech Republic is the proper and sole claimant in respect of these losses". This recommendation was adopted by the Governing Council Decision no. 56, S/AC.26/Dec.56 (1998), 2 October 1998.

"Czechoslovak Embassy and Embassy residence in Baghdad became the property of the Czech Republic".

The decision of the Panel was ultimately largely influenced by the existence of an agreement entered into between the two successor States (which, however, did not deal with the issue of wrongful acts committed before the dissolution). The Panel's Report therefore cannot be considered a general endorsement of the principle of the transfer of the right to reparation from the predecessor State to the successor State. At the most, it can be argued that the Panel did not reject the possibility of such transfer.

3.2.4 The Agreement on Succession Issues in the Context of the Dissolution of Yugoslavia (1991–1992)

As previously mentioned, the successor States to the former Yugoslavia (including the FRY) entered into in 2001 the *Agreement on Succession Issues*.[88] Article 1 of Annex F to the Agreement deals with the outcome of internationally wrongful acts committed by third States against the SFRY before its dissolution.[89] Under this provision, claims of the SFRY for reparation against other States before its dissolution are considered "rights and interests which belonged to the SFRY" and, as such, they should be "shared" among the successor States. The provision also indicates that the "division of such rights and interests" should be done under the direction of the Standing Joint Committee. It should be noted that the provision makes a direct reference to the division of the financial assets of the SFRY as a yardstick of the proportion of the "rights" to be shared among the successor States.[90]

This provision is a clear illustration of the acceptance *by the different successor States* of the validity of the principle that the successor States should be entitled to submit reparation claims for internationally wrongful acts

88 41 *ILM* 2002, 1–39. See, Part 2, Chapter 2, Section 4.3.3.2.

89 The provision reads as follows: "All rights and interests which belonged to the SFRY and which are not otherwise covered by this Agreement (including, but not limited to, patents, trade marks, copyrights, royalties, and *claims of* and debts due to *the SFRY*) shall be shared among the successor States, taking into account the proportion for division of SFRY financial assets in Annex C of this Agreement. The division of such rights and interests shall proceed under the direction of the Standing Joint Committee established under Art. 4 of this Agreement" (emphasis added).

90 The division of the SFRY's financial assets is indicated in Art. 5(2) of Annex C of the Agreement: Bosnia and Herzegovina: 15.5 %; Croatia: 23.0 %; Macedonia: 7.5 %; Slovenia: 16.0 %; FRY: 38.0 %.

committed against the predecessor State before the date of succession. This interpretation is, however, the object of some controversy.[91]

3.3 *Separation*

3.3.1 The Position Adopted in This Study and That of the Institute and the ILC

As a matter of principle, the continuing State (whose status as an independent State is not affected by territorial changes) is entitled to claim reparation against the third State responsible for the commission of any internationally wrongful act which occurred before the date of succession. Thus, the emergence of a new State does not *per se* jeopardise the continuing State's entitlement to compensation. This principle is recognised by scholars,[92] the Institute[93] and the ILC.[94] It is also illustrated by the 1997 Agreement entered into by Russia and France, examined in the next section. The question of whether this basic principle should apply in all situations remains. In my view, whenever the circumstances show that it is, in fact, the new successor State which is the "injured" State after the date of succession, it should be the one allowed to submit a claim for reparation to the responsible State. In such a case, the right to reparation "pass" to the successor State. There may also be situations where both the continuing and the successor States will be considered injured.[95]

The same approach has been followed by the Institute's Resolution. Under Article 5,[96] and Article 12(1), the right to reparation does *not* pass to the

91 See, Part 2, Chapter 2, Section 4.3.3.2 referring to letters sent to myself by Sir Arthur Watts and Professor Vladimir-Djuro Degan, who both took part in the negotiations.

92 Stern, Responsabilité, 354; Monnier, 67; Atlam, 31; Peterschmitt, 40.

93 Kohen & Dumberry, 92ff.

94 ILC Special Rapporteur Šturma, Third Report, 2019, paras 52, 45: "It is largely accepted that succession of States does not affect the right of the predecessor State that continues to exist to claim reparation from the wrongdoing State for its acts committed before the date of succession of States".

95 This possibility of shared responsibility is covered by Art. 12(4)(5) of the Institute's Resolution.

96 Just like Art. 4 mentioned above (Part 2, Chapter 2, Section 6.1), the Institute's Resolution includes a provision (Art. 5) providing for the general framework of analysis regarding matters involving succession to rights for three categories of State succession where the predecessor State continues to exist. Under Art. 5(1), the predecessor State can invoke the international responsibility of the perpetrator of a wrongful act committed against it and request reparation for the injury caused. Art. 5(2) provides for an exception to that general principle in the situation where the internationally wrongful act committed against a predecessor State "affect[s] the territory or persons" which, after the date of succession, are under the jurisdiction of the successor State. Whenever this is the case, the successor State may request reparation to the perpetrator for the injury caused by such act.

successor State.[97] The general rule is that the predecessor State that continues to exist keeps this right. One exception is found in Article 12(1): The right to reparation "pass" to the successor State "if there exists a direct link between the consequences of this act and the territory or the population" of the successor State.[98] The commentary provides some examples where such a link exists, for example, a wrongful act destroying property/infrastructures or affecting the environment/natural resources located in the territory over which the new State is now sovereign. The Final Report also provides a concrete illustration of a situation where there is a "direct link" between a wrongful act and the population of the successor State.[99] As noted in the commentary, while in these situations the acts were "undoubtedly committed against the predecessor State, it remains that, after the date of succession, the real and lasting consequences of the act are clearly suffered by the new State, and not by the continuing State".[100]

The same approach was initially followed by ILC Special Rapporteur Šturma in Draft Article 12. In 2022, the Drafting Committee adopted a new provision (Guideline 12) that is more explicit: "the predecessor State continues to be entitled to invoke the responsibility of the other State even after the date of succession, if the injury to it has not been made good".[101] Draft Article 12(2) put forward by the Special Rapporteur provided for an exception similar to that contained in the Institute's Resolution dealing with situations where there is a link between a wrong and the territory/population of the new State.[102] For the Special Rapporteur, in a situation where the injury caused by a wrongful act "affected primarily or exclusively" the territory which later became an independent State or where it "affected persons who subsequently became

97 Kohen & Dumberry, 92.

98 Ibid 98ff.

99 IIL, Final Report, Kohen, para 62: "Putting aside the fact that territorial rights are in general for the benefit of a given population, even though the legal holder may be the State concerned, it may occur that the wrongful act has a specific population as a direct victim. This is particularly relevant in cases of violations of human or minority rights. If the population directly concerned by the wrongful act becomes the population of the successor State, the situation also deserves to constitute an exception to the non-succession rule in cases in which the predecessor State continues to exist".

100 Kohen & Dumberry, 99.

101 ILC, Commentaries, 2022, para 89, Art. 12, sub-para 2, explaining that it considered referring "specifically to requesting reparation from the responsible State", but decided instead that "entitle[ment] to invoke" responsibility "was preferable because it is broader, encompassing not only reparation but also other obligations arising from the commission of an internationally wrongful act".

102 ILC Special Rapporteur Šturma, Third Report, 2019, paras 54, 58.

nationals of the successor State", "it is hard to imagine that the predecessor State could, after the date of succession of States, still claim reparation" for such injury.[103] Greece commented that the provision should explicitly cover "instances of removal of movable, cultural or other, State property from the territory which came under the jurisdiction of the successor State".[104] Under Draft Article 12(2), when there is such a link, the new State "may request" reparation to the perpetrator.[105] The Special Rapporteur explained that this "rather soft language" was used to indicate that "this is not an automatic succession but a mere possibility, under special circumstances, to claim reparation".[106] In fact, the goal was to "rebut any allegation of automatic succession" and "simply reflected the idea that a successor State is able to present a claim or request for reparation".[107] This soft language contrasts with the Institute's Resolution which refers unambiguously to a *right to reparation* that "pass" to the successor State when there is a "direct link" between a wrongful act and the territory/population of the successor State.

Guideline 12 (which was never formally adopted by the ILC) uses different wording: "a successor State may, in particular circumstances, be entitled to invoke the responsibility of the State that committed the internationally wrongful act". As mentioned above, it would have been preferable to use the more affirmative language contained in the Institute's Resolution. The Chair explained that the word "may" was used to reflect the "conditionality of the entitlement on the existence of the particular circumstances".[108] Yet, the provision no longer indicates what these "circumstances" are; it no longer contains a reference to the territorial or personal nexus. The Commentary does refer to this nexus, adding that this language was "intended, inter alia, to satisfy the interests of newly independent States": "It would be odd if a newly independent State would not be entitled to invoke the responsibility of a wrongdoing State for injury affecting its territory or population before it became

103 Ibid para 45.

104 Greece, letter sent to the UN GA Sixth Committee, Rep. 76th sess., Nov. 2021. See also, ibid, Rep. 77th sess., 2 Nov. 2022.

105 ILC Special Rapporteur Šturma, Fourth Report, 2020, para 63, explaining that whenever there is such a link, "it is possible for compensation to be requested (…) by the successor State provided that this State continues to (…) bear injurious consequences of the internationally wrongful act".

106 Ibid para 136.

107 ILC Report, 71st sess., 2019, A/74/10, 2019, chap. VII, paras 72–118, at para 84.

108 ILC, Statement, Park, 2022, 10. See also: ILC, Commentaries, 2022, para 89, Art. 12, subpara 7.

independent".[109] In my view, this comment also applies in the context of separation outside the specific context of decolonisation.

As further examined in the next section, State practice in the context of separation shows the existence of examples in favour of both principles of succession and non-succession. The first example, an agreement between Russia and France, is an illustration of the principle that the continuing State remains entitled to claim reparation for wrongs committed before the date of succession. Two other examples of State practice have been found where the successor States were allowed to claim reparation for internationally wrongful acts committed before the date of succession. In these two cases, the parties accepted that the right to reparation be transferred to a new State since it was considered the injured State.

3.3.2 The 1997 Agreement Entered into by Russia and France on Reparation for Expropriation of Bonds after the 1917 Russian Revolution

In the context of the break-up of the USSR, a final settlement of reciprocal financial and property demands was entered into in 1997 between Russia and France.[110] As explained above,[111] the Agreement provided for Russia to compensate France in the amount of US$ 400 million in exchange for guarantees that France would not exercise diplomatic protection for claims of French nationals and corporations against Russia arising out of the non-payment of bonds expropriated after the 1917 Revolution. Russia agreed not to pursue claims for reparation which the USSR had for many years against France. Article 2 (al. a) of the Agreement thus refers to the claims linked to the "Western intervention" of 1918–1922 and other military or hostile operations undertaken by Western States (including France) against the new Soviet government during that period.[112]

109 ILC, Commentaries, ibid sub-para 6.

110 *Accord du 27 mai 1997 entre le Gouvernement de la République française et le Gouvernement de la Fédération de Russie sur le règlement définitif des créances réciproques financières et réelles apparues antérieurement au 9 mai 1945*, Bill No. 97–1160 (*JORF* no. 295, December 1997, 18453) passed by the French National Assembly on 19 December 1997 approving the Agreement and the Memorandum (*JORF* 15 May 1998).

111 This Agreement was discussed in detail in Part 2, Chapter 2, Section 6.2.4.3.

112 These claims are analysed by Michel Cosnard, "Les créances au titre de l'intervention occidentale de 1919–1922", in: P. Juillard & B. Stern (eds), *Les emprunts russes et le règlement du contentieux financier franco-russe* (Cahiers internationaux n°16 2002) 121–149. Art. 2 (al. c) also deals with the renunciations by Russia of "claims" ("créances") including gold deposited in France. See, Geneviève Burdeau, "L'or russe dans le règlement du contentieux financier franco-russe", in: Juillard, ibid 151–169.

From the information available, it does not appear that France objected to the fact that such claims for reparation were part of the negotiations leading to the Agreement. This is certainly because France considered Russia to be the legal "continuator" of the USSR. As such, it remained entitled to submit a claim for reparation arising from damage which occurred before the break-up of the USSR.[113] This is an illustration of the basic principle of the continuity of claims to reparation adopted by both the Institute and the ILC.[114]

3.3.3 The 1946 Agreement on Reparation from Germany in the Context of the Separation of Pakistan (1947)

After the Second World War, an agreement was reached in 1946 for the establishment of an Inter-Allied Reparation Agency for the equitable distribution among several States of the total assets declared to be available as reparation from Germany.[115] The Dominion of India was a party to the Treaty, i.e. before India formally became an independent State (in August 1947) pursuant to the *Indian Independence Act (1947)*.[116] As mentioned above,[117] Pakistan has been viewed as having seceded from India in 1947.[118] The Governments of India and Pakistan reached an agreement on 22 January 1948 under which they agreed on the division of the share of reparation allocated to India under the 1946 Agreement. This agreement between India and Pakistan led to the conclusion of an *Additional Protocol* to the 1946 Agreement which was entered into on 15 March 1948. The *Additional Protocol* indicates that Pakistan "shall be deemed to have been a Government signatory of the [1946] Paris Agreement, as from

113 It should be noted that the USSR (which was officially created in 1922) was itself the continuing State of the Russian State which emerged after the 1917 Revolution. In that sense, the Russian Federation is the *continuing State* of the *continuing State* of the Russian State which existed between 1917 and 1922.

114 Kohen & Dumberry, 94–5; ILC Special Rapporteur Šturma, Third Report, 2019, para 53.

115 *Agreement on Reparation from Germany, on the Establishment of an Inter-Allied Reparation Agency and on the Restitution of Monetary Gold*, 14 January 1946, in force on 24 January 1946, 555 *UNTS* 69. The Agreement determined the percentage that each State would receive in terms of war reparation.

116 *Indian Independence Act (1947)*, 10 and 11 Geo. VI, c. 30; LR Statues 1947.

117 This example was discussed in Part 2, Chapter 2, Section 7.2.1.

118 India has generally been considered the *continuing State* of the British Dominion of India. See, *Indian Independence (International Arrangements) Order*, Gaz. India Extra, 14 August 1947. For this reason, this exemple involving Pakistan is examined in this Section dealing with separation.

the date of the entry into force of the said Agreement, with corresponding rights and obligations".[119]

This example shows that all Parties to the international treaty accepted that a new State (Pakistan) could claim reparation arising out of internationally wrongful acts committed by Germany during the Second World War at a time when that new State did not exist. This example is, in fact, also an illustration that *both* the continuing State and the successor State can in some circumstances be considered to be the injured States.[120]

3.3.4 The 1958 Protocol Entered into by the USSR and the GDR for the Restitution of Cultural Properties

As already mentioned,[121] the victory of the Soviet Red Army in 1945 was followed by the pillage of some 2.5 million works of art and cultural property which were transferred from Germany to the Soviet Union. The question of the restitution of these cultural properties is still not settled between Russia and "unified" Germany. Another solution prevailed with respect to the GDR, which was considered to have "seceded" from the rest of Germany in 1949.[122] A Protocol was entered into by the USSR and the GDR in 1958 for the restitution of some of the art treasures, books and archives which had been taken away by the Red Army from the territory of Germany.[123] It is estimated that some 1.9 million cultural objects belonging to German owners were returned by the USSR to the GDR.[124]

This is a clear example of State practice where the State responsible for the commission of an internationally wrongful act (the USSR) provided reparation (in the form of restitution) to a new State (the GDR) even if that State did not exist at the time when the act was committed.[125] It should be noted that the

119 *Additional Protocol to the Agreement on Reparation from Germany, on the Establishment of an Inter-Allied Reparation Agency, and on the Restitution of Monetary Gold of 14 January 1946*, 15 March 1948, in force on 15 March 1948, 555 *UNTS* 104.

120 ILC Special Rapporteur Šturma, Third Report, 2019, para 55.

121 This example is discussed in Part 2, Chapter 2, Section 6.2.4.2.

122 This point is discussed in Part 2, Chapter 2, Sections 6.2.3 and 6.3.3.

123 The Protocol was signed on 8 September 1958 and the Final Protocol on 29 July 1960. See, M. Boguslavsky, "Legal Aspects of the Russian Position in Regard to the Return of Cultural Property", in: Elizabeth Simpson (ed): *The Spoils of War. World War II and Its Aftermath: The Loss, Reappearance, and Recovery of Cultural Property* (Harry N. Abrams 1997) 189; Petra Kuhn, "Comment on the Soviet Returns of Cultural Treasures Moved because of the War to the GDR", *Spoils of War, Newsletter*, no. 2, 1996.

124 This figure is provided in: Kuhn, ibid.

125 The example is mentioned in: ILC Special Rapporteur Šturma, Third Report, 2019, para 56.

decision by the USSR to provide reparation was undoubtedly politically motivated in the context of the Cold War.

It should be added that during the debate at the ILC, one member, Professor Nolte, explained that he had "doubt" that the "case could be said to constitute a meaningful precedent in the context of the topic".[126] This is because, at the time, the USSR did not consider the pillage as a wrongful act, the GDR did not regard the return of the object as a form of reparation, and, finally, none of the States concerned had "regarded the matter as one that involved succession of States in respect of State responsibility".[127] Another member also noted that "from the text of the protocol, it was clear that the return of property thereunder was in no way interpreted as restitution in connection with an internationally wrongful act".[128] On the last point, it is very rare to find any example where the States involved openly refer to a matter of contention between them as one involving specifically an issue of State succession to responsibility. In my view, given the highly politically sensitive context of the Cold War (when the GDR was generally considered a "puppet" of the USSR), what matters is not so much what may have (possibly) been the perception of these States about the event, but rather what they actually did. Considering the completely imbalanced power relationship prevailing between the parties back then, it is not surprising that the agreement was not openly portrayed as one involving reparation to compensate a wrong done in the past. It is true, however, as noted by Nolte, that the fact many States did not consider the GDR a "new" State could suggest that it is not the strongest precedent involving secession. Yet, as mentioned above,[129] at the time the GDR *did* consider itself (since 1956) as a *new State*. It seems highly unlikely that this new position could have been taken without the approval of its "master" in Moscow. In other words, when the agreement was signed both parties considered the GDR as new State.

126 ILC, "Provisional Summary Record of the 3477th Meeting", 73rd sess., 10 July 2019, A/CN.4/SR.3477, statement by ILC Member Georg Nolte (Germany), addressing this example mentioned in the Third Report, ibid.

127 Ibid.

128 ILC, "Provisional Summary Record of the 3479th Meeting", 73rd sess., 12 July 2019, A/CN.4/SR.3479, statement by ILC Member Zagaynov (Russia).

129 See, scholarship mentioned in: Part 2, Chapter 2, Section 6.2.3.

3.4 *Newly Independent States*

3.4.1 The Position Adopted in This Study and That of the Institute and the ILC

As a matter of principle, the emergence of a Newly Independent State does not jeopardise *per se* the colonial State's entitlement to compensation as a result of internationally wrongful acts committed by a third State before the date of succession. The (continuing) colonial State should therefore remain entitled to claim reparation for such acts. This principle was adopted under Article 5(1) of the Institute's Resolution applicable to all cases where the predecessor State continues to exist after the date of succession.[130] The same solution was also adopted in ILC Guideline 12(1). This solution has been endorsed by writers.[131]

Is there any exception to this principle of non-succession? In my view, the right to reparation should pass to the new State when it is that State which is still injured after independence. Article 16(4) of the Institute's Resolution refers to a right to reparation arising from a wrong committed before the date of the succession "by the predecessor State or any other State against a people entitled to self-determination". That right "shall pass after that date to the newly independent State created by that people".[132] This solution has since been endorsed by writers.[133] The *Chagos* advisory opinion provides an illustration of this principle.[134] It could also potentially be used in the broader context of reparation claims regarding past crimes relating to slavery.[135] As mentioned

130 See, Kohen & Dumberry, 35ff.

131 Ruy & Baecke, 16.

132 Kohen & Dumberry, 139ff.

133 Jakubowski, State Succession, 267–268; Andrzej Jakubowski, "Cultural Heritage and State Succession", in F. Francioni & A.F. Vrdoljak (ed), *The Oxford Handbook of International Cultural Heritage Law* (OUP 2020) 602 ("Arguably, it may provide a newly independent State which has emerged in violent circumstances with a strong legal argument against its predecessor and/or another State to which a wrongful act can be attributed and give it the right to claim reparation for the violation of cultural heritage obligations, in particular those established by humanitarian rules for the protection of cultural property").

134 *Legal Consequences of the Separation of the Chagos Archipelago from Mauritius in 1965*, Advisory Opinion, ICJ Rep 2019, 95.

135 More generally, see, Buser, 445 ("the law of State responsibility does not provide rights to reparations for today's States if they are neither identical nor succeeding past subjects of international law. Neither can Caribbean States invoke the law of diplomatic protection as direct victims have died before they became nationals of modern Caribbean States"). See also, Ruy & Baecke; Katarina Schwarz, *Reparations for Slavery in International Law* (OUP 2022) 94ff (examining issues of continuity and succession); Ana Paola Vergara Lamadrid, "Nada se destruye, todo se transforma: la exigibilidad de la obligacion de reparar en el marco de una sucesion de Estados", 40 *Agenda Internacional*, 2022, 103ff.

above, ILC Guideline 12(2) (which was never formally adopted by the ILC) merely indicates that the new State "may, in particular circumstances, be entitled to invoke the responsibility of the State that committed the internationally wrongful act". The Commentary refers to the territorial or personal nexus as one such "particular circumstances" and specifically mention that this language was "intended, inter alia, to satisfy the interests of newly independent States".[136]

I have found several examples of State practice in the context of Newly Independent States where the new State was allowed to claim reparation for internationally wrongful acts committed before the date of succession. In these cases, the new State was deemed to be the injured State. It should be noted, however, that three of these examples of State practice[137] concern claims *between* the predecessor State and the successor State. They do not involve wrongs committed by a third State.[138]

3.4.2 The Peace Treaties Entered into by Japan with Indonesia, Malaysia and Singapore after the Second World War

After the Second World War, Japan entered into several peace treaties with its Asian neighbours. Three of these treaties are relevant in the context of the present discussion as they were entered into with States which did not exist when the internationally wrongful acts were committed by Japan during the Second World War. This did not prevent Japan from making reparation to these new States. It accepted, as a matter of principle, that the successor States may be entitled to receive compensation. This is because it was clear that these new States were the ones still injured. The wrongful acts had been committed by Japan on what was now their territories, and their own populations were the primary victims of these acts.[139]

One such treaty was entered in 1958 with Indonesia, a former Dutch colony, which became an independent State shortly after the end of the Second World War. In Article 4 of the treaty, Japan indicated that it was "prepared to pay reparation to the Republic of Indonesia in order to compensate the damage and

136 ILC, Commentaries, 2022, at para 89, Art. 12, sub-para 6.

137 One example is in the context of the independence of Nauru and another in the context of that of Vanuatu. A third example concerns the right of Namibia to claim reparation from South Africa for the illegal occupation and other human rights violations.

138 The reasons why such examples are of limited value in the context of the present study have already been explained in Part 1, Section 4.6.

139 Kohen & Dumberry, 138; ILC Special Rapporteur Šturma, Third Report, 2019, paras 60–62.

suffering caused by Japan during the [Second World] war".[140] Japan agreed to supply products and services for the next 12 years, worth an amount of some Yen 80.3 billion (i.e. some US$ 223 million).[141] In return, Indonesia waived all its claims against Japan.[142] Another similar treaty was signed in 1967 with Malaysia, a former British colony, which became an independent State in 1957.[143] This agreement dealt with what is oddly referred to as the "unhappy events" which took place in Malaysia during the Second World War and provided for Japan to pay reparation in the amount of Yen 2.94 billion.[144] Finally, another treaty was signed in 1967 with Singapore after its separation from Malaysia in 1965.[145] An interesting feature of this last agreement is the fact that in this case the damage which took place during the Second World War was not caused to the predecessor State (Malaysia) but to the predecessor of the predecessor State (i.e. the UK, the former colonial power).

140 *Treaty of Peace between Japan and the Republic of Indonesia*, in force on 15 April 1958, 324 UNTS 227; 3 *Jap. AIL* 1959, 158; Weston & Lillich, 158.

141 One interesting feature of this agreement is the acknowledgment in Art. 4 of the fact that "the resources of Japan are not sufficient, if it is to maintain a viable economy, to make complete reparation for all the damage and suffering for the Republic of Indonesia and other counties caused by Japan during the war and at the same time meet its other obligations". This is a consistent feature in Japan's post-Second World War treaties. On this aspect, see: A. Levy, "The Persian Gulf War Cease-Fire Agreement Compared with the Japanese Peace Treaty in Terms of Reparations and Reconstruction, 10 *Dick. JIL* 1992, 541–566. The implementation of Art. 4 of this agreement was the object of a separate agreement: *Reparations Agreement between Japan and the Republic of Indonesia*, 323 UNTS 248.

142 Art. 4(2). Japan also waived (in Art. 5) its claims against Indonesia. This provision has already been discussed: Part 2, Chapter 2, Section 7.2.5.

143 *Treaty of Peace between Japan and Malaysia*, 11 September 1967, in force on 7 May 1968, 13 *Jap. AIL* 1969, 209; Weston & Lillich, 349.

144 The content of the agreement is similar to the one entered into with Indonesia insofar as it provided for Japan to "supply in grants to Malaysia the products of Japan and the services of the Japanese people, the total value of which shall be Yen 2.94 billion". Under the Agreement, all questions arising out of these events are "fully and finally settled" between the two States.

145 *Treaty of Peace between Japan and Singapore*, 21 September 1967, in force on 7 May 1968, 13 *Jap. AIL* 1969, 244; Weston & Lillich, 121. The Treaty indicated that "an early and complete settlement of questions regarding the unhappy events in Singapore during the last war would contribute constructively to the furtherance of the friendly relations" between the two countries and that, consequently, "Japan shall supply in grants to the Republic of Singapore the products of Japan and the services of the Japanese people, the total value of which shall be Yen 2.94 billion". The Agreement "completely and finally" settled all questions arising out of WWII.

3.4.3 The *Certain Phosphate Lands in Nauru* Case (1992) in the Context of the Independence of Nauru (1968)

In the ICJ *Certain Phosphate Lands in Nauru* case, Nauru filed an Application in 1989 instituting proceedings against Australia in respect of a "dispute ... over the rehabilitation of certain phosphate lands [in Nauru] worked out before Nauruan independence".[146] From 1947 until its independence in 1968, Nauru was a United Nations Trust Territory jointly administered by Australia, Great Britain and New Zealand, with Australia having effective administration. Nauru alleged Australia's failure to make any (or adequate) provision for the rehabilitation of the phosphate lands worked out in Nauru while under Australian administration.[147] Nauru also maintained that Australia had failed to "comply with applicable international standards in respect of the preparation for transfer of control by a predecessor in title or a predecessor responsible for the control and administration of territory".[148] In its Memorial, Nauru referred expressly to the existing rights of a people entitled to self-determination: "the people of a trust territory are an already existing international entity to whom duties are owed by the Administering Authority, both under the Trusteeship Agreement or otherwise under general international law".[149] This is an example of a situation covered by Article 16(4) of the Institute's Resolution.[150]

146 *Certain Phosphate Lands in Nauru, Preliminary Objections* (*Nauru v. Australia*), Judgment, 26 June 1992, ICJ Rep. 1992, 240.

147 It was more specifically alleged by Nauru that Australia had breached many of its obligations under international law, including an "obligation to respect the right of the Nauruan people to permanent sovereignty over their natural wealth and resources" ("Memorial", Nauru, v. I, April 1990, third Subm.). Another ground invoked was the "principle of general international law that a State which is responsible for the administration of territory is under an obligation not to bring about changes in the condition of the territory which will cause irreparable damage to, or substantially prejudice, the existing or contingent legal interest of another State in respect of that territory" (ibid Sixth Sub., see also at para 458).

148 "Application Instituting Proceedings", Nauru, 10 May 1989, para 48. The reasoning is further explained in "Memorial", Nauru, ibid, para 464, as follows: "The 'transfer' of the Island of Nauru to the Applicant State on independence is not to be regarded as a case of State succession operating against an assumption of a clean slate". Nauru maintained ("Memorial", ibid, para 467) that the general duty owned by Australia to it was "confirmed by the settled international practice" of Decree N° 1 of the United Nations Council for Namibia (examined below in Chapter 5, Section 3.4.5).

149 "Application", ibid para 48. The reasoning is further explained in "Memorial", ibid para 464: "[t]he emergence of a new State from the status of a trust territory in accordance with the principle of self-determination embodied in the trusteeship arrangements is not the emergence *ab initio* of an entirely new legal entity, but the emergence from a state of dependence of a people whose rights and status are already distinctly recognized, and to which the predecessor State is in principle accountable".

150 Kohen & Dumberry, 140.

Australia submitted several objections to the jurisdiction of the Court over the dispute. However, Australia did not object, as a matter of principle, to the right of Nauru as a new State to submit a claim for damage which occurred before its independence.[151] The Court could have refused to hear this case on the ground that any such claim for reparation could not be submitted by a new State not existing at the time the damage occurred. It did not. As such, it can be argued that the Court also implicitly recognised this right for a new State.[152]

3.4.4 The 1984 Exchange of Notes between Vanuatu and the United Kingdom

The Island of Vanuatu became an independent State in July 1980.[153] On 13 March 1984, it entered into an Exchange of Notes with the UK concerning "civil disturbances on the islands of Santo, Tanna and Malekula between May and August 1980" which provided for the UK to make an "*ex gratia* contribution" of some VT 142,068,023 "to assist the Government of Vanuatu to meet the cost of admissible claims".[154] The Notes thus cover damage for events which took place before as well as after the independence of the Island.[155] No objection was raised against the right of Vanuatu, as a new State, to submit a claim for damage which occurred *before* its independence.

3.4.5 Namibia (1990)

Before the independence of Namibia in 1990, the United Nations explicitly recognised its right, upon its independence, to claim reparation for damage against South Africa as a result of its illegal occupation.[156] The United Nations

151 In fact, in its "Preliminary Objection" (December 1990) and its "Counter-Memorial" (29 March 1993) Australia does not mention this issue at all.

152 ILC Special Rapporteur Šturma, Third Report, 2019, para 59. *Contra*: ILC, "Provisional Summary Record of the 3479th Meeting", 73rd sess., 12 July 2019, A/CN.4/SR.3479, comment by ILC Member Zagaynov (Russia) noting that Nauru "had not based its position fully on the rules applicable to succession" and that Australia "had also not regarded the case as one relating to succession or to the rights and obligations that it entailed".

153 Before its independence Vanuatu was known as the New Hebrides (an Anglo-French "Condominium" since 1906).

154 *Exchange of Notes between the Government of the United Kingdom of Great Britain and Northern Ireland and the Government of Vanuatu Concerning the United Kingdom Contribution Towards Compensation Claims Arising out of Civil Disturbance in Vanuatu in 1980*, 13 March 1984, *UKTS* 1984, no. 55 (Cmnd. 9293); Weston et al., 289.

155 The Notes also mentions that the contribution is "without prejudice to the position of the United Kingdom and does not amount to the admission of past, present or future liability" on its part and that it is a "full and final settlement" of claims arising of these events.

156 The example is mentioned in: ILC Special Rapporteur Šturma, Third Report, 2019, para 63; Kohen & Dumberry, 140.

also recognised such right for Namibia against other States, individuals and corporations. These two different aspects will be examined in the following two sections. I will also examine the issue of claims made in relation to crimes committed against the Herero people.

The Right to Claim Reparation against South Africa for the Illegal Occupation and other Human Rights Violations. The UN General Assembly and the UN Security Council repeatedly reiterated the illegality of South Africa's continuous occupation of Namibia.[157] The ICJ, in its advisory opinion of 1971, also stated that South Africa incurred international responsibility arising from this continuing violation of an international obligation.[158] Subsequently, the UN Security Council declared that "South Africa remains accountable to the international community for any violations of its international obligations or the rights of the people of the territory of Namibia".[159] More specifically, two UN General Assembly resolutions stated that upon its independence the new State of Namibia would have the right to claim reparation for human rights abuses committed by South Africa during the period of illegal occupation.[160] These resolutions clearly accepted, as a matter of principle, that the successor State (Namibia) would be entitled to claim reparation for internationally wrongful acts which were committed at the time it did not even exist.[161]

157 On 27 October 1966, the UN GA adopted Res. 2145 (XXI), whereby it decided that the Mandate was terminated, and that South Africa had no right to administer the territory of Namibia. Subsequently, UN SC Res. 264 (1969), 20 March 1969, approved the decision of the GA to terminate the Mandate. UN SC Res. 276 (1970), 30 January 1970, declared illegal the continued presence of South Africa in Namibia.

158 *Legal Consequences for States of the Continued Presence of South Africa in Namibia (South West Africa) notwithstanding Security Council Resolution 276 (1970)*, Advisory Opinion, 21 June 1971, *ICJ Rep. 1971*, 16. The Court stated (at para 118) that South Africa was accountable for any violations of "the rights of the people of Namibia". It also held that South Africa had the obligation to end the occupation and to withdraw its administration from Namibia.

159 UN SC Res. 301 (1971), 20 October 1971, para 4.

160 UN GA Res. 36/121, 10 December 1981, para 25, demanding "that South Africa account for all 'disappeared' Namibians and release any who are still alive and declares that South Africa shall be liable for damages to compensate the victims, their families *and the future lawful Government of an independent Namibia for the losses sustained*" (emphasis added). The same content is also found in UN GA Res. 38/36, December 1983, para 42.

161 This seems to be the position adopted by the UN Group of Experts in its Report of 18 December 1990 (E/CN.4/1990/7, 67) which requested a study on the damage caused during the period of occupation and the establishment of a mechanism by which equitable reparation could be provided. See, Raymond Goy, "L'indépendance de la Namibie" 37 *AFDI* 1991, 404.

The Right to Claim Reparation for Internationally Wrongful Acts Committed by other States, Individuals and Corporations under "Decree No. 1 on the Natural Resources of Namibia Enacted by the United Nations Council for Namibia". In its 1971 advisory opinion, the ICJ explained as follows what were the binding obligations of States (other than South Africa) in the context of the illegal occupation:

> States members of the United Nations are under obligation to recognize the illegality of South Africa's presence in Namibia and the invalidity of its acts on behalf of or concerning Namibia and to refrain from any act and in particular any dealing with the Government of South Africa implying recognition of the legality of or lending support or assistance to such presence and administration.[162]

It is in this context that "Decree No. 1 on the Natural Resources of Namibia" was enacted on 27 September 1974 by the United Nations Council for Namibia.[163] The Council, which was established in 1967, was expressly authorised to "promulgate laws, decrees and administrative regulations as are necessary for the administration of [Namibia]".[164] There is some controversy as to the binding

162 *Legal Consequences for States of the Continued Presence of South Africa in Namibia (South West Africa) notwithstanding Security Council Resolution 276 (1970)*, Advisory Opinion, 21 June 1971, ICJ Rep. 1971, 16, 58.

163 "Decree on the Natural Resources of Namibia", Add. Report of the UN Council for Namibia, 29 UN GAOR Supp. 24A, 27–28, A/9624/add 1(1975). The Decree was endorsed by UN GA Res. 3295 (XXIX), 13 December 1974, 29 UN GAOR Supp. 31, 106, A/9631 (1975). See, N.J. Schrijver, "The Status of Namibia and of Its Natural Resources in International Law. A Report to the UN Council for Namibia", A/AC.131/GSY/CRP. 13 July 1984; H. Booysen & G.E.J. Stephan, "Decree no. 1 of the United Nations Council for South West Africa", 1 *South African YIL* 1975, 63–86; Caleb M. Pilgrim, "Some Legal Aspects of Trade in the Natural Resources of Namibia", 61 *British YIL* 1990, 249–278; George R, Shockey Jr., "Enforcement in United States Courts of the United Nations Council for Namibia's Decree on Natural Resources", 2 *Yale Stud. World PO* 1976, 285–339; François Rigaux, *Droit public et droit privé dans les relations internationals* (Pédone 1977) 279–293; N.J. Schrijver, "Namibian Decree in National Courts", 26 *ICLQ* 1977, 81–96; Itse Sagay, "The Right of the United Nations to Bring Actions in Municipal Courts in Order to Claim Title to Namibian (South West African) Products Exported Abroad", 66 *AJIL* 1972, 600–605; François Rigaux, "Le décret sur les ressources naturelles de la Namibie adopté le 27 septembre 1974 par le Conseil des Nations Unies pour la Namibie", 9 *RDH* 1976, 467–483.

164 UN GA Res. 2248 (S–V), 19 May 1967. The Council was dissolved after the independence of Namibia by UN GA Res. 44/243, 11 September 1990. On the Council, see: Karin Arts, "The Legal Status and Functioning of the UN Council for Namibia", 2 *Leiden JIL* 1989, 194–220; Lawrence L. Herman, "The Legal Status of Namibia and of the United Nations Council for Namibia", 13 *Canadian YIL* 1975, 306–322; Ralph Zacklin, "The Problems of Namibia

force of laws, decrees and regulations passed by the Council.[165] Decree No. 1 forbade the prospecting, mining, processing, selling, exporting, etc., of natural resources within the territorial limits of Namibia without permission from the Council.[166] Most importantly for the present discussion, Paragraph 6 of the Decree stated that the *future government* of an independent Namibia could hold liable for damages individuals and corporations contravening the Decree.

The Council took legal action against corporations breaching Decree No. 1 in one case: *UN Council for Namibia v. Urenco UCN and the Netherlands* before the District Court in The Hague, Netherlands.[167] The Council asked for a court order prohibiting Urenco from carrying out further enrichment of uranium originating from Namibia; it also sought a declaratory judgment.[168] The Council did not actively further pursue the court case in The Hague. As a result

in International Law", *Rec. des cours*, v. 171, 1981–II, 308–339; Andreas Julius, *Der United Nations Council for Namibia* (Peter Lang 1989).

165 N.J. Schrijver, *Sovereignty over Natural Resources: Balancing Rights and Duties in an Interdependent World* (Univ. Lib. Groningen 1995) 140, defining the binding nature of these instruments under international law as "less than that of a binding decision of, say, the Security Council, but greater than that of an 'ordinary' General Assembly resolution or a law of a foreign State". See also: François Rigaux, "Le décret sur les ressources naturelles de la Namibie adopté le 27 septembre 1974 par le Conseil des Nations Unies pour la Namibie", 9 *RDH* 1976, 473. It has been argued by others that, on the contrary, the Decree had no binding force on UN members: Ralph Zacklin, ibid 320–321; H. Booysen & G.E.J. Stephan, "Decree no. 1 of the United Nations Council for South West Africa", 1 *South African YIL* 1975, 68.

166 It also gave the UN Council the power to seize such materials as well as any vehicle, ship or container which transported these illegally-obtained resources.

167 "Writ of summons", *Nauta van Haersolte*, no. VM/1 W 3720817, in, "The URENCO Case", 2(7) *Namibia Bull.* 1988. In this case, the Council summoned in 1987 the Dutch corporations of Urenco Nederland v.o.f. and Ultra-Centrifruge Nederland N.V. (as well as the Netherlands) to appear in the District Court in The Hague. It was alleged that during the 1970s the companies based in the Netherlands were involved in the processing of uranium originating from Namibia in violation of the Decree prohibiting the processing and refining of natural resources of Namibia without the permission of the Council. This case is analysed in: N.J. Schrijver, "The UN Council for Namibia *vs.* Urenco, UCN and the State of the Netherlands", 1 *Leiden JIL* 1988, 25–48; N.J. Schrijver, *Sovereignty over Natural Resources: Balancing Rights and Duties in an Interdependent World* (Univ. Lib. Groningen 1995) 140–143; Caleb M. Pilgrim, "Some Legal Aspects of Trade in the Natural Resources of Namibia", 61 *British YIL* 1990, 263ff.

168 It should be noted that the Council did not ask the Court for any compensation because paragraph 6 of the Decree stipulates that only the "future Government of an independent Namibia" (and not the Council) could hold liable for damages corporations contravening to the Decree. This aspect is further discussed in: Pilgrim, ibid 261–262.

of the independence of Namibia on 21 March 1990, the case was withdrawn. Namibia did not pursue this case upon its independence.[169]

What is relevant for the present discussion is not so much the fact that the new State of Namibia did not continue the proceedings started before Dutch courts or that it did not submit any other claims against States as it could have had under the Decree. What is relevant is the Decree explicitly recognising the right of the "future government of an independent Namibia" to make such claim for reparation against States as well as against any "person, entity or corporation".[170] At the time of the enactment of Decree No. 1, no State contested the legitimacy of Paragraph 6 of the Decree and the fact that the future State of Namibia could take over the right to reparation arising from internationally wrongful acts committed before its independence.[171] In fact, the right of the (future) State of Namibia to claim reparation from individuals or companies for their economic activities in Namibia during the illegal occupation was explicitly recognised in two UN General Assembly resolutions, both stipulating that the Assembly:

> Declares that all activities of foreign economic interests in Namibia are illegal under international law and that consequently South Africa and all the foreign economic interests operating in Namibia are liable to pay damages to the future lawful Government of an independent Namibia.[172]

This right of the future independent State of Namibia[173] to claim reparation was also recognised implicitly by two resolutions of the

169 Pilgrim, ibid 278 (at footnote 94).

170 Raymond Goy, "L'indépendance de la Namibie" 37 *AFDI* 1991, 404; François Rigaux, *Droit public et droit privé dans les relations internationales* (Pédone 1977) 286; Pilgrim, ibid 252, 262.

171 Some objections were raised by several States but not with respect to this eventual right of claiming reparation. Thus, the US, France and the UK were not in favour of the wide range of powers given to the Council and did not specifically endorse the Degree. The one State that did support the Council and the Decree was the Netherlands. This explains why a complaint was filed before Dutch courts. See, George R., Shockey Jr., "Enforcement in US Courts of the United Nations Council for Namibia's Decree on Natural Resources", 2 *Yale Stud. World PO* 1976, 303–304; Ralph Zacklin, "The Problems of Namibia in International Law", *Rec. des cours*, v. 171, 1981–II, 323–324; H. Booysen & G.E.J. Stephan, "Decree no. 1 of the United Nations Council for South West Africa", 1 *South African YIL* 1975, 72ff.

172 UN GA Res. 40/52, 2 December 1985, para 14; UN GA Res. 38/36, 2 December 1983, para 42.

173 For instance, UN SC Res. 283 (1970), para 7, whereby the SC "[c]alls upon all States to discourage their nationals or companies of their nationality not under direct governmental control from investing or obtaining concessions in Namibia, and to this end to withhold

UN Security Council as well as by another UN General Assembly resolution.[174]

Decree No. 1 and the above-mentioned resolutions are clear examples where the international community explicitly endorsed the right of the successor State to claim reparation for internationally wrongful acts committed by other States (as well as corporations and individuals) before the date of succession.

Reparation Claims Regarding Crimes Committed Against the Herero People. One last example involves reparation claims made by a new State for wrongs committed by the colonial power against the local population many decades before independence. Scholars have argued that Namibia would have a right to claim reparation for the crime of genocide committed by Germany against the Herero people at the start of the 20th Century.[175] Other writers have debated whether the actions were illegal under international law at the time.[176] Some private lawsuits were filed in US courts by representatives of the Herero people against Germany and German companies.[177] In 2004, Germany's Development Aid Minister accepted Germany's "historical and moral responsibility" in the massacre of some 65,000 members of the Herero tribe by German troops in Namibia. Yet, she refused to provide any compensation; economic aid would be provided instead. It is only in 2015 that Germany began to qualify its actions against the Herero people as genocide and war crimes.[178] On 28 May 2021,

protection of such investment against claims of a future lawful Government of Namibia". See also, UN SC Res. 301 (1971), 20 October 1971, at para 12, whereby the SC "[d]eclares that franchises, rights, titles or contracts relating to Namibia granted to individuals or companies by South Africa after the adoption of GA Res. 2145 (XXI) are not subject to protection or espousal by their States against claims of a future lawful Government of Namibia".

174 UN GA Res. 36/121, 10 December 1981, para 11: "Calls upon all States to prohibit companies of their nationality not under direct governmental control from investing or obtaining concessions in Namibia and to announce that they will not protect such investments against claims of a future lawful Government of Namibia".

175 Lynn Berat, "Genocide: The Namibian Case Against Germany", *Pace Int'l L.Rev.*, 1993, 165, 201, "[i]t is apparent that because the present German state may be seen as a direct legal continuation of the old Germany instead of the creation of a new sovereign entity, it, rather than South Africa and Namibia, should be accountable for acts which took place in Namibia earlier in this century". See also: S.L. Harring, "German Reparations to the Herero Nation: An Assertion of Herero Nationhood in the Path of Namibian Development?", 104 *W. Va. LR* 2002, 393; Jeremy Sarkin, *Colonial Genocide and Reparations Claims in the 21st Century: The Socio-Legal Context of Claims under International Law by the Herero against Germany for Genocide in Namibia, 1904–1908* (Praeger 2009).

176 Buser.

177 These claims are examined in: R. Anderson, "Redressing Colonial Genocide under International Law: the Hereros' Cause of Action against Germany", 93 *Cal. LR* 2005, 1155–1189.

178 See, the article published by the President of the German parliament, Norbert Lammert, in *Die Zeit*, 9 July 2015.

German Foreign Minister, Heiko Maas, stated that Germany will formally recognize the atrocities against the Herero and Nama people as genocide. It pledged the equivalent of US$ 1.3 billion over 30 years for development projects. In June 2021, a joint declaration was made by Germany and Namibia indicating that "Germany accepts a moral, historical and political obligation to tender an apology for [the] genocide and subsequently provide for the necessary means for reconciliation and reconstruction".[179] But it does not refer to the term "reparation".

This example is noteworthy even if it is slightly less relevant as it does not involve a third State. It demonstrates that Germany did *not* consider that the fact that the crimes had been committed many decades before independence was *an obstacle* preventing a new successor State from claiming reparations. In other words, Germany did not invoke the "traditional" doctrine of non-succession.

4 Conclusion to Chapter 5

Until recently, very few scholars addressed the question as to whether a successor State could claim reparation for internationally wrongful acts committed *directly* against the predecessor State by another State before the date of succession. When the first edition of this book was published in 2007, writers generally answered the question in the negative. The prevailing view was that when the predecessor State *continues to exist* (e.g., separation), the continuing State should remain entitled to submit a claim for reparation against the third State responsible for the commission of the internationally wrongful act. Therefore, the right to reparation should remain with the continuing State, it should not be transferred to the successor State. Similarly, when the predecessor State *ceases to exist* (e.g. dissolution) the conclusion reached by many authors was that there can be no transfer of the right to reparation to any of the successor States.

I have explained in this Chapter that the application of a general theory of non-succession always denying any transfer of the right to reparation could lead, in some circumstances, to unfair results. This is the case whenever the

179 Catherine S. Namakula, "Reparations Without Reparation: A Critique of the Germany–Namibia Accord on Colonial Genocide", *African Yb. of Int. Hum. L*, 2021.

consequences of an internationally wrongful act committed before the date of succession *continue* to negatively affect the territory or the population of the new State after its independence. I believe that whenever a successor State is still "injured" as a result of the commission of such an act, it should be allowed to submit a claim for reparation to the State responsible for the act. This solution should prevail in cases where the predecessor State ceases to exist. It should also be accepted when the predecessor State continues to exist. This approach has since been endorsed by the Institute's Resolution. Under Article 5(2), when the injury caused by an internationally wrongful act committed against a predecessor State "affects the territory or persons" of a successor State, that State can request reparation for the injury suffered.

State practice and case law also supports this conclusion. In the context of the dissolution of Yugoslavia, all successor States agreed to the transfer of the right to reparation. I have found several examples where the successor State claimed compensation for internationally wrongful acts which occurred before the date of succession, at the time when it did not exist as an independent State. In some cases, the State responsible for the internationally wrongful act provided reparation to the new successor State.[180] In many other instances, while no compensation was ultimately paid, I have found no indication that the State responsible for the wrong objected to any such claim based on the ground that the new State did not exist at the time the wrong was committed. That may be explained by the fact that the new States involved in these examples have rarely based their claims on the specific argument of succession to the right to reparation. A good example is the *Gabčíkovo-Nagymaros* case where, given the language used in the *Compromis* to submit a dispute to the ICJ, the successor State (Slovakia) could have easily based its reparation claim on this doctrine of succession, but did not invoke such an argument.[181] At the end of the day, the right to reparation is rarely invoked by States in their practice and is almost never addressed by judicial bodies in their decisions.

180 For instance, the 1958 Protocol entered into by the USSR and the GDR for the restitution of cultural properties. See also, the peace treaties entered into by Japan with Indonesia, Malaysia and Singapore after WWII, and the 1984 Exchange of Notes between Vanuatu and the UK.

181 In fact, Slovakia explicitly rejected the existence of any principle of succession to the right to reparation: "Counter-Memorial", Slovakia, v. I, 5 December 1994, paras 3.60ff. It did so, however, for tactical reasons to avoid any *responsibility* for internationally wrongful acts committed by Czechoslovakia before the date of succession.

Most importantly, the fact that an internationally wrongful act was committed before the date of succession is *not* treated in State practice and case law *as an obstacle* preventing a new successor State from claiming (and sometimes) receiving reparation. Ultimately, these examples do not support the existence of any "rule" of non-succession to the right to reparation.

CHAPTER 6

The Commission of an Internationally Wrongful Act Affecting a National of the Predecessor State

1 Introduction

This chapter deals with the question whether the continuing State or the successor State can submit a claim for reparation for an internationally wrongful act committed by a third State (before the date of succession) which affected *a national of the predecessor State* who later became a national of the successor State. Because the internationally wrongful act affected a national of that State, the issue involves the concept of diplomatic protection. Section 2 examines scholarship and my own view on the matter. The next section (Section 3) examines relevant State practice and case law.

2 Analysis of Scholarship

2.1 *The Rule of Continuous Nationality in Diplomatic Protection*

It is a well-known principle of international law that by the mechanisms of diplomatic protection a State takes up on the international level the claim of one of its nationals who has suffered injuries as a consequence of the commission of an act by another State. By doing so, it is generally admitted that the State "is in reality asserting its own rights, its right to ensure, in the person of its subjects, respect for the rules of international law".[1] Since a State is, in fact, "asserting its own right" when protecting one of its nationals by exercising diplomatic protection, it needs to ensure that such person is indeed one of its nationals. Some scholars are very critical of this assumption.[2] Suffice it to note here that the debate involves "the argument that it is the individual itself against whom the internationally wrongful act is committed and not the

1 *Mavrommatis Palestine Concessions case* (Jurisdiction), Judgment, 30 August 1924, PCIJ *Series A*, no. 2. The same explanation is found in: *Panevezys-Saldutiskis Railway* case, Judgment, 28 February 1939, PCIJ *Series A/B*, no. 76 (hereinafter "*Panevezys-Saldutiskis Railway* case").

2 For instance, D.P. O'Connell, *International Law* v. II (Stevens & Sons 1970) 1034. I have discussed their views in the first edition of my book (see, 362ff).

 DOI:10.1163/9789004703810_010

State of nationality of this individual who is in reality injured".[3] Whatever the merits of this argument, the fact remains that the requirement mentioned in the *Mavrommatis* case is recognised in Article 44(a) of the ILC's *Articles on State Responsibility*, which states that the responsibility of a State may not be invoked if "the claim is not brought in accordance with any applicable rule relating to the nationality of claims".[4] At the end of the day, as noted by the ILC Special Rapporteur, "the rejection of the Vattelian (*Mavrommatis*) fiction is not the only possible theoretical basis for questioning the rule of continuing nationality in its *absolute* form".[5]

The traditional rule of diplomatic protection concerning the nationality of claims is the principle of "continuous nationality". A first essential condition for a State to exercise diplomatic protection on behalf of a person is that such person must have its nationality at the time of the *commission* of the internationally wrongful act by the third State.[6] The second condition is that such person remains a national of that State at least until that State *takes up his/her claim*.[7] There is limited support in doctrine,[8] as well as in case law,[9] for requiring continuous nationality *beyond* the moment of the presentation of the claim and extending such a requirement (as the *Loewen* Tribunal did[10]) until the date the award is *rendered*.[11] ILC Special Rapporteur Šturma considered this approach "to be exaggerated and not supported in practice".[12]

Support for the rule of continuous nationality is, however, far from being unanimous. It has been suggested that it is not a rule of international law.[13] This is, for instance, the position of Umpire Parker in the *Administrative*

3 ILC Special Rapporteur Šturma, Third Report, 2019, para 101, providing an overview of the argument without endorsing that position.
4 ILC's *Articles on State Responsibility*, 2001.
5 ILC Special Rapporteur Šturma, Third Report, 2019, para 106, emphasis in the original.
6 Monnier, 68.
7 Ibid.
8 Jenning & Watts, 512–513; Crawford, Brownlie's, 436.
9 *Affaire des biens britanniques au Maroc Espagnol* (*Great-Britain v. Spain*), case no. 36 "Benchiton", Award of Umpire Huber, 29 December 1924, *UNRIAA* v. 2, 706.
10 *The Loewen Group, Inc and Raymond L. Loewen v. United States*, ICSID case No. ARB (AF)/98/3, Award, 26 June 2003, para 225.
11 M. Mendelson, "The Runaway Train: the Continuous Nationality Rule from the Panevezys-Saldutiskis Railway Case to Loewen", in T. Weiler (ed) *International Investment Law and Arbitration: Leading Cases from the ICSID, NAFTA, Bilateral Treaties and Customary International Law* (Cameron May 2005), 15, 27.
12 ILC Special Rapporteur Šturma, Third Report, 2019, para 89. See also, para 98.
13 Ian Sinclair, "Nationality of Claims: British Practice", 27 *British YIL* 1950, 130; Verzijl, v. VI, 723.

Decision No. V case[14] and the position of some members of the Institute,[15] as well as the one defended by Judge van Eysinga in his dissenting opinion in the *Panevėzys-Saldutiskis Railway* case.[16] It should also be noted that the rule of "continuous nationality" was not adopted in the 1960 Harvard *Draft Convention on the International Responsibility of States*[17] or by the ILA Rapporteur Orrego Vicuña in his "Interim Report" on diplomatic protection.[18] Some authors have suggested that the traditional rule should be dropped altogether.[19] These criticisms are also echoed in the work of the ILC's Special Rapporteur Dugard on diplomatic protection, for whom "[t]he traditional 'rule' of continuous nationality has outlived its usefulness" and "has no place in a world in which individual rights are recognized by international law and in which nationality is not easily changed".[20]

---

14 *Administrative Decision No. V*, US-Germany Mixed Claims Commission, Decision of Umpire Edwin B. Parker, 31 October 1924, *UNRIAA* v. VII, 119, 140, 143 (also *AJIL* 1925, 614): "Those decisions which have adopted [the rule of continuous nationality] as a whole have recognized it as a mere rule of practice. Usually they have been rendered by divided commissions, with one member vigorously dissenting. When the majority decisions in these cases come to be analyzed, it is clear that they were in each case controlled by the language of the particular protocol governing the tribunal deciding them".

15 See, the position of N. Politis, *Annuaire IDI* 1933, 487–488, challenging the proposal of the Institute's Rapporteur Borchard endorsing the rule of continuous nationality. The debate held at the Institute is examined in detail in Chapter 6, Section 2.4.4.

16 *Panevezys-Saldutiskis Railway* case, 34–35. His opinion is examined in detail in Chapter 6, Section 3.3.1.

17 *Draft Convention on the International Responsibility of States for Injuries to Aliens*, 15 April 1961, Louis B. Sohn & Richard Baxter, Harvard, 55 *AJIL* 1961, 579, Art. 23(6).

18 F. Orrego Vicuña, "The Changing Law of Nationality of Claims", Interim Report, ILA, 2000, 28, see Rules 8–10. He is of the view (see 37) that "the retention of the rule of continuance of nationality does not seem to find any longer justification in the light of the changing role of nationality as a requirement of diplomatic protection".

19 Eric Wyler, *La règle dite de la continuité de la nationalité dans le contentieux international* (PUF 1990) 133–134; M. Bennouna, "La protection diplomatique, un droit de l'État?" in: *Boutros Boutros-Ghali Amicorum Discipulorumque Liber. Paix, Développement, Démocratie*, v. 1 (Bruylant 1998) 245; Matthew S. Duchesne, "The Continuous Nationality of Claims Principle: Its Historical Development and Current Relevance to Investor-State Investment Disputes", 36 *Geo. Wash. ILR* 2004, 783, 801–802.

20 ILC, "Addendum to First Report on Diplomatic Protection", by John R. Dugard, Special Rapporteur, 20 April 2000, A/CN.4/506/Add.1, para 24. He refers to the "dubious status of the requirement of continuity of nationality as a customary rule" (ibid para 12) which is "emphasized by the uncertainties surrounding the content of the alleged rule" and in particular the question of the "date until which continuous nationality of the claim is required" (ibid para 16).

2.2 *The Application of the Rule of Continuous Nationality in the Context of State Succession*

The application of the rule of continuous nationality in the particular context of State succession has important implications with respect to the possibility for both the continuing State and the successor State to submit claims on behalf of persons injured as a result of internationally wrongful acts committed before the date of succession. Two situations must be distinguished (and will now be examined): when the predecessor State ceases to exist; and when its existence is, on the contrary, not affected by territorial changes.

In situations where the predecessor State *ceases to exist* (incorporation, unification, dissolution), nationals of the predecessor State will become nationals of the successor State at the date of succession. At the time of the commission of the internationally wrongful act by the third State the individuals injured possessed the nationality of the predecessor State and not that of the successor State. The strict application of the rule of continuous nationality would prevent the successor State from exercising its diplomatic protection on behalf of its "new" nationals. They are sometimes referred to as "late" nationals. Writers recognise this state of facts.[21] This is indeed the

21 Stern, Responsabilité, 354; Monnier, 68–69 ("comme en cas de succession d'Etats les sujets de l'Etat prédécesseur deviennent les nationaux de l'Etat successeur, ce dernier ne pourra pas faire valoir le prétention qu'avait l'un d'eux contre un Etat tiers, du fait de la rupture du lien de nationalité"); Dupuy & Kerbrat, 84–5 ("[l]e principe est que l'Etat successeur ne peut faire valoir les prétentions d'un ancien ressortissant de l'Etat prédécesseur à l'encontre d'un Etat tiers"); Guggenheim, 474 ("le droit à la protection diplomatique à l'égard d'un Etat tiers, droit qui naît au moment où a lieu l'acte illicite, ne passe pas à l'Etat successeur"); Nguyen Quoc Dinh, Patrick Daillier & Alain Pellet, *Droit international public* (6th edn, LGDJ 1999) 550 ("[l]'Etat successeur n'est pas habilité à exercer la protection diplomatique, en vue d'engager la responsabilité d'un Etat tiers, à raison d'un fait antérieur à la succession et qui a causé un préjudice à un ressortissant du territoire muté", see, however the 8th edition, by Daillier, Forteau, Pelet, 618–9, indicating that this rule results in the interests of individuals been sacrified and explaining that the ILC has adopted an exception for State succession); Louis Delbez, *Principes généraux du droit international public* (3rd edn, LGDJ 1964), 275–276 ("[i]l n'existe pas … de succession au droit à réparation de l'Etat prédécesseur. Cela est vrai même s'il s'agit d'un préjudice subi par une personne privée. L'Etat successeur n'est pas fondé à exercer la protection diplomatique à l'égard de cette personne, passée au nombre de ses nationaux, car le délit est antérieur à la mutation territoriale et que ses droits n'ont pas été violés en la personne d'un de ses ressortissants"); David Ruzié, *Droit international public* (14th edn, Dalloz 1999) 90 ("[e]n principe, un Etat C (Etat successeur) ne peut faire valoir les prétentions d'un ancien ressortissant de l'Etat A (Etat cédant) contre un Etat B"). See also, the same assessment made by these other writers: Booysen, 213; I. Seidl-Hohenveldern, *Völkerrecht* (Carl Heymanns 1987) 288; A. Verdross, *Völkerrech* (4th edn, Springler 1959) 198 (who makes, however, an

conclusion reached by the PCIJ in the *Panevezys-Saldutiskis* case, further discussed below.[22]

In the other situation where the predecessor State *does not cease to exist* (separation, Newly Independent States, transfer of territory), the successor State would also not be able to exercise diplomatic protection for its "new" nationals. This is because at the time of the commission of the internationally wrongful act by the third State the individuals injured did not have its nationality but only the nationality of the predecessor State.[23]

It has been suggested that in cases where the predecessor State does not cease to exist, there are circumstances where at least in theory, the continuing State could exercise such diplomatic protection.[24] This is indeed true in the case of the existence of a right of option of nationality when the person injured before the date of succession decides to keep the nationality of the continuing State. In such a case, the continuing State may espouse the claim of such person because there is no break in the chain of nationality. However, such a right of option is not always available, and even in cases where it does exist, an individual may decide not to exercise it. In this last scenario, the individual injured before the date of succession would become a national of the successor State. The continuing State could not exercise diplomatic protection for such person for the simple reason that he/she would no longer be its national at the time the claim is submitted. Thus, the rule of continuous nationality would prevent the continuing State from exercising diplomatic protection for individuals who used to be its nationals but have since the date of succession become nationals of the successor State.[25] A good illustration of that principle is the *Henriette Levy* case, which was decided by a US-France Commission in 1881.[26] The only possible exception to that rule is when the continuing State's

exception for "continuous" internationally wrongful acts which continue after the date of succession); A. Verdross & B. Simma, *Universelles Völkerrecht, Theorie und Praxis* (Dunker & Humblot 1984) 633–634; Marcel Sinkondo, *Droit international public* (Ellipses 1999) 327.

22 *Panevezys-Saldutiskis* case, 16–17. See, Section 3.3.1.

23 Suzanne Bastid, *Droit international public* (Univ. Paris les Cours de droit, 1976–1977) 582: "Les règles relatives aux dates auxquelles doit exister la nationalité subsistent même lorsqu'il y a eu cession de territoires et changement de nationalité à raison de la cession intervenue. Pratiquement, la protection diplomatique devient impossible".

24 Eric Wyler, *La règle dite de la continuité de la nationalité dans le contentieux international* (PUF 1990) 117: "L'Etat dont le lésé possédait la nationalité à l'époque de l'acte illicite devrait conserver son droit d'intervention".

25 Nguyen Quoc Dinh, Patrick Daillier & Alain Pellet, *Droit international public* (6th edn, LGDJ 1999) 550. See also: I. Seidl-Hohenveldern, *Völkerrecht* (Carl Heymanns 1987) 288.

26 See, Moore, History, v. III, 2514ff. The case is examined below in Section 3.3.3.

"own national interest" has been affected by the original injury to one of its nationals (who no longer has such nationality).[27]

Therefore, the conclusion remains the same independently of the question whether or not the predecessor State ceases to exist. The application of the rule of continuous nationality in the context of State succession:

- would prevent the *successor State* from exercising diplomatic protection on behalf of its *new nationals* because they were not its nationals at the time the internationally wrongful act was committed; and
- would prevent the *continuing State* from exercising diplomatic protection on behalf of its *former nationals* for the reason that they are no longer its nationals at the time a claim is presented to the State responsible for the commission of the internationally wrongful act.

In other words, the application of the rule of continuous nationality in the context of State succession would result in neither the continuing State nor the successor State being able to exercise diplomatic protection on behalf of an individual injured as a result of an internationally wrongful act committed before the date of succession. ILC Special Rapporteur Šturma speaks of a "rupture of the nationality link".[28] Given that no State is entitled to seek redress against the State responsible, the internationally wrongful act would remain unpunished.[29] The same framework of analysis has been followed by both the Institute[30] and the ILC.[31]

2.3 *The Parties Are Free to Exclude the Application of the Rule of Continuous Nationality*

Since the rule of continuous nationality is *not* a peremptory rule of international law, the parties are always free not to apply it in the context of State succession (as in any other context). This is accepted by scholars, even by

27 This principle was recognised at Draft Article 9(3), "Addendum to First Report on Diplomatic Protection", John R. Dugard, Special Rapporteur, 20 April 2000, A/CN.4/506/Add.1, explaining (at para 29) that this provision was added to "ensures the right of the State of original nationality to bring a claim where its own national interest has been affected by the injury to its nationals". See also, comments by H. Rolin, *Annuaire IDI* 1933, 479, 519–520.

28 ILC Special Rapporteur Šturma, Third Report, 2019, para 91.

29 Monnier, 70–71: "En cas de succession d'Etats, la règle de la permanence de la nationalité, imperméable à toute exception, laisse sans remède la violation de la norme internationale".

30 Kohen & Dumberry, 66–7.

31 ILC Special Rapporteur Šturma, Third Report, 2019, paras 90–91.

the strongest supporters of the rule.[32] This was also recognised by Arbitrator Barge in the *Orinoco Steamship Company* case.[33] The same assessment was made by Umpire Parker in *Administrative Decision No. v*, where he indicated that the rule of continuous nationality was an "established rule of international law" which may, however, be changed "by mutual agreement between the two governments parties to a particular protocol creating a tribunal for the adjudication of claims and defining its jurisdiction".[34] Similarly, in the 1928 Arbitral Award in the *Pablo Nájera* case decided by the France-Mexico Claims Commission, President Verzijl observed that the rule of continuous nationality does not apply when the circumstances of the case show that it is the intention of the parties to exclude it.[35]

In the *Panevezys-Saldutiskis Railway* case before the PCIJ,[36] both the claimant (Estonia)[37] and the respondent (Lithuania)[38] agreed to this principle. The

32 E.M. Borchard, "La protection des nationaux à l'étranger et le changement de nationalité d'origine", 14 *RDILC* 1933(no. 3), 421, 446. See also, 463: "Il n'y a toutefois pas de raison pour que deux Etats ne puissent, s'ils le désirent, au cas où l'un d'entre eux succède à l'autre, convenir que l'Etat successeur, plutôt que l'ancien Etat, continuera à appuyer les réclamations internationales de ceux qu'il acquiert comme nationaux, sans le consentement de ceux-ci. Pareil traité modifierait le droit coutumier existant mais il peut y avoir quelque motif de procéder à ces modifications. Il n'est pourtant pas possible de forcer les Etats défendeurs à respecter semblable traité et à accepter les réclamations du ressortissant d'un Etat qui, par suite de cession de territoire, est devenu national d'un second Etat. Tout ce qu'on peut faire est d'exprimer l'espoir ou de formuler le voeu que pareils traités soient respectés et il se peut qu'avec le temps le droit résultant des traités deviendra droit coutumier". The same opinion is expressed by these authors: A. de Lapradelle & N. Politis, *Recueil des arbitrages internationaux*, v. III, 1872–1875 (Pedone 1954) 100–101 (footnote no. 1); Cecil Hurst, "Nationality of Claims", 7 *British YIL* 1926, 163, 182; Atlam 178; E.M. Borchard, "La protection diplomatique des nationaux à l'étranger", Rap. Suppl., *Annuaire IDI* 1933, Session of Oslo, 235ff, 244.

33 *Orinoco Steamship Company* case, US-Venezuela Mixed Claims Commission, *UNRIAA* v. IX, 180, 192.

34 *Administrative Decision No. v*, US-Germany Mixed Claims Commission, Decision of Umpire Edwin B. Parker, 31 October 1924, *UNRIAA* v. VII, 119, 140, 141. See also, the same view expressed by US Commissioner, Mr Anderson, in his sep. op.

35 *Pablo Nájera (France) v. Mexico*, Decision no. 30–A, 19 October 1928, *UNRIAA* v. V, 466, 488 (hereinafter "*Pablo Nájera* case"). This case is examined in: Section 3.1.1.

36 *Panevezys-Saldutiskis Railway* case. This case is examined in: Section 3.3.1.

37 "Observations et conclusions du gouvernement estonien", 20 April 1938, PCIJ, *Serie C, Pleadings, Oral Statements and Documents*, Judicial Year 1938–1939, no. 86, 176, 191–192.

38 "Pleadings ('Exposé') of Prof. Mandelstam, Agent for Lithuania", 13 June 1938, ibid 430, 434: "[D]'après le droit international … un gouvernement ne peut régulièrement porter un procès devant la juridiction internationale que si la demande est nationale au moment du préjudice subi. Il est vrai que tout gouvernement peut, par un traité, écarter cette règle. Mais, dans chaque cas particulier, il faut alors démontrer qu'un accord pareil est

Court also acknowledged that the rule applies "in the absence of a special agreement" between the parties and that there "are cases where the government concerned had agreed to waive the strict application of the rule" and to establish tribunals with jurisdiction to adjudicate claims "even if this condition as to nationality were not fulfilled".[39]

2.4 *The Rule of Continuous Nationality Is Not Appropriate in the Context of State Succession*

Many authors, the work of the ILC on diplomatic protection and that of the Institute, support the proposition that the application of a strict rule of continuous nationality is not appropriate in the context of State succession (Sections 2.4.2, 2.4.3, and 2.4.4). There is also support for this proposition in at least two decisions of international tribunals and in some individual and dissenting opinions of judges in two cases before the PCIJ and the ICJ (Section 2.4.1).

2.4.1 Case Law

The traditional rule of continuous nationality was firmly criticised by Judge van Eysinga in his dissenting opinion in the *Panevezys-Saldutiskis Railway* case before the PCIJ.[40] He was of the view that this rule of law which prevents the successor State from "espous[ing] any claim of any of its new nationals in regard to injury suffered before the change of nationality" leads to "inequitable results". This is the full paragraph of his reasoning:

> And in this connection the question also arises whether it is reasonable to describe as an unwritten rule of international law a rule which would entail that, when a change of sovereignty takes place, the new State, or the State which has increased its territory would not be able to espouse any claim of any of its new nationals in regard to injury suffered before the change of nationality. It may also be questioned whether indeed it is part of the Court's task to contribute towards the crystallisation of unwritten rules of law which would lead to such inequitable results. It follows from the foregoing that the Lithuanian Agent has not succeeded in establishing the existence, in the absolute form alleged by him, of the rule of international law to the effect that a claim must be a national

intervenu. Le Gouvernement lithuanien n'a conclu aucun traité avec le Gouvernement estonien et n'a pris aucun engagement envers ce Gouvernement, par lesquels il aurait renoncé à cette règle générale du droit international".

39 *Panevezys-Saldutiskis Railway* case, 16.

40 Ibid. His opinion is examined in: Section 3.3.1.

> claim not only at the time of its presentation but also at the time when the injury was suffered, and that this rule cannot resist the normal operation of the law of state succession.[41]

Judge Fitzmaurice, in his individual opinion in the *Barcelona Traction* case before the ICJ, also criticised the rule of continuous nationality and its application in the context of State succession. He indicated that when the change in nationality is involuntary (such as in cases of State succession) the rule "would work injustice", as it deprives new nationals of the successor State of any possibility of redress for past internationally wrongful acts.[42] In his view:

> too rigid and sweeping an application of the continuity rule can lead to situations in which important interests go unprotected, claimants unsupported and injuries unredressed, not on account of anything relating to their merits, but because purely technical considerations bring it about that no State is entitled to act.[43]

In his individual opinion in the same case, Judge Jessup agreed with the comments made by Judge Fitzmaurice and suggested that the rule of continuous nationality should not apply in the context of State succession.[44]

---

41 Ibid 35.

42 *Case Concerning the Barcelona Traction, Light and Power Company, Limited* (*Second Phase*) (Belgium v. Spain), Judgment, 5 February 1970, ICJ Rep. 1970, 3, ind. Op. Judge Fitzmaurice, 65, 100–101. This is the full paragraph of his reasoning: "Thus a rigid application [of the rule of continuous nationality], though justified where necessary to prevent abuses, should be eschewed where it would work injustice ... A clear case of this would be where the change in nationality was involuntary, e.g., because of a re-alignment of State boundaries ... Or again, why should the fact that a former dependent territory attains independence and become a separate State deprive whole categories of claimants in that State of all possibility of redress? Such would however be the effect of the continuity rule, for there would technically have been a change in the claimant's nationality, and the former sovereign or protecting State could no longer sustain the claim, while the new one also could not or, according to the doctrines involved, should not be able to do so, because the private claimant was not, at the time of the injury, its national,—or alternatively because, since the later State did not then exist as a separate State, it could not itself, *qua* what it now is, have suffered any wrong in the person of its national".

43 Ibid.

44 Ibid individual opinion of Judge Jessup, 162, 203: "Sir Gerald Fitzmaurice makes a forceful argument against any 'too rigid and sweeping' application of the continuity rule, but I believe his illustrative situation in paragraph 62 of his separate opinion may be covered by another rule deriving from the law of State succession, and on that basis would escape the application of the continuity rule for international claims which I consider to be generally binding—*specialia generalibus derogant*".

The proposition that the rule of continuous nationality should not apply in a strict manner in the context of changes of nationality occurring following a succession of States is also supported by President Verzijl in the *Pablo Nájera* case before the France-Mexico Claims Commission:

> Le cas présent diffère essentiellement des hypothèses dans lesquelles un individu, ressortissant de l'Etat A à l'époque des dommages, devient après cette époque et avant la date de la réclamation, ressortissant de l'Etat B de son propre fait. *Dans le cas de changements collectifs de nationalité en vertu d'un titre de succession d'Etats, la situation juridique doit être appréciée d'une manière beaucoup moins rigide* que ne le fait généralement la pratique arbitrale dans les hypothèses normales de changement individuel de nationalité par le fait volontaire de l'intéressé.[45] (emphasis added)

Echoes of the unjust consequences which might result from the application of a strict rule of continuous nationality can also be found in *Administrative Decision No. V* decided by Umpire Parker of the US-Germany Mixed Claims Commission.[46]

2.4.2 Scholarship

There is support for the proposition that the application of the rule of continuous nationality should depend on whether the change of nationality was

45 *Pablo Nájera* case, 488; AD 1927–1928, 52. This case is examined in detail in: Section 3.1.1.

46 *Administrative Decision No. V*, US-Germany Mixed Claims Commission, Decision of Umpire Edwin B. Parker, 31 October 1924, UNRIAA v. VII, 119, 140, 141–143: "The general practice of nations not to espouse a private claim against another nation that does not in point of origin possess the nationality of the claimant nation has not always been followed. And that phase of the alleged rule invoked by the German Agent which requires the claim to possess continuously the nationality of the nation asserting it, from its origin to the time of its presentation or even to the time of its final adjudication by the authorized tribunal, is by no means so clearly established as that which deals with its original nationality. Some tribunals have declined to follow it. Others while following it, have challenged its soundness. The application in all of its parts of the rule invoked by the German Agent to a privately-owned claim in which the nationality has changed by voluntary or involuntary transfer since the right accrued would deprive the claimant of all remedy for its enforcement through diplomatic intervention. The practical effect would frequently be to deprive the owner of his property. *As the rule in its application necessarily works injustice, it may well be doubted whether it has or should have a placed among the established rules of international law.* Those decisions which have adopted it as a whole have recognized it as a mere rule of practice" (emphasis added).

voluntary or involuntary.[47] Many scholars believe that the application of the traditional rule of continuous nationality may lead to unjust results when changes of nationality are *involuntary*, such as in cases of State succession.[48] This is indeed the position of ILC Special Rapporteur Šturma.[49] The application of the rule means that nationals of the successor State are left without any possible redress for internationally wrongful acts suffered at the time they were nationals of another State.[50] The fact that the application of the rule in

47 This is, for instance, the position of: Crawford, Brownlie's, 437; Atlam, 157, 180–182. *Contra*: O'Connell, *International Law*, v. II, Stevens & Sons, 1970, 1036 (for whom "a sharp distinction between voluntary and involuntary changes of nationality, with a limitation of the doctrine of continuous nationality to the former, seem of little value"); H.F. Van Panhuys, *The Role of Nationality in International Law: An Outline* (A.W. Sythoff 1959) 93 ("the tendency to make a distinction between a voluntary and an involuntary change of nationality must raise a host of problems").

48 Rousseau, v. V, 119 ("il est parfaitement inique de refuser toute réparation aux particuliers en raison de changements accidentels (décès) ou imposés (mutations territoriales) affectant leur statut juridique"); Atlam, 154, 182, see 184 ("[l]a distinction entre les changements volontaires et les changements collectifs de la nationalité conduit ainsi à neutraliser la règle de la continuité de la nationalité lorsqu'un tel changement se réalise du fait d'une succession d'Etats"). A. de Lapradelle & N. Politis, *Recueil des arbitrages internationaux*, v. III (Pedone 1954) 99–100 (footnote no. 1), discuss the case law supporting the rule of continuous nationality and mention that it mostly relates to voluntary acts of individuals to acquire a new nationality. The authors conclude that "il serait imprudent d'étendre cette jurisprudence au cas où le changement de la nationalité est le résultat de circonstances indépendantes de la volonté des intéressés et où l'application automatique de la règle conduirait à priver les individus et les Etats de la possibilité de faire valoir leurs droits actuels devant les juridictions internationales". The authors further indicate (101, footnote no. 1): "il suffit de constater l'abandon de la règle étroite de la persistance de la nationalité de la réclamation en présence de circonstances de droit et de fait qui auraient rendu la règle appliquée dans sa lettre souverainement injuste". This is also the position of Verzijl, v. V, 449, for whom the application of the rule in cases of "massive change of nationality" is not reasonable. See also: Ulrich Fastenrath, "Der deutsche Einigungsvertrag im Lichte des Rechts der Staatennachfolge", 44 *ÖZöRV*, 1992, 39; Ruth Donner, *The Regulation of Nationality in International Law* (2nd edn, Transnational 1994) 252, footnote 17. *Contra*: Schwarzenberger, 600–601; John Dugard, "Continuous Nationality", in *Max Planck Encyclopedia of Public International Law* (OUP online ed 2006) para 11. The position of writers is examined in: ILC Special Rapporteur Šturma, Third Report, 2019, paras 100ff.

49 ILC, ibid para 106: "the cases of involuntary changes of nationality because of the change of sovereignty (succession of States) support an exception to that rule". See also: Šturma, State Succession, 671.

50 This is, for instance, the position of O'Connell, *International Law*, v. II (Stevens & Sons 1970) 1035–1036, expressing doubts that the rule of continuous nationality "has or should have a place among the established rules of international law" partially based on the ground that "the wholesale change of nationality forced upon peoples in this century" would "leaves a substantial body of alien rights without a practical remedy if the rule

the context of State succession would ultimately deprive "large numbers and extensive categories of persons" of their rights has been described as "offensive to the modern conception of the role of international law in protecting the individual".[51] Others have argued that the application of the rule of continuous nationality in the context of State succession in fact rewards the wrongdoer State, as its wrong goes unpunished.[52] For all these reasons, a growing number of authors are of the view that the rule of continuous nationality should not apply in the context of changes of nationality resulting from State succession.[53] This is also my position.[54]

2.4.3 The Work of the ILC

The work of the ILC's Special Rapporteur on diplomatic protection has clearly adopted the position that the traditional rule of continuous nationality should not apply in the context of changes to nationality resulting from State succession. For Special Rapporteur Dugard, the rule of continuous nationality "may cause great injustice where the injured individual has undergone a *bona fide*

---

of continuous nationality [was] rigorously applied". This is also the position of Charles De Visscher, "Cours général de droit international public", *Rec. des cours*, v. 136, 1972–II, 166: "La grande vague de décolonisation des années 60 a mis clairement en lumière le caractère inéquitable de cette règle dont l'effet a été de priver des millions d'individus de toute protection du chef des dommages illicites subis avant la date de l'accession de leur peuple à l'indépendance". The writer is of the view that the rule should be abandoned for all cases of State succession (and not only for Newly Independent States).

51 O'Connell, State Succession, v. I, 538–539. This is also the conclusion reached by Atlam, 18.

52 Gabriele Salvioli, "Les règles générales de la paix", *Rec. des cours*, v. 46, 1933–IV, 125–127 ("je n'aperçois pas pourquoi le changement de nationalité du lésé devrait profiter à l'Etat coupable; je ne comprends pas pourquoi cette circonstance devrait aboutir à laisser sans réparation un acte internationalement illicite"); D.C. Ohly, "A Functional Analysis of Claimant Eligibility", in: R. Lillich (ed), *International Law of State Responsibility for Injuries to Aliens* (UP Virginia 1983) 286 ("by leaving such claims uncompensated, strict application of the continuous nationality doctrine allows wrongful international conduct to remain unretributed, rewarding the State whose actions gave right to the claim with additional incentive to conduct itself in a similarly wrongful manner in the future").

53 Erik J.S. Castren, "Aspects récents de la succession d'Etats", *Rec. des cours*, v. 78, 1951–I, 487–488; O'Connell, State Succession, v. I, 538–539; Wilhelm Wengler, *Völkerrecht*, v. I (Springer 1964) 602; Crawford, Brownlie's, 436–7. This position also seems to be defended by Verzijl, Jurisprudence, 567–568 (analysing the *Panevezys-Saldutiskis Railway* case). *Contra*: H.F. Van Panhuys, *The Role of Nationality in International Law: An Outline* (A.W. Sythoff 1959) 91, indicating that "international judicial bodies show little inclination to adopt [the] view" that any exception should be made to the rule of continuous nationality in the context of State succession.

54 See: Patrick Dumberry, "Obsolete and Unjust: The Rule of Continuous Nationality in the Context of State Succession", 76(2) *Nordic JIL* 2007.

change of nationality, unrelated to the bringing of an international claim, after the occurrence of the injury, as a result, *inter alia*, of … cession of territory or succession of States".[55] He even took the more radical view that it would be "preferable to reject the doctrine of continuous nationality as a substantive rule of customary international law".[56] This is reflected in Special Rapporteur Dugard's draft Article 9 (al. 1).[57]

The Report of the ILC mentioned that "most members" did not approve the Special Rapporteur's proposal to abandon the traditional rule of continuous nationality altogether. They preferred to maintain the traditional rule "albeit subject to certain exceptions aimed at those situations where the individual would otherwise have no possibility of obtaining protection by a State".[58] Members of the ILC agreed with the Special Rapporteur that a "basic exception" should exist regarding the rule of continuous nationality in cases of "involuntary changes of nationality of the protected person, arising from succession of States". Another exception should exist for "situations where it would be impossible to apply the rule of continuity owing to, for example, the disappearance of the State of original nationality through dissolution or dismemberment".[59] Final Article 5(2) provides for an exception to the traditional rule of continuous nationality in the context of changes of nationality resulting from State succession:

> A State may exercise diplomatic protection in respect of a person who is its national at the date of the official presentation of the claim but was not a national at the date of injury, provided that the person had the nationality of a predecessor State or lost his or her previous nationality and acquired, for a reason unrelated to the bringing of the claim, the

55 ILC, "Addendum to First Report on Diplomatic Protection", by Mr John R. Dugard, Special Rapporteur, 20 April 2000, A/CN.4/506/Add.1, at para 1. See also, para 21: "the doctrine of continuous nationality creates particular hardships in the case of involuntary change of nationality, as in the case of State succession".

56 Ibid at para 21.

57 Ibid. The provision reads as follows: "1. Where an injured person has undergone a *bona fide* change of nationality following an injury, the new State of nationality may exercise diplomatic protection on behalf of that person in respect of the injury, provided that the State of original nationality has not exercised or is not exercising diplomatic protection in respect of the injured person at the date on which the change of nationality occurs".

58 ILC, "Report of the International Law Commission on the Work of its Fifty-Third Session", 23 April to 1 June and 2 July to 10 August 2001, ILC Report, A/56/10, 2001, ch. VII, 507ff, at para 177.

59 Ibid.

> nationality of the former State in a manner not inconsistent with international law.[60]

The same approach was initially adopted by ILC Special Rapporteur Šturma's recent work. He refers to the "modern approach to State succession" which rejects the application of the principle of continuous nationality in the context of State succession "for theoretical, jurisprudential and practical reasons".[61] The conclusion of his Report is that "while it accepts such a rule as a traditional condition in the law of diplomatic protection, it rejects its strict and absolute interpretation", adding that "consistent with the modern State practice, case law and doctrinal views, the report maintains the exception to the rule of continuing nationality in cases of State succession".[62] His approach has been supported by some States.[63] He put forward Draft Article 15 (entitled "Diplomatic protection", attached to his Third Report), which he described as providing the "possibility" (emphasizing that "this is not an automatic succession but a mere possibility"[64]) for the successor State to request reparation "under special circumstances":

> 1. The successor State may exercise diplomatic protection in respect of a person who is its national at the date of the official presentation of the claim but was not a national at the date of injury, provided that the person or the corporation had the nationality of a predecessor State or lost his or her nationality and acquired, for a reason unrelated to the bringing of the claim, the nationality of the former State in a manner not inconsistent with international law.
> 2. Under the same conditions set in paragraph 1, a claim in exercise of diplomatic protection initiated by the predecessor State may be continued after the date of succession by the successor State.
> 3. Paragraphs 1 and 2 are without prejudice to application of rules of State responsibility relating to the nationality of claims and rules of diplomatic protection.

60 ILC, "Draft Articles on Diplomatic Protection with Commentaries, Text adopted at its fifty-eighth session", 2006, (2006) II(2) Yearbook ILC.

61 ILC Special Rapporteur Šturma, Third Report, 2019, para 99.

62 Ibid para 137.

63 Slovakia, letter sent to the UN GA Sixth Committee, 74th sess. Rep. 5 Nov. 2019; Estonia, ibid rep. 74th sess, undated.

64 ILC Special Rapporteur Šturma, Third Report, 2019, para 136.

Importantly, having been criticized by some States,[65] the content of this provision was later deleted. ILC Guideline 15 (never adopted) simply states that "The present draft guidelines do not address the application of the rules of diplomatic protection in situations of the succession of States".

2.4.4 The Work of the Institute

The Institute discussed on two different occasions (in 1931–1932 and in 1965) issues related to the rule of continuous nationality and the question whether it should apply in the context of State succession. It also did more recently under the rapporteurship of Marcelo Kohen at the session of Tallinn.

The Session of Oslo (1932). The debate at the Institute on the rule of continuous nationality and its application in the specific context of State succession first arose at the session of Cambridge (1931). Several members of the Institute objected to the strict rule of continuity of nationality presented by Rapporteur Borchard. They argued that its application would be unfair in the context of State succession as it would leave the injured person without any possibility of legal redress since neither the continuing State nor the successor State could take over his/her claim.[66] Some members argued, consequently, that the successor State should be given the possibility to take over the claims of its new nationals.[67]

The question was fiercely debated at the Institute's subsequent session of Oslo (1932), when Rapporteur Borchard presented a supplementary report to the one he had submitted at the previous session of Cambridge (1931).[68] The Rapporteur rejected the proposal made by some members to amend the rule of continuous nationality in the context of State succession.[69] Several members

65 Netherlands, letter sent to the UN GA Sixth Committee, rep. 74th sess. 5 Nov. 2019 (indicating that the content of the provision "contains an attempt at redefining the law applicable to State succession and diplomatic protection"); Austria, ibid rep. 71st sess. 5 Nov. 2019.

66 IIL, "La protection diplomatique des nationaux à l'étranger", *Annuaire IDI* 1931–II, Session of Cambridge, 201ff. See the remarks by N. Politis, 206–207.

67 See the comments by M.F.L. De La Barra, ibid 210; J. Brown Scott, ibid 212. See also, the letter sent by M.F.L. De La Barra to Rapporteur Borchard, *Annuaire IDI* 1933, Session of Oslo, 263, 264.

68 IIL, "La protection diplomatique des nationaux à l'étranger, Rapport supplémentaire", *Annuaire IDI* 1933, Session of Oslo, 235ff.

69 Ibid 243–244: "En ce qui concerne la suggestion suivant laquelle les changements de nationalité survenus par suite d'une circonstance légale internationale pourraient justifier l'intervention diplomatique du nouvel Etat en faveur de son nouveau citoyen, il est admis que cette suggestion est aussi contraire au droit et qu'elle ne devrait pas être défendue par l'Institut". Rapporteur Borchard also stated (ibid 246): "Au lieu de demander extension de la protection diplomatique en s'écartant de ses bases fondamentales, la solution devrait consister, je pense, à autoriser les particuliers à présenter leurs demandes

of the Institute still opposed the draft resolution. This is, for instance, the position of Politis, for whom the draft resolution "prive l'individu qui a changé de nationalité de toute protection diplomatique, pour le dommage qu'il aurait subi dans le passé".[70] He believed that the successor State should be given the right to claim reparation from the State responsible for the commission of internationally wrongful acts on behalf of its new nationals. However, he made an exception for three different cases.[71] Other members of the Institute also expressed similar views.[72]

Ultimately, some members (led by de Lapradelle) submitted an alternative draft resolution to the Institute which included a provision (Article 6) setting aside the traditional rule of continuous nationality: "le lien de droit entre la personne et l'Etat, qui conditionne l'exercice de la protection diplomatique, doit exister au moment de la présentation de la demande".[73] This new draft provision was condemned in the strongest terms by Rapporteur Borchard:

> L'article 6 contient une idée dangereuse: en établissant comme règle que l'Etat dont l'intéressé serait devenu le ressortissant, reprenne la protection exercée auparavant par l'Etat dont l'intéressé aura perdu la nationalité. Cet article consacre une vraie anarchie internationale.[74]

directement devant une juridiction internationale sous certaines conditions et restrictions à définir dans un traité".

70 N. Politis, *Annuaire IDI* 1933, Session of Oslo, 479, 487.

71 Ibid 488: "A la vérité, la protection doit pouvoir s'exercer en faveur de l'individu, malgré son changement de nationalité, sauf lorsque celui-ci agit contre son gouvernement d'origine, ou ne se décide pour une nationalité nouvelle que dans un but frauduleux, en recherchant la protection d'un gouvernement fort, capable de donner plus de prise à sa réclamation. L'objection faite par le Rapporteur de la difficulté de prouver cette fraude n'est pas déterminante. La pratique diplomatique offre de très nombreux cas où semblable preuve a pu être faite". To these two exceptions, Politis added (522) a third one: when the internationally wrongful act concerns a particular treaty violation to which the successor State is not a party.

72 See, for instance, the position of B. De Nolde, ibid 495: "[L]a nationalité devrait persister au moment de la présentation de la réclamation, sauf cependant dans le cas d'acquisition d'une nationalité nouvelle à la suite d'un changement territorial". See also, the position of A. De Lapradelle, ibid 516: "[I]l n'est pas nécessaire que l'individu lésé possède la nationalité de l'Etat requérant au moment où le dommage est né. La conséquence du contraire serait que, si l'on se trouve sans nationalité, on ne pourrait dans aucune circonstance, faire respecter ses droits". See also, the view held by H. Rolin, ibid 519–520, and the comments by A.N. Mandelstram, ibid 521.

73 Ibid 501–503.

74 E.M. Borchard, ibid 506. He also indicated (ibid 512) that in State practice no State would accept the proposal made by some members that a State may espouse the claim of a new national after a change of nationality. A *post facto* criticism of the arguments advanced by

Rapporteur Borchard nevertheless finally accepted the following amendment to his original draft text: "(...) si le changement de nationalité se fait par acte politique, indépendamment de la volonté de l'individu, il est à désirer, que les deux Etats s'entendent au sujet de la protection à lui accorder".[75] The draft resolution initially submitted by Rapporteur Borchard was rejected by members of the Institute by a slim majority of 2 votes.[76] The Institute ended up not adopting any resolution on this question.

The Session of Warsaw (1965). The question whether or not the rule of continuous nationality should apply in the context of State succession was dealt with by the Institute at its Session of Warsaw (1965).[77] The first draft resolution proposed by Rapporteur Briggs contained a classic endorsement of the traditional rule of continuous nationality.[78] Many members of the Institute argued that the rule of continuous nationality should be modified in the context of State succession.[79] It was also submitted that this rule should be more flexible for Newly Independent States in order to allow them to espouse claims of their nationals who did not have such nationality at the time the internationally wrongful act was committed.[80]

---

some members of the Institute against his draft resolution can be found in: E.M. Borchard, "La protection des nationaux à l'étranger et le changement de nationalité d'origine", 14 *RDILC* 1933, 421, 441–442.

75 Ibid 515.

76 Ibid 524–525.

77 IIL, "La protection diplomatique des individus en droit international. La nationalité des réclamations", Session of Warsaw, September 1965, 51–II *Annuaire IDI* 1965, 157ff.

78 Ibid 159. Art. 1 reads as follows: "Toute réclamation internationale présentée par un Etat en raison d'un dommage causé à un individu est irrecevable si elle ne possédait pas le caractère national de l'état requérant, tant à la date du dommage qu'à la date de la présentation de la réclamation". Art. 2(a) reads as follows: "Une réclamation présentée en faveur d'un individu possède le caractère national d'un Etat lorsque cet individu est un national de cet Etat ou une personne que cet Etat a qualité, en vertu du droit international, d'assimiler à ses propres nationaux aux fins de la protection diplomatique".

79 For instance, see the position taken by Sir Kenneth Bailey, ibid 180–181: "Le projet dans la rédaction actuelle, n'assure pas une protection complète des individus, notamment lorsqu'il y a un changement dans la structure de l'Etat susceptible d'affecter la nationalité des nationaux entre la date du dommage et la date de présentation de la réclamation diplomatique". He proposed the following amendment: "Si l'Etat, dont l'individu victime d'un dommage est le ressortissant au moment de la réclamation, faisait partie de l'Etat dont il était ressortissant lors du dommage, la réclamation est recevable". W. Wengler, ibid 168–169 (See also, 214) indicated that since in the *Lighthouse Arbitration* case the principle of succession to the obligation to repair was endorsed by the Arbitral Tribunal, the same solution should also be adopted for succession to the right to reparation.

80 This is the position of W. Wengler, ibid: "[d]ans [les cas de fusion et de démembrement d'Etats] les règles relatives à l'admissibilité de la réclamation devraient donc être

Members of the Institute proposed an amendment to the above-mentioned Article 1 with the addition of two paragraphs.[81] This amendment proposition was backed by many members of the Institute.[82] Several members, as well as the Rapporteur, were, on the contrary, of the opinion that this issue should not be dealt with in the present resolution and should be deferred for further analysis.[83] A compromise was finally reached; it was agreed that a new paragraph should be added to Article 1 to deal specifically with "new States".

The resolution adopted by the Institute clearly states that there is an exception to the principle of continuous nationality for Newly Independent States, whereby they can submit claims on behalf of their new nationals even if those persons were not their nationals at the time the internationally wrongful act was committed by a third State.[84] Although it was observed that it was not

---

assouplies; cela est très important dans le cas des nouveaux Etats". Q. Wright ibid 196, indicated that "Si l'on applique avec rigueur la règle de la nationalité continue depuis la date du dommage jusqu'à celle de la présentation de la réclamation, les Etats nouveaux se verront interdire le droit de présenter des réclamations pour des dommages causés dans un passé très récent". He therefore proposed that "l'on insère une disposition de *lege ferenda* prévoyant l'exercice de la protection diplomatique par l'Etat national quelle que fût la nationalité de la réclamation à l'origine". J. Spiropoulos, ibid 199, agreed with the proposition made by Q. Wright, which he described as establishing "la règle générale qu'un Etat peut présenter une réclamation diplomatique en faveur d'un de ses ressortissants quelle que soit la nationalité de la réclamation à l'origine". He referred to such a proposition as "quelque chose de tout à fait nouveau, voire de révolutionnaire" but mentioned that "le fait que cela soit nouveau ne saurait d'ailleurs suffire à repousser la proposition. Il est nécessaire d'adapter les normes juridiques aux exigences du temps". See also, the view held by I. Forster, ibid 181, who made reference to "le cas des millions d'Africains qui ont possédé la nationalité française avant l'indépendance de leurs pays respectifs et qui ont pu subir des dommages à l'époque de la période coloniale". The author also mentioned (218 & 236) that the Institute should avoid causing a denial of justice to these millions of Africans "qui ont faim et soif de justice".

81 The amendment was proposed by W. Wenger and J. Andrassy (ibid 213) and reads as follows: "Les conditions de l'article premier sont considérées comme remplies dans les cas: (1). Où l'individu victime du dommage ressortissait à la date du dommage d'un pays qui était alors lié de telle manière à l'Etat réclamant que ce dernier est responsable des violations de droit international causées par les organes de ce pays; (2). Où l'individu victime du dommage a changé de nationalité par suite des changements territoriaux ou des changements du statut international du pays auquel il appartient".

82 K. Bailey, ibid 215; A. De Luna Garcia, ibid 216; I. Forster, ibid 218.

83 See the position of the following members: E. Jiménez de Aréchaga, ibid 193, 214–215; R.L. Bindschedler, ibid 215; E. Castren, ibid 215–216; M.F. Bartos, ibid 216; S. Rosenne, ibid 216; J. Spiropoulos, ibid 217; F.-A.F. Von Der Heydte, ibid 217; R. De Nova, ibid 219.

84 Art. 1 of the final resolution adopted by the Institute entitled "Le caractère national d'une réclamation internationale présentée par un Etat en raison d'un dommage subi par un individu" (ibid 260) reads as follows: "(a) Une réclamation internationale présentée par un Etat en raison d'un dommage subi par un individu peut être rejetée par l'Etat auquel

always easy to clearly distinguish "new States" from other types of State succession,[85] and that ultimately the principle embodied in Article 1 (para b) could also be applicable to other cases of succession of States,[86] the resolution of the Institute applies only to Newly Independent States.[87] It was also decided that the other question of the applicability of the rule of continuous nationality to other types of succession of States should be reserved for a later time (and was, in fact, never followed up on).[88]

The Session of Tallinn (2015). The Institute's Resolution adopted in 2015 contains a clause dealing specifically with matters of diplomatic protection arising in the context of State succession to responsibility. Article 10, which will be examined in the next section, reads as follows:

---

elle est présentée si elle ne possède pas le caractère national de l'Etat requérant à la date de sa présentation comme à la date du dommage. Devant la juridiction saisie d'une telle réclamation, le défaut de caractère national est une cause d'irrecevabilité; (b) Une réclamation internationale présentée par un *Etat nouveau* en raison d'un dommage subi par un de ses nationaux avant l'accession à l'indépendance de cet Etat, *ne peut être rejetée ou déclarée irrecevable en application de l'alinéa précédent pour la seule raison que ce national était auparavant ressortissant de l'ancien Etat*" (emphasis added).

85 See, comments by L. Mbanefo, ibid 235.

86 See, comments by K. Bailey, ibid 236; W. Wengler, ibid 213.

87 For instance, see this comment by J. Zourek, ibid 237: "Le grand nombre des nouveaux Etats qui ont accédé à l'indépendance dans les anciens territoires coloniaux constitue un argument suffisant pour motiver cette façon de procéder. Il semble pleinement justifié à l'orateur de reconnaître, par exception à la règle posée dans le paragraphe a) de l'article premier, que la réclamation internationale présentée par un des Etats constitués dans les anciens territoires non autonomes ne peut pas être déclarée irrecevable pour la seule raison que le national qui avait subi le dommage n'avait pas la nationalité de l'Etat réclamant au moment du dommage subi. Cette exception visant le cas des nouveaux Etats accédant à l'indépendance ne saurait évidemment pas s'étendre, en l'absence d'une règle de droit international contraire, aux autres cas de la succession des Etats". This question is examined by Jean Salmon, "La cinquante-deuxième session de l'Institut de Droit international", *RBDI* 1966–2, 579, 582; Atlam, 190–191; Charles De Visscher, "Cours général de droit international public", *Rec. des cours*, v. 136, 1972–II, 1, 166.

88 See the proposition by P.C. Jessup (ibid 218) and the vote (ibid 220). See also, the explanation given by the Rapporteur, ibid 234: "Le rapporteur répond que le paragraphe b) de l'article premier traite du cas particulier des Etats nouveaux. La commission a considéré qu'il fallait reconnaître une exception immédiate en ce qui les concerne. Pour les autres questions de succession d'Etats cependant, la Commission a considéré qu'il fallait les réserver en vue d'un examen ultérieur par la Commission". The preamble to the Resolution (ibid 260) indicates: "réservant plus spécialement pour un examen ultérieur les cas où l'individu qui a subi le dommage a changé de nationalité … par la suite de modifications territoriales de l'Etat auquel il ressortissait".

1. A successor State may exercise diplomatic protection in respect of a person or a corporation that is its national at the date of the official presentation of the claim but was not a national at the date of injury, provided that the person or the corporation had the nationality of the predecessor State or lost his or her previous nationality and acquired, for a reason unrelated to the bringing of the claim, the nationality of the successor State in a manner not inconsistent with international law.
2. A claim in exercise of diplomatic protection initiated by the predecessor State may be continued after the date of succession of States by the successor State under the same conditions set out in paragraph 1 of this Article.
3. A claim in exercise of diplomatic protection initiated by a State against the predecessor State may be continued against the successor State if the predecessor State has ceased to exist. In the case of a plurality of successor States, the claim shall be addressed to the successor State having the most direct connection with the act giving rise to the exercise of diplomatic protection. When it is not possible to determine a single successor State having such a direct connection, the claim may be continued against all the successor States. The provisions of Article 7 apply *mutatis mutandis*.
4. Where the predecessor State continues to exist and the individual or corporation possesses the nationality of both the predecessor and the successor States, or the nationality of a third State, the question is governed by the rules of diplomatic protection concerning dual or multiple nationality.

2.5 *The Successor State Has a Right to Claim Reparation on Behalf of Its New Nationals for Internationally Wrongful Acts Committed before the Date of Succession*

Along with the long list of authorities referred to in the previous sections, I believe that the consequences of the application of the strict rule of continuous nationality in the context of State succession would create a blatant injustice for the new national of the successor State insofar as he/she could not obtain redress for damage suffered before the date of succession. This outcome would be unfair since, in most cases, the *consequences* of the commission of the internationally wrongful act on an individual before the date of succession will continue to affect this individual even after the date of succession. This person will often remain injured quite independently of his/her change of nationality.

It has been suggested that the unjust consequences which might result from the application of the rule of continuous nationality in the context of State succession are in practice limited by the existence of a "right of option" of nationality. It gives individuals the option (at the date of succession) to choose between the nationality of the continuing State and that of the successor State. According to some writers, if the injured individual opts to keep the nationality of the continuing State, the right to reparation would not be affected, as this State could exercise diplomatic protection on his/her behalf after the date of succession.[89] In my view, this theoretical "limitation" to the hardship caused by the application of the rule of continuous nationality is in reality of little help and is also morally reprehensible. Thus, it ultimately forces individuals to choose their nationality solely based on their willingness to keep alive their rightful claims against another State. This "limitation" is also very limited in scope. On the one hand, it is not widespread and is not available in all cases of State succession. On the other hand, it cannot apply in the context of dissolution, integration and unification of States (where the predecessor State ceases to exist).

Since the rule of continuous nationality should not apply in the specific context of State succession, the successor State should, consequently, be allowed to claim reparation on behalf of its new nationals. This position is supported by scholars.[90]

---

89 This is the position of Schwarzenberger, 600–601, who interprets the right of option as one solution, whereby the rule of continuous nationality cannot be deemed to be unjust. He, however, admits that such a right of option may "cause hardship" to an individual "for in order to keep his claim alive an individual may have to accept other, and disagreeable, consequences of such a choice". However, he states that "any such criticism of the nationality test misses the point". This is also the position of Giulio Diena, "La protection diplomatique en cas de décès de la personne lésée", *RDILC* 1934, 181: "On a cependant remarqué qu'il peut se faire que la personne lésée, après avoir subi le dommage, vienne à changer de nationalité, indépendamment de sa volonté. Mais il s'agit d'une hypothèse qui se réalisera bien rarement. En effet, même en cas de cession territoriale, la personne intéressée aura le plus souvent le moyen de manifester sa volonté en exerçant ou en n'exerçant pas le droit d'option". This argument is also referred to by H.F. Van Panhuys, *The Role of Nationality in International Law: An Outline* (A.W. Sythoff 1959) 93.

90 Crawford, Brownlie's, 436–7 ("the correct solution in principle is surely a rule of substitution, putting the successor [State] in charge of claims belonging to the predecessor [State]"); Eric Wyler, *La règle dite de la continuité de la nationalité dans le contentieux international* (PUF 1990) 117 ("[e]n dépit des réactions doctrinales, force est de constater qu'à défaut des dispositions spéciales, la règle de la continuité de la nationalité trouve application dans les cas de changement de souveraineté affectant la nationalité des habitants. Cet état de chose nous incite, ici encore, à recommander l'abandon de la règle: l'Etat dont le lésé possédait la nationalité à l'époque de l'acte illicite devrait conserver son droit d'intervention. Mais l'Etat prédécesseur ne survit pas toujours au changement de

In 2005, the Institute followed the position adopted by the ILC with the adoption of Article 10(1).[91] When the injury caused by an internationally wrongful act committed against a predecessor State affects "persons, which, after the date of succession, are under the jurisdiction of a successor State", that State can request reparation for the injury caused by such act. Under Article 10(1), a successor State may exercise diplomatic protection in respect of a person who is its national at the date of the official presentation of the claim, even if he/she did not at the date of the injury. This solution has been endorsed by ILC Special Rapporteur Šturma.[92] Contrary to the position adopted by Institute at its 1965 session, I believe that there is no reason to apply the principle only to Newly Independent States. A new successor State should be entitled to submit claims on behalf of its new nationals in *all* different types of succession.[93]

The same solution should certainly prevail whenever the State responsible for an internationally wrongful act has accepted *after* the date of succession that such right be transferred to the successor State. Section 3 examines several examples illustrating that point. There is support for the proposition that the right to reparation should also be transferred to the new State in cases when the predecessor State had already submitted a claim (before the date of succession) on behalf of its injured national.[94] This is indeed the solution followed under Article 10(2) of the Institute's Resolution. It provides that the

souveraineté; s'il disparaît, c'est à L'Etat successeur qu'il faudrait alors attribuer cette faculté"). See also, Gabriele Salvioli, "Les règles générales de la paix", *Rec. des cours*, v. 46, 1933–IV, 1–164, 125–127; Atlam, 184.

91 See, analysis, in Kohen & Dumberry, 69ff.

92 ILC Special Rapporteur Šturma, Third Report, 2019, para 112: "This article and the commentary thereto provide a thorough and convincing analysis of the doctrinal views and State practice that ultimately supports the development from the traditional (strict, absolute) to the modern (flexible) content of the continuing nationality rule".

93 *Contra*: David Ruzié, *Droit international public* (14th edn, Dalloz 1999) 90, who admits only an exception to the general rule of non-succession for Newly Independent States.

94 Guggenheim, 474, supports the general rule of non-succession: "Le droit à la protection diplomatique à l'égard d'un Etat tiers, droit qui naît au moment où a lieu l'acte illicite, ne passe pas à l'Etat successeur". However, he makes an exception (478, footnote 2) for cases where the claim was already espoused by the predecessor State before the date of succession: "L'Etat successeur a le droit de faire sienne la cause épousée pas l'Etat prédécesseur, même si au moment du préjudice seul ce dernier avait le droit de présenter la cause". The same reasoning is adopted by David Ruzié, *Droit international public* (14th edn, Dalloz 1999) 90. See also, Peterschmitt, 53–54. Others have, on the contrary, rejected this proposition. This is the case with Monnier, 71: "Que l'Etat prédécesseur eût ou non épousé déjà la cause de son ressortissant, l'Etat successeur, en la faisant valoir, soutiendrait une demande qui, n'étant pas nationale dès l'origine, devrait nécessairement être rejetée".

claim may be continued by the successor State under the same conditions set out in Article 10(1).[95]

It should be added that Article 10(3) of the Institute's Resolution deals with the different situation of a claim in exercise of diplomatic protection which was initiated by a *third State* (the injured State) *against* the predecessor State on behalf of one of its national before the date of succession.[96] In this situation, the question is whether or not such a claim may be continued (after the date of succession) by that State *against a successor State*. Under Article 10(3), such a claim can be pursued against the successor State in the event that the predecessor State has ceased to exist (such as in situations of incorporation, unification and dissolution).[97] Any claim in exercise of diplomatic protection initiated by a third State against a predecessor State which continue to exist after the date of succession (such as in situations of transfer of territory, separation and Newly independent States) is simply unaffected. Finally, Article 10(4) of the Institute's Resolution deals with the specific situation of persons having dual nationality.[98]

Some writers have argued that the successor State should not be allowed to submit a claim on behalf of its new national if it involves a breach of a *treaty obligation* to which the successor State *is not a party*.[99] This position was also

---

95 Kohen & Dumberry, 75ff.

96 Ibid.

97 One question arises in the context of a dissolution of State: against which of the different successor States may a claim be pursued by the injured State? Under Art. 10(3), in such a case of a plurality of successor States, the claim shall be addressed to the successor State "having the most direct connection with the act giving rise to the exercise of diplomatic protection". The provision also mentions that "when it is not possible to determine a single successor State having such a direct connection, the claim may be continued against all the successor States". Art. 10(3) further adds that "The provisions of Art. 7 apply *mutatis mutandis*".

98 According to this provision, in cases where the predecessor State continues to exist and the individual or corporation possesses both the nationality of the predecessor and the successor State, the question is governed by general rules of diplomatic protection concerning dual or multiple nationality.

99 For instance, O'Connell, State Succession, v. I, 538, indicates that "the successor State is incompetent to complaint of the breach of a treaty [by a third State] to which it was not a party". Charles De Visscher, "Cours général de droit international public", *Rec. des cours*, v. 136, 1972–II, 166, is of the view that "on concevrait difficilement que l'Etat nouveau puisse obtenir réparation de dommages causés en violation de traités auxquels il déclarerait, par ailleurs, ne pas vouloir succéder". This is also the position of Atlam, 196–197. *Contra*: E.M. Borchard, "La protection des nationaux à l'étranger et le changement de nationalité d'origine", 14 *RDILC* 1933 (no. 3) 421, 459.

supported by several members of the Institute at its session of Oslo (1932).[100] It is argued by these writers that the successor State should not be allowed to claim reparation for a breach of a treaty obligation that is not binding on it. It would seem illogical that a State not party to a treaty could nevertheless claim reparation for any breach of such treaty.[101]

In scholarship, reference is often made to the existence of one requirement: the individual for whom the new successor State espouses the claim needs to have changed his/her nationality for *bona fide* reasons unrelated to the bringing of an international claim. It is thus argued by some writers that a successor State should not take over the claim of a new national who has "fraudulently" changed his/her nationality in order to have his/her pre-succession claim be espoused by the successor State at the level of diplomatic protection.[102] This specific requirement finds its roots in traditional diplomatic protection. Thus, the rule of continuous nationality has been traditionally justified in order to prevent certain abuses by individuals who might be otherwise tempted to engage in State protection "shopping" and to acquire, for political reasons and solely for the sake of opportunity, the nationality of one powerful State in order to pursue their claims against another State.[103] This is the view of

100 This is, for instance, the position taken by E. Kaufmann, *Annuaire IDI* 1933, Session of Oslo, 479, 517–518 ("le changement de nationalité devrait être sans conséquence juridique au cas où le droit violé serait de caractère universel. Si, d'autre part, ce droit était de caractère spécial (p. ex. un traité conclu entre deux Etats), il n'y aurait aucune raison pour que le nouvel Etat fasse siennes les réclamations formulées jusqu'alors par l'ancien Etat protecteur"). This is also the view of A. Raestad, ibid 518–519 ("il y a des cas, dans lesquels le changement de nationalité ne peut, en raison de la nature du rapport juridique en cause, engendrer la transmission de la protection de l'ancien au nouvel Etat. Un premier de ces cas est constitué par le préjudice causé à un individu par la violation d'un traité entre deux Etats, par exemple, un traité de commerce"). See also, the comments by N. Politis, ibid 522.

101 It is argued by some writers that the question is different if the successor State does ratify the treaty. In such a case, nothing should prevent the successor State from being entitled to claim on behalf of its new nationals for breach of this treaty obligation. This is the position of Atlam, 197–198, who, however, seems to accept the right of the successor State to make reparation claim only in the context of Newly Independent States.

102 Atlam, 180; N. Politis, *Annuaire IDI* 1933, Session of Oslo, 479, 488 ("[à] la vérité, la protection doit pouvoir s'exercer en faveur de l'individu, malgré son changement de nationalité, sauf lorsque celui-ci … ne se décide pour une nationalité nouvelle que dans un but frauduleux, en recherchant la protection d'un gouvernement fort, capable de donner plus de prise à sa réclamation"). See also, the position of Gabriele Salvioli, "Les règles générales de la paix", *Rec. des cours*, v. 46, 1933–IV, 1–164, 125–127.

103 Moore, Digest, v. VI, 637, for whom the absence of the continuous nationality requirement "would allow [a person] to call upon a dozen Governments in succession, to each of which he might transfer his allegiance, to urge his claim". See also: Rousseau, v. V, 118–119;

Umpire Parker of the US-Germany Mixed Claims Commission in *Administrative Decision No. v*.[104] Some authors have indicated that there should be a presumption that changes of nationality in the context of State succession are made in good faith and are not fraudulent.[105] ILC's Special Rapporteur Dugard has rightly criticised the soundness of the argument of diplomatic protection "shopping" in contemporary international law.[106] The argument seems to be of little relevance in the context of State succession, where changes of nationality are, by their very nature, *involuntary*.[107] It is indeed not entirely obvious how an involuntary change of nationality by a person might possibly be considered to be a fraudulent attempt to pursue any pre-succession claim for damage.[108] In any event, Article 10(1) of the Institute's Resolution addresses any such concern in the context of *voluntary* change of nationality: the person must have lost its previous nationality and acquired the new one (of the successor State) for "reason unrelated to the bringing of the claim" and in a "manner not inconsistent with international law".[109] This is exactly the same language employed in Article 5(2) of the ILC *Articles on diplomatic protection*.[110]

E.M. Borchard, "La protection des nationaux à l'étranger et le changement de nationalité d'origine", 14 *RDILC* 1933 (no. 3) 421, 449.

104 *Administrative Decision No. v*, US-Germany Mixed Claims Commission, Decision of Umpire Edwin B. Parker, 31 October 1924, *UNRIAA* v. VII, 119, 140, 141: "Any other rule [then the rule of continuous nationality] would open wide the door for abuses and might result in converting a strong nation into a claim agency on behalf of those who after suffering injuries should assign their claims to its nationals or avail themselves of its naturalization law for the purpose of procuring its espousal of their claims".

105 This is, for instance, the position held by Atlam, 180. *Contra*: H.F. Van Panhuys, *The Role of Nationality in International Law: An Outline* (A.W. Sythoff 1959) 92, who speaks of an "irrebuttable presumption of bad faith" that is "assumed" in the context of voluntary changes of nationality, while there would be "rebuttable presumption" in other cases of involuntary changes of nationality.

106 In ILC, "Addendum to First Report on Diplomatic Protection", by Mr John R. Dugard, Special Rapporteur, 20 April 2000, A/CN.4/506/Add.1, at para 23, he refers to this argument as being "fanciful" and even "ridiculous" in contemporary international law.

107 O'Connell, State Succession, v. I, 537: "The explanation of the rule [of continuous nationality] is that, if it did not exist, persons would seek naturalization in States which were parties to arbitration agreements merely to get a hearing for their claims. If this is it only rationalization, then the rule obviously lacks cogency when the change of nationality is affected by transfer of territory and not by act of the claimant, and the conclusion should be drawn that States succession constitutes an exception to it".

108 *Contra*: H.F. Van Panhuys, *The Role of Nationality in International Law: An Outline* (A.W. Sythoff 1959), who is of the view that it is not "beyond doubt that in cases of State succession false motives may not influence the subsequent change of nationality".

109 The question is further examined in Kohen & Dumberry, 70–71.

110 ILC, "Report of the International Law Commission on the Work of its Fifty-Fourth session", 29 April–7 June and 22 July–16 August 2002, ILC Report A/57/10, 2002, chp. v, 120ff.

3 Analysis of State Practice and Case Law

Because of the limited number of relevant examples of State practice and case law dealing with this question, the present analysis is not based on the different types of succession.

The analysis of State practice and case law shows that different solutions have prevailed. The following tendencies can be highlighted:

- There are several examples of *international judicial decisions* where the traditional rule of continuous nationality was not applied and where the successor State submitted a claim for reparation on behalf of a new national even if this individual did not have the nationality of that State at the time the damage occurred (Section 3.1);
- There are several examples of *State practice* where reparation was provided to the successor State for its new nationals which did not have its nationality at the time the damage occurred (Section 3.2);
- There is only one significant decision of an international court where the application of the rule of continuous nationality prevented a *successor State* from claiming reparation for its new nationals concerning events which took place before the date of succession (the *Panevezys-Saldutiskis Railway* case, examined in Section 3.3);
- There is also one example where the application of the rule of continuous nationality by an international judicial body prevented *the continuing State* from exercising diplomatic protection on behalf of a person who was its national when the damage occurred but no longer had such nationality at the time the claim was submitted to the State responsible (the *Henriette Levy* case, examined in Section 3.3); and
- There is some support in case law (and in scholarship) for the proposition that the successor State does not have the right to claim reparation on behalf of its new nationals from the former State of nationality of such nationals (Section 3.4).

3.1 *Cases Where Successor States Have Submitted Claims on Behalf of Their New Nationals*

I have found four examples of international judicial decisions where the traditional rule of continuous nationality was *not* applied in the specific context of State succession.[111]

111 The same examples are examined in Kohen & Dumberry, 71ff; ILC Special Rapporteur Šturma, Third Report, 2019, para 119ff; Šturma, State Succession, 672.

The first example is the *Pablo Nájera* case of 1928 decided by the France-Mexico Claims Commission, where the Arbitral Tribunal held that the successor State (France) was allowed to submit a claim on behalf of a new national even if this individual did not have the nationality of that State at the time the damage occurred. Another similar situation arose in the 1934 Arbitral Award in the case of the *Claim of Finnish Shipowners against Great Britain in respect of the Use of Certain Finnish Vessels During the War*. In this case, the respondent (the UK) did not invoke the traditional rule of continuous nationality to deny the jurisdiction of the Sole Arbitrator over the case. The third and fourth examples are the consistent approaches adopted by the MATs established after the First World War and the United Nations Compensation Commission (UNCC) set up after the Gulf War (1990–1991). In both cases, it was deliberately decided to exclude the application of the rule of continuous nationality. This was done to prevent the unjust consequences that nationals of new States created after the conflicts could not seek redress for the damage they suffered during the conflicts. The new States were thus allowed to claim reparation on behalf of their new nationals which did not have such nationality at the time the damage occurred.

3.1.1 The *Pablo Nájera* Case (1928)

The *Pablo Nájera* case decided by the France-Mexico Claims Commission dealt with incidents which took place in 1916 in Mexico, when an Ottoman national (Mr Nájera, born in Lebanon in 1860) was injured as a result of the action of Mexican revolutionaries (during the Mexican Revolution which started in 1910).[112] At the time, Mr Nájera was still formally a national of the Ottoman Empire even though France had traditionally exercised diplomatic protection for Lebanese and Syrians abroad before the end of the First World War (and the break-up of the Ottoman Empire).[113] France filed a complaint on 15 June 1926 on behalf of Mr Nájera, whom it considered to be a French national, before

112 *Pablo Nájera* case 488. This case is mentioned in: Verzijl, Jurisprudence, 555, see 568, at footnote no. 10 (analysing the *Panevezys-Saldutiskis Railway* case). See also, A.H. Feller, *The Mexican Claims Commissions, 1923–1934; A Study in the Law and Procedure of International Tribunals* (Macmillan 1935) 102.

113 Following the defeat of the Ottoman Empire, the territory of Lebanon was placed under a French military administration and soon after became a French Mandate. In 1923, the League of Nations formally gave the Mandate for Lebanon and Syria to France. Art. 3 of the French Mandate provided that "les ressortissants de la Syrie et du Liban se trouvant hors des limites de ces territoires relèveront de la protection diplomatique et consulaire du Mandataire" (ibid 474). In other words, France could exercise diplomatic protection for Lebanese abroad.

the Claims Commission which was set up in 1923–1924 to examine claims for losses by French nationals against Mexico. In defence, Mexico objected, *inter alia*, that Mr Nájera was presently not a French national ("French protégés") under Article III of the *Compromis* under which the Commission was established. Mexico also objected that, at any rate, in 1916 (at the time the damage occurred) Mr Nájera was not a French national and that France could therefore not espouse his claim.

President Verzijl of the Tribunal held that Mr Nájera was included in the term "French protégés" under Article III of the *Compromis* at the time France espoused his claim and submitted its Memorial. The other important point remaining was that when the damage occurred, Mr Nájera was an Ottoman national and not a French national. President Verzijl first noted that the rule of continuous nationality did not apply when the circumstances of the case show that the parties had the contrary intention.[114] From his examination of the exchange of correspondence between the representatives of the two States, he concluded that it was indeed the intention of the Parties when they were negotiating the setting up of the Commission to consider Lebanese living abroad as "French protégés" under Article III of the *Compromis*.[115] The President also held that it was the intention of the Parties that Lebanese living abroad should benefit from this protection *retroactively* for damage suffered during the Mexican Revolution. Faced with such clear intention of the Parties,

114 *Pablo Nájera* case, 487–488: "Mais dans l'espèce ce dernier point se présente sous un jour particulier. Lorsque les deux Gouvernements correspondaient au sujet des Syrio-Libanais ou des protégés … ils savaient que tous les dommages auxquels se référaient les négociations avaient été causés pendant une période dans laquelle la qualité de 'protégé français' ne pouvait encore être appréciée à la lumière de la nouvelle situation juridique du Liban et de la Syrie … Ils savaient qu'un changement fondamental de la situation politique et juridique de ces régions était en train de se produire et que ce changement comporterait des conséquences juridiques pour les Syriens et les Libanais émigrés au Mexique. Ils pouvaient prévoir que la situation juridique de ces individus paraîtrait avoir changé entre l'époque des dommages et celle de l'introduction de la réclamation. Si, dans ces conditions, ils ont étendu quand même les bénéfices de la convention aux étrangers en question, sous la condition tacite que la Commission mixte à créer reconnaîtrait qu'ils peuvent être compris dans le terme 'protégé', il ne me semble pas loisible d'appliquer après coup aux réclamations de ces étrangers des règles techniques strictes, comme celles auxquelles je viens de faire allusion, ni d'exciper du fait qu'à l'époque des dommages ils étaient des sujets ottomans. L'intention évidente des Parties a été de faire bénéficier des avantages de la Convention des personnes originaires de Syrie et du Liban, qui auraient subi des dommages pendant les révolutions, pour autant que la France serait autorisée à les faire bénéficier de sa protection".

115 This was so because at the time of the negotiations, the Mandate over Syria and Lebanon had already been given to France.

President Verzijl decided that he could not apply the strict rule of continuous nationality and its requirement that the claim of Mr Nájera be "French" (in terms of nationality) at the time the wrongful act was committed.[116]

The reasoning was approved by the French Commissioner. In his dissenting opinion, the Mexican Commissioner refuted the position taken by President Verzijl. He maintained that the rule of continuous nationality should have found application in the present case and should have prevented France from espousing the claim of Mr Nájera:

> La doctrine juridique parfaitement claire qui s'impose de la date d'acquisition de la nationalité, est celle selon laquelle cette époque ne doit pas être postérieure à celle du préjudice subi pour que la réclamation soit recevable (...). [I]l est manifestement impossible que le demandeur Nájera et tous ceux qui se trouvent dans la même situation aient le droit de présenter une réclamation puisqu'ils ont acquis la qualité d'administrés français en 1924, après la signature du Traité de Lausanne, c'est-à-dire après avoir subi les dommages.[117]

This award is not the strongest precedent in support of the non-application of the rule of continuous nationality in the context of State succession. Thus, the outcome of this case was undoubtedly driven by the fact that President Verzijl considered that it was the intention of the Parties that the rule of continuous nationality should not apply.[118] This "intention" was, however, not self-evident. As a matter of fact, Mexico strongly objected that it ever had the intention to give the Commission jurisdiction over claims submitted by persons who were not French nationals when the damage occurred. In his dissenting opinion, the Mexican Commissioner also refuted (in strong terms) the position held by President Verzijl. Some quotes from the Award in fact show that President Verzijl was of the view that, as a matter of principle, the strict rule of continuous nationality should only apply in cases of *voluntary* changes of nationality and not when changes of nationality are involuntary.[119]

116 *Pablo Nájera* case, 487–488.

117 Ibid 503.

118 Kohen & Dumberry, 71.

119 *Pablo Nájera* case, 488: "Le cas présent diffère essentiellement des hypothèses dans lesquelles un individu, ressortissant de l'Etat A à l'époque des dommages, devient après cette époque et avant la date de la réclamation, ressortissant de l'Etat B de son propre fait. Dans le cas de changements collectifs de nationalité en vertu d'un titre de succession d'Etats, la situation juridique doit être appréciée *d'une manière beaucoup moins rigide* que

3.1.2 The Claim of Finnish Shipowners against Great Britain in Respect of the Use of Certain Finnish Vessels during the War (1934)

The case involved a claim submitted by Finland against Great Britain for damage suffered by Finnish nationals before the First World War.[120] At the time of the commission of the wrongful act, Finland was not yet an independent State (it became one after the Russian Revolution of 1917) and the victims had Russian nationality. In application of the traditional rule of continuous nationality, Great Britain (the respondent) could have easily argued that the claim should be rejected by the Sole Arbitrator because Finland could not, as a matter of principle, submit a claim on behalf of Finnish nationals who did not have such nationality at the time the damage occurred. Great Britain did not submit such defence. By not rejecting its own jurisdiction over the dispute, the Sole Arbitrator implicitly endorsed the validity of the proposition that a new State may be entitled to claim reparation for damage which occurred at a time the national (in this case a corporation) for which it is claiming did not have its nationality.[121]

It has been suggested that the silence of both the respondent State and the Sole Arbitrator on this point illustrates the fact that States rarely refer to the traditional rule of continuous nationality in the context of State succession and that judicial bodies do not apply it.[122] This is indeed a sound interpretation.

3.1.3 The Practice of Mixed Arbitral Tribunals Established after the First World War

Introduction. At the end of the First World War, several peace treaties were concluded between the victorious and the defeated States. The most important treaty was no doubt the *Versailles Peace Treaty* (28 June 1919) signed between Germany, on the one hand, and the Allies (the "Allied and Associated Powers" or "entente Powers", i.e. the British Empire, France, Italy, Japan, the US, etc.), on the other hand. Other separate peace treaties were also signed between

---

ne le fait généralement la pratique arbitrale dans les hypothèses normales de changement individuel de nationalité par le fait volontaire de l'intéressé" (emphasis added).

120 *Claim of Finnish Shipowners against Great Britain in respect of the Use of Certain Finnish Vessels During the War* (Finland v. UK), Award of Dr. Bagge, 9 May 1934, *UNRIAA* v. III, 1481.

121 Kohen & Dumberry, 72. The Sole Arbitrator had the power to examine its own jurisdiction *proprio motu* in this case even if the issue was not raised by the Parties in their respective submissions.

122 Atlam, 151; Peterschmitt, 50; Wengler, *Annuaire IDI* 1965–II, 168, 213; ILC Special Rapporteur Šturma, Third Report, 2019, paras 122, 125. Others have rejected this example as simply irrelevant: see comments by Castren, *Annuaire* ibid 215; Bartos, ibid 215.

the Allies and the "Central Powers" (Austria, Bulgaria, Hungary and Turkey).[123] These five treaties are known collectively as the "Paris Peace Treaties". They all provided for the establishment of Mixed Arbitral Tribunals (MATs) between each of the Allies, on the one side, and each of the "Central Powers" and Germany, on the other.[124] It should be noted that other MATs were also established separately: the US-Germany Mixed Claims Commission;[125] the Tripartite Claims Commission (US, Austria and Hungary);[126] and the Germany-Mexico Mixed Claims Commission.[127]

The tribunals (established under the so-called "Paris Peace Treaties") were all similar in content with respect to their provisions on reparation.[128] They had jurisdiction over three different types of claims for "material damage" suffered by individuals:[129]

123 The *Saint-Germain Peace Treaty* (1919) with Austria; the *Neuilly Peace Treaty* (1919) with Bulgaria; the *Trianon Peace Treaty* (1920) with Hungary; and the *Lausanne Peace Treaty* (1923) with Turkey.

124 See in general: Ellinor Von Puttkamer, "Versailles Peace Treaty", in: Bernhardt, 276; Norbert Wühler, "Mixed Arbitral Tribunals", in: Bernhardt, 143. The decisions of the tribunals are compiled in several volumes: *Recueil des décisions des tribunaux arbitraux mixtes* (hereinafter "*RDTAM*") (Sirey 1922–1930).

125 The US never ratified the *Versailles Treaty* and signed a separate peace treaty with Germany (*Treaty of Berlin* of 25 August 1921) which established a Mixed Claims Commission. Awards are found in *UNRIAA* v. 7, 13ff.

126 Awards of the Commission are in *UNRIAA* v. VI, 203.

127 The Commission was set up by a bilateral treaty of 16 March 1925.

128 Tribunals were set up under Art. 304 a), *Versailles Treaty*. See, Rudolf Blühdorn, "Le fonctionnement et la jurisprudence des Tribunaux Arbitraux Mixtes par les traités de Paris", *Rec. des cours*, v. 41, 1932–III, 220; Karl Strupp, "The Competence of the Mixed Arbitral Courts of the Treaty of Versailles", 17 *AJIL* 1923, 661–690; Karl Strupp, *Die zuständigkeit der gemischten schiedsgerichte des Versailles friedensvertrages* (Bensheimer 1923); J.C. Witenberg, *Etude sur la compétence des tribunaux arbitraux mixtes institués en vertu de l'article 304 b alinéa 1 du traité de Versailles, concernant les dommages causés par les enlèvements des biens des particuliers au cours de l'occupation allemande durant la grande guerre (1914–1918)* (Sirey 1925); J. Teyssaire & P. De Solere, *Les tribunaux arbitraux mixtes* (Ed. Internationales 1931); C. Carabiber, *Les juridictions internationales en droit privé. Histoire et société d'aujourd'hui* (Ed. de la Baconnière 1947) 216–228. For a recent analysis, H. Ruiz Fabri & E. Michel Erpelding (eds), *The Mixed Arbitral Tribunals: 1919–1939; An Experiment in the International Adjudication of Private Rights* (Nomos 2023).

129 Under Art. 297 of the *Versailles Treaty*, only "material" damage was compensable by the tribunals. Non-material damage, such as personal injuries, was excluded from the jurisdiction of the tribunals; they were dealt with by the State-to-State mechanism for settlement of disputes created by the Reparation Commission. See, Art. 232 and Annex 1 of the Treaty. See, Blühdorn, ibid 220. Also excluded from the jurisdiction of the tribunals were claims for damage caused by the German Empire and the other Central Powers to the Allied and Associated Powers which were dealt with by the Reparation Commission.

- claims between individuals originating from their pre-war relations, including debts and contract-related debts;[130]
- claims by nationals of the Allies against the German Empire and the other "Central Powers" for damage inflicted in German territories (as existing at the time of the beginning of the War in 1914) resulting from "exceptional war measures and measures of transfer taken by Germany [and other "Central Powers"] during the War with respect to the property, rights and interests" of individuals;[131] and
- claims by nationals of the "Central Powers" for measures (including confiscation/expropriation) taken by "new States".[132]

Thousands of claims were submitted by individuals and corporations before the different MATs established after the First World War.[133] One important feature of these MATs is that individuals had *direct access* to these tribunals (even if agents of the State of the claimants were always present at the hearings).[134] In that sense, the mechanisms set up departed from the traditional system of State-to-State dispute settlement where individual claims need to be endorsed by their State of origin under the umbrella of diplomatic protection. However, the nationality of claims remained the basis for the jurisdiction of these tribunals. For instance, the French-German MAT only had jurisdiction over disputes

130 Art. 296, *Versailles Treaty*. These claims were between nationals of "Allied and Associated Powers" and nationals of Germany and nationals of the "Central Powers".

131 Art. 297e, *Versailles Treaty*. It should be noted that claims by nationals of the German Empire and the other "Central Powers" for measures taken by "Allied and Associated Powers" were excluded from the jurisdiction of the tribunals. See, Karl Strupp, "The Competence of the Mixed Arbitral Courts of the Treaty of Versailles", 17 *AJIL* 1923, 661, 669ff.

132 Art. 297h, *Versailles Treaty*.

133 Norbert Wühler, "Mixed Arbitral Tribunals" in: Bernhardt, 145, provides the following figures: more than 20,000 cases were dealt with by the Franco-German MAT, about 10,000 cases by the Anglo-German MAT and over 10,000 cases by the German-Italian MAT. David J. Bederman, "The United Nations Compensation Commission and the Tradition of International Claims Settlement", 27 *NYU JIL & Pol.* 1994, 1, 17, 19–20, also indicates that over 10,000 cases were decided by the tribunal set up between Poland and Germany and that the US-Germany Mixed Claims Commission (1922–1939) disposed of 20,433 claims and rendered awards in 7,000 cases.

134 Art. 231, *Versailles Treaty*: "The Allied and Associated Governments affirm and Germany accepts the responsibility of Germany and her allies for causing all the loss and damage to which the Allied and Associated Governments and their nationals have been subjected as a consequence of the war imposed upon them by the aggression of Germany and her allies". The *Treaty* distinguished between reparation claims, which were to be determined by the Reparation Commission (Art. 233), and the settlement of claims of private individuals placed under the responsibility of the MATs (Arts. 297–303 of the Treaty).

involving German and French nationals. This question is dealt with in the next section.

Case Law. Following the end of the First World War and the break-up of the Russian Empire, the Ottoman Empire and the Austria-Hungary Dual Monarchy, several *new States* were created: Finland, Lithuania, Latvia, Estonia, Armenia, Georgia, Azerbaijan, Czechoslovakia, Poland and the Kingdom of the Serbs, Croats and Slovenes.[135] As mentioned above, the application of the traditional rule of continuous nationality in the context of State succession would require that individuals submitting claims to the MATs be nationals of a State Party to the *Versailles Treaty* when the damage occurred. The strict application of this rule would result in a great injustice. It would prevent nationals of these new States from submitting claims for reparation against Germany and the "Central Powers" because at the time the damage occurred, they were citizens of other States (the predecessor States: Germany, the Russian Empire, the Ottoman Empire, Austria-Hungary).

In order to prevent such an injustice, the MATs gave an interpretation of Article 304 (b, al. 2) of the *Versailles Treaty*[136] which is not in accordance with the traditional rule of continuous nationality. They indeed allowed nationals of the Allies to submit claims even if they were not nationals of those States at the time the damage occurred.[137] The US-Germany MAT also adopted a similar practical solution.[138] The consistent case law adopted by the different MATs

135 There were also some cessions of territory. Thus, former German Empire territories were ceded to France (Alsace-Lorraine), to the new State Poland (the Province of Posen, the east part of Upper Silesia, Eastern Pomerania, etc.), to Denmark (the northern part of Schleswig-Holstein), to the new State of Czechoslovakia (the Hulczyn area of Upper Silesia) and to Belgium (the cities of Eupen and Malmedy). Romania also gained some territories which formally belonged to the Russian Empire (Bessarabia) and the Austria-Hungary Dual Monarchy (Transylvania). The territories of South Tyrol and Trieste were granted to Italy.

136 This provision indicates that the MATs have jurisdiction over "all questions, whatsoever their nature, relating to contracts concluded before the coming into force of the present Treaty between nationals of the Allied and Associated Powers and German nationals".

137 For the same conclusion, see: ILC Special Rapporteur Šturma, Third Report, 2019, para 126; Kohen & Dumberry, 72.

138 The US-Germany MAT, which was not established pursuant to one of the five treaties known as the "Paris Peace Treaties", adopted, *as a matter of principle*, the traditional rule of continuous nationality. It thus decided that it only had jurisdiction over claims submitted by US nationals who had this nationality both at the time the damage occurred and when the Treaty of Berlin entered into force. See, *Administrative Decision No. V*, US-Germany Mixed Claims Commission, Decision of Umpire Edwin B. Parker, 31 October 1924, *UNRIAA* v. VII, 119, 140, 148 & 154. However, a different *practical solution* was in effect adopted in the context of changes of nationality resulting from State succession. Thus, the application of the traditional rule of continuous nationality would have prevented

established under the *Versailles Treaty* was that a person should be considered a "national of the Allied and Associated Powers" if at the time of the *entry into force of the Versailles Treaty* (January 1920) he/she had acquired such nationality.[139] One exception was made for cases where a person had changed his/her nationality from one Allies to another *after* the date of the entry into force of the *Versailles Treaty* but prior to the presentation of his/her claim.[140] The rule adopted by the MATs therefore allowed the submission of claims by nationals of new States which did not exist as independent States before the entry into force of the *Versailles Treaty*. These new States did not exist at the time the internationally wrongful acts were committed. Only two decisions deviated from this consistent case law.[141]

A good illustration of the principle adopted by these tribunals is the case of *Poznanski v. Lentz & Hirchfeld* before the Polish-German MAT arising from a contract entered into in 1914 by a German firm (Lentz & Hirchfeld) and a Polish

---

claimants from the Virgin Islands to submit claims since they were not US nationals at the time the damage occurred. The territory of the Virgin Islands, a Danish colony, was ceded to the US on 17 January 1917. In the case of *United Stated on behalf of Boyer v. Germany* (docket no. 276), it was, nevertheless, agreed by both agents of the US and Germany that the claimant should get some compensation for the damage resulting from the sinking of a US submarine in April 1916. No decision was rendered in this case. See, analysis in: John Hanna, "Nationality and War Claims", *Colum. LR* 1945, 301, 317; J.C. Witenberg, *Commission mixte de réclamations germano-américaine* (PUF 1927); A. Burchard, "The Mixed Claims Commissions and German Property in the US of America", 21 *AJIL* 1927, 472.

139 *Leontitos & Nicolas Arakas v. Bulgaria*, Greece-Bulgaria MAT, 3 April 1925, *RDTAM* v. V, 245; *National Bank of Egypt v. German Government and Bank fur Handel und Industrie*, UK-Germany MAT, 14 December 1923 and 31 May 1924, ibid v. IV, 233; *Meyer-Wildermann v. Hoirie Hugo Stinnes and others*, German-Romanian MAT, 6 November 1924, ibid, v. IV, 842, 846ff; *M. Kirschen Sr. v. Sobotka, ZEG & Empire Allemand*, German-Romanian MAT, 3 January 1925, ibid v. IV, 858, 862–863; *D'Esquevilley v. Aktiengesellschaft Weser*, French-German MAT, 27 October 1923, ibid v. III, 689, 692; *Mercier & cie. v. Etat Allemand*, French-German MAT, 26 October 1923, ibid v. III, 686; *Dame De Laire v. Etat Hongrois*, French-Hungarian MAT, 27 July 1927, *Ibid* v. VII, 825, 827–828; *O.V.C. v. R.A.A. (Dony)*, German-Belgian MAT, 18 July 1927, ibid v. VII, 548. For a recent analysis: Jakob Zollmann, "Nationality, Property, and the Mixed Arbitral Tribunals, 1914 to 1930", in H. Ruiz Fabri & E. Michel Erpelding (eds), *The Mixed Arbitral Tribunals: 1919–1939; An Experiment in the International Adjudication of Private Rights* (Nomos 2023) 133ff.

140 *Radziwill v. Etat Allemand*, French-German MAT, 26 January 1926, *RDTAM* v. IX, 81; *AD* 1925–1926, 238.

141 These two awards were rendered by the Austrian-Italian MAT. In one case, it was decided that the jurisdiction of the Tribunal was "determined by the nationality of the parties at the time of the contract" and that it should not take into account "any modification which might have successively happened in the nationality of the parties to said Contract": *Torrest Antonio v. Sami Spiegel & Etat fédéral Autrichien*, Italian-Austrian MAT, 27 June 1924, *RDTAM* v. V, 506.

firm (Poznanski).[142] The argument of the defendant (the German company) was that the Tribunal had no jurisdiction over the dispute pursuant to Article 304 (b, al. 2) of the *Versailles Treaty* since the Polish claimant company was not a national of the Allies when the dispute arose between the two companies but had Russian nationality at that time.[143] The Tribunal came to the conclusion that the question whether or not the company was a national of the Allies should be considered at the time the *Versailles Treaty* entered into force and not at the time when the contract between the parties was signed.[144] The Tribunal clearly adopted this solution because any other alternative would have left nationals of the new State of Poland with no right to redress for wrongful acts committed before the date of succession.[145] The Tribunal therefore decided that it had jurisdiction over the dispute since the company Poznanski was a Polish company at the time of the entry into force of the *Versailles Treaty* (and that Poland was an independent State at that time and was considered to be one of the Allies Powers).[146]

One delicate problem facing the MATs was that of individual nationals of States which became independent at the time of the entry into force of the *Versailles Treaty* but who only *formally* became nationals of these new States *after* the entry into force of *subsequent* peace treaties. In the context of claims submitted by Yugoslav nationals, the German-Yugoslav MAT consistently rejected its jurisdiction over claims involving this issue based on the ground that the claimants were not Yugoslav nationals at the time of the entry into force of the *Versailles Treaty* (in January 1920) since they only formally acquired such nationality later with the entry into force of the *Trianon Treaty* (26 July 1921).[147]

The exact same problem arose in the context of claims submitted by Czechoslovak nationals who were former nationals of Austria living in

---

142 *Poznanski v. Lentz & Hirchfeld*, Polish-German MAT, 22 March 1924, *RDTAM v.* IV, 353.

143 Ibid 356–357.

144 Ibid 358: "Le texte de l'art. 304, s'accommode également des diverses interprétations, et il n'y a aucune raison de rechercher depuis quelle époque les parties possèdent la nationalité exigée, du moment qu'elles la possèdent lors de la mise en vigueur du Traité".

145 Ibid: "A quoi l'on peut ajouter qu'en se plaçant au moment du contrat on diminuerait les prérogatives des ressortissants des Etats nouveaux sans pouvoir alléguer aucun motif à l'appui de cette restriction de leurs droits. Passe encore si la lettre du Traité n'admettait point d'autre interprétation, mais tel n'est point le cas".

146 Ibid. The Tribunal added, in an *obiter dictum*, that Poland existed anyway *before* the entry into force of the *Versailles Treaty*.

147 *Gabriel Radic v. Maschinenfabrik u. Mühlenbauanstalt G. Luther A.G.*, German-Yugoslav MAT, 1 October 1922, *RDTAM* v. II, 655, 660–662. See also: *Franz Peinitsch v. Etat Allemand; Etat Prusse Banque Bleichroeder*, ibid, 18 September 1922, ibid v. II, 610, 619ff.

territories now forming parts of the new State of Czechoslovakia (which was created by the *Versailles Treaty* of January 1920). These individuals formally became nationals of this new State only upon the entry into force of the *St. Germain Treaty* (16 July 1920).[148] The German-Czechoslovak MAT came to a different conclusion than the German-Yugoslav MAT. It decided that it had jurisdiction over these claims since a *de facto* Czechoslovak nationality had been created as a result of the *Versailles Treaty* and had, therefore, existed *before* the entry into force of the *St. Germain Treaty*.[149]

Another particularly sensitive problem concerned claims by individuals from the territories of Alsace-Lorraine against Germany for damage suffered during the War.[150] In accordance with Article 51 of the *Treaty of Versailles*, the territories of Alsace-Lorraine which were "ceded" by France to Germany in accordance with the Preliminaries of Peace and the *Treaty of Frankfurt* (1871) were "restored to French sovereignty as from the date of the Armistice of November 11, 1918". The population living in the territories of Alsace-Lorraine therefore "rebecame" French nationals on that date (provided that they had acquired no other nationality than German nationality before that date[151]).[152]

The question of the admissibility of such claims was first decided by the French-German MAT in the *August Chamant* case, where the claimant submitted a claim pursuant to Article 302(2) of the *Treaty of Versailles* against a judgment by default rendered by a German court during the War.[153] Germany

148 Art. 70, *Treaty of Peace between the Allied and Associated Powers, and Austria; Protocol; Declaration; and Special Declaration*, 10 Sept. 1919, in force on 16 July 1920, *UKTS* 1919, No. 11 (Cmd. 400).

149 *Loy & Markus v. Empire Allemand & Deutsch Ostrafrikanische Bank A.G.*, German-Czechoslovak MAT, 27 April 1923, *RDTAM* v. III, 998, 1007–1009. See also: *Gellert v. Kolker*, ibid 24 October 1923, ibid v. IV, 515, 524–525; *Goldschmiedt v. Heesch Hinrichsem & Cie*, ibid, 30 November 1923, ibid v. IV, 530, 533. The solution adopted by the MAT was criticised in: Rudolf Blühdorn, "Le fonctionnement et la jurisprudence des Tribunaux Arbitraux Mixtes creés par les traités de Paris", *Rec. des cours*, v. 41, 1932–III, 207–208.

150 These claims are discussed in: Blühdorn, ibid 209; Louis Cavare, *Le droit international positif*, v. I (2nd edn Pedone 1961) 284; Atlam, 150.

151 Art. 1(1), Annex to Section V of the Treaty. See, *De Luck v. Etat allemand*, French-German MAT, 31 March 1928, *RDTAM* v. VIII, 142, where the Tribunal declined its jurisdiction on the ground that the claimant had acquired Prussian nationality after the cession of territory in 1871.

152 One noteworthy provision of the Treaty is Art. 63: "For the purposes of the obligation assumed by Germany in Part VIII (Reparation) of the present Treaty to give compensation for damage caused to the civil populations of the Allied and Associated countries in the form of fines, the inhabitants of the territories referred to in Article 51 [i.e. Alsace-Lorraine] shall be assimilated to the above-mentioned populations".

153 *August Chamant v. Etat Allemand*, French-German MAT, 23 June 1921 & 25 August 1921, *RDTAM* v. I, 361. Art. 302(2) reads as follows: "If a judgment in respect to any dispute which

argued that the French-German MAT did not have jurisdiction over this claim as the claimant could not be considered a "national of an Allied Power" since he was *not a French national* but a German national at the time the damage occurred before the end of the War. The Tribunal rejected the argument submitted by Germany and decided that the words "a national of an Allied or Associated State" contained in Article 302(2) of the Treaty included persons from Alsace-Lorraine.[154] According to the Tribunal, it was the (rational and equitable) intention of the Parties that the fact that individuals from Alsace-Lorraine were not French nationals at the time the damage occurred during the War should not be prejudicial to their claims.[155] The Tribunal concluded that it had jurisdiction over the case.

The same French-German MAT had to deal with a similar claim in the *Veuve Heim* case, where the claimant requested, pursuant to Article 297e) of the Treaty, an indemnity for the confiscation of goods by the German authorities during the War.[156] The Tribunal also concluded that it had jurisdiction over

may have arisen has been given during the war by a German Court against a national of an Allied or Associated State in a case in which he was not able to make his defence, the Allied and Associated national who has suffered prejudice thereby shall be entitled to recover compensation, to be fixed by the Mixed Arbitral Tribunal provided for in Section VI".

154 Ibid 368. The Tribunal noted that: "aucune disposition spéciale à Alsace-Lorraine (partie III, section V et annexe) ne vient, sur ce point, déroger aux dispositions générales du Traités, ni leur apporter aucun tempérament, ni aucune modalité d'adaptation; qu'il faut, dès lors, appliquer celles-ci à l'espèce, conformément à l'esprit du Traité et à l'article 79, al. 2, en particulier; que la *sedes materiae* est l'article 302, al. 2; que cette disposition reconnaît indistinctement à tout ressortissant des Puissances alliées et associées le droit de réclamer la réparation du préjudice causé par un jugement rendu contre lui, en quelque nature que ce soit, par un Tribunal allemand, pendant la guerre, dans une instance où il n'a pas pu se défendre".

155 Ibid 368–369: "Que, dans l'espèce, la conclusion tirée des considérants qui précèdent ne blesse en aucune façon ni le bon sens ni l'équité; qu'il est au contraire rationnel d'admettre que l'intention des auteurs du Traité a été de placer au bénéfice de ses disposition tous les citoyens d'un même pays, sauf les cas où, pour des motifs spéciaux, il en décide autrement par une clause expresse; qu'il ne paraîtrait pas conforme aux principes de justice et d'équité que, de deux citoyens français considérés après la guerre, l'un, parce qu'il serait de Paris ou Marseille, aurait vis-à-vis de l'Allemagne un droit à la réparation d'un certain préjudice, droit qui serait refusé à l'autre, parce qu'il serait de Strasbourg ou de Metz".

156 *Veuve Heim v. Etat Allemand*, French-German MAT, 30 June 1921 & 19 August 1921, *RDTAM* v. I, 381. Art. 297 e) of Treaty allows the submission of claims to be determined by the MAT for "compensation in respect of damage or injury inflicted upon their property, rights or interests, including any company or association in which they are interested, in German territory as it existed on August 1, 1914, by the application either of the exceptional war measures or measures of transfer".

this case.[157] The Tribunal further added that individuals from the territories of Alsace-Lorraine had somehow never ceased to be "French nationals" in 1871 and that they were "virtual" French nationals from the date of the *Treaty of Frankfurt* (1871) until the end of the First World War (11 November 1918).[158] This last statement, which is in clear contradiction with Article 51 of the *Treaty of Versailles*,[159] was not endorsed in subsequent cases decided by the French-German MAT[160] and was strongly criticised by writers.[161]

Germany requested a revision of those two awards, but the MAT confirmed them.[162] The case law of the French-German MAT consistently held that individuals from Alsace-Lorraine could submit claims for reparation against Germany, even if at the time the damage occurred they were not nationals of the successor State (France).[163]

157 Ibid 387: "[Attendu] qu'il résulte de ce qui précède qu'un Alsacien-Lorrain a, comme tout ressortissant des Puissances alliées et associées, droit à une indemnité pour les dommages ou préjudices causés à ses biens, droits ou intérêts, sur le territoire allemand tel qu'il existait au 1er août 1914, par l'application tant des mesures exceptionnelles de guerre que des mesures de dispositions qui font l'objet des paragraphes 1 et 3 de l'annexe à la section IV de la partie X du Traité de Versailles et prises par l'Allemagne pendant la guerre; et que la requérante a droit à une indemnité pour le préjudice causé à ses biens par la confiscation ou l'expropriation de son linge, ainsi que par la réquisition de ses ustensiles de cuivre et de laiton".

158 Ibid: "[Attendu] que le Traité de Versailles considère les Alsaciens-Lorrains comme ayant une sorte d'indigénat distinct soit de la nationalité allemande, soit de la nationalité française jusqu'au jour de leur réintégration dans cette dernière; qu'il n'a pas voulu les assimiler aux ressortissants allemands pendant la guerre, mais qu'il les considère, comme des citoyens français virtuel et qu'il a voulu les placer, vis-à-vis de l'Allemagne, au bénéfice des mêmes droits que tous les ressortissants des Puissances alliées et associées, sous la seule réserve de certaines dérogations ou modalités d'application dictées par une situation spéciale et explicitement indiquées".

159 This provision indicates that persons from the territories of Alsace-Lorraine became French nationals only on the date of the Armistice of 11 November 1918.

160 In *Berger v. Etat Allemand*, 20 July 1924, *RDTAM* v. IV, 730, 732, the MAT spoke of the population of Alsace-Lorraine as being "réintégrées dans la souveraineté française".

161 Rudolf Blühdorn, "Le fonctionnement et la jurisprudence des Tribunaux Arbitraux Mixtes creés par les traités de Paris", *Rec. des cours*, v. 41, 1932–III, 209–210; Karl Strupp, "The Competence of the Mixed Arbitral Courts of the Treaty of Versailles", 17 *AJIL* 1923, 670 ("this conception is a monstrosity from the juridical point of view").

162 *Heim & Chamant v. Etat Allemand*, French-German MAT, 7 August 1922 & 25 September 1925, *RDTAM* v. III, 50, 57.

163 *Dietz v. Etat Allemand*, ibid, 11 April 1923, *RDTAM* v. III, 351; *Briegel v. Etat Allemand*, 19 May 1923, ibid v. III, 358; *Ruolt v. Etat Allemand*, 23 May 1923, ibid v. III, 361; *Berger v. Etat Allemand*, 20 July 1924, ibid v. IV, 730; *Rothbetz v. Etat Allemand*, 8 October 1924, ibid v. IV, 747; *Grande Carrières des Vosges v. Etat Allemand*, 11 December 1922, ibid v. III, 118.

3.1.4 The Practice of the UNCC

Overview. The UNCC was set up after the 1990–1991 Gulf War to deal with claims arising from the invasion and occupation of Kuwait by Iraq.[164] Decision no. 10 of the UNCC Governing Council provides in Article 5(1) that governments can make submission on behalf of their nationals and corporations which suffered damage as a result of the conflict.[165]

Decision no. 10 also indicates that "[i]n the case of Governments existing in the territory of a former federal State, one such Government may submit claims on behalf of nationals, corporations or other entities of another such Government, if both Governments agree".[166] This provision was expressly added to deal with the difficulties arising from the dissolutions of Yugoslavia and the USSR.[167] Governing Council Decision no. 10 was thus enacted in June 1992, i.e. *after* the break-up of the Soviet Union, *before* the dissolution of Czechoslovakia and in the midst of the break-up of Yugoslavia.[168] The provision was apparently adopted at the suggestion of the Russian delegation in order to "protect the interests of claimants in the former Soviet Union".[169]

---

164 On 2 August 1990 Iraq invaded Kuwait and occupied it until 27 February 1991. On 3 April 1991 the Security Council, acting under Chapter VII of the UN Charter, adopted Res. 687 which, *inter alia*, "reafirm[ed]" that Iraq was "liable under international law for any direct loss, damage—including environmental damage and the depletion of natural resources—or injury to foreign Governments, nationals and corporations as a result of its unlawful invasion and occupation of Kuwait". UN SC Res. 687 also decided (at para 18) to "create a fund to pay compensation for claims ... and to establish a commission that will administer the fund". The UNCC was created as a subsidiary organ of the SC by Res. 692 of 20 May 1991.

165 "Decision no. 10: Provisional Rules for Claims Procedure", UNCC Governing Council, S/AC.26/1992/10, 26 June 1992. Compensation was made available for individuals, corporations, governments and international organisations. More than 2.69 million claims were filed to the UNCC for a total amount of some US$ 350 billion claimed. A total of US$ 52.4 billion was awarded in compensation (see, Internet site UNCC, under "What we did": <https://uncc.ch/what-we-did>).

166 Ibid.

167 David J. Bederman, "The United Nations Compensation Commission and the Tradition of International Claims Settlement", 27 *NYU JIL & Pol.* 1994, 1, 31; J. Crook, "The United Nations Compensation Commission: A New Structure to Enforce State Responsibility", 87 *AJIL* 1993, 144 151–152; Norbert Wühler, "The United Nations Compensation Commission; A New Contribution to the Process of International Claims Resolution", *J.Int'l Econ.L.*, 1999, 247, 253–254.

168 According to the Badinter Commission, the break-up of Yugoslavia had already commenced in November 1991 ("Opinion no. 1", 29 November 1991, 92 *ILR* 1993, 166) and was concluded in July 1992 ("Opinion no. 8", 4 July 1991, 92 *ILR* 1993, 202).

169 David J. Berderman, "The United Nations Compensation Commission and the Tradition of International Claims Settlement", 27 *NYU JIL & Pol.* 1994, 1, 31. See also, J. Crook,

This provision recognises the right of a new successor State to submit claims for reparation against Iraq before the UNCC on behalf of its new nationals, even though these individuals did not have its nationality at the time of the commission of the internationally wrongful acts (i.e. at the time of the invasion and occupation of Kuwait by Iraq, which lasted from 2 August 1990 until 27 February 1991). This is clearly one example of international case law where the traditional rule of continuous nationality was not applied in the context of State succession.[170] The UNCC also had other features which clearly deviated from the traditional rule of continuous nationality.[171] This position adopted in the context of the UNCC was based on policy reasons, namely that a different rule would have been unfair and unjust as it would have left nationals of the new States with no right of redress for damage suffered. From the documentation available, it seems that Iraq, which strongly objected to the legality of the establishment of the UNCC and to many of its features, did not formally contest this particular aspect of the system.

Case Law. Before its dissolution (on 31 December 1992), Czechoslovakia filed several claims on behalf of its nationals. However, by the time (at the end of 1994) the UNCC Governing Council was to approve the recommendations made in the Reports of the Panel of Commissioners, Czechoslovakia had

"The United Nations Compensation Commission: A New Structure to Enforce State Responsibility", 87 *AJIL* 1993, 144, 151.

170 For the same conclusion, see: ILC Special Rapporteur Šturma, Third Report, 2019, para 127; Šturma, State Succession, 674–5; Kohen & Dumberry, 72.

171 Thus, the UNCC allowed States to exercise diplomatic protection for persons who became nationals *after* the events which result in a damage. Iraqi nationals having a "bona fide nationality of any other State" did not need to show that they had acquired that nationality of the claimant State at the time the damage occurred but only that they were nationals of that State on 2 August 1991 (i.e. one year after the invasion of Kuwait) or even later in some circumstances. The rule is established in: "Decision no. 1: Criteria for Expedited Processing of Urgent Claims", UNCC Governing Council, S/AC.26/1991/1, 2 August 1991, para 17. This rule is discussed in the following Panel Reports: *Report and Recommendations Made by the Panel of Commissioners Concerning the Sixth Instalment of Claims for Departure from Iraq of Kuwait (Category "A" Claims)*, UNCC Governing Council, S/AC.26/1996/3, 16 October 1996, at para 30; *Report and Recommendations Made by the Panel of Commissioners Concerning Part One of the Second Instalment of Individual Claims for Damages Above US$100,000 (Category "D" Claims)*, UNCC Governing Council, S/AC.26/1998/11, 2 October 1998, 10. This aspect is critically assessed in: D'Argent, 356. Another such feature is "Decision no. 7: Criteria for Additional Categories of Claims", UNCC Governing Council, S/AC.26/1991/7/Rev.1, 17 March 1992, at 5, para 26, which did not require that corporations had the nationality of the claiming State at the time of the submission of the claim or at the time of the rendering of the award but only at the "date on which the claim arose".

ceased to exist. One Governing Council Decision took the view that "[t]he claims were initially submitted by the Czech and Slovak Federal Republic" but that for reasons not indicated in its Decision, "[t]he award of compensation is to be paid to the Government of the Slovak Republic".[172] In another Decision, the Governing Council simply mentioned that:

> These claims were submitted before the Czech and Slovak Federal Republic ceased to exist. Awards of compensation are to be paid to the Governments of the Czech Republic and Slovak Republic, respectively.[173]

An agreement was eventually reached between the two successor States determining which of them should be compensated for the damage caused during the invasion and occupation of Kuwait.[174] The ILC Commentary considered this case as an illustration of the existence of a "personal link" between a wrong and a new State where "the injury was suffered by persons who became nationals of one successor State".[175] After the dissolution, the two successor States directly filed claims on behalf of their own new nationals. Annex 1 shows the total amount of compensation received by the two successor States.

The case of the integration of the GDR into West Germany is slightly different, since the date of succession (3 October 1990) occurred during the period of invasion and occupation of Kuwait by Iraq (2 August 1990 to 27 February 1991). However, in the different Panel Reports, no indication is given as to whether the damage was suffered before or after the date of succession. In other words, it is not clear from the documentation available whether any nationals of the GDR suffered from damage before the date of succession.[176] Annex 1 also indicates the amount of compensation received by Germany.

172 "Decision no. 20: First Instalment of Claims for Serious Personal Injury or Death (Category "B" Claims)", UNCC Governing Council, S/AC.26/Dec.20 (1994), 26 May 1994.

173 "Decision no. 22: First Instalment of Claims for Departure from Iraq or Kuwait (Category "A" Claims)", UNCC Governing Council, S/AC.26/Dec.22 (1994), 21 October 1994.

174 The Agreement is mentioned in: "Decision no. 28: Second Instalment of Claims for Departure from Iraq or Kuwait (Category "A" Claims)", UNCC Governing Council, S/AC.26/Dec.28 (1995), 22 March 1995. The same explanation is found in many subsequent Governing Council Decisions on Category "A" Claims.

175 ILC, Commentaries, 2022, para 89, Art. 14, sub-para 4.

176 The present author was told by a member of the Permanent Mission of Germany to the United Nations in Geneva (whose name should remain confidential upon his request) that Germany had no means to know the origin of the claims and whether the claimants were in fact from East Germany or West Germany. The position of the successor State was that this did not make any difference because all claims had been considered "Germans".

Annexes 2 and 3 show the total amount of compensation received by the different successor States in the context of the break-up of the USSR and Yugoslavia.

3.2 *State Practice Where Reparation Was Provided to the Successor State for Its New Nationals*

There are several examples of State practice where reparation was provided in an agreement to the successor State for its nationals, which did not have its nationality at the time the damage occurred:[177] the 1952 Agreement on reparation between the Federal Republic of Germany and Israel,[178] the 1982 Agreement between the UK and Mauritius,[179] the bilateral agreements entered into by Austria with Central and Eastern European States in the context of the 2000 *Austrian Reconciliation Fund Law*,[180] and the 2000 German *Law on the Creation of a Foundation "Remembrance, Responsibility and Future"*.[181]

In these examples, the fact that a new State claimed compensation for damage on behalf of its new nationals was not considered by the State responsible for the internationally wrongful act as an obstacle to reparation.[182] In fact, in these cases, the right to reparation was transfered to the new States.[183]

3.2.1 The 1952 Agreement on Reparation between the Federal Republic of Germany and Israel

On 10 September 1952, a reparation agreement (the *Luxembourg Agreement*) was signed by the Federal Republic of Germany and Israel calling for the former to provide annual fixed instalments of goods and services to the Jewish State over the next 11 to 13 years in compensation for the internationally wrongful acts committed by the Third Reich before and during the Second World

177 The same examples are examined in Kohen & Dumberry, 72ff; ILC Special Rapporteur Šturma, Third Report, 2019, paras 130ff.

178 *Agreement between the State of Israel and the Federal Republic of Germany on Compensation*, 162 *UNTS* 205; *BGBl*, 1953, v. II, no. 5, 37.

179 *Agreement between the Government of the United Kingdom of Great Britain and Northern Ireland and the Government of Mauritius*, 7 July 1982 and in force on 28 October 1982, *UKTS* 1983, no. 6 (Cmnd. 8785).

180 *Federal Law Concerning the Fund for Voluntary Payments by the Republic of Austria to Former Slave Laborers and Forced Laborers of the National Socialist Regime* (the "Reconciliation Fund Law"), 8 August 2000, in force on 27 November 2000, *ÖBGBl.*, I No. 74/2000.

181 *Gesetz Zur Errichtung Einer Stiftung "Erinnerung; Verantwortung Und Zukunft"*, *BGBl.*, 2000, v. I, 1263.

182 Kohen & Dumberry, 72.

183 For the same conclusion, see: ILC Special Rapporteur Šturma, Third Report, 2019, para 130.

War.[184] The Agreement provided for the amount of DM 3 billion (US$ 715 million) to be paid in reparation by Germany to the State of Israel. The vast majority of the reparation consisted not in payments in cash but in the shipment of goods of all kinds to Israel. In two separate parallel instruments (the *Hague Protocols*), Germany also committed to the amount of DM 450 million to be given to Israel for the Conference on Jewish Material Claims against Germany (or "Claims Conference", an umbrella Jewish organisation) to compensate Nazi victims.[185] It also called for Germany to enact laws to compensate Jewish victims of Nazi persecution.[186]

At the time of the commission of the internationally wrongful acts by the Third Reich, the victims were nationals of European States (Poland, Germany, etc.) and not nationals of Israel, which did not yet exist as an independent State. This did not prevent the new State of Israel from seeking reparation against Germany on behalf of its nationals as well as on behalf of non-Israeli Jews. In a Note dated 12 March 1951 addressed to the Four Allied Powers, Israel requested compensation in the amount of US$ 1 billion from the FRG and US$ 500 million from the GDR.[187] It should be added that in the Note Israel *did not* claim compensation for damage caused by the atrocious acts committed by the Third Reich *per se*; it claimed compensation for the consequences that such acts had on its economy, mainly the costs related to the reinstallation in Israel of an estimated 500,000 refugees who fled regions of Europe which had been under the control of Germany during the War.[188] In other words, the

184 *Agreement between the State of Israel and the Federal Republic of Germany on Compensation*, 27 March 1953, 162 *UNTS* 205; *BGBl*, 1953, v. II, no. 5, 37. See, E. Nathan, "Le traité israélo-allemand du 10 septembre 1952", *RGDIP* 1954, 375–398; Frederick Honig, "The Reparations Agreement between Israel and the Federal Republic of Germany", 48(4) *AJIL* 1954, 564–578; Nicholas Balabkins, *West German Reparations to Israel* (Rutgers UP 1971); Nana Sagi, *German Reparations: A History of the Negotiations* (Magnes 1980); Ronald Zweig, *German Reparations and the Jewish World: A History of the Claims Conference* (2nd edn, Westview 2001).

185 *Protocol II between the Federal Republic of Germany and the Conference on Jewish Material Claims against Germany*, 162 *UNTS* 205; *BGBl.*, 1953, v. II, 85.

186 *Protocol I between the Federal Republic of Germany and the Conference on Jewish Material Claims against Germany*, 162 *UNTS* 205; *BGBl.*, 1953, v. II, 85.

187 Note of 12 March 1951, in: P. Giniewski, "Il trattato tedesco-israelo per le riparazioni", *Riv. studi pol. Int.* 1954, 590; also in: *Documents Relating to the Agreement between the Government of Israel and the Government of the Federal Republic of Germany* (Ministry of Foreign Affairs of Israel, see doc. nos. 5 & 22).

188 This point is discussed in: E. Nathan, "Le traité israélo-allemand du 10 septembre 1952", *RGDIP* 1954, 379–380, for whom "le montant des dommages réclamés fut calculé en fonction des dépenses engagées et prévues pour la réinstallation des immigrants juifs

Agreement covered compensation for *survivors* of the Holocaust rather than for the victims who perished in the Holocaust.

This is an example of State practice where the traditional rule of continuous nationality was not applied in the context of State succession.[189] Thus, Germany did not require that the individuals on behalf of which Israel was now claiming reparation had Israeli nationality at the time of the commission of the internationally wrongful act. Germany also did not object to the fact that Israel submitted claims on behalf of former German nationals.[190] The special character of this Agreement has been highlighted.[191] It has been argued that this example was an exception to the "fundamental principle of international responsibility"[192] which could, however, be explained by its political nature,[193] by the *ex gratia* nature of the payments[194] and, finally, by the fact it was an agreement dealing with reparation for war crimes.[195] It should be added that during the debate at the ILC, one member, Professor Nolte, explained that it

---

en provenance des pays autrefois sous la domination allemande. Ces dépenses furent estimées à US$ 3,000 par tête".

189 For the same conclusion, Kohen & Dumberry, 72–3; ILC Special Rapporteur Šturma, Third Report, 2019, para 131.

190 Rudolf Dolzer, "The Settlement of War-Related Claims: Does International Law Recognize a Victim's Private Right of Action? Lessons After 1945", 20 *Berkeley JIL* 2002, 296, 324, believes that in this Agreement "the Federal Republic of Germany declared that compensation for the victims of persecution should not be dependent on their nationality, and that the Jews of German nationality were thereby included". For the author, "[t]his is one example of the government of the Federal Republic going beyond its legal obligations under public international law". This point is also discussed in: Bert-Wolfgang Eichhorn, *Reparation als völkerrechtliche Deliktshaftung: Rechtliche und praktische Probleme unter besonderer Berücksichtigung Deutschlands (1918–1990)* (Nomos 1992) 158.

191 E. Nathan, "Le traité israélo-allemand du 10 septembre 1952, *RGDIP* 1954, 384. See also, Karen Heilig, "From the Luxembourg Agreement to Today: Representing a People", 20 *Berkeley JIL* 2002, 176, 180: "The adoption [of the 1952 Agreement] was a revolutionary idea. In no previous case in history had a State paid indemnification directly to individuals, most of them not even its own citizens. Countries paid indemnification when they were defeated in war; the fact is as old as human history itself. But that a government should pay for crimes committed, not only to its own citizens, which was unusual enough, but to hundreds of thousands of non-citizens, or to another state, the State of Israel, which was not even in existence at the time the crimes were committed … was truly a revolutionary idea".

192 Rousseau, v. V, 118; Ch. Rousseau, "Chronique des faits internationaux", *RGDIP* 1990, 764–765.

193 Ibid.

194 This is the position of Czaplinski, 355–356.

195 Rousseau, v. V, 118. For David Ruzié, *Droit international public* (14th edn, Dalloz 1999) 90, reparation for crimes against humanity, such as this 1952 Agreement, is an exception to the rule of non-succession to the right to reparation.

was a "very specific form of global compensation in a special case that could not easily (…) be seen as supporting a general principle relating to succession of States".[196]

3.2.2 The 1982 Agreement on Reparation between the United Kingdom and Mauritius for the Ilois

In 1966, before Mauritius became an independent State (in 1968), the UK, the colonial power, separated the Chagos Islands from Mauritius and ceded (for a first period of 50 years, with an extension option) one of these Islands (the Island of Diego Garcia) to the US, which eventually built a military base there. The local population which lived on the Island of Diego Garcia (some 2,000 Ilois) were moved to Mauritius. A treaty was entered into between the UK and Mauritius in 1982 with the desire to "settle certain problems which have arisen concerning the Ilois who went to Mauritius on their departure or removal from the Chagos Archipelago after November 1965".[197] Article 1 of the Agreement provides that:

> The Government of the United Kingdom shall *ex gratia* with no admission of liability pay to the Government of Mauritius for and on behalf of the Ilois and the Ilois community in Mauritius in accordance with Article 7 of this Agreement the sum of £4 million which, taken together with the payment of £650,000 already made to the Government of Mauritius, shall be in full and final settlement of all claims whatsoever of the kind referred to in Article 2 of this Agreement against the Government of the United Kingdom by or on behalf of the Ilois.[198]

196 ILC, "Provisional Summary Record of the 3477th Meeting", 73rd sess., 10 July 2019, A/CN.4/SR.3477, statement by ILC Member Georg Nolte (Germany), addressing this example mentioned in the Special Rapporteur's Third Report. He believes that this was not a case of State succession and that the "nationality of the victims had played no role in the Agreement". This is indeed true. In my view, this example simply illustrates that the rule of continuous nationality was not applied and that Germany did not require that compensation be given only to those individuals who already had Israel's nationality when the wrongful acts were committed.

197 *Agreement between the Government of the United Kingdom of Great Britain and Northern Ireland and the Government of Mauritius*, 7 July 1982, in force on 28 October 1982, *UKTS* 1983, no. 6 (Cmnd. 8785); Weston et al., 283.

198 Art. 2 of the Agreement indicates that it only deals with claims for "the closure of the plantations in the Chagos Archipelago, the departure or removal of those living or working there, the termination of their contracts, their transfer to and resettlement in Mauritius and their preclusion from returning to the Chagos Archipelago". The Agreement deals with any incidents, facts or situation, whether past, present or future, occurring in the course of these events or arising out of the consequences of these events. In return for

In the *Chagos* advisory opinion, the ICJ noted that "the sum of approximately £4 million paid by the UK was disbursed to 1,344 islanders between 1983 and 1984", adding that "as a condition for collecting the funds, the islanders were required to sign or to place a thumbprint on a form renouncing the right to return to the Chagos Archipelago".[199] The Court also mentioned that the European Court of Human Rights declared inadmissible an application made by a group of 1,786 Chagossians against the UK for breach of their rights under the European Convention on Human Rights based on the ground that the claims had been settled by this 1982 agreement.[200] The ICJ held that "the peoples of non-self-governing territories are entitled to exercise their right to self-determination in relation to their territory as a whole, the integrity of which must be respected by the administering Power", adding that "any detachment by the administering Power of part of a non-self- governing territory, unless based on the freely expressed and genuine will of the people of the territory concerned, is contrary to the right to self-determination".[201] It concluded that "as a result of the Chagos Archipelago's unlawful detachment and its incorporation into a new colony", "the process of decolonization of Mauritius was not lawfully completed when Mauritius acceded to independence in 1968"[202] and that UK's "continued administration of the Chagos Archipelago" constitutes a wrongful act of a "continuing character".[203] This case is an illustration of Article 16(4) of the Institute's Resolution.

What matters for the present purposes is that the 1982 Agreement is an example of State practice where the strict rule of continuous nationality was not applied.[204] The UK did not object to the fact that the new State of Mauritius could submit claims on behalf of a group of people which did not

compensation, the Government of Mauritius will "use its best endeavours to procure from each member of the Ilois community in Mauritius a signed renunciation of its claims" (Art. 4). Finally, under the Agreement a trust fund will be established by Mauritius (Art. 6).

199 *Legal Consequences of the Separation of the Chagos Archipelago from Mauritius in 1965*, Advisory Opinion, ICJ Rep. 2019, 95, para 120, referring to the *Chagos Islanders v. United Kingdom* case.

200 Ibid para 128.

201 Ibid para 160.

202 Ibid para 174.

203 Ibid para 177. Therefore, the UK is under an obligation to "bring an end to its administration of the Chagos Archipelago as rapidly as possible, thereby enabling Mauritius to complete the decolonization of its territory in a manner consistent with the right of peoples to selfdetermination" (para 178).

204 For the same conclusion, Kohen & Dumberry, 73; ILC Special Rapporteur Šturma, Third Report, 2019, paras 134–5.

have its nationality at the time the damage occurred.[205] However, it should be noted that this example is one concerning claims *between* the predecessor State and the successor State.[206]

3.2.3 Bilateral Agreements Entered into by Austria with Other States in the Context of the Austrian "Reconciliation Fund Law" (2000)

The Austrian Reconciliation Fund was created with money from both the government and the private sector to provide compensation for persons who were deported from their home countries by the Nazi regime for forced or slave labour in the territory of Austria during the Second World War.[207] In the context of setting up this Fund, several bilateral agreements were signed on 24 October 2000 between Austria and six Central and Eastern European countries (Belarus, the Czech Republic, Hungary, Poland, the Russian Federation and Ukraine).[208] An Executive Agreement was also signed with the US. Along with these treaties was signed a Joint Statement stating Austria's "moral responsibility" for the internationally wrongful acts committed during the War.[209]

205 It should be noted that the Ilois people recently undertook legal action in the UK demanding their return to the Chagos Islands. In its Order of 3 November 2000 (*The Queen (ex parte Bancoult) v. Foreign and Commonwealth Office*, [2001] Q.B. 1067, 2000), the High Court decided that the UK acted unlawfully in sending the Ilois people in exile and that they could go back to the Chagos Islands. The UK government did not appeal the Court's Order and accepted the return of the Ilois people to the Chagos Islands, but not to the Island of Diego Garcia. Lawsuits were also filed in US courts for compensation.

206 For reasons why such examples are of limited value in the context of the present study, see: Part 1, Sections 4.6 and 4.7.

207 *Bundesgesetz über den Fonds für freiwillige Leistungen der Republik Österreich an ehemalige Sklaven- und Zwangsarbeiter des nationalsozialistischen Regimes* (*Versöhnungsfonds-Gesetz*) ("Federal Law Concerning the Fund for Voluntary Payments by the Republic of Austria to Former Slave Laborers and Forced Laborers of the National Socialist Regime" (the "Reconciliation Fund Law")), 8 August 2000, in force on 27 November 2000, *ÖBGBl.*, I No. 74/2000 of. All relevant documents can be found on this website: <http://www.reconciliationfund.at/>. See: Roland Bank, "The New Programs for Payments to Victims of National Socialist Injustice", 44 *German YIL* 2001, 307–352. About one million foreigners were forced by the Nazi regime to work on the territory of present-day Austria.

208 The Agreement with the Russian Federation was entered into on 27 November 2000.

209 *Joint Statement on the Occasion of the Signing Ceremony of the Bilateral Agreements Relating to the Austrian Reconciliation Fund*, 24 October 2000. The Joint Statement indicates that "Austria and Austrian companies acknowledge moral responsibility for and recognize the suffering of all victims of slave or forced labor who worked on the territory of the present-day Republic of Austria and who were exploited to contribute to the economy of that time". The Statement also notes that "Austria and Austrian companies wish to respond to and acknowledge moral responsibility and bring a measure of justice to the victims of slave or forced labor during the National Socialist era or World War II". In the Statement, reference is also made of the "common objective" of Austria and Austrian

What is interesting in the context of the present study is the fact that some of these bilateral treaties were entered into with new States: Belarus, the Czech Republic and Ukraine. When the damage occurred the individuals injured were not nationals of these new successor States. This did not prevent the State responsible (i.e. Austria in the context of the Fund) to provide compensation to the new successor States on behalf of these victims. This is therefore one example where the rule of continuous nationality was not applied in the context of State succession.[210]

3.2.4 The Joint Statement by Germany and other States in the Context of the German Foundation "Remembrance, Responsibility and Future" (2000)

Following the end of the Second World War, the Federal Republic of Germany decided to compensate victims of Nazi persecutions. Apart from the abovementioned 1952 reparation agreement entered into with Israel, many laws and funds were created over the years: The *Holocaust Indemnification* statute in 1953 (which was revised in 1956 and 1963),[211] the "Hardship Fund" in 1980,[212]

---

companies (including parents and subsidiaries as defined in Annex A of the Statement) to "receive all-embracing and enduring legal peace for all claims involving or related to the use of slave or forced labor during the National Socialist era or World War II". The Statement is also "recognizing that the establishment of the Reconciliation Fund does not create a basis for claims against Austria, Austrian companies, or Austrian nationals".

210 For the same conclusion, Kohen & Dumberry, 74; ILC Special Rapporteur Šturma, Third Report, 2019, para 133.

211 The statutes were collectively referred to as the "BEG" (*Bundesgesetzes zur Entschädigung für Opfer der nationalsozialistischen Verfolgung* or more simply *Bundesentschaedigungsgesetz*, e.g. the "Federal Law for the Compensation of the Victims of National Socialist Persecution"). The law of 1 October 1953 was revised on 29 June 1956 (*BGBl.*, 1956, v. I, 559) and on 14 September 1965 (*Zweiten Gesetzes zur Änderung des Bundesentschädigungsgesetzes-BEG-Schlußgesetz*, "Final Federal Compensation Law", BGBl., 1965, v. I, 1315). According to the US Foreign Claims Settlement Commission ("German Compensation for National Socialist Crimes", available at this website: <http://www.ushmm.org/assets/frg.htm#1>), more than four million claims were submitted to Germany under these different laws and Germany provided more than DM 72 billion in compensation.

212 Under Section 1 of the "Guidelines to Hardship Fund", published in Germany's Federal Register (14 October 1980), the Fund was created to compensate Nazi victims who "suffered several health damage" and were "therefore in a special hardship situation" and had not obtained any prior compensation because they had not met time deadlines or residency requirements of the BEG. The Fund, which was administered by the "Claims Conference" (the Conference on Jewish Material Claims Against Germany), was mainly set up to compensate Nazi victims living in the former USSR and Central and Eastern Europe.

the "Article 2 Fund" in 1992,[213] and, finally, the "Central and Eastern European Fund" of 1998.[214]

At the end of the 1990s, German companies were faced with numerous class action lawsuits brought before US courts by former slave and forced labourers of the Nazi era. It is in this context that several German companies took the initiative to set up a fund which would compensate victims. In August 2000, the Federal Republic of Germany passed the *Law on the Creation of a Foundation "Remembrance, Responsibility and Future"*.[215] The preamble to the Law indicated that the "German Bundestag acknowledges political and moral responsibility for the victims of National Socialism"[216] while remaining silent as to Germany's legal responsibility. The legislation established a fund of approximately US$ 5.2 billion to compensate those persons who performed forced labour in concentration camps or in another place of confinement (outside Austria) or a ghetto "under comparable conditions".[217] Under the Law, the

---

213 Under Art. 2 of the *Agreement on the Enactment and Interpretation of the Unification Treaty* of 18 September 1990, "[t]he Federal Government is prepared, in continuation of the policy of the German Federal Republic, to enter into agreements with the Claims Conference for additional Fund arrangements in order to provide hardship payments to persecutees who thus far received no or only minimal compensation according to the legislative provisions of the German Federal Republic". The "Article 2 Fund" was thus established in 1992 after the integration of the GDR into the FRG. The Fund was administered by the Claims Conference to provide pensions to needy Nazi persecutees who had received minimal or no compensation.

214 In January 1998, the Claims Conference and the German government entered into an agreement requiring Germany to contribute DM 200 million over a four-year period (beginning 1 January 1999) to directly compensate Holocaust victims in the former Soviet Union and Central and Eastern Europe. The "Central and Eastern European Fund" was established in May 1998 and is administered by the Claims Conference.

215 *Gesetz Zur Errichtung Einer Stiftung "Erinnerung; Verantwortung Und Zukunft"*, *BGBl.*, 2000, v. I, 1263. The Law was amended by the Law of 4 August 2001 (in force on 11 August 2001, *BGBl.*, 2001–I, 2036) as well as by the Law of 21 August 2002 (in force on 28 August 2002, *BGBl.*, 2002–I, 3347). All the relevant documents can be found at the official Internet site: <http://www.stiftung-evz.de>. See, Roland Bank, "The New Programs for Payments to Victims of National Socialist Injustice", 14 *German YIL* 2001, 307–352; Sean D. Murphy, *United States Practice in International Law, v. 1: 1999–2001* (CUP 2002) 136–144; Sean D. Murphy, "Implementation of German Holocaust Claims Agreement", 97 *AJIL* 2003, 692–695.

216 The preamble indicates that: "The National Socialist State inflicted severe injustice on slave laborers and forced laborers, through deportation, internment, exploitation which in some cases extended to destruction through labor, and through a large number of other human rights violations". It also stated that "German enterprises which participated in the National Socialist injustice bear a historic responsibility and must accept it".

217 Art. 11(1) al. 1, *Law on the Creation of a Foundation "Remembrance, Responsibility and Future"*. The Law also provides compensation for other types of personal injuries (such as

German government and German companies each provided half the funds for the Foundation. The fund was meant to be the exclusive forum for resolving such claims.

In the context of the Final Plenary Meeting concluding the preparation of the Foundation, a Joint Statement was signed by Germany, the US, Belarus, the Czech Republic, Ukraine, Israel, Poland, Russia, the Foundation Initiative of German Enterprises and the Claims Conference (a Jewish organisation).[218] It is noteworthy that this Statement was entered into by Germany and several States which did not yet exist at the time the internationally wrongful acts were committed. Germany did not invoke the rule of continuous nationality; it accepted that these States could negotiate a reparation agreement on behalf of individuals which did not have their nationality at the time the damage occurred. It should be added that during the debate at the ILC, one member, Professor Nolte, had doubts about the relevance of this example.[219] He explained that it was a "very specific form of global compensation in a special case that could not easily (...) be seen as supporting a general principle relating to succession of States".[220] For him, the parties simply "made a context specific special arrangement" and did not conceive it as a matter of State succession to responsibility. He also "doubted that it evidenced an *opinio juris* that affected traditional general rules relating to the nationality of claims".[221] It is true that the example involves a very specific context evidencing no *opinio juris* by the parties. In my view, the example is nonetheless interesting because it illustrates that the rule of continuous nationality was not applied by Germany.[222]

3.3 *Cases Where the Rule of Continuous Nationality Was Applied*

In only one significant case the traditional rule of continuous nationality was applied to prevent a new State from claiming reparation on behalf of its new nationals for damage arising out of events which took place before the date of succession.[223] This is the 1939 *Panevezys-Saldutiskis Railway* case decided

medical experiments and death or serious injuries to the health of a child, Art. 11(1) para 5) as well as some type of property damage where German companies were involved (Art. 11(1) para 1, item 3).

218 Joint Statement, 17 July 2000, *BGBl.*, 2000, v. II, 1383ff.

219 ILC, "Provisional Summary Record of the 3477th Meeting", 73rd sess., 10 July 2019, A/CN.4/SR.3477, statement by ILC Member Georg Nolte (Germany), addressing this example mentioned in the Special Rapporteur's Third Report.

220 Ibid.

221 Ibid.

222 For the same conclusion, Kohen & Dumberry, 74; ILC Special Rapporteur Šturma, Third Report, 2019, para 132.

223 For the same conclusion, Kohen & Dumberry, 74–75.

by the PCIJ (Section 3.3.1).[224] There are two other judicial decisions which are sometime referred to by writers but which, in fact, do not deal *per se* with the question whether a successor State has the right to claim reparation on behalf of its new nationals.[225] These are the 1849 *Sandoval and Others* case and the 1850 *Champion* case, both decided by the US Board of Commissioners in the context of the annexation of New Mexico and Texas by the US (Section 3.3.2). I have also found one example where the rule of continuous nationality was applied to prevent the *continuing State* from claiming reparation on behalf of its *former national* (Section 3.3.3).

3.3.1 The *Panevezys-Saldutiskis Railway* Case (1939)

The question whether the traditional rule of continuous nationality should apply in the context of State succession was dealt with in the *Panevezys-Saldutiskis Railway* case before the PCIJ.[226] In this case, Estonia (which declared its independence in February 1918 but was recognised by Russia only in 1920) exercised diplomatic protection on behalf of a company which had been expropriated by the Lithuanian authorities (which also declared its independence in February 1918 but was recognised by Russia only in 1920). Estonia claimed reparation for the expropriation.

The case is important even if the Court did not thoroughly address the application of the rule of continuous nationality in the context of State succession. Thus, the Court decided instead to join the Lithuanian objection on this point to the merits of the dispute. The question was nevertheless thoroughly debated by the Parties in their written and oral pleadings.[227] The issue was also raised and discussed in the individual opinions of some judges and, in particular, by Judge van Eysinga in his dissenting opinion.

---

224 *Panevezys-Saldutiskis Railway* case.

225 Eric Wyler, *La règle dite de la continuité de la nationalité dans le contentieux international* (PUF 1990) 115, also refers to the *Foucher* case (*Arthur Denis v. United States*, France-US Mixed Claims Commission, case no. 603, decision of June 1883) which arose in the context of the cession of Louisiana by France to the US in 1803. See, Moore, History, v. III, 2510; ibid v. II, 1152. However, a closer look at the facts of the case shows that the damage complained about by the heirs of Mr Foucher took place *after* the cession of territory in 1803. This case is therefore not relevant in the context of the present study.

226 *Panevezys-Saldutiskis Railway* case. This case is analysed in: Verzijl, Jurisprudence, 551–571. See also: Eibe H. Riedel, "Panevezys Saldutiskis Railway Case", in: Bernhardt, 224.

227 The present section contains large extracts of the arguments submitted by the Parties in their written and oral pleadings. It is pertinent to do given that scholars rarely refer to these documents.

The Facts of the Case. In 1892, a railway company named "First Company of Secondary Railways in Russia" (hereinafter referred to as the "First Company") was founded in St. Petersburg, Russia, and incorporated under the laws of the Russian Empire.[228] The company possessed railway lines and other assets in several Russian provinces. One such railway line was the Panevezys-Saldutiskis line, which passed through the Baltic provinces. The railway company was impacted by several dramatic sets of events after the Russian Revolution of 1917 and the end of the First World War. The company was first affected by a Soviet Russian decree of nationalisation in December 1917.[229] Soon after, both Estonia and Lithuania made declarations of independence in February 1918. As a result, different parts of the railway line were now under the sovereignty of the new States of Lithuania, Ukraine and Estonia. In September 1919, the new State of Lithuania confiscated (with no compensation in return) the assets of the First Company situated in Lithuania, which included the Panevezys-Saldutiskis line.[230]

In February 1920, the *Treaty of Tartu* was entered into between Soviet Russia and the new State of Estonia.[231] Under this Treaty, Russia transferred to Estonia all rights and all company shares of former private possessions (which had been nationalised by decree after the Revolution, such as those of the First Company) which were now situated in Estonia and "agreed" that the seats of those companies would be regarded as being transferred to Estonia.[232] Estonia then promulgated a series of provisional regulations regarding these joint-stock companies (which had undertakings in Estonia), stating that they would have to conduct shareholders' meetings within two months to be registered

228 For an overview of the facts, see: Verzijl, Jurisprudence, 555ff.

229 This was followed by a series of other Soviet decrees of nationalisation of all railway companies (from June 1918 to March 1919).

230 However, it should be noted that in October 1920, the railway line ceased to be under Lithuanian sovereignty and passed to the new State of Poland.

231 *Treaty of Tartu*, 2 February 1920, *LNTS* v. XI, 29–71.

232 Under Art. XI of the Treaty, Russia renounces to "all [its] rights to movable and immovable property of individuals, which previously did not belong to her, in so far as such property may be situated in Estonian territory". They became "the sole property of Estonia". In another supplementary article to this provision, it was stipulated that "the Russian government will hand over to the Estonian government *inter alia* the shares of those joint-stock companies which had undertakings in Estonian territory". The provision expressly referred to the First Company as one such company. Finally, the supplementary article to this provision also included the stipulation that the "Russian government agrees that the registered offices of [those companies] shall be regarded as transferred to [Tallinn, the capital of Estonia] and that the Estonian authorities shall be entitled to amend the statues of such companies in accordance with the rules to be laid down by those authorities".

under Estonian law. In the event of their failure to do so, the regulations indicated that they would be nationalised. In 1923, Estonia nationalised the part of the railway line of the First Company which was situated within its territory. In November 1923, the First Company held a shareholders' meeting in Tallinn: it proceeded to revise and amend its statutes in accordance with Estonian Law. It was also decided at that meeting that the company would be renamed "Esimene", with registered offices in Tallinn, Estonia. In 1923, the company "Esimene" was therefore formally Estonian by law.

The company "Esimene" subsequently requested compensation from Lithuania for the nationalisation which took place in 1919. These efforts were unsuccessful. In November 1937, Estonia submitted a claim before the PCIJ against Lithuania, on behalf of the company "Esimene", for reparation for the nationalisation of the Panevezys-Saldutiskis line.

The Arguments of the Parties. On the merits of the case, Lithuania maintained that it did not commit any internationally wrongful act. For Lithuania, the Russian company had ceased to exist as a consequence of the Soviet nationalisation decrees; it no longer existed in 1919 when the Lithuanian government took control of that part of the railway line situated on its territory.

In defence, Lithuania submitted two preliminary objections. One objection was that the company had not exhausted all local remedies under Lithuanian Law. The other objection submitted by Lithuania was that the Court had no jurisdiction over the present dispute since Estonia could not invoke any breach of obligation on behalf of the company because at the time the nationalisation took place, no legal relationship existed between Estonia and the company (which no longer existed).[233] Lithuania further argued that even if it was established that the company still existed (and that it had later become Estonian), Estonia should anyway be prevented from submitting this claim on behalf of the company in application of the rule of continuous nationality. Lithuania described this "well-established" principle in the following terms:

> Le Gouvernement lithuanien … reconnaît à chaque gouvernement le droit de prendre fait et cause pour ses ressortissants qu'il considère comme lésés par un acte émanant d'un autre gouvernement et contraire au droit international. Mais en même temps le Gouvernement lithuanien croit devoir rappeler le principe bien établi du droit international qui

233 "Contre-Mémoire", Lithuania, 30 August 1938, PCIJ *Serie C, Pleadings, Oral Statements and Documents*, Judicial Year 1938–1939, no. 86, 215, 265, 267.

> veut que le particulier en faveur duquel intervient un État ait été son ressortissant à la date du préjudice subi.[234]
>
> [D]'après le droit international ... un gouvernement ne peut régulièrement porter un procès devant la juridiction internationale que si la demande est nationale au moment du préjudice subi. Il est vrai que tout gouvernement peut, par un traité, écarter cette règle. Mais, dans chaque cas particulier, il faut alors démontrer qu'un accord pareil est intervenu. Le Gouvernement lithuanien n'a conclu aucun traité avec le Gouvernement estonien et n'a pris aucun engagement envers ce Gouvernement, par lesquels il aurait renoncé à cette règle générale du droit international.[235]

Thus, according to Lithuania, the company had already changed its nationality in 1919 and was not an Estonian national company at the time the damage occurred (when its assets were confiscated by Lithuania).[236]

On the merits of the case, Estonia submitted that the acts of nationalisation by Lithuania were illegal.[237] Estonia also maintained that the Russian

234 "Exceptions préliminaires", Lithuania, 12 March 1938, ibid 127, 138. See also, "Exposé", Prof. Mandelstam, Lithuania, 13 June 1938, ibid 430, 436ff.

235 "Exposé", ibid 430, 434.

236 "Exceptions préliminaires", Lithuania, 12 March 1938, ibid 127, 142. This is the argument developed by Lithuania: "L'application de la règle du droit international [i.e. the rule of continuous nationality] ci-dessus rappelée au cas actuel conduit logiquement à l'irrecevabilité de la demande du Gouvernement estonien. En effet, l'acte incriminé au Gouvernement lithuanien par la société estonienne est celui de la prise de possession du chemin de fer Panevezys-Saldutiskis. La règle plus haute démontrée exige, pour que le Gouvernement estonien soit qualifié à présenter au Gouvernement lithuanien des réclamations à ce sujet, qu'au moment où le Gouvernement lithuanien a pris possession du chemin de fer la personne qui se prétend lésée par cette mesure ait été un citoyen estonien. Or, le ministère des Communication lithuanien a commencé à exploiter ledit chemin de fer encore en septembre 1919. A cette époque, la Première Société était déjà nationalisée. Mais, admettant même *ex hypothesi* qu'en septembre 1919 la Première Société n'avait pas encore cessé d'exister, elle ne possédait pas, en tous cas, à cette époque la nationalité estonienne; en effet, l'assemblée générale des actionnaires de cette société, qui a pris la décision de transférer le siège social de la société de Pétersbourg à Tallinn, n'a eu lieu qu'en 1923. Il est donc parfaitement clair que le Gouvernement estonien n'a aucune qualité pour porter ses réclamations contre le Gouvernement lithuanien au sujet de la prise de possession du chemin de fer Panevezys-Saldutiskis devant la Cour Permanente de Justice Internationale, car si la société, pour laquelle le Gouvernement estonien a pris fait et cause, est à l'heure actuelle estonienne, elle ne l'était pas encore en 1919".

237 "Réplique", Estonia, 8 October 1938, ibid 288, 316ff, and 319: "Le gouvernement lithuanien ayant à maintes reprises refusé la restitution du chemin de fer à la Première Société, la demande du Gouvernement estonien est basée sur le simple principe qu'une indemnité correspondant au dommage que la Première Société a subi par suite d'un acte contraire au droit international doit lui être payée. Ce dommage est double: d'une part la mainmise

company had not ceased to exist as a consequence of the Soviet nationalisation decrees.[238] Such nationalisation would have been anyway impossible, since in 1918 all railway lines were situated *outside* the Russian territory as a result of the *Peace Treaty of Brest Litovsk* (3 March 1918) and the newly achieved independence of Lithuania, Ukraine and Estonia.[239] The position of Estonia was that even though the company had undergone some organisational transformation (it changed seats and its nationality), it was essentially the same company as the First Company, which was founded under (pre-Soviet) Russian Law.[240]

In response to the preliminary objection regarding nationality submitted by Lithuania, Estonia took two lines of argumentation, which will now be examined. The first argument put forward by Estonia was essentially factual, while the second one attacked the soundness of the strict rule of continuous nationality referred to by Lithuania.

Estonia first submitted some *factual arguments* which were aimed at making unnecessary the use of the rule of continuous nationality. Estonia maintained that, as a matter of fact, the company was already of Estonian nationality at the time the damage occurred. In order to prove this allegation, Estonia submitted three different (alternative, and to some extent conflicting) interpretations of events on the question of the proper date at which the damage occurred and on the question of the moment at which the company became Estonian:

– Because all legal issues concerning Estonia's relationship with Russia were only finally settled in February 1920 (*Treaty of Tartu*), Estonia argued that the company "Esimene" was *de facto* Estonian by nationality since the declaration of independence of Estonia (February 1918), i.e. *before* the damage occurred (in September 1919).[241]
– The company "Esimene" may have become Estonian only after 1919, but that does not matter since the initial internationally wrongful act of expropriation and the subsequent denial by the Lithuanian authorities that the company continue the exploitation of the railway line was of a *continuous character*. The illegal act which first occurred in 1919 continued to exist at the time the company formally became Estonian (in 1923).[242]

lithuanienne a dépossédé la Première Société d'un bien qui lui appartenait, et, d'autre part, depuis 1919 elle a été privée de la jouissance de sa concession".

238 Ibid 302ff, 316.

239 "Exposé", Baron Nolde, Estonia, 19–20 January 1939, ibid 532, 539.

240 Ibid 558.

241 "Observations et conclusions", Estonia, 20 April 1938, ibid 176, 185–186.

242 Ibid 184–185.

– The company "Esimene" in fact suffered damage only after September 1919, at a time when the company had clearly become Estonian (in 1923).[243]

Estonia presented two different *legal arguments* against the application of the rule of continuous nationality in the present case. The first main legal argument advanced by Estonia was that this rule (in its absolute form) did not exist as such in modern international law:

> [L]a règle rigide et absolue dont le Gouvernement lithuanien veut doter le droit des gens n'existe pas, et que tant la doctrine que la jurisprudence ont pu dégager de la diversité des circonstances dans lesquelles se posait le problème de la réclamation internationale de nombreuses exceptions à la règle en question.[244]

Estonia argued that the rule was not of strict application[245] and that scholarship (quoted by Lithuania in favour of the rule) had certainly not envisaged its application in the context of changes of nationality due to border changes.[246] In other words, it was submitted that the rule of continuous nationality should not apply in the context of State succession. In fact, Estonia sought to distinguish the present case from others where the doctrine of continuous nationality had been applied by arguing that in the case of the company "Esimene", the change of nationality had occurred *involuntarily* as a result of State succession. This is clear from these different extracts of its pleadings:

> Rien à objecter contre l'esprit de la règle: l'acquisition volontaire d'une réclamation étrangère par un ressortissant ou l'obtention par un réclamant étranger de la nationalité de l'État par voie de naturalisation dans le but d'acquérir la protection pour ses réclamations ne justifie pas

243 "Exposé", Baron Nolde, Estonia, 14–15 June 1938, ibid 469, 478.

244 "Observations et conclusions", Estonia, 20 April 1938, ibid 176, 194. See also, 186: "Le Gouvernement estonien estime enfin que la règle en question telle qu'elle est formulée dans l'exception n'existe pas en réalité dans le droit des gens moderne". More specifically, Estonia referred (ibid 187) to the above-mentioned debate at the Institute at its 1932 session of Oslo.

245 Ibid 189: "Ainsi, de tous côtés la tradition doctrinale que désire voir maintenir dans toute son intégralité le Gouvernement lithuanien s'effrite et cède la place à des règles plus nuancées et plus souples, qui tiennent compte des diversités de circonstances dans lesquelles se pose le problème de la responsabilité internationale". See also, "Exposé", Baron Nolde, Estonia, 14–15 June 1938, ibid 469, 475.

246 "Exposé", ibid.

> l'intervention de l'État: celui-ci serait alors un 'agent de recouvrement'. Mais les cas où la réclamation devient la propriété d'un ressortissant par la volonté de la loi et où l'acquisition d'une nouvelle nationalité est l'effet d'un changement territorial ne tombent évidemment pas sous l'empire de la règle prise dans son esprit.[247]
>
> On voit ainsi que l'ancienne jurisprudence arbitrale visait essentiellement les cas où le changement dans la nationalité de la réclamation provenait d'actes volontaires ou de manœuvres tendant à placer la réclamation sous les auspices d'un nouvel État, généralement plus puissant … Il serait imprudent d'étendre cette jurisprudence au cas où le changement de la nationalité de la réclamation de la réclamation est le résultat de circonstances indépendantes de la volonté des intéressés et où l'application automatique de la règle conduirait à priver les individus et les Etats de la possibilité de faire valoir leurs droits actuels devant des juridictions internationales.[248]
>
> Je ne crois pas qu'on puisse trouver dans le droit international positif de règle qui dise que, dans le cas où le changement de nationalité n'est pas volontaire—il ne s'agit pas ici de chercher une protection pour défendre un droit—que dans les cas où, sans sa volonté, l'individu est devenu sujet d'un autre pays, c'est fini: vous avez eu le malheur de changer de nationalité, vous n'avez plus de protection internationale, puisque la chaîne de la persistance de la nationalité a été brisée.[249]

The second legal argument of Estonia was to say that at any rate the rule of continuous nationality should not be applied *in the present case* because it would lead to inequitable results. It argued in favour of the abandonment of the rule "en présence de circonstance de droit et de fait qui auraient rendu la règle appliquée dans sa lettre souverainement injuste".[250] One unjust consequence resulting from the application of the rule was that the company, which had suffered damage, could not seek any redress solely because it (involuntarily) changed its nationality:

> Il s'agit d'une société qui devient estonienne, et on se demande si le droit de protéger cette société aurait disparu du fait de ce changement de nationalité. Je prends l'analogie très simple d'un Estonien, d'un individu

247 "Observations et conclusions", Estonia, 20 April 1938, ibid 176, 188.
248 Ibid 190.
249 "Exposé", Baron Nolde, Estonia, 14–15 June 1938, ibid 469, 474.
250 "Observations et conclusions", Estonia, 20 April 1938, ibid 176, 193.

> privé. Le traité de paix l'a fait changer de nationalité. Il a subi à l'étranger un préjudice au moment où il était encore russe, puisque la nationalité estonienne n'existait pas au point de vue international avant 1920, avant la reconnaissance de son indépendance par les Soviets. Ce préjudice porté à l'étranger ne donnerait lieu à aucune intervention diplomatique dans l'espèce: on dirait au ressortissant estonien: Vous avez changé de nationalité, personne ne peut plus protéger? Le résultat serait certainement injuste.[251]

According to Estonia, another unjust consequence of the application of the rule of continuous nationality in the present case would be that neither the continuing State (Russia) nor the successor State (Estonia) could provide diplomatic protection to the company:

> En succédant à la Russie dans l'exercice exclusif de la souveraineté à l'égard des sociétés reconnues estoniennes, l'Estonie a de ce fait même succédé dans son droit de protéger les droits et les intérêts de ces sociétés. Affirmer le contraire équivaut à reconnaître qu'aucun État n'a plus le droit de protéger ces sociétés en tout ce qui concerne la période où elles étaient encore russes. Car, d'une part, selon le Gouvernement lithuanien, l'Estonie n'a pas ce droit, les sociétés n'étant devenues estoniennes qu'en 1920, et, d'autre part, le Traité de paix de 1920 a manifestement privé la Russie du droit d'intervenir en faveur des sociétés. Un vide en résulterait qui ne saurait être justifié en droit. Une règle du droit des gens sanctionnant une solution négative de cette nature paraît difficilement concevable.[252]

In its pleadings, Lithuania refuted the arguments developed by Estonia and stated that scholarship and international case law did not support any difference of treatment between cases where changes of nationality were voluntary from those other collective changes imposed upon individuals by State succession.[253] Lithuania further argued that the distinction put forward by Estonia between cases of involuntary and voluntary changes of nationality was anyway not applicable in the present case since the seat of the company had not changed as a result of any border modification. Thus, Lithuania maintained

251 "Exposé", Baron Nolde, Estonia, 14–15 June 1938, ibid 469, 473–474.

252 "Observations et conclusions", Estonia, 20 April 1938, ibid 176, 186.

253 "Exposé", Prof. Mandelstam, Lithuania, 13 June 1938, ibid 430, 442–443. See also, "Réplique", ibid, 17 June 1938, ibid 497, 500–501.

that the seat of the company had remained in Russia after Estonia became an independent State.[254] Lithuania also submitted (alternatively) that the distinction referred to by Estonia between cases of involuntary and voluntary changes of nationality was of no help in the present case since the company had changed its nationality *voluntarily*.[255] Lithuania maintained that the company became Estonian in 1923 by its own voluntary acts, deciding to change its seat and move it to Tallinn, Estonia.[256] Estonia, on the contrary, held that the change of nationality of the company was not voluntary, as it resulted from the application of the *Treaty of Tartu* of 1920.[257]

Ultimately, Counsel for Estonia indicated that "je crois que la Cour de Justice internationale pourra, au moment où elle étudiera le fond du problème, tenir compte d'une tendance certaine à ne pas considérer la règle de la persistance de la nationalité comme une règle absolue".[258] To this argument, Lithuania responded that "les tribunaux internationaux n'appliquent pas des tendances, mais les règles du droit positif".[259]

The Decision of the Court. In its Decision, the Court first affirmed the classic rule of diplomatic protection. This is the relevant quote from the Decision:

> In the opinion of the Court, the rule of international law on which the first Lithuanian objection is based is that in taking up the case of one of its nationals, by resorting to diplomatic action or international judicial proceedings on his behalf, a State is in reality asserting its own right, the right to ensure in the person of its nationals respect for the rules of international law. This right is necessarily limited to intervention on behalf of its own nationals because, in the absence of a special agreement, it is the bond of nationality between the State and the individual which alone confers upon the State the right of diplomatic protection, and it is a part of the function of diplomatic protection that the right to take up a claim and to ensure respect for the rules of international law must be envisaged. Where the injury was done to the national of some other State, no claim to which such injury may give rise falls within the scope of the

254 "Réplique", ibid, 497, 503.

255 "Exposé", Prof. Mandelstam, Lithuania, 13 June 1938, ibid 430, 443.

256 "Duplique", Baron Nolde, Estonia, 18 June 1938, ibid 518, 521. See also, "Exposé", Prof. Mandelstam, Lithuania, 24–25 January 1939, ibid 591, 623–624.

257 "Exposé", Baron Nolde, Estonia, 14–15 June 1938, ibid 469, 475–476. See also, the answer given to a question asked by Judge Hudson: "Exposé", ibid, 19–20 January 1939, ibid 532, 591.

258 "Exposé", Baron Nolde, Estonia, 14–15 June 1938, 469, 475.

259 "Réplique", Prof. Mandelstam, Lithuania, 17 June 1938, ibid 497, 501.

> diplomatic protection which a State is entitled to afford nor can it give rise to a claim which that State is entitled to espouse.[260]

The Court noted that the rule of continuous nationality could be set aside by agreement between the parties and that there were examples of international adjudication where this had been done. However, it held that in the present case "no grounds exist for holding that the parties intended to exclude the application of the [continuous nationality] rule".[261] The Court then stated that "[t]he Lithuanian Agent is therefore right in maintaining that Estonia must prove that at the time when the injury occurred which is alleged to involve the international responsibility of Lithuania the company suffering the injury possessed Estonian nationality".[262] This is in fact the only passage from the Decision where the Court clearly seems to have endorsed the traditional rule of continuous nationality.

The Court did not further investigate the question. It decided instead that the question whether the company was indeed Estonian at the time the damage occurred could not be separated from issue of the ownership of the *Panevezys-Saldutiskis* railway line (which was also disputed by Lithuania). In other words, the preliminary objection raised by Lithuania could not be decided without a full examination of the case on the merits.[263] This aspect of the Court's decision was criticised by some Judges in their individual opinions[264] as well as in scholarship.[265]

Judge De Visscher and Count Rostworowski, in their common individual opinion, were of the view that the Lithuanian argument regarding the absence of Estonian nationality of the claim was "well-founded".[266] They explained that the "initial act of injury" was the seizure of the railway line in 1919 and then went on to say that at that time the First Company was not yet Estonian. According to the two Judges, the claim submitted by Estonia should have been

260 *Panevezys-Saldutiskis Railway* case, 16.

261 Ibid.

262 Ibid 16–17.

263 Ibid 17.

264 For instance, the position of Judge De Visscher and Count Rostworowski in their common individual opinion (ibid 24ff) concluding that the Court should have decided the preliminary objections raised by Lithuania in the first stage of the proceedings before dealing with the merits of the case. The same conclusion was reached by Judge Erich in his individual opinion (ibid 50ff). *Contra*: diss. op. Judge Hudson (ibid 46).

265 Verzijl, Jurisprudence, 555, 566; Atlam, 139; H.F. Van Panhuys, *The Role of Nationality in International Law: An Outline* (A.W. Sythoff 1959) 93.

266 *Panevezys-Saldutiskis Railway* case, 24.

rejected on the ground of the lack of the "bond of nationality required by international law". This is the full reasoning of the Judges:

> The Estonian Government has tried to prove that the rule of law underlying the objection is subject to various qualifications, but it has not claimed that in 1919 the interests damaged by the seizure had already acquired Estonian character. On its own admission, the First Russian Company, which is said to have survived the nationalization decrees, was only transformed into an Estonian company as a result of the Treaty of Tartu of February 2nd, 1920, and, to quote the words of the Estonian Agent: 'at the time and by the fact of the treaty of peace' (oral statement of the Agent for the Estonian Government, June 14th, 1938; Oral Statements, p. 40). Accordingly, even it could be agreed that the change of nationality dates back to the Treaty of Tartu, the change could still not operate in regard to a fact which the Parties agree in dating 1919. Finally, either the interests affected by the seizure were at that time still represented by the Russian company, according to the Estonian Government's theory of survival, or they were no longer represented by any company at all, according to the argument of the Lithuanian Government to the effect that the nationalization decrees destroyed the Company's legal personality. In either case—and this fact is alone decisive—there was in 1919 no Estonian company, and therefore the bond of nationality required by international law to have existed at the time the injury was suffered, was manifestly lacking.[267]

The Court finally upheld the second preliminary objections raised by Lithuania according to which the company had not exhausted all local remedies before Lithuanian courts. The case was therefore rejected.

The Dissenting Opinion of Judge van Eysinga. In his dissenting opinion, Judge van Eysinga argued that the Court should have first dealt with the two preliminary objections raised by Lithuania. He concluded that both objections were unfounded. His reasoning on the first objection (dealing with the nationality of the claim) will now be examined.

He first noted that it could not be denied that at the time the expropriation measures were taken by the Lithuanian authorities (in 1919) the First Company did not have Estonian nationality.[268] Lithuania was therefore right to invoke

267 Ibid 27.
268 Ibid 31.

the rule of continuous nationality. However, the Judge indicated that "there appears to be ground for serious doubt" that such rule of law exists "in the absolute form attributed by [Lithuania]".[269] He concluded that Lithuania had "not succeeded in establishing the existence of the rule" in its strict and absolute form.[270]

The Judge went on to explain that the rule of continuous nationality had been frequently used in the special context of Mixed Arbitral Commissions and that the logic of such rule in this context was "perfectly comprehensible", as these judicial bodies are aimed at treating only claims by nationals of both sides. He further admitted that "perhaps in this sphere it is possible to speak of a rule of international law [in favour of continuous nationality] in the sense that, in the absence of a definite treaty provision, it must be observed by the Mixed Commissions".[271] The Judge also mentioned that scholarship often quoted in support of the strict application of the rule of continuous nationality was in fact related to the work of these Mixed Commissions. He also made reference to the above-mentioned debate at the Institute at its 1932 Oslo session and, in particular, to the position taken by Politis during those debates. He said that the rule of continuous nationality "may be binding on a certain number of cases, [but] is by no means crystallised as a general rule".[272]

The Judge was of the view that the Court should not take part in the crystallisation of the rule because of its "inequitable results". This is his full reasoning:

> And in this connection the question also arises whether it is reasonable to describe as an unwritten rule of international law a rule which would entail that, when a change of sovereignty takes place, the new State, or the State which has increased its territory would not be able to espouse any claim of any of its new nationals in regard to injury suffered before the change of nationality. It may also be questioned whether indeed it is part of the Court's task to contribute towards the crystallisation of unwritten rules of law which would lead to such inequitable results. It follows from the foregoing that the Lithuanian Agent has not succeeded in establishing the existence, in the absolute form alleged by him, of the rule of international law to the effect that a claim must be a national claim not only at the time of its presentation but also at the time when

269 Ibid.
270 Ibid.
271 Ibid 33.
272 Ibid 35.

> the injury was suffered, and that this rule cannot resist the normal operation of the law of state succession.[273]

The conclusion reached by the Judge was that the existence of the rule of continuous nationality, in its "absolute form", had not been proven by Lithuania. Therefore, he indicated that such rule "cannot resist the normal operation of the law of State succession".[274] It seems that Judge van Eysinga believed in some sort of universal succession: "the legal life of the new State in all its aspects proceeds in succession to the legal life of the old State. Thus, in all matters where the Government of the latter had jurisdiction, its place is now taken by the Government of the new State. This holds good as regards diplomatic protection".[275] Therefore, the Judge was clearly of the view that there should be a succession to the right to exercise diplomatic protection for new nationals from the predecessor State to the successor State:

> [I]t is difficult to see why a 'claim' against a third State arising out of an unlawful act should not also pass from the old to the new State. Regarded from this aspect of the law of State succession—there is nothing surprising in the fact that Estonia should have had the right to take up a case which previously only Russia could have espoused. Such a 'succession' is an absolutely characteristic and even essential feature of the law of State succession. The successor State is continually exercising rights which previously belonged exclusively to the old State, and the same holds good as regards obligations. Accordingly it would be quite normal that in this case the successor State should have protected both diplomatically and before the Court a company the diplomatic protection of which formerly fell to Russia alone.[276]

Conclusion. This is a case where the classic rule of continuous nationality was endorsed by the Court in the context of State succession. However, the reasoning of the Court does not constitute the most solid foundation in support of the application of the traditional rule when changes of nationality result from succession of States.[277] The Court's reasoning is thus limited to one sentence, where it simply stated that Estonia "must prove that at the time when

273 Ibid.
274 Ibid.
275 Ibid 32.
276 Ibid.
277 For the same conclusion, Kohen & Dumberry, 75.

the injury occurred … the company suffering the injury possessed Estonian nationality".[278] The Court did not further examine the issue. The statement of the Court is also merely in the form of an *obiter dictum*. Thus, this statement was made in relation to an issue which was not involved in the determination of the case by the Court on its merits. The Court rejected the Estonian claim on another ground unrelated to the question of the nationality of claim. The claim was rejected by the Court on the ground that Estonia had not exhausted all local remedies before Lithuanian courts. In fact, in the operative part of the judgment, no mention is even made of the preliminary objection raised by Lithuania on the question of the nationality of the claim.

The only clear support for the application of the rule of continuous nationality in the context of State succession can be found in one paragraph of the common individual opinion of Judges De Visscher and Count Rostworowski.[279] The only judge who did thoroughly tackle the issue came to a completely different conclusion. In his dissenting opinion Judge van Eysinga clearly rejected the application of the rule when changes of nationality result from succession of States. His reasoning has found some support in scholarship.[280]

3.3.2 The *Sandoval and Others* Case (1849) and the *Champion* Case (1850)

The *Sandoval and Others* case arose in the context of the annexation of the territory of New Mexico, which had been part of Mexico, by the US in 1848.[281] The case of *Champion* arose in the context of the annexation of Texas (an

278 *Panevezys-Saldutiskis Railway* case, 16–17.

279 Ibid 24.

280 This is, for instance, the position of Verzijl, Jurisprudence, 555, see 568–569, who believes that there should be an "exception" to the rule of continuous nationality in the context of State succession. However, he maintains that such an exception should not have been applied in this case. Thus, he believes that there should have been no transfer of any right to claim reparation from the predecessor State (Russia) to the new State (Estonia), since the former had extinguished the rights initially belonging to the First Company by nationalising it in 1918. However, he is of the view that the case did not involve any question dealing with the nationality of the claim given that, in his opinion, the internationally wrongful act complained about by Estonia was not committed in 1919, but much later (i.e. when the Lithuanian government refused to pay any compensation). At which time, the company was undoubtedly Estonian by nationality. He believes that the preliminary objection raised by Lithuania on the question of the nationality of the claim should have been rejected by the Court.

281 See, Moore, History, v. III, 2323–2324. The case is mentioned in: *Administrative Decision No. V*, US-Germany Mixed Claims Commission, Decision of Umpire Edwin B. Parker, 31 October 1924, *UNRIAA* v. VII, 119, 140, 145 (footnote 9).

independent State since 1836) by the US in 1845.[282] In both cases, the territorial changes were dealt with in the *Treaty of Guadalupe Hidalgo*[283] between the US and Mexico, under which was established a US internal commission (the Board of Commissioners) to "ascertain the validity and amount" of claims of US nationals against Mexico which had their origin in events which took place before 1848.[284]

The claims by Mr Sandoval, Mr Francisco Saracina and Mr Clement Saracina were for services rendered as civil officers in the territory of New Mexico and for money obtained by means of a forced loan. These were claims against the Government of Mexico for damage which occurred at the time these individuals were residing in New Mexico and were therefore Mexican nationals. Mr Sandoval and the others became nationals of the US subsequent to the annexation of New Mexico in 1848 and filed their claims before the Board of Commissioners.[285] The Board dismissed the claims based on the application of Treaty provisions. The Board stated that the claims arose prior to the date of the entry into force of the 1848 Treaty and that Article 14 of the Treaty explicitly excluded such claims. The Board also took the view that these claims should fail since the claimants were not citizens of the US at the time of the entry into force of the Treaty and, therefore, not entitled to receive any compensation.[286]

282 See, Moore, ibid 2322.

283 *Treaty of Peace, Friendship, Limits, and Settlement*, 2 February 1848, ratified by the US on 16 March 1848 and by Mexico on 30 May 1848 and proclaimed on 4 July 1848, in: Malloy, v. I, 1107–1121.

284 Art. 14, indicating that the US "discharge the Mexican Republic from all claims of citizens of the US, not heretofore decided against the Mexican Government, which may have arisen previously to the date of the signature of this treaty". Art. 15 further provides that Mexico was exonerated from all demands of US nationals and that these claims were considered "entirely and forever canceled, whatever their amount may be".

285 The claimants were arguing that their "citizenship and allegiance [had] been totally changed from that of Mexico to that of the US, so that [they had] no recourse upon the Government of Mexico, nor means of asserting or enforcing [their] claim but through the Government of the US" (in: Moore, History, v. III, 2323–2324).

286 The Board also added this comment: "It would be a forced interpretation of the language employed in the treaty to regard the memorialists and others similarly situated as embraced within the provisions of the fourteenth articles, and as entitled to the indemnification thereby secured to citizens of the US whose claims originated anterior to that period, and which it is known had long been the subject of negotiation and discussion between the two governments. The Government of the US could have had no knowledge of the amount of claims of Mexican citizens within the ceded territory upon that republic, nor or their origin or validity; and could have had no purpose or intention of assuming their payment out of the limited fund provided for indemnities to its own citizens for claims which are generally understood to amount to a much larger sum. The treaty does not discharge the Mexican republic from claims of this character, and the US have

In the *Champion* case, two nationals of Texas (an independent State since 1836), Mr Edward Dwyer and Mr J.H. Grammant, were passengers on the US schooner Champion, which was illegally captured by a Mexican vessel of war in 1837. As Texan nationals, they claimed reparation from Mexico for injuries resulting from the capture. Mexico apparently never made any reparation before the date of succession. After the annexation of Texas, at which time the claimants became US nationals, they submitted a claim to the Board for compensation. The Board of Commissioners declined its jurisdiction over their claims on the ground that they were not citizens of the US when the injury complained of occurred.[287]

These two cases are of limited value to the present discussion. Thus, they do not deal with the question whether the successor State (the US) can take over the claims of its new nationals against the State responsible for the damage (Mexico). In fact, the issue dealt with by the Board had nothing to do with any question of diplomatic protection, as no claim was submitted against Mexico. The question at stake was solely whether the claimants could be deemed US nationals and whether the US should *itself* provide compensation to its own new nationals. The Board simply applied the Treaty provisions without making any assessment of the traditional rule of continuous nationality in the context of State succession.

3.3.3 The *Henriette Levy* Case (1881)

There is one example where the application of the traditional rule of continuous nationality by an international judicial body prevented the *continuing State* from exercising diplomatic protection on behalf of a person who was its national when the damage occurred but no longer had such nationality at the time the claim was submitted to the State responsible. This is the *Henriette Levy* case decided in 1881 by a US-France commission.

This case dealt with the claim by Mrs Henriette Levy, the widow of Mr Jacob Levy, for the seizure by US forces in Louisiana in 1863 of cotton belonging to Mr Levy and some associates of his firm.[288] Mr Levy was a French national at the time the damage occurred. He subsequently moved with his family to the city of Strasbourg (France), where he died in 1871. That year, the territories

---

done no act to invalidate them" (in: opinion of Messrs. Evans, Smith & Paine, Board of Commissioners, 30 November 1849, Moore, ibid).

287 Opinions of Messrs. Evans, Smith & Paine, Board of Commissioners, 9 December 1850, in: Moore, ibid 2322.

288 See, Moore, History, v. III, 2514ff; Eric Wyler, *La règle dite de la continuité de la nationalité dans le contentieux international* (PUF 1990) 113; Atlam,133.

of Alsace-Lorraine (where the city of Strasbourg was situated) were ceded by France to Germany. At that time, Mrs Levy did not make use of her right of option to keep her French nationality pursuant to Article II of the *Frankfurt Treaty* (of 10 May 1871). She therefore became a German national in 1871.

Upon the establishment of a US-France Commission in 1880, Mrs Levy submitted a claim for the damage sustained by her deceased husband (and his associates). The US argued that Mrs Levy had become a German national in 1871 and that the Commission had no jurisdiction over claims submitted by German nationals.[289] It was further argued by the US that the Commission should not make any distinction between voluntary and involuntary changes of nationality and that the motive, reason or the attending circumstances in the case of a change of nationality should not be considered.[290] Counsel for the claimant argued, on the contrary, that the Commission had jurisdiction over the dispute since at the time the damage was sustained by Mr Levy, he was a French national and continued to be a citizen of France all his life.[291]

In its decision of 25 June 1881, the Commission dismissed the claim based on the ground that it did not have jurisdiction over claims of individuals who were no longer French nationals.[292]

289 Moore, ibid 2515. This is the argument submitted by the US: "That it appears that the claimant and her children, about the year 1871, became citizens or subjects of Germany, and have ever since remained and are now such citizens or subjects, and have not since that year been citizens of the republic of France, and that this claim is therefore not presented by or on behalf of the citizens of that republic".

290 Ibid 2517.

291 Ibid 2516. It was further argued that any subsequent changes of nationality by Mrs Levy could not affect the rights acquired by the heirs of Jacob Levy while Alsace-Lorraine was an integral part of France. In other words, the claimant argued that the cession of Alsace to Germany in 1871 did not affect the private rights of these citizens, including the right to reparation for injuries committed prior to the cession.

292 Ibid 2517: "The commission, in this case, judges well-founded and admits the demurrer interposed by the agent of the US to the claim or memorial. In its opinion, it is beyond doubt that the claimant and her children, being natives of Alsace, and having always resided there, and not having made choice of the French nationality during the interim granted by the treaty of May the 10th, 1871 (which applied to persons of full age as well as to minors), are included in the collective naturalization, real as well as personal, which resulted to that country in consequence of its annexation to the German Empire, sanctioned by that treaty. And as German subjects, which they have become, they cannot in any manner have recourse to a commission created solely for the settlement of certain claims of French or American citizens. The French nationality of Jacob Levy, whose rights the claimant and her children have inherited, cannot be included in this inheritance. Possessed by him alone, it does not satisfy the requirements of the convention, which demands French nationality in those who actually present themselves before the commission".

3.4 *The Specific Problem of Reparation Claims against the Former State of Nationality*

There is support for the proposition that the new successor State does not have the right to submit a claim for compensation on behalf of its new nationals against the former State of nationality of such nationals.[293] This rule has been put forward by Rapporteur Borchard at the session of Oslo (1932) of the Institute.[294] This proposition was supported by several members of the Institute, even by those who were in favour of the non-application of the rule of continuous nationality in the context of State succession.[295] The rule was also mentioned by ILA Rapporteur Orrego Vicuña.[296] The same principle is also reflected in Article 5 (al. 3) adopted by the work of the ILC on diplomatic protection, which reads as follows:

> Diplomatic protection shall not be exercised by the present State of nationality in respect of a person against a former State of nationality of that person for an injury incurred when that person was a national of the former State of nationality and not of the present State of nationality.[297]

Article 10(1) of the Institute's Resolution does not contain any such limitation. Article 10(4) deals with the different situation of persons having dual nationality.

International case law and State practice is, however, far from being unanimously in support of this principle.

The rule was endorsed in the *Affaire des Forêts du Rhodope Central (Fond)* case.[298] This claim arose from Bulgaria's alleged deprivation of individuals'

293 O'Connell, State Succession, v. I, 538; E.M. Borchard, "La protection des nationaux à l'étranger et le changement de nationalité d'origine", 14 *RDILC* 1933, 421, 459; Sir Cecil Hurst, "Nationality of Claims", 7 *British YIL* 1926, 163, 182.

294 IIL, "La protection diplomatique des nationaux à l'étranger, Rap. Suppl.", *Annuaire IDI* 1933, Session of Oslo, 235ff.

295 See, remarks by N. Politis, *Annuaire IDI* 1931–II, 201, 206–207; De La Barra, ibid 211. See also, comments by N. Politis, *Annuaire IDI* 1933, 479, 488.

296 F. Orrego Vicuña, "The Changing Law of Nationality of Claims", Interim Report, ILA, 2000, 28, 43 (at points no. 8 and 10), for whom claims by the successor State "shall not be made against the former State of nationality". See also, 36: "It is quite evident that the new State of nationality should not be able to claim against the former State of nationality for wrongs that the individual might have suffered under the latter's jurisdiction".

297 ILC Report, 54th sess., 2002, A/57/10, ch. V, 120ff. The issue is also dealt with in: ILC, "Addendum to First Report on Diplomatic Protection", John R. Dugard, Special Rapporteur, 20 April 2000, A/CN.4/506/Add.1, para 30.

298 *Affaire des Forêts du Rhodope Central (Fond)*, Award, 29 March 1933, *UNRIAA* v. III, 1389. This case is referred to in: Atlam, 134.

property and exploitation rights over forests situated in Central Rhodope. This territory had become part of Bulgaria in 1913 (by the *Treaty of Constantinople*)[299] and was under Bulgarian sovereignty at the time of the commission of the internationally wrongful acts. It later became part of Greece.

In this case, the successor State (Greece) claimed on behalf of several of its nationals who had acquired property rights in the forests. The Arbitrator rejected the claim for two of these Greek nationals on behalf of which Greece submitted a claim. The reason given was that these two individuals had Bulgarian nationality at the time the damage occurred and that, therefore, Greece (the successor State) could not submit a claim for reparation on behalf of these two nationals against Bulgaria (the predecessor State). The Arbitrator rejected the argument submitted by Greece that preventing it from exercising diplomatic protection on behalf of these two nationals would "aller à l'encontre de la tendance actuelle du droit international de considérer la protection diplomatique comme un moyen nécessaire de sauvegarder les droits individuels dans les rapports internationaux".[300] This is the full reasoning of the Arbitrator:

> A l'époque où s'est produit le fait dommageable—la prétendue confiscation des forêts—ils étaient donc incontestablement ressortissants du pays qui prenait les mesures incriminées. Dans ces conditions, il ne saurait être admissible, selon le droit international commun, de reconnaître au Gouvernement hellénique le droit de présenter des réclamations à leur profit pour ces faits dommageables, étant donné que ceux-ci ont été causés par leur propre Gouvernement ... [L]a Grèce ne saurait baser une réclamation sur le fait qu'un ressortissant bulgare a été frappé de mesures de confiscation de la part du Gouvernement bulgare, même s'il est ultérieurement devenu sujet hellénique.[301]

The principle of non-succession was also applied by a US internal commission (the Board of Commissioners) in the above-mentioned *Sandoval and Others* case arising in the context of the annexation of the territory of New Mexico by the US in 1848.[302] In this case, the Commission did not allow claims by US nationals against Mexico.

299 *Treaty of Peace Between Bulgaria and Turkey*, 29 September 1913, 8 *AJIL* 1914, 27–45.

300 *Affaire des Forêts du Rhodope Central (Fond)*, Award, 29 March 1933, *UNRIAA* v. III, 1389, 1413.

301 Ibid 1421.

302 See, Moore, History, v. III, 2323–2324.

Conversely, the principle of succession was applied in the context of the MATs set up after the First World War.[303] Thus, the consistent case law of the French-German MAT allowed French nationals to submit claims against Germany (the predecessor State) even though they were German nationals (living in the territories of Alsace-Lorraine) at the time the internationally wrongful acts were committed by Germany.[304]

Similarly, in the 1952 Agreement between West Germany and Israel, compensation was given to Israel for internationally wrongful acts committed against Jews before and during the Second World War.[305] Germany did not object to the fact that the new successor State of Israel could submit claims on behalf of new Israeli nationals who were German nationals at the time the damage occurred.

The same observation can also be made regarding the above-mentioned 1982 Agreement between the UK and Mauritius.[306] This is a case where the successor State (Mauritius) claimed reparation on behalf of its new nationals against the former State of nationality of these individuals (the UK, the colonial power).

4 Conclusion to Chapter 6

The question whether the successor State may take over the right to claim reparation on behalf of its new nationals which were injured before the date of succession involves concepts of diplomatic protection. The important

303 See, Chapter 6, Section 3.1.3.

304 *August Chamant v. Etat Allemand*, 23 June 1921, 25 August 1921, *RDTAM* v. I, 361; *Veuve Heim v. Etat Allemand*, 30 June 1921, 19 August 1921, ibid v. I, 381; *Heim & Chamant v. Etat Allemand*, 7 August 1922 and 25 September 1925, ibid v. III, 50, 57; *Dietz v. Etat Allemand*, 11 April 1923, ibid v. III, 351; *Briegel v. Etat Allemand*, 19 May 1923, ibid v. III; 358; *Ruolt v. Etat Allemand*, 23 May 1923, ibid v. III, 361; *Berger v. Etat Allemand*, 20 July 1924, ibid v. IV, 730; *Rothbetz v. Etat Allemand*, 8 October 1924, ibid v. IV, 747; *Grande Carrières des Vosges v. Etat Allemand*, 11 December 1922, ibid v. III, 118.

305 *Agreement between the State of Israel and the Federal Republic of Germany on Compensation*, 162 *UNTS* 205; *BGBl.*, 1953, v. II, no. 5, 37. See also: *Protocol II between the Federal Republic of Germany and the Conference on Jewish Material Claims against Germany*, 162 *UNTS* 205; *BGBl.*, 1953, v. II, 85; *Protocol I between the Federal Republic of Germany and the Conference on Jewish Material Claims against Germany*, 162 *UNTS* 205; *BGBl.*, 1953, v. II, 85. This example is discussed in Chapter 6, Section 3.2.1.

306 *Agreement between the Government of the United Kingdom of Great Britain and Northern Ireland and the Government of Mauritius*, 7 July 1982, in force on 28 October 1982, *UKTS* 1983, no. 6 (Cmnd. 8785); Weston et al., 385. See, Chapter 6, Section 3.2.2.

question is whether or not the traditional diplomatic protection rule of continuous nationality finds application in the context of succession of States. As mentioned above, the strict application of this rule in this context would result in neither the continuing State nor the successor State being able to exercise diplomatic protection on behalf of individuals who suffered damage as a result of internationally wrongful acts committed before the date of succession.[307] Since no State would be entitled to seek redress for the damage suffered, a wrongful act would therefore remain unpunished. This is undoubtedly unfair from the point of view of the injured individual. This is especially the case if that person continues to be injured after the date of succession.

The conclusion that the application of the strict rule of continuous nationality is not appropriate in the context of State succession is supported by many authors and the ILC *Articles on diplomatic protection*. The successor State should indeed have the right to claim reparation on behalf of its new nationals against the State responsible for damage arising from an internationally wrongful act committed before the date of succession. The same approach has been endorsed by the 2015 Institute's Resolution (Article 10).

This conclusion is supported by the present analysis of case law and State practice.[308] I have found several examples of State practice where the State responsible for the internationally wrongful act committed before the date of succession did not raise any objection to a claim submitted by a new State for compensation on behalf of its new nationals which did not have its nationality at the time the damage occurred.[309] In fact, no example of State practice was found where a State made any objection on this ground. Two examples of international case law have also been found where the State responsible for the internationally wrongful act committed before the date of succession did not submit any objection (based on the rule of continuous nationality)

307 On the one hand, the rule prevents the *successor State* from exercising diplomatic protection on behalf of its *new nationals* because they were not its nationals at the time the internationally wrongful act was committed. On the other hand, it would also prevent the *continuing State* from exercising diplomatic protection on behalf of its *former nationals* because they are no longer its nationals at the time a claim is presented to the State responsible for the act.

308 Kohen & Dumberry, 74–75.

309 See, the position of the FRG in the 1952 Agreement entered into with Israel and the position of the UK in the 1982 Agreement with Mauritius. Other examples are the position of Austria which signed different bilateral agreements with several new States in the context of the 2000 Austrian "Reconciliation Fund Law" and the position of Germany in the context of its 2000 *Law on the Creation of a Foundation "Remembrance, Responsibility and Future"*.

against claims made by the successor State for its new nationals.[310] In all of these examples, the rule of continuous nationality was *not* considered by the State responsible for the internationally wrongful act as an *obstacle* preventing the successor State from receiving reparation.[311]

It is true that in a few other cases the State responsible for the internationally wrongful act committed before the date of succession *did object*, based on the traditional rule of continuous nationality, to a claim submitted by the successor State for its new nationals.[312] What is relevant, however, is the fact that such objections by the State responsible were not upheld by international judicial bodies.

In fact, there is *only one case*[313] where the classic rule of continuous nationality was endorsed by a judicial body, therefore preventing the successor State from claiming reparation on behalf of its new national.[314] This is the 1939 *Panevezys-Saldutiskis Railway* case decided by the PCIJ.[315] However, as previously observed, the reasoning of the Court in this case does not constitute the most solid foundation in support of the application of the rule. Thus, the Court's reasoning on the question is limited to one sentence (in the form of an *obiter dictum*),[316] which does not provide any explanation as to the origin, the content and the scope of application of the rule.[317] In fact, the only clear support for the application of the rule can be found in one paragraph of the common individual opinion of Judge De Visscher and Count Rostworowski.[318] In his dissenting opinion, Judge van Eysinga, on the contrary, concluded that the new successor State of Estonia should have been given the right to exercise diplomatic protection on behalf of the company even if the company did not have its nationality when the damage occurred.[319] As noted by ILC Special

310 See, the position of the UK in *Claim of Finnish Shipowners against Great Britain in respect of the Use of Certain Finnish Vessels During the War* (Finland v. UK), Award of Dr. Bagge, 9 May 1934, *UNRIAA* v. III, 1481. This is also the position of Iraq in the context of the UNCC.

311 For the same conclusion, Kohen & Dumberry, 74–75.

312 This is the position of Germany in the context of the MATs set up after WWI. This is also the position of Mexico in the *Pablo Nájera* case.

313 For the same conclusion, Kohen & Dumberry, 74–75.

314 In *Henriette Levy*, US-France Commission, 1881 (in: Moore, History, v. III, 2514ff), the rule of continuous nationality prevented the *continuing State* from exercising diplomatic protection on behalf of a person who was its national when the damage occurred but no longer had such nationality at the time the claim was submitted to the State responsible.

315 *Panevezys-Saldutiskis Railway* case.

316 Ibid 16–17.

317 For the same conclusion, Kohen & Dumberry, 74–75.

318 *Panevezys-Saldutiskis Railway* case, 24.

319 Ibid 35.

Rapporteur Šturma, "this decision supporting the non-succession approach marks at the same time the beginning of debates concerning the expediency of the principle of continuous nationality".[320]

It can therefore be concluded that there is *very limited* support in international case law and State practice for the application of the strict rule of continuous nationality in the context of State succession.[321]

320 ILC Special Rapporteur Šturma, Third Report, 2019, para 119.

321 For the same conclusion, Kohen & Dumberry, 74–75.

PART 4

General Conclusion

General Conclusion

The present study addressed the issue whether there is succession to rights and obligations arising from internationally wrongful acts committed before the date of succession. Any question of State succession involves two contradictory principles: continuity and break. The central issue is therefore whether the territorial changes affecting a State result in continuity or break of its legal rights and obligations existing prior to the date of succession. In the present study, the aim was to determine the point of equilibrium between the solution of succession or non-succession. There is simply no unique answer to this question. Any general theory either in favour of or against the *automatic* transfer of the right to reparation and the obligation to repair from the predecessor State to the successor State would be illusory. Similarly to any other question of State succession, the issue is much too complex to be resolved by any general all-inclusive theory.[1] Both the Institute[2] and the ILC[3] took the same approach as the point of departure for their works.

The analysis of any issue of State succession needs to consider the "eminently important role of factual situations".[4] This is precisely what the strict doctrine of non-succession fails to take into account in developing its general theory. Thus, quite apart from the weaknesses of the arguments put forward by writers supporting this general theory (which are still relied upon today[5]), their analysis of State practice and case law typically suffers from two other

1 P.M. Eisemann, "Rapport du Directeur de la section de langue française du Centre", in: Eisemann & Koskenniemi, 64: "Le phénomène de la succession d'Etats n'est nullement rebelle au droit mais il conduit naturellement vers des solutions spécifiques adaptées à la variété des situations plutôt que vers l'application automatique de règles générales".

2 IIL, Final Report, Kohen, 534; Kohen & Dumberry, 9ff.

3 ILC Special Rapporteur Šturma, Second Report, 2018, para 16; ibid, First Report, 2017, para 83; ibid, Third Report, 2019, para 35.

4 Stern, Concluding Remarks, 208. See also, Kaplane, 37.

5 Perhaps surprisingly, some of the old arguments of the doctrine are still used by States today. See, Austria, letter sent to the UN GA Sixth Committee, rep. 74th sess. 2 Nov. 2021: "As opposed to state debts, the responsibility for wrongful acts is a highly personal liability that is not transferable". See also: *Croatia Genocide Convention* case, sep. op. Judge Kreća, para 65.2, indicating that "responsibility *in personam* is too much linked with the legal identity and continuity of the State which makes it difficult to ascertain it in terms of *ipso iure* succession to responsibility without prejudice to the fundamental principles of equality and independence of States", adding that "The legal identity and continuity of a State appears to be the powerful argument in favour of the general principle of *action personalis moritur cum persona*". *Contra*: ILC Report, 69th sess., 2017, A/72/10, chap. IX, para 247, refers to the "strong disagreement" of the Special Rapporteur regarding this "old doctrine or fiction".

 | DOI:10.1163/9789004703810_011

important shortcomings. Firstly, they generally fail to conduct their investigation in light of the fundamental distinction between different *types of* succession of States. Secondly, they often fail to consider the important fact that the solution to the issue depends also on a variety of *factors and circumstances*. These factual situations have a direct impact on how one assesses matters of State succession to responsibility.

Ultimately, this study was aimed at responding to the affimation of ILC Special Rapporteur Crawford, made more than 20 years ago, that "[i]t is unclear whether a new State succeeds to any State responsibility of the predecessor State with respect to its territory".[6] More recently, Judge Xue in her Declaration in the *Croatia Genocide Convention* case also noted that "little can be found about State succession to responsibility in the field of general international law", adding that "rules of State responsibility in the event of succession remain to be developed".[7] In fact, the present analysis of relevant State practice, case law and scholarship, shows the emergence of several patterns, rules and principles. My general conclusions will now be examined. I believe that 8 points should be highlighted.

1 The Foundations of the Doctrine of Non-succession Are Not as Solid as They Appear to Be

Until recently, the "rule" of non-succession seemed so well-established, that O'Connell, who was one of the first scholars to be critical about this theory, opened the chapter on the topic in his 1967 two-volume book stating that "it has been taken for granted that a successor State is not liable for the delicts of its predecessor".[8] For years, almost all general international law textbooks seemed to have adopted this doctrine of non-succession.

Yet, the study of State practice and case law shows that the foundations of the doctrine of non-succession were never that solid in the first place. In fact, the doctrine of non-succession is not often invoked by States in their international relations. It is also rarely referred to or applied by judicial bodies. I have found several examples of State practice where the principle of the transfer of rights and obligations to the successor State has been accepted by States and applied by courts. It is also true that in each case there were specific circumstances which militated in favour of such transfer. One obvious example is of

6 ILC, Commentaries, State Responsibility, 2001, 119, para 3.

7 *Croatia Genocide Convention* case, Decla. Judge Xue, para 23.

8 O'Connell, State Succession, v. 1, 482.

course when the successor State has accepted to take over responsibility in a treaty or under its own laws. In other cases, the respondent State did not raise any objection to such a transfer. Other factors were also important, including preventing any unjust enrichment. The existence of a "territorial" or "organ" link between the successor State and the consequences of a wrong also played a role. In any event, the very fact that any such transfer of rights and obligations has taken place may have come to a surprise to the readers when I published the first edition of this book in 2007. It shows that the "traditional" doctrine of non-succession, which had been taken for granted for so many years, was never truly a solid all-encompassing principle of general application. In fact, the nature and extent of the exceptions to this (always improbable) general "rule" of non-succession may be considered the most important features of modern State practice and case law.

In this respect, it is quite telling that Crawford, who back in 2001 doubted the existence of any rule on State succession to responsibility, affirmed 10 years later that "there has been a certain shift in consensus, from what Dumberry refers to as the 'traditional' or 'absolute' approach of non-succession (…) to a more nuanced view that focuses on the facts of the succession in question".[9] He prefers the latter approach: "the fact-sensitive approach" to the issue "promoted in the *Lighthouse Arbitration*, and advanced by O'Connell, Verzijl and Dumberry, seems preferable to the negative succession rule posited by *Robert E. Brown, Hawaiian Claims* and the commentators such as Hurst".[10]

Yet, one needs to be careful when assessing what may be considered as a recent evolution of hearts and minds on the issue. The question is further examined in the next sections.

2 The Doctrine of Non-succession Remains Supported by Many States

In the first edition of my book, I explained that the doctrine of non-succession was not representative of contemporary international law. Others have since endorsed that view.[11] The affirmation is still true when one looks at the recent

9 Crawford, State Responsibility, 437. On this point, see Ruy & Baecke, 21.

10 Crawford, ibid, 455.

11 Šturma, State Succession, 653–678, 655: "This Article aims to demonstrate that the traditional view, according to which there is no succession in the field of State responsibility for internationally wrongful acts, no longer corresponds to the current status of international law". (also, at 677). See also, Vergara Lamadrid, 220–223, noting a change of paradigm in case law (see also, Ana Paola Vergara Lamadrid, "Nada se destruye, todo

State practice and case law showing that there are many examples supporting the solution of succession. Yet, in other ways the position I adopted in 2007 may have been somehow too optimistic.

When I wrote my book, there were few publicly available statements by States (outside judicial proceedings where they were involved as party) openly expressing their views on matters of succession to responsibility. Now, there are plenty. What they clearly show is that many States still consider that the doctrine of non-succession is in fact the only applicable principle.

This clash of opposite ideas could not have been clearer than what happened during the last sessions of the work of the ILC on State succession to responsibility. In fact, right at the outset, it seems that several ILC members were reluctant to study the question of succession to responsibility.[12] Thus, the 2018 Report to the ILC indicates that the "scarcity of State practice" and the fact that it was "diverse, context-specific and often politically sensitive" were mentioned as "difficulties" which "confirmed the initial misgivings expressed by some members as to the suitability of the topic for codification or progressive development".[13] A good example is the UK's position:

> The State practice identified by the Special Rapporteur in his report is highly context-specific and sensitive. It must be viewed in its historical, political and cultural context. Rather than revealing any discernible trends of universal application, the practice summarised in the report tends to demonstrate the contrary. The succession of State responsibility involves policy—and, indeed, political—decisions which go to the heart of the identity of the States involved.[14]

In response, the Special Rapporteur noted that he was "fully aware" that State practice was "diverse, context-specific and sensitive", but that this fact did "not allow the existence of the 'clean slate' principle to be asserted as a

---

se transforma: la exigibilidad de la obligacion de reparar en el marco de una sucesion de Estados", 40 *Agenda Internacional*, 2022, 89).

12 Some writers had doubts on whether this exercise of codification was really needed. See also, Kaplane, 42 ("the decision of the ILC to begin its own work on the same topic is somewhat unclear: the need for these rules exists, but is not urgent, and similar work has already been accomplished, albeit by a different organisation"). She examines the pros and cons of this codification effort.

13 ILC Report, 70th sess., 2018, para 234. See, letters sent to the UN GA Sixth Committee by, *inter alia*, UK (rep. 69th sess., 31 Oct, 1 Nov. 2017), Netherlands (rep. 74th sess., 5 Nov. 2019); Sierra Leone (rep. 74th sess., 5 Nov. 2019).

14 UK, ibid.

legal basis governing the relations between States".[15] In other words, the "non-conclusiveness of State practice does not mean that the responsibility for an internationally wrongful act 'stops at the door of succession of States'".[16] He also noted that the argument does not mean that the "work on this topic is impossible or cannot be useful",[17] nor should it "be abused in a way that makes virtually impossible not only codification, but also any meaningful debate on succession of States in relation to international responsibility".[18] In any event, given that the ILC's role is not limited to that of codification, "an exercise aiming at the clarification of rules applicable in these situations clearly meets criteria of progressive development of international law in the area overlapping with rules on State responsibility, which already have been successfully codified".[19] He is right.

Several States have also mentioned the same concern in their comments at the UN GA Sixth Committee about the suitability of the topic for codification.[20] Thus, Austria "questioned the contemporary relevance of the topic", which was "highly controversial"; it also noted the recent work of the Institute "with an outcome that Austria found difficult to accept".[21] The US was "not confident that the topic will enjoy broad acceptance or interest from States".[22] Other States complained that the Special Rapporteur was putting too much emphasis on the practice of Western States and should examine relevant examples from other continents.[23] In addition, the ILC Report also explained that "several members expressed caution at the heavy reliance of the report on academic writings and on the work of the Institute of International Law".[24]

15 ILC Special Rapporteur Šturma, Third Report, 2019, para 19.

16 Ibid, Fourth Report, 2020, para 19.

17 Ibid, Third Report, 2019, para 19.

18 Ibid, Fourth Report, 2020, para 20.

19 Ibid, Third Report, 2019, para 19.

20 See, letters sent to the UN GA Sixth Committee by, *inter alia*, UK (rep. 71th sess., 2019), Turkey (rep. 69th sess., 1 Nov. 2017), Italy (rep. 71th sess., 2019; rep. 72th sess. 2021), Romania (rep. 72th sess. 2021), Netherlands (rep. 71th sess. 2019), China (rep. 69th sess. 2017; 73th sess. 26 Oct. 2018), Israel (rep. 70th sess. 26 Oct. 2018), Austria (rep. 69th sess. 2017).

21 ILC Special Rapporteur Šturma, First Report, 2017, para 7.

22 US, letter sent to the UN GA Sixth Committee, rep. 72nd sess. 1 Nov. 2017.

23 Letters sent to the UN GA Sixth Committee by Malaysia (rep. 73rd sess. 31 Oct. 2018) and India (rep 76th sess. 2 Nov. 2021).

24 ILC Report, 70th sess. 2018, para 234. See, for instance, ILC, "Provisional Summary Record of the 3434th Meeting", 70th sess. 20 July 2018, A/CN.4/SR.3434, statement by ILC Member Huang (China): "The biggest difficulty lay in the scarcity of relevant State practice. To make up for that scarcity, the Special Rapporteur referred extensively in his report to legal writings and research outcomes, citing frequently, among others, the views of Patrick Dumberry of the Graduate Institute of International and Development Studies and the

Many States expressed the same concern about the undue reliance on such materials;[25] some of them being very specific indeed on that point.[26] As a result, many States considered that the work could only be treated as progressive development of the law, not an exercise of codification.[27]

Another important point is that the general approach which was adopted by Special Rapporteur Šturma (in line with the Institute's Resolution) was not shared by several ILC members. They openly supported the traditional rule of non-succession and ultimately rejected any approach that they considered to be favouring succession to obligations.[28] In their statements,

---

2015 resolution of the Institute of International Law on succession of States in matters of international responsibility. In fact, almost every draft article proposed by the Special Rapporteur corresponded to articles of the Institute's resolution and, in some instances, their titles and wording were almost identical". He also added that he was "deeply concerned as to how the Commission would be able to maintain its prestige and central position in the progressive development and codification of international law, as mandated by the General Assembly in accordance with the Charter of the United Nations, if its work relied excessively on existing outcomes of private academic groups or the international law community".

25 See, letters sent to the UN GA Sixth Committee by UK (rep. 74th sess. 5–6 Nov. 2019), Iran (rep. 74th sess. 2019), China (rep. 71st sess. 31 Oct. 2019), Israel (rep. 70th sess. 2018).

26 Russia, ibid, rep. 73rd sess. 31 Oct. 2018: "We also doubt that the departure from the 1978 and 1983 Vienna Conventions is methodologically correct. We also note that instead of relying on the achievements of the Commission relating to the succession of States, the report of the Institute of the International Law and a resolution adopted on its basis as well as the works of Mr. Patrick Dumberry were used as the main basis for this research". See also, Netherlands, ibid, rep. 74th sess. 5 Nov. 2019: "the Netherlands aligns itself with the caution expressed in the Commission with respect to the methodology applied by the Special Rapporteur. It seems the vast majority of the rapport, and the ensuing conclusions, is based on academic literature, in other words doctrine. Academic literature that qualifies as doctrine, that is as "teachings of the most highly qualified publicists of the various nations" is a subsidiary means for the determination of international law. It should therefore not be put at a more important level than sources that reflect customary international law, such as the Articles on State Responsibility and the Draft Articles on Diplomatic Protection. The Netherlands would urge the Special Rapporteur, and the Commission, to conduct a more thorough investigation into existing State practice and opinio juris, instead of the reliance on doctrine".

27 See, letters, ibid, by UK (rep. 71st sess. 2019), Romania (rep. 71st sess. 2019).

28 ILC Report, 69th sess. 2017, A/72/10, chap. IX, at para 231: "A number of members underlined that the 'traditional' rule of non-succession that the Special Rapporteur had outlined remained the prevailing position at the present time, with the possibility of automatic succession being limited to succession to State debts, and the potential for a limited range of clearly established possible exceptions to non-succession being available. Other members expressed doubt that the traditional rule of nonsuccession had changed, although the report of the Special Rapporteur suggested he saw it otherwise, and suggested that

Russia[29] and Austria[30] were probably the most virulent critics of the approach adopted by Special Rapporteur Šturma. They considered that he had, in fact, endorsed the rule of *automatic* succession to obligations. Thus, Austria had trouble with the title chosen by the ILC because it could "suggests that there may be situations in which a successor state automatically succeeds" to international responsibility.[31] For Austria, "what the Special Rapporteur has termed the 'traditional view' (...) reflects the existing state of international law".[32] In fact, it was suggested that he was replacing the "principle of non-succession by a principle of succession".[33] For Austria, such a "purported rule that responsibility passes from a predecessor state to a successor state would not be a welcome progressive development of law".[34] Similarly, Russia argued that Special Rapporteur Šturma had adopted a rule of automatic succession.[35] It also believed, perhaps more surprisingly, that matters involving obligations related to a continuing State was outside the scope of the work of the ILC and should not have been discussed.[36] These criticisms may seem exaggerated. The

---

any shift from the traditional rule must be supported by clear and unambiguous evidence of State practice and decisions of courts and tribunals".

29 Russia, letter sent to the UN GA Sixth Committee, rep. 73rd sess. 31 October 2018.

30 Austria, ibid rep. 69th sess. 2017. See also, Austria, ibid rep. 71st sess. 5 Nov. 2019.

31 Austria, ibid rep. 69th sess. 2017: "My delegation has noted that even the Special Rapporteur himself has been careful to state that it is unclear whether any general rules providing for succession into responsibility exist. Still, the title chosen by the Commission suggests that there may be situations in which a successor state automatically succeeds into the responsibility incurred by a predecessor state in regard to that other state's wrongful act. This implicit suggestion is unfortunate".

32 Austria, ibid rep. 69th sess. 2017. See also, rep. 72nd sess. 2021 ("We do not think that any rule asserting an automatic transfer of rights and obligations to successor states where the predecessor state does not continue to exist can be identified as lex lata, nor would we consider it a good candidate for progressive development of law").

33 Austria, ibid rep. 71st sess. 2019 ("In spite of the Special Rapporteur's disclaimer in paragraph 16 of his second report (...) the Special Rapporteur would in fact replace the principle of non-succession by a principle of succession").

34 Austria, ibid rep. 74th sess. 2 Nov. 2021.

35 Russia, ibid rep. 73rd sess. 31 Oct. 2018: "During the last session the Special Rapporteur decided to cardinally change his approach to the topic by changing the recognition as the general rule of a norm regarding automatic succession with regard to the responsibility for the norm of the absence of succession with potential exclusions".

36 Russia, ibid Rep. 72nd sess. 24 Oct. 2017, noting that it "became a continuator of the Soviet Union", but arguing that "continuation does not belong to this topic". See also, Russia, rep. 73rd sess. 31 October 2018. See also, ILC, "Provisional Summary Record of the 3479th Meeting", 73rd sess. 12 July 2019, A/CN.4/SR.3479, comment by ILC Member Zagaynov (Russia): "questions of succession did not arise in cases in which the responsibility or rights of a predecessor State that continued to exist were entailed, and in which the

Special Rapporteur referred to this idea of (a qualified and not absolute) "presumption of succession", in the context of dissolution, which could anyway be "confirmed, rebutted or modified by agreements".[37] But, most importantly, he had always *rejected* the application of any general theory of automatic succession.[38] In fact, many States did support the middle-ground approach favored by Special Rapporteur Šturma by rejecting both the rule of non-succession and that of automatic succession.[39] Yet, it is also undeniable that many others States clearly endorsed the traditional rule of non-succession.[40] Only a few States took the opposite view.[41]

---

successor State was not involved. It was important not to confuse the concepts of continuity and succession".

37 ILC Special Rapporteur Šturma, Second Report, 2018, para 148.

38 Ibid, First Report, 2017, para 83: "this does not mean that the opposite thesis, i.e. automatic succession in all cases, is true. At best, it is possible to conclude that it was succession in certain cases. The transfer or not of obligations or rights arising from State responsibility in specific kinds of succession needs to be proved on a case-by-case basis". This is also clear from this other passage: ibid, Second Report, 2018, para 16: "He does not suggest replacing one highly general theory of non-succession by another similar theory in favour of succession. Instead, a more flexible and realistic approach is needed. The outcome might well be a confirmation of non-succession in certain legal relations arising from State responsibility and a formulation of special rules (or possible exceptions) on succession in others".

39 Letters sent to the UN GA Sixth Committee by Italy (rep. 71th sess. 2019; 74th sess. undated; rep. 72th sess. 2021), Cameroon (rep. 76th sess. 2021), Portugal (rep. 71th sess. 2019; 74th sess. undated), UK (rep. 72th sess. 2–3 Nov. 2021), Netherlands (rep. 74th sess. 5 Nov. 2019), Slovenia (rep. 69th sess. 31 Oct. 2017; 74th sess. 5 Nov. 2019; 77th sess. Nov. 2022), Malaysia (rep. 77th sess. 2 Nov. 2022). See, ILC Special Rapporteur Šturma, Fifth Report, 2021, para 11, indicating that "most States agreed (or at least did not dispute)" this position and referring to: Brazil, Cameroon, Croatia, Denmark on behalf of the Nordic countries, Italy, Portugal, Sierra Leone, Slovenia and the UK.

40 See, letters, ibid, by Japan (rep. 69th sess. 2017), Vietnam (rep. 74th sess. 6 Nov. 2019; rep. 76th sess. 2021), Romania (rep. 72nd sess. 2021), Russia (rep. 69th sess. 2017).

41 The most explicit position was taken by the Czech Republic, ibid, rep. 69th sess. 1 Nov. 2017: "We believe that it is time to subject to the scrutiny the old doctrinal dogma according to which the possibility to invoke responsibility for an internationally wrongful act committed either by or against the predecessor State stops at the door of State succession. This view, common in traditional literature and having still some advocates, was largely based on an understanding of 'State responsibility' which was very different from the concept underlying the International Law Commission's Articles on responsibility of States for internationally wrongful acts. (...) We concur with the Special Rapporteur's preliminary conclusion and are of the view that contemporary international law does not preclude succession in respect of secondary rights and obligations arising from an internationally wrongful act of the State, and we would encourage the Special Rapporteur to consider formulating a general provision encapsulating this thesis. This, of course, would be only a starting point in the more complex exercise aimed at answering the question

These theoretical disagreements among ILC members would have some very practical consequences in terms of drafting. They ultimately led to the provisional adoption of "Guidelines" instead of "Draft Articles". (In 2024, the ILC decided to stop its work on the issue and the Guidelines have therefore never been formally adopted.) This is because "several members questioned whether the development of draft articles was the most appropriate outcome".[42] They preferred a document that "would be designed to serve as general guidance for States (as opposed to developing a set of binding rules)".[43] The content of the provisions initially put forward by ILC Special Rapporteur Šturma would be one by one completely diluted of any "binding" obligations. The language would be softened to the extent that what was left could no longer be considered "Articles". It should be recalled here that the original goal of the work undertaken by the ILC was to determine "whether there are *rules of international law* governing both the transfer of obligations and the transfer of rights arising from international responsibility of States for internationally wrongful acts".[44] It seems that no such clear "rules" have been found after five years of work. This is clear from the Third Report indicating that it "does not assert any automatic succession to rights and obligations arising from internationally wrongful acts (State responsibility), which would be the result of an automatic operation of rules of international law".[45] Special Rapporteur Šturma referred to "automatic" in this context to mean "the devolution of rights and obligations *in application of a rule* of international law".[46] In other words, there is no applicable "rule" indicating that, under international law, in one situation or another there is a transfer of rights or obligations to the successor State. This is obvious when considering that none of the Guidelines impose any *obligations* on States. Typically, the Guidelines merely suggest "the possibility for a successor State to raise the issue of reparation of injury caused to the predecessor State, which is now affecting the successor

---

whether there are emerging specific rules of international law supporting the devolution of secondary obligations or rights (as the case may be) arising from internationally wrongful acts of States in situations of State succession and what are the perspectives of their progressive development and codification". See also, Netherlands, rep. 72nd sess. 1st Nov. 2021: "the point of departure should be the principle that no legal vacuum in terms of State responsibility should emerge. (…) If such agreement cannot be reached, the legal vacuum should be avoided by transferring rights and obligations to the successor State or States".

42 ILC Report, 73rd sess., 12 August 2022, A/77/10, para 86.

43 Ibid.

44 ILC Special Rapporteur, Šturma, First Report, 2017, para 19, emphasis added.

45 Ibid, Third Report, 2019, para 34.

46 Ibid para 33, emphasis added.

State, with the wrongdoing State".[47] They only go so far as to encourage States to reach agreements on matters of succession to responsibility. But the possibility for them to reach any such agreement always exists anyway, with or without the Guidelines.

At the end of the day, while the final product is disappointing, Special Rapporteur Šturma should not be blamed for this outcome. He has written five very well-researched reports, which are of the greatest importance to scholarship on State succession. He should be praised for the balanced and generally satisfying approach adopted in the Draft Articles attached to his Second and Third Reports.[48] The ILC Secretariat also published a comprehensive and very useful survey of agreements dealing with succession to responsibility.[49] Many States' strong reluctance to any departure from the traditional rule of non-succession was simply insurmountable.

Ultimately, the recent debate at the ILC reveals what may be qualified as a certain backlash by some States (but not all of them[50]) against the very idea of succession to responsibility. In that sense, it was somewhat premature to say back in 2007 that the doctrine of non-succession was not representative of contemporary international law. It would be more prudent and accurate to say that "the traditional thesis of non-succession has been questioned by modern practice".[51] In any event, what is clear is that no doctrine of *automatic succession* to responsibility has emerged.[52]

47 Ibid para 34.

48 For a critical assessment of the Draft Articles initially put forward by him, see Kaplane, 39–40, 42–43.

49 ILC, "Succession of States in respect of State responsibility, Information on treaties which may be of relevance to the future work of the Commission on the topic", Memorandum by the Secretariat, A/CN.4/730*, 20 March 2019.

50 See, Netherlands, letter sent to the UN GA Sixth Committee, rep. 72nd sess. 1st Nov. 2021: "My Government would reiterate its position, as previously expressed, that the point of departure should be the principle that no legal vacuum in terms of State responsibility should emerge. (…) Whether rights or obligations be transferred in specific situations should be assessed on a case-by-case basis and be addressed in a succession agreement. If such agreement cannot be reached, the legal vacuum should be avoided by transferring rights and obligations to the successor State or States".

51 ILC Special Rapporteur Šturma, First Report, 2017, para 83. Agreeing: Slovenia, letter sent to the UN GA Sixth Committee, rep. 69th sess. 31 Oct. 2017: "Slovenia considers that the Special Rapporteur provided evidence that the traditional theory of nonsuccession has been challenged by modern practice, or at least that modern international law does not exclude the possibility of any transfer of obligations arising from state responsibility. In this light, Slovenia agrees with the Special Rapporteur that the examples of state practice and jurisprudence cited in the first report support his finding on the evolution of the traditional rule of non-succession".

52 Reyes Gajardo, 85–6; Vergara Lamadrid, 220–1.

3 Succession to the Obligation to Repair Essentially Depends on the Type of Succession Involved and on Whether the Predecessor State Continues to Exist

This is the basic assumption that I have adopted at the outset of this study. It has proven to be correct in light of State practice and case law. The solutions adopted in State practice and case law for different types of succession can be summarised as follows.

In the context where the predecessor State *ceases to exist* because of the events affecting its territorial integrity (integration, unification, dissolution), the tendency is clearly towards succession to the obligation to repair. This is undoubtedly the case of *modern* State practice and case law. Prime examples are the incorporation of the German Democratic Republic into the Federal Republic of Germany (1990) and the (much older) unification of the United Arab Republic (1958). The practice in the context of dissolution is less straightforward. While older cases followed the doctrine of non-succession, more modern practice provides many examples where the successor State has agreed to take over obligations arising from internationally wrongful acts committed by the predecessor State before its break-up. I have found such agreements between the injured State and the successor State[53] and among the successor States themselves.[54] It could be argued that the ICJ in both the *Gabčíkovo-Nagymaros* and the *Croatia Genocide Convention* cases, while not taking position on the issue, did not reject the possibility of the transfer of the obligation to repair to a new State. Interestingly, a few judges in their individual opinions rejected the reasoning of the Court in the last case on this point precisely because they considered that it was based upon a *presumption* in favour of succession to responsibility.[55]

In the context where the predecessor State *continues to exist* following the events affecting its territorial integrity, the overwhelming tendency is clearly toward non-succession to the obligation to repair. The continuing State remains responsible for *its own* internationally wrongful acts committed before the date of succession. This is the case regarding transfer of territory

53 See, examples in the context of the dissolution of the United Arab Republic (1961). See also, the *Compromis* between the parties to submit the *Gabčíkovo-Nagymaros* case to the ICJ.

54 2001 *Agreement on Succession Issues* in the context of the break-up of the former Yugoslavia.

55 *Croatia Genocide Convention* case, Decla. Judge Xue, para 22; Sep. op. Judge Skotnikov, para 5; Sep. op. Judge Kreća, paras 60–61.

and separation where I have found several examples of State practice and case law supporting this solution. There are also a few cases where the contrary solution of succession was adopted. Yet, they can be explained by special circumstances and factors (a point further discussed below). The examination of State practice and case law in the context of Newly Independent States shows a great variety of solutions supporting both the principles of succession and non-succession to international responsibility. Yet, there are strong reasons for supporting, as a matter of principle, a rule of non-succession (except for wrongs committed by insurrectional movements).

4 State Succession to the Obligation to Repair Depends on the Different Factors and Circumstances Involved in Each Case

One basic assumption adopted at the outset of this study was that *specific problems* of State succession to the obligation to repair require *specific solutions* which would depend on different *factors and circumstances* involved. The soundness of this assumption was confirmed by my analysis of State practice and case law.

Several specific circumstances have been identified where State practice and case law (as well as scholarship) support the application of the principle of succession, whereby the successor State takes over the obligations arising from internationally wrongful acts committed by the predecessor State before the date of succession. This is the case in the following three circumstances:

- The successor State has accepted to take over the obligations arising from the commission of the internationally wrongful act;
- The internationally wrongful act was committed by an insurrectional movement during an armed struggle which eventually led to the creation of the new State;[56]
- The successor State maintains and continues after its independence the internationally wrongful act which was initially committed by the predecessor State before the date of succession.[57]

56 However, as previously noted (Part 2, Chapter 3, Section 6), this is not a case of State succession *per se*. It should be added that the successor State is not responsible for obligations arising from internationally wrongful acts committed *by the predecessor State* during the struggle led by an "insurrectional movement" to establish that new State.

57 When the predecessor State no longer exists after the date of succession, the successor State should be responsible not only for its own internationally wrongful acts committed after that date but also for the obligations arising from the acts committed by the predecessor State before that date. However, this solution should not apply in the context

It could be argued that some of these principles are so well-established that they can be considered rules of customary international law. This is arguably the case for the second principle recognised in Article 10(2) of the ILC *Articles on State Responsibility*.[58] Yet, even if they were considered as such, they would be principles of State responsibility rather than rules specific to the field of State succession.[59] Pajnkihar refers to some of these principles as examples of "fictitious succession to international responsibility".[60] He distinguished between cases of "fictitious succession" and "real succession". In the context of "fictitious" succession, the rules of State responsibility apply, whereas "real" succession is based on the rules of State succession.[61]

---

where the predecessor State continues to exist (such as in cases of separation). In this last case, as a matter of principle, the continuing State should remain (after the date of succession) responsible for *its own* internationally wrongful acts committed before the date of succession. Yet, I also mentioned one exception. See, Part 2, Chapter 3, Section 5.

58 On this question, see Dumberry, Rebellions, 86ff, 303ff, citing many scholars taking position on the issue. In *Croatia Genocide Convention* case, paras 82, 102–3, the Court did not take position. It "consider[ed] that, even if Article 10(2) of the Articles on State Responsibility could be regarded as declaratory of customary international law at the relevant time, that Article is concerned only with the attribution of acts to a new State; it does not create obligations binding upon either the new State or the movement that succeeded in establishing that new State" (para 104).

59 Pajnkihar, 237, 314, 321.

60 One example of "fictitious succession" he mentioned is the successor State's "acknowledgment and adoption of a conduct as its own, when the State accepts as its own an act that is not otherwise attributable to it" (Ibid 321). Another example is wrongful acts committed by an insurrectional movement (317). Continuing breach is examined in the section of his book dealing with "real" succession to responsibility (at 326). Yet, at 328 he indicates that "The IDI and ILC effectively combined succession to this kind of breach with the acknowledgment and adoption of the act as one's own" and that "It is therefore a matter of *fictitious* succession", adding that "however, acknowledgment and adoption can provide a special link on which *real* succession can be based" (emphasis in the original).

61 Ibid 312, also at 314: "In cases of fictitious succession to international responsibility, the conduct is attributed directly to the successor State that was also bound by the primary legal norm at the time of the conduct. International responsibility arise directly in relation to it and not to the predecessor State. The successor State is therefore internationally responsible from the outset and does not succeed to the responsibility of the predecessor State. Thus, the wrongful act, international responsibility, and its consequences "belong" to the successor Stat according to the rules of international responsibility. The link to succession is only illusory and arises from the fact that international responsibility emerged *before* the date of succession and survived beyond it since it was not adjudicated before", emphasis in the original. See also, at 322 ("fictitious succession to international responsibility is only a virtual succession given that the rights and responsibilities arising from the international responsibility of States are not succeeded to but belong to the successor State from the outset"). See also, at 322: "Nevertheless, it can be confirmed that in these cases, the successor State is responsible for internationally wrongful acts that occurred

It should be added that while a few writers support the existence of a *general* customary rule in favour of succession to responsibility,[62] the better view is that no such general rule exists. This is the position of Czaplinski,[63] Stern[64] and others.[65] This is no doubt a sound approach. In any event, as further discussed below, the examples of State practice I have examined are based on the consent of the successor States to any transfer of the obligation to repair.

A few words should be added on the position taken by the ILC Special Rapporteur on custom. In response to the common theme mentioned by States about of the "paucity" of State practice which was "diverse, context-specific and sensitive", he noted that it was true that the "occurrence of succession of States is relatively rare or at least less frequent than" in other areas.[66] Yet, he also added that this "implies, quite obviously, that the requirement of general practice as an element of identification of customary international law cannot be applied too strictly" because "otherwise, no codified rules on succession of States would be possible".[67] As a result, he believes that "any general customary norms of international law crystallize and are established only slowly in this area".[68] He also noted that "the specific feature of law of State succession is that, in most cases, a solution of difficult legal problems was reached by agreements".[69] This is because "States prefer to have freedom to negotiate the conditions of succession, if necessary".[70] But, at the same time, these agreements "constitute State practice".[71] As such, they are relevant to assess whether any rule of custom has developed.[72] At the end of the day, he is right not to suggest

before the date of its formal creation, which makes them similar to the cases of State succession. However, secondary rights and obligations have not passed to it by virtue of the succession procedure".

62 Volkovitsch, 2162, supporting the establishment of "a customary norm of international law providing for a rebuttable presumption of succession to liability".

63 Czaplinski, 343, is of the view that State practice "shows a tendency to transfer delictual liability but it is not consistent" and that "the conclusion is that this practice does not prove the existence of a customary rule concerning the succession in respect of delictual obligations".

64 Stern, Responsabilité, 338, who believes that "en l'absence de précédents significatifs" it cannot be concluded that there "existe une règle générale de transmission de la responsabilité".

65 Ruy & Baecke, 21–2; Vergara Lamadrid, 227.

66 ILC Special Rapporteur Šturma, Fourth Report, 2020, para 20.

67 Ibid.

68 Ibid, First Report, 2017, para 85.

69 Ibid, Fourth Report, 2020, para 22.

70 Ibid, First Report, 2017, para 85.

71 Ibid, Fourth Report, 2020, para 22.

72 Ibid, para 31, noting that "that practice varies and is driven by many non-legal considerations", which makes it "difficult to draw inferences on customary international law from such agreements".

the existence of any specific customary rule on the question of succession to responsibility. There is indeed, to the best of my knowledge, no clear example of States' *opinio juris* on the transfer of rights and obligations arising from the commission of a wrongful act.[73] There is certainly no indication that States believe that they have any *obligation* on this matter.

There is some support in State practice and case law (as well as scholarship[74]) for the proposition that, depending on specific circumstances of each case, the obligation to repair may pass to the successor State:

- When there is a "direct link" between the consequences of an internationally wrongful act committed by the predecessor State and the territory or the population of the successor State;[75] and
- When the author of the internationally wrongful act was an organ of the predecessor State that later became an organ of the successor State.[76]

My analysis of State practice and case law also led to several other conclusions:

- I believe that there is no general principle of succession whereby the successor State is automatically responsible for obligations arising

73 The point was highlighted in ILC, "Provisional Summary Record of the 3434th Meeting", 70th sess., 20 July 2018, A/CN.4/SR.3434, statement by ILC Member Huang (China): "The Special Rapporteur listed some facts pointing to successor States' taking over the responsibility of reparation of the predecessor States, without dwelling on the legal position of the former in that process, which was however the core element of opinio juris. The simple act of taking over the responsibility of reparation of a predecessor State might reflect a voluntary decision of the State concerned or its reluctant acceptance of a decision of an international tribunal. It was not possible to deduce directly that such act was based on an opinio juris regarding the rules of the succession of State responsibility on the part of the successor State. In some instances, the States in question did not believe that they were required to assume the State responsibilities involved but for various reasons did so unwillingly. The existence of opinio juris regarding the rules of the succession of State responsibility could be questioned in such cases". See also on this point: Vergara Lamadrid, 220–1.

74 One recent example is Pajnkihar calling it a "special rule" (338–9), 341 ("A successor State that has a special link to the matter of succession (i.e., injury) shall fully succeed to the secondary rights and obligations of reparations relating to that matter, followed by conditional succession to other secondary rights and obligations").

75 See, examples in the context of the separation of Belgium from the Kingdom of the Netherlands (1830) and the dissolution of the United Arab Republic.

76 See, *Lighthouse Arbitration* and *Samos* cases, both in the context of transfer of territory and the *Bijelić* case involving separation.

from "odious" acts and other violations of *jus cogens* norms committed by the predecessor State before the date of succession;
- There is also no support for the proposition that the successor State that becomes party to a treaty by way of succession is automatically responsible for obligations arising from the breach of that treaty by the predecessor State before the date of succession.
- The successor State is not *automatically* responsible for the obligations arising from an internationally wrongful act committed by the predecessor State *solely based* on the fact that such act took place prior to its independence on what is now its territory. However, the successor State should nevertheless be held responsible for the obligations arising from internationally wrongful acts committed by the predecessor State that are *specifically linked* to what is now its territory, such as violations of territorial regime obligations.

Finally, several *factors* (the principles of unjust enrichment, equity, fairness and justice) need to be considered to determine whether there should be any transfer of rights and obligations. They are discussed in the next paragraphs.

5 The Issue of State Succession to the Obligation to Repair Should Ultimately Be Resolved Based on the Application of Three Fundamental Equitable Principles

I have identified three basic rules that are, in my view, fundamental to resolve problems of State succession to the obligation to repair:

- No wrong should be left unpunished;
- The State which participated in committing a wrong or benefited from it should be responsible for its consequences; and
- Any outcome of allocation of liability between the different States should be just, fair and avoid unjust enrichment.

First, the basic principle at the heart of this study is that no wrong should be left unpunished.[77] This is because there are situations where the *consequences* of an internationally wrongful act do not simply disappear after the date of

77 Agreeing: Netherlands, letter sent to the UN GA Sixth Committee, rep. 72nd sess. 1st Nov. 2021: "My Government would reiterate its position, as previously expressed, that the point of departure should be the principle that no legal vacuum in terms of State responsibility should emerge". See also, Czech Republic, 69th sess. 1 Nov. 2017.

succession: "These consequences continued to exist in a similar manner as territory, population, property or debts continued to exist in cases of succession".[78] Whenever this is the case, what matters is "not leaving the injured States or injured persons without any reparation".[79] As a matter of principle, an internationally wrongful act committed before the date of succession should not remain unpunished simply because a succession of States happened.[80] Judge Cançado Trindade acknowledged this point in his dissenting opinion in the *Croatia Genocide Convention* case.[81]

After the date of succession, an injured State victim of an internationally wrongful act should not be left with no debtor. The application of a strict rule of non-succession would be too favourable to the wrongdoer State and undoubtedly unfair for the injured State. The Institute has adopted the same basic position.[82] Yet, applying the opposite general rule of succession would

---

78 ILC Report, 70th sess., 2018, para 258.

79 Ibid. See also, Pajnkihar, 332: "At the date of succession, an injury exists as a factual situation in relation to which the predecessor State has (secondary) rights and obligations of reparation. If no succession had occurred, the predecessor State would have been obliged (or entitled) to provide (or request) reparations, that is, to erase the injury. Because the injury, as a factual situation, continues to exist after the date of succession, it is reasonable to argue that the rights and obligations related to it pass to the successor State just like the rights and obligations pertaining to other matters. The successor State replaces the predecessor State in its responsibility for the international relations of the territory, which implies an all- encompassing replacement and not merely a transfer of individual rights and obligations".

80 See also, IIL, Final Report, Kohen, para 53. Agreeing: M. Milanovic "The Tricky Question of State Succession to International Responsibility", *Ejil Talk!*, 16 Feb. 2009; Ralph Janik, "International Responsibility", in: Andre Nollkaemper, August Reinisch, Ralph Janik, and Florentina Simlinger (ed), *International Law in Domestic Court: A Casebook* (OUP 2019), 434–5; Reyes Gajardo, 85; Vergara Lamadrid, 225.

81 *Croatia Genocide Convention* case, Diss. op. Judge Cançado Trindade, para 31: "it would be unjust for the victims if no responsibility could be vindicated for the commission of internationally wrongful acts and their consequences extended in time. (...) An internationally wrongful act and its continuing consequences cannot remain unpunished and without reparation for damages".

82 Kohen & Dumberry, 10: "The sort of 'clean slate' rule applicable to all cases of State succession in the field of international responsibility, which is supported by some writers, would result in numerous situations where the consequences of illegality would simply be erased and unaccounted for. Such an outcome flies in the face of the requirement for stability in international relations as well as the very idea of equity and justice. Such an outcome would also be contrary to the interests of all States affected by an event of State succession, i.e. both the successor and predecessor States as well as third States. It would crucially affect the interest of the holder of a right to reparation following the commission of the wrongful act. In sum, the application of a strict non-succession rule would result in the victim no longer having any possibility of obtaining reparation if the wrongdoer State ceased to exist. Not only would such an outcome constitute a rather unusual way to end a

not be appropriate either. One must properly consider the variety of relevant circumstances and factors specifically involved in each case of succession.[83] Any global "rule" of succession would also sometimes lead to unjust results. A fact-sensitive approach is needed. As noted by the Arbitral Tribunal in the *Lighthouse Arbitration* case, "It is no less unjustifiable to admit the principle of transmission as a general rule than to deny it. It is rather and essentially a question of a kind the answer to which depends on a multitude of concrete factors".[84]

The second basic rule is that the State which has participated in the commission of a wrong or benefited from it should be responsible for its consequences. The first stage in this fact-sensitive investigation is to start with this basic proposition: the State which has *directly participated* in the act should be responsible for it. Thus, whenever the events affecting the predecessor State's territorial integrity *do not* lead to its extinction (separation, transfer of territory) the continuing State *remains* responsible for the internationally wrongful acts *it has* committed before the date of succession.[85] Whenever this is the case, the investigation should stop at this first stage.

But in some circumstances, one needs to ask further questions in order to properly identify which State should be held responsible for the consequences of the commission of a wrongful act. This is the second stage of the analysis. The most obvious situation where such an analysis should take place is when the predecessor State no longer exists, such as in case of dissolution. At this second stage, the guiding principle is that a State should not be held responsible for the consequences of internationally wrongful acts in relation to which it has simply nothing to do. This basic rule explains why in the context of dissolution *not all* the successor States should equally be held responsible for pre-succession damage. It also explains why in the context of separation, there are circumstances where the continuing State should *not* necessarily be responsible for wrongs committed before independence. In these situations, identifying the State which should be held responsible requires assessing its *participation* in the wrongful act. The questions that need to be asked are the following:

---

relationship of responsibility, it would also be, most importantly, fundamentally contrary to the principles of justice and equity governing international relations".

83 The Institute and the ILC have adopted the same basic position: IIL, Final Report, Kohen, 24; Kohen & Dumberry, 13–4; ILC Special Rapporteur Šturma, First Report, 2017, para 83; ibid, Second Report, 2018, para 16.

84 *Lighthouse Arbitration* case, at 91.

85 Pajnkihar, 338.

- Can the successor State be considered to have *indirectly* participated in the act, i.e. through the actions taken before independence by the "organs" of an autonomous government, or by a rebel group, with which the new State has some structural continuity?;
- Did the successor State maintain and continue, after its independence, the internationally wrongful act which was initially committed by the predecessor State before the date of succession?

In addition, identifying the State which should be held responsible also requires assessing who *benefited* from the consequences of the wrongful act. The following questions are relevant in this context:

- Can the successor State be considered to have, after its independence, benefited or gained anything (economically or otherwise) as a result of the wrong?;
- Is there a "direct link" between the consequences of an internationally wrongful act committed by the predecessor State and the territory or the population of the successor State?[86] When there is such a link, the new State will be considered to have benefited from it.[87]

A positive answer to any of these questions militates in favour of recognising that the successor State should take over responsibility. Thus, only the State which has *participated* (even indirectly) in the commission of a wrong or *benefited* from it should be responsible for its consequences.

The third basic rule is that when considering whether there is succession or not to responsibility, the principle of equity should be taken into account.

86 See, Pajnkihar calling this principle a "special rule" (338–9), 341: "A successor State that has a special link to the matter of succession (i.e., injury) shall fully succeed to the secondary rights and obligations of reparations relating to that matter, followed by conditional succession to other secondary rights and obligations".

87 IIL, Final Report, Kohen, para 96, indicating that "the question whether there is some benefit deriving from the wrongful act is covered by the notion of the existence of a direct link between the consequences of the internationally wrongful act and the territory or the population of the successor State". See also, this comment by Greece, letter sent to the UN GA Sixth Committee, Rep. 76th sess., Nov. 2021, referring to situations where "there is a 'clear direct link' either between the consequences of the act and the territory or the population of the successor State", and stating: "In our view, in such cases the successor State might be required to provide compensation based on the concept of unjust enrichment and also because the fact that it continues to enjoy the benefits of the wrongful act without any expression of eagerness to provide reparation to the injured State or its nationals".

Thus, the outcome of any allocation of liability between the different States (the continuing State and the successor State(s)) should be fair and equitable, not only from their perspective but also from the point of view of the injured third State.[88] As noted by Stern in the context of State succession in general, "the legal principles have to be applied with pragmatism, in order to arrive to a just and satisfactory result for the people concerned".[89] This observation applies *a fortiori* when issues of succession to responsibility arise. The goal is to avoid, as much as possible, any situation of unjust enrichment: "no State, including a successor State, should benefit from an internationally wrongful act".[90]

The rules identified above are based on principles of State responsibility, they are not unique to the realm of State succession.[91] One writer recently noted that these rules should not be considered as "exceptions" to a general rule of non-succession, but rather as "*solutions* to the unfair consequences of non-succession".[92] What matters is indeed not so much *where* these principles are coming from, i.e. whether they exist under general international law or whether they are specific rules of State succession.[93] What is important is that these principles do exist. What matters is that these different rules can be used, in practical terms, to *solve problems* of State succession to responsibility. They can be used to find solutions and to ensure that no wrong is left unpunished. For instance, the principle of unjust enrichment is a general principle of law[94] and, as such, it can be used by States and applied by tribunals to solve problems of succession to responsibility.

88 The importance of an equitable distribution of rights and obligations is recognised by the Institute's Resolution (Art. 7).

89 Stern, Concluding Remarks, 208–209.

90 ILC Special Rapporteur Šturma, Fourth Report, 2020, para 55.

91 Reyes Gajardo, 81.

92 Ibid 85, emphasis added.

93 On this point, see the comment by Austria, letter sent to the UN GA Sixth Committee, rep. 70th sess. 2018: "In our view, only in cases where a successor state acknowledges and adopts the unlawful acts of a predecessor state as its own, in line with Article 11 of the State Responsibility Articles, or is unjustly enriched as a consequence of such an act, the obligations arising from the internationally wrongful act of the predecessor state would be transferred to the successor state. However, it is doubtful whether this transfer of obligations is the consequence of a succession of states at all. Rather, it seems to be based on other rules of international law".

94 P. Dumberry, *A Guide to General Principles of Law in International Investment Law* (OUP 2020) 234ff.

6 Solutions to Problems of Succession to the Obligation to Repair Remain Largely Based on the Consent of the Successor State

Although there are many situations and circumstances where a transfer of the obligation to repair to the successor State should prevail, it remains that in all examples of State practice examined above, that State explicitly or implicitly *agreed* to such transfer.[95] In fact, like any other problems of succession of States, State practice remains largely based on *political opportunity* rather than anything else.[96] Some States believe that agreements based on consent are the only way to solve matters of succession to responsibility.[97] There is no doubt that States "prefer ad hoc political solutions rather than fixed and somewhat rigid rules" and that this "further increases the uncertain nature of the rules on treaty succession which, in turn, then lead to an even further increase in pragmatic political solutions".[98] States are reluctant to agree in advance to any document which includes binding obligations which will find (potentially) application only in the future. This explains the low number of States that have ratified both the 1978 and 1983 Vienna Conventions thus far. Codification of matters of State succession has always been a very complicated exercise.[99] The

95 This is a point highlighted by Reyes Gajardo, 80: "the case law does not show an automatic succession to international responsibility. State practice mostly manifests the willingness of successor States to assume the international obligations that, at first, are not held by them, but that they make their own by means of their consent to it" (see also, 85). See also; Vergara Lamadrid, 225.

96 Stern, Concluding Remarks, 209; O'Connell, The Law of State Succession, 1956, 272. O'Connell, Recent Problems, 117–118, identifies the limitation as follows: "The truth of the matter is that the 'practice' is likely to consist of decisions taken by public officials who have not achieved the necessary intellectual penetration of the problem to perceive the true issue, who may be more influenced by political or other ephemeral considerations than by juristic logic, who may even be ignorant of the nature of the problem, or of its ramifications, or may be equipped with obsolescent literature, or even no literature whatever" (see also, ibid 199). This is also the analysis of P.M. Eisemann, "Rapport du Directeur de la section de langue française du Centre", in: Eisemann & Koskenniemi, 33, for whom "la succession d'Etats est, avant tout, un phénomène politique" and States will "utiliser le droit international pour parvenir au but qu'ils se sont assignés plus qu'ils ne chercheront à appliquer des normes supposées 'objectivement' applicables". See also, Erik Castren, "Aspects récents de la succession d'Etats", *Rec. des cours,* v. 78, 1951–I, 402.

97 Russia, letter sent to the UN GA Sixth Committee, rep. 73rd sess. 31 October 2018.

98 A. Zimmermann & J.G. Devaney, "Succession to Treaties and the Inherent Limits of International Law" in C.J. Tams et al. (eds), *Research Handbook on the Law of Treaties* (Elgar 2014) 539.

99 A. Sarvarian, "Codifying the Law of State Succession: A Futile Endeavour?" 27(3) *EJIL* 2016, 789ff; Kaplane, 13–4.

recent work of the ILC on succession to responsibility is only the most recent example.[100]

There are very few cases where a judicial body *imposed* the solution of succession on the successor State which had previously denied any such succession based on the ground that it could not be held responsible for obligations arising from internationally wrongful acts which took place before the date of succession.

One such case is Claim no. 4 decided by the Arbitral Tribunal in the *Lighthouse Arbitration* case.[101] There is, however, a doctrinal controversy as to whether the Arbitral Tribunal in fact held the successor State (Greece) responsible for the obligations arising from the commission of internationally wrongful acts which took place *before* the date of succession or only for its *own acts* committed after that date. Another relevant case is the decision of a Greek municipal court of the Aegean Islands in the *Samos (Liability for Torts) case*.[102] The principle of the transfer of the obligation to repair to the successor State was also applied by the High Court and the Supreme Court of Namibia in the case of *Minister of Defence, Namibia v. Mwandinghi*.[103] Yet, in this case the courts were, in fact, simply applying a provision of the Namibian Constitution. They may also have been influenced by the political context in which Namibia became an independent State. Similarly, in the case of *Bijelić v. Montenegro*, the ECHR decided that the new State was responsible for wrongs which took place before its independence.[104] Yet, Montenegro had agreed to such transfer during the proceedings.

I have also found two cases decided by Dutch courts (the courts of the continuing State) where it was held that it was for the *successor State* to take over the consequences of internationally wrongful acts committed before the date of succession.[105] Yet, in these cases, the court simply applied a provision to that effect contained in the devolution agreement signed by Indonesia and the Netherlands. French municipal courts also consistently held that the new State of Algeria should be responsible to provide compensation to the victims of internationally wrongful acts committed by the FLN in its struggle to achieve

100 For a critical assessment of the Draft Articles initially put forward, see Kaplane, 39–40.

101 *Lighthouse Arbitration* case, 23 *ILR* 1956, 81.

102 *Samos* case, 70.

103 *Mwandinghi* case, Namibia, Supreme Court, 358.

104 *Bijelić* case.

105 *Poldermans v. State of the Netherlands*, Court of Appeal of The Hague (First Ch.), 8 December 1955, *NJ* 1959, no. 7, *ILR* 1957, 69; *Poldermans v. State of the Netherlands*, Supreme Court, 15 June 1956, ibid. *Van der Have v. State of the Netherlands*, District Court of The Hague, 12 January 1953, *NJ* 1953, no. 133, *ILR* 1953, 80.

independence.[106] Yet, Algeria never took part in these proceedings. These court decisions did not formally hold Algeria responsible for these wrongs. They simply held that France could not be responsible for such acts which only "concerned" ("*intéressent*") Algeria.

In sum, (almost) all instances where succession to responsibility took place are based on the consent of the successor State to such transfer of obligations.

7 The Successor State Has the Right to Claim Reparation for Internationally Wrongful Acts Committed by a Third State before the Date of Succession

State practice and case law in the context of State succession to the right to reparation (analysed at Part 3) is much more straightforward than the issue of succession to the obligation to repair. The fact that an internationally wrongful act was committed before the date of succession is generally (with very few exceptions) not considered by the State responsible for the act to be an *obstacle* preventing the successor State from receiving reparation. The doctrine of non-succession is in fact (almost) never invoked by States. Moreover, this so-called principle of non-succession to the right to reparation is not applied by international judicial bodies. The only exception is the *Panevezys-Saldutiskis* case.

It therefore seems established in both State practice and international case law that a successor State can claim reparation for internationally wrongful act committed by a third State before the date of succession. This principle applies both when the wrongful act directly affects the predecessor State and when it affects one of its nationals.

8 The Tendency in Favour of Continuity of Rights and Obligations Is in Accordance with Modern State Practice in Other Fields of State Succession

One cannot help but notice a modern trend towards the principle of succession to responsibility. The consequences arising from the commission of a

106 See, *Perriquet*, Conseil d'Etat, case no. 119737, 15 March 1995, *Rec. Lebon*; *Hespel*, Conseil d'Etat, 2/6 SSR, case no. 11092, 5 December 1980, *Rec. Lebon*; Conseil d'Etat, 2/4 SSR, case no. 5059, 25 May 1970, *Rec. Lebon; Etablissements Henri Maschat*, Conseil d'Etat, case no. 04878, 10 May 1968, *Rec. Lebon*; *Consorts Hovelacque*, Conseil d'Etat, 2/6 SSR, case no. 35028, 13 January 1984, *Rec. Lebon*.

wrong do not simply disappear whenever a succession of States takes place. There are plenty of examples where the successor State took over the rights and obligations arising from such wrongful acts. This conclusion is in line with a clear tendency towards the continuity of rights and obligations in other fields of State succession.[107] This is certainly the case, for instance, in the context of succession to multilateral treaties.[108]

This undeniable tendency towards continuity is dictated by the concern of the international community for the stability of international legal relations among States.[109] This requirement for stability has long been supported by O'Connell, for whom "the freedom of a successor State to pursue its goals is inherently limited by the responsibility of all States to promote the greater good of mankind" and "must not be at the expense of the principles of order and justice".[110] Stern also indicates that the new successor State "devient partie intégrante du système international préexistant, dont il se doit de respecter l'intégrité et la cohérence".[111] The stability of the international legal order requires that the interests of injured States be protected in the context of succession of States. The application of a strict and automatic doctrine of non-succession could hardly be considered to be serving that purpose. It is too favourable to the interests of the wrongdoer States and is detrimental to those of the injured States.

It is conceivable (and should be hoped) that rules of customary international law in favour of State succession to responsibility will eventually develop over time in specific circumstances.[112]

---

107 Stern, Succession, 422.

108 See, *inter alia*, Stern, ibid, 291–295; Photini Pazartzis, *La succession d'États aux traités multilatéraux à la lumière des mutations territoriales récentes* (Pedone 2002) 143–151, 158–159; ILA "Rapport final sur la succession en matière de traités", New Delhi Conference 2002, 14–15; Patrick Dumberry & Daniel Turp, "State Succession With Respect to Multilateral Treaties in the Context of Secession: From the Principle of Tabula Rasa to the Emergence of a Presumption of Continuity of Treaties", 13 *Baltic YIL* 2013, 27–65.

109 Rein Mullerson, "Law and Politics in Succession of States: International Law on Succession of States", in: Geneviève Burdeau & Brigitte Stern (eds), *Dissolution, continuation et succession en Europe de l'Est* (Cedin-Paris I 1994) 44.

110 O'Connell, Recent Problems, 120.

111 Stern, Succession, 119.

112 A similar conclusion is reached (in the context of State succession in general) by Stern, ibid 122: "il n'est pas exclu de penser qu'avec l'approfondissement de la solidarité internationale et donc de l'intérêt général aux dépens des intérêts particuliers des Etats, les cas dans lesquels le droit international posera des règles tendant à assurer la continuité des relations ne feront que croître".

Annexes 1 to 3

Annex 1

Number of claims submitted and amount of compensation awarded (in US$) by the UNCC governing council to the successor states in the context of the dissolution of Czechoslovakia[a]

	Claims by individuals (claims categories A, B, C, D)	Claims by corporations (claims category E)	Claims by government (claims category F)	Total amount in compensation awarded
Czech Republic	271 claims 2,132,630.37	16 claims 12,170,425.60	1 claim 4,733.00	288 claims 14,307,788.97
Slovakia	145 claims 1,087,047.40			145 claims 1,087,047.40

Number of claims submitted and amount of compensation awarded (in US$) by the UNCC governing council to Germany[b]

	Claims by individuals (claims categories A, B, C, D)	Claims by corporations (claims category E)	Claims by government (claims category F)	Total amount in compensation awarded
Germany	313 claims 7,598,388.97	167 claims 48,861,585.55	11 claims 7,059,571.00	491 claims 63,519,545.52

a These figures are taken from: "Addendum to the Report Submitted to the Executive Secretary to the Governing Council in Accordance with Art. 16 of the Provisional Rules for Claims Procedure (Report no. 42)", UNCC, S/AC.26/2003/R.1/Add.1, 28 January 2003. This is the last available compilation of claims established by the UNCC.

b Ibid.

 | DOI:10.1163/9789004703810_012

Annex 2

Number of claims submitted and amount of compensation awarded (in US$) by the UNCC governing council to the successor states in the context of the break-up of the USSR[a]

	Claims by individuals (claims categories A, B, C, D)	Claims by corporations (claims category E)	Claims by government (claims category F)	Total amount in compensation awarded
Armenia				0
Azerbaijan				0
Belarus				0
Georgia				0
Kazakhstan				0
Kyrgyzstan				0
Moldova				0
Russia	6,588 claims 28,198,841.00	7 claims 89,887,591.30	2 claims 1,916,352.00	6,597 claims 120,002,784.30
Tajikistan				0
Turkmenistan				0
Ukraine	183 claims 713,000.00			183 claims 713,000.00
Uzbekistan				0

a Ibid. As explained earlier, the three Baltic States (Estonia, Latvia and Lithuania) are not considered to be successor States to the USSR. They have, consequently, filed no claim before the UNCC. The only exception are 4 claims filed by Estonia, on behalf of its nationals, for which it was awarded a total of US $24,000 in compensation.

Annex 3

Number of Claims submitted and Amount of Compensation Awarded (in US$) by the UNCC Governing Council to the Successor States in the Context of the Dissolution of Yugoslavia[1]

	Claims by individuals (claims categories A, B, C, D)	Claims by corporations (claims category E)	Claims by government (claims category F)	Total amount in compensation awarded
Bosnia and Herzegovina	2,816 claims 10,251,855.10	10 claims 94,038,672.00		2,826 claims 104,290,527.10
Croatia	318 claims 1,684,016.72	15 claims 4,326,466.00		333 claims 6,010,482.72
Republic of Macedonia	573 claims 2,466,480.89	17 claims 8,398,750.00		590 claims 10,865,230.89
Serbia and Montenegro	2,600 claims 11,718,852.85	9 claims 24,433,577.00		2,609 claims 36,152,429.85
Slovenia	185 claims 934,508.81	3 claims 1,295,376.00		188 claims 2,229,884.81

1 Ibid.

Index

Printed in the United States
by Baker & Taylor Publisher Services